D1267306

THE ARCHAEOLOGY OF EGYPT IN THE THIRD INTERMEDIATE PERIOD

The Third Intermediate Period in Egypt (1076–664 BCE) has been characterised previously by political and social changes based upon the introduction of Libyan social and cultural influences. In this book, James E. Bennett analyses the concepts of 'transition' and 'continuity' within the cultural and societal environment of Egypt during the Third Intermediate Period and provides an up-to-date synthesis of current research on the settlement archaeology of the period. This is achieved through the assessment of settlement patterns and their development, the built environment of the settlements, and their associated material culture. Through this analysis, Bennett identifies several interconnected themes within the culture and society of the Twenty-First to Twenty-Fifth Dynasties. They are closely related to the political and economic powers of different regions, the nucleation of settlements and people, self-sufficiency at a collective and individual level, defence, both physical and spiritual, regionality in terms of settlement development and material culture, and elite emulation through everyday objects.

James E. Bennett is a scholar of Egyptian archaeology.

THE ARCHAEOLOGY OF EGYPT IN THE THIRD INTERMEDIATE PERIOD

JAMES E. BENNETT

CAMBRIDGE
UNIVERSITY PRESS

CAMBRIDGE
UNIVERSITY PRESS

University Printing House, Cambridge CB2 8BS, United Kingdom

One Liberty Plaza, 20th Floor, New York, NY 10006, USA

477 Williamstown Road, Port Melbourne, VIC 3207, Australia

314–321, 3rd Floor, Plot 3, Splendor Forum, Jasola District Centre,
New Delhi – 110025, India

79 Anson Road, #06–04/06, Singapore 079906

Cambridge University Press is part of the University of Cambridge.

It furthers the University's mission by disseminating knowledge in the pursuit of
education, learning, and research at the highest international levels of excellence.

www.cambridge.org
Information on this title: www.cambridge.org/9781108482080
DOI: 10.1017/9781108699488

First published 2019

Printed in the United Kingdom by TJ International Ltd, Padstow Cornwall

A catalogue record for this publication is available from the British Library.

Library of Congress Cataloging-in-Publication Data
NAMES: Bennett, James E. (Egyptologist), author.
TITLE: The archaeology of Egypt in the Third Intermediate Period / James Bennett.
DESCRIPTION: Cambridge, United Kingdom ; New York, NY, USA : Cambridge University Press,
2019. | Includes bibliographical references and index.
IDENTIFIERS: LCCN 2019008519 | ISBN 9781108482080 (alk. paper)
SUBJECTS: LCSH: Egypt – History – Third Intermediate Period, ca. 1071-ca. 650 B.C. | Egypt –
Antiquities. | Human settlements – Egypt.
CLASSIFICATION: LCC DT89 .B46 2019 | DDC 932/.015–dc23
LC record available at https://lccn.loc.gov/2019008519

ISBN 978-1-108-48208-0 Hardback

In Memoriam

Joyce Edna Jones (1922–2014)

Sharron Lynn Bennett (1954–2014)

CONTENTS

FIGURES

MAPS

TABLES

PREFACE

The Third Intermediate Period in Egypt (1076–664 BCE) has been characterised previously by political and social changes based upon the introduction of Libyan social and cultural influences.[1] Studies have so far focused primarily on the chronology, funerary practices, and ceramics, at the expense of the settlements and their associated material culture. This book analyses the concepts of 'transition' and 'continuity' within the cultural and societal environment of Egypt during the Third Intermediate Period and provides an up-to-date synthesis of current research on the settlement archaeology of the period. Simultaneously, the book creates a methodology to redefine the ways in which we view chronological phases of Egyptian history pertaining to the title 'Intermediate Period', specifically relating to the early first millennium BCE. This is done through the assessment of settlement patterns and their development, the built environment of the settlements, and their associated material culture. Through this approach several interconnected themes are identified within the culture and society of the Twenty-First to Twenty-Fifth Dynasty that relate to the political and economic powers of different regions, the nucleation of settlements and people, self-sufficiency at a collective and individual level, defence, both physical and spiritual, regionality in terms of settlement development and material culture, and elite emulation through everyday objects.

The book is divided into five distinct, yet interconnected chapters, each one dealing with a specific aspect of the settlement archaeology of the Third Intermediate Period. Chapter 1, 'Terminology and Chronology', refrains from entering into the complex debates on the chronology of the period but does provide a brief overview of the way in which the name 'Third Intermediate Period' developed in academic thought, while at the same time offering readers a basic up-to-date chronology of the period, to provide the skeleton from which to hang the settlement archaeology evidence within a relative chronology, and political environment. Chapter 2, 'Settlement Patterns and Land Policy', analyses landscape and settlements to identify zones of living and resources, the political mapping of settlements versus topographical pressures, and whether general trends in settlement patterns can be established based on the currently available evidence. Through the analysis of the datasets, this chapter also discusses the inherent problems within the available evidence base for the period, and explores characteristics such as regional settlement identities, settlement pattern development, population nucleation, and land management.

Chapter 3, 'Settlement Development and Built Remains of the Third Intermediate Period', provides a detailed analysis of intra-settlement archaeology to assess the way in which settlements were managed by the ruling elites and local domestic populations. This approach provides the cultural and physical setting from which Third Intermediate Period phases can be assessed in relation to the built environment. Through the analysis of the settlement data, this chapter also raises characteristics of regional settlement development, the maintenance and adaption of New Kingdom civic and religious structures, the self-sufficient nature of local populations to maintain the built environment, and to utilise the surrounding built environment to maintain their domestic lives. Chapter 4, 'Domestic Material Culture of the Third Intermediate Period', assesses the chronological framework of Third Intermediate Period material culture from typical domestic household assemblages to assess the potential to create object typologies. Analysis of the material culture raises characteristics of ceramic production and distribution, foreign trade, dining and drinking culture, the use of heirlooms, social status, the re-use of objects, elite emulation, domestic religion, and finally regional considerations. Analysis of this information identifies the specific social fabric and the living conditions during the Third Intermediate Period.

Finally, Chapter 5, 'Conclusions: Transition and Continuity in the Third Intermediate Period', evaluates the characteristics identified in Chapters 2 to 4 to understand themes of continuity and transition in Egypt during the Twenty-First to Twenty-Fifth Dynasty based on archaeological settlement material, the built environment, and the material culture. The conclusion redefines how we view the chronological phase of Egyptian history pertaining to the title 'Third Intermediate Period', to comprehend the everyday life and social practices of the people living at that time and highlight the period as a distinctly defined cultural element within Egyptian society and Egyptology as a whole. Ultimately, this book provides a scholarly, detailed, accessible, and up-to-date introduction to the settlement archaeology of the Third Intermediate Period, bringing together current archaeological research to reassess what is a poorly represented and understood period of Egyptian history within the academic and non-academic literature to provide a comprehensive analysis of the development of Egyptian settlement archaeology.

ACKNOWLEDGEMENTS

This work arises out of a doctoral study conducted at Durham University from 2012 to 2017, and the author would like to thank Durham University for its support during the duration of the work. I am most grateful to the many people who have aided me over the many years with discussions, information, and encouragement, and I am pleased to be able to thank them here. I may have forgotten some people and for that I can only offer my apologies.

Special thanks go to Penelope Wilson for her support, including her many comments and critiques throughout all stages of the work, and to Tom Moore for his contributions to the discussions and thoughtful advice during the research. I also wish to express my thanks to my colleagues and friends, as well as the staff and individuals in the UK and abroad who have provided access to their imagery, or shared information. These include Susan Allison, Manfred Bietak, Stephanie Boonstra, Jane Burkowski, Iain Calderwood, Aidan Dodson, Dina Faltings, Alice Ford Smith, Barry J. Kemp, Chris Kirby, François Leclère, Aurelia Masson-Berghoff, Lucia Ronolfi, Slawomir Rzepka, Eric W. Schnittke, Jacob Smith, Jeffrey Spencer, Neal Spencer, Elaine Sullivan, Christophe Thiers, Jonathan Tubb, and Robert Wenke.

I also wish to extend my gratitude to the various institutions and organisations that have allowed me to use their imagery. These are: the Egypt Exploration Society, the Trustees of the British Museum, University Museum, University of Pennsylvania, BAR Publishing, Mission française des fouilles de Tanis (MFFT), CNRS-CFEETK (Centre national de la recherche scientifique–Centre franco-égyptien d'étude des temples de Karnak), the Oriental Institute of the University of Chicago, and the Metropolitan Museum of Art, New York.

On a personal note, I wish to extend my gratitude and heartfelt thanks to my father, Michael, for his immense support throughout the preparation of this work, and support for my career to date. I thank my brother, Andrew, his wife, Jenette, and my niece, Marianne, for their support and continued enthusiasm for my work and research. I also wish to mention Pauline, Eileen, and Liza, and want to dedicate a special mention to Lauren who has been a tower of support and enthusiasm for the work. I also wish to thank Jeremy, Carol, and Jessica.

Finally, I would like to extend my thanks to Beatrice Rehl, Sarah Lambert, and Edgar Mendez at Cambridge University Press for their help and guidance in bringing this work to publication, and to my copyeditor, Carol Fellingham Webb, for her diligent work on the final text. I am grateful to the detailed and encouraging comments from the peer-reviewers, who have provided detailed feedback and no doubt improved the final form of the manuscript. Any remaining errors are of course my own.

FIGURE CREDITS

Figures in Chapter 2 were created using ArcGIS® software by Esri. ArcGIS® and ArcMap™ are the intellectual property of Esri and are used herein under licence. Copyright © Esri. All rights reserved. For more information about Esri® software, please visit www.esri.com.

Maps of Upper Egypt (Figs. 1–5, 16–17, 18) were created using Light Grey Canvas Map (Esri, DeLorme, HERE, MapmyIndia). Copyright © 2014 Esri.

Maps of the Nile Delta (Figs. 6–15) were created using Esri, HERE, DeLorme, MapmyIndia, © OpenStreetMap contributors, and the GIS user community. Overlay of Nile branches and associated waterways on maps of the eastern Nile Delta, courtesy of Prof. M. Bietak and Dr N. Spencer.

CHRONOLOGICAL TABLES

CHRONOLOGICAL OUTLINE OF ANCIENT EGYPT

Old Kingdom	2580–2120 BCE
First Intermediate Period	2120–2010 BCE
Middle Kingdom	2010–1660 BCE
Second Intermediate Period (Lower Egypt)	1700–1535 BCE
Second Intermediate Period (Upper Egypt)	1660–1545 BCE
New Kingdom	1540–1078/1079 BCE
Third Intermediate Period	1078/1076–664 BCE
Saite Period	664–525 BCE
First Persian Period	525–404 BCE
Late Dynastic Period	404–340 BCE
Second Persian Period	340–332 BCE
Macedonian Period	332–310 BCE
Ptolemaic Period	310–30 BCE
Roman Period	30 BCE–395 CE

CHRONOLOGICAL OUTLINE OF THE THIRD INTERMEDIATE PERIOD

Theban High Priests of Amun[2]	
Piankh	1079–1076 BCE
Herihor	1076–1071/1070 BCE
Herihor (King)	1071/1070–1062 BCE
Twenty-First Dynasty Tanite pharaohs[3]	
Smendes I	1076–1052 BCE
Amenemnisu	1052–1048 BCE
Psusennes I	1048–1000 BCE
Amenemopet	1002–992 BCE
Osochor	992–987 BCE
Siamun	986–968 BCE
Psusennes II	967–944 BCE

Twenty-First Dynasty Theban High Priests of Amun

Pinudjem I	1078–1061 BCE, as king = 1061–1040 BCE
Masaharta (A)	1060–1052 BCE
Djedkhonsuefankh	1052 BCE
Menkheperre (A)	1051–1001 BCE, as king = 1040–1001 BCE
Smendes II	1001 BCE
Pinudjem II	1001–976 BCE
Psusennes III = King Psusennes II (Tanite)	976–967 BCE, as king = 967–944 BCE

Twenty-Second Dynasty pharaohs[4]		Twenty-Second Dynasty pharaohs[5]	
Shoshenq I	ca. 943–923 BCE	Shoshenq I	ca. 943–923 BCE
Osorkon I	ca. 923–890 BCE	Osorkon I	ca. 923–890 BCE
Shoshenq IIa	ca. 890–? BCE	Shoshenq IIa	ca. 890–? BCE
Shoshenq IIc	?	Shoshenq IIc	?
Shoshenq IIb	?–888/885 BCE	Shoshenq IIb	?–877/874 BCE
Takeloth I	ca. 888/885–875/872 BCE	Takeloth I	ca. 877/874–864/861 BCE
Osorkon II	ca. 875/872–842 BCE	Osorkon II	ca. 864/861–831 BCE
Shoshenq III	ca. 842–804/799 BCE	Shoshenq III	ca. 831–793/788 BCE
[Shoshenq IV]	ca. 804/799–790 BCE	[Shoshenq IV]	ca. 793/788–782/779 BCE
Pamiu	ca. 790–783/780 BCE	Pamiu	ca. 782/779–773/770 BCE
Shoshenq V	ca. 783/780–747/744 BCE	Shoshenq V	ca. 773/770–736/733 BCE

Twenty-Third Heracleopolitan/ Theban Dynasty[6]		Twenty-Third Heracleopolitan/ Theban Dynasty[7]	
Harsiese A	ca. ?–834 BCE	Harsiese A	ca. ?–834 BCE
Takeloth II	ca. 834–810 BCE	Takeloth II	ca. 834–810 BCE
(Shoshenq III	ca. 810–793/788 BCE)	(Shoshenq III	ca. 810–793/788 BCE)
Osorkon III	ca. 793/788–766/761 BCE	Osorkon III	ca. 793/788–766/761 BCE
Takeloth III	ca. 770/765–758/753 BCE	Takeloth III	ca. 770/765–758/753 BCE
Rudamun	ca. 758/753–748/747 BCE	Rudamun	ca. 758/753–748/747 BCE
Shoshenq VIa	ca. 748/747–743/742 BCE	Shoshenq VIa	ca. 748/747–743/742 BCE
Peftjauawybast	ca. 743/742–733/732 BCE	Peftjauawybast	ca. 743/742–733/732 BCE
Ini	ca. 733/732–729/728 BCE	Nimlot D	ca. 733/732–? BCE
		Thutemhat	ca. ?–725/724 BCE
		Ini	ca. 725/724–721/720 BCE

Twenty-Third Tanite Dynasty[8]		Twenty-Third Tanite Dynasty[9]	
Osorkon IV	ca. 747/744–716 BCE	Osorkon IV	ca. 736/733–716/715 BCE
[Pedubast II]	ca. 716/715–694/693 BCE	[Pedubast II]	ca. 716/715–693/692 BCE
Pa-sen-n-X	?	Pa-sen-n-X	?
Sankhtawy Sekhemkare	?	Sankhtawy Sekhemkare	?

(continued)

(continued)

Twenty-Third Tanite Dynasty[8]		Twenty-Third Tanite Dynasty[9]	
Gemenefkhonsbak	?	Gemenefkhonsbak	?
Sehetepibre Pedubast [III]	?671–667/666? BCE	Sehetepibre Pedubast [III]	?671–667/666–? BCE
Neferkare P . . .	?–664? BCE	Neferkare P . . .	?–664? BCE

Twenty-Third Dynasty Theban Rebel Kings[10]		Twenty-Third Dynasty Theban Rebel Kings[11]	
Pedubast I	ca. 835–813 BCE	Pedubast I	ca. 824–802 BCE
Iuput I	ca. 821–810 BCE	Iuput I	ca. 810–799 BCE
[Shoshenq VI]	ca. 810–805 BCE	[Shoshenq VI]	ca. 799–794 BCE

Twenty-Fourth Dynasty[12]

Tefnakht I Shepsesre	728–721 BCE
Bakenrenef Wahkare	721–715 BCE

Twenty-Fifth Dynasty

Piankhy	747–716 BCE/744–714 BCE
Shebitku	714–705 BCE
Shabaka	705–690 BCE
Taharqa	690–664 BCE
Tantamani	664–656 BCE (final 8 years in Southern Egypt)

ABBREVIATIONS

Ä&L	*Ägypten und Levante, Internationale Zeitschrift für ägypische Archäologie und deren Nachargebiete*
ÄA	Ägyptologische Abhandlungen
ÄeDs	Ägyptische Denkmäler in der Schweiz
ÄF	Ägyptologische Forschungen
AfO	Archiv für Orientforschung: Internationale Zeitschrift für die Wissenschaft vom Vorderen Orient
AJA	*American Journal of Archaeology*
AmerAnt	*American Antiquity*
Ann Assoc Am Geogr	*Annals of the Association of American Geographers*
AnOr	*Analecta Orientalia*
APol	*Archaeologia Polona*
ARCE	American Research Center in Egypt
Artefact	*Journal of the Archaeological and Anthropological Society of Victoria*
ASAE	*Annales du Service des Antiquities de l'Égypte*
AttiFir	Atti e memorie dell'Accademia Toscana di Scienze e Lettere 'La Colombaria' (Florence)
ÄUAT	Ägypten und Altes Testaments: Studien zur Geschichte, Kultur und Religion Ägyptens und des Alten Testaments
AVDAIK	*Ärchäologische Veröffentlichungen, Deutsches Archäologisches Institut, Abteilung Kairo*
BACE	*Bulletin of the Australian Centre for Egyptology*
BAR IS	British Archaeological Reports International Series
BCE	*Bulletin de liaison du Groupe International d'Étude de la Céramique Égyptienne*
BdE	Bibliothèque d'Étude
BEHE SHP	Bibliothèque de l'École des Hautes Études, Sciences Historiques et Philologiques
BES	*Bulletin of the Egyptological Seminar*
BIFAO	*Bulletin de l'Institut Français d'Archéologie Orientale*

BM	British Museum
BM EA	British Museum Egyptian Archaeology
BMMA	*Bulletin of the Metropolitan Museum of Art*
BMSAES	*British Museum Studies in Ancient Egypt and Sudan*
BMusHongr	*Bulletin du Musée Hongrois des Beaux-Arts*
BN	*Biblische Notizen*
BSAE	British School of Archaeology in Egypt
BSFE	*Bulletin de la Société Française d'Égyptologie*
BSFFT	*Bulletin de la Société Française des Fouilles de Tanis*
B. TAVO	Tübinger Atlas des vorderen Orients, Beihefte Reihe B
CAJ	*Cambridge Archaeological Journal*
CCÉ	*Cahiers de la Céramique Égyptienne*
CCEM	Contributions to the Chronology of the Eastern Mediterranean
CdE	*Chronique d'Égypte; Bulletin périodique de la Fondation Égyptologique Reine Élisabeth, Bruxelles*
CENiM/ENiM	*Cahiers/Égypte Nilotique et Méditerranéenne*
CG	Catalogue Général
CGC	Catalogue Général des Antiquités Égyptiennes du Musée du Caire
CG JE	Catalogue Général des Antiquités Égyptiennes du Musée du Caire, Journal d'Entreé
CHANE	Culture and History of the Ancient Near East
Class	classical site name
CRIPEL	Cahiers de Recherches de l'Institut de Papyrologie et d'Égyptologie de Lille
DFIFAO	Documents de fouilles de l'Institut Français d'Archéologie Orientale du Caire
DGÖAW	Denkschriften der Gesamtakademie. Verlag der Österreichischen Akademie der Wissenschaften
EA	*Egyptian Archaeology: the Bulletin of the Egypt Exploration Society*
ECHO	Egyptian Cultural Heritage Organisation
ÉdÉ	*Études d'Égyptologie*
EEF	(Publications of the) Egypt Exploration Fund
EES	Egypt Exploration Society
EES ASE EES	Archaeological Survey of Egypt, Memoirs
EES EM	Egypt Exploration Society Excavation Memoirs
EES OP	Egypt Exploration Society Occasional Publications
EgUit	Egyptologische Uitgaven
EM	Egyptological Memoirs

ERA	Egyptian Research Account
EVO	Egitto e Vicino Oriente: Rivista della sezione orientalistica dell'Istituto di Storia Antica, Università degli Studi di Pisa
FIFAO	Fouilles de l'Institut Français d'Archéologie du Caire
Geneva	*Bulletin du Musée de Genève*
GLECS	*Comptes rendus du Groupe Linguistique d'Études Chamito-Sémitiques*
GM	*Göttinger Miszellen: Beiträge zur ägyptologischen Diskussion*
HÄB	Hildesheimer Ägyptologische Beiträge
HdO	*Handbuch der Orientalistik. 1. Abt. Bd. 1: Ägyptologie*
HPA	High Priest of Amun
HWJ	*History Workshop Journal*
IFAO	l'Institut Français d'Archéologie Orientale
JACF	*Journal of the Ancient Egyptian Chronology Forum*
JAEI	*Journal of Ancient Egyptian Interconnections*
J Anthropol Res	*Journal of Anthropological Research*
JAOS	*Journal of the American Oriental Society*
JARCE	*Journal of the American Research Center in Egypt*
J Archaeol Method Th	*Journal of Archaeological Method and Theory*
JAS	*Journal of Archaeological Science*
JEA	*Journal of Egyptian Archaeology*
JEgH	*Journal of Egyptian History*
JFA	*Journal of Field Archaeology*
JHS	*Journal of Hellenic Studies*
JNES	*Journal of Near Eastern Studies*
JSSAE	*Journal of the Society for the Study of Egyptian Antiquities*
Karnak	*Cahiers de Karnak*
KAW	Kulturgeschichte der Antiken Welt
Kêmi	*Revue de Philologie et d'Archéologie Égyptiennes et Coptes*
Ktèma	*Civilisations de l'Orient, de la Grèce et de Rome antiques*
LibStud	*Libyan Studies*
MÄS	Münchner Ägyptologische Studien
MDAIK	*Mitteilungen des Deutschen Archäologischen Instituts, Abteilung Kairo*
MEEF	Memoir of the Egypt Exploration Fund
MEES	Memoir of the Egypt Exploration Society
MIFAO	Mémoires publiés par les membres de l'Institut Français d'Archéologie Orientale
MIO	*Mitteilungen des Instituts für Orientforschung*

MMAF	Mémoires publiés par les membres de la Mission Archéologique Française au Caire
MRE	Monographies Reine Élisabeth
NEA	*Near Eastern Archaeology*
NHE	The Natural History of Egypt
OBO	Orbis Biblicus et Orientalis
OIP	Oriental Institute Publications
OIS	Oriental Institute Seminars
OLA	Orientalia Loveniensia Analecta
OMS	Oxbow Monograph Series
On.Am.	The Onomasticon of Amenemope
PAM	*Polish Archaeology in the Mediterranean*
P.BM EA	Papyrus British Museum Egyptian Archaeology
PdÄ	Probleme der Ägyptologie
PM	B. Porter and R. L. B. Moss, *Topographical bibliography of ancient Egyptian hieroglyphic texts, reliefs, and paintings*, 6 vols. (Oxford, Oxford University Press)
PSBA	*Proceedings of the Society of Biblical Archaeology*
RA	*Revue d'Assyriologie et d'Archéologie Orientale*
RAPH	Recherches d'Archéologie, de Philologie et d'Histoire
RdE	*Revue d'Égyptologie*
RT	*Recueil de Travaux Relatifs à la Philologie et à l'Archéologie Égyptiennes et Assyriennes*
SAAB	*State Archives of Assyria Bulletin*
SAGA	Studien zur Archäologie und Geschichte Altägyptens
Sahara	*International Yearly Journal on the Prehistory and History of the Sahara*
SAK	*Studien zur Altägyptischen Kultur*
SBAW	Sitzungsberichte der Bayerischen Akademie der Wissenschaften, Phil.-hist. Abteilung
SBL	Society of Biblical Literature Dissertation Series
SDAIK	Sonderschrift des Deutschen Archäologischen Instituts, Abteilung Kairo
SE	Shire Egyptology
SEAP	Studi di Egittologia e di Antichità Puniche
SMA	Studies in Mediterranean Archaeology
Sphinx	*Revue Critique Embrassant le Domaine Entier de l'Égyptologie*
StudAeg	*Studia, Aegyptiaca*
TOPOI	Berlin Studies of the Ancient World
TT	Theban Tomb
TTSO	Tut'ankhamūn's Tomb Series

UGAAe	Untersuchungen zur Geschichte und Altertumskunde Ägyptens
UPMJ	*University of Pennsylvania Museum Journal*
Urk	K. Sethe, H. W. Helck, H. Schäfer, H. Grapow, and O. Firchow (eds.), *Urkunden des ägyptischen Altertums*, 8 vols. (Leipzig and Berlin, 1903–57)
UZK	Untersuchungen der Zweigstelle Kairo des Österreichischen Archäologischen Instituts
VA	*Varia Aegyptiaca*
Wb	A. Erman and H. Grapow (eds.), *Wörterbuch der ägyptischen Sprache*, 7 vols. and 5 Belegstellen (Leipzig and Berlin, 1926–63; reprinted Berlin, 1992)
WdO	Die Welt des Orient: Wissenschaftliche Beiträge zur Kunde des Morgenlandes
WorldArch	*World Archaeology*
WVDOG	Wissenschaftliche Veröffentlichungen der Deutschen Orientgesellschaft
WZKM	*Wiener Zeitschrift für die Kunde des Morgenlandes*
ZÄS	*Zeitschrift für ägyptische Sprache und Altertumskunde*

CHAPTER ONE

TERMINOLOGY AND CHRONOLOGY

THE PERIOD 1078/6–664 BCE IS COMMONLY KNOWN AS THE 'THIRD
Intermediate Period' (the Twenty-First to Twenty-Fifth Dynasty). The
once unified government in the preceding Ramesside Period (Nineteenth to
Twentieth Dynasty, 1295–1078/6 BCE) was replaced by considerable political
fragmentation in the Twenty-First Dynasty. The pharaohs now ruled from the
north at Tanis, and a line of Theban High Priests of Amun (HPA) and army
commanders controlled the south from Thebes. Alongside this shift of power
was the re-emergence of local centres under the control of quasi-pharaohs and
local Libyan, or warrior-class, chiefs, starting in the Twenty-Second Dynasty,
and concurrently ruling from the mid-Twenty-Second Dynasty onwards. The
warrior-chiefs were of the Meshwesh and Libu tribes that had gradually entered
Egypt during the reigns of Ramesses II and Ramesses III as prisoners of war,[1]
and had subsequently been settled in the Delta and Middle Egypt.[2] The
demographic structure of Egypt also changed at this time as the incoming
peoples integrated with the native Egyptian population. Egypt itself became
a more politically inward-looking country, while its power hold over the
Levant and Nubia was reduced.[3] These factors had consequences for the
structure of Egyptian society.[4] This chapter begins by discussing how we
have come to view relative chronological phases relating to the period after
the New Kingdom, the origin of the term 'Third Intermediate Period', and the
political and cultural climate in which the term was devised. It then goes on to

outline the chronology of the period to anchor the data sources discussed in this book into a relative chronological framework.

TERMINOLOGY

Labels applied to periods of history often carry with them social connotations, such as the term 'classical', used in 'classical Greece', which indicates positivity and progression, while those of 'Dark Age' indicate negativity, and regression.[5] At the same time these labels demonstrate the views within previous archaeological thought and theory, which unless challenged through new analysis often go on to subconsciously shape the discussions and approaches to the archaeology, history, and culture of a specific time period. The term 'intermediate' has the inherent meaning of 'between two other related things', in the case of ancient Egyptian chronology, the New Kingdom (ca. 1540–1078/6 BCE) and the Saite Period (664–525 BCE), both of which are characterised by a central ruling authority. The term 'intermediate' within Egyptology has inherent implications of poverty and decline and implies that periods of strong centralised authority were superior. When the central authority is not visible within the archaeological record, for whatever reasons, and the historical sources (most importantly texts) created by the central authority fail to be preserved, then scholars are left with less certainty concerning what was going on. There are, however, only implications of poverty, as well as political and economic decline, in the final decades of the late New Kingdom, but these are primarily recorded around the Theban region. During the reign of Ramesses IX in years 10–15, there were incidents of tribes from the Western Desert coming into the Thebaid and elsewhere,[6] while in years 13–17 the royal tomb robbery scandal was uncovered. Coupled with high food prices, theft and corruption, and a loss of respect for kings, whether dead or alive, were factors that transformed the sporadic violation of Theban royal tombs into wide-scale pillaging in the following decades.[7] Later, in the reign of Ramesses XI economic conditions such as famine persisted, indicated by the so-called 'Year of the Hyenas'.[8] During such 'intermediate' times the socio-political and economic structures of the country may change, but people continue to survive by reorganising their communities, and continuing the day-to-day process of living. Such a process can be viewed as a return to a simpler socio-political structure.[9] It is argued that post-collapse societies are to many scholars an annoying interlude, their study a chore necessary to understand the renaissance that followed.[10] This attitude is nowhere more vividly portrayed than by William Matthew Flinders Petrie in the late nineteenth and early twentieth century, who, although the term 'Third Intermediate Period' was not yet in use during his time in Egypt, states in his diary entry in relation to his excavations at Lahun that: 'The cemetery at Illahun so far discovered is entirely re-occupied under the

XXIIIrd dynasty and of no historic value.'[11] Édouard Naville, who also worked in Egypt during the late nineteenth century, this time at Bubastis, also shared similar negative attitudes and did not consider the fine workmanship of the Hathor columns of Osorkon II as being a product of the Twenty-Second Dynasty and its craftspeople, and proposed they were usurped Twelfth or Eighteenth Dynasty works.[12] This lack of interest, presumptions of a lack of artistic quality, and the placing of a focus on to the periods of the Old, Middle and New Kingdoms created what Lantzas refers to in terms of Archaic Greek studies as an 'Academic No Man's Land'.[13]

An evidence-based analysis must be applied when we begin to observe the past objectively, consider what is available for observations and, fundamentally, critically assess how scholars approach the material.[14] To engage with the past objectively and conscientiously, divisions of 'Kingdom' (as in Old, Middle, and New) and 'Intermediate Period' (as in First, Second, and Third), whether based on absolute or relative chronology, or changes in material culture, must be considered as discrete periods of history, and the language used to define them should be absent of interpretational bias. There must be a critical awareness of the role of the researcher and the biases of cultural historians which have affected scholarly attempts to understand the past,[15] as evidenced by the views of early researchers such as Petrie and Naville in their treatment of the material of the Third Intermediate Period.

The term 'Third Intermediate Period', according to Cyril Aldred,[16] was first created by Georg Steindorff in his 1946 museum catalogue as a convenient name to be used in the cataloguing of Egyptian statuary between the New Kingdom, ending with the Twentieth Dynasty (1078/6 BCE), and the Late Period, beginning with the Twenty-Sixth (Saite) Dynasty (664 BCE),[17] while other scholars such as John Romer state that Kenneth Kitchen in his seminal work *The Third Intermediate Period in Egypt (1100–650 BC)*, first published in 1973, christened the period as the 'Third Intermediate Period'.[18] Despite the attributions to the naming of the period, 'Third Intermediate Period' has become fixed academic nomenclature to describe this complex period of Egypt's history. The term has survived and permeated most studies of Egypt's history, culture, and material studies regarding the Twenty-First to Twenty-Fifth Dynasty. There was a call to change the term to the 'Post-Imperial Epoch',[19] but Egyptologists did not adopt this, and the usage of the term 'Intermediate' has been retained. The implications of using labels such as 'intermediate' can create bias against the periods in question and assign a superiority to the preceding and succeeding phases, which is somewhat demonstrated by the wealth of studies focusing on all aspects of society in the New Kingdom, and even the Saite to Ptolemaic Period which is better defined culturally and chronologically. There are many reasons for the focus on other periods at the expense of the 'Intermediate Periods', as so little has survived in the way of monumental architecture, and the preservation of literature and textual data is limited at best compared with that in the preceding periods of the Old, Middle, and New Kingdoms. In the 'Third Intermediate Period' the arena of royal power was concentrated within the Delta nome capitals, of which hardly anything has survived as a result of the wetter environmental and ecological conditions. This is in striking comparison to the well-preserved and drier area of the desert fringes in Upper Egypt, particularly at Thebes, where tombs and temples are well preserved. While admittedly the material record so far gathered, no more so than the settlement remains, is sparse, like other post-collapse societies such as Archaic Greece, this should not deter scholarly interest. By their nature these periods exercise a fascination and present a challenge, to answer questions regarding what was happening in cultural, social, religious, political, and economic terms.[20] The growing corpus of settlement and domestic material culture remains can now begin to answer some of the most pressing questions regarding the development of settlements, and culture in general, from the perspective of this period of Egypt's history.

CHRONOLOGY

One of the main problems in understanding the Third Intermediate Period is providing a sound historical framework for the Twenty-First to Twenty-Fifth Dynasty, which has been more difficult to establish than for any other period of Egyptian history.[21] This book has included the Twenty-Fifth Dynasty as forming part of the Third Intermediate Period because the underlying political geography of Egypt from the time of Piankhy (747–716 BCE), and for almost another century later, was 'thinly veiled behind the purely superficial unity of rule presented by the Twenty-Fifth Dynasty'.[22]

Studies have concentrated on understanding the chronology and the sequence of kings and local rulers, and many scholars still do not agree on a wide range of chronological aspects.[23] There is a lack of a continuous series of dates for any ruler, and there can be no confidence in the suggestion that the highest known year date for any reign reflects its true length. Ultimately the chronology of the Third Intermediate Period is imprecise and uncertain in many respects.[24] Most of the king lists which have survived from ancient Egypt were written before this period. The only list to survive that includes the kings of the Third Intermediate Period is the list of the Greek historian Manetho who was writing in the third century BCE. Manetho acquired his sources from the High Priests of Ptah at Memphis and several other Delta sources. His king list therefore provides an incomplete picture for the country and contains a Lower Egyptian bias.[25] As well as Manetho's list, royal and private inscriptions have been used to establish the order of the kings, including the cross-referencing of Egyptian sources with Assyrian and other contemporary Near Eastern sources, including biblical references. The loss of data makes it difficult for a balanced historical picture of the country to be achieved,[26] which most seriously affects the Delta, where many of the important historical developments took place.

Libyan rule in Egypt began with the accession of the Twenty-First Dynasty, and the specific administrative system introduced at the outset of the dynasty continued during the Twenty-Second and the Twenty-Third Dynasty. In a more general cultural record there are clear differences between the Twentieth and Twenty-First Dynasty, but a close unity between the Twenty-First and Twenty-Second Dynasty. These included a changed conception of kingship. There was no longer one unique ruler over Egypt but rather several kings at the same time, all assuming full royal style and claiming full royal power, without challenging sets of claims. There was a division of the country and the capital of the Lower Egyptian kings of the Twenty-First and Twenty-Second Dynasty now became Tanis, where several of them were buried within the temenos of the Amun temple.[27] It is now generally agreed that the power of the founders of the Twenty-First Dynasty, Piankh and Herihor, was based on their capacity as army commanders, which may also have applied to Smendes I, the first pharaoh of the Twenty-First Dynasty, although we do not know which military, priestly, or civil titles he held. Piankh and Herihor may have been Libyan Great Chiefs whose mutual relations were determined in accordance with the Libyan social hierarchy where brothers and cousins are placed on equal social levels.[28] Furthermore, in this patrilineal system, descent and genealogical closeness was a determining factor, but at the same time brothers and patrilineal parallel cousins were structurally positioned to compete for access to resources, inheritance, and overall leadership, which most likely led fraternal succession to take precedence over father to son succession.

THE *WHM-MSWT* (REPEATING OF BIRTHS), THE THEBAN HIGH PRIESTLY SUCCESSION, AND TWENTY-FIRST DYNASTY HIGH PRIESTS OF AMUN

Owing to the weakness of centralised governmental control during the late Twentieth Dynasty from the reign of Ramesses IX to that of Ramesses XI, Upper and Lower Egypt changed from areas of administrative convenience into distinct political entities. The self-sufficient pride of the Theban hierarchy and the weakness of the northern Ramesside kings helped to form a political schism between the north and south. From Year 19 of Ramesses XI onwards a new regime was implemented called the 'Renaissance' (*whm-mswt*, lit. repeating of births), and from then on, the dateline is formed as Year 1 of X corresponding to Year 19 of Ramesses XI. The *whm-mswt* reached at least a Year 10 (= Ramesses XI Year 28), and probably a Year 12 (= Ramesses XI Year 30).[29] This political division saw a strong military command given to the High Priests of Amun at Thebes who controlled Upper Egypt, and to a new man hailing from Mendes, called Smendes, based on the newly elevated site of Tanis, replacing the now mainly defunct previous Ramesside capital of Piramesse (Qantir). To prevent further socio-political problems, the Viceroy of Nubia, Panehesy, was relieved of his post and the Nubian province was given to the High Priest of Amun at Thebes. However, Panehesy rallied his loyal troops in Nubia and successfully held off the forces of the High Priest of Amun, and it is likely that Panehesy held a practical border somewhere between Maharakka and Derr near Korosko, and maybe even made common cause with a rising new chiefdom in Kush, on whom he could draw for defence in a common interest against Egypt.[30]

Recent debate as to the sequence of the Theban High Priests of Amun (HPA) during the political transition at the end of the New Kingdom has led to the generally accepted order of Herihor then Piankh to be questioned, and the proposal put forward that Piankh preceded Herihor.[31] The theory has been both rejected by some[32] and endorsed by others.[33] The current arguments used for the reversal of the traditional order Herihor–Piankh have been widely debated.[34] The reversed order does, however, match the Libyan social hierarchy and the changed conception of kingship during this period.[35] The chronological models for the early inception of the Twenty-First Dynasty in Thebes are still debated, and there is still currently no clear consensus among scholars of the period.

There is general scholarly agreement on the number and reigns of the Twenty-First Dynasty, and a precise idea of the parallel sequence of HPA at Thebes and northern pharaohs. There are seven kings listed in Manetho and the Egyptian archaeological and textual evidence.[36] The Tanite pharaohs are Smendes I, Amenemnisu, Psusennes I, Amenemopet, Osochor, Siamun, and Psusennes II. The parallel priestly line in Thebes also has a fixed sequence of Pinudjem I, Masaharta, Menkheperre, Smendes II, Pinudjem II, and Psusennes III (who is almost certainly the same as the Tanite Psusennes II). Between the pontificates of Masaharta and Menkheperre was Djedkhonsuefankh, under the co-kingship of Pinudjem I with Psusennes II, and he was called 'son' of the royal Pinudjem (I).

THE EARLY TWENTY-SECOND DYNASTY: SHOSHENQ I TO OSORKON II

The most important chronological sources for the Twenty-Second Dynasty onwards in Upper Egypt are the Nile flood level records at Karnak, the annals of the priests of Karnak, the Chronicle of Prince Osorkon at Karnak, and the statues and other objects belonging to families which provide evidence of extensive genealogies, while for Lower Egypt they are the donation and

Serapeum stelae. The start of the Twenty-Second Dynasty has commonly been fixed by convention to 945 BCE with the accession of Shoshenq I, which saw the brief reunification of Upper and Lower Egypt. Recent analysis of lunar dates would suggest Year 1 of Shoshenq I now correlates to 943 BCE based on a lunar date from a stela of Shoshenq I found in the Dakhleh Oasis.[37] The lineage of the first part of the Twenty-Second Dynasty is relatively well known. Based on the stela of Pasenhor B (from Year 37 of Shoshenq V),[38] there is a definite father to son sequence: Shoshenq I, Osorkon I, Takeloth I, and Osorkon II. This sequence does not mean each one immediately followed the other into office, as the Manethoic list records three unnamed kings between Osorkon I and Takeloth I.

THE MID-TWENTY-SECOND DYNASTY TO THE TWENTY-THIRD DYNASTY

Since the reign of Osorkon II at the latest, the Twenty-Second Dynasty kings and their sons lost out to the powers of decentralisation when clearly defined separate spheres of power and local kinglets of non-Egyptian origin, including Chiefs of the Ma(shwesh) and Libu, appeared, mainly in Lower Egypt and northern Middle Egypt (Faiyum, Heracleopolis, Hermopolis, and possibly as far south as Asyut).[39] The dual kingships of the Twenty-First Dynasty recurred in the middle of the Twenty-Second Dynasty. It is not clear whether this regionalisation only came into existence at the outset of the Twenty-Second Dynasty or whether it already existed during the Twenty-First Dynasty, but only became explicit in the surviving sources.[40] The chronological model set out in Kitchen's seminal *The Third Intermediate Period in Egypt (1100–650 BC)*, originally published in 1973, stated that in the Twenty-Second Dynasty King Takeloth II directly succeeded Osorkon II. More than a decade later David Aston published an article in which he suggested Takeloth II was not a Tanite pharaoh as had always been presumed, and was in fact a king of a different, rival, Theban Twenty-Third Dynasty, and a contemporary of the Tanite Pharaoh Shoshenq III who followed the reign of Osorkon II.[41]

This newly proposed chronology used the Chronicle of Prince Osorkon, carved on to the Bubastite Gate at Karnak, to suggest that Year 22 of Shoshenq III was close to Year 24 of Takeloth II, and not twenty years later. Assuming Shoshenq III's Year 22 followed Takeloth II's highest known year date, Year 25, then Shoshenq III came to the throne in Tanis in Year 3 of Takeloth II.[42] The new chronology suggested that the civil war described in the Chronicle of Prince Osorkon, which broke out in Thebes in Takeloth II's Year 11, was caused by Pedubast Siese setting himself up in opposition to Takeloth as King of Thebes, and thus, Year 1 of Pedubast = Year 11 of Takeloth II = Year 8 of Shoshenq III. A detailed study of the burial assemblages of the descendants of

Takeloth, plus generation counting, suggested that Takeloth II should be dated from ca. 825–800 BCE, meaning that Osorkon II had to have reigned for around forty to forty-five years to fill in the chronological gap; this was justified by genealogies that indicate that the reign of Osorkon II covered more than one generation (twenty-eight to thirty years per generation), suggesting that Takeloth II must have reigned slightly earlier in time.[43] The new chronological model of Aston has since been adopted, modified, and added to,[44] but is still strongly criticised by Kitchen.[45] There are now two main rival competing chronologies for the mid-Twenty-Second and Twenty-Third Dynasty, those of Aston and Kitchen. The fragmentation of the Twenty-Second Dynasty and the emergence of the Twenty-Third Theban/Heracleopolitan Dynasty based on Aston's chronological model allowed the creation of a power vacuum, in which several local dynasts began setting themselves up within the important political centres. These political centres and local dynasts continued to function well into the end of the period, until the advent of Assyrian aggression and conquest.

THE KINGDOM OF THE WEST UNDER TEFNAKHT AND THE PROTO-TWENTY-FIFTH DYNASTY IN NUBIA

Political contact between Egypt and Nubia was renewed ca. 750 BCE when the ruler of Nubia, Kashta, of whom we have surviving contemporary records, appears to have been recognised as king throughout Nubia, and as far north as Elephantine, where a stela was found proclaiming him King of Upper and Lower Egypt.[46] This Nubian kingdom had come into existance in the late tenth or early ninth century BCE. The chiefs were buried in simple graves at el-Kurru.[47] The previous occupation of the Fourth Cataract area in the New Kingdom and the subjection to Egyptian culture had created an Egyptianised Nubian people, and it was under the rule of the Theban Pharaoh Osorkon III that Nubian power began to interact with the Theban state, although it was initially restricted to the southern border of Egypt at Elephantine.[48] Kashta, who died in ca. 747 BCE and was buried in a tomb at el-Kurru, was succeeded by his son Piankhy.[49] Within the first decade of his reign (ca. 747–737 BCE) Piankhy claimed to be the protector and ruler of Thebes, established garrisons along the southern sector of the Nile, and sought out the allegiance of local dynasts in Middle Egypt including Nimlot D of Hermopolis.[50]

In Egypt, two stelae found at Buto[51] state that by Year 36 of the Tanite Pharaoh Shoshenq V (ca. 732 BCE), a western Delta ruler called Tefnakht claimed to be Great Chief of the Ma, Army Leader, and Great Chief of the Libu, challenging the dynast and Chief of the Libu, Ankhhor in Mendes, who still claimed the title in Year 37 of Shoshenq V.[52] In Year 38 of Shoshenq V (ca. 730 BCE) Tefnakht added the title 'Great Chief of the Entire Lands' and the religious titles of Neith,

Wadjet, and the Lady of *Imaw* which reflected his rule in Sais, Buto, and Kom el-Hisn. Tefnakht was now in control of the entire western Delta, effectively creating a western kingdom, stretching from the Mediterranean coast to Memphis and *Itj-Tawy* in the south. From this power base Tefnakht extended his control south of Memphis by attacking Heracleopolis and advancing on Hermopolis. This rapid advance southward, bypassing the eastern Delta kings, would bring Tefnakht into open conflict with the Nubian state in the south, and the proto-Twenty-Fifth Dynasty now reigned over by Kashta's son Piankhy. The famous Piankhy Stela recounts how, after the defection of Nimlot D to Tefnakht, Piankhy came to Egypt and fought back against Tefnakht. The defeat of Tefnakht's forces at Memphis meant Piankhy could claim both the south and north of Egypt, and the rulers of Egypt now submitted to Piankhy. After the victory Piankhy returned to Napata never to return to Egypt, nor was he challenged in the Thebaid. Egypt still retained a politically divided series of mini-states that would remain for the next century. The Nubian conquest did not make Egypt into a united system and was only a superficial one for the remaining Twenty-Fifth Dynasty.[53]

THE TWENTY-FOURTH DYNASTY

With the return of Piankhy to Napata, there was no Nubian administration left in place and Piankhy had no intention of ruling as pharaoh. The power vacuum that was left allowed the local dynasts to continue to rule their settlements and hinterlands, especially in the Delta. The old Tanite dynasty had become no more than a petty chiefdom and the Middle Egyptian rulers and Chiefs of the Ma had all become subservient to Piankhy, but Tefnakht at Sais retained the entire united western Delta kingdom.[54] Tefnakht regained Memphis and became pharaoh in the north, and now has the cartouche of Shepsesre-Tefnakht. Shepsesre-Tefnakht did not attempt to remove Osorkon IV from the Tanite throne and claim the eastern Delta, nor did he move south for fear of Nubian aggression.

Directly after the rule of Tefnakht I came the official beginning of Manetho's Twenty-Fourth Dynasty. The Twenty-Fourth Dynasty was made up of one king called Bakenrenef ruling from Sais, and as he is listed by Manetho, it suggests that he officially ruled in Memphis, and was not de facto king like Tefnakht. The nature and extent of the rule of Bakenrenef is unknown, but he did nothing to eliminate the royal lines still presiding in Tanis-Bubastis or the Chiefs of the Ma outside the Western Kingdom. Furthermore, it is not known to what extent the other dynasts accepted and recognised the rule of Bakenrenef.[55]

THE TWENTY-FIFTH DYNASTY

After Piankhy's death in ca. 716/14 BCE he was succeeded by Shebitku, who reconquered Egypt. Shebitku was followed by Shabaka.[56] On the whole, during the Twenty-Fifth Dynasty from the time of Shebitku the internal affairs of Egypt were peaceful, but at Sais, a Stephanites may have become a local ruler. He may have been a descendant of Tefnakht, ruling from 695–688 BCE. After Shabaka came Taharqa, who was crowned at Memphis. It is widely agreed that the earliest event in Egyptian history that can be dated with relative precision is the accession to the throne of Taharqa in 690 BCE.[57] The first thirteen years of Taharqa's reign were peaceful, but local chiefs continued to rule their independent mini-states in the same way as in the previous Libyan Period. The portrayal of Nubian rule in the Twenty-Fifth Dynasty as sole rulers of Egypt particularly on Theban monuments provides a superficial impression that, from the reign of Shebitku, the Nubian rulers had created a united country and the era of the local mini-state dynasts was over, but this was not the case. The Twenty-Fifth Dynasty rulers had merely imposed a central rule based at Memphis, Thebes, and Napata. This form of rule was based upon the already existing series of Delta and Upper Egyptian chiefs and mayors compiled by the Assyrian records of local rulers by Assurbanipal in 667/6 BCE, and this is further confirmed by the Egyptian evidence.[58] In 674 BCE Esarhaddon of Assyria attempted to invade Egypt but was defeated by Taharqa's forces, but he invaded for a second time in 671 BCE, defeating Taharqa and driving him from Memphis. In 669 BCE Esarhaddon attacked Egypt again when trouble broke out, but he died en route. Again in 667/666 BCE Assurbanipal marched to subdue Egypt where Taharqa had re-established his rule since 671 BCE. Taharqa was defeated and he fled to Thebes. The Assyrians went as far south as Thebes, while Taharqa escaped to Napata, and Assurbanipal received the submission of the Upper and Lower Egyptian dynasts headed by Necho I of Sais. After Assurbanipal returned to Nineveh, the Delta chiefs conspired with Taharqa to co-rule with him, but the plot was discovered and the conspirators were sent to Nineveh. The conspirators were executed in the main centres of Sais, Mendes, and Pelusium as a warning. The chiefs were sent to Nineveh where they were all executed, apart from Necho I of Sais and his son. Necho I was appointed as a kinglet and was returned to Sais and Memphis as the Assyrian vassal, while his son Psammetik was appointed to rule Athribis.[59] In 664 BCE Taharqa's nephew Tantamani succeeded him and, claiming the kingship of Upper and Lower Egypt, sailed through Egypt and invaded the Delta. Necho I of Sais was the only resistance and was killed by Tantamani. The Delta chiefs recognised Tantamani as king, and since Necho I was now dead, sent a deputation to Tantamani led by Pekrur, the ruler of Saft el-Henna.[60] Assurbanipal invaded Egypt again in 664/663 BCE and caused Tantamani to flee to Thebes. The Assyrians followed Tantamani, sacked Thebes, and then probably went on to Napata.[61] This event was the end of Nubian control of Egypt and the Twenty-Fifth Dynasty, but in Napata Tantamani's rule went unchallenged. In the Delta, the start of the Saite Period (Twenty-Sixth

Dynasty) began, with Psammetik I king of the west from the Mediterranean to Memphis, with Athribis and Heliopolis. Psammetik I began imposing his primacy on other districts of the Delta, and by 656 BCE, through the presentation of his daughter Nitocris I to Amun in Thebes and the adoption of Nitocris I by Shepenwepet II and Amenirdis II as the future God's Wife of Amun, he gained the recognition of Thebes, creating a fully unified Egypt.[62]

CHAPTER TWO

SETTLEMENT PATTERNS AND LAND POLICY

As Chapter 1 established the basic relative chronological framework for the period, Chapter 2 establishes the theoretical and archaeological context for the study of landscape and settlements in the Third Intermediate Period. It discusses the approaches to and problems inherent in Egyptian settlement studies regarding landscape reconstruction, the preservation of ancient sites, and defining the concept of 'site'. This chapter also constructs a framework for the understanding of settlement archaeology in the Third Intermediate Period through the analysis of a dataset made up of Third Intermediate Period textual and archaeological material from landscapes and settlements. To work towards the framework for settlement pattern studies, archaeological theory regarding landscape archaeology is outlined in order to establish a methodology to set out the most effective way of approaching Egyptian settlement patterns and define the concept of what is a 'site' in Egyptian settlement archaeology. A comprehensive record of survey, excavation reports, artefacts, and texts must be used in constructing gazetteer data for the Third Intermediate Period site corpus, which simultaneously highlights the research agendas of previous projects and institutions. The 'site' corpus data can then be evaluated to assess its effectiveness for conducting landscape archaeology to see if settlement patterns are visible, the extent to which they are different from those of the New Kingdom, and the factors which may have influenced these patterns with due regard to the limitations of the data.

EARLY NINETEENTH- AND TWENTIETH-CENTURY APPROACHES TO
EGYPTIAN SETTLEMENT STUDIES OF THE THIRD INTERMEDIATE
PERIOD

Before the modern techniques and approaches to Egyptian settlement archaeology of the past few decades, there was a focus by Egyptologists and archaeologists at the end of the nineteenth century and in the early twentieth on the
discovery of objects of artistic beauty, or textual and historical documents
which were valued by museums or private collectors.[1] Work focused on the
temples and cemeteries, particularly those on the desert edges in which the
removal of windblown sand was much easier and more cost-effective compared with the excavation of stratigraphically complex settlements. The diffi-
culty and expense of excavating complex sites was a major factor in the lack of
interest, particularly in the exploration of the Delta region. The environmental
conditions in the Delta also provided difficult working conditions for excavators such as Naville and Petrie. The level of standing water hindered Naville's
excavations at Bubastis,[2] while Petrie's work in February 1884 at Tanis was
hampered by continual storms which created impassable mounds of mud. In
contrast, dust storms in the middle of June the same year, coupled with searing
heat and violent rain, closed Petrie's excavations.[3] Local environmental conditions also made it difficult to access Delta sites. In 1886 Petrie and Griffith
began working at Nebesheh, which was described as being situated in a marshy,
muddy district that was only accessible by wading or swimming in the canals.[4]
Sites on the desert edge, however, produced objects and information immediately, following a simple clearing operation instead of the extensive settlement excavations.[5] Since the 1970s, and especially from the end of the
twentieth century to the beginning of the twenty-first century, there has
been a focus on improving our knowledge of Egyptian settlements, with
emphasis on settlement excavations in the Delta and the Nile Valley. In 2000
at the International Congress of Egyptologists, the then Secretary General of
the Supreme Council of Antiquities, Gaballa Ali Gaballa, made a call for
excavators to focus on the Delta koms and tells. From 2000, applications for
new concessions in Upper Egypt were rejected, unless projects were already
underway, although this has since been reversed. Settlement archaeology has
now expanded to include the reconstruction of the local hydrology and
associated hinterlands using auger boring and geophysical survey, which has
been able to access the remains and extents of buried settlements underneath
both the Nile alluvium and desert sands.[6]

Prior to the new emphasis on Egyptian settlement archaeology, the only
dedicated research on the settlements of the Third Intermediate Period was by
Yoyotte.[7] This philological study discussed only the Delta toponyms documented on the monuments of the Libyan Chiefs of the Delta and Middle

Egypt, including their land donation stelae. Other sources analysed were toponyms listed on the Twenty-Fifth Dynasty Piankhy Stela, and the Assyrian War records of Esarhaddon and Assurbanipal. Yoyotte made several geo-political observations for the Delta, concerning the power bases of the various Delta chiefs and pharaohs. Later, Gomaà[8] focused on the Delta toponyms, building on the work of Yoyotte. Ultimately, both 'topographical' works by Yoyotte and Gomaà comprised a historical survey of local northern rulers using textual evidence, and the focus was restricted mainly to the Delta and on discussions of the toponyms at the expense of the archaeological remains of the settlements. The discussions of the settlements by Yoyotte and Gomaà were also located within the modern Egyptian landscape, as far as possible, but no further analysis was attempted regarding reconstructing the palaeo-topography, the patterns of settlement, or the layout and development of settlements throughout the period in the Delta. Subsequently, there is a large void in our knowledge of how the settlements and settlement patterns in the Delta developed during this period, while almost the entire region of Upper Egypt has been completely neglected. Recent work by Meffre[9] in the region between Heracleopolis and Hermopolis again focuses on the royal and elite monuments to provide a historical synthesis for the region and a detailed study of the local elites, chiefs, and religious clergy, but it does also provide a welcome study of some of the main military establishments in the region.[10] A decade after Gomaà's study on the settlements of the Delta, O'Connor put forward hypotheses regarding the development of Egyptian settlement patterns and internal settlement development.[11] These included the following hypotheses:

1 Settlement patterns probably reflected the way in which the map of real and symbolic power altered, as settlements began to reflect changing political circumstances and their cultural effects.

2 The general pattern of settlement may have changed in response to a new political system, the altered relations between the government and the governed, combined with a prevailing civic insecurity.

3 Settlement layouts may have changed as there were important developments in the sacred landscape, particularly in the royal and dynastic cemeteries, which now lay within the local administrative centre's temple precincts, rather than following the traditional New Kingdom precedent of burial in the Valley of the Kings.

4 The well-distributed settlement patterns of the New Kingdom may have become more concentrated into tighter urban units.

Since O'Connor made these hypotheses in 1983, the state of knowledge regarding the settlements of the Twenty-First to Twenty-Fifth Dynasty has been growing as a result of new archaeological investigations, and many of these hypotheses can now be assessed within the current settlement archaeology evidence. The following sections establish the theoretical and archaeological context for the study of landscape and settlements in the Third Intermediate Period, and discuss the approaches to and problems inherent in Egyptian settlement studies regarding landscape reconstruction, the preservation of sites, and how the concept of 'site' is defined within Egyptology. A framework for the understanding of settlement archaeology in the Third Intermediate Period is constructed through the analysis of the dataset or corpus comprising textual and archaeological material from landscapes and settlements.

THE THEORETICAL, METHODOLOGICAL, AND ARCHAEOLOGICAL CONTEXT FOR INTERROGATING EGYPTIAN SETTLEMENT LANDSCAPES

Methodologies have been developed for the interrogation of Near Eastern landscapes, especially those in alluvial floodplains, using integrated methods of culture historical, processual, and post-processual approaches, and by the assessment of the degree to which parts of the landscape have been lost or obscured as the result of physical transformations and cultural processes.[12] Although these methodologies were developed for Mesopotamia and the Near East, the later cultural and physical taphonomic conditions within the riverine landscape of the Near East have similarities with the development of the alluvial floodplain environments of the Nile Valley and Delta. The methodology for interrogating the landscape of Egypt, not just in the Third Intermediate Period but also for other periods of Egyptian landscape history, is

- identification of the natural environment, geology, and landscape of the Nile Valley and Delta, focusing on potential areas of settlement location and the rationale for their choices;
- establishment of the problems in identifying the ancient landscape due to modern constraints and changes, such as the limits of the cultivable land and its palimpsest character;
- analysis of the effects of the changing hydrological patterns of the Nile and its associated hydrological features, such as canals, on potential settlement patterns and site preservation, and the modern effects of sebakhin (farmers who extract fertiliser derived from the remains of ancient mud-brick buildings) and urbanisation;
- discussion of the way in which archaeologists have debated the concept of 'site';
- definition of the problems in producing a site corpus for Egypt which can be used to identify (or not) settlement patterns. These include off-site survey,

regional preservation rates, site size, and toponyms which cannot be associated with modern locations;

- assembling the datasets and creating a corpus of sites from survey and excavation data, and textual evidence (see Appendix 1);
- assessment of the quality of the evidence to construct a representative sample of sites from all regions in Egypt during a particular period, which will demonstrate the variability in the data, based on text-based versus data-driven (archaeological) evidence, regional site densities, and cemetery locations, and highlight, where possible, chronological developments of site types per region;
- assessment of the administrative documentation relating to systems of land control to determine if there were changes in the geo-economic policies of the administration, or whether there was a continuation of earlier land policies that may affect settlement patterns;
- plotting the militarised institutions and foundations of Egypt in comparison with the previous period, to assess change or adaptation within the internal military organisation and the defence of different regions in relation to local populations, resources, river traffic, and border security;
- providing regional case studies to test the potential for settlement pattern studies within Egyptian archaeology; and, finally,
- establishment of the characteristics of Egyptian settlement patterns at that time, and suggest best practices for the future in settlement pattern studies.

THE NATURAL ENVIRONMENT AND SETTLEMENT LOCATIONS

The natural environment, and in turn the landscape, of Egypt has changed considerably since antiquity. It is complex to reconstruct the palaeo-topography within a floodplain environment, but it is important to create an awareness of the stresses and risks in the landscape, as well as the resulting impact on any dataset of ancient 'sites'. The Nile Valley was carved into the African plateau by the river around 5 to 8 million years ago. After that, the Valley gradually refilled with sediments.[13] At the end of the Late Glacial Maximum, around 12,500 years ago, and the subsequent cooling until around 8,000 years ago, the ice caps melted, producing a rise in the sea level of up to 120 m.[14] The rise in the sea level caused the coastline of the Nile Delta to be further inland than it is today,[15] and created coastal marshes and brackish swamps in the Delta. As the rise of the sea level slowed down, the Delta apex moved seawards, creating the Delta landscape of the Pharaonic Period around 4000 BCE, or earlier, with its main channels, smaller distributaries, and levees meandering around large sand hills ('turtle backs' or geziras) rising above the floodplain. These geziras created high areas for settlements above the annual inundation. The 10 km wide Nile Valley is bounded on each side by large cliffs and is flat bottomed.[16] The desertification of the grasslands adjacent to the Nile Valley began from ca. 7000 BCE,[17] in the Saharan Neolithic. Sand from the Sahara was blown into the Nile Valley,[18] modifying the geography of the sides of the Nile canyon and causing the previous Palaeolithic settlements to move away from the marginal terraces of the Nile Valley into the floodplain, particularly on to the river levees.[19] Active levees on the erosional side of the river were not a rational choice for a settlement. The lateral migration of the Nile endangered the survival of these settlement types.[20] For example, the settlement of Thebes was situated on an active levee. The threat of the Nile, and the effect of high floods destroying settlements, are described in the Year 3 inscription of Osorkon III in Luxor temple.[21] This flood was ca. 70 cm higher than an abundant flood, which was considered ideal for agriculture, and it proved catastrophic for the mud-brick houses of Thebes.[22] The inscription states 'the inhabitants of his city are like swimmers in a wave'.[23] Later, in the reign of Taharqa in the Twenty-Fifth Dynasty, there was another high flood episode.[24] Repeated high flooding events are characteristic of the ninth to seventh century BCE compared with earlier periods,[25] with implications for settlements in general during the Third Intermediate Period throughout Egypt.

The sinuosity and braiding of the Nile had a fundamental effect on the landscape within fixed periods of time and led to dynamic and complex settlement pattern developments. The Nile had an important impact on both the choice of land for settlement and the subsequent destruction of field systems.[26] This has created a cyclical pattern of construction and destruction which occurred within relatively short but irregular periods of time, as the Nile began to move away from existing settlements that relied on proximity to the river to function. At the same time, the migration of the Nile caused other sites to become more prosperous as the river moved closer. In archaeological terms, the fluctuating sinuosity of the Nile and the braiding effects caused the destruction and concealment of settlements which make an accurate reconstruction of the different scales of habitation difficult for different periods.

There may have been more bars and islands in antiquity than in the modern Nile landscape.[27] The alluvial islands, created by the river's dynamics, were an important resource for agriculture: small-scale farming communities, animal grazing, and settlement extensions could become attached to the floodplain when minor channels silted up, thus allowing for settlement expansion.[28] Islands are as high as, if not higher than, the surrounding floodplain because their proximity to the river meant a greater sediment deposition occurred on them than on the surrounding floodplain. The advantages of islands, including their height, proximity to the river, preservation, and cosmological significance, made them an ideal location for the siting of a new settlement.[29] This type of dynamic landscape, with the foundation, development, and abandonment of settlements based on fluctuating hydrology, is a key theme for understanding the evolution of settlement patterns at regional levels, the development of political houses, and regional power plays.

In the Nile Delta, the most important settlements lay on 'turtle backs' (geziras) in the immediate vicinity of the main Nile branches. These sites developed as centres for their outlying hinterlands. Settlements distant from the main river branches were dependent on the larger settlements, and in exchange the smaller settlements would have probably supplied resources to the larger centres, which were located on the traffic routes.[30] The most important political settlements of Egypt would have depended on vast agricultural hinterland areas, and would have acted as 'magnets drawing in people and resources'.[31] The most important Delta settlements lay not only on, or near, a main river branch, along levees, and on spacious geziras, but on important points of junction. Many of the nome capitals were established where land routes met the main waterways.[32] Other nome centres developed at the junctions of land routes from the desert, especially to the east from Asia, at Tanis, and the Libyan Desert to the west, such as at Edfu, Huw, Akhmim, Asyut, and Hermopolis, while some were on wadi fans such as Hierakonpolis.

There was a strong element of geographical determinism in the location of settlements, leading the function and developmental history of settlements to differ. Some settlements were better suited as trade or staple market centres, or collection and distribution centres for the administration. The produce of smaller centres had to be moved from initial starting points to the main cities through an interactive riverine-lacustrine-marine system, which gave new powers to certain settlements along the way.[33] The system of settlements, water networks, and their focal destinations was flexible within a system of political change, but was often at the expense of settlements that diminished in size, or were abandoned when the waterways no longer served the larger centres.[34] Other settlements had military and strategic importance, while some settlements controlled trade to and from other countries, or areas away from the Nile Valley and Delta.[35]

The hinterlands of both the Nile Delta and the Valley were important for the economy and character of settlements.[36] The sites located at crossroads, trade centres, and staple market areas, nomes, or districts were a stimulus to the concentration of populations.[37] Placing the Third Intermediate Period settlements within the contemporary geological and hydrological settings, as far as is possible, is vital for understanding the roles settlements performed and the associated settlement patterns that developed.

CONSTRUCTING ANCIENT HYDROLOGY AND SETTLEMENT LOCATIONS

The river Nile acted as a trade network and water supply,[38] as well as a land barrier and territorial zone marker, which provided defensive capabilities. The alluvial landscape of Egypt was in a continuous state of flux owing to its dynamic hydrologic nature. Many ancient settlements are known thanks to their citations in ancient texts, but many of them are not archaeologically located on the ground because the waterways near the sites have changed since antiquity. The mobility of the settlements is inextricably linked to the fluctuating hydrological conditions of the Nile.

Although the Nile was one of the most important aspects for the functioning of a settlement, it was often the most uncontrollable part of the landscape, which in turn dictated the location, prosperity, and ultimately the eventual decline of many important settlements. The Nile migrates within its channels, but the Nile's migration, and its relationship to archaeological sites, remains little studied.[39] Before the construction of the Aswan High Dam in the 1960s, the migration of the Nile increased in rate during the high flood seasons until it burst its banks during the flood, but migration was negligible when the Nile was low.[40] Seasonal variations had important consequences for settlements. The medieval geographies of the Nile Valley confirm that the route of the main Nile through Upper Egypt from the First Cataract to Cairo was much as it is today, not perhaps at the level of every meander, but at least in its overall form and route.[41] Lateral migration of the main channel has been estimated at around 2 m per year over a period of one hundred years.[42] There has been a predominantly eastward migration of the Nile since the Ptolemaic Period. The course of the main Nile during the Ptolemaic Period was probably along the axis of the pharaonic Nile between ca. 2900 and 332 BCE.[43]

Research carried out so far does not provide a comprehensive picture of the position and fluctuations of the Nile in Upper Egypt, but detailed geological analysis of specific locations is useful in determining the factors which affected settlement location and the parameters for understanding settlement patterns. In the case of the Third Intermediate Period, with its settlements underneath modern towns and/or field systems, it is even more difficult to detect the towns and villages and their relationship to the Nile. Nevertheless, some key case studies have been undertaken in the regions of Akhmim,[44] Sohag,[45] Memphis,[46] and Thebes, where either a topographic feature or detailed geological analysis has been able to highlight the potential to understand the link between landscape and settlement dynamics.[47]

In association with the main Nile branch in Upper Egypt was the Bahr Yusef. The Bahr Yusef connected the Nile Valley with the Faiyum depression. The presence of a parallel waterway to the Nile in Middle Egypt is important for understanding the potential landscapes of the Third Intermediate Period in this area. Such a parallel waterway to the Nile suggests that, in between, a more discrete landscape and settlement network may have developed. The start point of the Bahr Yusef varies according to different geographical writers, suggesting a gradual movement upstream over time.[48] The Bahr Yusef ran parallel with the main Nile on its western periphery until it reached Lahun.[49] From Lahun, the Harawat canal continues into the Faiyum, much like it did in ancient times.[50] The presence of settlements bordering the Bahr Yusef, such as Oxyrhynchus, confirms the presence of this waterway in some form during the Third Intermediate Period.

In the Nile Delta, the situation is more complex because of several important river branches, smaller distributaries, and canals, and, as a result, the reconstruction of the floodplain is problematic for any one period, including the Third Intermediate Period. Later, Chapter 3 discusses the inter-regional settlement patterns of the Delta and provides a detailed discussion concerning the topography of the Third Intermediate Period Delta to better understand the settlement patterns and connections, with subsequent implications for political, socio-economic, and land management. The following sections discuss the cultural processes that directly resulted in the selective loss of the ancient landscape features. These include ancient and modern land reclamation projects, later taphonomic developments, sebakh extraction, and the impact of modern demographics and increasing urbanisation.

ANCIENT AND MODERN LAND RECLAMATION

Since the end of the Third Intermediate Period in 664 BCE, the limits of the cultivable land of the Delta and Nile Valley have been altered drastically by human intervention, although the area of the cultivable floodplain in Upper Egypt at times of reasonably good floods has remained similar to that of ancient times.[51] During the Ptolemaic Period (310–30 BCE), intensive reclamation projects were carried out in the Faiyum, as well as at the Delta margins, by Ptolemy II (282–246 BCE) and Ptolemy III (246–222 BCE).[52] The introduction of the *saqiya* (an animal-powered water wheel) and the Archimedes screw in the Ptolemaic Period caused an increase in the available arable land of the Nile Valley.[53] The modern process of land reclamation was initiated in the nineteenth century by Mohammed Ali al-Mas'ud Ibn Agha (Mohammed Ali) (1769–1849 CE).[54] Initial land reclamation schemes were limited to expanding the cultivable land adjacent to the ancient cultivated borders. Mohammed Ali initiated the digging of new canals which doubled the capacity of the irrigation canals. The cleaning of alluvial mud from the canals regularly allowed perennial irrigation of huge tracts of land in Lower Egypt, where, eventually, the basin systems of irrigation all but disappeared. The area of cultivated land increased between 1813 and the 1830s by around 18 per cent.[55] The first large-scale modern land reclamation projects, focusing on land away from the main river channels, began in 1948 with the Abis Project to the south-west of Alexandria.[56] After the Egyptian Revolution in 1952, the new government's policy was one of increased agricultural production through the horizontal expansion and reclamation of desert lands.[57] Abdul Nasser launched land reclamation projects to directly address the slow rate of expansion in cultivated land areas in a response to rapid population growth. The department of the Permanent Organization for Land Reclamation was established in 1952, and from 1966, it conducted these projects, along with several other agencies including the Egyptian Authority for the Utilisation and Development of Reclaimed Land (EAUDRL).[58] One such project was the 'Tahrir Province Project' (west of the Delta and south of Alexandria) run by Magdi Hassanein in 1954,[59] which reclaimed ca. 78,000 feddan (32,760 ha).[60] Between 1960 and 1970 almost 500,000 feddan (210,000 ha) was brought under cultivation. Most projects from 1952 to 1982, and especially prior to 1973, were conducted on the heavier soils of the northern Delta where the reclamation requirements were drainage and the desalinisation of water-logged and saline lands.[61] Later, in 1987, the Mubarak Project was initiated in which 80,000 feddans (33,600 ha) of land were reclaimed from the western side of the Delta.[62] In the eighty-five years from 1930 to 2015 the Foreign Agricultural Service (FAS) Cairo estimates land reclamation efforts in Egypt yielded an additional 2.6 million feddan (1.09 million ha) of agricultural land. This is equivalent to an increase of 44 per cent in those years. In 2009, the Ministry of Agriculture announced a land reclamation goal in which they laid out a plan to reclaim an additional 3 million feddan (1.26 million ha) by 2030. The political and economic situation in 2011 halted this project, but in 2014 Egyptian president Abdel Fattah el-Sisi announced the programme would move forward starting with 1.5 million feddan (4,200 ha) near the oasis of Farafa in the Western Desert.[63]

The modern reclamation projects have transformed the way in which the Delta and Nile Valley landscapes appear compared with ancient times. They have artificially enlarged the ancient cultivated land boundaries, reclaiming previous marshland and riverine environments, increased crop and fish farming, and reclaimed land for new urban projects. The ancient sites of Kom Abu Billo, Kom el-Hisn, and Kom el-Abqa'in in the western Delta that once bordered the fringes of the desert are now located in newly reclaimed zones of land for farming and urban expansion. Many sites, as well as the agricultural landscape, have been lost or reduced in size. The new environmental settings of sites have distorted and removed them from within their original topographical settings, affecting our understanding of the sites' original environmental setting and function. The same criteria apply to eastern Delta sites such as Tell Belim and Tell el-Balamun that were once located in the marshlands and coastal areas of the Mediterranean Sea. Both sites are now located inland in areas of saline march or desalinated Delta lands which provide a false sense of their original topographic and environmental location.

Nile Valley sites have also been affected by the shifting river channels, overbuilding, and land-grabbing, for example at Hermopolis, Qaw el-Kebir

(Antaeopolis), el-Hibeh, and Shutb. By reconstructing the approximate boundaries of the Nile Delta and Valley prior to the land reclamation projects begun by Mohammed Ali, the ancient settlements, and their functions, along with the settlement patterns, can be reconstructed more accurately within the contemporary ancient landscape. The cultivable land boundaries at the time of the Third Intermediate Period were more complex as they are obscured by Ptolemaic–Roman, Late Antique, and modern Egyptian adaptations to both the built and natural environment. The reconstruction of land use can be no more than an educated guess but provides a baseline for further analysis of Third Intermediate Period settlements and the associated landscape.

SEBAKHIN AND MUD-BRICK EXTRACTION

The activities of sebakhin (mud-brick farmers) who extracted vast quantities of mud-brick remains from ancient settlements have caused a devastating impact on our understanding of Egyptian sites. *Sebakh*, translated as 'manure/fertiliser', is derived from the remains of mud-brick buildings, which make up most ancient Egyptian settlement mounds. The bricks are mined out because they are rich in nitrogen from the Nile silt and occupational material from the ancient settlements.[64] The sebakh is spread over the fields to enhance the nitrogen levels in the soil, or it was used to create saltpetre in the manufacture of gunpowder. Sebakh farming was conducted on a large scale from 1830 to 1930, after which the digging of mud-brick by large industrial companies was officially banned, although mud-brick extraction still occurs in the present day, especially in the Nile Delta where settlement mounds are in remote and unprotected areas.[65] This threat to Egyptian sites was reiterated by Habachi in the mid-twentieth century when he stated, 'Many important ruins have not been excavated, but have been left to the sebakhin who are still very active. Sooner or later these ruins disappear, leaving a few traces or no traces at all of the importance of the old cities they used to represent.'[66] The Egyptian Antiquities Department, founded in 1858, could not prevent the removal of the sebakh and, in some cases, even licensed its extraction.[67] It was not until 1901 that the Antiquities Service presented to the Ministry of Public Works, the Ministry of the Interior, and the Ministry of Finances 'Instructions sur le sébakh'.[68] In 1910, the Ministry of Public Works issued a decree concerning the removal of sebakh, requiring that permission should be sought from the Antiquities Service, which would organise the observation and surveillance of the earth removal on ancient sites.[69] There were 545 tells/koms to which the decree applied and they were arranged by inspectorates and districts from the Delta to Aswan. Most of the sites were in the Delta, Middle Egypt, and the Faiyum and only a few were in Upper Egypt.[70] By the time the new regulations were enacted, the mounds at some sites had already been largely removed, for example at Sais, Sakha, and Naukratis. The work continued at others, although with supervision from regional inspectors such as Georges Daressy, who documented his work at these sites in the Annales du Service des Antiquités de l'Égypte from 1893 to 1930.

MODERN URBANISM

The urban demography of Egypt in the modern era has had an impact on the preservation of ancient sites. The population of Egypt in 1897 was approximately 10 million; it grew at a slow rate of 1.3 per cent per annum from 1897 to 1947, but accelerated to around 2.5 per cent from 1950 to 1970.[71] Following the Second World War, there was a new era of accelerated growth in urbanisation. The population of people living in cities in 1910 was 10 per cent and by 1975, had increased to 30 per cent. From 2010 to 2015 the annual urban population growth was 1.7 per cent, while the rural population growth was 1.6 per cent, with an overall urban population in 2014 of 43.1 per cent.[72] Egypt and the Arab world is now the most urbanised global region after Latin America. The growth in population was due to a natural increase within the cities themselves and the migration of people from rural to semi-rural areas. Improved medical technology from western Europe led to a steady decline in mortality, but left fertility rates at high levels. From 1975 to 1980 fertility rates increased to 2.5 per cent, and then 2.6 per cent in 1980–5. Between 2010 and 2015 there was an annual population growth of 1.6 per cent with approximate population density of 83.3 people per km^2.[73] Egypt is now the most populated Arab country with a population of around 83 million people in 2015,[74] growing by 1.76 per cent each year. The population is set to rise to 150 million by the year 2050, with continued growth through the end of the century. Egypt's total land area is 995,450 km^2, but only 3.6 per cent is arable land.[75] As the rural population grows this places pressures on the available amounts of cultivable land despite the numerous land reclamation policies. Urban populations have grown, and from 1984 to 2007 the rate of urban encroachment on arable lands was 13,000 ha per year and, since January 2011, this has increased to 21,000 ha per year. The lack of habitable space in the floodplain has caused many modern settlements to encroach upon the ancient sites in search for available land, further affecting the original setting and the preservation of the sites within their associated landscapes.

THE CONCEPT OF SITE IN EGYPTOLOGY

To progress to the discussion of settlements and how they have been recognised within the Egyptian archaeological record, it is first necessary to understand what constitutes a site, as this has implications for survey and artefact find-spot data. Site identification creates a baseline for the different types of empirical data analysed for the Third Intermediate Period. Archaeologists have long considered the concept of site within archaeology. The designers of regional surveys have each defined the concept of what constitutes a site, as this is commonly a unit, if not the unit of analysis. Explicit definitions of what sites are were routinely lacking until the mid-twentieth century. Sites can be defined as 'any place, large or small where there are to be found traces of activity, where artefacts were present'.[76] The site was recognised as an empirical unit, offering it as a special cluster of cultural features or items, or both.[77] The formal characteristics of a site are defined by its form, context, and the spatial and associated structure of the population's cultural items and features present. There are two contrasting extreme views of the concept of site: some archaeologists view sites as composing the entirety of the archaeological record, with the areas in between them constituting archaeological voids. Conversely, sites are only one manifestation of archaeological remains, appearing as high densities of artefacts to be distinguished from off-site areas of low density.[78] The site as an empirical notion was discarded by Dunnell[79] in favour of a site-less concept of the archaeological record which views an artefact as the basic unit of observation in a world of varying concentrations of artefacts on or near the surface. Most definitions of site recognise a site as a valid empirical unit expressed as a spatial phenomenon. A site is a finitely bounded place, though often its extent is difficult to determine.[80] There are seven different demarcations of site category outlined by Tainter:[81]

1 *behavioural*: any locus intentionally used by human populations;
2 *arbitrary*: a place which meets the criteria of (artefact) density or presence;
3 *inclusive*: any archaeological manifestation, including isolated items or activity;
4 *research potential*: a place whose information potential cannot be fully explored at the time of discovery;
5 *research objective*: varies with the research goals of different projects;
6 *content-based*: excludes or includes sites based on a list of conditions; and
7 *density-based*: varies with local abundance, i.e. if there are fewer archaeological materials, requirements are lower and a greater proportion of sites are recorded.

These definitions of site may not be inclusive or sensitive enough, however, particularly in areas of low artefact density. They are not operationalised or consistently defined for heritage managers and rely too much on the arbitrary definitions of the person classifying the areas.[82] For this study on settlement patterns, the author has chosen to define 'site' by the presence of physical material culture and textual evidence of human habitation and occupation activity, whether this was for short or sustained periods of time, and this activity can be conducted at the domestic, administrative, military, cultic, or funerary level.

The concept of site within Egyptology has gradually developed from a monument or place where antiquities were extracted, to become valued in the social, scientific, and cultural aspects of the ancient Mediterranean world.[83] Over time Egyptian sites have become legal entities, the boundaries of which are continually negotiated and at times reified by Egyptologists and government officials. By the mid-twentieth century, academic methods of site recording and mapping accommodated questions concerning short- and long-term dynamic human and environmental processes, questions which necessitated tighter spatial control of artefacts, deposits, and measurements.[84] Sites, or more properly archaeological lands, have only recently emerged in the bureaucratic sphere as a spatial entity bounded on cadastral maps and established by decree.[85] The potential parameters and problems for understanding sites in Egypt can be illustrated in the following ways, such as fragmented landscapes, off-site surveys, and site size.

FRAGMENTED LANDSCAPES IN MODERN EGYPT

The impact of the sebakhin and the land reclamation projects fragmented ancient sites into smaller units which may have once formed part of the same politically administered area or constituted elements of the same site. This has occurred mainly in the Nile Delta; for example, Tell Gadiya, which once belonged to the tell of Leontopolis, is now a small, disconnected mound.[86] Land fragmentation therefore poses a problem in constructing regional site densities, whereby large sites could have had satellite elements, on the same tell area or associated hinterland. Equally, Tell Gadiya could have been part of the same urban area of Leontopolis which was spatially disengaged and fragmented due to modern sebakhin or land reclamation activity. This identifies the problem of quantifying such sites as they may distort the real number of settlements in an area. Tell Gadiya may indicate nome centres had districts and subsidiary elements around them, when and where the landscape permitted. Sites may have comprised districts or multiple differently named areas designated in the literature as appearing to be separate settlement locations, which cannot be defined as they have not yet been located archaeologically. Sites may have had multiple different topographical designations associated with them and were not designated by a single toponym. For example, Edfu is referred to as both 𓉐𓂝𓏤𓊖 Djebau and 𓊍𓈖𓏏𓊖 Behedet on the Twenty-First Dynasty Onomasticon of Amenemope. Site names can also change over time. The 'Five Great Fortresses of the Sherden' changed to the 'Five Great Fortresses of the Ma' based on a new political order at the start of the Twenty-Second Dynasty.[87] Different scribes may have recorded the same place but spelled it differently using different phonetic hieroglyphic signs. Sites may be abbreviated, given informal names, or named in regional dialects in nonadministrative texts. Religious texts may refer to sites differently using sacred toponyms or using names for sacred areas as the name of the whole site. This means there can be a mismatch between site survey data, ancient site complexes, and between textually attested and archaeological 'sites'.

'OFF-SITE' SURVEYS AND EGYPTIAN ARCHAEOLOGY

Off-site surveys have been used effectively in Mesopotamian landscape archaeology.[88] They have allowed for the assessment of landscape phenomena, the degree of population concentration, and the intensity of agricultural and pastoral land use in between nucleated tell sites, particularly of the early Bronze Age. The assumption that any artefact scatter represented a settlement or tomb is a historical by-product, the details of which are only known through excavation.[89] Off-site surveys entail walking systematic transects between sites or grid patterns of sample points. Through the collection of field scatters and pinpointing minor artefact scatters, off-site surveys have enabled survey data in north Mesopotamia to be compared with intensive survey data from around the Mediterranean.[90] Early Bronze Age sites in Mesopotamia are surrounded by low density scatters of abraded artefacts classified as field scatters. These scatters are interpreted as the result of agricultural intensification in which settlement-derived debris was spread on fields around the settlement as manure in attempts to increase crop yields.[91] Off-site surveys preserve traces of ancient road systems radiating out of tell sites that connected them with their satellite sites, as well as their associated agricultural and pasture land.[92]

Conducting off-site surveys in Egypt is problematic owing to the nature of the post-depositional effects of the sedimentation of the Nile and the spreading of sebakh-waste on the surrounding agricultural land. The Egypt Exploration Society (EES) Delta Survey utilised this material culture sampling strategy and has produced good results for the chronology of some Delta sites. Caution, however, must be applied to the assumption that there is a relationship between what is found on the surface and what is actually below the ground. This may be the case in European and American field survey, but the taphonomic nature of site development in Egypt means that correlating what is found in surface survey and what is beneath the ground can be problematic. Studies have shown that fieldwalking on tell sites and surface collections of sherds are biased in favour of later periods,[93] unless sites were abandoned at specific periods and never resettled, such as the New Kingdom city of Amarna in Middle Egypt. The under-representation of the earlier periods and over-representation of the later periods can be slightly mitigated by scraping the surface by 50 mm to collect potsherds,[94] although the earlier dated sherds will only be expected if the level of occupation is less than 0.5 m from the surface. The interpretation of site signatures from disturbed contexts, such as ploughzones (where the top

0.3 m of archaeology is destroyed), provides other biases.[95] Those artefacts and sherds found in plough soil will only represent between 0.3 per cent and 15 per cent (usually ca. 5–6 per cent) of the artefacts present at a site. Fieldwalking must be complemented by exploratory excavation techniques if the site is to be assessed for its archaeological potential and site stratigraphy.[96] The presence of surface pottery only indicates a site was active at a certain point in time, and it is not possible to ascertain what level of occupation there was, or whether it was expansive, long-term human habitation, or a small area and short-time nomadic activity. The current state of pottery studies for the Third Intermediate Period further compounds the problem. Without explicit reference to royal objects associated with the assemblages, the close dating of Third Intermediate Period pottery to dynasties or reigns is difficult to establish. The re-use of stone monuments can also create an effect of a false-positive in a site chronology. Monuments created at earlier points in time with earlier royal names, and also those of private individuals, were sometimes transported to other sites to embellish new settlements; they can create the false impression of royal and monumental activity at sites which were founded at later dates. The classic cases are the transfer of the monuments of the Ramesside capital at Qantir to Tanis in the Third Intermediate Period, and the re-use of pharaonic monuments primarily from Delta sites in the building of the new Ptolemaic capital at Alexandria.[97]

TELL FORMATION IN EGYPT

The nature of tell formation and the subsequent taphonomic developments such as biological, chemical, and mechanical destruction prompted by both human and climatic factors have had an impact on the post-depositional processes that have affected how we interpret tell development and stratigraphic preservation.[98] Tell sites can be equated with major 'settlements' and provided prominent and immobile features of the landscape even after they had been abandoned. The taphonomic development of tell sites can affect the way in which site chronologies are obtained. Tells are the long-term effect of repeated human occupation on a single site, with composite occupation strata, destruction levels, and naturally deposited sediments.[99] They represent multiple, partly superimposed settlement phases. After the Third Intermediate Period, new occupations of the Late Period, Ptolemaic–Roman, and Late Antique Period partially or totally cover Third Intermediate Period levels, so that only a small percentage of surface deposits are visible and available for analysis, providing a reduced data area for interpretation such as at Buto, Sais, and Dendera. This scenario is especially prevalent on tell sites in Egypt, as the surrounding floodplain limits occupation space, forcing later occupations to build on top of the earlier periods. The partial or complete levelling of previous structures, entire tell surfaces, pit digging which interferes with the underlying stratigraphic matrix, and irregular rebuilding phases create a smaller horizontal area over time as the tell becomes taller.[100] The building material used on tells is predominantly mud-brick, with some fired brick from the Late Dynastic to Ptolemaic–Roman Period, and stone is used for temples and tombs. The mud-brick structures are mixed in with redeposited silts, stratified settlement deposits, and the debris of their own collapse and decay. Other depositional and erosional processes in operation since the end of the Third Intermediate Period include erosion of tell surface and climatic effects. Tell sites in Egypt are also exposed to wind, rainfall, ground water, and humidity, which are the most destructive natural threats for mud-brick.[101] These factors have eroded tell sites so that many are now reduced to the modern ground level.[102] The gradual deposition of alluvial sediments around the bases of tells, particularly those in the Delta, has raised the surrounding ground level. Since the construction of the Aswan High Dam in the 1960s, these sedimentation levels have probably reduced. The full horizontal and vertical limits of tells are visually obscured by the modern floodplain, but can be assessed through non-invasive methods such as magnetometry and coring.

THE SIZE OF 'SITES' IN EGYPT

One of the most important types of information collected for the analysis of site distributions, which leads to a better understanding of settlement patterns, is an estimate of the overall size of each site. The larger the site area was should indicate its position within the hierarchical system of political and economically important settlements. Ranking of size estimates is one of the critical initial steps of analysis necessary before more sophisticated levels of distributional analysis can be conducted.[103] The problem of site area sizes distorts the documentation of regional settlement systems, which can be observed in Aegean settlement pattern studies.[104] Drill augering in conjunction with local ceramic and material culture datasets can be used to define the horizontal limit and the vertical depth of the longevity of the occupation of a site. This approach is demonstrated at Buto through a long-term drill coring programme which provided good results regarding the accumulation of different activity phases.[105] The ancient landscapes in Egypt, however, are not as well preserved as those in Mesopotamia and the Aegean. The same detailed analysis as performed for Mesopotamian and Aegean landscape studies is not possible, so expectations of what can be achieved in Egypt are lower. The Third Intermediate Period evidence at this moment regarding settlement pattern studies can only provide a broad indication of the chronological range of all sites. Better-defined and specific diagnostic ceramic forms, more complete stratigraphic records of individual sites, and individual and restricted time phases based on artefact analysis are required to define dynastic attributions for most sites in this study. For the purposes of Chapter 2 of this book, the analysis will focus on the settlement distribution for the Third Intermediate Period within a geographical and regional context rather than detailed intra-site comparisons. Intra-site comparisons are discussed in Chapter 3 using a well-defined chronological group of sites to assess the development of the built environments of different settlements in different geographical and political regions.

ARCHAEOLOGICAL SURVEY IN EGYPT

Archaeological surveys in Egypt since 1798 have contributed different sets of information and types of data to the archaeological picture of the Third Intermediate Period, particularly in relation to the identification of Third Intermediate Period settlements and burial grounds. In 1798 Napoleon conquered Egypt and the subsequent expedition of the savants led to the creation of the multi-volume *Description de l'Égypte*. It mapped the political condition, natural history, and antique wonders of Egypt for a European audience.[106] The efforts of the savants to document the entire country were broad in scope and relied upon the compilation of cartographic maps and plans from limited, ground-based measurements.[107] The plates in the catalogue positioned toponyms on maps with special attention to their biblical and classical connotations, with the savants building on earlier travellers' accounts. Ancient sites were documented with their approximate position recorded on a regional map at 1:100,000 scale, or larger. Most details were rendered in impressionistic fashion as if they were viewed from the ground. Temple walls, columns, pylons, modern houses, and debris mounds were plotted with the aid of Gunter's chains and a plane table.[108] A result of Napoleon's campaign was the discovery of the Rosetta Stone, a bilingual inscription which played a role in the decipherment of the Egyptian scripts by Jean-François Champollion (1790–1832 CE). Most texts were not repositories of esoteric knowledge but dealt with historical, administrative, and secular matters, and routine aspects of religious cults.[109] Ippolito Rosellini (1800–43 CE), in 1829, and Karl Lepsius (1810–84 CE), between 1849 and 1859, led further expeditions to Egypt to record the temples and tombs, and the monumental inscriptions associated with them.[110] John Gardner Wilkinson visited Egypt in 1821, a year before Champollion, and remained in Egypt for the next twelve years, returning in 1842, 1848–9, and finally 1855–6. Wilkinson visited many sites and copied the inscriptions and scenes, and much of his archive still awaits evaluation. Consulting Wilkinson's copies has solved many problems as they show the monuments as they were between 1821 and 1856. Many of the Theban non-royal tombs have been damaged or destroyed since Wilkinson's recording, while others, including entire tombs, still await publication, or are now inaccessible.[111] Later, between 1905 and 1907, James Breasted (1865–1935 CE) extended the recording of monuments and texts throughout Nubia.[112]

The British Survey of Egypt from 1898 to 1948 was a systematic cadastral survey of the countryside. The main purpose was to gain topographic data for tax revenues from the agricultural economy base of the country.[113] The ruins, tells, and other ancient features were demarcated and labelled and placed on the maps, which varied in scale from 1:500 to 1:250,000 from 1903 to 1947. These maps remain the authoritative source for identifying, naming, and delineating archaeological sites in Egypt. In the twentieth century the Service des Antiquities implemented the policy of mapping out site boundaries with reference to the Survey of Egypt maps.[114]

In the late nineteenth and early twentieth century the Egypt Exploration Fund (EEF), later to become the Egypt Exploration Society (EES), conducted rescue excavations and survey work at sites which were disappearing because of sebakh mining and the agricultural expansion in the Nile Delta.[115] Naville[116] and Petrie[117] worked at Nebesheh, Tanis, and Naukratis, mainly because of the biblical or classical connections of sites. George Hogarth visited sites in Kafr el-Sheikh province which were mentioned on papyri and in classical sources. Many sites were inaccessible owing to the marshlands surrounding them.[118]

In the Delta, there was infrequent archaeological interest in survey work until relatively modern times. The local offices of the Egyptian Antiquities Organisation (EAO) (later the Supreme Council of Antiquities (SCA), and now the Ministry of State for Antiquities (MSA)) conducted a large amount of work in the Delta, reported through the *Annales du Service des Antiquités de l'Égypte*. A survey of the western Delta to identify ancient sites was conducted by André Bernand using cartographic and Ptolemaic–Roman lexicographical sources,[119] while toponyms mentioned in Christian and Islamic sources of the Arab Period were studied by Stefan Timm.[120]

The archaeological and geological survey of the Austrian–German team at Tell el-Daba/Qantir demonstrated that detailed regional survey alongside geological work could result in the identification of important buried archaeological strata.[121] Since Bietak's work at Tell el-Daba/Qantir in 1975, archaeological surveys have shown the archaeological potential of the Delta sites. Surveys were conducted in the western Delta at Naukratis and its surrounding hinterland.[122] The University of Liverpool surveyed an area in Sharqiya province, around the modern city of Zagazig.[123] Surface surveys in Sharqiya province were conducted by the University of Amsterdam directed by van den Brink in a 30 km² area around Qantir.[124] This survey produced good results for the Predynastic/Early Dynastic periods and the New Kingdom. The Italian Archaeological Mission of the CSRL-Venice to the eastern Delta in 1987 surveyed from Mendes and Gezirat Sangaha to Tanis.[125] In the easternmost part of the Delta, especially the coastal area by the mouth of the Pelusiac branch, forty sites from different periods were surveyed by a French mission interested in the eastern frontier.[126] In the central Delta, as part of the Buto concession, Ballet and von der Way visited and conducted a pottery survey of nearby sites.[127] At Mendes, SPOT (System pour l'Observation de la Terre), a remote sensing multispectral imaging technology, was utilised to determine the settlement patterns in the surrounding area and to locate buried tell sites with positive results.[128] Remote sensing assisted survey techniques were used to understand the geology and hydrology in the south-western Delta.[129] In the modern province of Beheira, sixty-three sites were surveyed,[130] with further survey work in the region of Lake Mareotis to the west of Alexandria and along the northern coast.[131]

In the eastern Delta, the Polish archaeological survey in the Sharqiya governate built upon the previous work by the University of Amsterdam, the CSRL-Venice, and the University of Liverpool by surveying Tell el-Murra and the surrounding hinterland.[132] In 2006, the EAIS GIS project was established and the 'GIS Center' became an official department within the Ministry of State for Antiquities (MSA). This department collected and analysed spatial data of all registered archaeological sites in Egypt. The database contained information on the location, legal status, archaeological contents, and current threats to the sites. So far two volumes have been published, those of Sharqiya province and Rosetta.[133] The EES's comprehensive Delta Survey Project begun in 1997–8 was developed by Jeffrey Spencer as a way of collating a photographic, bibliographic, and descriptive catalogue of Delta sites.[134] The project makes the information available to researchers and archaeologists via a dedicated website.[135] The aim of the project was to focus on the inspection of remote or less well-known sites, identified from various editions of the Survey of Egypt maps.[136] As a first stage of information gathering, visits were made to ascertain whether the sites still existed, and then the survey teams assessed their current size, the nature (and if possible the date) of archaeological deposits, at least of the surface layer, and any other ancillary information from local sources.[137] So far, hundreds of sites have been documented in the provinces of Beheira, Kafr el-Sheikh, Minufiyeh, Daqhaliya, Qalubiya, and Sharqiya, and more are regularly added to the Delta Survey online database.[138] In Middle Egypt, remote sensing and coring survey in the area around Amarna has located thirty-seven previously unknown sites and potential ancient river courses.[139]

Modern survey methods are utilised within Egyptology to complement traditional non-destructive techniques. The methods include geophysical survey and remote sensing using satellite imagery along with drill auger coring. Geophysical surveys have been used widely in Egypt at different site types[140] and the magnetic method has been successful at defining site plans at the upper levels,[141] owing to the presence of magnetic iron oxides in the Nile silt, which was the primary building material in the Nile Valley and Delta.[142] Archaeologists have been able to access the remains and extents of buried settlements in the Delta,[143] the Faiyum,[144] and the Oases.[145]

Remote sensing surveys using satellite imagery (CORONA, Landsat, SPOT), Shuttle Imaging RADAR-C (SIR-C), X-Band Shuttle Aperture RADAR (X-SAR), and multispectral and high-resolution satellite images,[146] as well as open source software such as GoogleEarth, can trace defunct waterways and define topographical features on the ground, including ancient buildings and settlements concealed by the alluvium and sand.[147] They can be used to track the rate of site destruction due to population growth, urban expansion, and looting.[148] Auger boring has been used in conjunction with these new methods to access the vertical stratigraphy of the settlements underneath the Nile alluvium and the desert sands to provide taphonomic data as to how these sites developed as well as associated hydrological information.[149] Early results from electrical resistance tomography and ground penetrating radar at Thebes (Karnak Waterways Project)[150] and Quesna[151] suggest that combinations of techniques can build up palaeo-topographies into which archaeological data can be fitted.

ANCIENT TEXTS OF THE THIRD INTERMEDIATE PERIOD

Surveys and archaeological excavation data relating to the identification of settlements can be supplemented by texts found on papyrus documents, as well as in royal, private, and administrative texts from monuments. The vast majority of ancient texts that survive from the Third Intermediate Period are papyri that relate to burial rituals, such as the Book of the Dead and the Book of Gates, most of which have been found in elite burials at Thebes.[152] As well as the funerary papyri, oracular amuletic decrees, or 'divine deliberations' transcribed on to papyri, were popular in the theocratic state of Amun at Thebes,[153] while statues deriving from the cachettes at Karnak and elsewhere in Thebes, as well as those found in Upper Egypt, focus on aspects of genealogy, religious rituals, and the local cults of the period. Despite this imbalance between religious/cultic/funerary and administrative data, several texts dated to the Third Intermediate Period which specifically document toponyms are known. They are the Twenty-First Dynasty Onomasticon of Amenemope, the Twenty-Second Dynasty Cairo Block JE 39410 of Shoshenq I from Heracleopolis, several land registers, land donation stelae, the Twenty-Fifth Dynasty Piankhy Stela, and the war records of Assyria.

The Onomasticon of Amenemope

The Onomasticon of Amenemope is preserved on nine papyrus copies and dates to the Twenty-First Dynasty.[154] The Golénischeff Onomasticon, found at el-Hibeh in Middle Egypt, is the most complete version and preserves a list of settlements, cultic locations, geographical regions, river branches, and quarries in the Nile Valley, but becomes less clear when describing the Delta. The text provides a detailed picture of the most important sites and locations at the outset of the Twenty-First Dynasty. The text also creates a topographical skeleton on to which additional archaeological and textual data can be added to assess future developments and inter-regional settlement systems. The text provides an image of how Egypt was visualised in geographical terms by a scribe from Thebes or el-Hibeh and addresses the issue of local and regional perspectives, although being regionally biased.

Cairo Block JE 39410 (Shoshenq I)

Cairo Block JE 39410 was found at Heracleopolis and dates to the reign of Shoshenq I.[155] This temple block was inscribed in hieroglyphs, and documents, in cadastral style, individuals, settlements, and institutions required to offer sacrificial bulls to the temple of Heryshef at Heracleopolis.

Land Registers

Land registers related to the land holdings of the Theban temples in the Tenth Upper Egyptian Nome include the Twenty-First/Twenty-Second Dynasty Papyrus Reinhardt[156] and Papyrus Louvre AF 6345, dated at the earliest to either the reign of Ramesses IX or Ramesses XI,[157] although the palaeography is closer to administrative documents of the Twenty-First Dynasty.[158] These documents demonstrate a link between the Theban temples and other nomes in an economic context. They include several settlements of the Tenth Upper Egyptian Nome, which is poorly represented in the wider archaeological evidence.

Land Donation Stelae

Land donation stelae record gifts of land to temples and their personnel, and provide historical and economic information over and above their significance for the study of Egyptian cults and associated belief systems.[159] Many of these stelae not only have dates, which aid in the chronological debate for the period, but also provide a wealth of knowledge regarding the toponyms, including obscure examples active during the Third Intermediate Period, and evidence for land administration.

The Piankhy Stela

The Twenty-Fifth Dynasty Piankhy Stela records the conquest of Egypt by the Nubian king Piankhy.[160] The stela documents sixty-nine toponyms, locations, or geographical areas. The text, owing to the historical situation, focused on settlement locations in Middle Egypt and the Delta. The most important political and strategic locations are recorded, and the text omits most smaller and more obscure locations that must have been encountered on Piankhy's conquest of Egypt.

The Campaign Records of Assyria

The records of Assyria from the reigns of Esarhaddon and Assurbanipal document several politically and strategically important settlements in Egypt at the end of the Third Intermediate Period. Like the Piankhy Stela, the texts record the most important Delta sites.[161]

AN EVALUATION OF THE THIRD INTERMEDIATE PERIOD SETTLEMENT DATA: TEXT-BASED VS ARCHAEOLOGICAL DATA

The partial nature of the Third Intermediate Period evidence highlights the problem of interpreting texts in which only one sector of society is literate. The texts were recorded by the hand of the state, the ruling authorities, the priests, or the literate elites. These texts have imparted a bias to the written record,[162] and economic or political factors may have been the reason for their creation. A further problem in assessing regional site densities and changes over time in the development of settlement patterns and relational networks is that some place names survive over long periods, while others change based on political, religious, and economic influences, and can be hard to track, or even mistaken for new locations. Toponyms recorded in texts are presumed to be active prior to their documentation. Locations recorded on monuments, or in texts, unless explicitly stated as being new foundations of a monarch, such as on the New Kingdom boundary stela of Akhenaten at Amarna or the Twenty-Second Dynasty settlement of Per Sekhemkheperre, are older than the earliest recorded spellings. The sites recorded on Papyrus Louvre AF 6345, Papyrus Reinhardt, and Cairo JE 39410 will have been active prior to their first recorded spelling, but how much earlier is as yet unknown. Sites known exclusively from texts and monuments may be older than the first attested textual attestation or monument attribution, unless further archaeological evidence can be used to fill in the chronological gaps and provide evidence of the earliest occupation levels independent of the monuments and texts.

The distribution of settlements based on the different document types raises elements of document bias. Those settlements documented on the Twenty-Fifth Dynasty Piankhy Stela and the Assyrian campaign inscriptions relate to important centres of military infrastructure and strategic importance. Those listed on the Onomasticon of Amenemope are related to the economic and administrative system, while those recorded on Cairo JE 39410 are linked with obligations to the local cult centre of Heryshef at Heracleopolis. The recorded texts and sites have different biases, but as a collective they suggest different levels of settlement 'importance'. The preservation of site types recorded in the texts depends on the individuals' or institutions' own bias for their recording. In comparison, archaeological data removes the categories of bias found in texts, but such data reflects a bias to site preservation rates. In total, 241 Third Intermediate Period sites in Upper and Lower Egypt are documented from both textual and archaeological data. Of these, 109 sites (45.23 per cent of the Upper and Lower Egyptian corpus) cannot yet be equated with modern Arabic toponyms and are only mentioned in texts, while 54.77 per cent can be equated with modern toponyms and are in geographically fixed locations.

UPPER EGYPT

Upper Egypt has 158 (65.56 per cent of the total) known Third Intermediate Period sites (Table 1). Approximately 53 per cent of Third Intermediate Period Upper Egyptian sites are not equated with modern Arabic toponyms and 17.72 per cent of textually attested toponyms come from the Tenth Upper Egyptian Nome, while 25.95 per cent of textual attested toponyms come from the Heracleopolitan/Faiyum region.

These figures show an under-representation of the real situation regarding settlements in general and may reflect the interest in what was worth recording by the state. Military locations are almost exclusively known from texts, with most not found archaeologically, especially in the border regions in the Tenth Upper Egyptian Nome and those clustering in the Heracleopolitan/Faiyum region. The cadastral lists of Papyrus Louvre AF 6345,[163] Papyrus Reinhardt,[164] and Cairo JE 39410 create a textual over-representation in the Tenth Upper Egyptian Nome and the Heracleopolitan hinterland. Specific texts like this can thus skew the data. The Onomasticon of Amenemope focuses on the most important economic and political centres (such as the nome capitals), mainly in Upper Egypt, which may explain why almost all of them have been located and identified with modern Arabic toponyms owing to their continued strategic, political, economic, and geographical desirability from the Third Intermediate Period onwards, and into the modern era.

Regional site density comparisons between the New Kingdom[165] and Third Intermediate Period based on text and monument attributions must be taken with some caution, particularly for the Heracleopolitan and Faiyum regions. Other regions show a general correlation of stable regional site densities

TABLE I *Percentage differences of settlements between the New Kingdom and Third Intermediate Period. Third Intermediate Period regional site density is calculated by the number of attested settlements within one region of Upper Egypt as a percentage of 158 (total number of Upper Egyptian sites).*

Region	New Kingdom settlements	Third Intermediate Period settlements	Third Intermediate Period regional density (%)	Site difference (%)
1st UE	7	7	4.43	0
2nd UE	2	1	0.63	−50
3rd UE	11	10	6.33	−9.09
4th UE	11	9	5.70	−18.18
5th UE	4	5	3.16	+25
6th UE	2	1	0.63	−50
7th UE	4	5	3.16	+25
8th UE	13	6	3.80	−53.84
9th UE	3	4	2.53	+33.33
10th UE	6	30	18.99	+400
11th UE	1	1	0.63	0
12th UE	9	3	1.90	−66.66
13th UE	7	3	1.90	−57.14
14th UE	1	2	1.27	+100
15th UE	11	4	2.53	−63.63
Akoris to Atfih	160	67	42.4	−58.13
Total	252	158		−37.30

throughout the two periods, but again the incorporation of these sites with the documents is based on political, economic, and religious factors and is unlikely to represent the wider intra-regional site networks of smaller economically, politically, and cultically less important sites such as those that may be equivalent to the modern Arabic Ezbets.

LOWER EGYPT

The site evidence for Lower Egypt is different to that from Upper Egypt and is supplied mainly by archaeological excavations and surface survey (Fig. 1). The Delta evidence is lacking in detail and number compared with that from Upper Egypt as only 83 (34.44 per cent) known Third Intermediate Period sites are recorded for Lower Egypt. In the Delta, 30.12 per cent of the 83 sites are attested through texts, but not identified with modern Arabic toponyms. There are 19 (22.89 per cent) sites where the ancient name of the site is unknown, but there is archaeological data of the period and they are mainly found in the eastern Delta, in the ancient Tanitic and Pelusiac branch region. This contrasts with evidence from Upper Egypt for which 12 (7.59 per cent) of 158 sites are known exclusively from archaeological excavations and, so far, do not have an

LOWER EGYPT REGIONAL DISTRIBUTION

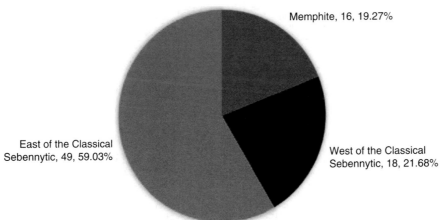

Memphite, 16, 19.27%

East of the Classical
Sebennytic, 49, 59.03%

West of the Classical
Sebennytic, 18, 21.68%

Fig. 1 Regional density of sites for Lower Egypt during the Third Intermediate Period.

identified ancient name. The Delta evidence based on these figures is lacking in added textual detail and site quantity compared with Upper Egypt. The eastern Delta has the largest site density with 49 sites (59.03 per cent). Only 18 sites (21.68 per cent) are attested in the western Delta sector and 16 sites (19.27 per cent) from the Memphite region.

SPATIAL ANALYSIS AND QUANTIFICATION OF THIRD INTERMEDIATE PERIOD SITES

The application of statistical analysis and quantitative techniques to analyse archaeological distributions based on the category of 'site' in Egypt, which relate to their economic relationships, has received little attention. Location-Allocation covering frameworks have been used to simulate the spatial pattern of the top levels of the settlement hierarchy (the nome system) for the Ramesside Period and showed that the Ramesside administration maximised the control of the Nile Valley population.[166] There was a close correspondence between the spatial efficiency and the choice of important sites such as nome capitals to control these regions. The Location-Allocation model focused on the nome centres and cannot be used to assess other settlement distributions located within the nome regions. Where a representative sample of sites from well-recorded regions is available, settlement prediction models can be used to fill geographic voids. These approaches have been beneficial to studies of settlement patterns on Crete.[167] However, the Cretan landscape offers a different ecological and geographical scenario compared with Egypt, and focuses on overland routes, whereas in Egypt transport was conducted on the hydraulic networks. The nature of the Third Intermediate Period site data and the regional inconsistencies in site preservation, with almost 50 per cent of the corpus not located, do not allow for such a spatial analysis study to be conducted at this current time.

THE DEVELOPMENT OF AN EGYPTIAN SETTLEMENT PATTERN MODEL

The model developed within this book is a multi-approach system that enables Egyptian settlement patterns to be assessed within the boundaries of current archaeological research, thought, and theory. This is achieved through the identification of the natural environment, geology, and landscape of the Nile Valley and Delta in order to identify potential areas of settlement location, and from there, establish the problems in identifying the extent and subsequent development of the landscape from ancient to modern times, through natural and cultural factors. Egyptian 'sites' can be defined by the presence of physical material culture and textual evidence of human habitation and occupation activity over short or sustained time periods, at domestic, administrative, military, cultic, or funerary levels. Only once these fundamental processes have been finalised for each project or research question can a comprehensive assessment be undertaken of the academic literature, along with excavation and survey data, to develop a corpus of sites representative of each region, which can be plotted on geographical maps. For meaningful conclusions to be made regarding chronological developments of settlement patterns in particular regions, a secondary corpus of sites from the preceding time phase must be constructed for comparison on both a geographical (spatial) level and at the site density ratio level. These regional maps can then demonstrate the variability in the data, such as text-based versus data-driven (archaeological) evidence, regional site densities, and cemetery locations, and where possible, chronological developments of site types in particular geographic regions. Finally, the model requires regional case studies to be performed to test the potential for settlement pattern studies within the distinct chronological framework being studied, which is the focus of the next sections.

The results of the initial macro-analysis of sites in large geographical areas of Upper and Lower Egypt – showing that regional density studies and site identification for Upper Egypt are derived from texts for nearly 50 per cent of the corpus – highlight the need for increased archaeological survey and archaeological excavations in Upper Egypt. There needs to be a shift in attitude and research focus away from tomb and temple excavations to look for textual and monumental data that can help refine chronologies of the period, and to target areas of domestic settlement layers before they are lost to modern pressures. This is particularly the case in Upper Egypt where survey and excavation are still largely confined to the desert fringes and focus on cemetery or temple areas such as at Thebes. The regional density study has shown a lack of Third Intermediate Period site attestations particularly in the Second, Sixth, and Eleventh Upper Egyptian nomes, and the region of Middle Egypt in general. Regional nome studies are required to fill in the knowledge gap particularly in Middle Egypt, while excavations at nome capitals may add further evidence to regional and local polities such as the possibility of identifying additional regional rulers that may reflect the further political and administrative division of regional centres. Off-site survey and fieldwalking, on and between tell sites, are not sufficient to define site chronology. Therefore, when conducting fieldwalking one must complement it by exploratory excavation techniques if the site is to be assessed for its archaeological potential and site stratigraphy.[168] This can be done through a focused study of coring, resistivity, and magnetometry studies on exposed tell areas. In general, the Third Intermediate Period, as stated in Chapter 1 of this book, is still largely concerned with the establishing of a relative chronology for the period, with a focus on texts, artwork, and funerary culture, while settlement studies for the period in general are not focused on or dominated by text-based analysis, without an integrated approach, or are found isolated within larger multi-phase archaeological reports, with little or no focused regional analysis of Third Intermediate Period settlement development.

The Third Intermediate Period data is not representative enough at a regional level for statistical and spatial analysis, unlike studies in the Near East and Aegean. Furthermore, the number of small centres recorded may not be accurate for the region, based on the regional site density analysis. This indicates that the general pattern of settlement found in the regions of the Tenth Upper Egyptian Nome and the Heracleopolitan/Faiyum region, based on textual evidence from the earlier Wilbour Papyrus, the Twenty-First Dynasty Papyrus Louvre AF 6345, and the Twenty-Second Dynasty Cairo JE 39410, was likely to have been replicated to some extent in other large cultivated areas in the country, such as the Third Upper Egyptian Nome. The evaluation of the data has highlighted several interesting areas, particularly the divisions of site data between Upper and Lower Egypt, with Upper Egypt represented by textual attestations and archaeology, and the Delta being mainly represented by archaeological evidence. The multi-approach model is an effective way of assessing the settlement patterns of the Third Intermediate Period based on the variability of the surviving data and demonstrates the potential and limitations of the data for conducting landscape and settlement pattern studies during the Third Intermediate Period using an integrated process of culture historical, processual, and post-processual approaches. The model allows flexibility within the data, removes hierarchical bias of sites, and provides scope for future revisions of site attributes and economic and political importance by using the unique site identification system. Utilising this model, the following sections evaluate settlement dynamics and processes within the Third Intermediate Period landscapes and settlements in a series of regional case studies.

SETTLEMENT PATTERNS IN THE THIRD INTERMEDIATE PERIOD: THE CASE STUDIES

Utilising the settlement pattern model developed above, and the associated archaeological and textual data, the following sections determine whether settlement patterns are visible within the Third Intermediate Period landscape, to what extent they are different from the New Kingdom, and the factors that may have influenced these patterns. The evaluation of the potential for and limitations of landscape archaeology in Egypt provides an overall assessment of whether, considering the current evidence and access to Egyptian sites, landscape archaeology can be conducted and what we can aim to learn from regional thematic approaches. The following case studies demonstrate the diverse ways in which settlement studies can be approached in different areas, as no single approach will work for all areas of Egypt. In the eastern and western Delta, the approach will combine hydrological reconstruction, textual documents, archaeological survey, and excavation of settlements/cemeteries to document settlement networks. In Upper Egypt and the Memphite area, the approach is more text based, including Egyptian philological designations and archaeological material. The following sections establish that regional settlement systems were a characteristic of the period, and document the impact of the military on regional settlement networks and then what these characteristics indicate regarding Third Intermediate Period society.

UPPER EGYPT: THE FIRST AND SECOND UPPER EGYPTIAN NOMES

The southern nomes of Upper Egypt represent a different geographical situation compared with the rest of Upper Egypt (Maps 1 and 2). The area around Aswan is characterised by low desert hills coming down to the river, with cataracts of the river forming impassable barriers to fluvial transport. The lack of habitable space on either side of the Nile caused by the sandstone cliffs made organically developed settlement difficult. In the First Upper Egyptian Nome, a 5 km long area between the modern towns of Naga el-Hamdlab and Naga el-Hajar, where the Valley is reduced to the Nile itself, created limited space for the alluvium to rest during the annual inundation. The lack of available arable land made it difficult for settlements to develop, until cultivation started around the modern town of Naga el-Hajar, ca. 14.5 km to the south of the nome capital Kom Ombo. To the north of Gebel el-Silsila the Eastern Desert borders the Nile closely, sometimes leaving no room for agriculture to take place. On

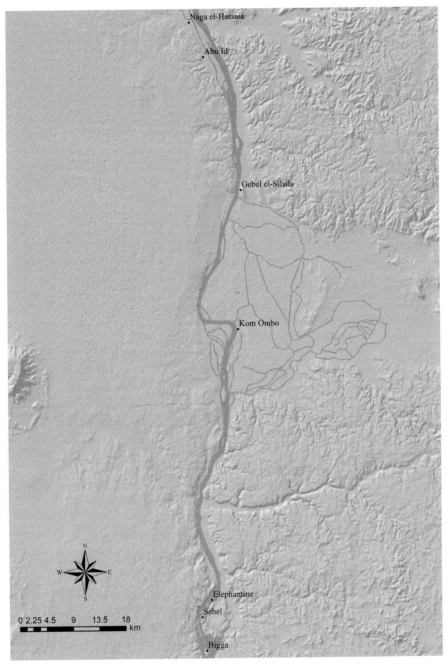

Map 1 Third Intermediate Period sites in the First Upper Egyptian Nome. Copyright © 2014 Esri.

the West Bank, sandstone mountain ranges border the Nile closely from the villages of Naga el-Hamam to Naga el-Aqabiyya, an almost 12 km long area with little vegetation or modern settlement. The region of the First and Second Upper Egyptian nomes is characterised by the lack of settlements during the

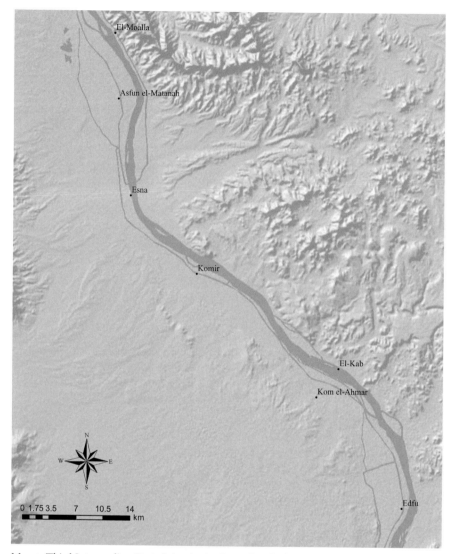

Map 2 Third Intermediate Period sites in the Second and Third Upper Egyptian nomes.
Copyright © 2014 Esri.

Third Intermediate Period. This lack of settlement activity is attested for both the
Third Intermediate Period and New Kingdom, when, as in the Third Intermediate
Period, the main centres of activity lay in the frontier forts of Bigga, Sehel, and
Elephantine. Further north beyond Elephantine, the lack of evidence for settlements within the region corresponds to the much-reduced cultivated area, as there
is a long 40.5 km stretch of Nile Valley between Elephantine and Kom Ombo with
no evidence of settlement activity for the period.

The high proportion of border forts (Bigga, Sehel, Elephantine, Abu Id) in
the First Upper Egyptian Nome no doubt creates an illusion of a higher density

of settlement compared with the other less populated region, the Second Upper Egyptian Nome. The high preservation of settlement numbers in desert environments affects site density ratios compared with those in more arable areas of the country, where settlements are located above the floodplain and have had continued occupation. This region should not be viewed as a highly dense region of organically developed settlement with a large population density, compared with the regions in Middle Egypt, as the high frequency of fortress locations creates an illusion of a region with a well-developed settlement pattern. As control of the First Cataract region began to decline during the Third Intermediate Period and the security of the First Upper Egyptian Nome was not guaranteed, people may have moved out of the smaller settlements and into the frontier settlement of Elephantine and the cultivated region of Kom Ombo to gain security and guaranteed food supplies. The area around the Second Upper Egyptian Nome capital Edfu has a wide floodplain with a large hinterland area for the potential development of satellite settlements. The evidence so far suggests a sparsely settled area in the Third Intermediate Period, which is confirmed by, and corresponds with, the New Kingdom data. The hydrology of the area in the New Kingdom indicates the Nile had a minor channel between Kom el-Farahy and Hagar Edfu, probably with a larger channel to the east of Kom el-Farahy.[169] During the New Kingdom, the Nile still deposited silts around Kom el-Farahy. The occupation history of Kom el-Farahy is not clear, but there may have been continuous activity on the Kom or a hiatus after the New Kingdom, and after the New Kingdom the Nile migrated to the east.[170] The evidence suggests that, as a result of a change in the local hydrology at around the end of the New Kingdom, a new settlement pattern may have developed in the region around Edfu, as Kom el-Farahy may have been abandoned at the start of the Twenty-First Dynasty.

THE THEBAN NOME

The Theban Nome is one of the most studied areas of Egypt thanks to the good preservation of religious and funerary monuments, along with a large corpus of textual material. Most evidence, particularly texts, for the Third Intermediate Period is derived from the temples and tombs in the area, but the archaeological settlement evidence is lacking in comparison (Map 3). On the East Bank, there is evidence of Third Intermediate Period settlement activity to the west of the Mut Complex at Karnak,[171] and in the area of Abu el-Gud with Third Intermediate Period settlement found built over the top of a small temple of Ramesses II,[172] while a Twenty-First Dynasty stela of the High Priest of Amun, Menkheperre,[173] describes the encroachment of the Theban settlement into the walls of the Amun temple,[174] suggesting some form of expansion of the

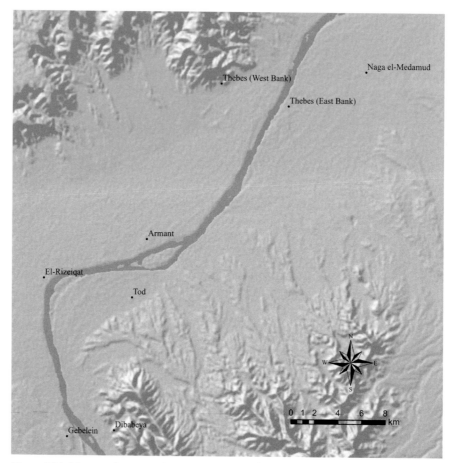

Map 3 Third Intermediate Period sites in the Theban region. Copyright © 2014 Esri.

New Kingdom settlement to the north-east of the Amun temple of Karnak in the early Twenty-First Dynasty. On the West Bank, a settlement developed within the Great Enclosure wall of the temple of Medinat Habu,[175] and numerous necropoli have been located within the New Kingdom mortuary temples.[176] The settlement distribution for the Third Intermediate Period in the Theban Nome corresponds largely to that of the preceding New Kingdom. Many of the settlements of the New Kingdom continued to function and retained their political importance, with Armant and Naga el-Medamud maintaining their significance throughout the period. The number of recorded settlements is approximately equivalent to that of the New Kingdom, while the New Kingdom texts provide a much more varied and detailed description of the surrounding sacred landscape and religious buildings, which is lacking from the Third Intermediate Period texts.

The Twentieth Dynasty Papyrus BM 10068, which records the robberies of the royal tombs in the Valley of the Kings, provides information regarding the settlement patterns on the West Bank of Thebes during the Twentieth Dynasty, which can be tracked into the Third Intermediate Period. Papyrus BM 10068 has the title 'Town register of the west of Thebes from the temple of Menmaatre to the settlement of Maiunehes'. This text preserves a list of houses, with the names and occupations of their owners. It begins with the temple of Menmaatre (the temple of Seti I at Gurna), followed by ten houses, the majority of which were occupied by priests, likely a priestly community in connection with the temple.[177] The text then mentions the temple of Usermaatre Setepenre (the Ramesseum), followed by fourteen more houses occupied by priests, no doubt connected to the Ramesseum.[178] Finally, the temple of Medinat Habu is listed, with 155 houses that form a real community with mixed occupations and not a reduced temple staff.[179] The settlement of Maiunehes is likely to refer to the settlement inside the Medinat Habu temple. The communities from the West Bank had nucleated to Medinat Habu and the West Bank population density had now increased within the single confines of the temple; settlement density decreased across the wider West Bank floodplain as the mortuary temples were utilised as large burial grounds. The increase in tribal raids and the decreased security on the West Bank facilitated the move behind the walls of Medinat Habu, following concerns for security and protection.

Beyond Thebes itself, Tod has so far produced no monumental or textual evidence of the Third Intermediate Period, although some form of settlement activity continued as Third Intermediate Period ceramics have been found in fills in the temple area.[180] The omission of Tod from the Onomasticon of Amenemope could indicate that, by the Twenty-First Dynasty, the settlement had lost some of its political and administrative status. Its omission corresponds with the cessation of activity at el-Salamiya to the west of Tod. El-Salamiya was probably an associated burial ground and possible settlement associated with Tod, with burials dating from the Middle Kingdom[181] until the Twentieth Dynasty.[182] The cessation of the burial activity in the late Ramesside Period would correspond with the reduced monumental activity at Tod and its omission from the preserved texts of the period. These factors indicate Tod had lost its prominence in the Third Intermediate Period, and it is possible that elite tomb construction also ceased at el-Salamiya at the same time.

UPPER EGYPT: AKORIS TO ATFIH

The region from Akoris to Atfih encompasses the Sixteenth to Twenty-Second Upper Egyptian nomes (Maps 4 and 5). These nomes have been grouped together to form a coherent geographic region to assess the potential for an analysis of settlement patterns regarding the earlier Twentieth Dynasty cadastral

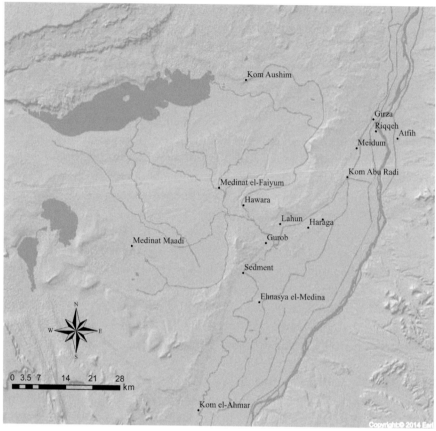

Map 4 Archaeologically located Third Intermediate Period sites in the Akoris to Atfih region (north part). Copyright © 2014 Esri.

survey of the region recorded on the Wilbour Papyrus. This approach allows for a quantitative and comparative analysis to be achieved with the Third Intermediate Period data. The grouping of these regions into one unified district is in line with the geo-political boundaries of the Third Intermediate Period and allows for the large number of unlocated settlements to be placed within a specific regional area. The error percentage in the placement of unknown locations in one nome or another is reduced.

The evidence from the cadastral lists of the Twentieth Dynasty Wilbour Papyrus and the Twenty-Second Dynasty Cairo JE 39410 allow for a snapshot of the development of a settlement system in the Akoris to Atfih region based on textual evidence. These documents can provide a chronological progression of a specific site type development that indicates changes in the organisation of the settlement networks during the transition between the end of the New Kingdom and the start of the Twenty-Second Dynasty. The Wilbour Papyrus lists 142 locations in this region for the reign of Ramesses V (ca. 1149–1145

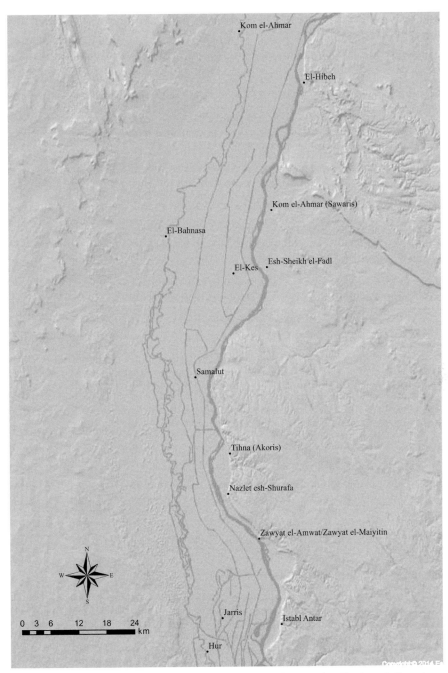

Map 5 Archaeologically located Third Intermediate Period sites in the Akoris to Atfih region (south part). Copyright © 2014 Esri.

BCE).[183] This is no more than 75 years before the start of the Third Intermediate Period, and ca. 206 years before the reign of Shoshenq I in 943 BCE. There are 67 sites recorded on Twenty-First and Twenty-Second Dynasty monuments and texts in this same region. There is a 52.82 per cent decrease in recorded sites from the end of the New Kingdom and into the Third Intermediate Period. Whether this scenario represents a nucleation of settlement into the larger regional centres and a reduction in small sites from the end of the New Kingdom into the Third Intermediate Period is at this moment unclear. The Wilbour Papyrus may represent the wider network of settlements for the region and is a model for other large floodplain regions in Upper Egypt and the Delta. Most of the sites recorded on the Third Intermediate Period records are newly recorded toponyms and may suggest either new settlements being created in this region and the declining importance of others, a changing of settlement names in conjunction with a new political regime in the region, or the bias of textual documents towards specific site types that were chosen to be recorded, while omitting a large majority of the smaller sites. The recording of toponyms of Cairo JE 39410 from the reign of Shoshenq I for religious reasons and not on an administrative papyrus may reflect only the most important sites for the region in a cultic setting of offering bulls, while those smaller settlements that may have been listed in large administrative cadastral surveys have been omitted.

One site type which allows for a glimpse at the development of the settlement system in this region and can shed light on this site type in Third Intermediate Period Egypt is the iꜣt sites. In the Twentieth Dynasty, the Wilbour Papyrus records several locations formed with the writing 𓇌𓈈, a late writing of 𓈐. The hieroglyph depicts a mound and should be equated with the modern Arabic term *kom* or *tell*.[184] The Wilbour Papyrus records eleven locations with the old writing of 'mound'. In the Third Intermediate Period, none of the five attested iꜣt locations are to be identified with sites previously listed in the Wilbour Papyrus, while all five of the Third Intermediate Period settlements exhibit the later writing 𓇌𓈈 instead of 𓈐. What is noticeable regarding the writing of the term 'mound' is that the Twenty-First Dynasty documents all exhibit the later form 𓇌𓈈, while the Twenty-Second Dynasty document exhibits the earlier writing of 𓈐. It is possible the document of Shoshenq I is a re-copying of an earlier text in which the early form of 𓈐 has been retained, or it could be that an archaising form of language was adopted for the temple inscription of Heryshef.

The five 'mound' locations make up 7.46 per cent of the recorded Akoris to Atfih region settlements, but cannot be equated with any modern Arabic toponyms. In the Third Intermediate Period the five 𓈐 settlements are all newly named settlements, and there is limited evidence for other 𓈐 settlements for Egypt in the Third Intermediate Period, with the only other examples being 𓈐𓈓 iꜣt-tꜣmt, from the Memphite region, and the settlements of 𓈐 tꜣ iꜣt pꜣ bik 'The Mound of the Falcon' in the Theban Nome and 𓈐 iꜣt-ity from the Tenth Upper Egyptian Nome. Ultimately 𓈐 settlements only occur in Upper Egypt and the Memphite region.

Other Third Intermediate Period sites in the region are el-Hibeh, el-Bahnasa (Oxyrhynchus), and Atfih. Beyond the main temple and the royal necropolis at Heracleopolis,[185] the evidence for domestic settlement in this region is lacking, with only limited early Third Intermediate Period settlement at Lisht North[186] and Akoris.[187]

The archaeology for the region beyond Heracleopolis, Lisht North, Akoris, and el-Hibeh is almost entirely made up of cemeteries, which are predominantly situated on the West Bank of the Nile but are likely to have had some form of associated settlement. The cemeteries include Sedment,[188] Gurob,[189] Lahun,[190] Haraga,[191] Hawara,[192] Meidum,[193] Riqqeh, and Girza, with possible evidence of a funerary stela from Kom Abu Radi (north-east of Abusir el-Meleq and 6 km south of Meidum),[194] and a textual attestation of activity at Abusir el-Meleq on Cairo JE 39410. It was proposed that the cemetery of Lahun had been abandoned at the end of the Middle Kingdom and was re-used between the Twenty-Second and Twenty-Fifth Dynasty for the burials of the people of the fortress of Per Sekhemkheperre.[195] Only one military burial was found in the necropolis, while no monument from Lahun mentions Per Sekhemkheperre.[196] A re-analysis of so-called Twenty-Second to Twenty-Fifth Dynasty burials at Lahun by Aston has led to the re-dating of these burials to no earlier than the seventh century BCE and would place them at the end of the Third Intermediate Period, probably sometime in the Twenty-Fifth Dynasty; this would suggest that if Lahun was re-used, then the associated burial ground of the Twenty-Second Dynasty has not been discovered, or Per Sekhemkheperre is not in the vicinity of Lahun. Although the Faiyum is named in the Third Intermediate Period, little else is known concerning the wider region and its settlements compared with the Nile Valley to the east. Evidence is limited to a small number of royal and private monuments at Medinat el-Faiyum (Crocodilopolis) and Medinat Maadi, while it is possible that there was some settlement or funerary activity at Kom Aushim (Karanis), as two cartonnage mummies in anthropoid wooden coffins were found during excavations in the 1980s.[197] At Medinat Maadi, the Middle Kingdom temple (Temple A) has a preserved decoration of a King Osorkon (I?) in the portico (Second Hypostyle Hall),[198] while a statue of proposed Third Intermediate Period date, probably of the Twenty-Second Dynasty, comes from Medinat el-Faiyum.[199]

Owing to the lack of survey and excavation in the region to the north of the settlement of Akoris, and the early excavations of the cemeteries bordering the West Bank, the settlement pattern situation in this region is difficult to interpret, while the settlement patterns for the smaller order settlements of the Third Intermediate Period are not possible to assess. The overall nature of the evidence from this region is reliant on textual sources, instead of archaeology, but should not be dismissed out of hand. The documentation of this region within the papyri and the temple inscriptions indicates its importance from both a political and economic viewpoint from the start of the Third Intermediate Period. What is notable within the region of Akoris to Atfih is that, in conjunction with the prosperous cultivable region, there is a proliferation of fortified outposts, no doubt controlling access in and out of the most economically valuable regions, as well as access to and from the wadi routes. Several wadi routes lead out to the Eastern Desert, including the Wadi Lishyab, the Wadi Arhab, and the Wadi Sannur, while desert routes leading out to the Western Desert in the region of Heracleopolis were the Wadi Ruwayar and the Wadi Muweilih, heading out towards the Bahariya Oasis. These routes would need securing as they were one of the main access routes into and out of the Western Desert for the Heracleopolitan region.

THE MEMPHITE REGION

Apart from the indication of East Bank quarry activity at Turah, the active cemeteries at Giza and Saqqara, and the main centres of settlement at Memphis and Heliopolis, the settlement network of the Memphite region is poorly recorded, and sites are only documented within the ancient texts. The modern city and suburbs of Cairo probably now cover many of the settlements of the Third Intermediate Period, which are thus inaccessible.

The ancient settlement of ⟨hieroglyphs⟩ ḥwt-šd-ꜣbd (Hut-Shedabed)[200] was located south of ⟨hieroglyphs⟩ pr-ḥꜥpy (Per Hapy), the modern Atar en-Naby.[201] The same Per Hapy was again recorded later on the Piankhy Stela, written as ⟨hieroglyphs⟩. The toponym ⟨hieroglyphs⟩ ḥr-ꜥḥꜥ (Her-aha) is in Old Cairo at Babylon, while ⟨hieroglyphs⟩ pr-psḏt (Per Pesdjet), 'The House of the Ennead', was another name for Babylon.[202] Near Memphis was the settlement of ⟨hieroglyphs⟩ ꜣt-ṯꜣmt (Iat-Tjamet),[203] and to the south of the Memphite Nome was a cult centre of Amun at ⟨hieroglyphs⟩ ḫnt-nfr (Khent-Nefer).[204] Finally, on a block statue of Nespaqashuty from Thebes dated to Shoshenq III,[205] a district to the north of Heracleopolis called ⟨hieroglyphs⟩ ww pgꜣ (W-Pega), 'The District of Pega', is recorded. This district had a main settlement called ⟨hieroglyphs⟩ pr-pgꜣ (Per-Pega), 'The House of Pega'.

HYDROLOGY AND SETTLEMENT IN THE CANOPIC REGION DURING THE NEW KINGDOM AND THIRD INTERMEDIATE PERIOD

The western Delta perhaps had a low settlement density possibly caused by the associated hydraulic situation (Maps 6 and 7). New Kingdom evidence for water-ways in the western Delta record 'The Western River'.[206] In the New Kingdom, Min, a governor of Abydos under Thutmose III, had the title 'Commander of Troops of the Western River'.[207] An ostracon dated to the early Ramesside Period and the Onomasticon of Amenemope also record this river.[208] The 'Western River' is now understood to be the modern Canopic branch of the Nile.

Map 6 Archaeologically attested New Kingdom settlements in the western Nile Delta. The route of the Canopic (Western Nile) and (proposed) Canopic Nile distributary is based on Spencer, 2014: fig. 1. (Kom Firin Project: Courtesy of the Trustees of the British Museum). An alternative course for the New Kingdom Canopic distributary channel based on the position of New Kingdom sites in the landscape, or possibly even another parallel New Kingdom channel, is proposed by the author.

In the western Delta, Kom Firin was situated upon a Nile distributary to the west of the Canopic branch.[209] The presence of a waterway along the south of Kom Firin is corroborated by Corona satellite imagery.[210] The Canopic branch may have passed 10 km to the north-east of Kom Firin, and therefore Kom Firin may not have had convenient access and transport links to other major

Map 7 Archaeologically attested Third Intermediate Period sites in the western Nile Delta. The route of the Canopic (Western Nile) and (proposed) Canopic Nile distributary is based on Spencer, 2014: fig. 1. (Kom Firin Project: Courtesy of the Trustees of the British Museum).

centres such as Memphis to the south and the Mediterranean coast to the north. The distributary associated with Kom Firin, to the west of the Canopic Nile, formed part of the landscape during the Third Intermediate Period. Identifying the course of the Canopic Nile (Western River) within the area for the Third Intermediate Period has proved problematic. There are, so far, no New Kingdom or Third Intermediate Period sites situated along the course of the projected Canopic river, despite allusions to them in the texts.[211]

The local aquatic environment at Kom Firin was exploited as a food source. These secondary Nile channels were good places for fishing, flora, and fauna. The pottery from the cores at Kom Firin in these areas, and topographical surveys, suggest activity in the late Ramesside and Third Intermediate Period. There may have been temporary small-scale activity associated with light industry, or a harbour prone to seasonal flooding.[212] The successive temple enclosure layouts at Kom Firin indicate the landscape changed from the late second millennium BCE to the seventh century BCE. In the Late Period, the temple enclosure was extended into the western area of the tell, where flooding had once occurred, suggesting the waterways had migrated to the north of the tell, leaving the area permanently above the annual flood.[213]

Additional information regarding waterways comes from a block of Shoshenq III that mentions the 𓄓𓈗 ḫns canal,[214] which had a strong connection with Kom el-Hisn. The ḫns canal lay downstream and also, possibly, upstream of Kom el-Hisn.[215] Several channels are visible on Corona satellite images to the north-west and west of Kom el-Hisn, as well as at Kom el-Abqa'in and Kom Firin. These channels suggest a bifurcation of the waterway just west of Kom el-Hisn. The Western River may have been the name for all the river channels and canals in the western Delta and the 𓄓𓈗 ḫns canal did not exist prior to the Twenty-Second Dynasty.[216] The Onomasticon of Amenemope may confirm this hypothesis as it mentions only the 'Western River' for the Twenty-First Dynasty and not the 𓄓𓈗 ḫns canal, which is first attested under Shoshenq III. The hieroglyphic writing of the word 𓄓𓈗 ḫns, with the double-headed lion glyph meaning 'to traverse', may have been a visual pun relating to the splitting and merging, meandering and anastomosing portions of the river in the south-western Delta.[217]

The mention of the canal on the 𓈗 block of Shoshenq III at a time when there was increased royal patronage in the settlements of the western Delta at Kom el-Hisn and Kom Firin, with which the 𓄓𓈗 ḫns canal had a direct connection, could indicate that the new channel allowed the settlements to prosper economically and provided the optimal conditions for the principality of the Western Kingdom to develop. The tendency for new channels created by avulsions, perhaps assisted by human actions, would result in the extension of the river channel network, and thereby would have allowed or encouraged the growth of new settlements and populations along the new branch channels, and extended the network of transport and trade arteries.[218] The need for increased labour would have facilitated the creation of new irrigated farmland.

The avulsion of the rivers could be managed so both the old and new channels could be used for transport and water access for settlements along their banks. This would have extended the potential irrigation of the plain and the new channels would operate as a safety valve by receiving surplus water from the original channel.[219] In the Late Period, an increase of settlements in the western Delta at Naukratis, Kom Kortas, and Kom Abu el-Tubul may reflect the importance of river avulsions for the creation of new urbanised landscapes. In the Late Period, there is now evidence of occupation along the Canopic branch,[220] which was absent in the previous Third Intermediate Period.

THE WESTERN DELTA UNDER SHOSHENQ III AND SHOSHENQ V

Shoshenq III was the first king since Ramesses II to extend his temple-building programme into the western Delta, from his initial place of power at Tanis in the eastern Delta. At Kom el-Hisn there was sustained settlement activity throughout the Third Intermediate Period, but there is no evidence that the Ramesside religious structures were added to, or modified, until approximately four hundred years later in the mid-eighth century BCE, when Shoshenq III built a new temple pylon. Shoshenq III's son Padibehenbast in Year 28 set up a stela in which he donated land to the temple, which could have been for the provision of the new temple foundation.[221] A second donation stela set up by Ankhpakhered, who was a lesser chief in Year 32 of Shoshenq III, four years after Padibehenbast's stela, indicates the growing prosperity of the temple estates at Kom el-Hisn under Shoshenq III. Shoshenq III began to re-use the works of Ramesses II and started adding to existing Delta temples, at Tell Umm Harb and Bindariya. Four stelae also provide evidence of continued elite patronage and land donation by the chiefs of the Libu at the temple, or temples, at Kom Firin in the reign of Shoshenq V. Whether this referred to the pre-existing Ramesside temple or a new foundation is not yet known. Finally, at Kom Abu Billo, Shoshenq V dedicated land to the temple.[222]

Shoshenq III initiated a new land management policy in the western Delta through the construction of new temples and the renovations of existing structures, combined with donations of land for these foundations. Shoshenq III still had some control over the western Libyan chiefs and was free to dedicate monuments to his own kingship in various parts of the Delta, while not having full territorial control over such areas. Shoshenq V began to consolidate settlements around the capital at Kom el-Hisn to bring them back under the nominal control of the Tanite kings in response to the mounting geo-political pressure of the period from the growing power of the Libyan chiefs in the west. The growing interest and influence of the region suggests it had some strategic, and perhaps symbolic, importance for the rulers of the

Twenty-Second Dynasty. The riverine access to these settlements and their connection with the Mediterranean were important to the Tanite kings as they could access trade goods coming from the Western Desert and the Mediterranean Sea and have access to important cattle and grazing regions.

THE CENTRAL-WESTERN DELTA

This area comprises the lands between the Western River or Canopic branch and the Sebennytic branch through the centre of the Delta. The main settlements in the area were Sais, Buto, and Sakha. Central Delta hydrology during the Third Intermediate Period can be discussed in relation to the settlements of Sais and Buto. Sais and Buto are situated to the east of the ancient 'Waters of Ptah', which ran partly on the course of the modern Rosetta branch.[223] Geological investigations and associated Landsat imagery analysis at Buto identified several undated palaeochannels. By extending the palaeochannel course to the south, the relationship with the Saite hinterland can be suggested.[224] Older river channel systems may have been subsumed into the modern canals such as the Qodaba and Nashrat canals, but there is scope for further investigations into the sedimentology of the Basyun/Sais area.[225] A major buried channel exists approximately 7.5 km to the east of the modern Rosetta branch, but no date could be provided for when it was active.[226] This channel may have been the main channel for Sakha. The prominence of Sais was determined by the presence of associated river channels, which may have surrounded the site, providing strategic and economic potential to its positioning,[227] no more so than the elevation of Sais into the capital of the Western Kingdom of Tefnakht in the later Third Intermediate Period. The same can be said for Buto, which was resettled in the Third Intermediate Period, developing into an important political centre, no doubt on the basis of a shift in the associated local hydrology, and perhaps the emergence of the Saitic branch.[228] Recent excavations at Sais have found the remains of a Third Intermediate Period settlement,[229] and coring surveys at Buto show extensive resettlement of the site in the early phases of the Third Intermediate Period,[230] while textual evidence from numerous monuments indicates that Buto was an important political centre. Buto and Sakha are both attested in the Twenty-First Dynasty and continue to be active into the Twenty-Fifth Dynasty, developing under the control of local leaders. Sais, unlike Buto and Sakha, is not recorded in the early Third Intermediate Period texts and this may indicate that it was not yet a political power in the western Delta. Beyond the settlement, there is little evidence of royal activity or monumental building at Sais for the early Third Intermediate Period, with the only evidence perhaps two armbands[231] belonging to Prince Nimlot of the Twenty-Second Dynasty.[232]

THE EASTERN DELTA: THE MENDESIAN BRANCH OF THE NILE

Herodotus and Pseudo Skylax both say the Mendesian branch connected to the Sebennytic branch. Later authors do not provide a connection point, perhaps reflecting its disappearance during the Ptolemaic Period.[233] The pharaonic evidence for the Mendesian branch prior to Herodotus is lacking. During the ninth to the seventh century BCE the Mendesian branch, like the Tanitic and Pelusiac branches, began to migrate towards the north-west as the western Delta began to subside.[234] Throughout antiquity the Mendesian branch flowed near Mendes, while the Third Intermediate Period port of Tell Tebilla was located close to its mouth.[235] The Mendesian branch changed course during the Pharaonic Period. Bietak suggested the creation, sometime before the first millennium BCE, of a new nome located a few kilometres west of Mendes, with Hermopolis Parva as its capital, owing to the presence of the Mendesian branch between the two sites.[236] Nome territory was defined in ancient times by Nile branches and its major distributaries.[237] Bietak's hypothesis has since been confirmed by the discovery of the Old Kingdom Mendesian temple of the ram god Banebdjed, which was bordered by waterways running north, west, and east of Mendes.[238] During the Third Intermediate Period, Mendes and Hermopolis Parva were reunited as part of the Mendesian Nome. The administrative reunification suggests a progressive eastward migration of the Mendesian branch, whereby the river no longer flowed between the two sites, but rather east of Mendes. The later fifth-century BCE reference of Herodotus to both a Mendesian and a Thmuite Nome would confirm this scenario (Map 8).[239]

Third Intermediate Period settlement along the suggested course of the Mendesian branch has not been identified until 8.85 km downstream of the bifurcation point in the region of Tell Muqdam (Map 9). Evidence of New Kingdom activity in the southern Mendesian branch region is only attested at Barakim on the East Bank, some 3.5 km away from the Mendesian branch itself and 25.75 km downstream, and this continues in the Third Intermediate Period (Map 10).

The ancient site of 𓈖𓉻𓏏𓂋𓇳 *t3šnt r*ᶜ (Ta Shunet Re), 'The Granary of Re', may be found near Barakim at Shon Yusef, but closer to the Nile and nearer the border of the Mendesian and Leontopolite nomes. Third Intermediate Period evidence has not been found at Shon Yusef, which is now levelled to cultivation.

Opposite Barakim, on the West Bank of the Mendesian branch, is Tell Tambul with occupation dates in the New Kingdom. Based on the Mendesian branch trajectory, Tell Tambul lies ca. 6.3 km away from the Mendesian branch. The el-Buhiya canal flows past the eastern side of Tell Tambul, indicating either a connecting canal in the New Kingdom linked to both the main central Nile Delta branch and the Mendesian branch, or that the

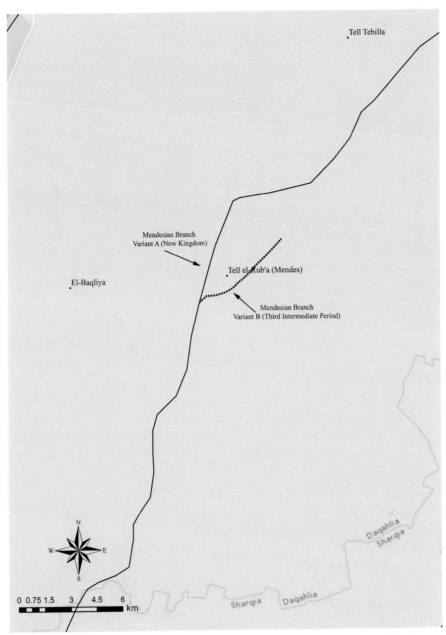

Map 8 Variant positions of the Mendesian branch from the New Kingdom to the Third
Intermediate Period. Variant A position of the Mendesian Nile based on Bietak, 1975: plan 4.

Mendesian branch in the New Kingdom was further to the north-west. To the
north, at a distance of 11.3 km, both Bilgai and Hermopolis Parva are in
connection with a proposed linking canal.[240] This canal as stated by Bietak
connects to the modern Damietta branch to the south of Busiris.[241] The canal
may have been located between the modern villages of Shubrawish and Kafr el-

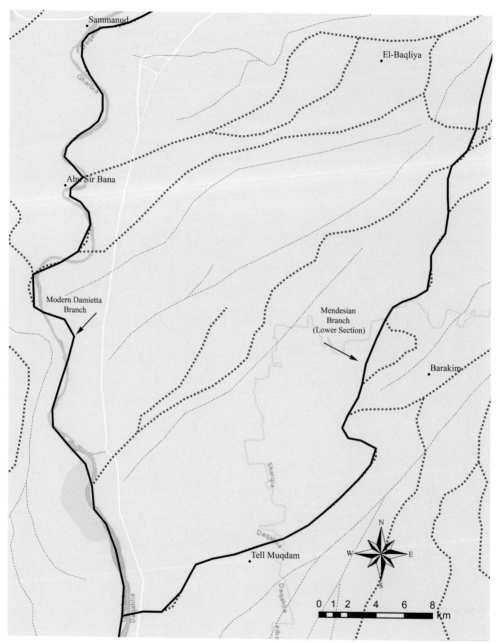

Map 9 Lower section of the Mendesian branch region during the Third Intermediate Period. Position of Nile branches based on Bietak, 1975: plan 4.

Mandara on the east bank of the Damietta branch. The canal would have run in the region of the modern villages of Ezbet el-Jummayzah, Kafr Abu Shawarib, and Ezbet el-Sabkha, and to the north of Hermopolis Parva (el-Baqliya), and connected again with the Mendesian branch to the north of Mendes,[242] in the region of the modern villages of Mit Luzah, Ezbet el-Dawarani, and Ezbet el-

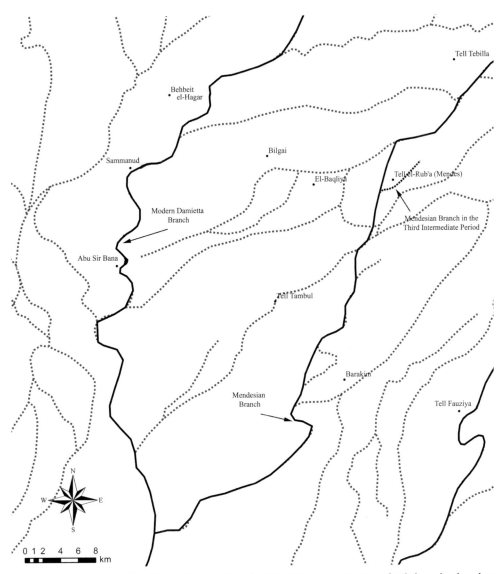

Map 10 Lower section of the Mendesian branch in the New Kingdom. Position of Nile branches based on Bietak, 1975: plan 4.

Sheikh Youssef. The settlement evidence from this region of the Mendesian branch indicates Third Intermediate Period settlement only continued at el-Baqliya and at Mendes, and not at Tell Tambul (Map 11).

North of Mendes the settlements of Tell Tebilla, Tell Buweib, and Tell Bahr Mahed date to the New Kingdom. Settlement continued at Tell Tebilla and Tell Buweib in the Third Intermediate Period. There is no evidence of Third Intermediate Period settlement north-east beyond Tell Buweib along the East Bank of the Mendesian branch. A 16.5 km stretch of the Mendesian branch's west bank from Tell Tebilla to Tell Bahr Mahed has no evidence of settlements

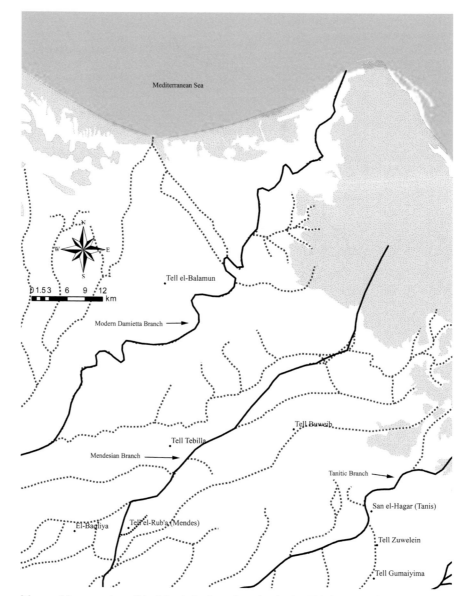

Map 11 Upper section of the Mendesian branch region in the Third Intermediate Period. Position of Nile branches based on Bietak, 1975: plan 4.

of either New Kingdom or Third Intermediate Period date. On the East Bank north of Mendes, there is another long 24.9 km gap between Mendes and the next settlement of Tell Buweib. The placement of Tell Buweib on the Bahr Hadrus drainage canal, which runs to the south of Thmuis (Tell Timai), may indicate that Tell Timai could have been active in the Third Intermediate Period, creating an island formation for Mendes and Thmuis, with Tell Timai on the south acting as a potential military site defending the Bahr Hadrus waterway which led out into the Mediterranean Sea. The projected waterway of the Bahr Hadrus, as stated by Bietak,[243] would join with the canal that linked the Mendesian branch and the Central Nile branch (Damietta), on which the New Kingdom settlement of Tell Tambul was located. It was only in the Third Intermediate Period, when a shift in the local waterway to the east of Mendes removed the hydraulic boundary between the two nomes, that the settlements were reunited into one geo-political area. In the Third Intermediate Period, the area around Mendes was under the control of a local line of Libyan chiefs, who made Mendes their regional capital, thus elevating it into a major political and economic centre. This is also the case further to the south, as Leontopolis was now a major political centre with its own local ruler. There is no further evidence of smaller settlements within the hinterlands at either Mendes or Leontopolis.

THE EASTERN DELTA: TANITIC AND PELUSIAC BRANCHES OF THE NILE

The ancient authors Herodotus, Pseudo Skylax, Diodorus Siculus, Strabo, Pliny the Elder, and Pomponius Mela are consistent in naming the seven principal Nile branches of the Delta. There are some divergences, particularly regarding the presence of the Tanitic branch. By the time Herodotus visited Egypt ca. 450 BCE there were only three principal Nile branches – the Pelusiac, Sebennytic, and Canopic – while the other branches, including the Tanitic, had diminished in importance and were artificially maintained.[244] Both Herodotus, who was writing no more than two hundred years after the end of the Third Intermediate Period, and the later Pomponius Mela, in 43 CE, omit the presence of a Tanitic branch in their writings.[245] Pseudo Skylax in the mid-fourth century BCE (ca. 338–337 BCE) states that the Tanitic branch connected to the Pelusiac branch, but not where, and no later author indicates where it connected. Strabo suggests the mention of a Saitic branch by Herodotus was an alternative name for the Tanitic branch, but modern scholarship now rejects this theory,[246] and the Saitic branch should be associated with Sais, or the Saite Nome. Owing to the position of the Tanitic branch within the textual ordering of the Delta branches, modern scholarship has regarded the otherwise unknown Cataptystic branch of Pomponius Mela as a direct substitution for the Tanitic branch, but other than the position within the texts there is no other reason to make such an identification.[247] The later writings of Ptolemy Claudius ca. 43 CE identify a mouth bearing the Tanitic name but no associated waterway, and indeed no author after Pseudo Skylax connects the mouth to the wider river network. The geological evidence indicates that, by the time of Ptolemy Claudius, the Tanitic branch had disappeared.[248] The Busiris river of Ptolemy Claudius is sometimes suggested to be Ptolemy's nomenclature for the older Tanitic branch. The settlements mentioned by Ptolemy indicate a trajectory which does not pass close to Tanis, or the Tanitic Nome.

Ptolemy has the Tanitic branch debouch through the Phatnitic mouth and not the Tanitic, with which he does not associate a distributary. Both Pseudo Skylax and Ptolemy suggest the Tanitic branch was a distributary of the Pelusiac branch, and that it was connected to the Busiris river. Such an association with the Busiris river is therefore tenuous, and again we are left with a waterway which resembles no earlier channels, and indeed no later representation of the eastern Delta.[249]

The nature of the evidence prior to the fifth century BCE adds to the problem of locating the Tanitic branch in the Pharaonic Period. The texts and monuments of the Third Intermediate Period do not explicitly attest to a Tanitic branch or provide any definitive nomenclature which could be equated with such a feature. The Onomasticon of Amenemope still refers to 'The Waters of Pre' (the Pelusiac branch) as the dominant waterway of the eastern Delta in the Twenty-First Dynasty, even though the capital had moved away from Qantir to Tanis as a result of the silting up of the Pelusiac branch in the region of Qantir. The consistent omission in the Third Intermediate Period texts and monuments of any reference to a Tanitic branch is striking, as this has been assumed as the major Nile branch in connection with the new capital at Tanis. One term, 𓈎𓏲𓂋𓏭𓈗, wryt, is mentioned in association with the region during the Ramesside Period.[250] The translation of this term 𓈎𓏲𓂋𓏭𓈗 is 'High Water',[251] or 'Great Water'. The associated determinative suggests it is a channel and may reflect a river run-off channel in high flood episodes. This term may be evidence for the Tanitic channel in the region of Tanis during the Ramesside Period, but as it is no longer mentioned after the Ramesside Period, and is absent in the Third Intermediate Period sources, along with any mention of associated Nile channels for the region, it is difficult to provide evidence of a 'Tanitic branch' within the hydraulic landscape of the Third Intermediate Period. The original function of Tanis was as a port in the late New Kingdom, indicating the area was most likely a swampy/lacustrine region where it was difficult for large settlements to develop, and it may have been served by an interconnected system of canals rather than a main Nile tributary. Finally, the mention of the region of 𓂋𓈖𓅱𓈊 r3-3ḫt, 'The Opening of the Fields', on the Twenty-Second Dynasty statue of Gerew from Tanis[252] would indicate that there were large areas of arable and cultivated land around Tanis. A zone of agricultural land around Tanis called 'The Opening of the Fields' was already documented in the previous New Kingdom on an obelisk of Neshey.[253]

The New Kingdom settlements of Tanis, Gezirat el-Faras, Tell Fauziya, and Tellein situated on the projected trajectory of the Tanitic branch are no more than 1.6 km away from the branch itself on the West Bank (Map 12).[254] From Tanis, Gezirat el-Faras was ca. 19.5 km upstream. From Gezirat el-Faras, Tell Fauziya was another 20.9 km upstream, with the final most westerly settlement of Tellein lying another 40.2 km along the channel. There is a possible

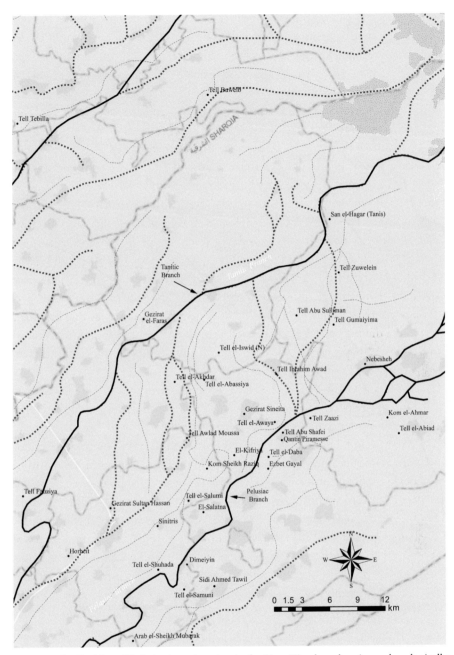

Map 12 The Tanitic and Pelusiac branch region in the New Kingdom showing archaeologically attested settlements. Position of Nile branches based on Bietak, 1975: plan 4.

progressive staggering of settlement locations from Tanis to Tell Fauziya, based on the equidistant nature of each of the sites. In the Third Intermediate Period, there is no evidence of settlement along the projected Tanitic branch's West Bank (Map 13). Third Intermediate Period ceramic evidence has not been

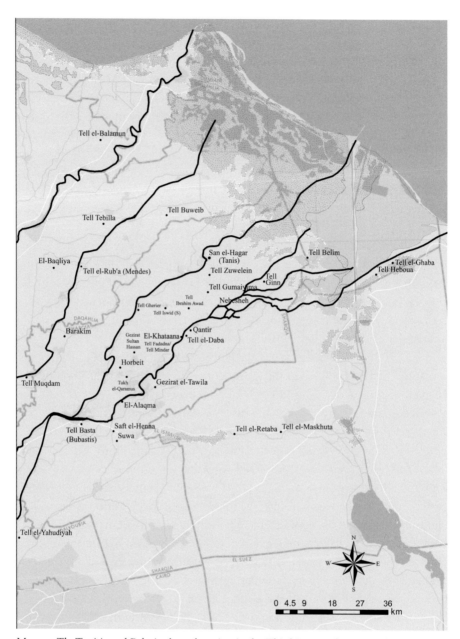

Map 13 The Tanitic and Pelusiac branch region in the Third Intermediate Period. Position of
Nile branches based on Bietak, 1975: plan 4.

found at Gezirat el-Faras, Tell Fauziya, or Tellein. There is also no evidence of
Third Intermediate Period settlement on the east bank of the projected Tanitic
branch. The only settlement of the period within 1.6 km of the projected
Tanitic trajectory is Tell Gherier, which itself is located on the intersection of
the Tanitic branch and one of the canals which form the canal network
between the Pelusiac and suggested Tanitic course. The canal network

proposed by Bietak linked the Tanitic and Pelusiac branches.[255] This canal system supported fifteen New Kingdom sites. The number of sites is reduced in the Third Intermediate Period, when a maximum of nine are attested, with Tell Gherier the closest to the proposed Tanitic course. At the time when Qantir was in decline and the eventual movement of the capital to Tanis was in process, an increase of Third Intermediate Period activity may be expected in association with Bietak's[256] proposed trajectory of the Tanitic Nile branch and the hinterland of Tanis. The archaeological and textual evidence so far does not support such a scenario. The problems of locating a Tanitic branch in the Third Intermediate Period landscape suggest the hypothesis that there may have been a different hydrological development in play during the Third Intermediate Period.

Bietak suggested that during the Twenty-First to Twenty-Second Dynasty a branch of the Pelusiac river flowed into the Tanitic arm.[257] The modern Bahr Faqus may follow the same trajectory and runs for 17.2 km. The canal runs to the west side of both Tell Zuwelein and Tell Gumaiyima. An ancient waterway in this channel could have supported contact between the old capital of Qantir and the Third Intermediate Period capital at Tanis.

Tell Zuwelein is located ca. 4.8 km south of Tanis and has New Kingdom remains[258] and a substantial burial ground of the Third Intermediate Period.[259] Tell Gumaiyima is located around 4.5 km to the south of Tell Zuwelein and has a late Ramesside cemetery,[260] while late nineteenth-century excavations at the site indicated the presence of a Third Intermediate Period enclosure and temple.[261] The presence of both late Ramesside and Third Intermediate Period burials at each site is paralleled with the taphonomic development of Tanis, which has late Ramesside burials as the earliest activity at the site prior to the settlement's development into the Third Intermediate Period capital. The equidistant nature of Tell Zuwelein and Tell Gumaiyima from Tanis indicates that they may have been founded along a route leading from Tanis to another settlement such as Nebesheh or the old capital of Qantir.

This possible scenario of population increases and site density growth may mirror that observed in the western Delta river network at the end of the Third Intermediate Period and in the Late Period with the creation of new settlements along the Canopic branch. The avulsion of the Pelusiac branch around Qantir and the resulting extension or adaptation of the river network in the area could have led to the establishment of new settlements along what is now the Bahr Faqus canal. The creation of new channels by avulsion, perhaps assisted by human action, would have encouraged the growth in populations in the region. The labour forces required for the excavation of longitudinal canal systems would have taxed the available pool of labour which would already have been busy with the maintenance and clearance of the existing canal network as well as normal agricultural tasks. The movement of labour into these areas, either from elsewhere in Egypt or as settled captives, would have raised local population numbers on either a temporary or permanent basis.[262] The creation of new canals would set into motion a positive feedback requiring more irrigated farmland, which would contribute to urbanisation and potentially further growth in the existing irrigation system in the region.[263]

Elsewhere in the region, settlement activity continued at Tell Ibrahim Awad, Gezirat Sultan Hassan, and Pharbaitos. New settlement activity for the Third Intermediate Period is found at Tell Gherier, Tell Iswid (S),[264] and Tell Fadadna/Tell Mindar, while at Tukh el-Qaramus there is only limited evidence of New Kingdom activity.[265] There is a significant decrease in the number of attested settlements for the Third Intermediate Period in this region. This may be due to the preservation of the archaeological and textual material. It could reflect a movement out of the previous Ramesside settlements and into a more nucleated form of urbanised settlement and larger communities. In contrast, the pattern and form of habitation may have differed considerably between the Tanitic and Pelusiac regions. The large number of satellite sites clustering around the main centre of Qantir appears to contrast with the large tell mound site type which focused all settlement in one nucleated area, instead of dispersing the settlement on to smaller tell sites that clustered around the main nucleus of Qantir.

THE EAST BANK OF THE PELUSIAC BRANCH

The Pelusiac branch was the main waterway which supported the New Kingdom capital of Piramesse. New Kingdom settlement activity increased on the projected course of the Pelusiac branch at the time of the construction and lifetime of the Ramesside capital at Qantir.[266] Along the Pelusiac branch, on the East Bank, ten New Kingdom sites can be identified. In the Third Intermediate Period there was limited low-level settlement at Qantir, but the New Kingdom settlements of Tell Zaazi, Ezbet Gayal, Sidi Ahmed Tawil, Dimeyin, Tell Samuni, and Arab el-Sheikh Mubarak all show an absence of Third Intermediate Period ceramics. Two new Third Intermediate Period settlements appear at el-Alaqma and Gezira el-Tawila. El-Alaqma is 4.8 km upstream of the New Kingdom settlement of Arab el-Sheikh Mubarak, while Gezira el-Tawila is 4.8 km downstream. The evidence from the East Bank suggests new settlements were developed upstream of the capital at Qantir and may indicate that the Pelusiac branch had only moved in the region of Qantir.

In the far south of the Pelusiac branch, New Kingdom settlement was found at el-Shobak, el-Birkawi, el-Shagamba, Bilbeis, and Minayar, while the main settlements of Tell el-Yahudiyah, Bubastis, and Saft el-Henna all show evidence of New Kingdom and Third Intermediate Period activity (Maps 14 and 15).

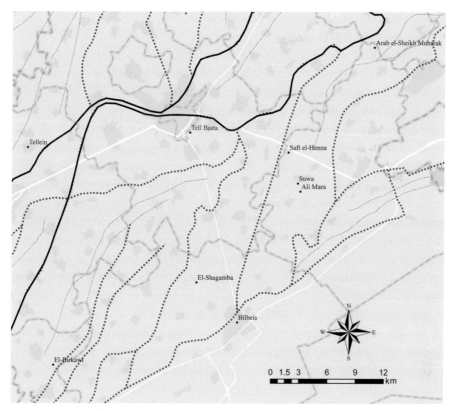

Map 14 New Kingdom sites in the region of Bubastis and the Wadi Tumilat. Position of Nile branches based on Bietak, 1975: plan 4.

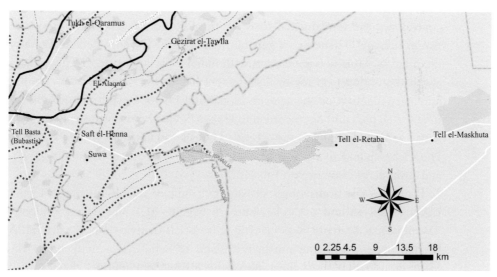

Map 15 Third Intermediate Period sites in the region of Bubastis and the Wadi Tumilat. Position of Nile branches based on Bietak, 1975: plan 4.

Suwa, associated with Saft el-Henna, is the only other site to preserve Third Intermediate Period occupation.

The proposed waterways of Bietak indicate that there was probably a minor channel in the New Kingdom which flowed in the area of the modern el-Bahr el-Shirini as it flows past Bilbeis, while Minayar and el-Shobak both border it closely on the East Bank.[267] Two more possible hydrological variants of canals probably connected with the el-Bahr el-Shirini based on Bietak's hydraulic maps,[268] with el-Shagamba on a western waterway and Saft el-Henna, Suwa, and Ali Mara on the easternmost channel. The presence of concentrated Third Intermediate Period activity on the eastern channel suggests this was active during the Third Intermediate Period only. The Wadi Tumilat during this period saw continued activity at Tell el-Retaba and Tell el-Maskhuta, while the entrance of the Wadi Tumilat around Saft el-Henna may have been fortified by the new military foundation of 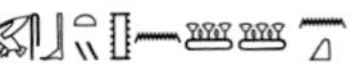 *pꜣ-sbty-n-ššnḳ*, 'The Walls of Shoshenq III', to control traffic into and out of the Eastern Desert.

The settlement patterns in this region indicate that there was a reduction in settlement from the New Kingdom into the Third Intermediate Period. The archaeological data may reflect a real-world picture of settlement at this time in this area during the Third Intermediate Period, and settlement had contracted or nucleated to the main centre at Bubastis.

THE MILITARY LANDSCAPE OF THE THIRD INTERMEDIATE PERIOD

After the end of the New Kingdom, military power rather than bureaucratic control was the fundamental basis for royal authority. The High Priests of Amun ruling at Thebes were generals, while in the Twenty-Second Dynasty the rulers were army commanders with military backgrounds.[269] The military also had an impact on regional settlement networks. Forty-two sites exhibit a military function or character in Upper and Lower Egypt; of these, thirty-nine (92.86 per cent) are recorded in Upper Egypt almost exclusively through texts and situated in the Tenth Upper Egyptian Nome and the Heracleopolitan/Faiyum region; only three are recorded in Lower Egypt, and again derive from texts (Table 2).

There are few archaeologically attested military establishments in Upper Egypt (Maps 16 and 17). The southern frontier of Egypt during the early Twenty-First Dynasty was at Bigga and has activity under the HPA Menkheperre.[270] To the north, the island of Sehel has activity under the HPA Pinudjem I.[271] At the time of the HPA Menkheperre, the southern border of Egypt was still considered to be at Bigga, but afterwards, there is no longer any evidence of elite or royal inscriptions south of Elephantine. From the reign of the HPA Menkheperre, Elephantine became the main southern

TABLE 2 *Regional site density of Third Intermediate Period military locations in Upper Egypt.*

Nome	Military locations	% Distribution
1st	4	10.26
2nd	0	0
3rd	1	2.56
4th	2	5.13
5th	1	2.56
6th	0	0
7th	0	0
8th	1	2.56
9th	0	0
10th	8	20.51
11th	0	0
12th	0	0
13th	0	0
14th	0	0
15th	1	2.56
A–A 16th–22nd	21	53.85

frontier and authorised control point of Egypt. In the Twenty-Fifth Dynasty, the zone of the Nile in the First Upper Egyptian Nome was fortified most likely by Piankhy with several military installations aimed at a policy of controlled access between Upper Egypt and Nubia. These forts allowed Piankhy to launch his assault on Egypt. So far only one fort has been located, at Abu Id.[272]

A feature of the Theban region in the Twenty-First Dynasty was the erection of a series of forts by HPA Menkheperre. The first was at Gebelein on the southern Theban border, and the second was at Higazeh, which lay on the northern Theban border. Both forts were part of a fortified checkpoint system designed to control river traffic in and out of the nome,[273] while Gebelein also controlled any foot traffic into and out of the nome leading to the Kharga Oasis. Evidence for activity in the Kharga Oasis is attested for the Twenty-First Dynasty, under HPA Pinudjem I.[274] Gebelein was supplemented by the fortified structure at Higazeh, which provided extensive views of the entire Fifth Upper Egyptian Nome. Higazeh would have provided the same primary function as Gebelein by controlling river traffic and foot traffic, this time at the entrance to the Wadi Hammamat. The construction of both these forts allowed the Theban pontiffs to have a full view of the Theban Nome territory, which was not possible from the Gebelein fortress alone. Furthermore, the construction of these forts demonstrates the need to control populations, trade, and economic resources from the deserts. Inscriptions on elite statuary indicate that the fortifications of the Theban Nome were

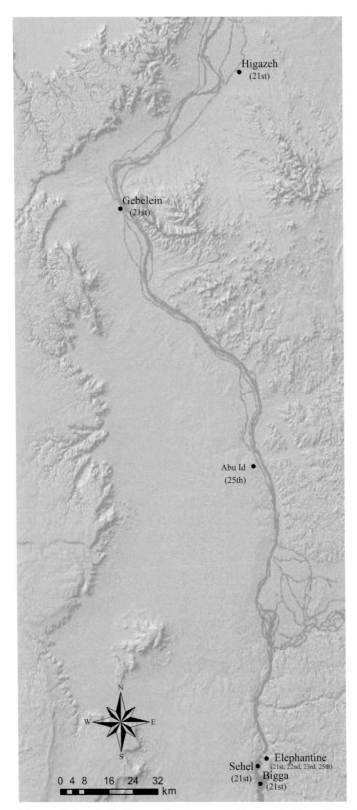

Map 16 Archaeologically attested military establishments in Upper Egypt (southern section).
Copyright © 2014 Esri.

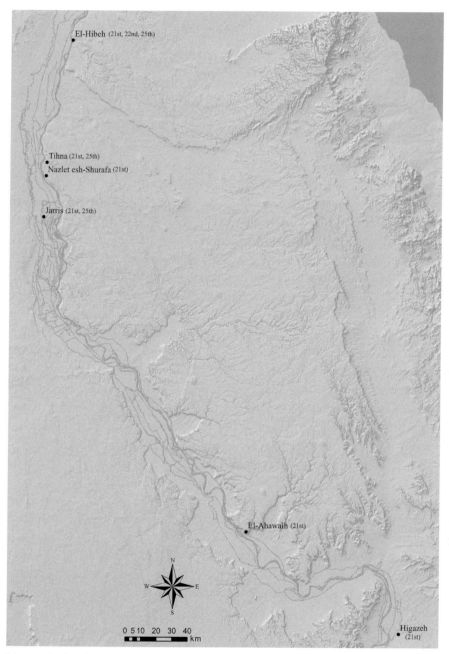

Map 17 Archaeologically attested military establishments in Upper Egypt (northern section).
Copyright © 2014 Esri.

supplemented by an additional military location in the centre of the nome
called 'The Seat Beloved of Thoth'. This site is first mentioned during the reign
of Merenptah in the New Kingdom.[275] It is located near Medinat Habu
(possibly underneath the Ptolemaic temple of Thoth at Qasr el-Aguz). The
fort was maintained into the Twenty-Second Dynasty, like the forts of Mer

Meshaf and Usermaatre in the Heracleopolitan region. Finally, a second possible military location was that of the Twenty-First Dynasty 'Mound of the Falcon' listed on the Onomasticon of Amenemope and it may have had some connection with 'The Seat Beloved of Thoth'.

From the Eighth Upper Egyptian Nome to the Heracleopolitan region there are again few archaeologically attested military forts. In the Eighth Upper Egyptian Nome, close to the northern border, was the fort of el-Ahawaih. El-Ahawaih was founded in the late New Kingdom and continued to be utilised in the Third Intermediate Period. It is suggested that el-Ahawaih is a well-suited candidate for the location of *tꜣ dḥnt*, 'The Promontory', which was a toponym recorded on numerous fragments of the el-Hibeh archive dated to the reign of HPA Menkheperre.[276] El-Ahawaih had views of the wider Abydene West Bank, the associated burial grounds, and the floodplain region, and could also view the entrance to the Wadi Umm Araka which led out to the Western Desert. This fortification would have been part of the military landscape maintained by the HPA Menkheperre in the control of access to the Nile Valley.

North of el-Ahawaih, HPA Menkheperre constructed or maintained forts at Nazlet esh-Shurafa and el-Hibeh. There may have already been some Ramesside Period activity at Nazlet esh-Shurafa prior to the constructions of Menkheperre, as a statue of Khaemwese, the son of Ramesses II, was found at the site.[277] The Onomasticon of Amenemope records that the fort of Neferusy at Jarris was still in use and continued so into the Twenty-Fifth Dynasty as Piankhy records it as one of the main centres which he assaulted. This string of military locations reflects the Twenty-First Dynasty policy of river traffic control extending from the Theban Nome into Middle Egypt as far north as the Heracleopolitan/Faiyum region, representing the limits of the territorial control. In the Twenty-Second Dynasty, el-Hibeh became an important military centre, but the monumental and textual evidence goes silent on the other forts constructed by HPA in the Twenty-First Dynasty. In the Twenty-Second Dynasty the overall picture of the military landscape for the period apart from el-Hibeh is reliant on texts, which can fill in the gaps within the archaeological record.

Military establishments dominate the settlement landscape of the Tenth Upper Egyptian Nome and the Heracleopolitan region. Four main military site types are recorded: 𝄞 *nḫtw*, 𓏏 *sgr*, 𓉻 *bḫn*, and 𓉐 *iḥw*, with Per Sekhemkheperre attributed to be the main controlling military centre in the area.

𝄞 *nḫtw* 'fortress' are all restricted to the Heracleopolitan/Faiyum region. These include 𝄞 *pꜣ nḫtw n mr-mšꜥ.f* 'The Fortress of Mer Meshaf', 𝄞 *pꜣ nḫtw ꜥꜣ (n) wsr-mꜣꜥt-rꜥ* 'The Fortress of Usermaatre', 𝄞 *(m) ḥꜣt pꜣ 5 nḫtw ꜥꜣ n n(ꜣ) mꜥ* 'The Head of the Five Great

Fortresses of the Ma', which is the same fortress as the New Kingdom 'Five Great Fortresses of the Sherdan',[278] and ⛩ *p3 nḫtw n mk-kmt* 'The Fortress of the Protector of Egypt'. 🏯 *nḫtw* forts are only found in the Nile Valley. None of these military toponyms has been identified with a modern Egyptian site.

There are nine recorded 🏯 *sgr* locations in the Nile Valley for the Third Intermediate Period. They are so far only documented for Upper Egypt, indicating *sgr* locations were exclusive to the Nile Valley like the 🏯 *nḫtw* forts. In the New Kingdom, seven *sgr* locations are documented on the New Kingdom Wilbour Papyrus in the region corresponding to the area between Akoris and Atfih.[279] In the 152 km stretch of the Nile Valley recorded on the Wilbour Papyrus, 9.94 per cent of the sites mentioned are *sgr* foundations. In the Third Intermediate Period only two *sgr* locations are recorded in the Akoris–Atfih region. They are both recorded on the Twenty-Second Dynasty Cairo JE 39410. One is 🏯 *dmi p3-sgr-n-ḥwt-ty* 'The Village of "The-Fort-of-the-Estate-of-Tiy",'[280] and the other 🏯 *dmi p3-sg-n-ꜥr(t)* 'The Village of "The-Fort-of-the-Goat".'[281] Both toponyms are recorded on the Wilbour Papyrus and demonstrate either a continuation or re-founding of two *sgr* locations in the Twenty-Second Dynasty. Papyrus Louvre AF 6345 records seven *sgr* locations in the Tenth Upper Egyptian Nome at the start of the Twenty-First Dynasty. A *sgr* fort called 🏯 *sgr-šk* was situated at, or near to, the boundary between the Ninth and Tenth Upper Egyptian nomes. 🏯 was linked with 🏯 *pr-ḥr-nb-mḏ3iw* 'The House of Horus, Lord of the Medjay',[282] which was a garrison force of 'Desert Police Officers'. Both toponyms are associated with the defence and control of individuals between the two regions, and the control of movement throughout, and into, the Nile Valley. A third defensive location, called 🏯 *p3-sgr-ti-nt-inh*, was situated close to the border zone and north of 🏯 *ḥwt k3=k*. 🏯 *p3-sgr-ti-nt-inh* and 🏯 *sgr-šk* may have been located on opposite sides of the Nile Valley to increase control from both banks of the Nile, suggesting both desert sides were covered as well as the river.

Three 🏯 *bḫn* sites are recorded on Cairo JE 39410. They are 🏯 *dmi p3-bḫn-n-p3-nhsy* 'The Castle of Panehesy',[283] 🏯 *dmi p3-bḫn-n-nfr-rnpt* 'The Castle of Neferenpet',[284] and an undefined name for another *bḫn* location, possibly that of the 'Castle of the Vizier'(?).[285] Both the Castle of Panehesy and the Castle of the Vizier are recorded on the Wilbour Papyrus. 'The Castle of Neferenpet' is not recorded on the Wilbour Papyrus, indicating that this *bḫn* may have been a new foundation of the Third Intermediate Period. Unlike 🏯 *nḫtw* and 🏯 *sgr*, 🏯 *bḫn* sites are documented in Lower Egypt. The Lower Egyptian examples include 🏯 *p3 bḫn n bỉw*,[286] an unknown location but likely to be associated with the Memphite Nome,[287] and a place simply called *bḥn* in association with Tukh el-Qaramus in the north-eastern Delta.

In the New Kingdom, eight military camp (also translated as stables or storehouses) settlements are documented on the Wilbour Papyrus. This figure is low compared with the frequency of the title of 'Stable Master' in the text if one translates it as 'stable'.[288] The lack of 𓇋𓎛𓅱𓉐 *iḥw* settlements in the Twentieth Dynasty is continued into the Third Intermediate Period. There are five 𓇋𓎛𓅱𓉐 *iḥw* sites recorded in the Third Intermediate Period toponyms and these represent 8.06 per cent of all Heracleopolitan region settlements. The first 𓇋𓎛𓅱𓉐 *iḥw*, 𓊪𓇋𓎛𓅱𓉐 *pꜣ iḥw n ḥꜣt* (The Stable of the Front), is recorded in the Twenty-Second Dynasty and occurs again in the Twenty-Third Dynasty in Year 10 of Peftjauouybast 𓂧𓏤𓇋𓊪𓇋𓎛𓅱𓉐 as *dmi pꜣ iḥw n ḥꜣt*. No Third Intermediate Period 𓇋𓎛𓅱𓉐 *iḥw* sites are found in New Kingdom documents and all are probably new foundations. This shows a reduction in this type of site and may also indicate a new set of 𓇋𓎛𓅱𓉐 *iḥw* sites for the region.

Finally, 𓉐𓏤𓊹 Per Sekhemkheperre was a royal foundation of Osorkon I, but no contemporary documents of Osorkon I record the foundation.[289] Per Sekhemkheperre is mentioned on nine documents dating from the reign of Osorkon II to Piankhy. The toponyms do not refer specifically to a fortified foundation. The assumption that this was a military site is based upon the military titles of people who were associated with it.[290]

DOMESTIC MILITARY POLICY

The evidence shows that there was a concentration of a military presence in the First Upper Egyptian Nome, the Theban region, the Tenth Upper Egyptian Nome, and in the region from Akoris to Atfih. In Upper Egypt, the military landscape of the Ramesside pharaohs was adopted by the rulers of the Twenty-First and Twenty-Second Dynasties and adapted to fit the needs of the new geo-political landscape, which they now controlled. There was a preference for fortifications on the borders of nomes, and at the entrance to important wadi routes, trading zones, and agricultural regions. The military establishments in the Theban region have Ramesside precursors, while the changing of the name of the Ramesside 'Five Great Fortresses of the Sherden' to that of the Third Intermediate Period 'Five Great Fortresses of the Ma' corresponds to the re-use of Ramesside forts into the Third Intermediate Period. The pre-existing built military environment was added to and developed by Osorkon I in the Heracleopolitan region with the military foundations of Per Sekhemkheperre and Mek Kemet which controlled the access routes into Lower Egypt, the Oases, and the Memphite area. These fortresses added military security to the region, which was most likely the ancestral home of the Twenty-Second Dynasty. The large amount of fortifications in and around Heracleopolis reflects the military lineage of the Libyan pharaohs and their desire both to secure themselves within the Heracleopolitan region and to ensure their influence over the Delta capitals. It may also have been to control traffic to the west and east without having to go down the western and eastern Nile Delta branches. This would explain why the greatest proportion of military establishments are documented in northern Upper Egypt and the Delta apex. In Lower Egypt, apart from the Memphite region with some limited references to a *bḫn* establishment, and a *bḫn* at or around Tukh el-Qaramus, the usage of military terminology such as *nḫtw, bḫn*, and *sgr* is missing from the Third Intermediate Period literary evidence. The Piankhy Stela, although a military campaign record, is silent on the different military foundation types for the Delta, but they are recorded for the Memphite region in the text. This indicates either that settlements of this type were not encountered during Piankhy's campaign in the Delta, that they were defined using different terminology, or that different types of military settlements found in Upper Egypt do not exist in Lower Egypt during the Third Intermediate Period, or they just did not exist in the Delta.

DEVELOPMENTS IN THE SETTLEMENT PATTERNS OF EGYPT IN THE THIRD INTERMEDIATE PERIOD

Despite the nature of the landscape and its taphonomic development since the end of the Third Intermediate Period, a combination of historical texts, regional archaeological and environmental case studies, and the landscape itself can be used in conjunction to understand aspects of the political, social, and economic relationships of settlement systems in Egypt. The regional studies on the Deltaic settlement systems have raised several issues such as the location and emergence of active Nile Delta branches during the period. The Mendesian branch during the Third Intermediate Period should be located between Mendes and Thmuis (Tell Timai), while there is so far no evidence to suggest the presence of the Canopic branch in the western Delta at this time, and the overall density of settlements in the western Delta for this period remains low. There appears to be a new hydraulic system developing in the western Delta with the presence of the 𓂧𓏤𓈖𓈗 *Khenes* canal under Shoshenq III and the subsequent development of the political centres in that region, which facilitated the increased settlement numbers attested in the Late Period. There is a general absence of Third Intermediate Period settlement evidence along the previously proposed Tanitic branch location. The settlement systems in the eastern Delta favour a continuation of settlement along the Pelusiac branch, while there is no meaningful change in the settlement pattern of the region despite the movement of the capital to Tanis. This calls into question the level of political power of Tanis during the Twenty-First Dynasty, as it has no associated donation stelae, and the rulers were still residing in Memphis during the early Twenty-First Dynasty, while the royal residence was at Heracleopolis in the Twenty-Second Dynasty. The region around Bubastis appears to have a low regional settlement density. The evidence suggests that settlement density appears to have contracted or nucleated to the main centres at Bubastis, Tanis, Mendes, and Leontopolis. The growing territorial pressures exercised by the increased fragmentation of the state and inter-regional territory annexation could have caused this scenario.

The military institutions of the New Kingdom in Upper Egypt appear to have been maintained with subsequent additions and fortifications erected in areas of important strategic and politico-economic junctures based on new political borders, particularly in the Theban Nome and the Heracleopolitan/Faiyum region. The lack of identifiable military settlements in the Delta may suggest a different military organisation or military site terminology was in place. When the First and Second Upper Egyptian nomes are studied, the proliferation of archaeologically attested military site types and the lack of potential for cultivation can be seen, thanks to the high site preservation rates in desert regions, which is a feature observed in Near Eastern archaeology.[291] The Theban case study shows the importance of comparing texts with the archaeological record to track the prosperity of settlements during political changes: the texts would suggest that Tod had lost some of its political or economic power, and as the temple showed no sign of additions compared with other sites such as Armant and Naga el-Medamud, this might agree with this hypothesis. Finally, comparing and chronologically tracking place names through the administrative texts shows the political and economic importance of certain site types over different phases, something which has been demonstrated with the 𓉐 settlements in the Heracleopolitan/Faiyum region.

The characteristics of the Third Intermediate Period identified through the settlement pattern evidence and regional cases studies suggest that Egypt in general at this period was a country that was fragmented in an administrative sense. This gradual fragmentation of the geo-political landscape is seen in the choice and geographical extent of settlements mentioned on early Third Intermediate Period administrative and cadastral documents. The gradual retraction of Twenty-First Dynasty influence on the southern border to Elephantine and the focus on fortifying military locations in the south of Egypt along a checkpoint system indicates a more inward-looking attitude among the political elite. The decrease in overall site numbers compared with the New Kingdom may be reflective of a bias in site preservation rates, but may be representative of a more inward-looking regional policy of local populations, and the need to be clustered in more close-knit kin groups, following Libyan social influence. This is especially visible in the Delta where Libyan influence was most felt, while the growing power of regional centres may have influenced the urbanisation of the country, creating a hinterland pull out of the small settlements and more urbanised centres under strong powerful local leaders.

LAND MANAGEMENT AND LOCAL ECONOMIES

Discussions regarding the economic relationships of sites encounter several difficulties, including the incomplete nature of the site corpus and the unknown levels of social complexity for the smaller settlements, many of which are only known from cadastral or onomastic surveys or are yet to be discovered. An assessment of the administrative documents and archaeological material does, however, bring to light several issues regarding the way Third Intermediate Period pharaohs and local chiefs administered the land and provides some indications as to the structure of the economy of the period. This section reviews land management policies to characterise the different mechanisms of land administration and land holdings, which are then compared with New Kingdom policies. In addition to the wider state-level land management and economies, this section also discusses the evidence for local domestic economies such as manufacturing and object creation by craftspeople and artisans.

Land Registers

Several land registers dated to the Third Intermediate Period provide evidence as to the nature and extent of land holdings of temple institutions. The evidence documented in Papyrus Reinhardt[292] and Papyrus Louvre AF 6345[293] deals with the Theban temples' land holdings in the Tenth Upper Egyptian Nome. These documents demonstrate that the Theban temples continued to hold and administer large amounts of land as far away as the Tenth Upper Egyptian Nome at least up until the Twenty-Second Dynasty. The texts record the size of each field, its location, and the names of the individuals responsible for its farming or direct oversight, the number of grain sacks produced or taxed from each plot of land, and the institution associated with the plot owner. Land parcels in Papyrus Reinhardt can be as small as half an aroura and up to 30 arourae in area.[294] This shows that not only were the Theban temples administering wealth, generated by the Theban area or gifted by the king, but they were collecting revenues gained from what was an extensive hinterland.[295] Twenty-First Dynasty benefices of female members of the families of the HPA provide evidence of Theban land holdings in the agriculturally rich Third Upper Egyptian Nome and at Girga, el-Atawla, and Akhmim. This indicates that the administrative systems of the Theban temples continued to be well organised to manage such a complex and wide-ranging system of land ownership. This pattern of land administration in the early Third Intermediate Period follows the traditions documented in the earlier Twentieth Dynasty Wilbour Papyrus, with a recorded 2,800 plots of land and tenures located in Middle Egypt associated with cult centres distributed over a 150 km strip of land from the area of Akoris to Atfih.[296]

The Twenty-First Dynasty Onomasticon of Amenemope can also be used to understand the bureaucratic and economic rationale for choosing certain sites over others to be recorded in the administrative text. The onomasticon is written from a Theban administrative perspective, is didactic in nature, and was, no doubt, used as an important scribal exercise.[297] An analysis of the place names in association with known land holdings, royal benefices, and the construction dates of monumental architecture attributed to the early Twenty-First Dynasty HPA families indicates that this document was compiled most likely in the reign of Pinudjem I.[298] It seems to have developed out of a survey of the available land holdings and important administrative and religious foundations, as most of them are found in political areas controlled by the Twenty-First Dynasty HPA and benefices of their families. These included prominent cultic or function-specific sites such as economically important quarries and animal rearing institutions for cattle and fowl, which were prominent in temple ritual and offerings. By cross-referencing the textual documents and archaeological evidence, it becomes clear that some sites lost economic importance while others rose to prominence during the transitional phase between the end of the New Kingdom and the early years of the Third Intermediate Period. The most prominent example of a settlement's possible reduction in economic and political power may be seen at Tod, just south of Thebes, which is no longer recorded on the Onomasticon of Amenemope despite being one of the most important political, religious, and economic centres in the Theban region during the New Kingdom. Another example that demonstrates the usefulness of employing the Onomasticon of Amenemope as part of an economic discussion is the entry 𓉐𓏏𓄤𓂋𓈉𓈖𓇋𓈙𓈇 pr-nḥb-n-iš 'The House of the Opened Land of Isha' or 'The Newly Opened Land of Isha'.[299] The absence of this toponym which is clearly related to agricultural donations and land tenure from the earlier economic Papyrus Louvre AF 6345 indicates that 'The House of the Opened Land of Isha' was likely to have been a new domain, and was one of the most important locations in the Tenth Upper Egyptian Nome for the Theban administration at the time of the compilation of the Onomasticon of Amenemope. The mention of this new toponym could indicate that the sites listed in Papyrus Louvre AF 6345 had lost some of their economic importance, and that, upon the advent of political change, the sites in the onomasticon had become the dominant political and economic centres in the area and controlled the distribution of land and resources to the Theban state. Finally, the Dakhleh Stela of Shoshenq I mentions the existence of a cadastral register, which has not survived, for Year 19 of a King

Psusennes (possibly Psusennes II?).[300] The mention of this cadastral survey indicates the continued tradition of land surveys into the Twenty-First and Twenty-Second Dynasty following the New Kingdom tradition of Papyrus Harris and the Wilbour Papyrus.

The lack of evidence for Theban land holdings north of the Tenth Upper Egyptian Nome suggests that, by the end of the Twenty-First and start of the Twenty-Second Dynasty, the limit of Theban control was at the Tenth Upper Egyptian Nome. After the Twenty-Second Dynasty no similar land registers have survived for the period to provide us with a view of the land holdings of Upper Egyptian temple institutions. The temple cadastral block of Shoshenq I from Heracleopolis (Cairo JE 39410), documenting the personnel, institutions, and individuals that had to provide sacrificial bulls for the temple of Heryshef, seems to have served a different function, coming from a cultic background.

Libyan Delta Land Management: Donation Stelae

During the New Kingdom, the Delta land occupation appears to be systematised by the Ramesside pharaohs, being confined mainly to the eastern Delta with the construction of the new capital at Qantir. Fortress construction on the western fringes of the Delta would have also opened the area up for urbanism and state-run settlements.[301] Furthermore, in New Kingdom Nubia, the existing cult centres and small shrines had the opportunity to reassign land.[302]

Beyond the Twenty-First Dynasty, evidence for land administration in the Delta comes primarily from land donation stelae, which are an important resource for understanding the economic relationships of settlements in the Delta with one another from the Twenty-Second to Twenty-Fifth Dynasty.[303] The majority of donation stelae originate in the Delta, with only a handful coming from Middle Egypt and the Thebaid. They are clearly a Delta development and form a counterpart to the Abnormal Hieratic land lease documents of the late Twenty-Fifth Dynasty, in which the landowner and cultivator made an agreement discussing the terms of a lease of land.[304]

Land donation stelae are one of the most characteristic groups of monuments of the Third Intermediate Period. The inscriptions record gifts of land to temples, or to their personnel.[305] The endowments concerned commonly come from the hand of an important dignitary and are usually dated. The donation stelae suggest a devolution of power to local chiefs who administered the royal territory on behalf of the king and controlled those regions that were important economic assets.[306] The provenance of some of the donation stelae suggests that they may have been set up in the settlements, perhaps in the temple they are related to, or set up in the fields as boundary markers.[307]

Not all donation stelae have the amount of land donated preserved in their inscriptions. Of those stelae that have an amount preserved (twenty-five stelae), an estimated 320 arourae of land (ca. 87.52 ha)[308] was donated to the eastern Delta settlements in the regions of Bubastis and Mendes, while in the western Delta region, 270 arourae (74.145 ha) of land were donated in the areas around the settlements of Kom Firin, Kom Abu Billo, Buto, Sais, and Busiris (Table 3).

In total ca. 590 arourae were donated, the equivalent of 161.665 ha, but not all stelae found record the amount of land donated. In the donation stelae, land at Tanis is conspicuous by its absence. There are no Twenty-First Dynasty Tanite donation stelae and this raises the question of the level of political power Tanis had, if any.[309] This may be reflected in the general lack of attested settlements in the Tanite hinterland for the period. In the Twenty-Second and Twenty-Third Dynasty there is an increase in donation stelae in the Delta, with

TABLE 3 *Land donation stelae: geographical locations and recorded amounts of land in chronological order for the eastern and western Delta.*

Land donation	Stela number and data	Reign	Arourae	Hectares
Eastern Delta				
Bubastis	Stela Berlin 8437 + Aberdeen Stela 1337	Takeloth I	30	8.205
Bubastis	Cairo Stela JE 31653	Takeloth I	10	2.735
Bubastis	Stela Cairo Temp 2/2/21/13	Pamiu	10	2.735
Bubastis	Stela Cairo JE 45779	Shoshenq V	42	11.487
Bubastis	Stela Florence 7207	Pedubast I	3	0.8205
Mendes	Stela Brooklyn Mus. 67–118	Shoshenq III	10	2.735
Mendes	Cairo Stela Geneva MAH 23473	Iuput II	5	1.3675
Pharbaitos	Stela Louvre E.10571	Shabaka	5	1.3675
Hermopolis Parva	Strasbourg Stela 1588	Unnamed king	5	1.3675
Tukh el-Qaramus	Cairo Stela 11/1/25/13	Shoshenq III	200	54.7
Totals			320	87.52
Western Delta				
Busiris	Stela Louvre E.20905	Shoshenq III	40	10.94
Buto	Stela Ancient Farouk Collection	Shoshenq V	10	2.735
Buto	Michaïlidis Collection	Tefnakht	10	2.735
Buto	Stela New York Met. Mus. 55.144.6	Shabaka	20	5.77
Buto	Stela Tell el-Fara'in	Shoshenq V	10	2.735
Kom Firin	Cairo JE 85647	Shoshenq V	5	1.3675
Kom Firin	Stela IFAO Store Registration No. 14456	Shoshenq (V?)	5	1.3675
Kom Firin	Stela Brooklyn Museum 67.119	Shoshenq V	10	2.735
Kom Firin	Stela British Museum EA 73965	Shoshenq V	10	2.735
Kom Abu Billo	Cairo JE 30972	Shoshenq V	10	2.735
Sais	Athens Stela (Athens Nat. Mus. 32)	Tefnakht	10	2.735
Western Delta	Cologne Stela, Private Collection	Shoshenq (?)	100	27.35
Western Delta	Stela Leningrad Ermitage 5630	Shoshenq IV	10	2.735
Western Delta	Stela Chicago Oriental Museum	Shoshenq III	10	2.735
Western Delta	Stela Moscow I 1a 5647	Shoshenq III	10	2.735
Totals			270	74.145

Shoshenq III and Shoshenq V being the proponents of a policy of settlement and land development in the western Delta settlements in the Twenty-Second Dynasty. The donation stelae of the Twenty-Second and Twenty-Third Dynasty are essentially concerned with lands in association with settlements concentrated on the edges of the eastern and western Delta, while in the central Delta they are rare, and those that do survive date to the Twenty-Fifth and Twenty-Sixth Dynasty. It is suggested that the absence, or scarcity, of royal or large economic chiefdoms in the central Delta indicates that these areas did not provide economic opportunities for land development, and that this absence allowed the Twenty-Fifth Dynasty kings to take advantage of these under-developed economic areas.[310] The general preservation of monuments from the central Delta makes such an assumption difficult to confirm. There is evidence from Bindariya and Tell Umm Harb of monumental works of Shoshenq III, while Busiris, Athribis, Behbeit el-Hagar, and Sebennytos, situated near the banks of the modern Damietta branch, do show increased evidence of economic and political power in the later stages of the period. It is more likely that the lack of royal monuments and settlement density is down to poor preservation rates and research focus, rather than the Twenty-Second and Twenty-Third Dynasty rulers not favouring this area as an economic and politically important region.

It is suggested that the distribution of donation stelae reflects a slow progression linked to a systematic, intensive, east–to–west land reclamation project in the wetland areas of the Delta in line with the influx of new people occupying the remaining free land.[311] The land areas being donated at Bubastis, Tukh el-Qaramus, Buto, and Mendes actually indicate that the parcels of land were relatively small compared with the overall land area of the Delta and the region/sites in which they were being donated. Based on the estimated land areas, the results do not support an 'intensive' land reclamation policy by these kings as a response to housing new populations in new land parcels. These stelae are likely to have been symbolic, rather than 'real' attempts by the local rulers to align themselves with the earlier New Kingdom system of land donation. It is likely that these stelae reflect a reorganisation of the 'old land' areas in a new partnership between the kings and temples. This reorganisation and elevation of old lands into new power bases is observed at Buto and Sais where new land donations were received in this period. In the eastern Delta, the centres of Mendes, Pharbaitos, Bubastis, and Tukh el-Qaramus received land donations and became important political centres of the period.

Libyan Land Policy in the North

At the end of the New Kingdom, the socio-political developments that led to a decrease in the wealth of Egypt did not initially impede the role of the temple economies permanently.[312] The policy of land registers continued in the Twenty-First Dynasty and administrators continued to levy taxes and assess the land holdings of the major institutions in line with the earlier New Kingdom traditions of land registry. Many of the most important temple institutions continued to hold land in extensive hinterlands, particularly that of Thebes up to the Tenth Upper Egyptian Nome and as far south as the Third Upper Egyptian Nome. The continued evidence for cadastral registers shows a continuity in the administrative functioning of land organisation and quantifying the levels of tax that each area was capable of giving. There is evidence that the New Kingdom land donation policy already employed in the Delta in the Ramesside Period continued through the Twenty-First Dynasty in Upper Egypt, albeit at a reduced level. During the Twenty-Second Dynasty the evidence from Upper Egypt for land administration declined and was replaced by the increased use of donation stelae in the Delta and Middle Egypt, where local chiefs administered the royal territory on behalf of the king and controlled those regions that were important economic assets. These areas were small parcels of land and they reflect the rejuvenation of 'old land' areas in a new partnership between the kings and temples: through political links with the monarch, the rejuvenation of the sacred landscape drove new urbanism in these areas and created politically powerful new settlements.

LOCAL AND HOUSEHOLD INDUSTRIES

Within the settlements, there is the continued evidence for state and household industries including the manufacture of pottery, metal, faience, and stone tools. This section assesses some of the different industrial areas from across Egypt to analyse their locations within the settlement; the presence or not of raw material storage spaces or fuel; the seasonality of the areas; the amount of use of the areas; and what happened at the end of their use life. In the absence of tomb scenes or wooden model representations, which form the core basis for our understanding of the way in which these industries were performed in the Old Kingdom to New Kingdom, the Third Intermediate Period relies solely on small amounts of archaeological evidence which can be compared with the previous periods to assess continuities or changes in the development of the industries from the New Kingdom, and shed light on the local and household industries and associated economies of the Third Intermediate Period.

The best representation of industrial areas for the Third Intermediate Period comes from pottery kilns overlying the small Ramesside temple of Ptah and 'Tombs V–Z' at Memphis. The mud-brick-constructed kilns were situated along the exterior face of the enclosure of the Ptah temple (Fig. 2).[313] At least six more-or-less circular kilns were found, on average 2–3 m in diameter. The kilns had a short life span since they overlap one another stratigraphically and re-used baked kiln bricks were found being used among the unbaked bricks from which the kilns were made. The Third Intermediate Period kilns at Memphis outwardly resemble the only New Kingdom scene of pottery manufacture, in the tomb of Kenamun (TT 93) at Thebes, but there are no traces of ladders or stairways at Memphis, which may have been constructed with wood[314] and, thus, did not survive. The kilns appear to have had subsidiary buildings comprising some thin-walled, round or rectangular structures made of mud-brick with beaten earth floors.[315] These structures were thought to be pottery magazines for the temporary storage of pottery before and after firing.[316] In earlier periods, pottery kilns appear to have been situated outside the settlement, but close to other industries

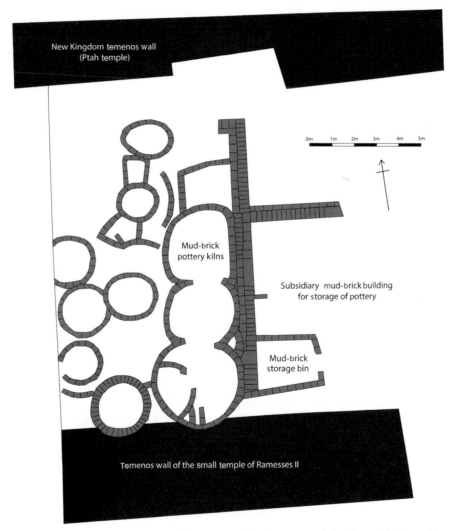

Fig. 2 The pottery production complex in Memphis Area D4 overlying the small Ramesside Ptah temple next to the Ptah temple temenos wall (redrawn, after Jacquet, 1965: pl. 9). (Courtesy of the University Museum, University of Pennsylvania.)

such as carpentry, metal working, and stone vessel manufacture, and are often associated with baking and brewing.[317] The small disused Ramesside Ptah temple provided an opportune space for the construction of the Third Intermediate Period kiln complex, with the existing walls providing support for the kilns, and suggesting that the previously uninhabited or unused area adjacent to the southern face of the Ptah temple became a designated industrial area, much like the kiln complexes behind the mortuary temple of Amunhotep son of Hapu on the West Bank of Thebes.[318] The construction of kilns had to be a carefully thought-out process, as kilns would have produced intense heat and smoke, and if they were placed near to or to the south of any residential areas then the smoke would have been blown in the direction of the wider settlement. The position of the kiln complex at Memphis would have meant that the smoke would be blown up against the temenos wall, up into the air, and be dissipated. The direct relationship between the kiln complex and the temenos wall, and its proximity to the temple, may indicate some form of continued local settlement production controlled or regulated by the Ptah temple. In the eastern sector of Memphis, at Kom el-Qala over the area of the temple of Merenptah, a faience production area may be indicated by the discovery of approximately one thousand clay moulds for faience objects and amulets. Some moulds are from Third Intermediate Period strata, but whether these are contemporary with the Kom el-Qala moulds cannot be determined.[319] Petrie found moulds which he states were later than the Merenptah temple but earlier than the houses,[320] suggesting faience production was carried out during the late Twentieth and early Twenty-First Dynasty.[321] The two zones of industrial activity at Memphis in the early Third Intermediate Period show industrial production centres were set up in previously uninhabited areas of religious complexes, indicating that, as the temples ceased to function, the inhabitants adapted the sacred space for industrial purposes. In the small Ramesside Ptah temple there was evidence of flint tool production alongside the pottery kilns, while the presence of pounders, rubbing stones, and drill handles indicated a 'stone manufactory' area in the neighbourhood of the kiln complex.[322] Metal working also reached its peak during the Third Intermediate Period, while many of the workshops must have been centred within the temple temenoi and controlled by the local elites.

While the archaeological evidence from the Third Intermediate Period for industrial areas is limited, and in turn that for local and regional economies, the evidence from Memphis does shed some light on the development of settlement space in which to accommodate and develop new industrial areas of industry, a pattern which may have been adopted in other settlements of the period. At a more basic sustenance level, fishing continued to be an important part of local economies as it had been in the New Kingdom, indicated by the continued presence of small copper alloy hooks at Memphis,[323] Gurob,[324] Tell el-Ghaba,[325] Akoris,[326] Hermopolis,[327] and Lisht.[328] At Akoris, fish, mainly catfish, were stored and prepared in designated buildings, alongside the storage of fishing equipment such as harpoons, fishhooks, weights, and nets.[329] As well as catfish, Nile perch were caught, while the larger harpoons would have been used in the pursuit of hippopotami and crocodile. Farming and the production of crops and animal by-products also remained a vital part of local and regional economies.

OBSERVATIONS ON THIRD INTERMEDIATE PERIOD LAND POLICY AND LOCAL ECONOMIES

The general policy of land administration was a continuation of New Kingdom policies with extensive hinterland connections with the major temple institutions, along with land donations. A characteristic of the Third Intermediate Period is that land administrators appear to have developed a policy of a reorganisation of old lands, which were brought under the powers of new political centres. These settlements subsequently developed throughout the period into important independent political and economic centres. Those regions with the most economic value based on agricultural surplus are consistently mentioned in the administrative documents of both the New Kingdom and the Third Intermediate Period, while other nomes and their capitals such as Shutb and Dendera are absent within the texts. The economies at the local and domestic level, such as areas of craft and production, were maintained, while specific industries such as pottery, metal working, and faience manufacture, especially for funerary use, were conducted in open-air walled enclosures and away from the main settlements. These new industrial areas were constructed on the disused open spaces of earlier temples and other administrative structures as uninhabited spaces for new industrial ventures were sought. Faience figurine and amulet production at Memphis appears to be at the domestic level as hundreds of moulds were found within the houses, but kilns were also built within the courtyard of the Merenptah temple; it is not clear whether this temple continued to function alongside the new domestic activity and therefore whether the industry could still be classed as temple workshops. Finally, the production of flint tools by local communities also appears to have been a primary site economy.

CHAPTER THREE

SETTLEMENT DEVELOPMENT AND BUILT REMAINS OF THE THIRD INTERMEDIATE PERIOD

C HAPTER 2 HAS ALREADY EXAMINED THE QUESTION OF SETTLEMENT patterns and regional policies of land management through regional case studies and several characteristics of the period were explored. The characteristics included the increasing territorial pressures created by the fragmentation of the state and inter-regional territory annexation; the maintenance and adaptation of New Kingdom military institutions, and the creation of new fortresses in areas of important strategic and politico-economic junctures based on new political borders; the establishment of a more inward-looking regional policy of local populations and the need for populations to be clustered in more close-knit kin groups, following a Libyan social influence, particularly in the Delta where Libyan influence was most felt; and finally, the growing power of regional centres may have influenced the urbanisation of the country and created hinterlands with more urbanised centres under strong powerful local leaders. This chapter moves on to assess the built archaeological remains of the Third Intermediate Period and moves from a macro-analysis (settlement patterns) to a micro-analysis (the settlements themselves) by discussing these remains. The archaeological remains of the Third Intermediate Period settlements are made up of two main types of material culture: the built environment, consisting mainly of mud-brick and stone structures, and the ceramics and wider object world. This chapter discusses the former, while the latter will be discussed in Chapter 4.

The chapter begins by establishing the locations of preserved Third Intermediate Period domestic settlement remains to assess the different regional built environments of settlements and the way in which settlements developed spatially over time. The settlements are further analysed to define the way in which Late Period urban policies affected the development and preservation of Third Intermediate Period urban topography within the archaeological record. The maintenance of or changes in urban topography of the Third Intermediate Period are discussed in the light of the top-down policies of a new political regime in a re-unified government and state in Late Period Egypt. Based on the characteristics identified previously in Chapter 2, the present chapter assesses whether the settlements in the Third Intermediate Period developed as independent entities within specific regions or if there was a general pattern of settlement policy across different political boundaries and geographical regions. It also assesses characteristics of new ideologies, both political and religious, and the economic limitations of different regions through examination of the construction of monumental architecture (walls, temples, and palaces), the nucleation of domestic architecture around monumental constructions, the development of architectural design in administrative, religious, and domestic architecture, and the self-sufficient nature of local populations by way of grain storage and food supply. The case studies at the outset of the chapter describe the development of habitation within Third Intermediate Period settlements and are discussed in geographical order from south to north (Map 18).

THE SPATIAL DEVELOPMENT OF THIRD INTERMEDIATE PERIOD SETTLEMENTS

1 Thebes

The New Kingdom and Third Intermediate Period settlement on the East Bank of Thebes lies buried beneath the modern city of Luxor, as shown in the excavations at Abu el-Gud,[1] and to the west of the Mut temple at Karnak (Fig. 3),[2] and probably stretched between the temples of Luxor and Karnak. A Twenty-First Dynasty stela of the HPA Menkheperre[3] describes the encroachment of an Asiatic domestic population into the walls of the Great Amun temple at Karnak,[4] which indicates early Third Intermediate Period settlement in the south-east area of Karnak. After the construction of Menkheperre's wall, based on associated excavation plans, the area was utilised for the construction of small chapels to Osiris. The area is now built over by the Late Dynastic temple enclosure (Fig. 4). On the West Bank, a New Kingdom papyrus[5] indicates that small settlements grew up

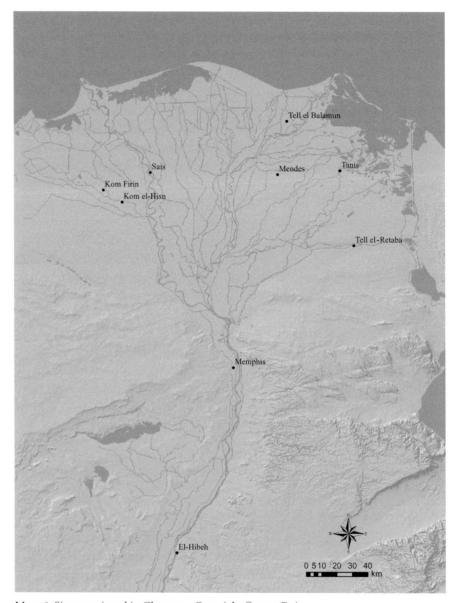

Map 18 Sites mentioned in Chapter 3. Copyright © 2014 Esri.

in the areas in between the New Kingdom mortuary temples, acting as local support service communities, while many others flourished as Thebes grew in prosperity under the New Kingdom pharaohs, particularly at Deir el-Medina and Malqata. By the early Third Intermediate Period, the communities on the West Bank had moved into the temple of Ramesses III at Medinat Habu (Fig. 5). As a result, the West Bank population density had increased within the confines of Medinat Habu and the density

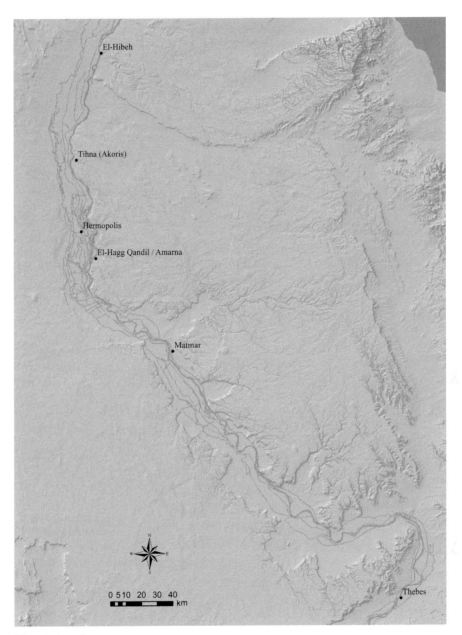

Map 18 (cont.)

of the settlements most probably decreased across the wider West Bank floodplain, although the exact development of wider floodplain settlement systems is difficult to assess with the current evidence. The increase in tribal raids and the decreased security on the West Bank would have facilitated a move behind the walls of Medinat Habu, over concerns for safety and protection.

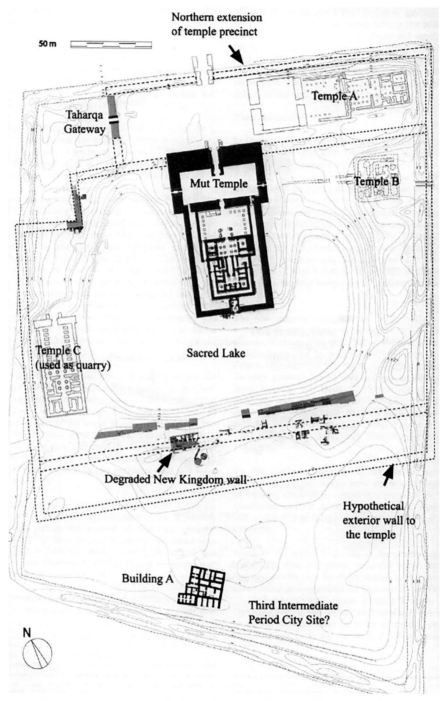

Fig. 3 Area of Third Intermediate Period settlement to the west of the Mut temple at Karnak. (Sullivan, 2013: fig. 6.4). (Courtesy of BAR/ Prof. E. Sullivan.)

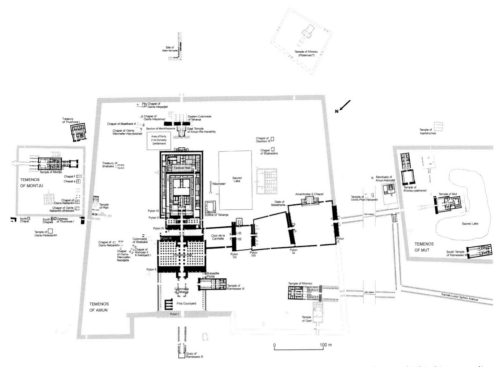

Fig. 4 Map of Karnak showing the location and extent of the known New Kingdom and Third Intermediate Period temple landscape (Dodson, 2012: xxiv, map 7). (Courtesy of Dr A. Dodson.) Location of bastion of Menkheperre and early Twenty-First Dynasty settlement area added by the author.

2 Matmar

At Matmar, the Third Intermediate Period domestic structures found within the Seth temple of Ramesses II were aligned to the southern mud-brick enclosure wall, and the east–west axial alignment area of the limestone chippings represented the former position of the temple (Fig. 6).[6] The presence of circular grain silos on the exterior of the temenos wall may suggest some form of settlement outside the enclosure.

3 Hermopolis

At Hermopolis the Third Intermediate Period population continued to live in a settlement in an already established New Kingdom occupation sector to the west of the Amun temple (Fig. 7).[7] British Museum excavations traced the Third Intermediate Period settlement in the north-west at 'Site W'.[8] Early German excavations, particularly in 'Graben IV', located to the east side of 'Site W', found Third Intermediate Period settlement remains stretching for 170 m in a north-westerly direction from the exterior of the New Kingdom temple enclosure wall, but these were labelled as 'Spätzeit' (Late Period). These 'Spätzeit' layers had Third

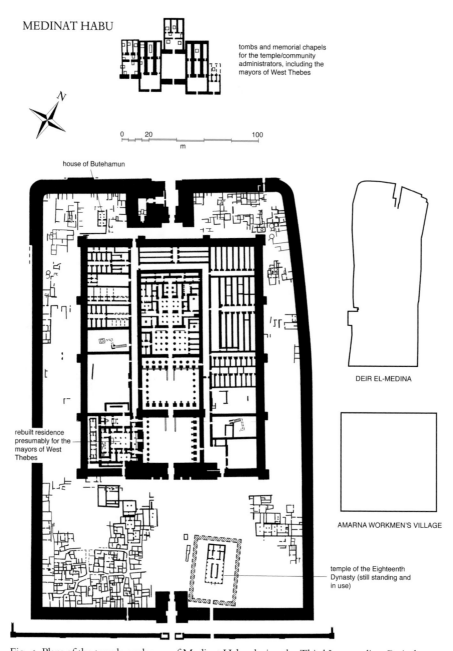

Fig. 5 Plans of the temple enclosure of Medinat Habu during the Third Intermediate Period, compared with the sizes of the New Kingdom settlement of Deir el-Medina and the workmen's village at Amarna (Kemp, 2018: fig. 8.17). (Courtesy of Prof. B. J. Kemp.).

Intermediate Period material mixed within them.[9] Other deposits designated 'Spätzeit' were present in Graben II further south of the enclosure. In Graben II, the Third Intermediate Period buildings were themselves constructed over occupation levels of the New Kingdom. The deep stratigraphy of Graben II suggests the

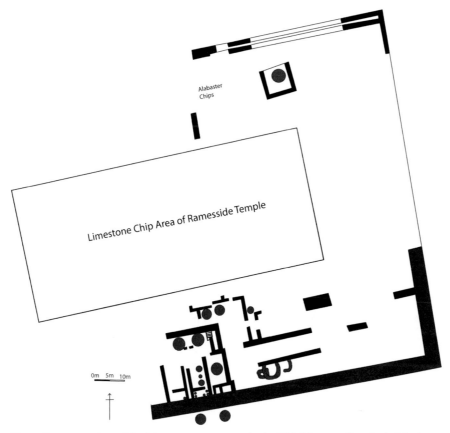

Alabaster
Chips

Limestone Chip Area of Ramesside Temple

0m 5m 10m

Fig. 6 Reconstruction of the Matmar temenos area in the Third Intermediate Period (redrawn after Brunton, 1948, pl. xlv).

ancient settlement during the dynastic period was located in the south-eastern part of the tell.[10] Evidence of the Third Intermediate Period settlement was found to the south-east of the high mound of Kom Qassum (Test Area 2). The presence of Third Intermediate Period ceramics in the surface dumps suggests the Third Intermediate Period settlement extended to the south-west of the New Kingdom temenos for a considerable distance.[11]

4 Memphis

There is a small amount of evidence for temple construction and funerary structures at Memphis during the Third Intermediate Period (Fig. 8). The Third Intermediate Period occupation levels excavated by the EES at Memphis (Kom Rabia) in the southern-western corner of the Ptah temple were, however, poorly preserved, with only some areas of flooring and walls remaining, but they do provide evidence for the spatial orientation of the Memphite settlement around the outside of the Ptah temple. The builders of the Third Intermediate Period

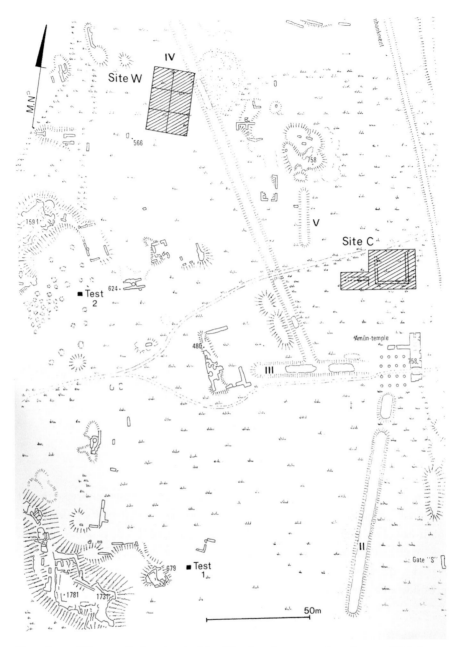

Fig. 7 Map of Hermopolis showing the New Kingdom Amun temple and areas of Third Intermediate Period settlement in the north-west of the tell (Site W), Graben II–IV, and test pit 2 (Spencer, 1993: pl. 1). (Courtesy of Dr A. J. Spencer/The Trustees of the British Museum.).

settlement placed the walls in shallow foundation trenches cut into a relatively uniform deposit covering the remains of the earlier Ramesside structures. It is possible that the deposit into which the Third Intermediate Period walls were cut was levelled flat as a preparation for the new buildings. By the time the

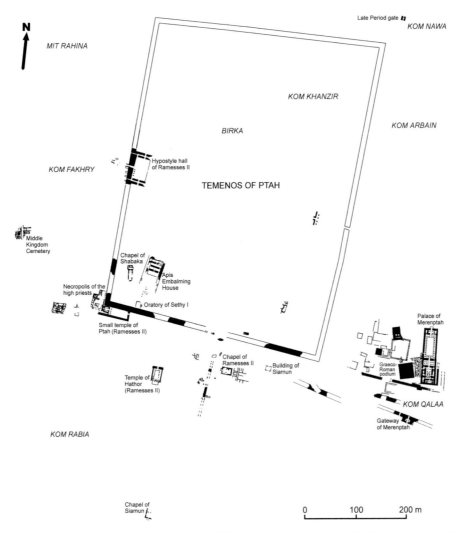

Fig. 8 Third Intermediate Period temple and funerary structures at Memphis (Dodson, 2012: xxi, map 5). (Courtesy of Dr A. Dodson.).

Third Intermediate Period houses were built, the Ramesside ground plan had partially or entirely disappeared.[12] The Third Intermediate Period structures, based on the small area excavated, appear to follow the architectural orientation of the New Kingdom, or they lie slightly more south-east–north-west.[13] The walls no longer respected the open space of an earlier Ramesside courtyard, but the New Kingdom Ptah temple enclosure, or the small Ptah temple of Ramesses II outside the main temenos wall, dictated the uniformity of the Third Intermediate Period settlement. The New Kingdom Memphite temples therefore preserved the original alignment of the New Kingdom ground plan into the Third Intermediate Period.[14] The temple of Merenptah at Kom el-Qala dictated the axial alignment of later domestic structures, as they were aligned to the western side of the temple courtyard. The alignment of the Kom el-Qala houses in a south-east–north-west direction corresponds with the Third Intermediate Period Kom Rabia houses, suggesting a general south-east–north-west alignment of houses at Memphis in conjunction with the New Kingdom temples.

5 Kom Firin

Along the western exterior wall of the Ramesside temple at Kom Firin, but within the temple enclosure, early Third Intermediate Period occupation was found, along with early Third Intermediate Period settlement in the north-east and north-west of the temple enclosure (Figs. 9–11).[15] The magnetic survey along the route from the Ramesside gateway to the temple forecourt suggests this area may have been relatively clear of civic buildings. If this was the case, then it would suggest that any post-New Kingdom structures, built here after the Ramesside enclosure and temple fell out of use, were destroyed, or the original Ramesside processional route remained clear throughout the Third Intermediate Period.[16] A similar scenario is observed at Medinat Habu, where the route from the gateway of the temple of Ramesses III was kept clear, while the Third Intermediate Period settlement developed on both sides.

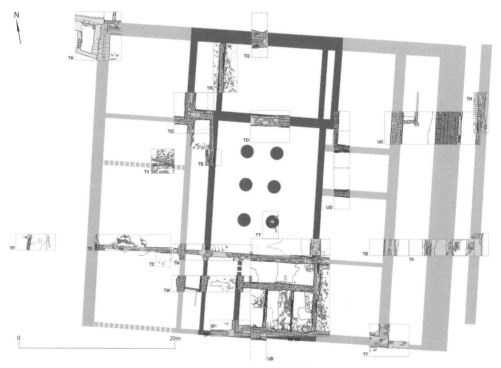

Fig. 9 Kom Firin showing the location of the Ramesside temple and enclosure and the Third Intermediate Period settlement (Spencer, 2008: fig. 2). (Kom Firin Project: Courtesy of the Trustees of the British Museum.)

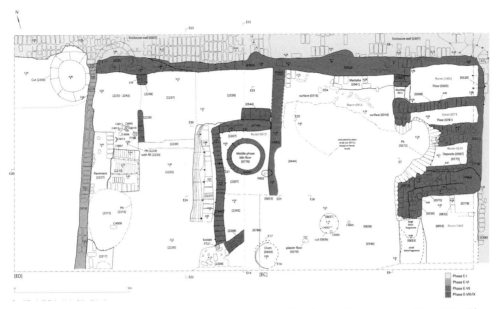

Fig. 10 Tripartite house structure in the north-east corner of the Ramesside temenos at Kom Firin, Phase E V–VI (Spencer, 2014: fig. 30). (Kom Firin Project: Courtesy of the Trustees of the British Museum.)

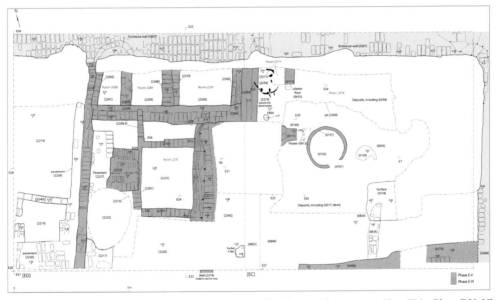

Fig. 11 Tripartite house structure in the north-east corner of the Ramesside temenos at Kom Firin, Phase E V–VI (Spencer, 2014: fig. 31). (Kom Firin Project: Courtesy of the Trustees of the British Museum.).

6 Mendes

At Mendes, the Third Intermediate Period settlement was located to the south of the temple of Banebdjed, while to the north and west of the temple there is, so far, no evidence of Third Intermediate Period settlement. The wider settlement, therefore, retained its axial layout as it would have existed in the twelfth century BCE.[17] Nineteenth- and twentieth-century farming has reduced the ninth- and eighth-century BCE occupation levels in the south of the tell, but there is evidence of sub-floor basements in the houses. These basements overlay houses of the First Intermediate Period settlement, indicating a re-use of old districts of the settlement which may have fallen into ruin.[18] The New Kingdom enclosure wall was already in a state of disrepair and was being cut into for both domestic and funerary purposes. To the south of the Banebdjed temple, along its western side, there was a Third Intermediate Period/Saite Period casemate building pre-dating the Twenty-Ninth Dynasty burial of Pharaoh Nepherites I. This building may have been a monumental tomb of the Libyan Period. Further to the west of this casemate structure, it is tentatively suggested that the area was used for mud-brick tomb chambers of the Mendesian Third Intermediate Period elite,[19] but the area was destroyed by Late Period redevelopment.

7 Kom el-Hisn

A survey of Kom el-Hisn in 1996 by the EES demonstrated that part of the Third Intermediate Period settlement was located to the west of the early Ramesside/Third Intermediate Period temple of Sekhmet-Hathor. Auger boring and test pitting in the area showed there to be substantial settlement deposits dating from the late New Kingdom, the Third Intermediate Period, and into the early Saite Period (Fig. 12).[20] Test Pit 4 on the western edge of the kom revealed late New Kingdom and Third Intermediate Period deposits. The auger coring taken across an east–west axis of the tell demonstrated the development of the settlement in the west from the early Ramesside Period. Moving slightly to the west of the temple there was a relatively deep series of deposits which may represent the early Ramesside settlement that grew up alongside the western wall of the temple of Ramesses II. The survey and excavations could not define whether the entire settlement was within the walls of the temple enclosure, or if there had been additional settlement outside. The isolated nature of late New Kingdom and Third Intermediate Period deposits, and the distinct difference in deposit depths compared with those further west, could indicate a concentrated area of settlement for an extended period. There is a distinct decrease in the depth of the settlement deposits further to the west.[21] The alignment of the Third Intermediate Period walls in Test Pit 4 in association with the back wall of the temple and the earlier Ramesside houses attests to the ongoing usage of the New Kingdom built environment as a basis for the layout of succeeding building phases.[22]

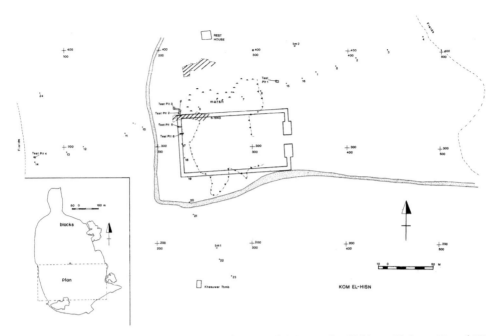

Fig. 12 Plan of the New Kingdom/Third Intermediate Period/Saite temple of Sekhmet-Hathor at Kom el-Hisn with coring and test pit locations (Kirby, Orel, and Smith, 1998: 24, pl. 1). (Courtesy Dr Chris Kirby/Egypt Exploration Society.).

8 Tell el-Balamun

A widespread domestic occupation consisting of mud-brick houses and grain silos dating to the late New Kingdom/early Twenty-First Dynasty was found within the New Kingdom temple enclosure (Fig. 13). This settlement was later removed to build a new temple of Shoshenq III.[23] By the time of the early Third Intermediate Period, the New Kingdom temenos wall was already in a state of disrepair, while there is evidence for a new Third Intermediate Period enclosure to the south–east, enclosing the Shoshenq III temple. To the south-east of the Third Intermediate Period enclosure a small section of settlement dating to the end of the eighth or the start of the seventh century BCE was found,[24] but the stratigraphic connection between the Third Intermediate Period enclosure and the settlement cannot be ascertained as the later temple of Psammetik I cut through the deposits between the two areas (Fig. 14). Therefore, it is not known whether this settlement was located within the temple enclosure or outside it. The south-western part of this settlement area had fewer traces of buildings than the northern part, suggesting this was an area relatively free of structures, containing deposits of rubbish and builder waste instead.[25]

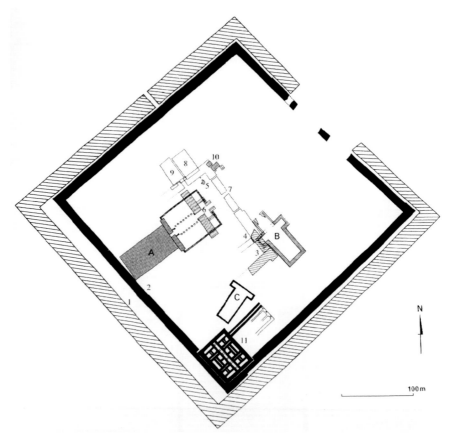

Fig. 13 Temple enclosure of Tell el-Balamun (Leclère, 2008: pl. 6.3). (Courtesy of Dr Fr. Leclère.).

DEVELOPMENTS IN THE SPATIAL LAYOUT OF THIRD INTERMEDIATE PERIOD SETTLEMENTS

The spatial layout of Egyptian settlements in the Third Intermediate Period continued to be formed by the construction of domestic buildings which nucleated around the main temple enclosures. These buildings retained the axial alignment of the earlier New Kingdom settlements in relation to the main cult temple. In the Delta, as a result of the limitations of tell space, new domestic areas were built on earlier abandoned domestic and funerary zones. This shows a reorganisation of domestic settlement into new areas. In the late New Kingdom and early Twenty-First Dynasty, ephemeral settlements saw the development of domestic communities within the New Kingdom temple enclosures as responses to local civic insecurity, while attempts at domestic encroachment on religious and civic areas in the main political centres are demonstrated at Thebes and Memphis.

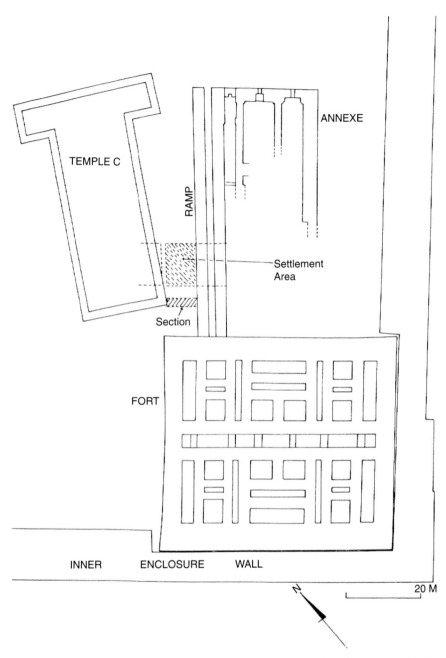

Fig. 14 Location of Third Intermediate Period settlement between the subsidiary temple of Psammetik I and the Saite fort ramp at Tell el-Balamun. (Spencer, 1996: pl. 32). (Courtesy of Dr A. J. Spencer/The Trustees of the British Museum.)

THE LATE PERIOD PALIMPSEST

The evidence for Third Intermediate Period settlement remains, such as complete housing plans and religious and secular civic buildings, is limited. Reasons for the lack of surviving remains include the natural progression of tell sites and the taphonomic nature of their development. The research focus for many archaeological missions was on temple enclosures that since the Third Intermediate Period have undergone substantial adaptations in the built environment, through the enlargement and rebuilding of temenoi walls, the re-use of monuments, and the complete redesign of temple complexes in later periods.

At Thebes, the Third Intermediate Period settlement to the west of the Mut temple at Karnak was enclosed by a Late Period wall,[26] which no doubt levelled a large area of Third Intermediate Period settlement including administrative buildings associated with the temple. At Hermopolis the construction of the new Thirtieth Dynasty temple enclosure also removed a large amount of the Third Intermediate Period settlement which was located to the west of the New Kingdom temple.[27] In the Delta at Kom Firin, as part of a change in the sacred topography of the settlement, the Twenty-Sixth Dynasty builders constructed a new enclosure wall which levelled a large area of ground inside the previous Ramesside enclosure wall, and in turn levelled a substantial part of the Third Intermediate Period settlement.[28] In the eastern Delta at Tell el-Balamun, the Saite ruler Psammetik I redeveloped the entire area of the Third Intermediate Period temple complex.[29] As at Kom Firin, this was done as a result of the change in the sacred topography of the settlement, with the new enclosure extending over much of the southern part of the tell[30] and most likely destroying vast areas of Third Intermediate Period settlement to make way for the new temple enclosure. Finally, at Tanis, the new Saite enclosure will have levelled a large part of the Third Intermediate Period settlement outside the enclosure of Psusennes I (Fig. 15).

At the juncture between the end of the Third Intermediate Period and the reunification of the country under the Twenty-Sixth Dynasty, those temples which were ruined or had squatters or domestic encroachment provided an important reason for the renewal of temple buildings and a chance to redevelop the sacred topographies of the settlements. The encroachment of domestic and industrial structures on New Kingdom temples in the Third Intermediate Period is clearly visible in the archaeological and textual evidence, but for other temples there may have been other motives for renewal and redevelopment, perhaps dictated by royal ideology. The Third Intermediate Period temples were taken down and levelled ready for new temples to be built on their foundations, such as at Tell el-Balamun[31] and Tanis,[32] while others were extended, replaced, or their blocks used in other temples like those at Bubastis[33] and Tanis.[34] This means that the reason Third Intermediate Period settlements known to us are so poorly preserved, both above ground and within the vertical deposits, is down to the subsequent Saite Dynasty's policy of sacred landscape change. Previous settlement layouts, including those of the New Kingdom and Third Intermediate Period, were obliterated to accommodate new built environments. The Late Period cityscapes now facilitated the removal of large

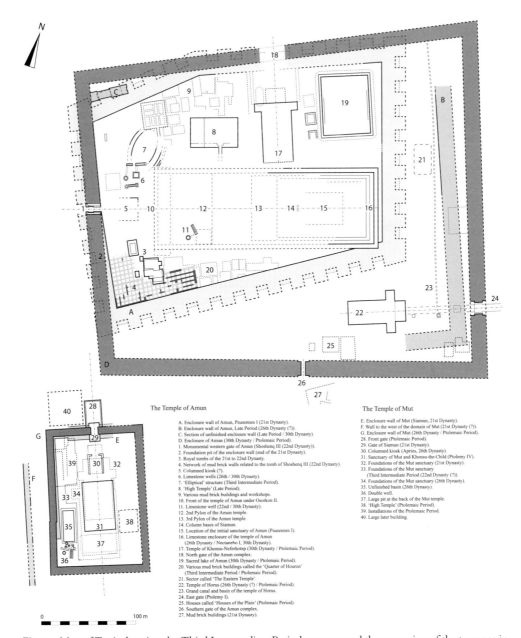

The Temple of Amun

A. Enclosure wall of Amun, Psusennes I (21st Dynasty).
B. Enclosure wall of Amun, Late Period (26th Dynasty (?)).
C. Section of unfinished enclosure wall (Late Period / 30th Dynasty).
D. Enclosure of Amun (30th Dynasty / Ptolemaic Period).
1. Monumental western gate of Amun (Shoshenq III (22nd Dynasty)).
2. Foundation pit of the enclosure wall (end of the 21st Dynasty).
3. Royal tombs of the 21st to 22nd Dynasty.
4. Network of mud brick walls related to the tomb of Shoshenq III (22nd Dynasty).
5. Columned kiosk (?).
6. Limestone wells (26th / 30th Dynasty).
7. 'Elliptical' structure (Third Intermediate Period).
8. 'High Temple' (Late Period).
9. Various mud brick buildings and workshops.
10. Front of the temple of Amun under Osorkon II.
11. Limestone well (22nd / 30th Dynasty).
12. 2nd Pylon of the Amun temple.
13. 3rd Pylon of the Amun temple.
14. Column bases of Siamun.
15. Location of the initial sanctuary of Amun (Psusennes I).
16. Limestone enclosure of the temple of Amun
    (26th Dynasty / Nectanebo I, 30th Dynasty).
17. Temple of Khonsu-Neferhotep (30th Dynasty / Ptolemaic Period).
18. North gate of the Amun complex.
19. Sacred lake of Amun (30th Dynasty / Ptolemaic Period).
20. Various mud brick buildings called the 'Quarter of Houron'
    (Third Intermediate Period / Ptolemaic Period).
21. Sector called 'The Eastern Temple'.
22. Temple of Horus (26th Dynasty (?) / Ptolemaic Period).
23. Grand canal and basin of the temple of Horus.
24. East gate (Ptolemy I).
25. Houses called 'Houses of the Plain' (Ptolemaic Period).
26. Southern gate of the Amun complex.
27. Mud brick buildings (21st Dynasty).

The Temple of Mut

E. Enclosure wall of Mut (Siamun, 21st Dynasty).
F. Wall to the west of the domain of Mut (21st Dynasty (?)).
G. Enclosure wall of Mut (26th Dynasty / Ptolemaic Period).
28. Front gate (Ptolemaic Period).
29. Gate of Siamun (21st Dynasty).
30. Columned kiosk (Apries, 26th Dynasty).
31. Sanctuary of Mut and Khonsu-the-Child (Ptolemy IV).
32. Foundations of the Mut sanctuary (21st Dynasty).
33. Foundations of the Mut sanctuary
    (Third Intermediate Period (22nd Dynasty (?)).
34. Foundations of the Mut sanctuary (26th Dynasty).
35. Unfinished basin (26th Dynasty).
36. Double well.
37. Large pit at the back of the Mut temple.
38. 'High Temple' (Ptolemaic Period).
39. Installations of the Ptolemaic Period.
40. Large later building.

Fig. 15 Map of Tanis showing the Third Intermediate Period temenos and the expansion of the temenos in the Saite Period. (Courtesy of Dr Fr. Leclère/MFFT.)

proportions of the population from settlement zones that had grown up inside and around the New Kingdom and Third Intermediate Period temple enclosures. These removals included both administrative and religious buildings, including elite burials. The Saite Period and Late Dynastic policies contrast sharply with the Third Intermediate Period policy of the adaptation and continued re-use of the settlement plans and structures of the previous New Kingdom. As a result, the discussion of the spatial development of settlements seems limited, but when the Late Period restructuring is taken into account, the spatial changes may have been more extensive and involved a larger population than seems to be the case at first sight. The small-scale Third Intermediate Period remains could thus be considered as a proxy for larger datasets, but the actual size of the Third Intermediate Period settlement data is unknown.

THE BUILT ARCHITECTURE OF THE THIRD INTERMEDIATE PERIOD

This section focuses on the monumental architecture of the Third Intermediate Period, including walling, temples, and palaces. Monumental walls documented in both the archaeological record and ancient texts are analysed to understand the nature and extent of the monumental wall building policy for the period at political, economic, and social levels. The section assesses the condition of the existing built environment of the New Kingdom urban wall projects and its integration into the settlements of the Third Intermediate Period. It discusses the way in which New Kingdom walls were adapted, whether through extensions, reinforcements, and re-orientation, or if they were demolished to make way for new Third Intermediate Period structures. The processes identified will highlight aspects of pragmatic settlement design, and raise issues of regional economies and ideology, as well as regional security, as reasons to construct walls around the important resources of the settlement.

This section goes on to examine the structures inside and outside the walled enclosures to establish whether there are clear divisions between the New Kingdom and the Third Intermediate Period, the extent to which they represent a continuity or change over time, and the implications for the social and economic lived experience of the Third Intermediate Period population. Temple building is assessed to see if there were changes in the design and construction of religious buildings, and the extent to which new temples and shrines were constructed in the settlements. Following on from the discussion of temples, the other primary institution within the settlement, the royal palace, is documented. The location of Third Intermediate Period palaces is discussed to assess whether New Kingdom palaces continued to be used by the Third Intermediate Period rulers, or if new palaces were constructed. Furthermore, the taphonomic processes within the settlements are determined for both the lived experience of the population and the post-occupational phases of Third Intermediate Period houses. This is done to understand the way in which taphonomic processes have affected the way we understand the living conditions and development of domestic lifecycles. The architectural plans of

surviving houses that were occupied in the Third Intermediate Period are
compared to see whether there are parallel housing designs and architectural
developments across the country as a response to specific political, historical,
and environmental regions, or whether there was a continuation of the New
Kingdom house format. Finally, other intramural physical and social structures
of the Third Intermediate Period settlements – grain storage, cemetery
positions, waste disposal, and livestock husbandry and rearing areas – are
analysed to identify the social fabric and living conditions during the Third
Intermediate Period.

Enclosure Walls

The urban wall traditions of ancient Egypt were first developed and favoured
in the third millennium BCE at el-Kab, and Elephantine.[35] Settlement walls
often invite functionalist approaches, with defence the most common reason
quoted, but often the underlying reasons and rationale for their construction
can be multi-faceted.[36] Prior to the Third Intermediate Period, in the second
millennium BCE most large-scale enclosure walls were built around temples
rather than the wider settlement, with many of them incorporating buttresses
and crenulations into the design which mimicked contemporary defensive
architecture.[37] The temple enclosure walls represented a large investment of
resources but are difficult to explain as defensive in nature, and unlike
settlement walls, temple enclosures were not an optional extra within the
settlement's built landscape, but an essential part of the architecture of the
shrine.[38] The evidence suggests that except for planned settlements such as
Deir el-Medina, there were no enclosure walls constructed around urbanised
areas during the New Kingdom, unlike in the third millennium BCE at
Elephantine and Edfu.[39] Protection in response to a physical threat was
therefore not a primary concern and this is reflected in the political situation
for most of the New Kingdom.[40] The temple walls, however, provided
protection against both potential physical (inundation waters, *khamsin*
winds, 'natural' dangers) and metaphorical dangers, but more importantly
in the New Kingdom, the wall acted to separate the sacred space within from
the world around it.[41] The separation of the shrine by way of these walls
would have acted as a social exclusion barrier between the sacred and the
profane.

Third Intermediate Period Wall Terminology

There are several terms used during the Third Intermediate Period to denote
walls or walling elements. Those identified within the texts are 𓊃𓃀𓏏𓉐 *sbty*, 𓋴𓄿𓏏𓉐
s3(t), and to a lesser extent � 𓂝 *ỉnt* and 𓍿𓋴𓏏 *tsmt*. The term 𓊃𓃀𓏏𓉐 *sbty* is attested in
the New Kingdom,[42] and can be translated as 'wall/ramparts',[43] or 'enclosure

wall'.[44] This term can be used to indicate the wall of a settlement or a temple,[45] and is the most frequently used term for walls during the Third Intermediate Period. The Twenty-First Dynasty stela of Menkheperre[46] records that in his Year 48, *sbty ꜥꜢ wr* 'a very great wall' was built on the north side of the temple of Amun at Karnak. The HPA Menkheperre made this new wall as *bḫn* 'a citadel', 'fortress'. The function of this 'wall/rampart', if the restoration of the text is precise, should be read as *sḥꜢp*, which has the meaning 'conceal, cover or hide',[47] and can be translated as 'to protect/save'.[48] The wall constructed by the HPA Menkheperre was intended not to conceal the Amun temple at Karnak from view, but to mark the boundary between the sacred and the profane in the same way as the earlier New Kingdom walls around shrines.[49] Furthermore, the wall was constructed to *twr r ḥꜢw-mrw* 'purify (get rid of) the Haou-merou', who were an Asiatic group of people who had built their houses encroaching on to the temple,[50] indicating a social exclusion. Later, in the Twenty-Second Dynasty, the term [hieroglyphs] is used in the title of the settlement *pꜢ-sbty-n-ššnk* 'The Walls/Ramparts of Shoshenq III', documented on the donation stela Cairo JE 45610 found near Heliopolis.[51] The possible location of this settlement near the strategically important entrance of the Wadi Tumilat, the fact the Army Leader Bakennefi A dedicated the stela, and that the construction of the name of the settlement is similar in style to the important military checkpoint of the Middle Kingdom 'Walls of the Ruler', would indicate this settlement and its walls had a primary defensive/security function. [hieroglyphs] is frequently used in the Piankhy Stela,[52] where the text refers to many [hieroglyphs] 'walls/ramparts' in the settlements across Middle Egypt. [hieroglyphs] *sbty* walls are documented at Meidum, Per Sekhemkheperre, Medinat el-Faiyum, Bahnasa, Kom el-Ahmar, 'all the nomes of the South', and all of the [hieroglyphs] 'towns' of the west. Later we learn, prior to the Kushite invasion, Nimlot the ruler of Hermopolis had destroyed the [hieroglyphs] *sbty* of Jarris (Neferusy).[53] The section of the narrative which deals with the invasion of the Kushite forces uses the term [hieroglyphs] for the walls at Hermopolis,[54] and Memphis,[55] while Piankhy also found the [hieroglyphs] of *Itj-Tawy* sealed.[56] There is a deliberate distinction between the *sbty* at *Itj-Tawy*, which was the main fortified enclosure, and the *inbw*-walls of the buildings, which were full of soldiers.[57]

The next term, [hieroglyphs] *sꜢ(t)*, can be translated as 'wall',[58] while others define the term as 'ramparts' like [hieroglyphs].[59] The assault of Piankhy on Egypt states that el-Hibeh had its [hieroglyphs] demolished or overthrown,[60] at Per Sekhemkheperre [hieroglyphs] were built up,[61] and at Heracleopolis [hieroglyphs] were recorded in the context of each allied chief knowing which section of it (the wall) to man and protect.[62] The settlement at Memphis, in addition to [hieroglyphs], had [hieroglyphs];[63] Piankhy's troops are ordered to mount the [hieroglyphs] and enter them.[64] During the New

Kingdom, and from the Eighteenth Dynasty onwards, the term *s3(t)* designated a stone wall which could be inscribed, and this continued to be the case into the late New Kingdom.[65] During the Third Intermediate Period the term was used less accurately, and by the time of the Twenty-Fifth Dynasty *s3(t)* was used as a non-specific term for a 'wall', not differentiating between mud-brick and stone.[66]

A third term used during the Third Intermediate Period to refer to a type of boundary is recorded on the Twenty-First Dynasty stela of Smendes I. The term is the compound term ⟨hieroglyphs⟩ *ꜥ int*. Previously this stela has been interpreted as documenting the reconstruction of a Theban 'canal wall' of Thutmose III which formed the limits of Thebes after a catastrophic flood.[67] The text preserved is inaccurately published, making the certainty of the reading doubtful. The first word group is ⟨hieroglyphs⟩ *ꜥ*, which refers to a dyke or riverbed,[68] and the second word ⟨hieroglyphs⟩ *int* is a doubtful reading. The word is probably a mistranscription of ⟨hieroglyphs⟩ *int*, 'desert/valley',[69] with the omission of the ⟨hieroglyph⟩ phonetic sign. The structure Smendes refers to is a 'valley/desert dyke' that surrounded and protected the settlement of Thebes on its East Bank, which had fallen into disrepair as a result of a catastrophic flood.

The final term, ⟨hieroglyphs⟩ *tsmt*, can be translated as bastions.[70] This term comes from the Piankhy Stela where it described the besiegement of Memphis. The *sbty* walls of Memphis had been reinforced by the construction of ⟨hieroglyphs⟩, which were controlled by strong men. On the New Kingdom Israel Stela of Merenptah, messengers are sheltered from the sun by ⟨hieroglyphs⟩, while on the Onomasticon of Amenemope, ⟨hieroglyphs⟩ are listed between *sbty* and *inb*, suggesting they were a prominent feature of walls. In the Twenty-Fifth Dynasty, the mayor of Thebes, Montuemhat, rebuilt the *sbty* of the Amun temple at Karnak and re-erected in brick ⟨hieroglyphs⟩ which had fallen to the ground.[71]

The texts show that during the Third Intermediate Period, *sbty* was the most commonly used term for 'wall' and it most likely relates to the enclosure wall of the temple or the wider settlement. The terms *sbty* and *s3(t)* could be used synonymously and do not appear to denote specific types of wall construction, or material type, as was the case in the New Kingdom with *s3(t)* referring to the inscribed stone temple walls. Without additional qualifiers to these terms, any attempt at defining specific zones of walling through an analysis of the ancient settlements of the Third Intermediate Period cannot, at this moment, be achieved. Other terms include ⟨hieroglyphs⟩, which referred to a wall designed to prevent flood waters coming from the wadis and destroying settlements, while ⟨hieroglyphs⟩ refers to the large corner towers on mud-brick enclosures.

Third Intermediate Period Walling: Archaeological Evidence

Newly built monumental walls of the Third Intermediate Period are known at Tanis, el-Hibeh, Nazlet esh-Shurafa, Gebelein, Higazeh, Thebes, and Elephantine.

In the Twenty-First Dynasty, King Psusennes I constructed a new enclosure for the Great Temple of Amun at Tanis. The wall formed an elongated pentagon and enclosed around 6 ha. The width of the wall is 26–27 m at the corner towers, with buttresses along the wall.[72] The southern section of wall may have been built to avoid a pre-existing building, hydrological feature, or a break in the natural gezira. The foundation of Psusennes' enclosure follows the natural topography of the gezira, but the nature of the terrain and the high elevations could have caused the builders to abandon a straight-sided enclosure, to conserve as much space in the temenos as possible.[73] In Middle Egypt, at el-Hibeh, a new enclosure wall was constructed by the Twenty-First Dynasty HPA Pinudjem I, and subsequently either later repaired or added to by the HPA Menkheperre (Fig. 16). The preserved section of wall of Pinudjem I had a convex design and ran for ca. 600 m on its eastern side and was 12.6 m thick, with a surviving height of 10 m. The wall was built on top of earlier New Kingdom occupational strata and enclosed the existing settlement.[74]

Menkheperre also constructed monumental walls at Nazlet esh-Shurafa, Gebelein, and Higazeh as part of a chain of fortified positions securing access into and out of Middle Egypt. Another wall of the Twenty-First Dynasty was constructed by Menkheperre at Karnak and formed part of the thick (10 m wide) corner of the temenos of the Amun temple (Fig. 17). The wall was destroyed and levelled during the Ptolemaic Period.[75] The wall is most likely the same wall recorded on the Year 48 stela of Menkheperre,[76] built to prevent the houses of the Asiatic population from encroaching the Amun temple.[77] In the far south at Elephantine, the New Kingdom settlement does not appear to have had a wall, but in the Twenty-First Dynasty, a new encircling wall was constructed. It was replaced by a second wall, dated by ceramics as having a terminus post quem of the Twenty-Fourth Dynasty, possibly as a reaction to an unsecured border and the threat of Kushite invasion, or the result of an undocumented assault during the Third Intermediate Period. In a third phase, the wall was subsequently buttressed in the Twenty-Fifth Dynasty.[78] The refortification of Elephantine in the Twenty-Fifth Dynasty would correspond to the erection of the Kushite fort at Abu Id as part of a chain of southern forts in the First Upper Egyptian Nome.

Representational Evidence of Third Intermediate Period Enclosure Walls

The only pictorial relief that provides evidence for the design of Third Intermediate Period Egyptian walls is from a relief slab from the palace of Assurbanipal at Nineveh dated to ca. 660 BCE (Fig. 18).[79] The scene shows the siege and assault of an unknown Egyptian settlement. The walls depicted in this scene show evidence of bastions and corner towers with walkways along the tops of the walls. Emanating from the walls are what appear to be spears angled down towards the ground to prevent either siege towers getting close to the walls or

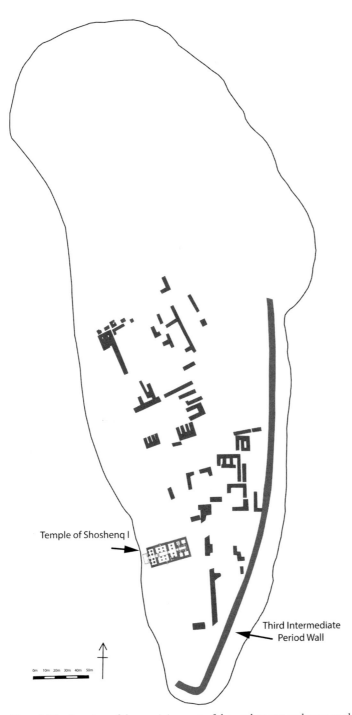

Fig. 16 The location of the surviving part of the settlement enclosure at el-Hibeh with the remains of ancient buildings of different dates. The small temple of Shoshenq I (redrawn from Wenke, 1984: 3, map 1.2). (Courtesy of Prof. R. Wenke.)

Fig. 17 The enclosure wall of the High Priest of Amun Menkheperre at Karnak (Coulon, Leclère, and Marchand, 1995: pl. xiiib). (Courtesy of CNRS-CFEETK 84477/Dr Fr. Leclère.).

Fig. 18 Relief showing the siege of an Egyptian settlement by the Assyrian army, from the palace of Assurbanipal at Nineveh (Hall, 1928: 44, pl. xl). (Courtesy of the Trustees of the British Museum.).

siege ladders being flush to the wall. Finally, there appears to be a central tower or secondary gateway complex located behind the main wall. A ladder rests on the main walls of the settlement to reach the higher tower complex.

Enclosure Walls as Defence

The Piankhy Stela and the relief of Assurbanipal both indicate that Third Intermediate Period walls were required to take on a more focused role in terms of defensive capabilities, alongside the cultic and symbolic aspects of the walls which were a prominent reason for their construction in the New Kingdom. One aspect identified by the movement of populations into some of the New Kingdom Egyptian enclosure walls was the need for refuge from attack. Many scholars now see walls as also having a symbolic function and this is certainly one aspect of the Egyptian New Kingdom and Third Intermediate Period constructions.[80] It is likely the aspect of symbolism and symbolic protection, which was prominent in the New Kingdom, was retained but now expanded into the need for a physical protection of the local communities and the civic structures during the Third Intermediate Period. The status of both a settlement and a ruler can be expressed through the creation of a large wall, which demonstrates the ability to invest in labour forces to work on these large projects. The intra-regional perception of threat developed throughout the transitory phase at the end of the Twentieth Dynasty and into the Twenty-First Dynasty, with evidence coming from the West Bank of Thebes during the reign of Ramesses IX. There were skirmishing and pillaging groups of 'Libyans' (the Meshwesh, Rebu, and Desert People/Foreigner groups) who conducted razzias. The ability to conduct these raids was no doubt a result of the break-down of security, which had caused some members of the communities to become frightened of the presence of these groups on the fringes.[81] A systematic and gradual breakdown of law and order occurs in Years 13–17 of Ramesses IX, seen in the robbing of royal tombs in the Valley of the Kings, alongside the degeneration of temple buildings through the re-use of the stone and mud-bricks for new temples, administrative buildings, and in domestic settings.

Walls constructed for defensive purposes are now evident around military settlements such as Per Sekhemkheperre, the walls of Shoshenq III in the north-eastern Delta, and at el-Hibeh, Nazlet esh-Shurafa, Higazeh, Gebelein, and Elephantine. These walls were intended for the defence of local populations and the control of access into politically crucial junctures of the country, while they may have fulfilled important secondary roles of food storage, live-stock, and other resource protection such as precious metals and luxury goods for trade.

The settlements at Kom Firin, Matmar, and Medinat Habu were in strate-gically exposed locations leading out into desert routes and at important traffic junctures, which caused people to live inside the walls. The concentration of new wall constructions at the start of the Third Intermediate Period is con-temporary with the high possibility of raids in the Twenty-First Dynasty in the regions around the wadi entrances into the Eastern and Western Desert. This is the case at Thebes, where there had been brigand raids from 'Libyan' tribes earlier, combined with a general breakdown in security such as tomb robbing. If the Meshwesh and Libu tribes were military in nature, then they may have influenced the construction policy in settlements such as the erection of high fortified walls, and brought a new mentality to security having observed walled settlements elsewhere. The threat and realisation of interstate warfare from the Twenty-Second Dynasty onwards in functionally specific military settlements may be observed in the new military foundations of the walls of Shoshenq III, most likely in the region of the entrance to the Wadi Tumilat, and Per Sekhemkheperre around the Faiyum entrance. The underlying threat of warfare between the Libyan extended family networks is explicitly expressed by Osorkon II on a stela which was erected in the temple of Amun at Tanis.[82] Osorkon II petitions Amun regarding his family, requesting:

> [You will fashion] my issue, the seed that comes forth from my limbs, [to be] great [rulers] of Egypt, princes, high priests of Amunresonther, great chiefs of the Ma, [great chiefs] of foreigners, and prophets of Arsaphes . . . You will turn their hearts towards the Son of Re, Osorkon II, you will cause them [to walk] on my path. You will establish my children in the [posts] [which] I have given them, so that brother is not jealous (?) of brothe[r].

The statement of Osorkon II clearly shows his concern that his children may become jealous of each other with the potential for conflict. Prior to the reign of Piankhy, the nature of intra-state Egyptian warfare is characterised by a preference for avoiding hand-to-hand contact; instead raiding and besieging is the preferred method. The military technology used by the Egyptians for siege warfare comprised ladders to scale walls. In the early Middle Kingdom, mobile wooden siege towers were used, as shown in the tomb of the general Intef (TT 386) at Thebes.[83] There is no evidence of siege warfare conducted between Egyptian settlements and different political houses during the Third Intermediate Period. Egyptian settlements were only subject to siege warfare by the Kushite and Assyrian invading forces. During the early Iron Age, new forms of weapon technologies and battle tactics developed in the Near East which could have created environments of aggression within which Egyptian fortifications had to be adapted. The Piankhy Stela provides textual evidence of new siege technology being used against Egyptian settlements, such as 𓉻𓏤𓈖𓏇𓋴𓏤 *iwn n ms*, siege towers,[84] 𓎼𓂋𓂋𓇋𓇋𓀜 *trry*, siege mounds,[85] and 𓃀𓄿𓎡 *bꜣk*, siege platforms,[86] and shows a development of military technology during the early first millennium BCE. The large walls which were erected around the most valuable assets of the Egyptian settlement indicate that one feature of the wall was to protect the economic foundations of the settlement. These included the temples themselves which controlled large aspects of the economy because of their storage facilities. The temple also represented the cultic engine of the settlement, and the population could identify with this sacred ancestral area and the locations which featured prominently in the mythic cycles of the settlement.[87] The temple was closely connected with the local elite who had a personal stake in maintaining its integrity and that of the storage magazines. The walls enclosed and defended the royal and elite burials like those at Tanis, Heracleopolis, and Medinat Habu. The enclosed locations emphasised places vital to the social wellbeing of the settlement and required defending through physical means.[88] The walls protected the royal palace and residences of the local leaders, including people who might be taken away as prisoners or killed, which in turn would create social unrest and perhaps conflict. The Piankhy Stela explicitly mentions the female royal family members of Nimlot at Hermopolis who were housed behind the walls. Other important individuals in danger of abduction or death included government officials and religious personnel who were tasked with keeping both the economic, political, and religious life of the settlement intact. Military units were housed within the walls, with, for example, stabling such as at Tell el-Retaba and the housing of soldiers in barracks if attacked. The enclosures housed the large grain silos in association with large houses that supplied and controlled the distribution of the grain supply to smaller family units, for example at Kom Firin and Matmar, while livestock would have been secured for primary and secondary consumption products. Temple workshops and production centres may have been protected along with the raw materials and finished products for external and internal trade. The enclosure walls provided the minimum requirements to maintain life in the settlement and those institutions which had to be defended to prevent the social disintegration of the settlement.[89]

Enclosure Walls as Reflections of Royal Strategy and Ideology

The construction of a wall was one of the most expensive and time-consuming civic projects a community could undertake. Large urban walls were one of the most visible and enduring physical objects, and must have held a considerable significance for the local community.[90] No government or regulatory body of any period or location would allow the construction and expenditure of resources and human labour without explicit approval.[91] An analysis of Third Intermediate Period walling allows one to understand the rationale for wall programmes and policies, to detect political motives and policies, and to understand how the processes of 'walling' reflects on the political framework, the allocation of power, and the accessibility of resources for settlement building.

The size of the walls could be used to project not only an urban community's status but the self-image and status to which it aspired.[92] In the New Kingdom, it was the role of the pharaoh to proclaim and authorise the construction of new wall programmes. The New Kingdom attests to such proclamations at Thebes,[93] and they continued in the early Twenty-First Dynasty under Smendes I and HPA Menkheperre. The policy of building walls, or inscribing proclamations concerning wall building, appears to be abandoned after the early Twenty-First Dynasty as there are no edicts from local pharaohs or chiefs proclaiming new urban wall projects until the Twenty-Fifth Dynasty under Taharqa and Shabaka. In the Twenty-Fifth Dynasty, Shabaka donated a stela[94] which documents the restoration of the ꜣ 'wall/fortification/rampart' at Dendera, and Taharqa proclaimed at Medinat Habu that he restored the ꜣ of the mound of Djeme.[95] The earlier stela of Shabaka provides an indication of a general restoration of all ꜣ of the country. This royal edict may have been because of the general lack of maintenance during the Twenty-Second to Twenty-Fourth Dynasty, and the later edicts because of the damage the wars of Tefnakht and Piankhy had caused in the urban centres of the Egyptian settlements, or as a reaction to the growing threat of Assyria. There is clear evidence of this in Thebes as Montuemhat rebuilt the *sbty* walls of the Amun temple and re-erected the bastions which had fallen, no doubt because of Assyrian aggression. The lack of wall building proclamations for the Twenty-Second to Twenty-Fourth Dynasty highlights the political nature of the local chiefs and rulers. They were restricted from building either politically, or by lack of resources, such as wood for beam slots and sand for casemate void fillings. Although access to and provision of mud-bricks would have been possible, the corvée workers necessary may not have been available for some reason. The large walling programmes would have needed large numbers of people to build these walls. The New Kingdom Papyrus Anastasi does shed some light on the details of a ꜣ *sṯ*,[96] which was a mud-brick casemate construction, the same type as those documented on the Piankhy Stela for scaling the high enclosure walls. The papyrus documents that to cut down on mud-brick production, casemates were filled with wooden beams and reeds. While it does not provide details of the amount of mud-bricks used in these construction types or the workforce such a construction would have required, it does state that those who were employed or tasked with the creation of these large casemate structures were soldiers. Unlike in the New Kingdom, there is no evidence of the military class being involved in civic construction work during the Third Intermediate Period. In most settlements, it would have been easier to use farmers, during off-periods, and either coerce or engage them in mud-brick manufacture on newly irrigated lands or beside the river. The evidence suggests there were many crumbling walls in a constant state of decline in the Third Intermediate Period, in politically important settlements such as Mendes, Tell el-Balamun, and even Thebes itself, and further suggests that even under the control of powerful local leaders, renovations were not conducted. Conversely, many settlements may have had no justification for incurring the expense of constructing or maintaining walls to create a protective boundary, such as at Kom Firin, where the population began to dismantle the enclosure for the re-use of the mud-bricks for domestic purposes, indicating there were no perceived threats at certain periods, or in certain regions.

Palaces

In the New Kingdom, pharaohs had multiple palaces operating concurrently, each with its own unique form and special duty.[97] The main types of palaces included ceremonial, governmental, and residential types, while in many cases the boundaries between the different forms were indistinct.[98] The two most important types can be identified as non-residential and residential. The non-residential palace represented a place of pre-eminent political and ideological importance which was the stage of the king's activities when he was not engaged in foreign wars or religious duties.[99] The non-residential palaces acted as seats of governance, where the pharaoh received foreign visitors and bureaucrats, addressed the court, issued decrees and orders, and took part in the administration of the country, but the structure did not function as a permanent residence for the royal family, and often had private apartments for short-term usage.[100] This type of palace was therefore mostly ceremonial or symbolic. The residential palaces differed from the ceremonial and governmental types, as they would serve as a more permanent house for members of the royal family.[101] The standard form for the New Kingdom royal residence included the same elements (with the addition of the throne room) identified in the large New Kingdom houses at Amarna.[102] During the New Kingdom, the pharaohs had access to a network of palaces across the country, both residential and ceremonial. The geo-political situation of the Third Intermediate Period would have prevented the rulers from using this network at times of political fragmentation. The different political houses would have utilised the local palaces for their own family networks. The palaces may have been redesigned to facilitate the combination of both a residential and ceremonial palace. They were likely to have been situated in the same location as the New Kingdom palaces, inside the temenos walls and situated to the east of the main temple. It was assumed that palaces of the Third Intermediate Period maintained the same general elements and layout of the New Kingdom;[103] however, there are no surviving ground plans of Third Intermediate Period palaces, so assuming clear links to New Kingdom palatial structures is somewhat premature.

Third Intermediate Period Palace Terminology
During the Third Intermediate Period, texts that describe the physical location of a royal 'palace' are limited.

Previously in the New Kingdom the terms 𓉐 ꜥḥ,[104] 𓉐 pr ꜥꜣ,[105] 𓊪𓉐 stp sꜣ,[106] and 𓉐𓏏𓊪 pr nswt[107] can all be translated as 'royal house/palace', while the term 𓍿𓈖𓏥 ẖnw is commonly translated by Egyptologists as 'residence' or even as 'capital city', but it is difficult to define to what extent our modern notions of a national capital are applicable to the Egyptian state in the first millennium BCE.[108] The terminology used during the Twenty-First to Twenty-Fourth Dynasty to refer to a royal palace/residence is 𓍿𓈖𓏥 ẖnw. The first example is recorded on the Twenty-First Dynasty Dibabeya inscription of Smendes[109] where Smendes issued decrees from 𓍿𓈖𓏥𓆑 ẖnw=f, 'his residence' in Memphis, and not from Tanis, the new capital. The text does not refer to a specific 'palace' structure from which the decree was issued, but merely to the presence of Smendes at 'his residence', Memphis. The decree on the stela records that Smendes I received news of the flooding of the Luxor temple while he was in the columned hall, most likely of the main Ptah temple of Memphis. This indicates that Memphis was still the political capital of the period, where all state business was conducted, and therefore the king may have had some form of residence at Memphis, but there is no indication as to its location within the settlement. The second example is on the early Twenty-Second Dynasty Gebelein inscription of Shoshenq I,[110] which mentions 𓍿𓈖𓏥𓊪𓂋𓏏𓇋𓊨𓏏 pꜣ ẖnw ist pꜣ kꜣ ꜥꜣ ḥr ꜣḥty, 'the Residence of the Temple Estate of Per Iset (The House of Isis), the Great Ka of Re Horakhty'. Again, this indicates not a specific 'palace' structure, but a central political centre. Later in the Twenty-Fifth Dynasty, the Piankhy Stela documents the terms 𓉐 ꜥḥ and 𓉐𓏏𓊪 pr-nsw for the 'palace'.[111] The two terms are used interchangeably for the term 'palace'. In the late Twenty-Fifth Dynasty and Saite Period the terminology to describe the royal residence emerges as a prototypical image of royal authority. The palace was defined by the presence of the king and can be circumscribed by expressions such as *bw ẖrỉ ḥm=f*, 'the place where his majesty dwells'.[112]

Archaeological Evidence for Third Intermediate Period Palaces

The New Kingdom palace of Ramesses III at Medinat Habu was redesigned in the Twenty-First Dynasty on the same spot for the mayors of Thebes,[113] and a palace of the Chiefs of the Ma was identified at Mendes. The Twenty-First Dynasty 'palace' at Medinat Habu reflects a pragmatic and legitimising approach to palace construction through the utilisation of the already existing New Kingdom space and association with an earlier Ramesside sacred and political building. At Mendes, the palace identified to the east of the temple of the ram god Banebdjed was built in the eleventh century BCE (based on ceramic analysis), at the time of the rise to power of Smendes I who, based on the name (Egyptian: Nesubanebdjed), most likely came from Mendes. The palace continued to function into the Saite Period. It was a rectangular structure measuring ca. 30 m from east to west and ca. 30 m or more from north to south. In some places the walls were 2 m thick, indicating that it had a second storey. The entrance was most likely on the northern side, while a modern road on the palace's western side has covered a passage that connected with the main ram temple. A door jamb rests on top of the mound bearing the outline of a Libyan chief.[114] The south side of the compound, downwind of the rooms for habitation, was for food production, and contained ovens and hearths. The final function of the building, after its near-destruction by the Persians, was as a place of pottery preparation.[115] The Great Chiefs of the Ma may have refurbished the temple and their accommodation in the palace,[116] but there was evidence of neglect to the main temenos walls within which the palace and temple stood. At Hermopolis the Piankhy Stela states that, as the temenos walls of Hermopolis were overrun, the local ruler Nimlot went from his palace and proceeded to the temple of Thoth to make offerings.[117] This indicates the palace was inside the main temenos, as Nimlot would not have been able to exit the main temple enclosure while it was being besieged.

Temples

In the absence of large amounts of religious written evidence, the most obvious physical reflection of the condition of the state religion, and the continuity in the religion of the New Kingdom pharaohs, is the construction of new temples and shrines across the country and the preservation of these institutions within the built landscape. The Third Intermediate Period has long been viewed as a period of stagnation in temple construction, but the lack of investment in temple building can be traced from the late New Kingdom. The last great temples of the New Kingdom were constructed under Ramesses III, and after the reign of Ramesses IV the construction of new monumental royal mortuary temples declined and finally ceased;[118] the demolition of existing temples and the robbing of stone began, while the mud-brick temple enclosures were collapsing at many of the main political centres such as Medinat Habu, Mendes, Tell el-Balamun, and Kom Firin. The temple landscape inherited by the Twenty-First Dynasty administration was in a poor state, and economic as well as new geo-political factors meant that access to resources for new temple buildings, such as quarries located in the south, was difficult. As a result, many earlier monuments were re-used, most evidently at the new northern capital of Tanis, which was constructed from dismantled monuments of Piramesse. It was not until the country once again became briefly unified under the early Twenty-Second Dynasty that temple construction resumed on a more substantial scale (see Appendix 2). The main temple builders of the period were those of the Twenty-Second Dynasty, Shoshenq I, Osorkon I, Osorkon II, and Shoshenq III, while other rulers contributed small ephemeral structures and refurbishments to temples across Egypt. The emerging evidence shows that temple building was not stagnant in the Third Intermediate Period and, in many cases, temples were constructed in the Delta in the arenas of northern power.

The Twenty-Fifth Dynasty Kushite rule of Egypt implemented a grand policy of temple building activity in Thebes and Upper Egypt, but only modest temple constructions in the north.[119] The temple remains that have survived for the Twenty-First to Twenty-Fourth Dynasty in the south suggest that little changed between the Ramesside and the Third Intermediate Period. The temple structures made during this period show that the builders and architects continued New Kingdom traditions as closely as possible, and political, religious, and cultural changes in the wider society did not have an impact on the construction and design of new temple buildings.[120] Only one architectural element indicates a future development in the temple architecture of the period, and this comes from the temple of Shoshenq I at el-Hibeh. This innovation was a freestanding sanctuary within the interior of the temple at the rear, which was to become a common feature in the later Ptolemaic and Roman periods.[121]

The Third Intermediate Period rulers constructed new temples at Tanis, Bubastis, el-Hibeh, and Tell el-Balamun. Alongside these new temples, they enlarged the existing New Kingdom temples in several different ways, such as the addition of columned forecourts, pylon entrances, small gateways, screen walls, and small external shrines, all of which could be inserted into the pre-existing temple complexes and temenoi with less overall expense.

Defining Third Intermediate Period Housing Phases

It is a common feature of Egyptology to break down typological studies of artefacts and architectural features into rigidly structured dynastic divisions based on the Manethoic tradition. Such divisions may be appropriate for ruling families, or political phases, but they are perhaps less appropriate when applied to material culture in the same way, and especially architectural elements in organically created settlements, as has been already indicated by the continuation of New Kingdom traditions in the design of religious architecture from the New Kingdom into the Third Intermediate Period. Time and divisions are fundamental to the study of history as these divisions organise and form the framework by which events and material culture are organised. Discussing domestic architecture through dynastic attributions may be appropriate in the case of state-planned settlements in their initial stages, such as Deir el-Medina or Amarna, but even the finished form of any house may only have lasted for a limited period.[122] The inhabitants' rapid reworking of the spaces in which they lived caused them continuously to reshape the urban landscape which they inhabited.[123] The reworking of space constitutes an organic development and immediately disguises the original architectural plan. Both the existing urban and natural environments shaped the development of housing, while it is also possible that the desires of the current inhabitants brought the primary changes, and what they believed to be both essential and achievable within the built environment and their own social and economic boundaries.[124] The change of a house plan would correspond to the changing household's circumstances, and would have often occurred rapidly, or repeatedly with seasonal variations.[125] The replacement and development of houses (or substantial areas) were conditioned by the 'use-life' as dictated by both the construction material and the household activities which occurred within the buildings.[126] A study of mudbrick housing in Syria has indicated an expected use-life of thirty to fifty years,[127] which is broadly consistent with that of modern mud-brick houses at Amara West in Nubia,[128] while modern Egyptian mud-brick houses could be fifty to sixty years old, and such houses in Gurna may have been even older.[129] It can also be difficult to define physical house boundaries in Egypt owing to the surviving nature of the remains, because of environmental and sebakhin effects, as well as the nature of the taphonomic development of urban areas on tells with restricted space. Egyptian houses often shared walls, and the subsequent remodelling makes it difficult to distinguish the edges of a single house, or phase of a house. The counting of courtyards, assuming each family had access to one open air space, has been one method of calculating housing units.[130] By contrast, many small villages and 'houses' contain a single-family group but with several family units, and using 'family' may not be a useful indicator for defining house boundaries. The issue of socio-economic status, household composition (presence of servants), and multiple floor levels make defining house division complicated.[131] A further problem is that most of the evidence for the housing of the Third Intermediate Period was collected in the early twentieth century. The excavations at that time occurred before standard scientific recording techniques were widely used in household archaeology studies. The detailed recording of the phases, assemblages, strata, and microarchaeological contexts of the structures was poor compared with modern standards. One of the most important aspects of interpreting household archaeology is defining floor levels, boundaries, contemporary living surfaces (and associated artefacts), and the general taphonomic process of the development of the house, particularly at the point of abandonment and collapse. The boundaries of single house units in organically developed settlements can be difficult to define. Some ethnographical studies in the Middle East have begun to provide clues for locating house boundaries, but the issue is still unresolved.[132] At Amarna, the larger New Kingdom residential establishments show evidence for the nesting or embedding of smaller households within the grounds of a larger unit enclosed by a boundary enclosure.[133] How much this practice may have continued into the Third Intermediate Period is so far unknown.

These issues mean that the primary problem is the location of contemporaneous housing layers and phases. The houses at Medinat Habu and Matmar demonstrate the problem in separating occupation phases from early excavations. It was stated for the Medinat Habu houses that 'due to the extensive destruction of the settlement it was impossible to distinguish between buildings of the Twenty-First to Twenty-Fourth Dynasty while only a relative dating was applied'.[134] Similarly, the original recording of the Matmar houses by Brunton documented a few walls with no indication of the phasing of the structures.[135] The perpetual re-layering and restoration of architectural features such as mud floors, walls, living spaces, subterranean floors, ceilings, and multiple storeys make defining floor levels complicated. Defining these layers and occupational phases is particularly difficult in the case of collapsed buildings.[136] Ceilings in kitchens and animal rearing areas were also lower than those in sitting and storage rooms, and so it was difficult to differentiate the structures when they collapsed together.[137] When mud-brick houses collapse, the elements of the house may be compacted and combined, including the rooftop living spaces with the ground floors, the interior wall elements such as windows, hanging food produce, niche emplacements, or the gypsum covered walls. It is possible that after the initial occupation phases, the function of the house was changed, and the abandoned structure was used as space for the grazing of animals, or children may have played there, collecting various objects such as rocks, seeds, and toys. Abandonment of the house would accelerate the deterioration; wind erosion and a lack of maintenance would undermine the walls.[138] The abandoned buildings would affect surrounding houses and become a danger, thus speeding the eventual restricting or abandonment of the area owing to structural insecurities, as many houses shared architectural elements such as boundary and partition walls. The new post-occupation phases might become a new living (or activity) surface which could be separated by one or more generations from the original household phase,[139] thus complicating observations on the way in which the household developed.

Amarna from the Eighteenth Dynasty has been the representative dataset for an analysis of different house types within Egypt. The house types were probably a broad sample of Egyptian houses of the New Kingdom, although the houses may have been more regular and less dense than was often the case in longer-lived settlements because there were fewer spatial constraints.[140] Typologies of houses from Amarna have been developed along with other house types from workmen's villages at both Amarna and Deir el-Medina. When looking at a longer-lived organically developed settlement, matters are more complicated. Relying on architecture is problematic as the ground plan of an excavated house is commonly used for the classification of houses within an overall settlement. Such reliance on architectural plans is not a problem at Amarna, Deir el-Medina, Deir el-Ballas, and Malqata where settlements have relatively short life spans or a single occupation phase. Understanding house plan and thus type becomes difficult when dealing with settlements with long phases of continuous occupation for many generations. During this time the size of the household, the composition of the family, the function of the house, and the changing activities over time can produce changes in the house plan. The later phases could completely differ in function, which may be the case in the Karnak priestly houses: there we cannot be sure as to the original ground plans, and whether Late Period alterations have distorted the Third Intermediate Period building plans or choice of layout for specific architectural elements. The choice of location for a house may affect its design and scope for development. For example, the construction of a new design of house on a previously uninhabited part of the settlement not bounded or spatially limited by a pre-existing built environment allows for more flexibility and scope in a horizontal plan such as those at Amarna. Houses constructed within a temple enclosure or in an already organically developed settlement bounded by pre-existing fixed structures, such as between the walls of Medinat Habu, which is restricted within a horizontal plan, are dictated by the availability of space in which new extensions and designs can occur. The production of architectural typologies must consider these factors. Otherwise, the assumption is that no change occurred of any kind from the original foundation until the final abandonment of the house.[141]

A secondary problem, and one of the most important in developing typologies, is that few, if any, Egyptian settlements have been excavated in their entirety, while the most important, such as the capitals of Memphis and Thebes, have a limited amount of domestic architecture preserved for the entirety of the Pharaonic Period. A lack of a wider settlement plan is problematic as the ground plans of a few excavated houses are not necessarily representative of the whole variety of existing house types across the country. Therefore, interpretation of house typologies should not be based on a single house and should not be taken as characteristic of the whole settlement, or country as a whole.[142] Finally, the transposition of results from one region to another should not be undertaken without a detailed consideration of the potential for regional variation, particularly in the Delta and Nile Valley. Consequently, the construction and modification of house plans was a fluid and flexible development, which may have continued across different dynasties. Analysis based on dynastic divisions is, therefore, not appropriate for house plans of organically developed settlements, and it may be better to classify the structures into occupation and architectural phases based on adaptation and change.

HOUSEHOLD ARCHAEOLOGY AND EGYPTOLOGY

Household archaeology differs from the study of the built environment in the way it infers behaviour from the archaeological record. It comprises the social, material, and behavioural components, the demographic unit based on kinship, the dwelling, its installations, and artefacts found therein, and the activities conducted by the household inside the housing.[143] Several contributions have been made to the creation of a methodological groundwork for household studies in the Mediterranean,[144] with discussions on several important issues relating to the terminology being used and innovative future approaches, mainly using computer-aided archaeological methods to analyse buildings.[145]

The first attempt to assess a settlement in Egypt, including finds and ethnographic records and considering the themes of the household, was conducted in the Middle Kingdom–Second Intermediate Period settlement on Elephantine.[146] The significance of the associated artefacts in the context of an abandoned settlement was rejected, and the analysis was built around the functional analysis of the layout of the rooms, the built-in features, and the details of the construction. Evidence from the workmen's village at Deir el-Medina and Amarna was reviewed by comparing the house models and the textual data to come to a functional separation of rooms in the different house types.[147] Many other studies have also provided contributions to household studies in Egypt, mainly for the New Kingdom.[148] Themes have focused on the potential status symbols in domestic architecture, the socio-economic background, the subsistence strategies at the household level, the question of gender-specific areas, the three-dimensional experience, including climate control and heating of areas, household lifecycles, and the access route(s) in houses. In the Late Period, family archives and the tracking of household lifecycles by linking them to the archaeological record have become new fields of research.[149]

Much of the analysis has focused on Amarna, Deir el-Medina, and Kahun and was restricted to the earlier periods such as the Middle and New Kingdoms. The analysis presented here provides a countrywide coverage of Third Intermediate Period housing and aims to offer conclusions on aspects of Third Intermediate Period domestic architectural developments within the framework of the household and assess the potential of an integrated approach in examining the archaeological evidence of domestic architecture.

REVIEW OF THE EARLY EXCAVATIONS AT THIRD INTERMEDIATE PERIOD SITES

As with any dataset, there are limitations to the evidence and the nature and extent of observations and conclusions, and this is particularly true when assessing complete ground plans of Third Intermediate Period domestic structures to assess the development and continuation in architectural styles and the introduction of new elements. The countrywide preservation of complete house plans is poor and does not allow for overall house area sizes to be calculated to assess social ranges across different regions of Egypt.

Plans of domestic structures and contexts that have construction and occupation dates of the Third Intermediate Period have been found in both Upper Egypt and the Nile Delta and provide a good dataset with which to assess architectural developments across the period and to compare with the previous New Kingdom. Examples of Third Intermediate Period domestic architecture which preserve enough of the overall ground plan of domestic structures for them to be assessed and compared have been found in the Delta at Kom Firin, Tell el-Retaba, and Memphis, while in Upper Egypt house plans have been found at Lisht North, Amarna (el-Hagg Qandil), Hermopolis, and Medinat Habu and in Luxor at Abu el-Gud. Other excavations, at Tell el-Balamun, Sais, and Buto in Lower Egypt and at Matmar, Akoris, and Elephantine in Upper Egypt, have uncovered domestic remains of the period but insufficient evidence is preserved of an overall ground plan or only fragments are preserved, such as partial remains of domestic walls or installations such as silos and workshop areas. These examples do not form part of the discussion on house plans but are used in the comparisons of ancillary elements of domestic settlements, while their associated domestic material culture is discussed later in Chapter Four. Modern excavations, such as at Kom Firin, Tell el-Retaba, Memphis, and Hermopolis, have provided more detailed evidence sets for household archaeology of the period, particularly in regard to the artefact contexts and micro-archaeological analysis, but supply only fragmentary ground plans. Conversely, early twentieth-century excavations at Medinat Habu and Lisht North used an expansive digging strategy, leading to evidence composed almost exclusively of the ground plans of the 'house', but the excavators did not systematically record the artefacts well, and contexts and micro-archaeological analysis were largely absent. Through a combination of both approaches, an analysis of the development of Third Intermediate Period domestic architecture can be conducted. A re-analysis of the earlier excavated domestic evidence shows that some of the structures from Karnak, Medinat Habu, and Memphis used to analyse house plans in the past must be viewed with caution.

The Karnak Priestly Houses

The re-analysis of early excavations, particularly the pottery assemblages found within some of the priests' houses south-east of the sacred lake at Karnak, has enabled the re-dating of some of them, at least the last occupational phases and post-depositional activity, to later in the Saite Period (Fig. 19).[150] These houses have been one of the main sources for architectural comparisons of the Third Intermediate Period and have influenced interpretations of housing design for the period. The houses were built up against the enclosure wall of Thutmose

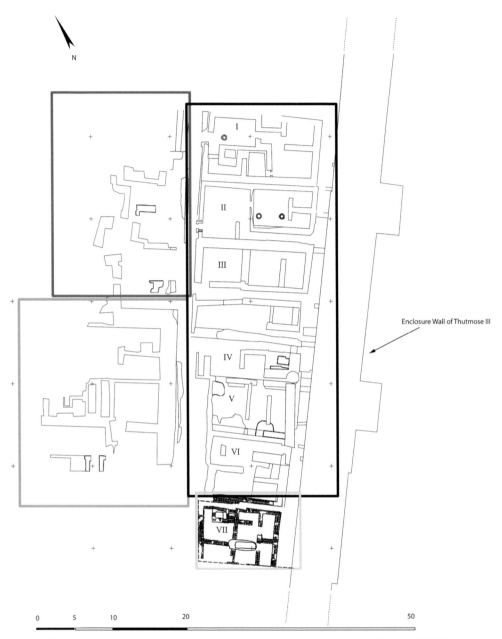

Fig. 19 Plan of the priests' houses at Karnak (Masson, 2007: pl. 1). (Courtesy of CNRS-CFEETK/Dr A. Masson-Berghoff.).

III, with six of the houses excavated between 1969 and 1970,[151] and a seventh house in 2001 as part of a follow-up reassessment of the area's stratigraphic and chronological development.[152] The first six houses were originally dated to the Twenty-First Dynasty based on the finds in House II. This was based on a stamped mud-brick of the HPA Menkheperre found at the ground level of the house,[153]

while an onomastic survey of an in situ door post found in House II belonging to
the Priest Ankhefenkhonsu gave the excavators reason to believe the house had
a Twenty-First Dynasty construction and occupation date.[154] House II was
entirely filled with rubble and the items in the fill phase of the building represent
not the original date of the construction of the houses, but a phase of later
occupation and collapse from the surrounding structures or of later dumping of
material into the houses. The re-analysis of the objects from within the houses in
2001 argued that the doorpost of Ankhefenkhonsu was not guaranteed evidence
for precise dating and the lintel could have belonged to a priest much later in date,
as there was no associated royal name.[155] The re-dating of the ceramics from the
1969–70 excavations also does not support an occupation phase in the Twenty-
First Dynasty.[156] Although a date in the later Twenty-Sixth to Twenty-Seventh
Dynasty was suggested, it must be acknowledged that the owners of the houses
may have modified them over the intervening five hundred years into the Saite
Period.[157] The case for modifications is hard to confirm with the available
evidence. The 2001 excavation of House VII provided some clarification to the
original occupation dates for the house compound. The ceramics from House VII
provided a date range from the Saite to Persian Period.[158] The early dating for the
construction of the priestly houses is now highly debatable, based on the door lintel
with no associated royal name and the ceramic data from the Saite/Persian Period,
and there is no justification for the buildings to be dated to the Twenty-First
Dynasty; however, it does not rule out the possibility of the presence of an earlier
Third Intermediate Period priestly quarter somewhere around the Sacred Lake
based on the associated finds.[159] It is not appropriate to use the Karnak priestly
housing plans in this architectural study as a comparative resource for securely
dated Third Intermediate Period structural remains and occupational phases.

The Memphite Doorways in the South-west of the Ptah Temple

At Memphis, the remains of architectural elements of buildings were found in
a trial trench cut at the back of the small Ramesside Ptah temple. The only
items published were the stone doorways (Fig. 20).[160] One of the doorways was
inscribed by the priest of Ptah and the House of Osiris, Lord of Rostau, Ptah-
Kha, and was erected for his father, Ashakhet, while the other more fragmentary example did not preserve the owner's name. Both stone doorways were
erected during the Twenty-First Dynasty in the reign of Psusennes I. There is
debate as to the function of these buildings. Originally the doorposts were
encased in brickwork and were interpreted as possible chapels[161] or tombs.[162] It
is suggested that they represent the doorways to priests' houses like the Karnak
examples discussed above.[163] As the evidence now suggests the construction
date of the Karnak doorposts and the priestly houses was not in the early Third
Intermediate Period, a comparison of the two sets of buildings therefore cannot

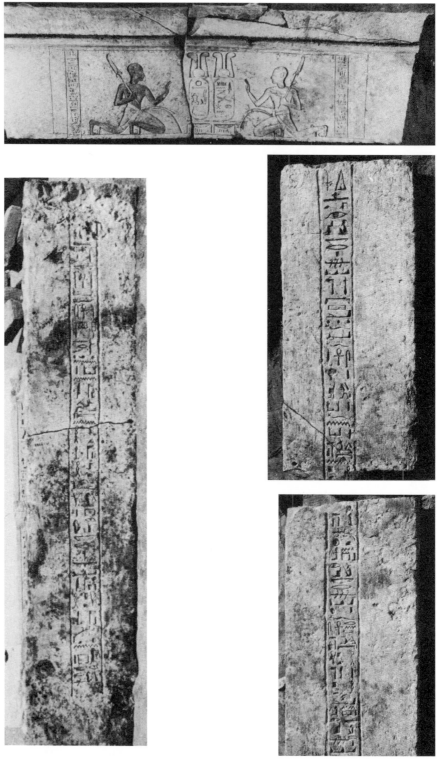

Fig. 20 Doorway of Ptah-Kha (lintel originally cut away in publication photos) (Anthes, 1965: pl. 321 a. 26–8). (Courtesy of the University Museum, University of Pennsylvania.)

be made, and the function of the building these doorposts belonged to cannot be determined at this moment. An assessment of these structures as houses is not achievable as no mud-brick walls or rooms were associated with the doorposts.

The House of Butahamun at Medinat Habu

At Medinat Habu, the best-preserved structure near the Western Fortified Gate belonged to the Overseer of the Treasury, Butahamun. It is the only known house of the period so far found which is associated with a named individual. This building has the potential, in combination with the associated architecture, to provide an insight into the role of the person and the household agency. The presence of an associated name with the house, in general, is a rarity, because the lack of individuals associated with house architecture is a 'near universal problem', particularly within household archaeology.[164]

The building dates to the reign of Ramesses XI or Smendes I, as Butahamun is last attested in Year 13 of Smendes I and by Year 16 was succeeded by his son Ankhefenamun.[165] The remaining structural elements of Butahamun's building were in a fragmentary state of preservation. The house plan shows a wide doorway into the first (transverse/court) room before the main room. Only the sill of the door was extant. Inside the room were two stone columns. The mud-brick foundations were all that remained of the room. From this room, one would enter the main (or secondary court) room. Four columns were regularly spaced across the room supporting a roof. All four of these columns still stood upright. The rear (western) wall of the room had the remains of two stone pilasters. There were the remains of a rectangular stone dais against the west wall. To the right of the dais there was a narrow doorway. Unfortunately, the rear rooms were not preserved. There was the possibility of a secondary doorway on the left-hand side of the dais.[166] Other remains in the vicinity may well have belonged to additional rooms of the building.[167] The assessment of the architecture, particularly its position within the Medinat Habu enclosure next to the entrance of the West Fortified Gate and the central room arrangement, which has a four-columned central hall with raised stone dais, calls into question the identification of this structure as the house of Butahamun. The structure was compared to the 'South' or 'Queen Tiy's' palace at Malqata, which was suggested to be an administrative office connected with the palace stores. If the structure of Butahamun was an office, it would correspond with his position as the 'Overseer of the Royal Treasury'.[168]

Based on the current analysis of the housing at Karnak, Memphis, and Medinat Habu, the problems in analysing architectural plans and elements assumed to represent houses from previous excavations become clear. Therefore, these so-called 'house plans' are unreliable for analysis and should not be used within the analysis of Third Intermediate Period house architecture.

ARCHITECTURAL HOUSE PLANS OF THE NEW KINGDOM

This section documents the architectural design of domestic houses in the preceding New Kingdom to provide a baseline for housing design prior to the Third Intermediate Period. Only then can the houses found in settlements with Third Intermediate Period occupation phases be analysed to see whether there was a continuation of New Kingdom architectural styles or whether new designs and architectural elements were introduced into the Third Intermediate Period domestic architectural repertoire.

In the early New Kingdom, there was a continuation of the Middle Kingdom style of housing which comprised a large rectangular, columned central hall, flanked by two smaller rectangular side rooms.[169] In the Amarna Period, there was a transition to the central hall house.[170] The houses at Amarna show a large variety of scale, with areas ranging from less than 10 m^2 to more than 400 m^2 (Fig. 21).[171] The larger of these houses were set within their own enclosures, which included several ancillary structures, among them other smaller houses. The Amarna houses exhibit a strict patterning of spatial layout from both the smallest and the largest structures, and show a tripartite division, with only the smallest houses lacking front rooms.[172] The central hall house style comprised a square, central hall living space with a brick dais against one wall and smaller rooms radiating from it. A rectangular pillared antechamber or reception fronted the central square room.[173]

Examples of tripartite houses are found in Egypt as early as the Old Kingdom, while staircases were a prominent feature of the New Kingdom Amarna houses.[174] After the Amarna Period, it was suggested that the house style reverted back to the traditional style of the Middle Kingdom; however, this is not observed across the country.[175] At the Ramesside capital of Qantir, the Nineteenth Dynasty houses had a tripartite layout in a continuation of the Amarna house style.[176] This was also the case in Thebes where the Nineteenth Dynasty houses behind the 'temple palace' of Medinat Habu were based on the Amarna architectural style, with a rectangular vestibule, a square central room surrounded by two rooms, and an antechamber.[177] Other houses at Medinat Habu, except for the so-called 'house'

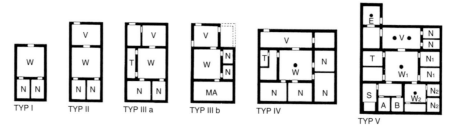

Fig. 21 Amarna house types (Bietak, 1996: 24). (Courtesy of Prof. M. Bietak.).

of Butahamun, reverted to the conventional Middle Kingdom style.[178] At Thebes, the Ramesside houses at Abu el-Gud were in the Amarna style,[179] but at the late New Kingdom/early Third Intermediate Period fort of el-Ahawaih, the houses do not show a continuation of the Amarna middle court plan.[180] The Ramesside Period houses at Deir el-Medina had similar designs to Amarna housing, with their square, columned main room, while the larger houses at Deir el-Medina had rooms surrounding the main room, a plan reminiscent of the Amarna style.[181] Finally, at Memphis, the Ramesside Period housing followed a similar plan to the Amarna style, but at the same time the Ramesside phase was founded upon and copied the earlier Eighteenth Dynasty house design. The Ramesside phase, there-fore, was influenced in its design by the earlier Eighteenth Dynasty structures, while the area showed a large amount of continuity from the New Kingdom.[182] The design of housing after the Amarna Period shows a preference for a continuation of the Amarna styles in many regions of the country, but at the same time architects reverted to the Middle Kingdom style.

Although the evidence is limited, the review of Nineteenth Dynasty/late New Kingdom house designs shows different architectural styles were con-current with each other, and no dominant architectural style was used across the country. The concurrent use of different housing styles may reflect the contemporaneity of space within more urbanised settlements, as new styles were built next to old styles, but had contemporary occupational phases. The late New Kingdom settlements were made up of a multiplicity of different housing styles, which were subject to adaptation and change over time based on the needs and socio-economic restrictions of the owners.

THE ARCHITECTURAL STYLES OF THE THIRD INTERMEDIATE PERIOD IN UPPER EGYPT

1 The Central Room with Double Column and Dais

There is considerable evidence to suggest the central room with double column and dais found in the Amarna Period houses continued to be a prominent feature in Third Intermediate Period house architecture. This style is observed in a late New Kingdom/early Third Intermediate Period house at Amarna itself (el-Hagg Qandil) (Fig. 22)[183] and throughout the period at Medinat Habu (Figs. 23–25),[184] but this combination of elements has not been documented at other settlements for the period beyond the Twenty-First Dynasty.

2 Amarna Style House Plans

At Lisht North, after the end of the Eighteenth Dynasty, the casing of the pyramid of Amenemhat III was removed and used as a source of building

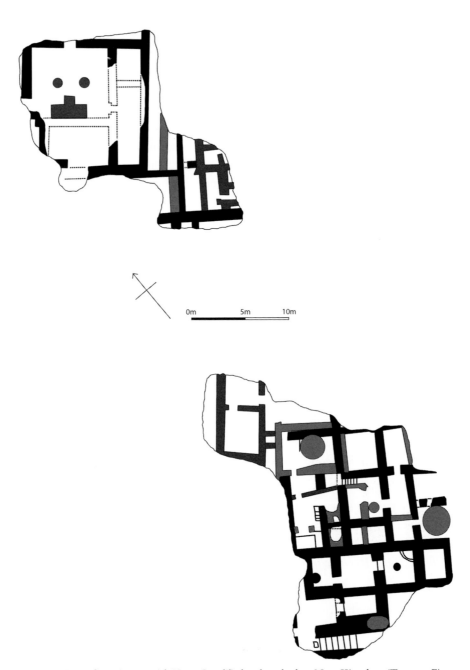

Fig. 22 House from Amarna (el-Hagg Qandil) dated to the late New Kingdom/Twenty-First Dynasty, showing the central columned room and dais (redrawn from Peet and Woolley, 1923: pl. XLI). (Courtesy of the Egypt Exploration Society.).

material, creating large rubbish heaps around the base of the pyramid. During the Twentieth Dynasty, a settlement grew up on top of the rubble mounds and was inhabited by a low social class, probably the workpeople who were tasked with removing the casing of the pyramid.[185] The housing itself was built up

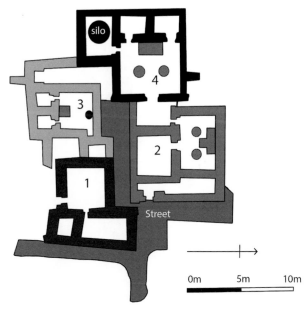

Fig. 23 Medinat Habu second phase houses, showing the central columned hall and dais (redrawn, after Hölscher, 1954: fig. 6). (Courtesy of the Oriental Institute of the University of Chicago.).

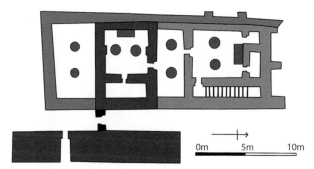

Fig. 24 Two houses side by side at Medinat Habu second phase house, showing central columned hall and dais (redrawn, after Hölscher, 1954: fig. 5). (Courtesy of the Oriental Institute of the University of Chicago.).

against the west side of the pyramid.[186] The objects found in the houses suggest the inhabitants were farmers who had a cottage industry manufacturing glass and beads, although the primary occupation was tomb robbing.[187] The extent of the occupation phases remains uncertain as there were no controlled excavations carried out on the settlement when it was excavated by Mace between 1906 and 1922.[188] The evidence suggests the settlement continued to be in use until its abandonment during the Twenty-Second Dynasty. The architectural plans were described as 'haphazard in design with walls at any angle and of no conceivable plan, and with narrow streets that terminated in people's private courtyards'.[189] A reassessment of the house plans in the 1990s showed the

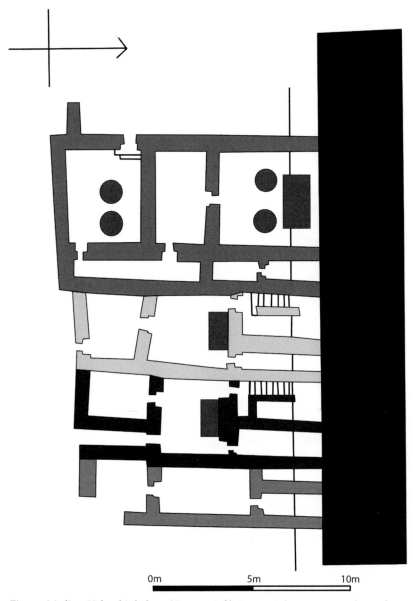

0m   5m   10m

Fig. 25 Medinat Habu third phase (Twenty-Fifth Dynasty): houses against the enclosure wall showing the central columned hall and dais (redrawn, after Hölscher, 1954: fig. 19).

houses conformed to the lower end style layouts of the middle-class houses from Amarna and Deir el-Medina, and represent the typical house plans of the Amarna Period.[190]

At Abu el-Gud, 120 m to the south of the Mut Complex at Karnak, a neatly planned series of mud-brick houses of the Nineteenth Dynasty were excavated, with wide entrances with stone door jambs and thresholds,[191] and a rectangular twelve-roomed storage magazine, or casemate for a stone structure. The structure seems to have related to a small temple of Ramesses II with an open court, followed by a colonnade, and behind that a sanctuary.[192] No plans of the complex were published, but based on the combination of buildings it appears to represent a small temple complex of Ramesses II. Directly on top of the Nineteenth Dynasty temple complex were large domestic structures dated by the excavators to the Third Intermediate Period/Late Period. It is not known if the Ramesside temple continued to function after the New Kingdom. The Mut Complex houses were centred around a main room, each house supplied with a pair of pillars to support the ceiling.[193] The descriptions of the architectural layout would suggest an Amarna style house, but this cannot be confirmed without published plans.[194] At Medinat Habu, at some point in the Twenty-Fifth Dynasty, several new houses were constructed. These newly built houses retained the New Kingdom dais element as discussed above, but now resembled the long narrow houses of the New Kingdom at Deir el-Medina, with a front room and a main room followed by two rear rooms or a staircase, all along the same line.[195] The long narrow house style of the New Kingdom can be observed to some extent in the house built on the so-called 'pomerium' of Ramesses III, which dates to the Twenty-Second–Twenty-Fourth Dynasty phase (Fig. 26).[196]

In the Twenty-Fifth/Twenty-Sixth Dynasty, at Medinat Habu a group of larger houses in Phase III were constructed within the temple's inner enclosure wall and retained parts of the Amarna type plan. Houses 1–2 and 5–6 had two square central rooms in a variety of layouts (Fig. 27). Several houses, of suggested Twenty-First Dynasty date, built upon the palace of Merenptah at Kom el-Qala were excavated by Fischer, but they remain unpublished.[197] An additional group of houses were also found upon the nearby temple of Merenptah at Kom el-Qala by Petrie in the early twentieth century (Fig. 28).[198] The houses were all of small size and built close by one another. The

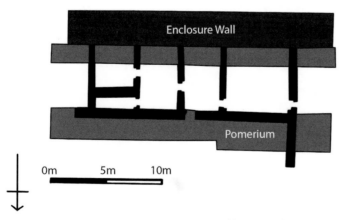

Fig. 26 Second phase Third Intermediate Period house on the pomerium of Ramesses III, resembling the long narrow houses of Deir el-Medina (redrawn after Hölscher, 1954: fig. 8). (Courtesy of the Oriental Institute of the University of Chicago.).

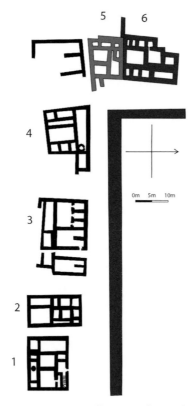

Fig. 27 Twenty-Fifth Dynasty houses from Medinat Habu (redrawn after Hölscher, 1954: fig. 19). (Courtesy of the Oriental Institute of the University of Chicago.)

Fig. 28 Plan of the Third Intermediate Period houses overlying the temple of Merenptah at Memphis (redrawn from Petrie, 1909: pl. XXVII).

ground plans of these houses were similar to the second phase houses (tenth to eighth century BCE) from Medinat Habu and the late New Kingdom/early Third Intermediate Period houses at el-Hagg Qandil (Amarna).[199] Considering these comparisons, it is argued that the nearby houses, which Fischer found at Kom el-Qala with similar designs and dating to the Twenty-First Dynasty, may be of a later Twenty-Second Dynasty construction date.[200] Without a detailed stratigraphic analysis of the structures found by Petrie and Fischer, combined with artefact contexts and micro-archaeological analysis, any assumed dating of these houses to a Twenty-Second Dynasty occupation phase must be taken with caution. The partial nature of the plans of many of the structures makes it difficult to assess whether there were different styles of housing used concurrently at Kom el-Qala, while the evidence from other settlements across the country shows different housing types could be contemporary with one another.

Excavations carried out by the EES at Kom Rabia found domestic remains dating to the Third Intermediate Period.[201] The remains overlaid the settlement of the New Kingdom, with approximately 20 m² of Third Intermediate Period stratigraphy preserved; they seem to have followed the same Amarna style layout of the previous New Kingdom phase.

Excavations at Kom Firin found early Third Intermediate Period parts of houses along the eastern wall of the Ramesside temple and, in Phases 5 and 6 (EV–I), in the north-eastern sector of the temenos area. A full house plan was not preserved, which makes it difficult to understand the spatial arrangement of the whole house. The inhabitants of the house conducted developments and adaptations of the house between Phases 5 and 6. The houses in the north-eastern sector of the Ramesside enclosure wall were built after successive silo installations of the early Third Intermediate Period. The rooms of the house were built against the interior faces of the temple enclosure, indicating the redevelopment of space. The use of the enclosure wall to provide support for housing is like the second phase domestic occupations of Ramesside temple enclosures at Matmar and Medinat Habu. The partial plans of the structure were consistent with a house, such as the small three rooms against the enclosure wall, preceded by a central space with perhaps a staircase to one side. The arrangement of the rooms of the Kom Firin house would fit with the broadly tripartite arrangement of New Kingdom houses.[202]

3 Other Domestic Architectural Designs

Several Third Intermediate Period houses from across Egypt, based on the preserved remains, do not incorporate known architectural elements such as the columns or dais, or adhere to the styles of architecture and housing layout of the previous Middle and New Kingdom traditions, particularly those of Amarna.

The first set of these houses were those found in grid square E5 at Medinat Habu (tenth to eighth century BCE), situated on an angular, hilly street, with various steps at short intervals to connect different occupation levels. Four complete houses were identified (Fig. 29). The first house, 'House 1', had two rooms but no subsidiary chambers, while House 2 had two rooms and a small courtyard in the front. The corresponding part of House 3, as far as can be ascertained, was not closed off from the street and behind it was a stairway that led up to the socle of the Great Girdle Wall. Based on this evidence it can be said that House 3 had a second storey. House 4 had its main room paved with baked bricks, while there was a second, now destroyed room to the east. House 4, based on the trapezoidal form at the front with its thin walls, was most likely an open court.[203] Secondly, at Medinat Habu, as well as some of the larger Twenty-Fifth Dynasty houses having Amarna style layouts, a new style was found (Houses 3–4) that diverged from the square central hall pattern and instead had a large rectangular main room surrounded by a series of three small rooms, and two long rectangular rooms making an L-shape around the first grouping.

In the Wadi Tumilat at Tell el-Retaba, in Area 3, two houses were partly excavated; one, 'House 2', had walls approximately 1 m thick. The wall thickness suggests a second or even a third storey. This structure was interpreted as the basement of the house, which was accessed by the upper floor as

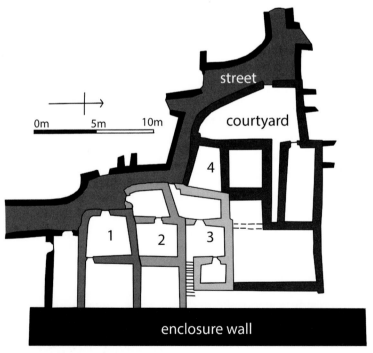

Fig. 29 Group of houses at Medinat Habu (redrawn, after Hölscher, 1954: fig. 7). (Courtesy of the Oriental Institute of the University of Chicago.).

no doors or windows were found.[204] A main road running from the large western gate of the fortress which led to the main temple divided Area 3 from a second area of housing, 'Area 5', but the houses on this side of the road were markedly different in design, with much thinner walls (0.3 m wide and smaller). The road appears to have separated two functionally different parts of the settlement, but it is possible the much larger and thicker-walled house represents a later phase of house design at Tell el-Retaba corresponding to the larger thicker-walled houses found at Hermopolis and in the later larger Twenty-Fifth Dynasty structures at Medinat Habu. In Area 9 at Tell el-Retaba, a third area of Third Intermediate Period structures again represented a different form of housing, consisting of small houses that have so far been attributed a general Third Intermediate Period phase dating. The initial stages of the Area 9 housing had only two rooms like in the smaller houses at Medinat Habu.[205] Finally, at Hermopolis in Grabung I and Graben IV there were domestic occupation levels of the Third Intermediate Period (Figs. 30–32).[206] The publication is of limited use for understanding the housing plans of the period because the ceramics collected all dated from the Eighteenth Dynasty to the Ptolemaic Period, and the described pottery is only partially illustrated.[207] Later excavations discovered the remains of Third Intermediate Period housing in 'Site-W'. Three construction phases were identified. Level 3 (the earliest phase) dates to before the eighth century BCE, Level 2 dates to the late eighth century BCE, and Level 1, which consisted of a large housing foundation overlying the foundations of the Level 2 house, dates from ca. 700–600 BCE, placing its construction at the end of the Third Intermediate Period and the transition phase into the

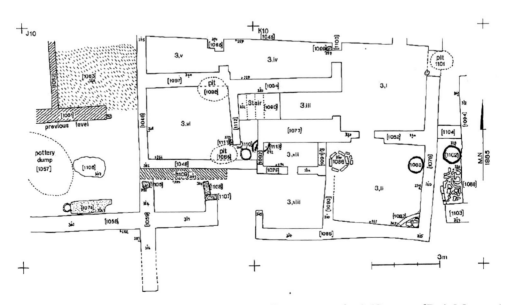

Fig. 30 Level 3 house at Hermopolis in squares J.10–K.10 (Spencer, 1993: pl. 10). (Courtesy of Dr A. J. Spencer/ The Trustees of the British Museum.).

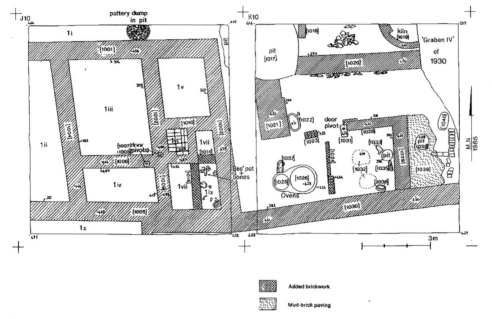

Fig. 31 Level 1 house at Hermopolis in squares J.11–K.11 (Spencer, 1993, pl. 18). (Courtesy of Dr A. J. Spencer/The Trustees of the British Museum.).

Saite Period.[208] The Level 3 (pre-eighth century BCE) house had eight rooms designed without a central hall, as in the standard Amarna plan, while the houses in Levels 2b–1 did not exhibit an Amarna style and appear to be random in their layout. The final phase (Level 1b) consisted of a large square house foundation of mud-brick and was built as single project with only a few minor later additions.[209] The brickwork formed a network of walls without interconnecting doorways, which appears to be similar to Late Period tower-house architecture.[210]

The preserved architectural plans of Third Intermediate Period housing demonstrate the maintenance of the New Kingdom Amarna design, with the central columned room and dais, while in some settlements a less regular architectural design began to be developed. These non-Amarna plans developed in response to increasing spatial limitations within the settlements and the requirements of the family group, and the economic and social hierarchy of the occupants of the household.

OTHER ARCHITECTURAL DOMESTIC FEATURES

Staircases, Columns, Stone Fittings, Ovens, Wall Decoration, and Mud-bricks

In some excavations, smaller elements from houses can be useful in understanding the capacity of settlements in the Third Intermediate Period. Staircases

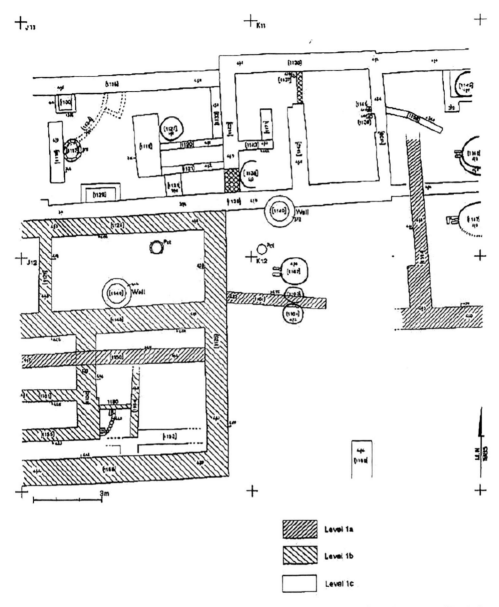

Fig. 32 Level 1b house at Hermopolis in squares J.10–K.10 (Spencer, 1993, pl. 3). (Courtesy of Dr A. J. Spencer/The Trustees of the British Museum.).

within homes demonstrate the need for vertical expansion of the household, indicating a spatial horizontal restriction within the settlement. Furthermore, they provide economic indications of individual households and the financial ability to build multi-storey dwellings. The presence of ovens within designated houses indicates food production within the home, and not being reliant on external, government-run food preparation areas, which again provides an economic indicator to the family unit and the self-sufficient nature of the domestic population in specific areas of the settlement. Finally, the application of wall decoration indicates the financial ability to afford coloured and decorated walls and expresses a desire by the family to express aesthetic and cultural trends and elite emulation.

Staircases have been found in several Third Intermediate Period houses throughout the period at Hermopolis,[211] Medinat Habu,[212] and Kom Firin.[213] An assessment of whether they were for accessing a second storey or a roof area is difficult, but if the walls had widths of 1 m or more, then a second storey could have been supported. The roof spaces would have been open areas in which craft work and storage areas would have been located, as is common in modern Egyptian houses.[214]

The rooms and courtyards of the early Third Intermediate Period settlement at Kom Firin were fitted with limestone architectural elements, which was typical in middle and high-ranking formal buildings: door jambs, lintels, thresholds, and column bases. Thirteen examples of limestone door sockets were found, including a fired clay example. The diameter of the pivot holes varied from 3.2 cm to 14 cm. The pivot holes are sometimes cut into slab-shaped pieces of stone, perhaps suggesting re-use, although others are no more than chunks of stone. The presence of multiple depressions may indicate re-use of the stone for a second doorway, and these door sockets could be made from recycled stone.[215] At Memphis, limestone blocks were used as thresholds or sills.[216]

At Kom Firin, the limestone fragments found in the domestic houses may have once been part of tables, seats, and stools.[217] At Memphis, four examples of limestone tables were found. They all exhibit the same features, with upper and outer surfaces which are flat and smooth.[218] Low tables of this type were used in the New Kingdom at Amarna, with one example still in situ on a mud-brick bench (mastaba),[219] while shallow limestone tables or stools with three legs 25 cm in diameter and 5–7 cm thick were found at Medinat Habu.[220]

Fragments from New Kingdom temples are also re-used in domestic contexts, and as architectural features of the houses, showing that temple structures were accessible as quarries. Large amounts of limestone fragments were found in the early Third Intermediate Period occupation phases at Kom Firin, but inscribed fragments were rare. One fragment bears the bottom of a Ramesside cartouche and was likely to have been part of a door jamb or lintel. It may have come from the temple, an official building, storeroom, or even a private house, but it was re-used in the Third Intermediate Period occupation phase as a door socket, along with other limestone fragments probably coming from earlier monumental Ramesside buildings, most likely the monumental gateway to the Ramesside enclosure.[221] Column bases were well carved but of quite poorly preserved stone. One example had the base drilled with a shallow depression in its upper surface, possibly to secure a wooden column, or as part of some secondary re-use.[222] There was no evidence that well-dressed slabs from the

Ramesside temple were used in the Third Intermediate Period occupation phases at Kom Firin.[223] At Matmar, there is evidence the local Ramesside temple was robbed of its stone to be used as architectural supports for the grain silos.[224] At Hermopolis a pivot block from the 700–600 BCE house phase had re-used an Amarna block from the New Kingdom temple.[225] The re-use of stone reflects the economic pressures of the period regarding access to stone supply and the provision of stone by royal and governmental agencies. This is the case in the Delta as the geo-political restrictions created by regional political and administrative fragmentation would have restricted access to quarries in Upper Egypt, forcing the population to recycle the stone elements around them. This applied to local rulers in their efforts to construct new temples.

The Third Intermediate Period houses continue to retain designated areas for cooking and the preparation of food, with small brick ovens identified in the domestic levels at Sais, Kom Firin, and Hermopolis, and it can be assumed that these housing areas were open to the air to allow the smoke to escape, although they may have been in designated spaces as in the case of some modern Egyptian village houses. Evidence of wall decoration in the domestic settlements of the period rarely survives, but there is evidence the walls were coated in mud plaster at Matmar[226] and in the Phase 5 house at Tell el-Retaba.[227] Mud plaster permitted the formation of a smooth flat surface which could be decorated, but the extent of painted decoration is debated because not enough has survived across the dynastic period. Representations of houses from tomb models and scenes indicates they were most likely coated in a whitewash, which would have helped reflect the heat, particularly in the summer months.[228]

As in the New Kingdom, Third Intermediate Period houses continued to be constructed of mud-bricks, as well as considerable quantities of re-used mud-bricks from earlier New Kingdom buildings, particularly New Kingdom temple enclosure walls. Mud-bricks can be analysed through a systematic recording of brick sizes,[229] while mud can to some extent be distinguished through its chemical components.[230] Measuring the sizes of bricks can allow the identification of brick factories or batches or manufacturing teams, for the purpose initially of internal comparison for a site chronology. Brick size analysis has many factors, which must be considered when using them for statistical analysis. Each brick has its own unique complex topography, and the reasons for the irregularity, even though made in moulds, include the amount of shrinkage during the drying process and disturbance during the drying process from the removal of the moulds.[231] The measuring of a brick to the nearest millimetre cannot be done as the brick's axis does not represent the true planes,[232] and the measurements collected for the Third Intermediate Period, as for all other periods, are a compromise.

After the Old Kingdom, and up until Late Antiquity, the broad spread of brick size values seems to have been around 15 x 30 cm.[233] The corpus of brick sizes collected from across the country in this analysis of the Third Intermediate Period is derived from average brick sizes taken from walls at Medinat Habu, Tell el-Balamun, Hermopolis, Elephantine, Karnak, Akoris, Matmar, and Tell el-Retaba. Two examples of stamped bricks exist, not in situ: one, with the name of the HPA Menkheperre, comes from the priestly house (House II) at Karnak and measured 27 x 15 x 7 cm, representing a fairly small size; the other, a large mud-brick with the name of Ini from Elephantine, measured 40 x 18 x 10 cm and may even have been longer.[234] This brick is most likely to have come from a monumental structure or even part of a floor, like the large 40 x 40 x 7 cm mud-bricks found in the floor of Houses 1 and 2 (Grid G12–13) at Medinat Habu. The remainder of the mud-brick examples from across the period all come from walls in domestic contexts and fit well within the norm for domestic brick sizes of the period, showing no deviation away from normal brick size averages for the Old Kingdom until Late Antiquity. The average brick size for the period is 33 x 16 x 9 cm, which fits well within the average domestic brick size of dynastic Egypt, and therefore differentiating chronological time phases based on brick sizes is not possible for the Third Intermediate Period.

Granaries and Storage Areas

The presence of storage facilities is a major feature in the urban makeup of pharaonic settlements, particularly those for the storage of grain and other agricultural commodities. Secure magazines were constructed for high-value items, such as precious metals, stones, and weaponry.[235] The Third Intermediate Period shows a continuation from the New Kingdom with the construction of circular grain (wheat and barley) silos as they are found in association with almost every domestic structure so far excavated, and there is no evidence for a fundamental change in grain silo design. What does become apparent is the quality of the construction of the smaller family unit sized silos. Successive smaller silos, which were on average around 1.5–2 m in diameter, were built one on top of the other over short spaces of time. This suggests that silos were maintained more frequently, or silo construction at the lower-class domestic scale was rudimentary and of a poorer construction quality, resulting in short use-lives, which required the constant construction and rebuilding of silo installations; therefore they are a prominent feature of Third Intermediate Period domestic architecture. The period sees large numbers of smaller silos built in previously open spaces, and at the same time they were constructed over and upon the remains of earlier housing phases, such as earlier walls and rooms, or even in disused or crumbling religious and administrative buildings of the New Kingdom, showing that grain storage for family units was a priority. These large areas of small, successively built family unit silos are a characteristic of the Third Intermediate Period.

Grain silo capacities can indicate their function and whether they were used by a self-sufficient single or extended family, or by the wider community as part of a governmental redistributive system. The circular granaries found in Third Intermediate Period settlements have no preserved heights recorded, and to estimate their fill capacities, this book adopts the approach of Kemp who suggests an estimated 2.5 m maximum fill height for domestic and administrative grain silos.[236] Using the grain ration estimates of one soldier per day can provide an approximate weight of grain needed for an average person. A male soldier required 0.375 kg of wheat and 0.225 kg of barley per day, which was a total of 0.6 kg of grain per day.[237] Circular grain silo capacity estimates are derived from silos at Matmar,[238] Kom Firin, Akoris, Kom Rabia (Memphis), Medinat Habu, and el-Hagg Qandil (Amarna).

The Kom Firin and Akoris (Areas L and M) silos were made of fragmentary and whole mud-bricks laid predominantly in stretcher-bond formation and only a single brick thick; the bonding and thickness of the other silos was not recorded in the excavation reports. The inhabitants of Matmar took stone from the Ramesside temple to construct supports for the silos. It is unclear from the reports whether the stone was used as an external structural support to the silo owing to its size, or if the stone was placed under the silo as a raised base. If it were the latter, then having the stones under the silos would have acted to reduce moisture and prevent rodents and insects from eating the grain.

The silo capacity estimates (Tables 4 and 5) show the maximum amount of grain required for the needs of the associated population of the settlement, because the grain was put to multiple uses including as surplus in the event of famine and surplus for the year ahead. The estimated capacities of the silos found in the silo courts of the large houses in the temple temenoi at Kom Firin and Matmar indicate their part in the taxation and ration system of the earlier New Kingdom, in which the workers were given a ration of grain as a form of payment.[239] Small group housing complexes of extended families and communities, such as at Medinat Habu, had one large grain silo in a designated room leading off from the central pillared hall with dais. The position of the silo indicates that those who wanted access to the grain had to go through the main room and past the owner/scribe/administrator seated on the dais, possibly indicating a level of control over grain resources for a small housing complex from the patriarchal head of the family or family group. Clusters of small family grain silos were constructed within walled areas which offered more protection of family stores and indicate that, unlike in the larger house groups which provided specific rooms for the protection of grain bins, these smaller silos were owned by families with restricted space in their own homes, so they had to

TABLE 4 *Grain silo capacities for individual silos from Matmar, Akoris, Kom Firin, Medinat Habu, and el-Hagg Qandil.*

Location of silo	Diameter (m)	Height (m)	Total volume (m³)	Wheat (kg)	Barley (kg)	People per year: wheat ration	People per year: barley ration
Matmar (near temenos entrance in designated room)	4.00	2.0	30	24,000	19,000	175	231
Matmar (outside main silo court)?	2.30	2.1	10	8,000	6,000	58	73
Matmar (outside silo court)	3.20	2.5	23	18,000	14,000	131	170
Matmar (outside silo court)	2.94	2.5	19	15,000	12,000	109	146
Matmar (outside silo court)	2.94	2.5	19	15,000	12,000	109	146
Matmar (silo court)	3.74	2.5	32	25,000	20,000	182	243
Matmar (silo court)	3.47	2.5	27	21,000	17,000	153	207
Matmar (silo court)	3.20	2.5	23	18,000	14,000	131	170
Matmar (silo court)	1.87	2.5	7	6,000	5,000	43	60
Matmar (silo court)	1.11	2.5	3	2,000	2,000	14	24
Matmar (outside temenos enclosure)	3.47	2.5	27	21,000	17,000	153	207
Matmar (outside temenos enclosure)	3.47	2.5	27	21,000	17,000	153	207
Matmar (other eastern silos)	4.09	2.5	38	30,000	24,000	219	292
Matmar (other eastern silos)	3.34	2.5	25	19,000	16,000	138	194
Kom Firin (top left silo, Phase EII)	2.94	2.5	19	15,000	12,000	109	146
Kom Firin (central silo, Phase EII)	4.00	2.5	36	28,000	23,000	204	280
Kom Firin (bottom silo, Phase EII)	3.24	2.5	23	18,000	15,000	131	182
Akoris Area L	1.00	2.5	2	2,000	1,000	14	12
	1.25	2.5	3	3,000	2,000	21	24
	1.50	2.5	5	4,000	3,000	29	36
	2.00	2.5	8	7,000	5,000	51	60
	2.00	2.5	8	7,000	5,000	51	60
	2.00	2.5	8	7,000	5,000	51	60
	2.00	2.5	8	7,000	5,000	51	60
	2.00	2.5	8	7,000	5,000	51	60
	2.00	2.5	8	7,000	5,000	51	60
	2.00	2.5	8	7,000	5,000	51	60
	2.00	2.5	8	7,000	5,000	51	60
	2.00	2.5	8	7,000	5,000	51	60
	2.00	2.5	8	7,000	5,000	51	60
	2.00	2.5	8	7,000	5,000	51	60
	2.00	2.5	8	7,000	5,000	51	60
	2.10	2.5	9	7,000	6,000	51	73
	2.10	2.5	9	7,000	6,000	51	73
	2.50	2.5	13	11,000	9,000	80	109
	2.50	2.5	13	11,000	9,000	80	109
	3.00	2.5	20	15,000	12,000	109	146
Akoris Area M	1.00	2.5	2	2,000	1,000	14	12
	1.50	2.5	5	4,000	3,000	29	36
	2.00	2.5	8	7,000	5,000	51	60
	2.00	2.5	8	7,000	5,000	51	60
	2.00	2.5	8	7,000	5,000	51	60
	2.50	2.5	13	11,000	9,000	80	109

(continued)

TABLE 4 *(continued)*

Location of silo	Diameter (m)	Height (m)	Total volume (m³)	Wheat (kg)	Barley (kg)	People per year: wheat ration	People per year: barley ration
Akoris large house	6.80	2.5	115	90,000	73,000	657	888
	6.80	2.5	115	90,000	73,000	657	888
	6.80	2.5	115	90,000	73,000	657	888
Medinat Habu house in G7	2.00	2.5	8	7,000	5,000	51	60
El-Hagg Qandil (Room 8)	3.00	2.5	20	15,000	12,000	109	146
El-Hagg Qandil (Room 25)	2.00	2.5	8	7,000	5,000	51	60
El-Hagg Qandil	1.00	2.5	2	2,000	1,000	14	12
El-Hagg Qandil	1.00	2.5	2	2,000	1,000	14	12

TABLE 5 *Total grain silo capacities from Kom Firin, Akoris, Matmar, and el-Hagg Qandil.*

Total grain storage capacity	Wheat (kg)	Barley (kg)	People per year: wheat ration	People per year: barley ration
Matmar	243,000	195,000	1,775	2,374
Kom Firin Phase EII	61,000	50,000	445	608
Akoris Area L	151,000	113,000	1,098	1,362
Akoris Area M	38,000	28,000	276	337
Akoris large house	270,000	219,000	1,972	2,666
El-Hagg Qandil	26,000	19,000	189	231

resort to communal protected grain storage. The grain silo analysis has demonstrated the continuing function of the New Kingdom bureaucratic system of taxation and grain rationing to the wider community, and shows that small family groups maintained control over grain supplies within their own homes, while families with limited domestic space could secure their grain supplies in group silo areas.

Animal Stabling and Husbandry Areas

Chapter 2 identified a reduction of stable establishments outside the main political centres controlled by kings and local leaders within the Akoris to Atfih region from the end of the New Kingdom into the Third Intermediate Period. It is possible that the stables had, by the end of the Third Intermediate Period, been removed from the hinterland settlements and were concentrated in large civic stables inside the main temenos walls, as at Tell el-Retaba, and at Hermopolis as documented on the Piankhy Stela. The Piankhy Stela also indicates that civic stabling at Memphis was for horses as well as oxen.[240] The only archaeological evidence of stabling dated to the Third Intermediate Period is at Tell el-Retaba in Area 6 within the mud-brick enclosure (Fig. 33),[241] while a royal stable at Qantir dating from the late Nineteenth to late Twentieth Dynasty, and probably extending into the early Third Intermediate Period, is of the same type as that discovered at Tell el-Retaba;[242] this shows a continuity in the architectural design of stables between the New Kingdom and Third Intermediate Period. Excavations at Sais in the Third Intermediate Period levels have also found considerable amounts of horse bones, which may suggest the presence of stables in the area.[243] The range of animals which were part of the domestic life of the Third Intermediate Period Egyptians can be gauged from the faunal evidence from the settlements of Kom Firin and Sais in the Delta. The animals included ducks, geese, cattle, dogs, cats, goats, donkeys, horses, and pigs.[244] Domesticated animals are likely to have been kept in two main locations: within the house, as is observed in the modern Egyptian village at Sa el-Hagar, where donkeys and goats are kept within the house, and near the house in designated grazing areas. Evidence from before the Third Intermediate Period shows that at Tell el-Daba, Memphis, and Amarna pigs

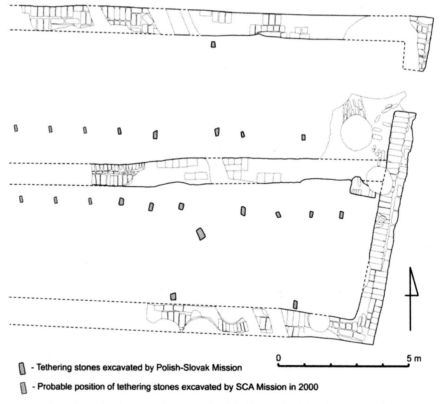

☐ - Tethering stones excavated by Polish-Slovak Mission

☐ - Probable position of tethering stones excavated by SCA Mission in 2000

0   5 m

Fig. 33 Plan of the Third Intermediate Period stables from Tell el-Retaba (Jarmužek, 2011: 132, plan 4). (Courtesy of Dr S. Rzpeka.).

were farmed, and depictions of swine herds show them outside the settlement, but it is possible that pigs were reared within the settlements, including at the larger houses of the Middle Kingdom settlement of Wah-Sut at Abydos.[245] In the Delta, the faunal assemblages of the Third Intermediate Period suggest that pigs were the main source of protein within the diet of the inhabitants of Sais (39.3 per cent) and Kom Firin (43.43 per cent),[246] and pigs also constituted an important part of the diet at Akoris in Middle Egypt.[247] Faunal reports from other Third Intermediate Period settlement phases are not yet published and this makes it difficult to see whether this was a countrywide development.

The presence of designated areas for the grazing of animals during the period has been suggested at Akoris in the 'South Area', in association with the many small silos. Large amounts of hay and dung accumulation in Area M indicate that this was an animal pen area.[248] Defined animal penning areas would have accommodated many of the domesticated animals of the household including goats and even donkeys. At Kom Firin, 1.136 per cent of the identified taxa was donkey bones, while horses (4.54 per cent) were common at Sais.[249] As horses were exclusively related to the elite classes, donkeys would have remained the working animals of the domestic settlements and agricultural families. The best evidence of donkey usage comes from the New Kingdom, when they were used for a wide variety of purposes and would have transported goods such as water, wood, grain, hay, and firewood, and pulled carts. Dung would have been removed from the settlements by the donkeys, and at night, the donkeys would have been stabled within the home for protection.[250]

Evidence of the keeping of animals within the home, no doubt for protection at night from predators or even theft from surrounding families or external thieves, is found at Sais and Hermopolis. The Third Intermediate Period house phase at Sais showed evidence of a storehouse or animal pen with a small 50 cm door threshold.[251] Just outside the doorway was a pile of pottery including some jar bases which still contained substantial amounts of chaff, perhaps from dried and partly decomposed manure.[252] Samples from the deposits were dominated by wheat glume bases, and represent charred material cleaned out of a domestic oven/hearth, in which cereal processing waste was used as the primary fuel.[253] This material had been dumped outside the house. The pottery had been thrown upon the ground surface at the base of a stone door pivot for the door to a small circular feature. The presence of the broken sherds may imply they were used in some way inside the animal pen, perhaps to cover the floor. If the building was an animal pen, then the circular shape may have been typical as well as the dividing cross wall of the structure.[254] In the central part of the Level 2b house at Hermopolis was a long open space that may have housed animals as there was an animal fodder bin present.[255]

It is likely that most Egyptian households had a dung heap within or immediately adjacent to the enclosed housing space occupied by a household or inter-related family, often in the courtyard, where the valuable sources of animal nutrition and agricultural manure would remain under the control of the family or families inhabiting the area and owning the yard.[256]

Areas for Refuse Disposal with the Settlements

The Egyptian diet was dependent on cereals, dried legumes, and preserved foods, alongside cheese, fruit, vegetables, fish, meat, grains, aromatic seeds, and condiments, with garlic and onions available all year round. Most of the ancient food waste was created during the preparation stage of the meals. In the nineteenth century, the amount of domestic waste produced per person, excluding sullage, was estimated at 567 kg a year,[257] equivalent to 1.5 kg a day. Leftover edible food after a meal was likely to have been minimal, as in modern rural villages. The females of the house, again as in modern times, were most likely responsible for the food management and the clearing of the food waste.[258] If leftovers were present they were likely to have been incorporated into the next meal. The hot climate did not always make it safe for leftovers to be consumed later, as food-spoiling microorganisms, some of which caused gastroenteritis and food poisoning, would quickly reach unacceptable levels for human consumption.[259] The food waste created by the families during the food-processing stages would have been thrown out deliberately and would have caused rubbish to accumulate within the household if not dealt with daily and removed from the property. The organised disposal of organic and inorganic waste is a vital part of the functioning of any settlement. The ability to remove waste and refuse from the home and the surrounding environment has an impact upon the health and quality of the life of the inhabitants. This section discusses the methods and practices by which the Third Intermediate Period population disposed of their household and human waste. Developments in house design from the courtyard style house into a roofed hall during the Second Intermediate Period at many settlements in Egypt enhanced the cleanliness of the large central space of the house through measures such as the separation of the street.[260] The separation of the street reduced the amount of dust settling in the former courtyard area, and enhanced the impetus to keep the space clean.[261]

Auxiliary parts of the house were the waste-producing activity areas, with the large mansions of the Middle Kingdom at Kahun exhibiting this division as well as small-scale New Kingdom houses.[262] At the workmen's village of Amarna, quern emplacements, mortars, ovens, and animal troughs were in the front and back of rooms of the small houses, but they were never in the central living room, where there was a bench and hearth for heating.[263]

In the Third Intermediate Period, the Level 1b (late Third Intermediate Period) house at Hermopolis shows that domestic waste was swept to the edge of what appears to be an outer room, possibly a courtyard, of the main house to the west, where it was left to accumulate, rather than removing it from the house itself. The accumulation of refuse along the edges of the walls is common in Egyptian settlements.[264] In smaller Third Intermediate Period dwellings, damaged or uninhabitable rooms were used as makeshift refuse areas. In other instances, entire houses which were uninhabitable were utilised as containers for local refuse. For example, at Tell el-Retaba, after the inhabitants of the Area 9 house left, the house was turned into a refuse area and filled with large quantities of bone and pottery.[265] Finally, at Sais (Kom Rebwa) in the 'Phase II' early Third Intermediate Period levels, pottery vessels were used to collect waste from inside the building, which was then dumped outside the main building door.[266]

The evidence suggests that auxiliary parts and external areas of the house were the place where refuse was dumped. Uninhabited and abandoned settlement zones and tell areas were prime locations for refuse disposal during the period, while movable elements such as vessels were used as refuse collection points. Food waste created during the preparation and cooking process was deliberately fed to animals, particularly pigs, as an efficient use of the waste products.

The pig has a similar range of nutrient requirements to those of humans and can recycle nutrients from food consumption, which was of considerable benefit in the removal of gone-off and non-edible (for humans) food waste.[267] Evidence for animals such as pigs being used within settlements to aid in waste removal comes from Abu Salabikh in Iraq, which suggests juvenile pigs ran free in the streets, disposing of waste and garbage thrown out of doors.[268] Further ethnographic observations in Greek villages suggest pigs could run free. If the pigs are let out during the day from a pen, where buckets of water and feed are available for them to return to as needed, they can forage up to a radius of ca. 1.6 km from where they are kept.[269]

Evidence from Egypt suggesting that pigs were an essential part in the waste refuse process comes from the previous New Kingdom. Several tomb scenes show pigs being driven into the open by swineherds.[270] They could have passed through the streets going to and from home on their way to the fields.[271] The degree to which pigs were free to roam or restricted is impossible to define. Pigs certainly belonged to temples during the New Kingdom, but areas such as inner parts, where even people were not allowed, would probably have been off limits to pigs scavenging through the heaps of waste immediately adjacent to the enclosure walls. While not all waste would be of nutritional value to domestic scavengers, the ability of pigs to consume both garbage and faeces would mean human pathogens would be removed from public areas, limiting the opportunity for the transmission of some faecally transmitted diseases.[272] Human and animal faeces could have been used to make dung cakes for fuel, and stored away for when the climate became colder, particularly in the winter months. The removal of waste would reduce the infestation of houses by rodents and insects which spread disease. On the other hand, pigs consume human waste, and in parts of Asia, there are incidents of excreta disposed of into pig-pens. A palaeo-biological study of waste found in animal enclosures suggests this practice occurred in the New Kingdom workmen's village at Amarna.[273] The presence and continuation of pigs within the Third Intermediate Period domestic settlements is indicated by the faunal remains from the western Delta at Kom Firin and Sais.[274] Mobile scavengers such as dogs and poultry could look after themselves and, ranging freely, feed from open areas.[275]

Despite waste removal, there is evidence that, later in the Third Intermediate Period, large amounts of rubbish accumulated within walled enclosures, particularly at Matmar where refuse layers as much as 80 cm deep were used as foundations for new domestic housing inside the temple enclosure. A similar scenario occurs at Medinat Habu during the second housing phase. In the New Kingdom, there is evidence for refuse collections located immediately outside the residential enclosures of Deir el-Medina, the Amarna workmen's village and Malqata,[276] and in the Third Intermediate Period, the outer walls at Kom Firin show evidence of rubbish dumping up against the walls of the enclosure,[277] indicating that the population was dumping refuse over the side of the temple's mud-brick enclosure wall.

The evidence for refuse disposal during the Third Intermediate Period, albeit limited, suggests refuse was deposited in abandoned areas of the house, disused or structurally unsafe buildings, and unused tell zones. Refuse built up inside the temple enclosures at Medinat Habu and Matmar, with the previous late New Kingdom domestic phases and temple areas now being encroached by refuse mounds. These areas of refuse provided foundations for new organically developed domestic settlements to build up on top of them, while at the same time walled communities were dumping refuse over the tops of the temenos walls, creating refuse mounds against the outer temenos walls. This was an easy option and would have meant the inhabitants of a walled settlement did not have to go outside with their refuse.

CEMETERY AND BURIAL LOCATIONS

After the New Kingdom there were significant changes in both tomb architecture and the burial assemblages with which the population chose to be buried. A substantial number of studies of the period have been dedicated to these changes, but mainly focus on the analysis of material discovered from the

Theban region owing to its good survival rates, while in the Delta and Middle Egypt little survives thanks to either ecological conditions, ancient looting, or poor early recording techniques. This Theban regional bias may have therefore created an unbalanced view of the changes in burial and funerary customs across the country. The evidence does, however, show that elite Thebans developed a new set of funerary values compared with the New Kingdom. The focus for the Theban elites was no longer a large decorated rock-cut tomb, but a space-efficient burial, which included the minimum essential burial goods for the rebirth of the individual.

The funerary landscape of the Third Intermediate Period is largely absent from the archaeological record. In all, thirty Third Intermediate Period cemeteries have so far been identified in Upper Egypt,[278] while only a few isolated burial grounds and individual elite and royal tombs are known from the Delta, particularly at Tanis and Tell Muqdam; the picture for the Delta is, however, severely hampered by ancient looting and modern urbanism. Third Intermediate Period cemetery phases are difficult to classify into dynasties from the mid-Twenty-Second Dynasty onwards. Most cemeteries in both Upper Egypt and the Delta are those of the elite population and royalty. Non-elite funerary sites are mainly unknown or poorly recorded, and in Upper Egypt there are no cemeteries recorded for the Fifth, Seventh, Eleventh, and Fourteenth Upper Egyptian nomes, while in the Delta huge geographic zones particularly in the central and western Delta are so far lacking any Third Intermediate Period funerary material.

Several factors may explain this under-representation of cemeteries in the archaeological record. Firstly, owing to the poorly documented early excavations of cemetery sites in Egypt, Third Intermediate Period cemeteries may have been misclassified and/or misdated in the academic literature. Many earlier necropoli were re-used in this period and may have been misclassified as earlier burials. The paucity of burial items with the poorer population may have led to these burials being mixed with earlier burials with clearly datable tomb assemblages. Many cemetery sites are likely still to be discovered, or large areas of previously known cemeteries which have Third Intermediate Period interment zones have yet to be excavated. Large numbers of elite and royal burials of the Third Intermediate Period were interred within the temenos walls of the main temples, and many of these temple temenoi have not been discovered or still await full excavation. Later sacred landscape changes initiated by the Late Period kings also destroyed many of the monumental tombs of the period. Many of the non-elite populations may have interred their dead on the settlement mounds, and successive taphonomic changes will have obscured the burials under thick settlement phases or sediment. Finally, the dynamic nature of the hydrological system, particularly in the Delta, along with ancient/modern looting and urban encroachment, may have destroyed many cemetery areas.

The evidence from surviving cemetery sites does show a general chronological progression of Twenty-First to Twenty-Fifth Dynasty burials from the First to the Tenth Upper Egyptian Nome. From the Eleventh to the Fourteenth Upper Egyptian Nome there is no evidence, so far, of Twenty-Second to Twenty-Fifth Dynasty burial grounds, but only examples of Twenty-First Dynasty interments. From the Akoris to Atfih region (Heracleopolitan/Faiyum region) the data shows the absence of Twenty-First Dynasty burials, and the region is characterised by Twenty-Second to Twenty-Fifth Dynasty burial grounds.

The locations of the cemeteries within the wider settlements show that the New Kingdom temples influenced the position and place of burial grounds during the Third Intermediate Period.[279] The rulers of Third Intermediate Period Egypt now constructed their tombs within the temple precincts, for example at Tanis, while other family members had tombs located near the cult temples at Tell el-Balamun, Memphis, Heracleopolis, and Hermopolis, or in the case of Harsiese A, in the temple of Ramesses III at Medinat Habu.[280] The tombs of the Gods Wives of Amun from the late tenth century BCE onwards are located behind the Ramesseum, or were in tomb chapels erected at Medinat Habu. The royal cousins Nesterwy and Djedptahefankh D were buried within or behind the temple of Ramesses III, while other members of Takeloth III's family had tombs within the temple of Hatshepsut. The cult temple at Matmar was a focal point for some burials, while at Thebes, the old temples of Hatshepsut, Ramesses II, Tauseret, Amenhotep II, Seti I, and Ramesses III all had Third Intermediate Period burials. Temple blocks were also found with the deceased in a few graves at Gurob and Matmar.[281] The non-elite populations appear to have chosen a more nucleated form of burial closer to the temples, instead of in the detached funerary and cultic zones of the New Kingdom, such as at Mendes, where crumbling enclosure walls of the temple were used for poor status burials.[282]

THE CONTINUITY AND TRANSITION OF THIRD INTERMEDIATE PERIOD SETTLEMENTS

After the end of the New Kingdom, Egyptian settlements within different political and environmental regions developed differing patterns of settlement management. The political centres of Thebes, Memphis, Mendes, and Kom el-Hisn continued the nucleation of domestic buildings around the main temple enclosures, retaining the axial alignment of the earlier New Kingdom settlements in relation to the main cult temple. In the Delta, at Sais and Mendes, owing to the limitations of tell space, new domestic areas were built on earlier abandoned domestic and funerary zones, showing a reorganisation of domestic settlement into new areas. This was also the case for tomb construction, which utilised the earlier tombs and cemeteries, while at the same time making use of the earlier civic and religious buildings as secure zones of interment. In the late New Kingdom and early Twenty-First Dynasty, ephemeral settlements such as Kom Firin, Matmar, and Medinat Habu saw the development of domestic communities within the New Kingdom temple enclosures as a response to local civic insecurity, while attempts at domestic encroachment on religious and civic areas in the main political centres such as Thebes had to be combated through new wall constructions. The temenoi of almost every settlement show some form of degradation, so much so that domestic installations and poor and elite burials were placed in the collapsing exterior sides of the walls, while the interior areas remained secure. The walls were only modified and maintained during the Third Intermediate Period to suit the needs of the existing population, and renovations were dictated by the resources the region could provide. Local kings and chiefs focused their attention on the civic and religious buildings within the main temple enclosures, such as temples, palaces, tombs, storage areas, and military installations.

The degeneration of a national temple building policy was already happening long before the start of the Third Intermediate Period and was a result of economic pressures and a general breakdown in efficient governmental controls rather than a significant change in the expression of state religion through physical building projects. The local chiefs and rulers focused their temple building within their own settlements and associated hinterlands and zones of power. Access to stone and precious metals for temple construction was not available to many rulers thanks to the geo-political boundaries of their realms. This, in turn, led them to further recycle the monuments of the previous religious built environment that they saw around them, to placate the gods and their own subjects within their own economic limitations. The surviving temple buildings show a continuation of Ramesside styles and designs, apart from the invention of the freestanding temple sanctuary during the reign of Shoshenq I, reminiscent of the temple sanctuaries from the Ptolemaic Period onwards.[283]

A pragmatic re-use of New Kingdom palace buildings can be observed in relation to the temple which would have retained the religious topography of the New Kingdom temenoi zones. Settlement management of many New Kingdom civic and secular buildings outside the main temenoi suggests that they ceased to function and were taken over by domestic and industrial architecture. The population became self-sufficient and adapted the built environment around them to suit their needs, utilising what was available to continue their domestic lives, despite the changing political and, perhaps, economic circumstances. Many domestic houses continued to adhere to the New Kingdom Amarna style, while less regular architectural styles were developed as a response to space limitations, the personal adaptation and needs of the family unit, the economic and social hierarchy of the occupants of the house, the settlement type and its location, or as a result of a decentralised government not dictating architectural conformity as in earlier periods, leading to unique regional plans developing at Medinat Habu, Hermopolis, and Tell el-Retaba. Local populations were self-sufficient at the family level in the storage of grain and food commodities, while grain surplus was stored within larger houses and temple enclosures for redistribution to the wider community, indicating the self-sufficient nature of the political centres. This suggests that family units had access to fields and agricultural facilities, and so long as they could grow produce they had a certain amount of self-sufficiency.

CHAPTER FOUR

DOMESTIC MATERIAL CULTURE OF THE THIRD INTERMEDIATE PERIOD

OBJECT ASSEMBLAGES FOUND WITHIN THIRD INTERMEDIATE Period settlements can determine whether there were chronological changes or regional differences within the material culture, and the ways in which the assemblages can be used to reconstruct changing lifestyles. This chapter demonstrates links back to Ramesside object preferences, and to precursors of Late Period typologies. The material culture of everyday life and the social practices of the people living at that time demonstrate the Third Intermediate Period as a distinctly defined cultural element within Egyptian society and Egyptology. There were changes in artefact usages and material culture, and implications for understanding characteristics of the object world of the period and the lifecycles of the Third Intermediate Period population. It must be noted at the outset that the completeness of the cultural assemblages is not uniform across the country, owing to the ecological conditions of the Delta. Large amounts of organic material are not preserved, such as textiles, wood, and matting, which would provide a more complete picture of the domestic assemblages. The site type, social status of the excavated area, tapho-nomic changes of different sites, and the poor levels of recording of objects in earlier excavations affect the completeness and variation of Third Intermediate Period domestic assemblages. The domestic material culture also demonstrates aspects of regionality in relation to the political fragmentation of the country. The ceramics of the period identify continuity or changes in the storage, dining, and drinking cultures. Alongside ceramics, this chapter also includes objects of personal adornment, tools, weapons, and re-used and salvaged stone. The artefacts and object world of the settlements aid the exploration of the social status of the population, the extent of elite emulation and self-sufficiency regarding elite object replication, the extent of object re-use and recycling, and the creation and availability of materials for object manufacture. Furthermore, in line with elite culture and social status, the objects found within the homes of the people can reflect a use of heirlooms to show social status, elite emulation, and links back to the genre of ancestor cult. An analysis of the physical manifestation of domestic religion through the terracotta figurines of the period assesses changes in form and type, and regional variations, including how geo-political considerations may be considered in looking for choices in the physical expression of domestic and state worship.

POTTERY

In the New Kingdom, it is possible to draw on well-dated ceramic assemblages from all parts of the Nile Valley, but despite this advantage there are still several problems in assigning precise dates to pottery after the start of the Nineteenth Dynasty.[1] This is because the ceramic chronologies are mainly based on cemetery material. There are too few closed groups in the core material habitually used for reference, and this core material is not published in enough detail to facilitate comparisons with newly excavated assemblages.[2] These concerns and problems with the late New Kingdom ceramics are the same, if not worse, for the Third Intermediate Period.

Most of the Third Intermediate Period ceramic assemblages that have provided cross-comparisons with domestic assemblages come from royal and elite burials such as those at Tanis, Heracleopolis, and Memphis, while other assemblages date from early excavations, many of which were poorly documented and recorded, such as those from Medinat Habu, Lisht North, and Memphis. There is so far only a small corpus of recently published settlement assemblages to compare, and these come mainly from the Delta in small excavation areas at Sais (Fig. 34), Tell el-Ghaba, and Tell el-Balamun, while others come from Hermopolis. However, recent excavations in the Theban region such as from Karnak and the Theban necropolis are beginning to provide new insights into the development of Third Intermediate Period ceramics. Despite these problems in the study of Third Intermediate Period ceramics, it is suggested that there was a general decline in the quality of ceramics, with more Nile silt and coarse wares and a large reduction in the number of marl wares, while there was an absence of fresh ideas and new forms which failed to stimulate new fashions in ceramic technologies.[3] It must be noted that no domestic settlement assemblage, even if large, can be assumed to represent all the vessels in use at any given moment in time, because whole

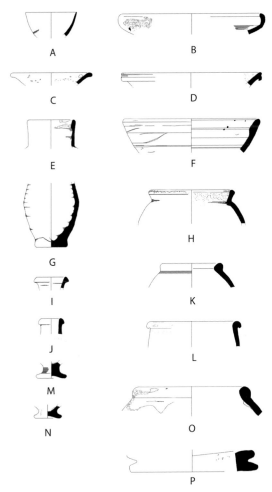

Fig. 34 Representative domestic sample of Third Intermediate Period ceramics from Sais. (Courtesy of Dr P. Wilson.)

and/or valued vessels would have been removed prior to an area being abandoned, cleaned, or its function changed.[4]

Ceramic Phasing

Despite these issues there are four distinct phases of ceramic development identified based on studies of the ceramics from the late Twentieth/Twenty-First Dynasty to the end of the Twenty-Fifth Dynasty. These phases are briefly outlined below.[5]

Phase One: Third Intermediate Period

In general, most ceramics of the late Twentieth and early Twenty-First

Dynasty are manufactured in Nile silt, with marl clay types attested but in small quantities. Phase One can be broken up into two distinct internal phases, named 1A and 1B.[6]

1A *Twentieth to Twenty-First Dynasty*

There is a conformity in the types and styles of ceramics manufactured between the end of the New Kingdom and the start of the Third Intermediate Period,[7] with a continuation of the use of forms of the New Kingdom.[8] Surface treatments on jars in Phase 1A include a thick orange or white slip, while small cups are covered by a thick red polished slip which disappears in the subsequent phase (1B).

1B *End of the Twenty-First to the First Part of the Twenty-Second Dynasty*

There are some morphological changes in the ceramic repertoire, but it remains relatively similar to Phase 1A, albeit with the disappearance of some 1A types, such as the cups with red polished slip and some carinated marl cups with black decorations.[9]

Phase Two: The Mid-Eighth Century BCE

In opposition to the situation in the north of Egypt, ceramic developments in the Theban region in the mid-eighth century BCE show several important morphological and technical developments.[10] The majority of the ceramics continue to be made from Nile silt, with the surface treatment predominantly of white slip and white bands on the upper part of jars, while the orange slip and red rims of Phase One are rare.[11] Phase Two witnesses the development of vessels being manufactured in Marl A4 Variant 2 fabric.[12]

Phase Three: End of the Eighth to the Start of the Seventh Century BCE

Phase Three[13] saw the increase in marl clay forms, particularly in the Theban region, while in general the marl forms develop more complex profiles with an increase in the marked rims and carination. Several forms also show a continuity with mid-eighth-century BCE forms (Phase Two), while the Nile silt forms also show continuities with ceramic traditions of the previous phases, such as many chalices or goblets. In this phase the orange slip applied to the Nile silt forms disappears.[14]

Phase Four: The Seventh Century BCE (End of the Twenty-Fifth to the Start of the Twenty-Sixth Dynasty)

This phase shows continuities from Phase Three, with some morphological evolution of forms, and the start of specific forms characteristic of the

Twenty-Sixth (Saite) Dynasty,[15] with marl clay becoming popular compared with its usage in the previous phase, while the Nile clay production shows a continuity with the previous forms, with similar surface treatments to the previous phase.

Domestic Manufacture and Distribution

The presence of the same vessel forms across the country, particularly in phases, combined with a stagnation in new vessel types being developed, may suggest that people were making their own vessels, but not in great quantities. They were also copying forms they were familiar with, rather than introducing new forms. This created the stagnation in new types until the rise in new forms and the increase of marl wares in the mid-eighth to seventh century BCE, possibly as a result of increased contact with Greece and the Levant. The presence of many small ovens in domestic contexts during the period may suggest that pottery manufacture was a household industry alongside faience amulet manufacture. The large centralised kilns such as those at Memphis would have been impractical for large vessels, or vats, and it is likely that these vessels were made closer to the place where they would be used. The large numbers of simply made open forms, such as the everted bowls and simple direct rim bowls, indicate that these were heavily manufactured in the settlements and probably had multifunctional uses.

As far as ceramic production and distribution is concerned, it is possible that, as in the New Kingdom, pottery production between 1200 and 800 BCE was concentrated in a few production centres and then traded throughout the country.[16] The geo-political considerations created through the regionalism of the period appear to have played little part in pottery production between 1200 and ca. 750 BCE, with the same forms turning up across the country over that time.[17] In the mid-eighth to seventh century BCE, there was a visible increase in the number of different forms being introduced, particularly in terms of storage vessels.

The use of marl clays for ceramic forms also began to increase again, particularly for closed forms. During the Twenty-Fifth Dynasty the Upper Egyptian ceramic production of marl vessels is distinctive compared with that in the north of the country, and was driven by the economic growth in the region marked by the distribution of ceramic production attested at sites across Egypt during the Twenty-Fifth Dynasty.[18] Theban Phase Three marl clay pottery has been found at Tanis, suggesting ceramic traditions were not so divided geographically as once thought, although future research will aid understanding of the extent of ceramic trade with Upper Egypt under the Twenty-Fifth Dynasty.[19]

Foreign Trade

The evidence suggests that during the Twenty-First to Twenty-Fourth Dynasty foreign trade was maintained with the Levant and the Aegean but on a much-reduced level compared with during the New Kingdom, which saw the importation into Egypt of large quantities of transport amphorae from the Levant[20] and fine pottery from the Aegean[21] and Cyprus,[22] while New Kingdom tomb scenes depict the arrival of foreign envoys bringing tribute and tradable goods.

Within the Third Intermediate Period settlements, Levantine amphorae are present in large numbers and were no doubt used to transport resins, oils, wine, honey, and other liquids.[23] At Hermopolis, Phoenician juglets (first half of the eighth century BCE) as well as a fragment of a Cypriote flask dated to 1050–850 BCE were found,[24] but imports were rarely found at Memphis, with only four body sherds found belonging to Phoenician and Canaanite jars.[25] At Sais, in early Third Intermediate Period layers, imported fabrics were again rare, with only two possible imported types, most notably Canaanite amphora types.[26] Foreign pottery continued to be used within burial contexts. Juglets, spherical jugs, and pilgrim flasks from Palestine are found in eleventh- to tenth-century BCE burials. In eighth-century BCE contexts, there are Phoenician juglets and storage vessels, while Cypriote barrel jugs have been found at Tell el-Retaba.[27] Finally, imported fabrics are not found in the Third Intermediate Period levels at the Anubieion at Saqqara, but only in the New Kingdom levels.[28] Perishable transport containers such as wooden boxes and sacks and perishable trade goods do not survive well within the archaeological record. They may be preserved in desert and arid locations, but the epicentre of foreign trade contacts would have been in the Delta capitals, where the ecological climate means such items do not survive. Foreign trade began to increase again from the late eighth to seventh century BCE with Aegean and Levantine vessels commonly found in late Third Intermediate Period assemblages, particularly in the Delta. It was the ports of Ashkelon and Ruqeish that would have played a key role in this re-connection of trading routes. Ashkelon and Ruqeish provided a connection that combined both land and sea routes into Egypt.[29] The economic expansion of Ashkelon was linked to its participation in Phoenician maritime trade, and Ruqeish was an intermediate stop for vessels departing from Ashkelon and a starting point for the caravan route through the Sinai.[30]

Ceramics as Indicators of Dining and Drinking Developments

Pottery can provide insights into the dining and drinking culture or foodways of the period and the way in which food and drink were produced and consumed.[31] In the Third Intermediate Period food was displayed and presented in large bowls, covered with lids made from either everted vessels or wicker baskets. The large numbers of straight rim bowls found were suitable for eating food taken from the communal family bowls. There is a lack of plates, while cutlery was absent in the assemblages, indicating the food in the bowls was eaten with bread as the agent to scoop it up, or meat was picked apart with the fingers. Some small microliths may have been used for cutting meat or fish, and people may have had individual knives or spoons which would not have survived within the domestic refuse assemblages. The food was likely to have all been served together in separate bowls, allowing one to choose what one wanted to eat. Condiments, dips, and spices were made available at dining and probably served in the small incurved bowls. Ethnographic evidence from modern Egyptian domestic contexts suggests the act of communal dining was a regular part of the dining culture of the period and would have reinforced communal and family social bonds. The location of the dining is difficult to assess, but in the Ramesside house at Sais, food was consumed in the columned central hall,[32] or in the largest open floor space. It is unclear, owing to the organic preservation, whether reed mats were placed on the floor and the food bowls set on them, or if they were placed directly on to the hard mud floor and stands were used for the vessels. The position of the diners is indicated by small, low, limestone tables which could have been used for the large serving trays, indicating that people would have been seated on the floor around the food.

The ceramic evidence also suggests that there was a change in the choice of the preferred drinking vessel during the Third Intermediate Period, from bowls and cylindrical beakers in the New Kingdom, to the goblet and footed drinking bowls. The goblet and footed bowl forms were the main drinking vessels from both domestic and burial assemblages. These forms are found in early domestic Third Intermediate Period layers at Kom Firin,[33] with faience types of vessels well known in contexts of the late eighth to seventh century BCE and found at Tell el-Balamun, Amarna, Hermopolis, Matmar Cemetery 900, and Karnak North.[34] Recent excavations at the Mut temple at Karnak have recovered footed bases from mid-eighth to seventh century BCE contexts, and a red washed example dating to the tenth to mid-eighth century BCE,[35] while goblets or footed bowls of this type occurred frequently throughout the excavations at Hermopolis.[36]

The size and capacity of these open shaped vessels show they are for individual servings and consumption.[37] The height of the goblets' stem from the base indicates that they were to be held in one hand while reclining and could be rested on flat surfaces when not in use. There is an increase in the usage and manufacture of the so called 'pilgrim flasks/bottles' which likely held wine and were used by servers to decant it into the small bowls and goblets. The presence of communal bowls designed to hold liquids may indicate that these acted as large wine containers from which people scooped wine using the goblets, while flat red slipped non-porous lids could have acted as wine covers.

The Egyptian goblets and footed bowls found in domestic contexts are made from pottery and appear alongside faience versions. The manufacture in pottery of lotiform goblet forms previously only found in faience indicates the demand for these types of vessel during this period by the non-elite society. The faience examples were a higher status object and the ceramic forms were trying to imitate a luxury item, indicating aspects of aspiration among local communities. Prototypes of these pottery goblets have their origins in New Kingdom royal and elite culture. The factors which had previously inhibited cultural communication between different social strata now ceased to operate in the new Libyan socio-political system.

STONE VESSELS

Calcite and limestone were the preferred choice of material for manufacturing stone vessels during the Third Intermediate Period, with many small bowl, vase, and alabastron types found in domestic assemblages.[38] The typical New Kingdom trussed-duck dishes continued to be used,[39] or were retained for considerable amounts of time within Third Intermediate Period domestic assemblages. Alongside these forms were many re-used stone bowls from the early Dynastic Period, the Old Kingdom,[40] and the New Kingdom. The mechanism by which these earlier bowls were acquired is unknown, but one potential source could have been the re-used Old and New Kingdom cemeteries, as bowls, particularly from the settlement at Memphis, do not show signs of reworking, or repair,[41] which may suggest that the old bowls were in a good condition when they were acquired.

FAIENCE VESSELS

Faience vessels, which were common in domestic contexts of the New Kingdom, for example at Memphis,[42] are rarely found in the settlements of the Third Intermediate Period.[43] The decline in the quantity of faience vessels from the New Kingdom into the Third Intermediate Period is evident in the domestic assemblages at Sais and Akoris, while at Kom Firin there are no intact examples of such vessels, with only a few fragments, all of which come from small vessels with poorly preserved glaze.[44] Vessels that are preserved are primarily of a green or blue glaze, and exhibit decoration consisting of black lines, animal or plant life, and geometric designs.[45] Most examples of published faience vessels, however, come from funerary contexts.[46] Although there is a lack of evidence for bowls and small vessel types in faience, there are more examples of faience lotiform goblets (Fig. 35). Lotiform goblets first appeared in

Fig. 35 Twenty-Second Dynasty chalice, MMA 13.182.53. (Courtesy of the Metropolitan Museum of Art.)

the New Kingdom during the reign of Thutmose III and continued to be manufactured into the Third Intermediate Period.[47] Lotiform goblets were manufactured at the domestic level in Memphis during the Third Intermediate Period,[48] possibly for a funerary function as so many are found in the upper-class burials of the period, particularly those of the royal families.[49] They continued to be used and manufactured at Hermopolis ca. 950–750 BCE with additional non-composition forms in the 950–600 BCE levels.[50] As the ceramic forms of pilgrim flasks are found throughout the Third Intermediate Period, it is probable that they were imitated in faience too; however, evidence of faience pilgrim flasks in domestic contexts is rare.[51] The settlement evidence so far does not suggest that faience pilgrim flasks were a common feature of the Third Intermediate Period domestic material culture, although they are known from burial contexts dated to after the middle of the eighth century BCE based on their morphology.[52] The evidence so far suggests that faience vessel usage in settlement contexts continued in the Third Intermediate Period, but the faience vessels are not preserved well, particularly within domestic contexts of the Delta compared with the Upper Egyptian and desert burial contexts. In the Late Period, settlements begin again to show an increase in faience vessel usage, suggesting there may be a connection with state-organised production, even at a cottage industry scale.

METAL VESSELS

Metal vessels, particularly copper alloy bowls, are common in New Kingdom domestic contexts,[53] but are so far absent in Third Intermediate Period domestic contexts. The evidence for metal vessel usage within Third Intermediate Period settlements has not survived well, and metal was constantly recycled within the settlements, or access to metal within domestic contexts of the Third Intermediate Period was limited. Metal vessels are so far known only from Third Intermediate Period burial contexts, and only from royal and elite burials at Tanis and Deir el-Bahari.[54]

STATUE FRAGMENTS AND THE RE-USE OF NEW KINGDOM INSCRIBED AND UNINSCRIBED STONES IN DOMESTIC STRUCTURES

Statue fragments found in domestic and funerary contexts are extremely rare in the Third Intermediate Period. Those that have been found all appear to date to the New Kingdom. Examples of royal statuary in Third Intermediate Period domestic contexts are known from Memphis[55] and Hermopolis.[56] Neither the example from Memphis nor that from Hermopolis shows any signs of reworking or re-use as a grinder or pounder. The presence of statue fragments in burial contexts of the Third Intermediate Period is so far unique to the burial of Tehuwymes at the Ramesseum, as several fragments of black granite or diorite Sekhmet statues in the burial may be explained as having an apotropaic function for the deceased.[57] The preference of Sekhmet statues in the burial of Tehuwymes is reinforced by the popularity during this period of Sekhmet amulets in the domestic lives of the people discussed later in this chapter. The presence and possible re-use of statue fragments in domestic contexts may reflect a desire to own and keep sacred objects for apotropaic uses in the household; however, more utilitarian uses for these objects cannot be excluded, although none of them exhibits usage in domestic activities such as evidence of rubbing or grinding.

Alongside the presence of New Kingdom statuary within Third Intermediate Period domestic contexts, New Kingdom stone temple fragments are also found in burial contexts. When they are found re-used in burial contexts, they have been ascribed as having an apotropaic function.

Examples of New Kingdom temple blocks are known from three burials, one at Gurob and two examples of local Ramesside temple fragments in burials at Matmar. This shows the influence that New Kingdom temples exercised on the burials of the Third Intermediate Period.[58] Similar to the statue fragments, temple blocks are used in domestic contexts and re-used as architectural features of the houses, showing that temple structures were accessible as quarries.

JEWELLERY: EARRINGS, EAR-STUDS, BRACELETS, RINGS, AND PERFORATED SHELLS

Jewellery made of precious stones is mainly found in royal burials at Tanis, Leontopolis, Buto, and Memphis, and the burials of the HPA at Thebes, and the presence of jewellery in domestic contexts is rare. Earrings and ear-studs are rarely found in Third Intermediate Period domestic phases, which is in direct contrast to the situation in the New Kingdom when they are common. No examples of earrings or ear-studs were found in the EES excavations at Memphis,[59] while early excavations at Memphis show items of personal adornment were restricted to faience pendants, beads, and finger rings,[60] which are more evident in the domestic assemblages of the period. Earrings have also not yet been found at Akoris, Kom Firin, or Sais. Similarly, no bracelets were found in Third Intermediate Period settlement contexts at Sais, Memphis, or Akoris. This contrasts with the burials of the period which show that the poor tended to be buried with necklaces and bracelets made of beads, shells, or amulets.[61]

Finger rings as a class of personal adornment overlap with other object types, notably the scarab-shaped objects, which can be used as ring bezels. Distinguishing the shanks of finger rings from other types of rings, notably earrings and possibly wig-rings, is nearly impossible to achieve, especially given the fragmentary nature of such objects from settlements.[62] The presence of finger rings in secure Third Intermediate Period occupation levels is rare. Examples of mainly green and green/blue faience finger rings have been found at Tanis from a Twenty-Second Dynasty elliptical structure and consisted of narrow rings, plain, with or without decoration of parallel straight lines, and openwork examples.[63] The manufacture of the bezel and shank on turquoise faience rings from Memphis[64] and Sais[65] was the same. Both rings date to the early Third Intermediate Period, and the similarity in design and manufacture may suggest some form of typological similarity between the early Third Intermediate Period ring designs in Memphis and Sais, although more evidence is needed to confirm this.

The burial assemblages of the period do provide evidence of finger rings in higher numbers as they were attached to bodies, and some dating criteria for finger ring development can be noted. The finger rings show a marked change at the end of the Third Intermediate Period. In the seventh century BCE, rings with bezels appear to have the bezel raised high above the shank, and often the bezel is undercut to leave room for the finger. In addition, bead rings, particularly those of glazed faience, begin to exhibit open fretwork designs at the end of the Third Intermediate Period,[66] but the lack of rings from Third Intermediate Period domestic contexts makes this development difficult to trace in the settlements.

Perforated cockleshells were used as personal adornment during the Third Intermediate Period, most likely for necklaces, as well as for spoons, mixing palettes, or as raw materials for inlays and smaller beads.[67] The evidence for perforated shells in Third Intermediate Period domestic contexts is limited, but the dates of the levels in which they have been found would suggest they were used in the early part of the period. Examples of other shells, such as cowrie shells, used for personal adornment in settlements are known from Kom Firin,[68] while at Hermopolis in the surface dumps a blue glazed cowrie shell amulet of unknown date was found.[69]

Shells are also used in poor Third Intermediate Period burial contexts and provide some context for their usages and functionality in the settlements beyond being used as items of personal adornment. Shells occur in 118 poor burials at Tell el-Yahudiyah, Saft el-Henna, Tell el-Retaba, Saqqara, Meidum, Lahun, Matmar, Abydos, Esna, and Thebes.[70] Apart from four spatha shells which were found on top of a coffin at Matmar, all other shells have been found inside the coffin, often being tied together to form necklaces, bracelets, and anklets,[71] similar to the example of the cowrie necklace from the domestic context at Kom Firin, which includes beads of faience and carnelian.[72] Of burial contexts, ninety-eight of them contained cowrie shells.[73] Cowrie shells were brought in from the Red Sea and most likely had fertility and 'female' properties and acted as protective amulets. Cowrie shell usage reflects the age of the individual who wore them. Of the sixty-five cases where such details have been published, fifty-two were children, eleven were females, and only one male, with one case of a woman and child buried together. This would indicate that cowrie shells were important for protection of children.[74]

Beads continue to play an important part in the personal adornment of the Third Intermediate Period population. The most diverse assemblage of beads comes from Tell el-Ghaba. Almost two hundred examples of different bead types were found in nearly every level of the excavations, but it was noted that they could have constituted part of other objects or large necklaces or bracelets.[75] Seven bead types were recorded: conical, disc, wafer, spacer, lozenge, spherical, and teardrop. Most of the beads were in faience, but they also occurred in bone, shell, glass, chert, agate, alabaster, steatite, carnelian, quartz, quartzite, and gold.[76] Beads also continue to be an important part of the personal adornment of the inhabitants of Memphis, with eleven examples, although there is a considerable drop in the number compared with the New Kingdom which had a hundred examples. The Third Intermediate Period Memphite beads were predominantly made of faience (white, turquoise, and blue),[77] but pottery and glass (blue and white) were also used.[78] A reduction in bead numbers from the Ramesside Period is also seen in the Sais material, as beads are only found in Ramesside levels, while beads have not been found in secure early Third Intermediate Period phases at Sais. Similarly, at Hermopolis there are no beads in later Third Intermediate Period phases (950–700 BCE), where scarabs and amulets are preferred. At Kom Firin, early Third Intermediate Period phase occupation does include spacer beads, disc beads, and a cylinder bead, all having blue glaze, as well as carnelian beads of both disc and cornflower form.[79]

TERRACOTTA FIGURINES

Terracotta figurines in Egypt have long been ignored owing to their simplicity or because they were viewed as crude products of less accomplished artisans. There is a growing awareness that terracotta has the potential to reveal more about the daily life, thoughts, beliefs, and cult practices of the non-elite.[80] Terracotta figurines are typical of, and best represented in, the Ptolemaic–Roman Period; however, terracottas are documented for all periods of Egyptian dynastic history, indicating that they were an enduring feature of dynastic Egyptian life and religion.[81] Terracotta figurines are known from the early Dynastic Period, Old Kingdom,[82] Middle Kingdom, and Second Intermediate Period.[83] They continued to be a common feature of New Kingdom settlements through to the Late Period.[84] Most terracotta figurines were used as votive offerings, indicated by the large amounts found at the shrines.[85] Terracotta was a quick and inexpensive medium for manufacturing and indicates the figurines' apparent value in the cult.[86] They may have been made and sold at cultic centres or buildings. Their presence in domestic contexts suggests that they had a wider function, or that domestic contexts provided opportunities for cultic practices and personal beliefs. Terracotta figurines in the Third Intermediate Period represented females and different types of animals such as birds, including geese and ducks, and quadrupeds, while the previously popular types of figure such as cobras seem to go out of favour.

Cobra Figurine Manufacture

In the New Kingdom, terracotta cobra figurines are one of the most distinctive aspects of the domestic material culture. Cobra figurines have been found in

Egypt at Amarna,[87] Deir el-Medina, Qantir, Kom el-Hisn, Tell el-Abqa'in,[88] Kom Rabia (Memphis),[89] Kom Firin,[90] Kom Rebwa (Sais),[91] Akoris, and Zawiyet Umm el-Rakham.[92] They have been found outside Egypt at Kamid el-Loz in Syria and Beth Shan in Israel.[93]

At Memphis (Kom Rabia) there is a significant reduction in cobra figurines at the end of the New Kingdom,[94] and it is likely that cobra figurines were not used at Memphis, at least near the Ptah temple after the end of the New Kingdom.[95] The significant reduction in cobra figurines after the end of the New Kingdom is also reflected in the Delta at Sais as those found in situ all belonged to the Nineteenth and Twentieth Dynasty levels,[96] while at Tell el-Ghaba and Kom Firin the post–tenth-century BCE settlements also show an absence of cobra figurines. The situation is the same in Upper Egypt at Akoris, as cobra figurines have primarily been found in the late New Kingdom layers, with some residual fragments in the early Third Intermediate Period settlement deposits, while at Hermopolis, Medinat Habu, and Karnak they are also absent after the New Kingdom phases. Despite the reduction and eventual cessation of cobra figurines after the New Kingdom, other terracotta figurine types were still common.

Terracotta Quadrupeds and Other Figurine Types

Quadrupeds and other animal figurines are not uncommon in Egyptian settlements, but are rarely considered by Egyptologists, being poorly represented in museum displays and catalogues.[97] Animal figures have the potential to elucidate more about the portion of society which made and used them, namely the non-elite who left such a scant record and are critical for our understanding of the full range of ancient life and belief systems. Quadrupeds are the most common examples of terracotta figurines so far found in the Third Intermediate Period domestic settlements at Memphis,[98] Kom Firin,[99] Sais,[100] Medinat Habu,[101] Hermopolis (Fig. 36),[102] and Tell el-Ghaba,[103] while a few geese or ducks are also attested.[104]

Assessing the function of animal figurines with little contextual or textual information is difficult. The presence of terracotta animal figurines in domestic contexts fits well with the evidence from the New Kingdom. These figurines were used in household rituals, perhaps to invoke prosperity, particularly the bovine figurines,[105] and a non-elite perception of their protective deities and links to the local rulers and military. There were many cattle cults around the Delta, including the Apis Bull, and they may have related to general aspects of fertility. If, however, the figurines represented cows, then an association with Hathor cults could be possible: at Kom el-Hisn, Hathor was worshipped and the settlement was suggested to be a cattle-rearing centre. Identifying terracotta animals, particularly bovines, with a specific deity is problematic, and, in fact,

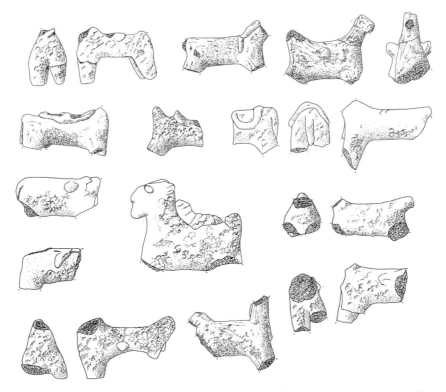

Fig. 36 Third Intermediate Period terracotta bovines from Hermopolis (Spencer, 1993: pl. 37, nos. 186–98, 200). (Courtesy of Dr A. J. Spencer/The Trustees of the British Museum.)

some figurines may have had multiple roles.[106] They may also have been used as toys,[107] but there is no evidence for this in the Third Intermediate Period contexts.

Most of the quadruped types found in the Third Intermediate Period are identified as horses. Prior to the Third Intermediate Period, images of horses appeared on New Kingdom ostraca,[108] but they are not associated with a specific deity. Horses appeared as the mount for Astarte and Harpocrates[109] and became extremely popular in the Ptolemaic–Roman Period.[110] An association with deities is probably a better explanation for the horses, rather than all figurines being used as toys. The popularity of horses in the figurative art of the period at the domestic level may be related to the natural attraction that horses have as large, powerful animals.[111] The faunal evidence at Sais attests to an increased presence of horses in the settlement in the Third Intermediate Period,[112] with art perhaps reflecting a daily reality. The importance of horses to the local rulers of the major political centres during the Third Intermediate Period is clearly demonstrated in the Piankhy Stela, particularly at Hermopolis. Piankhy was outraged as Prince Nimlot had neglected the treatment of his horses at Hermopolis.[113]

The dating and contexts of the horse figurines may provide a reason for their sudden abundance compared with other animal types. Of the fifty-four horse figurines from Hermopolis, only six fragments were found in the 950–850 BCE occupation phase, corresponding approximately to the limited number of quadruped types found in other early to mid-Third Intermediate Period occupation layers. There was a clear increase in quadruped (horse) figurine manufacture and usage at Hermopolis starting ca. 850 BCE (Table 6). This is also observed at Tell el-Ghaba, as all the terracotta animals are quadrupeds and they date from around the eighth century BCE onwards.[114] The increase in horse figurine manufacture at Hermopolis would correspond with the rise of local chiefdoms in Middle Egypt under the Hermopolite Dynasty and that of Prince Nimlot, and may reflect the horse as an important military and strength status symbol for local elites, which was depicted in domestic figurative material culture. The growing impact of Kushite influence in Upper Egypt in the late eighth century BCE, the invasion of Piankhy and his entering of Nimlot's stables ca. 728 BCE, and the subsequent anger at the condition of Nimlot's horses further attest to the importance of horses within the social fabric of elite culture at that time, and their importance to Kushite rulers. Evidence shows horse iconography became increasingly important for the Kushite pharaohs, with horses depicted on Piankhy's victory stela at Napata and the reliefs on the Gebel Barkal temple of Amun featuring horses. Piankhy initiated the custom of burying horses in a cemetery near his tomb at el-Kurru.[115] The descriptions of the treatment of and importance of horses for military and elite culture on the Piankhy Stela may be a rare example of a historical text reflecting a changing trend in figurative domestic material culture of Third Intermediate Period Egypt.

Horses were important not just to native Egyptian rulers but also to foreign powers. The Assyrians prized Egyptian horses, and Osorkon IV (730–715 BCE) sent twelve large horses to Sargon II (721–705 BCE).[116] Inscriptions of Sargon II

TABLE 6 *The increase in quadruped figurines in late Third Intermediate Period layers at Hermopolis.*

Site	Date range	Number
Sais (Excavation 1)	early Third Intermediate Period	1
Kom Firin	early Third Intermediate Period	5
Memphis (Kom Rabia)	early Third Intermediate Period	1
Tell el-Ghaba	eighth century BCE	6
Hermopolis	950–850 BCE	6
Hermopolis	850–750 BCE	17
Hermopolis	700–600 BCE	19
Hermopolis	late Third Intermediate Period/early Saite	12

mention that gifts of Egyptian horses trained to drive chariots were presented at the inauguration of his new capital at Dūr-Šarrukīn.[117] Horses were listed as booty that Esarhaddon (680–669 BCE) took from Egypt during his campaign. They also counted as part of the annual tribute imposed on Egypt.[118] Later, Assurbanipal (668–627 BCE) included horses among the booty captured when he conquered Egypt.[119]

The high proportion of terracotta horse figurines is possibly an indicator of the increased rise in importance of horses for the Egyptian rulers, influencing the choice of terracotta figurines being manufactured. The density of quadrupeds found at Hermopolis may be an important regional distinction in terracotta figurine choice which was driven to some extent by the non-elite perception of their protective deities and links to the local rulers and military. The manufacture of terracotta figurines, including quadrupeds, continued into the Saite Period at Kom Firin,[120] Naukratis,[121] Mendes,[122] and Edfu.[123] Later in the fifth century BCE, in association with Achaemenid rule, the simple quadruped figurines which were popular in the Third Intermediate Period are largely replaced in popularity by the so-called 'Persian horsemen' types with riders on their backs. 'Persian horsemen' are common in Lower Egypt, with examples from Memphis, Tanis, Bubastis, Athribis, Tukh el-Qaramus, Tell Dafana, and Herakleion.[124]

Terracotta Female Figurines

There are few published corpora of female figurines from settlements, but there is evidence to suggest female figurines were a common feature of the New Kingdom, continuing into the Third Intermediate Period with associated typologies. Figures of naked women with their arms down by their sides and the palms of their hands pressed against their thighs are found in Early Dynastic Egypt, and Middle Kingdom examples in faience have been suggested as the embodiment of the human sexual nature, buried with the dead to ensure continued sexual activity and fertility in the afterlife. The notion of such figurines being regarded as erotica or 'concubines for the dead' is now generally a discredited theory.[125] The women are not in sexual poses, and scenes of males and females together are not found in this genre of terracotta.[126] A connection with the goddess Hathor has been suggested,[127] as well as their roles as fertility deities.[128] The extensive usage of terracotta females in ancient Egypt has resulted in numerous typologies (Fig. 37).[129]

The long-legged, slender-hipped female figurines mirror the contemporary New Kingdom to late New Kingdom two-dimensional representations, while the fleshy, rounded bodies of the female figurines dated to the Third Intermediate Period correspond to the contemporary stelae,[130] as well as statues of the elite, suggesting considerable communication between the artisans of the elite and

Fig. 37 Terracotta female figurines: (1) Type A; (2) Type B; (3) Type C; (4) Type D; (5) Type E; (6)–(7) Type F. ((1)–(6) Teeter, 2010: pls. 1a, 9a, 13, 15, 16b, 22b; Courtesy of the Oriental Institute at the University of Chicago; (7) Spencer, 1993: pl. 40, no. 172; Courtesy of Dr A. J. Spencer/The Trustees of the British Museum.)

non-elite, and non-elite exposure to formal art styles.[131] At Memphis, in the settlement excavations by Anthes and the EES, terracotta figurines of women lying on beds, often with a small child, were found throughout the Third

Intermediate Period strata.[132] At Medinat Habu, the large numbers of females on beds may have also acted as votive offerings in the cults of the Gods Wives of Amun. What is striking is that in contemporary levels at both Sais[133] and Kom Firin, no examples of any female terracotta figurines have been found in either the New Kingdom or Third Intermediate Period levels. The variation in the different types is best documented at Medinat Habu, and like the diverse range of architectural styles found in the economically and socially diverse settlement, may reflect the economic status of the owner of the figurine, combined with the cultic/ritual and apotropaic needs of the individual who commissioned or bought it.

Terracotta Votive Beds: a Theban Tradition of the Twenty-Second and Twenty-Third Dynasty

'Terracotta votive bed' is a term used to refer to a narrow bench-like structure of clay with a rectangular front panel (Fig. 38). Most of the beds were impressed with a scene of a woman, or woman in a boat, flanked by figures of the god Bes. Two legs on the opposite side allowed the bed to stand upright.[134] The top and decorated front panels were separate slabs of clay joined with slip. The bed may have legs which flank the decorated panel, but more often the legs were subsumed into the front panel, whose lower edge supports the front of the bed. Two narrow legs could be attached to the back of the bed, and bars which connected the front and back legs may be represented.[135] The front of each bed was impressed with a mould-made design, and some preserved significant amounts of pigment. The top surface was painted with dark red lines or grid

Fig. 38 Votive bed: Twenty-Second Dynasty, Upper Egypt, Thebes, Assasif, Tomb MMA 825, MMA excavations, 1929–30, MMA 31.3.108. (Courtesy of the Metropolitan Museum of Fine Arts.)

patterns, while some had white washes.[136] Most votive beds from Medinat
Habu came from the Third Intermediate Period settlement within the enclosure walls, and they ranged in date from the Twenty-Second to Twenty-Third
Dynasty and from the Twenty-Fifth to Twenty-Sixth Dynasty, while there is
no evidence of stylistic chronology.[137] So far, all examples of votive beds come
from Thebes, suggesting they were a local tradition, and the large numbers of
beds found indicate that they were in high demand by the inhabitants of Thebes
in the Twenty-Second to Twenty-Third Dynasty,[138] but they quickly went
out of fashion. Their functions no doubt encompass the living, the dead, and
the domestic and funerary realms, as they have been found in settlements,
temples, and tombs.[139] The function of the beds is difficult to define. They may
have been used as altars, possibly in association with the terracotta female
figurines,[140] but the figurines are small in comparison with the beds.[141] The
decoration of the bed was only on the front, meaning it was to be looked at
from the front.[142] The beds may be a commemoration of a birth, and an object
that celebrated sexuality, fertility, and the protection of the child.[143] The
association with birth beds is emphasised by the figures of Bes flanking the
central decoration, in imitation of birth beds found on ostraca.[144] They may be
associated with rebirth and the veneration of deceased ancestors,[145] in the same
fashion as the earlier Eighteenth to Twentieth Dynasty *akh iqer n Re* busts and
stela, most of which are again from the Theban area.

Other Terracotta Model Types

Impressions of children's feet, or representations of them in clay, are found
during the Third Intermediate Period. Two were found at Kom Firin, while
a single example from Medinat Habu had been worked with a tool to empha-
sise the form of the toes and was dated to the Twenty-Fifth Dynasty. This
Twenty-Fifth Dynasty date was attributed based on similar examples coming
from the pyramid in Nuri, of a queen Anlamani (623–592 BCE).[146] However, an
exact date in the period cannot be defined for the Medinat Habu impressed foot
owing to the poor nature of the stratigraphy and associated artefacts within it.
The two examples from Kom Firin probably date to sometime in the early
Third Intermediate Period and suggest that this form of terracotta object was
used throughout the period. The graffiti of feet and their role in the devotion of
pious individuals to the gods suggest these items may have been to show the
veneration for a god in return for the birth of a child. The footprint as indicated
by the graffiti on the roof of the Khonsu temple at Karnak was closely associated
with an individual's being, and hence, it served to symbolically dedicate the
child to the god.[147] These dedications may be related to the theophoric names
that linked an individual and a patron deity, which were so common in the
Third Intermediate Period.[148]

In the South Area at Akoris in the late New Kingdom and early Third Intermediate Period phase, seventy fragments of a terracotta figurine type, so far not identified in other settlements, were determined to be deliberately broken. The figurines were small handmade human figures with no particular physical features such as breasts or genitals. The figurines were naked, and there was no hair or additional appliques such as jewellery. A circular projection placed around the torso was the only decoration, and was interpreted as a navel and the figurines to symbolise children, especially infants.[149] All the figurines were damaged around the head, and it is suggested they were broken ritually as part of an execration ritual and belonged to a genre used in secular beliefs which was a phenomenon of the Akoris region.[150] The execration ritual usually comprises the writing in hieratic of a magical spell which identified the object with a hostile, or potentially hostile, person, animal, or group of people. They were then smashed to nullify the threat posed.[151] The distribution of the figurines at Akoris is not defined, but they derive from the domestic areas.

SCARABS

Assigning dates to scarabs is problematic, even when dealing with excavated examples. Some of the major catalogues of scarabs avoid using dates at all.[152] Interpreting scarabs on stylistic grounds can also provide incorrect dating criteria.[153] Some studies, however, give close date ranges supported by detailed criteria for the date.[154] Other studies assign broad date ranges such as 'New Kingdom' or 'Eighteenth to Twentieth Dynasty'.[155] The date ranges provided in these studies span many centuries and it appears there are no precise parameters for the dating of scarabs.[156] Outside Egypt, Egyptian scarabs have been used in the dating of Levantine contexts, and in turn can provide further dating criteria for Egyptian sites, particularly in the Third Intermediate Period.[157]

One major problem is the lack of a clear typology of scarabs and the variability of decoration,[158] and another problem is the issue of heirlooms, that is scarabs which are stylistically older than their archaeological contexts. For example, at Malqata, scarabs of Thutmose III were made in the reign of Amenhotep III, or they may have been heirlooms passed from generation to generation.[159] Even if a scarab has the name of a king on it, it may not indicate the date of the scarab's manufacture.[160] This type of issue is evident in the Third Intermediate Period burial assemblages, where scarabs bearing the name Hedjkheperre Setepenre (Shoshenq I) were issued in the reign of Takeloth I or Takeloth II.[161] The greatest problem is the category of scarabs bearing the name Menkheperre (the prenomen of Thutmose III). The name Menkheperre was a decorative motif common long after the death of Thutmose III. The popularity of the name occurred because Thutmose III assumed a role as protector of the necropolis, and because his name functioned as a cryptogram for the name of the god Amun.[162] The name 'Menkheperre' was a common motif on scarabs of the Third Intermediate Period with examples from Tell el-Ghaba,[163] Kom Firin,[164] Hermopolis,[165] and Medinat Habu.[166] Another problem with scarabs is their small size, which means that they can work their way up through strata as residual objects, and at the same time can also drop from upper levels into lower strata, which makes it difficult to assess their original context.

Scarabs have been found in numerous Third Intermediate Period tomb groups of the poorer members of society, most frequently at Matmar and Lahun,[167] and like amulets, their use as dating criteria is somewhat limited owing to the multiplicity of different types, and the inability to date accurately most of the tomb groups in which they occur.[168] A few scarabs with named kings occur, but only those of Pedubast (I?) and Shoshenq III (both from Gerzeh) are unambiguous. All others bear the name of Hedjkheperre Setepenre or Menkheperre. The scarabs inscribed for Menkheperre are difficult to date, although many found in tomb groups at Matmar refer to Menkheperre Khmuny (Piankhy),[169] while others cannot be so readily attributed to any given reign.[170] In the Twenty-First Dynasty, there are few scarabs of either the Tanite or the Theban line, while it was in the Twenty-Second Dynasty and afterwards that the use of the scarab was revived.[171] This is demonstrated within the domestic contexts of the Third Intermediate Period, where the assemblages show the usage of scarabs continued to be a popular method of personal adornment into the Late Period, with steatite and faience being common materials used for their manufacture. The Third Intermediate Period domestic contexts so far excavated do not preserve scarabs in large quantities unlike in the New Kingdom. Scarabs have been found in domestic contexts at Kom Firin,[172] Akoris,[173] and Hermopolis.[174] The name 'Menkheperre' continued to be a common motif in the Third Intermediate Period at Tell el-Ghaba, Kom Firin, and Hermopolis (Fig. 39).[175]

AMULETS

There was a diverse range of faience amulet types used in the Third Intermediate Period, most of which were manufactured in blue or green faience, a characteristic of the period. The amulet types found in domestic assemblages correspond to the developmental phases of the same amulet types found in datable burial contexts. The domestic assemblages suggest that amulets were used within domestic contexts for apotropaic functions as part of the domestic religion of the household, but so far they are only preserved in small numbers. Most faience amulets that survive were used in

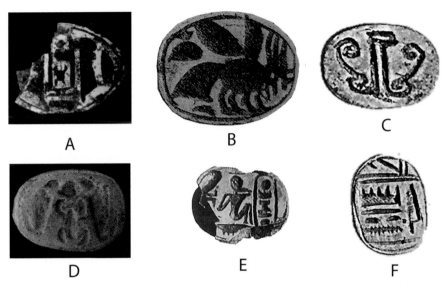

Fig. 39 Selection of Third Intermediate Period scarabs from domestic contexts. A and D from Kom Firin (A = Spencer, 2014: 57, pl. 286, F720; D = Spencer, 2014: 57, F676, pl. 72; Kom Firin Project: Courtesy of the Trustees of the British Museum). B, C, E, and F from Hermopolis (B = Spencer, 1993: pl. 35, no. 139 (Phase 2b–1b); C = Spencer, 1993: pl. 36, no. 147 (Phase 3); E = Spencer, 1993: pl. 36, no. 143; F = Spencer, 1993: pl. 36, no. 146 (Phase 1c); Courtesy of Dr A. J. Spencer/The Trustees of the British Museum).

funerary assemblages, predominantly for royal/elite burials, and those of women and children,[176] while they were manufactured in temple work-shops and small-scale industrial and domestic production centres. Numerous studies have been conducted on the chronology, typology, and function of Egyptian amulets (both those found within Egypt and those in the Near East).[177] Amulets are most commonly found in burial assemblages of the period, where 86 different types have been documented in 700 burials.[178] Within those burials only seven different types (Wadjet eyes, Bes, Sekhmet, other cat goddesses, Ptah–Sokar, Isis, and sows) appear in more than twenty-five tomb groups.[179] In domestic contexts, the preservation of faience amulets is limited and they have so far only been found at Memphis,[180] Hermopolis, Akoris, and Tell el-Ghaba.[181] Within domestic assemblages the most popular amulets are Wadjet eyes, Ptah–Sokar, Sekhmet, and Bes. Other amulet types preserved, albeit in lower numbers and in burial contexts, include amulets of the fish-goddess Hat-Mehyt,[182] baboons and apes,[183] sows,[184] cobra heads,[185] falcons,[186] aegi or protective collars,[187] Taweret, Isis and Child, Shu, Anubis, ram heads, Nefertum,[188] frogs,[189] and cats,[190] while a terracotta mould from Tanis dated to the Twenty-Second Dynasty shows evidence for a seated Isis with a Hathoric crown holding Horus on her knees.[191] As so few of these amulet types exist in domestic contexts, little can be said regarding discussions of dating criteria and typological changes.

WEAPONRY: METAL AND FLINT SPEARHEADS, METAL BLADES, AND ARROWHEADS

The problem of identifying spearheads is the corrosion of the metal, which sometimes makes it difficult to determine their original function. Metal spearheads are defined by sockets into which the haft is inserted; this is formed by wrapping around a sheet of metal to create the socket. Most metal weapons from both the New Kingdom and Third Intermediate Period are from burial contexts; however, in the New Kingdom settlement of Qantir an arms factory produced daggers and spearheads around the reign of Ramesses II for the purposes of warfare.[192] The presence of clearly defined spearheads in both flint and metal in Third Intermediate Period domestic and funerary contexts is rare (Fig. 40). The main problem is the differentiation between the function of these objects as either knife blades or spearheads. In the New Kingdom, flint examples from Qantir described as 'Lanzenspitzen'[193] may be spearheads as they were found in association with arrowheads, but identification is still questionable.[194]

In New Kingdom settlements, stone and metal spearheads are rarely found, with two possible unillustrated flint examples coming from Kom Rabia (Memphis).[195] They are described as crude and bifacial, which may indicate they were unfinished or heavily sharpened.[196] Finally, a New Kingdom bifacial tool described as a spear was found at Hermopolis;[197] however, it may also be a knife blade.[198] The only positively identified metal spearhead from a stratigraphically controlled excavation of a Third Intermediate Period settlement comes from the level 2b house phase at Hermopolis. Otherwise, metal spearheads are found only in burial assemblages of the Third Intermediate Period. A bronze example comes from Abydos, in the late Twenty-Fifth Dynasty tomb of Turu and Pagettereru *m nfr* Iri-pa-ankhkenkenef son of Paabetameri (Mace Cemetery D tomb 9),[199] while at Nebesheh, bronze spearheads are found in tomb groups TG 13–16 dated to the twelfth to eleventh century BCE.[200] The Nebesheh tomb group spearheads all belong to Petrie's fin blade types H128–130,[201] and this is also the case for the seventh-century BCE Abydos example. The metal example from Hermopolis has similarities in form with the fin blade typology but is much thinner and longer in design. It is not clear whether this reflects a change in morphology or regional difference, and, in any case, different metal spearhead designs may have been used concurrently, as in the case of arrowheads. There are attestations of five bronze spearheads from Abydos (Mace Cemetery D tomb 98) dated from ca. 950–750 BCE.[202] Other examples come from the unpublished Cemetery 500 burials at el-Ahawaih. Based on the scarce findings of both flint and metal spearheads in both the domestic and funerary assemblages, defining a morphological assessment of spearhead design is not possible at this stage. The fin blade type is used throughout the Third Intermediate Period, as it is found from the twelfth/

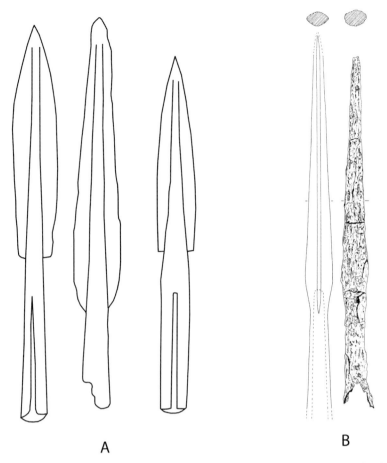

A   B

Fig. 40 Metal spearheads of the Third Intermediate Period. (A) bronze spearheads, Petrie Fin Blade types h128–130 (redrawn, after Petrie, 1917b); (B) long heavy spear point of narrow form from Hermopolis, the blade of approximately oval section and a deep socket for the haft, length 31 cm, width 2.6 cm, from K.10 Level 2b (Spencer, 1993: fig. 54). (Courtesy of Dr A. J. Spencer/ The Trustees of the British Museum.)

eleventh century BCE into the seventh century BCE in tomb groups, but other designs are seen at Hermopolis in the eighth century BCE. The usage of the fin blade types appears to continue into the early Saite Period, as similar examples have been found in the Saite enclosure at Tell Dafana.[203]

OTHER TOOLS: METAL AND FLINT

Flint tool assemblages from settlements are rarely published. At Memphis, most examples of flint tools excavated by both Petrie and Anthes were scrapers and cutting tools, particularly sickles and knives.[204] New Kingdom settlements show flint tools were a common part of the domestic artefact assemblages. Flint assemblages of the New Kingdom have been found at Qantir,[205] Gurob (mostly sickle blades and scrapers),[206] Amarna,[207] Deir el-Medina,[208] and

Matmar.[209] In the New Kingdom assemblages, the most common tools are the sickles, knife blades, and scrapers. Flint tools became the dominant type of tool into the Third Intermediate Period. Flint nodules are found in limestone,[210] which meant disused limestone temples and tombs could be broken down to access the nodules and produce tools. Flint was more accessible than metal and tools could be created at a domestic level, indicating self-sufficiency in material procurement and tool manufacture. Flint tools also have better preservation rates compared with those of metal and wood, which degrade in Deltaic conditions. Metal can be reconstituted and melted down to make new items, while broken wooden tools could have been used as fuel after their use-life. The artefact assemblages from Third Intermediate Period settlement layers at Sais,[211] Kom Firin,[212] Memphis,[213] Hermopolis,[214] and Akoris[215] all provide evidence for the continuation of the usage of flint tools in domestic assemblages, and the manufacture and repair of flint tools within the communities. The Third Intermediate Period flint corpora from across Egypt show sickle and knife blades were the most common type of tool, with other awls and scrapers an important feature of the domestic tool set. There was extensive flint debitage across all domestic levels, indicating a constant re-knapping and sharpening of flint tools. Evidenced by the large amounts of flint debitage found in the domestic levels at Sais, the working of flints may have been one of the daily activities of the community.[216] The re-use of many of the flint tools suggests that, although the raw material was available, it was carefully husbanded and small tools were preferred, as they may have been more economical.[217] The fragility of flint tools, compared with metal ones, means they would break or chip much more easily, so they were in constant need of retouching.[218]

Owing to the corrosion of copper alloy tools in Third Intermediate Period domestic phases, particularly in the Delta, and the re-use of metal, the identification of metal tools and the associated functions is problematic. It is likely that many of the remains represent borers, tweezers, hair curlers,[219] bodkins, or objects associated with piercing.[220] The predominance of copper alloy fragments at Sais[221] and Kom Firin[222] would suggest that copper was the preferred metal in the Third Intermediate Period occupation phases for small metal implements.[223]

ENTERTAINMENT (BOARD GAMES)

The game of *senet* was popular from the Old Kingdom onwards. Prior to the Seventeenth Dynasty, the game boards which are preserved appear inscribed or painted on slabs of stone, or as graffiti, and it is not until the start of the Seventeenth Dynasty that *senet* boxes (playing boards) are found in the archaeological record; they subsequently become increasingly popular in the New

Kingdom. There are forty-one *senet* boards securely dated to the New Kingdom, many of which preserve the popular 'game of twenty'.[224] None of the surviving *senet* boards from Third Intermediate Period funerary contexts was on a game box of the type known from the New Kingdom, and none of them contains the 'game of twenty' on the opposite face as this game appears to have disappeared after the end of the New Kingdom. Instead a new game is preserved on the opposite side of *senet*, 'the game of thirty-three', which is attested on the verso of five *senet* boards. The game is poorly understood, and the origins may lie in the Near East.[225]

So far, no examples of the *senet* gaming boards have been found in Third Intermediate Period domestic contexts. Within the domestic assemblages so far excavated for the Third Intermediate Period, the large numbers of gaming pieces do suggest that the playing of games was a favourite pastime in these communities, and as many of the *senet* boards were made from wood, faience, and ivory with glass inlays, it is likely that they do not survive well within domestic contexts, particularly in the Delta. This lack of *senet* boards may also indicate an economic restriction on the population in terms of access to wood and ivory products to construct such boards. Other, simpler media could be used for the creation of *senet* grids within domestic communities, such as being drawn on the ground or on ostraca, or scratched on to stone, such as in the example of a re-used stone for the door lintel in the Ramesside house at Sais which had what appears to be a crudely scratched *senet* grid consisting of three or four by twenty rows of squares.[226]

In the Third Intermediate Period, graffiti from the north colonnade of the first court of the temple of Medinat Habu depict two *senet* boards side-by-side.[227] Side-by-side boards are also scratched into the small boat ramp of Taharqa at the temple of Amun at Karnak.[228] As these are the only examples where players use two *senet* games at the same time, both the Medinat Habu and Karnak examples can be dated to around the Twenty-Fifth Dynasty.[229] In the Late Period, *senet* board examples from Tell Dafana were simply pottery plates adapted by the scratching on of a rough grid after firing,[230] and this may have been the common way of making a quick *senet* board in Third Intermediate Period domestic contexts. A ceramic object found at Kom Firin bearing four rows of holes – nine, ten, eight, and six (perhaps originally seven or eight) – was a simple gaming board in which pin-like pieces were moved along the holes.[231] This object was used for the game of 'Hounds and Jackals'. It used pegs in the shape of hounds and jackals that would have been placed in the indentations, but the rules of the game are not recorded. They may have been played with sticks or reeds as pegs, but they could also have been used to teach a child counting skills.[232]

'GAMING PIECES'

In the early Third Intermediate Period phase at Sais there were found twenty-nine examples of what may be counters for gaming.[233] The true function of these objects is debated, with possible associations with the textile industry as 'bobbins', spools, and winders of reels.[234] These so-called 'bobbins' may in fact have been ear gauges which were inserted into the pierced skin of the ear lobe. The weight and shape of the bobbins would have stretched the lobe, which may have been to indicate a higher social status of the wearer. Of the twenty-nine examples from Sais, fourteen were found in the overburden and are likely to be out of context, but were probably brought up from the earlier New Kingdom or Third Intermediate Period phases of occupation. A further ten examples were from New Kingdom levels. The main types of this object are: reel or bobbin, and possibly disc-shaped. The materials used to manufacture them were mainly baked clay and limestone, with the colour ranging from black to white and brown-red, and in some cases, the colours are particular to the shape of the object.[235] Two styles can be differentiated: 'bobbin' or 'reel' type, and cylinder 'bobbin' types.[236] The bobbin or reel type is shaped like a squat reel (or bobbin), with a concave waist around the centre of a cylindrical piece of clay. They are often flattened, and the pieces are squat and circular. They are usually made from fired clay, normally untempered Nile silt, without the addition of other tempers.[237] At Sais, the outer surface is treated with black paint or charcoal, which is then heavily polished, giving a glossy surface.

At Akoris a single example of this type of bobbin made from clay was found in the South Area, and tentatively identified as a gaming piece. It was unfired, but was black-polished like the Sais examples.[238] At Karnak, bobbins of this type have been found and identified as whorls, of which one had a black burnished surface.[239] At Tanis, green and blue green faience examples of the bobbin type were found.[240] At Kom Firin similar pottery bobbin types were found in early Third Intermediate Period levels. One example was made of Nile silt and fired to a pale brown with black core, with fine sand and chaff temper.[241] Like the other examples of this type from Sais it had a smoothed surface and was blackened in some areas, which may indicate it once belonged to a black bobbin set as suggested for the examples at Sais. The other example of the same type[242] exhibited a smoothed surface.[243] It is difficult to divine whether this class of object had a function related to gaming, textile manufacture, or body piercing and modification. If the identification of body piercing/modification is accepted, the different decorative styles and materials used to create them in pottery, stone, and faience could reflect emulation of elite body art and personal adornment styles. This form of body modification is not unique to the Third Intermediate Period, as ear-studs were common in New

Kingdom layers, particularly at Memphis,[244] while numerous statues and tomb scenes depict both males and females with stretched ear lobes. The Third Intermediate Period examples would have provided the same effect on the ear lobe, and therefore they provide a continuation in the stretching of the ear lobe from the New Kingdom into the Third Intermediate Period.

Other types of object which are classed as gaming pieces and have a conical or draughtsman style are found at Hermopolis in the 850–700 BCE occupation layers, while pyramidal types are found at Sais. Tall draughtsman versions on circular bases from Hermopolis all exhibit blue glazes.[245] The game pieces from the Third Intermediate Period layers have a similar shape to those which appear in the New Kingdom, have similarities with pieces used on *senet* boards,[246] and may be compared to a faience example from the Ramesside phase at Memphis.[247] At Sais, in early Third Intermediate Period layers, the gaming pieces are made out of both Nile silt and limestone, while a conical gaming piece of the same type was found in the 700–600 BCE phase at Hermopolis made out of calcite, with slightly convex surfaces and flat base on which there is a slight shallow depression from a drill.[248] In the Twenty-Sixth Dynasty at Tell Dafana, a similar green glazed conical-shaped gaming piece was found.[249] Faience versions of the conical type were found at Tell el-Ghaba and were considered, like the draughtsman versions, to belong to the game of *senet*.[250]

TESSON

Pottery tesson have been found in large numbers in both New Kingdom and Third Intermediate Period settlements, and they only occur in settlement contexts.[251] They consist of flat circular discs made from pottery sherds, from either the bases or bodies of vessels.[252] They can be found with their sides roughly broken, with their edges smoothed down, or entirely smoothed, so there is some differences in the appearance of the tesson.[253] Recut potsherds are found in settlements of the New Kingdom and continue to be used throughout the Third Intermediate Period at Sais,[254] Kom Firin,[255] Hermopolis,[256] Tanis,[257] and Memphis.[258] Pottery tesson have been interpreted in a number of different ways and may have fulfilled multiple different functions. The range of suggested functions includes counters,[259] amphora stoppers and plugs,[260] scrapers, scoops/spoons,[261] weights,[262] discs for wrapping spun flax thread around,[263] filters,[264] and burnishers.[265] However, it is most likely that they were used as gaming counters.[266] In the Twenty-Sixth Dynasty east annexe C, chamber 9 at Tell Dafana in the Qasr a *senet* board was found,[267] while in the same deposit were a number of pottery tesson,[268] which were interpreted as being part of the game of *senet*.

HEIRLOOMS, SOCIAL STATUS, ELITE EMULATION, AND
THE RE-USE OF SACRED OBJECTS

Several themes have emerged following the discussion of the domestic material culture of the Third Intermediate Period and can now be used to assess the nature of the lifecycles of the Third Intermediate Period populations in regard to cultural, social, and political changes, and the impact on the material culture of the period. During the Third Intermediate Period the political structures of Egypt had effectively developed into mini-chiefdoms. This was due to the impact and adoption of Libyan tribal characteristics in which collateral lines of relatives could seize power.[269] In these chiefdoms, it was the link to the ancestral past which defined the resources, power, and responsibilities the chief could have in his lifetime. The emphasis on ascribed, in contrast to achieved, characteristics and status governed the social order of chiefdoms.[270] Despite the apparently secure nature of these mini-chiefdoms, they were vulnerable, and failure by the chief to maintain his power and prestige, or a failure to maintain the appearance or illusion of his right to power, could lead to demotion. The origins of these chiefdoms are to be found in the control of resources. These resources included land, productive technology and labour, and the ideology of rank and of an inherited difference from other social groups around them.[271] One way in which elite members of chiefdom societies could transmit the construction of social inequality and hereditary rank was through the ownership of heirlooms.[272] At the same time, these object groups embody or preserve a sense of the past and serve as a vehicle for memory, which has links and continuities with New Kingdom ancestor cults, and the passing down of objects earlier in the Third Intermediate Period such as the Ramesside royal burial objects in the Twenty-First Dynasty tombs at Tanis.

The filtration of these chiefdom characteristics through the Third Intermediate Period social spectrum may be suggested in the object assemblages with the keeping of scarabs, Old Kingdom stone vessels, and the re-used New Kingdom temple stone work and statuary within both domestic and funerary contexts. The scarabs with the inscribed royal names of Menkheperre (Thutmose III) and of Shoshenq I found within both domestic and funerary assemblages would have embodied elements of prestige as the royal name, or the memory of an elite member of New Kingdom society, would have pervaded the object and created a bond with its owner; the royal and elite ancestral link infuses it with ancestral characteristics.[273] The heirlooms serve as memories and histories, acting as mnemonics to remind the living of their link to the distant ancestral past. Not everyone had access to this ancestral past, as these heirlooms were not available or equally accessible to all members of the community, and possession of them showed the inherited differences between different social classes.[274]

The amulets which appear as heirlooms within the Third Intermediate Period, most notably those of Shoshenq I (who attempted to regain the Levantine Empire), are highly valued as they refer to a ruler who had considerable prominence and distinction within the Egyptian politico-military memory of the people.

As most of the scarabs from the domestic contexts were made of steatite, they were not made in the royal workshops. It was the addition of the royal connection that added prominence and standing to the object.[275] People would have retained these scarabs within the immediate family unit to distinguish their social standing and link back to the ancestral past of the New Kingdom and early Twenty-Second Dynasty. The inclusion of these royal named scarabs in both domestic and funerary contexts allowed the pharaoh to have a significant symbolic impact on the other social worlds, even though he was not there in person.[276]

Finally, the objects from Third Intermediate Period contexts demonstrate that lower-class society began to emulate the elite material culture through the production of similar items in ceramic form. These include the pilgrim flasks, goblets, ear gauges, and the crudely modelled versions of females on beds.

TERRACOTTA REPRESENTATIONAL FIGURES

There was a continuation of animal figurine usage across the New Kingdom and Third Intermediate Period settlement deposits which reflects the possibility that indigenous Egyptian traditions remained unchanged over generations; it also shows the continuity of themes in domestic and state religion and the methods of material expression. The continuity of themes makes it difficult to provide date ranges and even associated typological developments within the animal figurine corpora.[277] Figurines share stylistic attributes from more than one period and phase.[278] There are several important changes over time and in respect to place, however, which may indicate social, religious, or economic developments in the Third Intermediate Period, showing an underlying baseline in cultural processes, although there are distinct changes in the practice and form of belief.

The first significant observation is a cessation in the manufacture of terracotta cobra figurines at some point in the early Third Intermediate Period. The reason for this sudden break in the manufacture of such figurines, which were a common feature in Ramesside domestic settlements, is at the moment unknown. It's possible that the lack of cobra manufacture may reflect a change in domestic religion at the time; a change in the apotropaic interior decoration schemes of houses in relation to the visual nature of the home, where cobra figurines would have been so prominent; or a change in the votive offerings on festival days when cobras are suggested to have been deposited on processional routes. Such a change may have been finalised with the advent of the 'Libyan' Twenty-Second Dynasty as, so far, no domestic contexts from that date onwards exhibit terracotta cobra figurines. This change in material culture may have wider implications regarding the processes in social life in the Third Intermediate Period.

A second significant trait is that with the cessation of the cobra figurines there is a rise in quadruped (horse/bovine) manufacture. Quadruped manufacture alongside other animal types was common in the New Kingdom, but at some time after the Twenty-Second Dynasty the presence of quadrupeds in the domestic assemblages increased, a feature which continued into the Late Period with the popularity of the horse and rider type (Persian riders). The increase in bovine/quadruped figurines may reflect a Libyan or Kushite influence on the choice of animals and could be a chronological marker for domestic settlements in which large concentrations of quadruped types are found. Animal terracottas show signs of ritual breaking in both the New Kingdom and Third Intermediate Period, demonstrating that aspects of domestic rituals continued. The large number of horses found at Hermopolis could indicate that certain subjects had regional popularity in line with political and Libyan warrior ideologies in which the horse was an important feature, while the importance of horses to the military makeup of Hermopolis in the Third Intermediate Period is vividly mentioned on the Piankhy Stela.

A third significant trend is in female figurine types which continue to be used into the Third Intermediate Period and are best represented at Memphis and Thebes, while so far there is an absence of such figurines in the Third Intermediate Period Delta settlements, apart from two examples at Tell el-Ghaba in the north-eastern Delta. These figurines may reflect a southern culture or the fact that the figurines were related to female cults in the important political and religious centres of the period. The use of terracotta votive beds is a Theban/southern object culture. Incidents of isolated domestic religious object types are also encountered at Akoris, while the manufacture of terracotta votive footprints, which may relate to childbirth, is seen in both Upper and Lower Egypt.

The religious terracotta objects from across Egypt suggest there was specificity in form and type across the country. There is a favouring of bovine and horse types in Middle Egypt in the Libyan ancestral zones and the military forts areas, indicating that horse types were linked to aspects of local military elite culture and of political power, while the different forms of females on beds, popular in Thebes, are probably related to the Gods Wives of Amun and to previous New Kingdom types. Other female forms do occur elsewhere, but are crudely made, local forms and reflect local versions of females and male/female fertility. The idea of regionalism in the choice of terracotta figurine is seen at Akoris in the so far unique execration figurines. The evidence of terracotta religious forms indicates that the political, social, and previous regional styles of religious material culture of a region could influence the nature of the domestic religious material expression.

THE USE OF AMULETS

During the Third Intermediate Period, the wearing of amulets continued as in the New Kingdom, but there was an increase in the quantity and type of forms, particularly divine beings, with large amounts of amulets being placed on the dead. The temple and funerary workshops produced large numbers of amulets for the funerary industry, and this was also done at the domestic level in 'cottage-industry' style faience production, particularly at Memphis and Tell el-Ghaba. Most amulets are made of blue and green faience, which is a good hallmark of the Third Intermediate Period. Wadjet eye typologies from burial contexts correspond to the domestic assemblages and are the most common amulet type in Third Intermediate Period settlements. Sekhmet amulets, which make their appearance in the Third Intermediate Period,[279] are common in domestic contexts across the country and no doubt reflect the protective and healing aspect of the deity, and her role in the warding off of pestilence. The presence of Sekhmet statue fragments in the burial of Tehuwymes at the Ramesseum reinforces the popularity of Sekhmet and her apotropaic function for the deceased and for the living. Ptah-Sokar amulets are common and the presence of the scarab on the head occurs in domestic contexts from around the tenth century BCE onwards, while Bes amulets become much more elaborate from the tenth to ninth century BCE. They were used in an apotropaic function, primarily to protect children.

The increase in the range and number of amulet forms suggests there was an increased perception among people for a need for protection from the physical and spiritual world. Amulets were also used to pass on the powers of that divinity to the wearer,[280] and therefore the amulets reflect on the choices of deity to be represented and those who were considered the most important apotropaic support to different communities at different time periods. Furthermore, the mass production of amulets at Memphis, and even in ephemeral settlements such as Tell el-Ghaba, indicates that there was a high demand for amulets, which suggests that the local populations were emulating the elite funerary culture for individual prestige. It also reflects on individuals' social status within the community, as faience was easily made compared with the higher status raw materials of semi-precious stones and metal used for amulet manufacture in the New Kingdom and the royal and elite burials.

RE-USE OF STONE: PRAGMATIC ECONOMIES VS SYMBOLIC ATTACHMENT

The homes of the Third Intermediate Period were furnished with stone door lintels and sills, while lower status dwellings may have used baked clay versions, or ceramic vessels acting as jambs. Inside the houses, re-used stone was made into tables and stools. Many of the stone elements of the houses were re-used, probably from surrounding buildings, most likely temples, tombs, and administrative structures that may have been systematically dismantled following poor preservation, abandonment, disuse, or general lack of upkeep by governmental bodies. The re-use of stone from temples and tombs for use in everyday domestic elements and for tools provides insights into the views and restrictions of the Third Intermediate Period people on acquiring new objects. This suggests that the population was of a poorer status than in the New Kingdom as they did not have access to high quality and 'new' raw materials. The people still required an expression of prestige, but their expectations were not matched by the economic reality in which they now found themselves. The people were pragmatic in nature and used the damaged and crumbling tombs and temples as ready-made stone quarries. In re-using stone from old tombs, they encountered the burial items themselves, as at Lisht North and Medinat Habu, where ancient burial goods were found in the settlements. The ancient burial goods would have been reconstituted in the Third Intermediate Period object world as many of them will have been luxury items such as the stone vessels. In addition, acquiring these objects would have provided a direct connection with the past and the ancestors. In re-using the stone and goods of old tombs, people would not have had to make or acquire new items, or gone out and quarried stone fittings themselves. They had everything they needed to create, rebuild, and add to their domestic environments in the immediate vicinity. This sheds light on the economic restrictions faced by the local populations and local regional governments regarding access to newly made goods and accessible stone quarrying areas. The local populations saw the local rulers were re-using burial items for their own purposes and re-using old temples for their own constructions, and the population followed suit. The local populations seem to have been self-reliant in acquiring new tools and objects for themselves and their homes, and were less reliant on the regional governmental systems to supply these for them. Stone was re-used for grinders and pounders, common objects in the residential houses in both the New Kingdom and Third Intermediate Period. Many were made from hard stone and came in loaf, disc, dome, brick, and cube types. Querns of slab, saddle, boat, and flat types attest to the processing of cereals, with most of them made from quartzite and granite. Flint tools were an important part of the domestic tool assemblages and were used for scrapers, sickles, blades, and cutting tools. The large amounts of flint debris indicate the inhabitants would engage in repair and manufacture of these flint tools on a regular basis.

CHAPTER FIVE

CONCLUSIONS: TRANSITION AND CONTINUITY IN THE THIRD INTERMEDIATE PERIOD

A SUBSTANTIAL AMOUNT OF EVIDENCE HAS BEEN SURVEYED AND analysed in the preceding chapters of this book, covering many aspects of Egyptian culture and society, and it is now an appropriate time to discuss its overall significance for the understanding of the development of Egypt during the Third Intermediate Period. Throughout the book a series of interconnected characteristics have been identified within Third Intermediate Period culture and society which relate to the political and economic power of regions, the nucleation of both settlements and people, self-sufficiency at a collective and individual level, defence, both physical and spiritual, regionality in terms of settlement development and material culture, and finally elite emulation through objects. Each of these characteristics will now be discussed in association with the themes of continuity and change/transition compared with the previous New Kingdom, and also within aspects of the socio-cultural and socio-geographical divide between the (Libyan) north and (Egyptian) south.

POLITICAL FRAGMENTATION AND REGIONAL ELITES

Starting at the end of the New Kingdom, the mechanisms for the political fragmentation of the Egyptian state in the early years of the Third Intermediate Period can be compared to the situation at the end of the Old Kingdom and during the emergence of the First Intermediate Period (ca. 2160–2055 BCE).

The previous centralised system of the pharaonic state of the Old Kingdom was firmly installed within a centralised capital as had been the case in the New Kingdom. The Old Kingdom social elite and the administrative expertise of the country controlled the traditions of Egyptian high culture, including the installations of the state religion, the cult of the king, and the divine ancestors who were in the immediate vicinity of the capital. The country was controlled by royal emissaries, who retained their attachment to the royal court and regarded themselves as members of the elite society of the capital, while there was large social and cultural inequality between the country and its rulers.[1] From the Sixth Dynasty onwards, the provincial administrators were appointed to single nome areas and took up residence in their districts, with offices frequently passed down to members of the same family, which created a change in the socio-economic patterns of the centralised system. This meant that economic resources that were originally held at the capital and redistributed to the local areas were now under the control of the local elites who resided in their provinces and had direct access to those resources.

This fragmentation of the centralised power into regional centres is mirrored with the rise of the Libyan chiefs and kings in their local seats of power, particularly in the Delta and Middle Egypt. The growing opposition between the local elites of the Old Kingdom and the centre became a differentiating factor, and the provincial aristocracy aimed to emulate the royal court in their new way of life,[2] which is again mirrored in the development of the Third Intermediate Period. The local elites now acted as separate centres within the political organisation and kept a large amount of local production within the provinces rather than having it exploited by the royal court; this led to a change in the social and economic patterns of the provinces, with rural Egypt becoming culturally more complex.[3] The retention of resources within the main centres is again mirrored within the political and resource management structure of the Third Intermediate Period and is a primary factor in the development of the regional power centres and the breakdown of centralised control.

SETTLEMENT PATTERNS CREATED OUT OF POLITICAL FRAGMENTATION

The political fragmentation of Egypt is shown clearly through the ethnicity of the country, where Lower Egypt as far south as the Faiyum and the Western Oases was 'Libyan', while Middle Egypt and Upper Egypt remained 'Egyptian'. This is indicated in several ways. The first is that most of the recorded names of Libyan elite members of society come from the Delta, while names that can be recognised as being distinctively Libyan are rare in Upper Egypt. The evidence from the donation stelae also shows that the central and eastern Delta was settled by the Meshwesh, the southern Delta by the

Mahasun, and the western Delta by the Libu. These ethnic divisions are not recognisable within Upper Egypt.[4] The consequences of these social divisions within Egyptian society are to some extent visible within the surviving settlement pattern data.

The general pattern and density of settlement during the Third Intermediate Period in Upper Egypt, which was fundamentally still 'Egyptian' based on the surviving data, was retained from the New Kingdom and unaffected by the developing political fragmentation in the country. Some regional centres, particularly that of Tod, appear to diminish in political and economic power during the early years of the Third Intermediate Period, while the settlements in the 'Libyan' centres of the Heracleopolitan and Faiyum region developed into important political entities; these centres also became the focus of an increased military network to secure the region.

In the 'Libyan' Delta, the developing political centres and regions show evidence for the resettlement of earlier sites, for example at Buto, along with the expansion and growth in the size of settlements upon abandoned areas and funerary zones as at Sais and Mendes. Such resettlements and urban expansions could indicate the growth of population in the Delta in line with an increased number of refugees entering from the Western Desert throughout the period, as evidenced by the settling of groups of the Meshwesh and Libu on the Delta geziras, which was initiated in the Ramesside Period. At the same time, the changing hydrological situation in the Delta seems to have created opportunities for previously under-developed regions to become more intensively settled and exploited agriculturally. The nome capitals of those regions and their hinterlands became optimal locations for new political and economic centres to consolidate land holdings and build up strong foci for local rulers, for example at Bubastis and Tanis. Centres like these began to thrive during the Third Intermediate Period, driving the settlement of the hinterland, facilitating new areas of settlement growth, and bringing the agricultural areas into a centrally organised system which continued into the Late Period, for example at Sais. The eastern Delta remained the most settled area in Lower Egypt, with continued occupation on the Pelusiac branch despite the rise to power of Tanis, suggesting that the Pelusiac branch was still active even if new distributaries had formed. The western Delta transitioned into a more urbanised and economically prosperous region through the development of the new hydraulic system in the reign of Shoshenq III. New towns/city centres at Kom el-Hisn and Kom Firin attest to this development and the interest of rulers in erecting stone monumental structures there. The political fragmentation of the Delta in the Third Intermediate Period was also due to growing territorial pressures exercised by the increased fragmentation of the centralised state. The inter-regional territory annexation may have facilitated the movement of smaller settlements into the main centres, such as the repopulation of Buto and the transferral of populations from Piramesse to Tanis. These factors could have increased population numbers in the main centres and created more urbanised settlements such as at Medinat Habu. The central towns provided a level of control and security for the population, perhaps based on the military and police nature of the local chiefs of the Meshwesh, for example in the heavily militarised zone of Libyan influence in Middle Egypt around Heracleopolis and the Faiyum.

These regional territorial pressures saw the transition of Egypt in the Third Intermediate Period into an inward-looking state created out of the need for the locally based political elites to control inter-regional land boundaries and resources. The reduction in attested sites from the New Kingdom to the Third Intermediate Period may reflect the new inward nucleated settlement patterning, especially in places such as the eastern Nile Delta and at Thebes, and the need for regional security systems to control populations by clustering them into small tight-knit groups such as at Medinat Habu and Matmar, perhaps based on Libyan tribal/military influences. An inward-looking policy of control is reflected in the continued use of old fortresses, for example in Middle Egypt and Thebes, and the construction of new ones on land borders and points of juncture, as at Per Sekhemkheperre and the Walls of Shoshenq in the eastern Delta, in effect controlling populations, trade routes, and resources into and out of the Nile Valley and Delta.

There are significant gaps in the knowledge of certain geographical regions during the Third Intermediate Period that require more detailed survey and excavation that can add to the understanding of the nature and density of Third Intermediate Period settlement and material culture, and the development and regionality of burial customs and funerary assemblages. The evidence for Upper Egypt in the Third Intermediate Period is based primarily on textual evidence and archaeology, with Lower Egypt mainly represented by archaeological evidence. There are still gaps in our understanding of the networks of the smaller towns and villages of the wider hinterlands, as records of these locations do not survive within the limited bureaucratic recording of the period.

LAND ADMINISTRATION AND ECONOMY

Land developments and the growth of political power favoured the 'Libyan' Delta region during the Third Intermediate Period as political power had shifted to the north more completely than in the Ramesside Period. The available lands of the Delta and the complex hydrological situation allowed for the creation of new individually ruled regions and states that could be developed to support these new political centres, in contrast to Upper Egypt which had relatively fixed geographical demarcations based on the hydrological and geological systems.

Land was administered in much the same way as in the New Kingdom, with a network of extensive hinterland connections with major temple institutions, while in the Delta a characteristic of the Third Intermediate Period was the reorganisation of old lands brought under the power of new rulers and settlements, which, based on the new economic power derived from these lands, allowed them to develop into important political and economic centres.

The economic benefits of foreign trade networks developed in the New Kingdom were drastically reduced during the Third Intermediate Period. The inward-looking policies of the Third Intermediate Period rulers and the economic restrictions put on different regions through geo-political pressures affected the economic outlook of Egypt. The opportunity for the development of trading contacts with the Aegean and the Levantine states, originally established under the palatial system through elite–elite contacts, was now disrupted by the restrictions on access to trade routes for large numbers of the elite. This probably affected those in Upper Egypt and the western Delta the most as they were potentially unable to access the eastern borders and the caravan routes across the Sinai into the Levant. Without a centralised elite within Egypt or the Near East working out of centralised capitals, as had been the case in the New Kingdom at Piramesse and Memphis, a sustained and controlled trade network would not be possible.

The strength of the regional economies is also reflected through the policies of the rulers and the pragmatic re-use of buildings and items, not just by the local populations, but by the elites as well. In many political centres it becomes clear that economic restrictions, alongside restriction of access to quarries, stifled the erection of new large temple complexes. The main temenoi of many settlements were not regularly repaired, indicating a potential lack of funds to repair even the most important administrative structures in the settlements. An apparent abandonment of maintenance of previously important religious and administrative buildings outside the temenoi walls, possibly because of dilapidation, was most likely the result of insufficient funds to keep them functioning.

The re-use of everyday domestic items such as stone and mud-brick from the temples, tombs, and administrative buildings that may have gone out of use owing to poor upkeep, disuse, or abandonment by local government, indicates an economic restriction on the local populations who could no longer afford to acquire new objects, and suggests that the Third Intermediate Period elites and non-elites were significantly poorer than those of the New Kingdom.

It is only when the international trading networks begin to gradually increase again at the end of the Third Intermediate Period, under the control of the Assyrians as part of their wider empire, and then become fully established again with the founding of Greek trading colonies at Naukratis under the Saite kings of the unified Twenty-Sixth Dynasty, that the material culture of the settlements becomes richer. There is an increase in imported goods and luxury items from the wider Mediterranean and Levant. The new economic stability of the state in the Twenty-Sixth Dynasty allowed for considerable renovations and new temple building across the country, as well as, in some cases, the total remodelling of the urban landscapes and their buildings in many of the important political centres.

DEFENCE POLICIES

There appears to be a heightened desire by the population to be protected by both physical structures and religious or spiritual objects. The physical manifestation of defence within the settlements was through the walled enclosures that were prominent features within the Third Intermediate Period built environment and were also consistently recorded in the inscriptions of conquering forces. Those settlements in areas which were exposed to potential infiltration by physical attacks, particularly those at the access to wadi routes, for example at Matmar, and on the edges of the cultivation leading into the Libyan desert, saw the population concentrated within the walled enclosures of the New Kingdom. These ephemeral populations moved into the enclosure walls where they could feel safe, and probably formed close-knit communities such as at Medinat Habu. The ability of these populations to move within what was previously a segregated religious zone indicates a breakdown in political control of many of the more ephemeral communities and settlements. This situation can be compared with Thebes and the enclosure of the Karnak temple, where populations were actively encroaching upon the sacred zones of the temple to construct domestic dwellings and were subsequently removed. This shows that in areas where a political elite resided, an authority of social and sacred segregation was still actively enforced, whereas in other regions, where this political control was weakened, the local population could dictate their own domestic settlement needs free from administrative control.

The most important civic and religious buildings were now concentrated within the main temple temenoi, as at Hermopolis, as there was now a focus on defending important structures such as temples, palaces, the royal and elite burials, as at Tanis and Tell el-Balamun, the central granaries, storerooms, and military buildings, which allowed the rulers to centralise power within one area where they could be monitored. The earlier New Kingdom civic and religious buildings outside the main temenos were abandoned and left to fall into ruin.

The reliance on and reference to physical defence as a characteristic of the period may indicate a form of underlying regional tension between different political centres and family lines, with the insecurity filtering its way down through the elite political classes into the wider population, as can be seen in the movement into high-walled secure zones in the settlements. This filtering down of tension and insecurity, and the potential for conflict, can be seen as people seem to show a heightened desire for protection both from the walled enclosures and from the closer-knit family and housing groups. There is also an increase in the quantity and range of amulet forms, especially of divine beings, which shows people thought there was a heightened danger to themselves, their families, and communities in both the physical and spiritual worlds. The local theocracies, from which the local rulers gained political power and legitimation, also gave people a local sense of self and protection from their local deity.

REGIONALISM

The development of Egypt into a theocratic state in the Third Intermediate Period was one of the most important driving factors in the creation of regionalism. The model of the theocratic state in Thebes was exported throughout the country into different regions, whereby each settlement and the associated hinterland, or the extent of the main centre's territory, developed into what could effectively be described as a 'city-state' culture,[5] along the same line as 'city-state' development in the wider Near East. Each 'city-state' in Egypt was now effectively under the control of the local deity, whether that be Amun in Thebes or Heryshef in Heracleopolis, and from these theocracies the local ruler would derive his autonomous political power and legitimation within a wider Libyan political structure. These theocracies allowed the local rulers to develop their own regional style of government and control, including resource management and the autonomy to dictate settlement development within the main political centre. The populations within these settlements and their links to the local gods developed intense religious identities, while their links to ancestral burial grounds drew them into a sense of continuity within the funerary landscape, in which they would need a connection with the dead to continue the afterlife rites.

At the macro-level, individual geographic and political regions exhibited different forms of settlement development and regionality influenced by the political, economic, and geographical conditions in which they were situated. Settlements in the main political centres, such as Memphis, continued to develop organically on top of the previous New Kingdom phases, retaining the axial alignments of the New Kingdom settlements in relation to the main temple enclosures around which they were concentrated.

The fragmented political nature of the country and the subsequent regionality created by this is expressed not only through divisions in the written scripts – with the development of abnormal hieratic in the more Egyptian areas of Middle Egypt and the south at Thebes, while Demotic developed in the Faiyum, northern upper Egypt, and the Delta – but also through the diverse choice of deities represented within domestic religion. This included the increased usage of quadruped terracotta figurines in Middle Egypt, particularly at Hermopolis, while female figurine types are commonly found in the political centres of Memphis and Thebes, reinforcing the suggestion of a southern object culture, which is so far absent in the Delta settlements. This division in material culture between the 'Libyan' north and the 'Egyptian' south is seen in the development of the material culture of burial assemblages. For example, shabti figurines from the north are better modelled than southern examples,[6] along with differences between northern and southern coffins,[7] while towards the end of the period, differences begin to appear in the ceramic development for the country, although to what extent is still to be fully determined.[8]

SELF-SUFFICIENCY

The governing bodies of each settlement do not appear to have interfered with the development of domestic settlements outside the temenos walls, as there is no evidence for new state-planned settlements or the creation of new axial alignments within the previous New Kingdom urban landscape, while in some cases even the exteriors of the temenoi were developed for burials and domestic purposes with the inside remaining secure, as at Mendes. Each settlement had the potential to be self-sufficient in its functioning, and this can be linked back to the political autonomy of the regions, and the advent of the theocratic 'city-states'.

The focus was now on the self-preservation of the settlement and the region, and on maintaining the institutions within the political and economic boundaries that the rulers possessed to ensure their power and keep the settlement functioning both religiously and bureaucratically. This can be seen as a local reaction to the removal of the centralised authority of the New Kingdom, and a need to re-establish at local and regional levels some form of managing control, which is reminiscent of the development of regional self-sufficiency at the end of the Old Kingdom and the development of the First Intermediate Period.

With the retraction of the local elites to within the large temenoi walls, the population outside the walls in the main political centres now took over the abandoned religious and administrative buildings outside. They utilised the buildings for domestic purposes, whether this was dismantling them for building material, primarily the mud-bricks for the construction of new housing, or building new homes within the courtyards or enclosures of the buildings, using the monumental architecture as an added defensive perimeter to the domestic complex and allowing the formation of discrete communities. They could also use these buildings as areas of industry, and again form discrete walled complexes to produce goods, also using the existing complexes as secured zones of manufacture. This process of re-use is an aspect that is paralleled in the re-deployment of earlier burial grounds for new interments, for example with burial shafts at Thebes and Saqqara.

The process of the re-use of earlier settlement areas was not stopped by the ruling elites, who firmly focused their activities within the temenos itself and on the protection of the structures within. Those people outside the walls were left to be self-sufficient, as indicated by multiple family and communal grain silos, for example those excavated at Akoris. The urban structures used New Kingdom house designs at Thebes and developed more organic-type house designs at Hermopolis to suit the needs of the families within their own economic and spatial limits.

The local population, at least prior to the mid-eighth century BCE, may have been self-sufficient in producing their own pottery because of the economic restrictions on purchasing new wares from a centralised source, while the lack of a trading connection with the wider Mediterranean created a stagnation in the development of new forms until the end of the period, when contacts with the Mediterranean region began to increase again. They also appear to have been self-sufficient in acquiring new stone tools and now became less reliant on local government to provide items of daily life, instead utilising the urban environment to manufacture and re-use items.

SOCIAL STATUS THROUGH MATERIAL CULTURE AND ELITE EMULATION

The material culture from the Third Intermediate Period domestic settlements is reflective of the political fragmentation of the country through the regionality of the choice of objects and themes represented, the economic limits of the settlements, the self-sufficient nature of the people living in the settlements, and the aspirations of people to elite culture. The pottery forms show little differentiation that would indicate the social status of the owner. The pottery production and types of vessels during this period were homogeneous despite the fragmented political nature of the country which created regionalism and diversity in several areas of social life. The baseline in the material culture shows a limitation of pottery forms compared with the New Kingdom, which also reflects the utilitarian needs of the population. The vessel types indicate a focus on group dining and communal drinking across the different social spectra, while storage was a primary function of most of the vessels. This again reinforces the self-sufficiency of local populations and family groups and centralised storage within both the settlement and the home.

Third Intermediate Period people appear, based on the pottery assemblages, to be eating, processing, and storing foods the same way as the New Kingdom population. It is likely that the everyday lifecycles of the inhabitants within the settlements did not fundamentally change from the New Kingdom, despite being poorer. The population continued to express social status using heirlooms linking themselves to important military rulers such as Shoshenq I, perhaps again showing a connection with warrior class ideologies of a Libyan influence.

Even though the Third Intermediate Period population were poorer than those of the New Kingdom, there was an aspiration among local populations to emulate elite culture through certain aspects of the material culture. The people still required a way of expressing social status and prestige, but they no longer had the economic means to do so, and therefore had to find new methods. The elite faience goblets were adapted into pottery versions and footed bowl types from around the Twenty-Second Dynasty onwards, reflecting the trickle-down of elite material culture to the non-elite population.

The surviving archaeological remains from the Third Intermediate Period indicate that it was not a time of perpetual disorder and chaos as so many have previously interpreted it. Granted there were substantial changes in the socio-economic conditions of the country in which the new powers had to adapt, but the people of Egypt continued their daily lives bounded by the new situations in which they found themselves. The new world order of the early first millennium BCE allowed the freedom and opportunity to develop new aspects of political structure, economic conditions, aspects of culture, elite emulation, a more multicultural Egypt, and self-sufficiency. It also created an isolationism at both the state and local levels, which only began to break down and become more outward looking at the start of the Twenty-Sixth Dynasty through re-establishment of connections with the new political powers of the Greek and Near Eastern states.

APPENDIX 1

GAZETTEER OF THIRD INTERMEDIATE PERIOD SITES

This appendix is a gazetteer of Third Intermediate Period 'sites' which are utilised within the analysis and discussions of this study. This appendix also incorporates Third Intermediate Period locations which have not been utilised in the discussions, but have contributed to the overall quantified site data statistics. It provides, where appropriate, detailed documentation and discussion of the sites, including discussions on the potential locations of toponyms not associated with modern Arabic toponyms. In addition to 'sites', this appendix will list wider geographic locations and regional toponyms, including thematic excursi in relation to groups of related toponyms, such as royal residences, administrative districts, and specific topographic features such as roads and waterways. The site of Tell Tennis, which preserves a statue base of Psusennes I,[1] has not been included in this gazetteer, as it is likely that this monument was brought to the site in the Late Antique Period, while Mut el-Kharab and other oasis sites have not been included as this study focuses on sites within the Nile Valley, Faiyum, and Delta.[2]

DATA LAYOUTS FOR UPPER EGYPTIAN SITES

- ID: ThIP_UE.1 = Identification Number ThIP (Third Intermediate Period)
- Nome + Ordinal Number (and Capital designated)
- Bank: West/East/Island
- GEOREF: geographic co-ordinates
- ArabicNAME: modern Arabic name of the site
- AEN_Hiero: ancient Egyptian name in hieroglyphs
- AEN_Trans: ancient Egyptian name transliterated
- Discussion: site discussion and available data
- A–A (HH) = Akoris to Atfih (Heracleopolitan Hinterland)

DATA LAYOUTS FOR LOWER EGYPTIAN SITES

- ID: ThIP_LE.1: Identification Number ThIP (Third Intermediate Period)

- GEOREF: geographic co-ordinates
- ArabicNAME: modern Arabic name of the site
- AEN_Hiero: ancient Egyptian name in hieroglyphs
- AEN_Trans: ancient Egyptian name transliterated
- Discussion: site discussion and available data

For sites documented on the Piankhy Stela, see the relevant sections in Grimal, 1981 and Lichtheim, 1980: 66–84.

UPPER EGYPT

ID: ThIP_UE.1 **NOME:** 1st **BANK:** Island   **GEOREF:** 24°0'55.46"N 32°53'40.10"E

ArabicNAME: Gezirat Bigga **AEN_Hiero:**   **AEN_Trans:** *sn-mt*

Discussion: Gezirat Bigga is the first site mentioned on the Twenty-First Dynasty Onomasticon of Amenemope indicating the administrative importance of this border for the early Twenty-First Dynasty High Priests of Amun.[3] An inscription of the HPA Menkheperre was left here.[4] Whether a small garrison force was retained here after the pontificate of Menkheperre is unknown, but after his pontificate the southern border most likely retracted back to Elephantine which was now the southern border for the remainder of the Third Intermediate Period.

ID: ThIP_UE.2   **NOME:** 1st **BANK:** Island   **GEOREF:** 24°3'39.76"N 32°52'15.50"E

ArabicNAME: Gezirat Sehel   **AEN_Hiero:**   **AEN_Trans:** *Stt*

Discussion: An inscription was left here by the HPA Pinudjem I.[5]

ID: ThIP_UE.3   **NOME:** 1st **BANK:** Island   **GEOREF:** 24°5'4.66"N 32°53'8.33"E

ArabicNAME: Gezirat Aswan   **AEN_Hiero:**   **AEN_Trans:** *3bw*

Discussion: From the reign of the HPA Menkheperre, Gezirat Aswan (Elephantine) became the main southern frontier and authorised control point of Egypt, with continous occupation under the Twenty-Second Dynasty with royal monuments of Osorkon II.[6] A number of private land donations to the Khnum temple were made in the Twenty-Second Dynasty,[7] and a number of private and royal monuments of the Twenty-Second to Twenty-Third Dynasty have been found,[8] along with a monument of the proto-Twenty-Fifth Dynasty ruler Kashta.[9] A settlement of the Third Intermediate Period also continued to function in the area of the New Kingdom Khnum sanctuary.[10]

ID: ThIP_UE.4   **NOME:** 1st **BANK:** West   **GEOREF:** 24°49'16.97" N 32°52'44.73"E

ArabicNAME: Abu Id   **AEN_Hiero:** NA   **AEN_Trans:** NA

Discussion: In the Twenty-Fifth Dynasty, most likely in the reign of Piankhy, the zone of the Nile in the First Upper Egyptian Nome was fortified by a number of military installations aimed at a policy of controlled access. Only one fort so far has been located, near the small modern village of Abu Id.[11]

ID: ThIP_UE.5   **NOME:** 1st **BANK:** East   **GEOREF:** 24°27′7.61″N
                   Capital   32°55′42.88″E
ArabicNAME: Kom Ombo   **AEN_Hiero:** 𓂋𓏤𓇋𓇋𓊖   **AEN_Trans:** *nbyt*

Discussion: There is evidence of Twenty-First Dynasty burial activity within a re-used Middle Kingdom tomb during the reign of the HPA Menkheperre.[12] The New Kingdom temple may have been functioning to some degree as there was a hieratic inscription of the Twenty-First Dynasty carved into it,[13] which may indicate some form of settlement was still active in relation to the temple activity. There is, so far, no evidence to suggest the character or form of development of Kom Ombo after the early Twenty-First Dynasty.

ID: ThIP_UE.6   **NOME:** 1st **BANK:** East   **GEOREF:** 24°38′31.05″N
                                                             32°56′4.73″E
ArabicNAME: Gebel el-Silsila   **AEN_Hiero:** 𓈖𓏤𓇋𓇋𓊖   **AEN_Trans:** *ḫny*

Discussion: Quarrying was resumed at Gebel el-Silsila in Year 21 of Shoshenq I to extract stone for his ambitious building projects at Thebes and Memphis.[14]

ID: ThIP_UE.7   **NOME:** 1st **BANK:** West   **GEOREF:** 24°52′11.03″N
                                                             32°51′25.62″E
ArabicNAME: Naga el-Hassaia   **AEN_Hiero:** NA   **AEN_Trans:** NA

Discussion: Naga el-Hassaia is a cemetery site where numerous funerary stelae were found that dated stylistically and philologically to the Twenty-Second Dynasty.[15] It is unclear with which settlement this cemetery was associated.

ID: ThIP_UE.8   **NOME:** 2nd **BANK:** West   **GEOREF:** 24°58′37.73″N
                   Capital   32°52′20.91″E
ArabicNAME: Edfu   **AEN_Hiero:** 𓍑𓂉𓊖   **AEN_Trans:** *ḏbȝ*

Discussion: The Onomasticon of Amenemope mentions Edfu twice, once as 𓍑𓂉𓊖 *ḏbȝ* and the second time as 𓅓𓊖 *bḥd.t*.[16] These two toponyms are unlikely to refer to the same physical location. This is the only time a duplication of a settlement name occurs in the entire document: the most important settlements of Tanis, Thebes, and Memphis are written only once. These two toponyms relating to Edfu probably refer to different settlement districts, or divisions of space. It is clear from the location listings for Egypt in the onomasticon that each nome has either one or two second-order cities or locations associated with it; therefore it is likely that 𓍑𓂉𓊖 *ḏbȝ* is the primary settlement of Edfu itself and 𓅓𓊖 *bḥd.t* is the overall name for the settlement and its districts. This would suggest that settlements may have had overall names for the wider settlement and then individual names for districts located within the wider named settlement. Therefore, the toponym 𓅓𓊖 *bḥd.t* has been listed as a geographical zone and not part of the settlement site list, as 𓍑𓂉𓊖 *ḏbȝ* fulfils this role and represents the wider 'site' of Edfu.

Regarding the settlement longevity throughout the period, several non-royal statues have been found dating from the Twenty-Second to Twenty-Fifth Dynasty. These include a funerary stela of Nesamun,[17] a stela of Horimai,[18] and a kneeling statue of Nespaqashuty.[19] During the Twenty-Fifth Dynasty, Edfu began to be redeveloped by Taharqa. A new gate was added to the New Kingdom temple, most likely standing on the access road to the temple.[20] Finally, from the Twenty-Fifth Dynasty reign of Shabaka was a statue of a man called Amenemhat who was Prophet of Amun at Karnak.[21] The statue mentions his wife before Mut of Ashur and Apet as a Hippopotamus.[22]

The late Third Intermediate Period settlement was identified in excavations to the west of the Ptolemaic Horus temple that revealed traces of walls of the Twenty-Fifth to

Twenty-Sixth Dynasty.[23] They rest upon a large 2.6 m ash deposit of the New Kingdom that covered the silo court of the Second Intermediate Period after the New Kingdom administrative activity moved to another area of the settlement. Extremely thin walls only 58 cm thick, large open courtyards, and square magazines built into the ground and used as cellars characterise the new domestic buildings of the Twenty-Fifth to Twenty-Sixth Dynasty.[24] This all suggests some reworking and redevelopment of the settlement in the Twenty-Sixth Dynasty, a feature that is common at other sites. The cemetery of Edfu, located at Hagar Edfu (24°58'25.43"N 32°50'27.29"E), has revealed Third Intermediate Period burial activity in the area around the 'Pyramid' tomb. To the south of the 'Pyramid' tomb was termite-eaten wood and white plaster that may have belonged to a coffin, and four 'sausage jars' containing embalming materials.[25] The ceramics associated with the coffin and other ceramics found on surface surveys in Area 5 would indicate a Third Intermediate Period date for this part of the cemetery.[26] Third Intermediate Period pottery is common all along the desert escarpment from north to south in areas 0–9. The cemetery at Hagar Edfu has a general Third Intermediate Period date as the ceramic sequence has yet to be defined. Funerary stelae found at Edfu suggest that the cemetery was active in the Twenty-Second to Twenty-Fifth Dynasty at least.

ID: ThIP_UE.9   **NOME:** 3rd   **BANK:** West   **GEOREF:** 25°5'23.89"N
Capital   32°46'20.38"E
ArabicNAME: Kom el-Ahmar   **AEN_Hiero:** ☉⊚   **AEN_Trans:** *Nḥn (Mḥn)*

Discussion: The site of Kom el-Ahmar, the ancient Hierakonpolis, is mentioned only on the Onomasticon of Amenemope during the Third Intermediate Period.[27] No more is known regarding this site for the Third Intermediate Period after the early Twenty-First Dynasty.

ID: ThIP_UE.10   **NOME:** 3rd   **BANK:** East   **GEOREF:** 25°7'7.80"N
32°47'52.21"E
ArabicNAME: El-Kab   **AEN_Hiero:** 🦅⌐🪶⊗   **AEN_Trans:** *nḥb*

Discussion: Little archaeological evidence survives from the site beyond a Twenty-First Dynasty obelisk.[28] The discovery of this small obelisk indicates that the temple of Nekhbet was adorned at this time. There is further evidence of temple adornment as a foundation deposit was found from either the late Ramesside or Twenty-First Dynasty, indicating some substantial addition to the New Kingdom temple. The presence of the Twenty-First Dynasty obelisk may indicate the foundation deposit is most likely of Twenty-First Dynasty date too, as part of the temple addition. El-Kab is documented on the Onomasticon of Amenemope,[29] and Istemkheb D, the sister wife of Pinudjem II, was given the title of Prophetess of Nekhbet, which was then inherited by her daughter Nesitanebtashru.[30] These benefices indicate the Twenty-First Dynasty had a direct interest not just in the religious aspect of the settlement but in the associated benefices and income that the settlement and hinterland could provide.
The Old Kingdom cemetery at el-Kab was re-used during this period.[31] A mastaba of the Third Dynasty was excavated by a Belgium expedition in which a yellow varnished coffin of the classic Theban type was found among later burials.[32]

ID: ThIP_UE.11   **NOME:** 3rd   **BANK:** West   **GEOREF:** 25°12'50.92"N
32°38'1.48"E
ArabicNAME: Komir   **AEN_Hiero:** 🏠🦆✶   **AEN_Trans:** *pr-mrw*

Discussion: The site of Komir, the ancient *pr-mrw*, is mentioned only on the Onomasticon of Amenemope.[33] No more is known regarding this site for the Third Intermediate Period after the early Twenty-First Dynasty.

ID: ThIP_UE.12   **NOME:** 3rd   **BANK:** West   **GEOREF:** Esna and Hagar Esna (NW of Esna) (25°17′ 51.09″N 32°30′49.77″E)

ArabicNAME: Esna and Hagar Esna   **AEN_Hiero:** 𓊖𓏤𓉐𓈖   **AEN_Trans:** *iwnyt*

Discussion: Esna is documented on the Onomasticon of Amenemope.[34] No more is known about the settlement until the Twenty-Fifth Dynasty when the temple is added to by Shabaka and a new naos installed.[35] Evidence for cemetery activity during the Third Intermediate Period is from material that is said to have derived from excavations conducted by John Garstang during 1905–6 that were only published in a brief report.[36] Garstang did not attribute any of the tomb groups to the Third Intermediate Period, stating that the Esna necropolis (Hagar Esna) dated from the Twelfth to Twentieth Dynasty, apart from one limestone sarcophagus of the Singer of Amun Inshu originally dated by Garstang to the Twenty-Second Dynasty. The sarcophagus of Inshu found in the cemetery is more likely dated to the Nineteenth Dynasty and not the Twenty-Second Dynasty.[37] The burial groups found by Garstang have a date range of the late Eighteenth to the Twenty-Second Dynasty, and several of the burials should be dated to the late Third Intermediate Period or Late Period,[38] more precisely the second half of the eighth century BCE or later.[39] In addition, Tomb Group 643 (Esna 250),[40] inside a large Nineteenth Dynasty superstructure with two storeys and six vaulted burial chambers, had been burnt on more than one occasion. There was evidence of Third Intermediate Period re-use, with cartonnage fragments possibly dating as early as ca. 930–700 BCE.[41] The cemetery is likely to have been used ca. 750 BCE and later, possibly spanning back at the earliest to ca. 900 BCE.

ID: ThIP_UE.13   **NOME:** 3rd   **BANK:** NA   **GEOREF:** NA
ArabicNAME: NA   **AEN_Hiero:** 𓂝𓊖𓃭𓆱𓊖   **AEN_Trans:** *ꜥgn*
Discussion: The ancient site of *ꜥgn* is documented on the Onomasticon of Amenemope.[42] The site was a benefice of Nesikhons A and is mentioned on the Twenty-Second Dynasty stela of Neseramun from the Karnak cachette.[43] *ꜥgn* is most likely to be found near the sites of Esna and Asfun el-Matanah.

ID: ThIP_UE.14   **NOME:** 3rd   **BANK:** West   **GEOREF:** 25°23′29.44″N 32°32′30.07″E

ArabicNAME: Asfun el-Matanah   **AEN_Hiero:** 𓉗𓏏𓊃𓈖𓆳𓊖   **AEN_Trans:** *ḥwt-snfrw*

Discussion: *ḥwt-snfrw* is listed on the Onomasticon of Amenemope.[44] So far, it is only in the Twenty-Fifth Dynasty that evidence of royal activity has been documented at this site, with the erection of a red granite stela of Taharqa, offering to the god Hemen.[45]

ID: ThIP_UE.15   **NOME:** 3rd   **BANK:** East   **GEOREF:** 25°27′29.53″N 32°32′13.01″E

ArabicNAME: El-Moalla   **AEN_Hiero:** 𓉐𓏲𓐍𓄿𓊖   **AEN_Trans:** *pr-ḥꜣt*

Discussion: *pr-ḥꜣt* is considered to be the modern el-Moalla.[46] The site is listed on the Onomasticon of Amenemope,[47] and is listed directly after *ḥwt-snfrw* and *ꜥgn*. El-Moalla has a direct connection to both ʿ*ḥwt-snfrw* and *ꜥgn*. El-Moalla is mentioned on a fragment of a Twenty-First Dynasty papyrus which was in Alan Gardiner's possession, and is also mentioned on the block statue of Neseramun,[48] as Neseramun is prophet of both *ḥwt-snfrw* and *ꜥgn*.[49] El-Moalla is a well-known cemetery of the First Intermediate Period, but three Twenty-First Dynasty coffins are reputed to have been found here. One of them belongs to a woman,[50] and is reminiscent of Twenty-First Dynasty coffin styles from Thebes, while two other coffins are both unpublished,[51] but have been reported as originating from here.[52] It is likely that there was a connected settlement of which Neseramun was the prophet of the local temple.

ID: ThIP_UE.16   **NOME:** 3rd   **BANK:** East   **GEOREF:** 25°29′40.65″N 32°31′12.56″E

ArabicNAME: Dibabeya   **AEN_Hiero:** NA   **AEN_Trans:** NA

Discussion: A stela from the reign of Smendes I was inscribed in the quarry at Dibabeya near to Gebelein, giving orders to repair damage caused to the temple of Luxor after a high flood.[53]

ID: ThIP_UE.17   **NOME:** 3rd   **BANK:** Island   **GEOREF:** NA

ArabicNAME: NA   **AEN_Hiero:** 𓊖   **AEN_Trans:** iw-m-itrw

Discussion: iw-m-itrw (lit. Island in the River) is an island near Gebelein with a cult of the god Sobek, listed on the Onomasticon of Amenemope.[54]

ID: ThIP_UE.18   **NOME:** 3rd   **BANK:** West   **GEOREF:** 25°29′24.02″N 32°29′1.32″E

ArabicNAME: Gebelein   **AEN_Hiero:** 𓉐   **AEN_Trans:** pr-ḥw.t-ḥr

Discussion: Mud-bricks of both the Twenty-First Dynasty HPA Menkheperre and his wife Queen Istemkheb were found at Gebelein and may be from a fort enclosing the temple of Hathor.[55]

ID: ThIP_UE.19   **NOME:** 4th   **BANK:** West   **GEOREF:** 25°35′44.26″N 32°27′55.65″E

ArabicNAME: El-Rizeiqat   **AEN_Hiero:** 𓊖 or 𓊖   **AEN_Trans:** sw-mnw

Discussion: El-Rizeiqat is listed on the Onomasticon of Amenemope.[56] Early twentieth-century excavations at el-Rizeiqat found funerary items from the New Kingdom, but there is, so far, no evidence of continued burial activity at el-Rizeiqat dating to the Third Intermediate Period. Its inclusion on the Onomasticon of Amenemope indicates its importance for the early Twenty-First Dynasty administration.

ID: ThIP_UE.20   **NOME:** 4th   **BANK:** West   **GEOREF:** 25°37′18.83″N 32°32′40.48″E

ArabicNAME: Armant   **AEN_Hiero:** 𓊖   **AEN_Trans:** iwny

Discussion: Armant is listed on the Onomasticon of Amenemope.[57] At Armant there was activity in the temple area in the Twenty-Second Dynasty. A Twenty-Second Dynasty statue of Djedkhonsuefankh was added,[58] along with a granite statue of Osiris dedicated by Shepenwepet II in the Twenty-Fifth Dynasty.[59] So far there have been no associated cemeteries for Armant that date to the Third Intermediate Period.

ID: ThIP_UE.21   **NOME:** 4th   **BANK:** East   **GEOREF:** 25°34′58.97″N 32°32′0.34″E

ArabicNAME: Tod   **AEN_Hiero:** 𓊖   **AEN_Trans:** ḏrti

Discussion: Tod is not listed on the Onomasticon of Amenemope, but Third Intermediate Period pottery has been found in the temple area.[60]

ID: ThIP_UE.22 **NOME:** 4th   **BANK:** West   **GEOREF:** For Medinat Habu:
25°43′11.09″N 32°36′2.86″E

ArabicNAME: Luxor (West Bank)

Intra-Site List

ThIP_UE.22.1.1 Medinat Habu (Domestic)

ThIP_UE.22.2.2 Wadi el-Malikaat (Cemetery)

ThIP_UE.22.2.3 Wadi el-Maluuk (East Valley) (Cemetery)

ThIP_UE.22.2.4 Wadi el-Maluuk (West Valley) (Cemetery)

ThIP_UE.22.2.5 Deir el-Bahari (Cemetery)

ThIP_UE.22.2.6 The Ramesseum (Cemetery)

ThIP_UE.22.2.7 Sheikh Abd el-Gurna (Cemetery)

ThIP_UE.22.2.8 Valley South of Deir el-Bahari (Cemetery)

ThIP_UE.22.2.9 Deir el-Bahari (Cemetery)

ThIP_UE.22.2.10 Assasif (Cemetery)

ThIP_UE.22.2.11 Dra Abu el-Naga (Cemetery)

Discussion: The Theban West Bank has been taken as one 'site' but
with multiple functions across the area. Each functional area has been
given an additional suffix to the ThIP_UE.22 designator for the
Theban West Bank area.[61]

ID: ThIP_UE.23   **NOME:** 4th **BANK:** West   **GEOREF:** NA
ArabicNAME: NA   **AEN_Hiero:** 𓏏𓊖   **AEN_Trans:** *tꜣḏḥwty st mry*

Discussion: *tꜣḏḥwty st mry* 'The Seat Beloved of Thoth' was a military base on the
Theban West Bank.[62] This military base is mentioned on the statue of the Vizier
Nespaqashuty,[63] and is dated by the cartouche of Shoshenq III and the name of the
HPA Harsiese B.[64]

ID: ThIP_UE.24 **NOME:** 4th **BANK:** West   **GEOREF:** NA
ArabicNAME: NA   **AEN_Hiero:**   **AEN_Trans:** *tꜣ*

tꜣ iꜣt pꜣ bik

Discussion: The site of *tꜣ iꜣt pꜣ bik* 'The Mound of the Falcon' is attested for the Theban
Nome in the Twenty-First Dynasty and is listed among the settlements of
Amenemope.[65] This location is not mentioned again in the Third Intermediate Period,
but on a later Ptolemaic papyrus,[66] there is record of the priests of the 'Resting Place of
the Ibis and Falcon' in the Theban Nome.[67] The tombs of the Ibises are recorded on
another Ptolemaic papyrus as being on the 'Mountain of Djeme',[68] and it is possible
that the later Ptolemaic name could be equated with the Twenty-First Dynasty name.[69]
This location may have an association with the fortress 'The Seat Beloved of Thoth' in
the area of Medinat Habu, which was first mentioned under Merenptah and maintained into the Twenty-Second Dynasty, and it could have an associated military
function.[70]

ID: ThIP_UE.25   **NOME:** 4th **BANK:** East   **GEOREF:** 25°42′40.29″N
Capital   32°39′5.39″E
ArabicNAME: Thebes (East   **AEN_Hiero:**   **AEN_Trans:** *nw.t*
Bank) between the Karnak and
Luxor temples

Monument and Textual Activity Date:

The full writing of the settlement of Thebes on the Onomasticon of Amenemope is
nwt wꜣst nt imn ḥnwt n dmi nb.[71] There is
a considerable amount of archaeological data attested for Third Intermediate Period works

within the temples at Karnak and Luxor, which it is beyond the scope of this book to document.[72] The main settlement of Thebes was situated around the Karnak temple enclosures.[73]

ID: ThIP_UE.26   **NOME:** 4th   **BANK:** West   **GEOREF:** 25°44′1.91″N 32°42′37.12″E

ArabicNAME: Naga el-Medamud   **AEN_Hiero:** 𓈘𓆓𓅱   **AEN_Trans:** *mꜣdw*

Discussion: The ancient site *mꜣdw* is listed on the Onomasticon of Amenemope.[74] The HPA Menkheperre added to the main temple of Naga el-Medamud, in effect fortifying the temenos walls, while bricks stamped in his name were found in the temple itself.[75] Twenty-First Dynasty building activity was followed up with new building works in the northern kiosk by Shepenwepet, Amenirdis I, and Shepenwepet III.[76]

ID: ThIP_UE.27   **NOME:** 4th   **BANK:** West   **GEOREF:** NA

ArabicNAME: NA   **AEN_Hiero:** 𓁷𓁷𓏤𓄿𓇋𓅓𓈖𓊖   **AEN_Trans:** *ḥr (=i) ḥr imn*

Discussion: Within the Theban Nome there is mention of a site called 𓁷𓁷𓏤𓄿𓇋𓅓𓈖𓊖 *ḥr (=i) ḥr imn* 'My Face is Upon Amun', which is listed on the Onomasticon of Amenemope.[77] The name for the site can be used in personal names of the Eighteenth Dynasty.[78] The site must have been significant to be mentioned alongside Armant, Naga el-Medamud, and Thebes, but has not been positively located. The name of the settlement indicates that the site was in view of the Great Temple of Amun at Thebes (Karnak), and the inhabitants of this town could view the front pylons of the Amun temple. This indicates that it was most likely situated on the West Bank, but still within the borders of the Theban Nome. The settlement is mentioned on the temple list of Anena behind the Montuhotep temple at Deir el-Bahari and is mentioned in the Ramesside tomb of Amenemhab (TT 44), who was a priest in 'My Face is Upon Amun'. In the list of Puyumre there is an 'Amun of Herihoramun', which is listed before Amun of Deir el-Bahari.[79] A reference to the site of Herihoramun is recorded in tomb TT157 of Nebwenenef, a Ramesside official, who was called Overseer of the Prophets of *ḥr (=i) ḥr imn*.[80] *ḥr (=i) ḥr imn* may be in the area of the temple of Amenhotep I and Queen Ahmose-Nefertari.[81] Evidence from around the temple suggests that there was some votive activity within the temple during the Twenty-First Dynasty, as a headless granite scribe statue of Amenmose was found in its ruins,[82] along with a votive block depicting Ahmose-Nefertari dated to the Twenty-Second Dynasty.[83]

ID: ThIP_UE.28   **NOME:** 5th   **BANK:** East   **GEOREF:** 25°50′15.61″N 32°49′47.18″E

ArabicNAME: Higazeh   **AEN_Hiero:** NA   **AEN_Trans:** NA

Discussion: The HPA Menkheperre erected a new fortification on the northern boundary of the Theban Nome at Higazeh. Bricks with the cartouches of Queen Istemkheb, wife of Menkheperre, attest to this new building work.[84]

ID: ThIP_UE.29   **NOME:** 5th   **BANK:** East   **GEOREF:** 25°54′58.00″N 32°45′50.05″E

ArabicNAME: Qus   **AEN_Hiero:** 𓎼𓋴𓇌𓊖   **AEN_Trans:** *gsy*

Discussion: The ancient site of *gsy*, the modern-day Qus, is listed on the Onomasticon of Amenemope.[85] Little survives from the Third Intermediate Period from this site, apart from a plaque bearing the name of a King Usermaatre that preserves the writing of the name of Qus.[86] The plaque probably comes from a foundation deposit of an unknown temple in the settlement.[87]

ID: ThIP_UE.30   **NOME:** 5th   **BANK:** West   **GEOREF:** 25°58′24.31″N
                                                                32°43′56.94″E

ArabicNAME: Tukh   **AEN_Hiero:** 𓊪𓏏𓈖𓊖   **AEN_Trans:** *nbt*

Discussion: The ancient site of *nbt*, the modern Tukh, is only listed on the Onomasticon of Amenemope.[88] Nothing else is known about this site for the remainder of the Third Intermediate Period.

ID: ThIP_UE.31   **NOME:** 5th   **BANK:** East   **GEOREF:** 25°59′44.08″N
                      Capital   32°49′1.12″E

ArabicNAME: Quft   **AEN_Hiero:** 𓎼𓃀𓏏𓇌𓅱   **AEN_Trans:** *gbtyw*

Discussion: The Fifth Upper Egyptian Nome capital is located at modern-day Quft (ancient: Coptos). The site has preserved most of the datable material from the Fifth Upper Egyptian Nome for the Third Intermediate Period. The Twenty-First Dynasty is limited to a re-used limestone fragment with the remains of an oracle text datable to the HPA Pinudjem I[89] and a stela of Pinudjem I representing Henttawy A.[90] In the Twenty-Second Dynasty Osorkon I placed his name on a gate of Thutmose III in the north chapel.[91] A granite basin bearing the name and titles of King Harsiese was found at Quft.[92] Finally, the Twenty-Fifth Dynasty at Quft is represented by a stela of Taharqa[93] that corresponds to another stela from his Temple T at Kawa in Nubia.[94]

ID: ThIP_UE.32   **NOME:** 5th   **BANK:** East?   **GEOREF:** NA

ArabicNAME: NA   **AEN_Hiero:** 𓊃𓏏𓆑𓊖   **AEN_Trans:** *stf*

Discussion: 𓊃𓏏𓆑𓊖 *stf* is listed on the Onomasticon of Amenemope.[95] So far there is no proposed site for this settlement. It must have lain between the sites of Quft (Coptos) and Dendera.

ID: ThIP_UE.33   **NOME:**   **BANK:** West   **GEOREF:** 26°8′29.66″N
                      6th Capital   32°40′14.14″E

ArabicNAME: Dendera   **AEN_Hiero:**   **AEN_Trans:** *iwn.t*
                                 𓏏𓈖𓏏𓂋𓏏𓊖

Discussion: Archaeological material from throughout the Third Intermediate Period has been found at 𓏏𓈖𓏏𓂋𓏏𓊖 *iwn t3 ntrt*, the modern Dendera. Dendera was the capital of the Sixth Upper Egyptian Nome. It is mentioned on the Twenty-First Dynasty Onomasticon of Amenemope.[96] Excavations by the IFAO working on the foundations of the Ptolemaic–Roman temple of Hathor have recovered archaeological evidence for occupation strata of the Twenty-First Dynasty.[97] The surface survey at the site conducted in 1995–6 found no evidence of ceramics of the Twenty-First to Twenty-Second Dynasty within the Ptolemaic–Roman temenos area or the area outside the temenos wall known as the ancient settlement located to the east.[98] Excavations against the temple's outer western wall were conducted to determine the construction of the temple's foundations (Sondage 98.1). In doing so, ceramics dated to the Twenty-First and Twenty-Second Dynasty were found in two layers. The first was in Layer C and in the fill of a silo. The ceramics were used as backfill for an occupational layer; underneath this layer was a new layer of occupation of compacted earth with ceramics exclusively of the Old Kingdom. Therefore, the discovery of ceramics as a fill layer does not provide any evidence for the location of the town during the Third Intermediate Period at Dendera. The original temple of the Ramesside Period was in this area as large amounts of Ramesside blocks, primarily of Ramesses III, were found in the foundations of the Ptolemaic–Roman temple of Hathor. It is possible that the temple of the Ramesside Period continued to function into the Third Intermediate Period. No re-used blocks of the Third Intermediate Period have been found in the Ptolemaic–Roman structure, which may indicate that it was not added to in the Third

Intermediate Period. Several objects from Dendera are dated to after the Twenty-Second Dynasty. This may indicate that the backfill of the earlier structures using Twenty-First and possible Twenty-Second Dynasty material may have coincided with the spatial reorganisation of the settlement, and the development of a new zone of the city. We do not have an exact provenance of the post-Twenty-Second Dynasty material from Dendera, but it was most likely used to adorn the temple of Hathor. These objects included a Twenty-Fifth Dynasty stela of Shabaka before Hathor and Harsomtus, along with a statue of Hor, who was overseer of works of Amun at Thebes; the statue gives hymns to the divinities and has a broad date range of the Twenty-Second to Twenty-Fifth Dynasty.

One such object was a block statue of Basa dated to the mid-Twenty-Second to Twenty-Third Dynasty.[99] Additional evidence of religious structures comes from an animal cemetery, which can be dated to the Twenty-Second and Twenty-Third Dynasty; this is further added to by a cache of copper vessels found in Mastaba 340 now in the Ashmolean Museum, dated from the Twenty-Third to Twenty-Fifth Dynasty.[100] No Third Intermediate Period tombs are known from Dendera, and Petrie's[101] dating of the burial of the singer in the temple of Hathor, Mutirdis, to the Twenty-Fifth Dynasty should be corrected to ca. 650–620 BCE.[102]

ID: ThIP_UE.34   **NOME:** 7th   **BANK:** East   **GEOREF:** 26°3′31.08″N
                                                              32°18′25.28″E
ArabicNAME: Kasr el-Sayed   **AEN_Hiero:**   **AEN_Trans:** *nꜣ-šny-n-stḥ*

Discussion: The ancient site of *nꜣ-šny-n-stḥ* 'The Trees of Seth' (classical: Khenoboskian; modern: Kasr el-Sayed) is listed on the Onomasticon of Amenemope.[103] The region around Kasr el-Sayed may have been a location where fugitives escaped to, as a Twenty-First Dynasty letter that was addressed to the chief taxing master, Menmarenkakhte, from the mayor of Elephantine, Meron, discussing unjust tax demands, mentions 'The Trees of Seth', Tukh, and the neighbourhood of Edfu.[104] A second letter of the same date documents a criminal or a fugitive who had escaped, and those involved in his capture consulted an oracle (possibly Hathor of Dendera and the God of Sheniset/Khenoboskian) to see if they would be successful.

ID: ThIP_UE.35   **NOME:** 7th   **BANK:** NA   **GEOREF:** NA
ArabicNAME: NA   **AEN_Hiero:**   **AEN_Trans:** *pr-binw*

Discussion: During the Third Intermediate Period, the site of *pr-binw* is only listed on the Onomasticon of Amenemope.[105] No more is known about this site for the period.

ID: ThIP_UE.36   **NOME:**   **BANK:** West   **GEOREF:** 26°1′3.44″N
                    7th Capital   32°16′56.89″E
ArabicNAME: Huw   **AEN_Hiero:**   **AEN_Trans:** *ḥw.t-sḥm*
Discussion: The site of Huw is the ancient *ḥw.t-sḥm* and is listed on the Onomasticon of Amenemope.[106] The site retained its political importance throughout the Third Intermediate Period as attested by several stelae found at the site.[107]
Activity increased in the Twenty-Fifth Dynasty when the number of stelae being dedicated increased, including those of Nesmin,[108] Tasherimut,[109] and Tadiamenipet.[110]

ID: ThIP_UE.37   **NOME:** 7th   **BANK:** NA   **GEOREF:** NA
ArabicNAME: NA   **AEN_Hiero:**   **AEN_Trans:** *pr-imy-r-ꜥb*
Discussion: The site of *pr-imy-r-ꜥb* is listed on the Onomasticon of Amenemope,[111] and is translated as 'The House of the Overseer of Horns'. This toponym is likely to

have been associated with the title 𓍿𓊪𓍯 that was common in the Middle Kingdom, the Eighteenth Dynasty, and from the Ramesside Period when the title became rare.[112] There is a reference made to herds being created for Osiris by Seti I on a stela from Abydos, which mentions a man named Hor as 'Overseer of the Horns of the Mansion of Menmaare, whose Heart is Pleased in Abydos'.[113] An inscription of Shoshenq I mentions 𓌳𓂝𓍿𓄿𓄿𓏤𓇯𓏥𓊃𓂋𓍿𓄿𓄿 *pȝ mr ꜥbn ꜥnḥwt n pr ḥr-š.f*, 'The Overseer of Horned Cattle and Goats of the House of Heryshef'.[114] This place should be located in the region of Heracleopolis and not in the Seventh Upper Egyptian Nome.[115] The toponym 𓉐𓂋𓄿𓃀𓄿𓄿 could have been a distinctive foundation or centre that was set up as a breeding location for cattle, with an associated satellite settlement. The geographic location would place it south of the ancient 𓉐𓂋𓂦𓂦𓏤𓊖 *pr-dȝdȝ* (modern Abu Tisht), on the border between the Seventh and Eighth Upper Egyptian nomes, in an area that was highly fertile and a prime location for the grazing and rearing of cattle. This location could be related to the routes between the oases, in which cattle were brought up the oasis route from Nubia into the Nile Valley at this point to be fattened up for distribution to royal centres.

ID: ThIP_UE.38 **NOME:** 7th **BANK:** West   **GEOREF:** 26°7'7.21"N
                                                              32°5'47.31"E

ArabicNAME: Abu Tisht   **AEN_Hiero:** 𓉐𓂋𓂦𓂦𓏤𓊖   **AEN_Trans:** *pr-dȝdȝ*

Discussion: The settlement of 𓉐𓂋𓂦𓂦𓏤𓊖 *pr-dȝdȝ* is listed on the Onomasticon of Amenemope[116] and is referenced on a Thirtieth Dynasty statue of Harwodj who was a Prophet of Amenemopet of *pr-dȝdȝ*.[117] The explicit nature of the connection between the nome capital Huw (*ḥw.t-sḥm*) and the settlement of Abu Tisht is affirmed on the Twenty-Second Dynasty Dakhleh Stela,[118] which dates to Year 5 of the reign of Shoshenq I.[119] This stela documents how the governor of Huw, Weheyset, was sent to the Dakhleh Oasis to resolve an uprising in the settlement of Sa-Wehet, which is not located.[120] This stela confirms that the centres in this area of the Nile Valley at the start of the Twenty-Second Dynasty were linked with activity in the Western Oases, which is seen in the proliferation of fortified centres and checkpoints set up from the late Ramesside Period onwards to control access in and out of the oases in the Heracleopolitan and Theban regions. The stela makes mention of a land or cadastral register in Year 19 of a King Psusennes, possibly Psusennes II.[121]

ID: ThIP_UE.39 **NOME:** 8th **BANK:** NA   **GEOREF:** NA
ArabicNAME: NA   **AEN_Hiero:** 𓍿𓂝𓃀𓏤𓊖   **AEN_Trans:** *nḫt*

Discussion: The ancient site of *nḫt* listed on the Onomasticon of Amenemope[122] was originally suggested to be joined to the toponym of Abydos.[123] It is likely that the location was the same as that found in the epithet of a god whose name and figure are now lost, who was 𓌓𓈖𓏏𓈖𓃀𓃀𓏏𓊖 *ḥnty-nȝwt*, 'Foremost in the Town of Female Ibexes'.[124]

ID: **NOME:** 8th **BANK:** West   **GEOREF:** 26°11'23.27"N
ThIP_UE.40   31°54'26.42"E
ArabicNAME: NA   **AEN_Hiero:**   **AEN_Trans:** *nȝ mḫr n ṯn*
                         𓈖𓄿𓅓𓐍𓂋𓈖𓏤𓍿𓈖𓊖

Discussion: The ancient toponym of *nȝ mḫr n ṯn* 'The Storehouses of This' is listed after that of the main cemetery and pilgrimage site of el-Arab el-Madfuna (classical: Abydos).[125] Therefore the settlement must be located to the north of Abydos, but before the modern village of Nag el-Meshayikh (ancient: *Pr mḥt wbn*) and the capital of the nome, Girga (ancient: *ṯnі*). The toponym *nȝ mḫr n ṯn* is found on a stela found at

Abydos[126] relating to the Twenty-First Dynasty HPA family, where Psusennes, the son of Menkheperre A, dating from the Twenty-First Dynasty, has, besides the title of HPA, the attributes of Min-Hor and Isis of Quft (Coptos), Prophet of Amun-Her of Makher (or <of> *n-makher*), and Prophet of Amun of Tiy.[127] Černy was tempted to take the writing of Tiy as an erroneous writing of *ṯni* (ancient: This; modern: Girga), and in view of the provenance of the stela it is difficult not to connect the previous name with the *n mḫr-n-ṯn* of the Onomasticon of Amenemope.[128] Another attestation of the location comes from two papyrus fragments in Turin,[129] which join and bear on the recto a text of a Year 8 of a king of the Twentieth Dynasty, giving a list of people in connection with the royal tomb as they are in the charge of the foreman of the royal tomb Nekhemmut.[130] One of the men on this list comes from the 'Storehouses of This' and in the same fragment a proper name 'He of This' occurs.

ID: ThIP_UE.41   **NOME:** 8th   **BANK:** East   **GEOREF:** 26°20′17.30″N 31°56′18.39″E

ArabicNAME: Nag el-Meshayikh   **AEN_Hiero:**   **AEN_Trans:** *pr mḥt wbn*

Discussion: This location known as the 'Eastern Behdet' is listed on the Onomasticon of Amenemope.[131] Eastern Behdet can be identified with the modern village of Nag el-Meshayikh, which borders the desert edge on the East Bank of the Nile.[132]

ID: ThIP_UE.42   **NOME:** 8th   **BANK:** West   **GEOREF:** 26°11′0.30″N 31°54′57.93″E

ArabicNAME: El-Arab el-Madfuna   **AEN_Hiero:**   **AEN_Trans:** *ꜣbḏw*

Discussion: The ancient site of *ꜣbḏw* is listed on the Onomasticon of Amenemope and is identified with the modern el-Arab el-Madfuna (classical: Abydos).[133] *ꜣbḏw* was an important necropolis for much of Egyptian history, being linked with the worship of Osiris.[134] The burials of the Third Intermediate Period are divided into three types. The first were brick-built structures situated in the Western Cemetery, part of the northern sector of the Abydos necropolis.[135] The second type were intrusive burials,[136] while several royal family members of the Twenty-First, Twenty-Second, and Twenty-Fifth Dynasty were buried in brick and stone-built tombs, as well as several elite burials.[137] The burials of the Third Intermediate Period are to be found along the processional valley leading to the Umm el-Qaab, where the tomb of Osiris was supposed to be located.[138] A revival of the cultic activity took place at the tomb of Djer in the Twenty-Fifth Dynasty after the initial peak in the Ramesside Period.[139] The ceramics of the Twenty-First to Twenty-Fourth Dynasty produced a minimum of 10 per cent of the ceramic material, which is comparable to the amount for the Eighteenth Dynasty. The Twenty-First to Twenty-Second Dynasty percentage may increase substantially when other assemblages are assessed.[140]

ID: ThIP_UE.43   **NOME:** 8th Capital   **BANK:** East   **GEOREF:** 26°20′15.98″N 31°53′27.08″E

ArabicNAME: Girga   **AEN_Hiero:**   **AEN_Trans:** *ṯni*

Discussion: The ancient site of *ṯni* (classical: This; modern: Girga) was the capital of the Eighth Upper Egyptian Nome. Girga is almost unknown for the period, apart from a mention on the Onomasticon of Amenemope.[141]

ID: ThIP_UE.44   **NOME:** 8th   **BANK:** East   **GEOREF:** 26°21′2.10″N
                                                                31°56′35.50″E

ArabicNAME: El-Ahawaih   **AEN_Hiero:**   **AEN_Trans:** *t3 dhnt*

Discussion: The toponym *t3 dhnt* is translated as 'The Promontory',[142] while other forms of the writing occur.[143] There was more than one town during the Third Intermediate Period with the name *t3 dhnt*.[144] It is possible that this toponym *dhnt* could be associated with the HPA Piankh as P. Berlin 23231 recto x+3 says 'within that *dhnt* of Piankh'. It is likely that the *dhnt* recorded in the el-Hibeh archive is to be equated with the fortress of el-Ahawaih.[145]

ID: ThIP_UE.45   **NOME:** 9th   **BANK:** West   **GEOREF:** 26°28′30.17″N
                                                                31°48′5.40″E

ArabicNAME: El-Menshah   **AEN_Hiero:**   **AEN_Trans:** *nšyt*

Discussion: The toponym *nšyt* is listed on the Onomasticon of Amenemope and is possibly identified with the ancient Ptolemais Hermiou.[146] The Abydos list of Ramesses II and the Ramesside Papyrus Harris both place *nšyt* before *hnt-mn* (modern: Akhmim), but on the Onomasticon of Amenemope it is listed after Akhmim.[147]

ID: ThIP_UE.46   **NOME:**   **BANK:** East   **GEOREF:** 26°33′53.44″N
                    9th Capital   31°44′47.58″E

ArabicNAME: Akhmim   **AEN_Hiero:**   **AEN_Trans:** *hnt-mn*

Discussion: The capital of the Ninth Upper Egyptian Nome, *hnt-mn* Akhmim is listed on the Onomasticon of Amenemope.[148] A cartouche of Smendes was found on a re-used block from a small temple that he erected there, suggesting that the Twenty-First Dynasty at Tanis continued to erect temples in Upper Egypt. This is only the second monument of Smendes I that has been found this far south, as his only other monument comes from his stela at the Gebelein quarry. This indicates that Smendes' authority may have stretched as far as Akhmim in the early Twenty-First Dynasty.[149] Pinudjem I, Psusennes II, or Pamiu may have continued building activity at Akhmim, indicating a continued policy of conserving and restoring buildings in the area.[150] There are several Twenty-First Dynasty burials[151] and a limestone stela of Hor dated from the Twenty-Second to Twenty-Fourth Dynasty.[152] The settlement of Akhmim had a strong connection to the settlement of Thebes and the Twenty-First Dynasty family of the HPA, as Nesikhons A became the Prophetess of Min-Hor and Isis in *ipw* 'Ipu', which was an alternative name for Akhmim.[153] This allowed Nesikhons A to collect a substantial benefit for herself and the HPA at Karnak.

ID: ThIP_UE.47   **NOME:** 9th   **BANK:** NA   **GEOREF:** NA
ArabicNAME: NA   **AEN_Hiero:**   **AEN_Trans:** *pr sngr*

Discussion: The ancient site of *pr sngr* or *šngr* is listed on the Onomasticon of Amenemope.[154]

ID: ThIP_UE.48   **NOME:** 9th   **BANK:** West?   **GEOREF:** NA
ArabicNAME: NA   **AEN_Hiero:**   **AEN_Trans:** *dˁ rwh3*

Discussion: The ancient toponym of *dˁ rwh3* is translated as 'Evening Storm'.[155] In a relative north to south sequence, the toponym is to be located closer to the vicinity of Akhmim than to Qaw el-Kebir.[156] The settlement of *dˁ rwh3* was the location for a large irrigation or pleasure pool of Queen Tiy in the Eighteenth Dynasty and was a benefice in which she could draw revenue.[157] The settlement is later recorded on the Amiens Papyrus from the late Ramesside Period in relation to grain taxation, so we know it was an important centre economically before the Twenty-First Dynasty.[158] The title of governor of $ḏꜥ$ $rwḥꜣ$ is mentioned on a statue of Mermaat.[159] The location of the settlement is still unable to be assessed at this point. The mention of 'storm' in the name may indicate that it was subject to storms coming in from the desert, like the similarly named settlement of $ḏꜣnt$ 'Tanis' (modern: San el-Hagar) on the eastern Delta fringes. The Amiens Papyrus provides a small clue as to the geographical location in terms of the bank on which the settlement should be located. The text mentions that the corn was collected from the riverbank of 'Evening Storm', while the second location that grain was taken from was 'in the island to east of Evening Storm'.[160] This indicates that the settlement of Evening Storm was located close to if not on the banks of the Nile and that an island was located east of the settlement, which would indicate that the settlement was located on the West Bank of the Nile between Akhmim and Qaw el-Kebir.

ID: ThIP_UE.49 **NOME:** 10th **BANK:** NA   **GEOREF:** NA
ArabicNAME: NA   **AEN_Hiero:** 𓄤𓏛𓈖𓈏𓏥𓊖 **AEN_Trans:** sgr-$šk$
Discussion: Located near to the boundary of the Tenth Upper Egyptian Nome. Probably acted as a border fort establishment.[161]

ID: ThIP_UE.50 **NOME:** 10th **BANK:** NA   **GEOREF:** NA
ArabicNAME: NA   **AEN_Hiero:**   **AEN_Trans:** pr-$ḥr$-nb-$mḏꜣiw$
          𓉐𓂋𓅆𓈖𓃀𓏏𓈖𓏥𓊖
Discussion: This site was most likely linked with 𓄤𓏛𓈖𓈏𓏥𓊖 sgr-$šk$ in the region of the nome's southern border. 𓉐𓂋𓅆𓈖𓃀𓏏𓈖𓏥𓊖 pr-$ḥr$-nb-$mḏꜣiw$ 'The House of Horus, Lord of the Medjay' was a garrison force of police officers. Both sgr-$šk$ and pr-$ḥr$-nb-$mḏꜣiw$ 'The House of Horus, Lord of the Medjay' can be associated with defence and the control of individuals between the two regions and of movement throughout the Nile Valley in the region of the Tenth Upper Egyptian Nome.[162]

ID: ThIP_UE.51 **NOME:** 10th **BANK:** NA   **GEOREF:** NA
ArabicNAME: NA   **AEN_Hiero:**   **AEN_Trans:** $pꜣ$-sgr-ti-nt-inh
          𓉐𓄤𓃀𓏤𓈖𓋹𓊖𓉗𓏥𓊖
Discussion: $pꜣ$-sgr-ti-nt-inh is documented on P. Louvre AF 6345 and situated close to the southern border of the Tenth Upper Egyptian Nome and north of the site of 𓉗𓂓𓈎 $ḥwt$ $kꜣ$=k.[163] Both this sgr fort and 𓉐𓂋𓅆𓈖𓃀𓏏𓈖𓏥𓊖 pr-$ḥr$-nb-$mḏꜣiw$ 'The House of Horus, Lord of the Medjay' may have been located on opposite banks of the Nile Valley to increase control of river traffic.

ID: ThIP_UE.52 **NOME:** 10th **BANK:** NA   **GEOREF:** NA
ArabicNAME: NA   **AEN_Hiero:** 𓉗𓂓𓈎 **AEN_Trans:** $ḥwt$ $kꜣ$=k
Discussion: P. Louvre AF 6345 confirms that the site of 𓉗𓂓𓈎 $ḥwt$ $kꜣ$=k was located within the Tenth Upper Egyptian Nome.[164] The site of 𓉗𓂓𓈎 $ḥwt$ $kꜣ$=k is economically linked to the temple of Menkheperre-Chepsy, Prince in Hut-Kak, which suggests a foundation of Thutmose IV in Karnak or Thebes. It is important economically to note that one of the gods of the Tenth Upper Egyptian Nome benefited from a religious foundation at Thebes, as Chepsy was known as Lord of $ḥwt$ $kꜣ$=k.[165]

ID: ThIP_UE.53   **NOME:** 10th Capital   **BANK:** East   **GEOREF:** 26°52'59.09"N 31°29' 53.84"E Approximate location of the ancient settlement of Antaeopolis in 1820. Cemetery locations of the Twenty-Second and Twenty-Fifth Dynasty are located ca. 26°54'0.89"N 31°31'22.40"E.

ArabicNAME: Qaw el-Kebir   **AEN_Hiero:** 𓈎𓏤𓏤𓈍𓏤𓊖   **AEN_Trans:** ṯbw

Discussion: The ancient site of ṯbw is listed on the Onomasticon of Amenemope and is identified with the modern Qaw el-Kebir.[166] The ancient settlement was washed away by the Nile in the first half of the nineteenth century, and the Ptolemaic temple blocks re-used in a palace at Asyut.[167] The main settlement and the earlier Third Intermediate Period remains are not likely to have survived the flood, but the site is mentioned on P. Louvre AF 6345 in addition to the Onomasticon of Amenemope. Excavations at Qaw el-Kebir by the BSAE discovered several cemeteries in which a few tombs were dated to the Third Intermediate Period.[168] The tombs were divided into two groups termed 'Group A' dated to the Twenty-Second Dynasty.[169] The burials of Group B dated to the Twenty-Fifth Dynasty.[170]

ID: ThIP_UE.54   **NOME:** 10th   **BANK:** NA   **GEOREF:** NA
ArabicNAME: NA   **AEN_Hiero:** 𓉐𓏤𓊪𓏭𓏛𓊖   **AEN_Trans:** pr-[ḫn]m [...]bs

Discussion: Documented on P. Louvre AF 6345.[171] An unknown location in the Tenth Upper Egyptian Nome.

ID: ThIP_UE.55   **NOME:** 10th   **BANK:** NA   **GEOREF:** NA
ArabicNAME: NA   **AEN_Hiero:** 𓉗𓏏𓏤𓆑𓏏𓊖   **AEN_Trans:** ḥwt-ḫft

Discussion: Documented on P. Louvre AF 6345.[172] This settlement has no connection with the ḥwt-ḫft mentioned on P. Wilbour.[173]

ID: ThIP_UE.56   **NOME:** 10th   **BANK:** NA   **GEOREF:** NA
ArabicNAME: NA   **AEN_Hiero:** 𓏤𓈖𓏥𓎡𓏤𓈐𓊖   **AEN_Trans:** pȝ-kȝ-tȝ

Discussion: Documented on P. Louvre AF 6345.[174] An unknown location in the Tenth Upper Egyptian Nome.

ID: ThIP_UE.57   **NOME:** 10th   **BANK:** NA   **GEOREF:** NA
ArabicNAME: NA   **AEN_Hiero:** 𓏤𓂋𓏤𓃀𓏛𓊖   **AEN_Trans:** inr-mry

Discussion: Documented on P. Louvre AF 6345.[175] An unknown location in the Tenth Upper Egyptian Nome.

ID: ThIP_UE.58   **NOME:** 10th   **BANK:** NA   **GEOREF:** NA
ArabicNAME: NA   **AEN_Hiero:** 𓈖𓏤𓏏𓏤𓃀𓊖   **AEN_Trans:** [i]ȝt bȝ

Discussion: Documented on P. Louvre AF 6345.[176] An unknown location in the Tenth Upper Egyptian Nome.

ID:ThIP_UE.59   **NOME**: 10th   **BANK**: NA   **GEOREF**: NA
ArabicNAME: NA   **AEN_Hiero**:   **AEN_Trans**: *iȝt-ity*

Discussion: Documented on P. Louvre AF 6345.[177] An unknown location in the Tenth Upper Egyptian Nome.

ID:ThIP_UE.60   **NOME**: 10th   **BANK**: NA   **GEOREF**: NA
ArabicNAME: NA   **AEN_Hiero**:   **AEN_Trans**: *Pȝ-nḥsy*

Discussion: Documented on P. Louvre AF 6345.[178] An unknown location in the Tenth Upper Egyptian Nome.

ID:ThIP_UE.61   **NOME**: 10th   **BANK**: NA   **GEOREF**: NA
ArabicNAME: NA   **AEN_Hiero**:   **AEN_Trans**: *pr-nḥb-n-išȝ*

Discussion: *pr-nḥb-n-išȝ* 'The House of the Opened Land of Isha' or just 'The Newly Opened Land of Isha' is listed on the Onomasticon of Amenemope.[179]

ID:ThIP_UE.62   **NOME**: 10th   **BANK**: West   **GEOREF**: 26°50′36.04″N
                                                                                      31°25′19.62″E
ArabicNAME: Kom Ishkaw   **AEN_Hiero**:   **AEN_Trans**: *wȝḏt*

Discussion: *wȝḏt* is only mentioned on the Onomasticon of Amenemope.[180] There is, so far, no more evidence for the settlement of *wȝḏt* for the remainder of the Third Intermediate Period.

ID:ThIP_UE.63   **NOME**: 10th   **BANK**: NA   **GEOREF**: NA
ArabicNAME: NA   **AEN_Hiero**:   **AEN_Trans**: *tȝ-nt-ḥry-ṯbw*

Discussion: *tȝ-nt-ḥry-ṯbw* is listed on P. Louvre AF 6345.[181] This toponym is so far unidentified with a modern location. It must have been near ṯbw.

ID:ThIP_UE.64   **NOME**: 10th   **BANK**: NA   **GEOREF**: NA
ArabicNAME: NA   **AEN_Hiero**:   **AEN_Trans**: *mw.t nb.t*
                                                                                      mgb

Discussion: The goddess Mut was worshipped in the Tenth Upper Egyptian Nome as a Middle Kingdom/Second Intermediate Period statue mentions Mut as *mw.t nb.t mgb* 'Mut Mistress of Megeb,[182] which is mentioned on the Onomasticon of Amenemope but has the writing *pr-mwt-nbt-mgn* 'The House of Mut Mistress of Megen'.[183] It is likely that this is a faulty writing of Megeb and that we have here reference to one of the cult centres of Mut that was active in the early Twenty-First Dynasty.

ID:ThIP_UE.65   **NOME**: 10th   **BANK**: Island   **GEOREF**: NA
ArabicNAME: NA   **AEN_Hiero**:   **AEN_Trans**: *in-mwt*

Discussion: The second most economically important settlement on the P. Louvre AF 6345 taxation list at the start of the Third Intermediate Period is that of *in-mwt*.[184] The Chronicle of Prince Osorkon mentions this toponym in connection with a benefaction of one *heqat* of grain to be given daily to a temple of Amenemope in Year 24 month 4 of Takeloth II.[185] The text provides additional geographic evidence, saying that it was *iw n in-mwt* 'The Island of Inmut'.

ID: ThIP_UE.66 **NOME:** 10th **BANK:** NA   **GEOREF:** NA
ArabicNAME: NA   **AEN_Hiero:** ☐𓏤𓇌𓄿𓊱☐ **AEN_Trans:** *pr-wḏy*

Discussion: A town that appears to have retained a large amount of both its economic and political importance during the start of the Twenty-First Dynasty was that of ☐𓇌𓄿𓊱☐ *pr-wḏy* 'The Village of the Stela', which is listed on P. Louvre AF 6345.[186] The site of *pr-wḏy* is recorded again later on the Onomasticon of Amenemope,[187] but has the writing ☐𓇌𓄿. This location is mentioned on the tomb robbery papyrus where there is a mention of *pr-wḏy*.[188]

ID: ThIP_UE.67 **NOME:** 10th **BANK:** NA   **GEOREF:** NA
ArabicNAME: NA   **AEN_Hiero:** 𓂋𓈖𓏤𓏤𓍿 **AEN_Trans:** *mḥw-n-'ntywy*

Discussion: This toponym is listed only on the Onomasticon of Amenemope.[189] It is not identified with any modern toponym.

ID: ThIP_UE.68 **NOME:** 10th **BANK:** NA   **GEOREF:** NA
ArabicNAME: NA   **AEN_Hiero:** 𓆑[▨▨▨]�� **AEN_Trans:** NA

Discussion: This toponym has an uncertain reading. It is listed on P. Louvre AF 6345.[190]

ID: ThIP_UE.69 **NOME:** 10th **BANK:** NA   **GEOREF:** NA
ArabicNAME: NA   **AEN_Hiero:**   **AEN_Trans:** *idb pȝ dšr /*
                            ��𓎛𓈖𓏤𓈗𓂋𓏺   *pȝ dšr*

Discussion: *idb pȝ dšr / pȝ dšr* is listed on P. Louvre AF 6345.[191] The writing is unclear, possibly *idb pȝ dšr* or 𓈖 serves as the determinative for the previous word and we are to read the toponym as *pȝ dšr* 'The Red'.[192]

ID: ThIP_UE.70 **NOME:** 10th **BANK:** NA   **GEOREF:** NA
ArabicNAME: NA   **AEN_Hiero:** 𓉐𓂓𓅓𓅓𓏥 **AEN_Trans:** *pr kmkm*

Discussion: *pr kmkm* is listed on P. Louvre AF 6345.[193] This *pr kmkm* is not to be associated with the toponym of *pr kmkm* in relation to the site of Armant.[194]

ID: ThIP_UE.71 **NOME:** 10th **BANK:** NA   **GEOREF:** NA
ArabicNAME: NA   **AEN_Hiero:**   **AEN_Trans:** *[. . .] mȝ mntw*
                            𓈗𓂋𓈖𓇳𓆄𓏤𓈗   *nb [. . .]*

Discussion: *[. . .] mȝ mntw nb [. . .]* is listed on P. Louvre AF 6345.[195] *[. . .] mȝ mntw nb [. . .]* may be read 'The New [Foundation] of Montu Lord of [. . .]'. This toponym has not been identified with a modern toponym.

ID: ThIP_UE.72 **NOME:** 10th **BANK:** NA   **GEOREF:** NA
ArabicNAME: NA   **AEN_Hiero:**   **AEN_Trans:** NA
                            𓈖𓈗𓂋𓈖𓊃𓏤𓎟𓆄

Discussion: This toponym with an uncertain reading is listed on P. Louvre AF 6345.[196]

ID: ThIP_UE.73 **NOME:** 10th **BANK:** NA   **GEOREF:** NA
ArabicNAME: NA   **AEN_Hiero:**   **AEN_Trans:** *[. . .]š-m-r-ky*
                            𓈗𓈖𓂋𓈒𓊃𓏤𓐍

Discussion: *[. . .]š-m-r-ky* is listed on P. Louvre AF 6345.[197] The final part of the name is translated as ' . . . shemerki', but this toponym is not identified with a modern Arabic toponym.

ID: ThIP_UE.74 **NOME:** 10th **BANK:** NA   **GEOREF:** NA
ArabicNAME: NA   **AEN_Hiero:** 𓊪𓈖𓏏𓂝𓈖 **AEN_Trans:** *sgr-ᶜn*
Discussion: *sgr-ᶜn* is listed on P. Louvre AF 6345.[198] This *sgr* fort has not been identified with a modern toponym.

ID: ThIP_UE.75 **NOME:** 10th **BANK:** NA   **GEOREF:** NA
ArabicNAME: NA   **AEN_Hiero:** 𓊪𓈖𓏏𓂝𓈖 **AEN_Trans:** *sgr-h₃nw*
Discussion: *sgr-h₃nw* is listed on P. Louvre AF 6346.[199] *sgr-h₃nw* is located to the north of the unidentified 𓊪𓈖𓏏𓂝𓈖 *inr-mry* 'Inermery', which is listed on P. Louvre AF 6345.[200]

ID: ThIP_UE.76 **NOME:** 10th **BANK:** NA   **GEOREF:** NA
ArabicNAME: NA   **AEN_Hiero:** 𓊪𓈖𓏏𓂝𓈖 **AEN_Trans:** *sgr-sk*
Discussion: *sgr-sk* is listed on P. Louvre AF 6346,[201] but is not identified with a modern toponym.

ID: ThIP_UE.77 **NOME:** 10th **BANK:** NA   **GEOREF:** NA
ArabicNAME: NA   **AEN_Hiero:** 𓊪𓈖𓏏𓂝𓈖 **AEN_Trans:** *Sgr* . . .
Discussion: *Sgr* . . . is listed on P. Louvre AF 6345.[202] The remaining part of the name is missing. This site has not been identified.

ID: ThIP_UE.78 **NOME:** 10th **BANK:** NA   **GEOREF:** NA
ArabicNAME: NA   **AEN_Hiero:** 𓊪𓈖𓏏𓂝𓈖 **AEN_Trans:** *sgr-š₃g* . . .
Discussion: *sgr-š₃g* . . . is listed on P. Louvre AF 6345,[203] but is not identified with a modern toponym.

ID: ThIP_UE.79 **NOME:** 11th **BANK:** West   **GEOREF:** 27°8′41.67″N
                   Capital   31°14′21.15″E
ArabicNAME: Shutb   **AEN_Hiero:** 𓊪𓈖𓏏𓂝𓈖 **AEN_Trans:** *š₃-ḥtp*
Discussion: The ancient capital of the Tenth Upper Egyptian Nome, *š₃-ḥtp* (modern: Shutb) is listed on the Onomasticon of Amenemope,[204] but apart from this no more is known about the settlement for the Third Intermediate Period.

ID: ThIP_UE.80 **NOME:** 12th **BANK:** East   **GEOREF:** 27°14′18.66″N
                   Capital   31°12′55.52″E
ArabicNAME: El-Atawla   **AEN_Hiero:** 𓊪𓈖𓏏𓂝𓈖 **AEN_Trans:** *pr-nmty*
Discussion: The ancient settlement of 𓊪𓈖𓏏𓂝𓈖 *pr-nmty* (modern: el-Atawla) is synonymous with 𓊪𓈖𓏏𓂝𓈖 *dw-fyt* as there are several attestations to the god Nemty and this ancient toponym in the New Kingdom,[205] and later in the reign of Psammetik I.[206] During the Twenty-First Dynasty the Greenfields Papyrus records that the daughter of Pinudjem II, Nesitanebtashru, is given the benefice and title of Prophetess of 𓊪𓈖𓏏𓂝𓈖 *dw-fyt*, like her mother, Nesikhons, before her.[207]

ID: ThIP_UE.81 **NOME:** 12th **BANK:** East   **GEOREF:** 27°6′14.56″N
                                                           31°19′58.08″E
ArabicNAME: Matmar   **AEN_Hiero:** NA   **AEN_Trans:** NA
Discussion: A considerable amount of evidence for Third Intermediate Period burials and burial customs of a non-elite population were found at Matmar, along with domestic evidence found within the New Kingdom temple temenos walls.[208]

ID: ThIP_UE.82 **NOME:** 12th **BANK:** NA   **GEOREF:** NA
ArabicNAME: NA   **AEN_Hiero:** 🏠 **AEN_Trans:** *pr-mwt*

Discussion: The ancient settlement of *pr-mwt* is listed on the Onomasticon of Amenemope,[209] but no more is known about this settlement for the rest of the Third Intermediate Period.

ID: ThIP_UE.83 **NOME:** 13th **BANK:** West   **GEOREF:** 27°10′43.96″N
                    Capital   31°11′13.02″E
ArabicNAME: Asyut   **AEN_Hiero:** 🦅 **AEN_Trans:** *s3wty*

Discussion: The ancient capital of the Thirteenth Upper Egyptian Nome, *s3wty* is listed on the Onomasticon of Amenemope,[210] but little is known about the settlement for the Third Intermediate Period. At least two coffins are dated stylistically to the Third Intermediate Period and find the closest parallels from the tomb of Iurudef at Saqqara, which can be dated to the Twentieth to Twenty-First Dynasty.[211] These dates for a Twenty-First Dynasty cemetery would correspond to the mention of the settlement on the Onomasticon of Amenemope. Asyut may have developed into an important regional political centre in the late Third Intermediate Period. There is evidence of a possible local ruler called Padinemty (cartouche), known from a copy of his Book of the Dead, but this is not confirmed.[212]

ID: ThIP_UE.84 **NOME:** 13th **BANK:** NA   **GEOREF:** NA
ArabicNAME: NA   **AEN_Hiero:** 🏠 **AEN_Trans:** *pr-sḥmy*

Discussion: *pr-sḥmy* is listed on the Onomasticon of Amenemope,[213] but no more is known about this settlement for the remainder of the Third Intermediate Period.

ID: ThIP_UE.85 **NOME:** 13th **BANK:** NA   **GEOREF:** NA
ArabicNAME: NA   **AEN_Hiero:** 🏠 **AEN_Trans:** *pgs*

Discussion: The ancient settlement of *pgs* is listed on the Onomasticon of Amenemope,[214] but no more is known about this settlement for the remainder of the Third Intermediate Period.

ID: ThIP_UE.86 **NOME:** 14th **BANK:** West   **GEOREF:** 27°26′19.78″N
                    Capital   30°49′10.70″E
ArabicNAME: El-Quseyah   **AEN_Hiero:** 🏠 **AEN_Trans:** *ḳis*

Discussion: The ancient capital of the Fourteenth Upper Egyptian Nome, 🏠 *ḳis* (modern: el-Quseyah) is listed on the Onomasticon of Amenemope,[215] but no more is known about the capital for the remainder of the Third Intermediate Period.

ID: ThIP_UE.87   **NOME:** 14th   **BANK:** NA   **GEOREF:** NA
ArabicNAME: NA   **AEN_Hiero:** 🏠 **AEN_Trans:** *snnḳ*

Discussion: The settlement of 🏠 *snnḳ* is listed on the Onomasticon of Amenemope,[216] but no more is known about this settlement for the remainder of the Third Intermediate Period.

ID: **NOME:**   **BANK:** East   **GEOREF:** El-Hagg Qandil (27°
ThIP_UE.88 15th   37′37.74″N 30°53′2.68″E) (Amarna
                                                    Cemetery) 27°38′37.54″N 30°53′
                                                    54.16″E
ArabicNAME: El-Hagg   **AEN_Hiero:** 🏠 **AEN_Trans:** *pr-šs*
Qandil (+ Amarna)

Discussion: A domestic area was identified at el-Hagg Qandil 'The House of Alabaster' (?). The site of *pr-šs* 'The House of Alabaster' may lie to the south of Amarna at el-Hagg Qandil, where the remains of Twenty-First Dynasty domestic activity have been located.[217] It has also been positioned at the site of el-Sheikh Sa'id.[218] It was argued that *pr-šs* was the ancestral place name of the modern el-Bersheh, and it may have originally designated an industrial site at the entrance of the Wadi Zabayda close to where the Sheikh Sa'id tombs are, a place in which alabaster was worked. Recent excavations have produced evidence of a calcite quarry closer to the site of el-Bersheh, which suggests that the name *pr-šs* may have been a designation for this quarry.[219] The absence of Twenty-First Dynasty material at the site of el-Bersheh would suggest that, for the Third Intermediate Period, the location of this *pr-šs* should be located closer to the site of Amarna and the tombs at Sheikh Sa'id. Cemetery area (*Amarna*): An intact burial from the workmen's village has been dated on stylistic grounds of the coffin to the late twelfth or early eleventh century BCE, whilst the pottery comprises well-known Twentieth and Twenty-First Dynasty types.[220] Pottery thrown out of the south tombs at Amarna has shown that these tombs were re-used at some point in the Twenty-Fifth Dynasty.[221]

ID: ThIP_UE.89 **NOME:** 15th **BANK:** West   **GEOREF:** 27°46'53.29"N
                  Capital   30°48'9.89"E
ArabicNAME: El-Ashmunein   **AEN_Hiero:** 🦉 **AEN_Trans:** *wnw*

Discussion: The ancient capital of the Fifteenth Upper Egyptian Nome was at 🦉 *wnw* (classical: Hermopolis), the modern el-Ashmunein. 🦉 *wnw* became the seat of a series of local kings in the latter part of the Third Intermediate Period and was an important strategic location in the invasion stela of Piankhy. Excavations at the site by both the German Expedition to Hermopolis in 1929–39 and the British Museum excavations between 1980 and 1990 have produced evidence of the Third Intermediate Period settlement to the west of the New Kingdom temple of Thoth.[222] Numerous Third Intermediate Period monuments from the site attest to the settlement's political importance throughout the period. The monuments from el-Ashmunein include fragments of a Year 15 stela of Osorkon III,[223] and blocks of Osorkon III, all found in the temple of Thoth.[224] Other monuments, probably of the reign of Osorkon III, include a statue base of the king from the Thoth temple.[225] From the reign of Rudamun, a fragment of a faience royal statue was found,[226] along with a fragment of a faience sistrum.[227] About 1 km to the north of the main ruin field of Ashmunein, at the site of Ezbet el-Idara, a fragment of a Middle Kingdom royal statue was re-used for Thutemhat.[228] The small village now borders the ancient ruin mound and has been taken as being part of the wider ruin field. Finally, excavations inside the Thoth temple found the remains of what are likely to be the burial chapels in the forecourt of the temple that belonged to local elites, high priests of Ptah, or even the local rulers.[229]

ID: ThIP_UE.90 **NOME:** 15th **BANK:** West   **GEOREF:** 27°54'52.60"N
                                                             30°45'37.09"E
ArabicNAME: Jarris?   **AEN_Hiero:** 𓈖𓆑𓂋𓅱𓋴𓇌𓊖 **AEN_Trans:** *nfrw-sy*

Discussion: The fortress of *nfrw-sy* is listed on the Onomasticon of Amenemope.[230] The location of the fort has been said to be 7 km away from Hur to the north of el-Ashmunein,[231] in the area of Sheikh Abada,[232] opposite el-Ashmunein on the East Bank of the Nile,[233] at the modern site of Itlidem,[234] or at Jarris, 16 km to the north of el-Ashmunein.[235] The nature of the site is likely to be militarised, and has been defined as a fortress.[236] Neferusy continued to be used throughout the Third Intermediate Period, as it is one of the fortresses that Piankhy had to defeat in the battle for Middle Egypt, and is again located close to the Nome border between the Fifteenth and the Sixteenth Nome. A reassessment of the material relating to the location of Neferusy came no closer to the conclusion of where this site was located within Middle Egypt.[237]

ID: ThIP_UE.91 **NOME:** 15th   **BANK:** West   **GEOREF:** 27°51′34.76″N
                                                                    30°43′52.59″E
ArabicNAME: Hur   **AEN_Hiero:** 𓉐𓉐𓄿𓎛𓏏   **AEN_Trans:** *ḥwt wrt*
Discussion: *ḥwt wrt* is listed on the Onomasticon of Amenemope,[238] and the Piankhy
Stela, and is located near the desert to the north of el-Ashmunein and to the south of
Itlidem.

Region of Akoris to Atfih (Sixteenth to Twenty-Second Upper Egyptian Nomes): Approximate Boundaries of P. Wilbour

ID: ThIP_UE.92 **NOME:**   **BANK:** NA   **GEOREF:** NA
                  A–A (16th)
ArabicNAME: NA   **AEN_Hiero:** 𓉐𓂋𓈙𓏤𓅱   **AEN_Trans:** *pr wḏy*
Discussion: A 𓉐𓂋𓈙𓏤𓅱 *pr wḏy* is mentioned, but unlike the previous settlement
located in the Tenth Upper Nome, this one has no external geographic evidence to
suggest a location. It is likely to be situated to the south of the Speos Artemidos,[239] or
near Tahnasa.[240]

ID: ThIP_UE.93 **NOME:**   **BANK:** East   **GEOREF:** 27°54′13.87″N
                  A–A (16th)   30°52′17.84″E
ArabicNAME: Istabl Antar   **AEN_Hiero:** 𓉐𓈖𓃀𓏏   **AEN_Trans:** *pr-nbt-in(t)*
Discussion: In 1902–4 rock-cut tombs in the cliffs to the north of the Speos Artemidos
were excavated and dated to the Twentieth to Thirtieth Dynasty.[241] They have since
been re-dated to the Twenty-Second to Twenty-Fifth Dynasty.[242] *pr-nbt-in(t)* is
recorded on the Onomasticon of Amenemope and may have formed a small cultic
settlement associated with the cemetery to the north of Speos Artemidos.

ID: ThIP_UE.94 **NOME:** A–A   **BANK:** East   **GEOREF:** 28°2′40.09″N
                  (16th Capital)   30°49′50.05″E
ArabicNAME: Zawyat el-Amwat/   **AEN_Hiero:** 𓍛𓏤   **AEN_Trans:** *ḥbnw*
Zawyat el-Maiyitin.
Discussion: *ḥbnw* was the ancient capital of the Sixteenth Upper Egyptian Nome. It is
mentioned on the Onomasticon of Amenemope,[243] and again on the Piankhy Stela,
but no more is known about the development of this nome capital throughout the
period.

ID: ThIP_UE.95 **NOME:**   **BANK:** East   **GEOREF:** 28°7′5.38″N
                  A–A (16th)   30°46′21.35″E
ArabicNAME: Nazlet   **AEN_Hiero:** NA   **AEN_Trans:** NA
esh-Shurafa
Discussion: Stamped bricks of the HPA Menkheperre[244] suggest the presence of
a fortress at this site. A statue of Khaemwese, son of Ramesses II, was also found here,[245]
which may indicate Menkheperre was continuing the construction and use of
a Ramesside fortress in this area.

ID: ThIP_UE.96 **NOME:**   **BANK:** East   **GEOREF:** 28°11′2.50″N
                  A–A (17th)   30°46′34.81″E
ArabicNAME: Tihna   **AEN_Hiero:** 𓉐𓂸𓈘𓅱   **AEN_Trans:** *pr-mꜣiw*
Discussion: The Onomasticon of Amenemope lists Tihna (classical: Akoris) as *pr-
mꜣiw*.[246] The fortified site of Tihna (Akoris) has substantial evidence of Third
Intermediate Period domestic activity. The site is located on the border of the

Sixteenth Nome, placing it in a good strategic location in the Heracleopolitan region. A cemetery of the period was also found,[247] along with temple building activity at the site, as is indicated by a foundation inscription of Osorkon III.[248]

ID: ThIP_UE.97 **NOME:** A–A (17th) **BANK:** West **GEOREF:** 28°18′32.74″N 30°42′42.09″E

ArabicNAME: Samalut **AEN_Hiero:** 𓏴𓏏𓊖 **AEN_Trans:** *mn-ꜥnḫ*

Discussion: *mn-ꜥnḫ* is listed on the Onomasticon of Amenemope and is equated with the modern Samalut.[249]

ID: ThIP_UE.98 **NOME:** A–A (17th) **BANK:** NA **GEOREF:** NA

ArabicNAME: Unknown **AEN_Hiero:** 𓃛𓅱𓉔𓇌𓏏𓈖𓇌𓂋𓇌𓊨𓏏 **AEN_Trans:** *tꜣwḥy.t-n-iry-st*

Discussion: *tꜣwḥy.t-n-iry-st* is an unknown location listed on the Onomasticon of Amenemope, but geographically it should be located between el-Kes and Kom el-Ahmar, near Sharuna.[250]

ID: ThIP_UE.99 **NOME:** A–A (17th Capital) **BANK:** East **GEOREF:** 28°29′17.93″N 30°50′54.99″E

ArabicNAME: Esh-Sheikh el-Fadl (Hardai) **AEN_Hiero:** 𓃞𓂧𓊖 **AEN_Trans:** *ḥr-di*

Discussion: *ḥr-di* documented on the Onomasticon of Amenemope is equated with the modern esh-Sheikh el-Fadl.[251]

ID: ThIP_UE.100 **NOME:** A–A (17th Capital) **BANK:** West **GEOREF:** 28°28′49.14″N 30°47′4.66″E

ArabicNAME: El-Kes **AEN_Hiero:** 𓊽𓆑𓎡𓏤𓊖 **AEN_Trans:** *sꜣ-kꜣ*

Discussion: *sꜣ-kꜣ* is the modern el-Kes. It is listed on the Onomasticon of Amenemope.[252]

ID: ThIP_UE.101 **NOME:** A–A (18th Capital) **BANK:** East **GEOREF:** 28°34′51.61″N 30°51′27.53″E

ArabicNAME: Kom el-Ahmar (Sawaris) **AEN_Hiero:** 𓉗𓈖𓇓𓊖 **AEN_Trans:** *ḥwt – nsw*

Discussion: *ḥwt – nsw* is located at Kom el-Ahmar near Sharuna in the Eighteenth Upper Egyptian Nome and was the capital of the nome. It is documented on the Piankhy Stela.[253] Kom el-Ahmar (Sawaris) is an extensive kom in the region of the village of Ezbet el-Kom el-Ahmar, about halfway between el-Gharabi in the south and Sharuna in the north. Parts of the original koms have been removed for the recovery of farmland. The whole area is scattered with many ceramics, which can be dated primarily to the Late Antique Period. Fragments of relief blocks mostly come from a temple of the early Ptolemaic Period.[254] Remains of a temple that may be the same as the Ptolemaic temple were observed by Nestor l'Hote in the early nineteenth century.[255] The standing masonry was demolished in the late nineteenth century for the production of building materials.[256] On flat land east of the kom lies an extensive necropolis, which takes the name el-Kom el-Ahmar Sawaris.[257] The necropolis is covered in burials and shafts. It has tombs of the Ptolemaic–Roman Period,[258] and also many important tombs of the Old Kingdom.[259] Only evidence from textual sources confirms that the site of *ḥwt – nsw* was active as an important settlement during the Third Intermediate Period as, so far, no archaeological evidence has been located for a presence on the preserved parts of the mound and burial ground.

ID:	**NOME:**	**BANK:** NA	**GEOREF:** NA
ThIP_UE.102	A–A (18th)		
ArabicNAME: NA		**AEN_Hiero:** 🪶⊚	**AEN_Trans:** *ḥwt-rdw*

Discussion: *ḥwt-rdw* 'The House of the Redu Bird'[260] is documented on the Piankhy Stela in association with el-Hibeh. *ḥwt-rdw* is in the Eighteenth Upper Egyptian Nome but has so far not been identified. The settlement of *ḥwt-rdw* was an important settlement on the East Bank of the Nile and the name has been known from the Old Kingdom. The settlement name is recorded on a stela of Bebi from the necropolis of Kom el-Ahmar near Sharuna, citing Anubis as Lord of *ḥwt-rdw*.[261] In three other tombs belonging to Iuhi, Sabi, and Mentinefer of the same necropolis, this is a title given to Anubis.[262] There is a hiatus of the name in the Middle Kingdom, but it appears again in the Twenty-Fifth Dynasty with the invasion of Piankhy.[263] Some scholars place the location of the settlement at the modern Sharuna,[264] while others place it between el-Kom el-Ahmar in the north and esh-Sheikh el-Fadl in the south.[265] The presence of the titles in association with *ḥwt-rdw* in the necropolis of el-Kom el-Ahmar indicates the site is close to the necropolis, probably directly opposite *ḥwt – nsw* in the area of Ezbet Kom el-Ahmar; in any case, closer to here than to Sharuna or south of Kom el-Ahmar. Both cities of *ḥwt – nsw* and *ḥwt-rdw* were originally two adjacent places that grew together over the course of history.[266]

ID:	**NOME:**	**BANK:** East	**GEOREF:** 28°47′12.27″N
ThIP_UE.103	A–A (18th)		30°55′16.98″E
ArabicNAME: El-Hibeh		**AEN_Hiero:** 𓄿𓈖𓈙𓏏𓏏𓊖	**AEN_Trans:** *ꜣyw-ḏꜣyt* and
		or 𓄿𓏤𓎡𓈖𓐍𓏏𓈅𓈇	*wr ḏhnt wr nhtw*

Discussion: El-Hibeh was the territorial land boundary for the HPA in the Twenty-First Dynasty. It is documented under two names during the Third Intermediate Period. The first name was *Tꜣyw-ḏꜣyt* 'Their Walls', which is documented on the Piankhy Stela, and the second is 𓄿𓈖𓈙𓊖 *tꜣ(y.w)-ḏꜣy(t)* from a wooden fragment found at either el-Hibeh or Thebes, dated to the Libyan Period.[267] The identification of el-Hibeh with the Coptic ΤΕΥΧΟ or ΤΟΥΧΟΙ has been known for a long time and can be considered secure.[268] Later in the period Piankhy engages the *tꜣ-thn-wr-nhtw* 'The Crag Great of Victories'. The later Prince of the West, Tefnakht, on the invasion of Piankhy, had entrusted two fortresses to his sons in Middle Egypt, one of which was el-Hibeh.[269] This signifies the continuing importance of this region as a heavily fortified and strategic location for the duration of the Third Intermediate Period. This site highlights the nature of site names changing as the period goes on, and the problems of assuming only one toponym relates to one site. An Italian expedition working in the cemeteries of el-Hibeh also found many late Third Intermediate Period coffins.[270]

ID:	**NOME:**	**BANK:** West (west of	**GEOREF:** 28°32′22.74″N
ThIP_UE.104	A–A (19th)	the Bahr Yusef)	30°39′25.84″E
ArabicNAME: El-Bahnasa		**AEN_Hiero:** 𓉐𓏤𓄓𓊖	**AEN_Trans:** *pr-mḏd*

Discussion: *pr-mḏd* (classical: Oxyrhynchus; modern: el-Bahnasa) is first attested on the Piankhy Stela, but there is evidence from P. Wilbour of a Per Medjay which may have been an earlier spelling of the settlement in the Twentieth Dynasty.

ID: ThIP_UE.105   **NOME:** A–A (19th)   **BANK:** West (west of Bahr Yusef)   **GEOREF:** 28°52′21.82″N 30°47′55.66″E

ArabicNAME: Kom el-Ahmar   **AEN_Hiero:** 𓎛𓊖   **AEN_Trans:** *ṯkꜣ-nš*

Discussion: Another toponym associated with Kom el-Ahmar (Sawaris) is 𓎛𓊖 *ṯkꜣ-nš*, just to the north of Oxyrhynchus.[271] The affiliation of Kom el-Ahmar near Mazura with the Coptic TAKINAW, the Greek Takova and the ancient Egyptian *ṯkꜣ-nš*, can be regarded as secure.[272]

ID: ThIP_UE.106   **NOME:** A–A (19th Capital)   **BANK:** West (near Bahr Yusef)   **GEOREF:** NA

ArabicNAME: NA   **AEN_Hiero:** 𓂋𓊪𓂋𓅱𓊖   **AEN_Trans:** *spr-mrw*

Discussion: Spermeru, the capital of the Nineteenth Upper Egyptian Nome, is only documented on the Onomasticon of Amenemope.[273] No more is known about this location for the Third Intermediate Period.

ID: ThIP_UE.107   **NOME:** A–A (20th Capital)   **BANK:** West   **GEOREF:** 29°5′7.84″N 30°56′15.26″E

ArabicNAME: Ehnasya el-Medina   **AEN_Hiero:** 𓇗𓆑𓈖𓊖   **AEN_Trans:** *nn-nsw*

Discussion: The capital of the Twentieth Upper Egyptian Nome was *nn-nsw* (classical: Heracleopolis Magna), now the modern Ehnasya el-Medina. This was one of the main political centres of the period. In addition to the main settlement and necropolis, the cultic toponym 𓃻𓈖𓆑𓊖 *nꜣrf* Naref[274] is mentioned on other Third Intermediate Period monuments, all in association with the Heracleopolitan region.[275] The toponym Naref is associated with the god Osiris in religious contexts and is confined to the Heracleopolitan Region. The toponym was conceived under the dual nature of an aspect of the god Osiris in the Heracleopolitan region and a mythical local place name.[276] Another cultic toponym associated with Heracleopolis is 𓃒.[277] The final toponym is 𓈐𓎡𓎡𓏭𓊖 *iꜣt kyky* 'The Mound of the Kyky Plant'.[278] This location is either a religious neighbourhood or location of another settlement temple of Heracleopolis.[279]

Sites in Association with the Heracleopolitan Hinterland (No Additional Evidence to Place in Geographical Order)

ID: ThIP_UE.108   **NOME:** A–A (HH)   **BANK:** NA   **GEOREF:** NA

ArabicNAME: NA   **AEN_Hiero:** 𓌉𓄿𓉐𓅓𓂝𓊖   **AEN_Trans:** *pꜣ nḫtw n mr-mšꜥ.f*

Discussion: *pꜣ nḫtw n mr-mšꜥ.f* 'The Fortress of Mer-Meshaf' is mentioned on five documents dating from between the reigns of Ramesses III and Shoshenq I.[280] Two of the five monuments date to the Third Intermediate Period. The first is from a block of Shoshenq I and has the writing 𓌉𓄿𓉐𓅓𓂝𓊖 *pꜣ nḫtw n mr-mšꜥ.f* 'The Fortress of Mer-Meshaf'.[281] The second is from a stela found in the temple of Heracleopolis belonging to a Sethemheb, dating to either the end of the New Kingdom or the Twenty-First Dynasty.[282] Sethemheb is described as being 'head of 𓌉𓄿𓉐𓂻𓉐𓊖 *pꜣ nḫtw n mr-mšꜥ.f* The Fortress of Mer-Meshaf'. The Fortress of Mer-Meshaf originally comprised a temple along with a fortress, and was originally founded by Ramesses II.[283]

A donation stela of Ramesses III records the name 𓃀𓏤𓉐𓏤𓇳𓁐𓎛𓏏𓊹𓊹 *r ḥwt-nṯr rꜥ-ms. sw mry-imn mr-mšꜥ.f* 'The Temple of Ramesses beloved of Amun of Mer-Meshaf',[284] and the name is met again on P. Wilbour as 𓉐𓏤𓇳𓁐𓈖𓏥𓎛𓏏𓊹𓊹 *ḥwt-nṯr rꜥ-ms. sw mry-imn ꜥnḫ wḏꜣ snb mr-mšꜥ.f* 'The Temple of Ramesses beloved of Amun, Life, Prosperity, Health, Mer-Meshaf'.[285] By Year 17 of Ramesses IX the name of Ramesses II is lost from the title and it is simply called Mer-Meshaf,[286] a name which is retained into the Third Intermediate Period and on the monuments of Shoshenq I and Sethemheb. There is no evidence in the Ptolemaic–Roman toponyms that indicates a precise location for the fortress,[287] but the mention on the Heracleopolitan monuments indicates that it was near Heracleopolis. The toponym has been suggested to be at several locations including Barmacha (south of Heracleopolis (Minya Province) to the west of Maghagha),[288] near to the Faiyum entrance,[289] and to the north of Heracleopolis, not far from Gurob where it could act as a way of controlling Western Desert peoples entering the Nile Valley.[290]

ID:	NOME:	BANK: NA	GEOREF: NA
ThIP_UE.109	A–A (HH)		
ArabicNAME: NA		AEN_Hiero:	AEN_Trans: *pꜣ nḫtw ꜥꜣ (n)*
		𓉗𓂝𓏏𓎛𓈖𓄿𓏛𓇳𓊃𓂝	*wsr-mꜣꜥt-rꜥ*

Discussion: Two monuments document the existence of the 'Fortress of Usermaatre'. The first is a stela dated to either the end of the New Kingdom or the start of the Twenty-First Dynasty, which mentions a Sherden soldier called Pa-Djesef of 𓉗𓂝𓏏𓎛𓈖𓄿𓏛𓇳𓊃𓂝 *pꜣ nḫtw ꜥꜣ (n) wsr-mꜣꜥt-rꜥ* 'The Great Fortress of Usermaatre', which was found in the temple at Heracleopolis.[291] The fort is also mentioned on the block of Shoshenq I in relation to 𓉗𓂝𓏏𓇳𓊃𓂝 *pꜣ ꜥꜣ n twḥr n wsr-mꜣꜥt-rꜥ* 'The Great of the Touher of Usermaatre'.[292] The fortress was likely founded in the reign of Ramesses II,[293] and the monuments recovered indicate that soldiers were stationed there, as there is mention of Pa-Djesef the Sherden, linking him to the Sea Peoples, and the block of Shoshenq I mentions the Great of the Touher of Usermaatre, indicating that by the Twenty-Second Dynasty the fortress was home to the elite chariot drivers of possible foreign origin.[294] The fortress has not been found, but like 'The Fortress of Mer-Meshaf', it should be located in the Heracleopolitan region based on its association with Heracleopolitan monuments and individuals.

ID: ThIP_UE.	NOME:	BANK: NA	GEOREF: NA
110–114	A–A (HH)		
ArabicNAME: NA		AEN_Hiero:	AEN_Trans: *(m) ḥꜣt pꜣ 5*
		𓂧𓈋𓏤𓏭𓏤𓈖𓏏𓏥𓊖	*nḫtw ꜥꜣ n n(ꜣ) mꜥ*

Discussion: The Five Great Fortresses of the Ma is a toponym that is unknown before the Third Intermediate Period. The location is mentioned on two monuments. The first is a door found in the cemetery at Heracleopolis belonging to the general and first prophet of Heryshef, Amenhaemopet, who is 𓂧𓈋𓏤𓏭𓏤𓈖𓏏𓏥𓊖 *(m) ḥꜣt pꜣ 5 nḫtw ꜥꜣ n n(ꜣ) mꜥ* 'at the Head of the Five Great Fortresses of the Ma'.[295] The second is a lintel from the cemetery at Heracleopolis, which is made for the son of the Chief of the Ma, Osorkon, which states that Osorkon, like Amenhaemopet, was 𓂧𓈋𓏤𓏭𓏤𓀀𓏏𓏥𓊖 *(m) ḥꜣt pꜣ 5 nḫtw ꜥꜣ n n(ꜣ) mꜥ* 'at the Head of the Five Great Fortresses of the Ma'.[296] The Five Great Fortresses of the Ma was proposed to be equivalent to 'The Five Great Fortresses of the Sherden', a toponym, which is documented on two monuments dating to the end of the New Kingdom or Twenty-First Dynasty.[297] The first was a block from the tomb of Menmaatrenakht who was a general and chief of troops who lived at the time of Ramesses XI. The associated titles indicate that

Menmaatrenakht was 〈hieroglyphs〉 *ḥзt pз 5 nḫtw š̠r(d)зnз* 'at the Head of the Five Great Fortresses of the Sherden'. The provenance of the tomb block is unknown, but it is known that Sherden troops were grouped into institutions at the end of the New Kingdom in various fortified networks, especially around the Hermopolis and Spermeru.[298] There is, however, no geographical evidence to link the block of Menmaatrenakht to the region of Heracleopolis.[299] The second monument was that of a stela of Sethemheb found in the temple of Heryshef at Heracleopolis.[300] The titles associated with Sethemheb state that he is 〈hieroglyphs〉 *ḥзt pз ꜥз nḫtw ꜥз š̠rdзnз* 'at the Head of the Three Great Fortresses of the Sherden'. The three singular lines after the definitive article 〈glyph〉 *pз* are restored to 〈glyph〉 as they are unevenly spaced.[301] The absence of the mention of the Five Great Fortresses of the Sherden on the monument of Shoshenq I[302] suggests that the fortress chain no longer existed by the time of the Twenty-Second Dynasty.[303] The alteration of the Sherden to the Ma resulted from a political change at the start of the Twenty-Second Dynasty when the Egyptian fortresses passed under the control of the Libyan troops.[304]

ID:	NOME:	BANK: NA	GEOREF: NA
ThIP_UE.115	A–A (HH)		
ArabicNAME: NA		AEN_Hiero: 〈hieroglyphs〉	AEN_Trans: *pз nḫtw n mk-kmt*

Discussion: A limestone statuette found at Atfih dated to the reign of Osorkon I preserves the toponym 〈hieroglyphs〉 *pз nḫtw n mk-kmt* 'The Fortress of the Protector of Egypt'.[305] The preserved toponym is an abbreviation of the name of a royal foundation; however, the royal name is missing. The term *mk-kmt* 'Protector of Egypt' is a frequently used phrase in the preceding Ramesside Period.[306] Based on the proliferation of the terminology in the Ramesside Period and the founding of other forts by Ramesside kings in the region of Heracleopolis, the foundation of this fort should date to the same period; however, there is no evidence to support such a claim.[307] The mention of the fort under Osorkon I and the founding of the fort of Per Sekhemkheperre on the opposite bank of the Nile near the Faiyum could indicate that it was another foundation of Osorkon I and the fortification of the northern area of Middle Egypt.

ID:	NOME:	BANK: NA	GEOREF: NA
ThIP_UE.116	A–A (HH)		
ArabicNAME: NA		AEN_Hiero: 〈hieroglyphs〉	AEN_Trans: *dmi pз-bḫn-n-pз-nḥsy*

Discussion: The Castle of Panehesy is documented on Cairo JE 39410 and is found on the Twentieth Dynasty Wilbour Papyrus written as *p-n-nз-nḥsy*.[308] The location of this toponym has been suggested as being at Bilhasa.[309]

ID:	NOME:	BANK: NA	GEOREF: NA
ThIP_UE.117	A–A (HH)		
ArabicNAME: NA		AEN_Hiero: 〈hieroglyphs〉	AEN_Trans: *dmi pз-bḫn-n-nfr-rnpt*

Discussion: The ancient site of *dmi pз-bḫn-n-nfr-rnpt* 'The Castle of Neferenpet' is documented on Cairo JE 39410, but cannot be equated with an Arabic locality and it is not mentioned on the Wilbour Papyrus, indicating that this may have been a new foundation after the end of the Ramesside Period.[310]

ID: **NOME:** **BANK:** NA **GEOREF:** NA
ThIP_UE.118 A–A (HH)
ArabicNAME: NA **AEN_Hiero:** NA **AEN_Trans:** *bḥn*

Discussion: This toponym is recorded on Cairo JE 39410.[311] The term possibly equated with the 'The Castle of the Vizier' is again mentioned on the Wilbour Papyrus,[312] but no more is known about its location within the Heracleopolitan hinterland.

ID: **NOME:** **BANK:** NA **GEOREF:** NA
ThIP_UE.119 A–A (HH)
ArabicNAME: NA **AEN_Hiero:** **AEN_Trans:** *dmi p3-sg-n-ḥwt-ty*

Discussion: 'The Village of the Fort of the Estate of Tiy' is mentioned on Cairo JE 39410,[313] and is also mentioned in P. Wilbour, with a similar writing, but it is not possible to locate it exactly.[314] It is probably located to the north of Heracleopolis as the fields associated with the village in P. Wilbour were then under the authority of a man called Hori who was a priest of the temple of Ramesses beloved of Amun at *Pa-tjesy-hor*, a locality that is associated with Memphis.[315]

ID: **NOME:** **BANK:** NA **GEOREF:** NA
ThIP_UE.120 A–A (HH)
ArabicNAME: NA **AEN_Hiero:** **AEN_Trans:** *dmi p3-sg-n-ᶜr(t)*

Discussion: 'The Village of the Fort of the Goat', documented on Cairo JE 39410,[316] is also attested in the Wilbour Papyrus but under various different writings.[317] The fort must have been situated close to Heracleopolis as P. Wilbour shows that some of its fields belonged to the temple of Heryshef.[318] The village could have been named as 'The Southern Goat'.[319]

ID: **NOME:** **BANK:** NA **GEOREF:** NA
ThIP_UE.121 A–A (HH)
ArabicNAME: NA **AEN_Hiero:** **AEN_Trans:** *rbn*

Discussion: *rbn* is listed on the Onomasticon of Amenemope,[320] and is equated with the *brn* of the Wilbour Papyrus.[321]

ID: **NOME:** **BANK:** NA **GEOREF:** NA
ThIP_UE.122 A–A (HH)
ArabicNAME: NA **AEN_Hiero:** (Twenty-Second Dynasty) **AEN_Trans:** *p3 iḥw n ḥ3t*
(Twenty-Third Dynasty) *dmi p3 iḥw n ḥ3t*

Discussion: *p3 iḥw n ḥ3t* 'The Military Camp/Stockyard/Storehouse/Stable of the Front' is listed on stela Cairo JE 39410 (Twenty-Second Dynasty). The toponym is later documented on a Year 10 stela of King Peftjauawybast (A) (Twenty-Third Dynasty) from Heracleopolis as *dmi p3 iḥw n ḥ3t*.[322]

ID: **NOME:** **BANK:** NA **GEOREF:** NA
ThIP_UE.123 A–A (HH)
ArabicNAME: NA **AEN_Hiero:** **AEN_Trans:** *dmi p3 iḥw n pn-rᶜ*

Discussion: 'The Village of the Military Camp/Stockyard/Storehouse/Stable of Pen-Re' is documented on stela Cairo JE 39410.[323] It is an unknown location in the region.

ID:	NOME:	BANK: NA	GEOREF: NA
ThIP_UE.124	A–A (HH)		

ArabicNAME: NA **AEN_Hiero:** 𓉐𓏤𓂻𓈈𓏤𓂋𓏤𓏛𓉐 **AEN_Trans:** *dmi pꜣ iḥw*
n nb-smn

Discussion: 'The Village of the Military Camp/Stockyard/Storehouse/Stable of Neb-Semen' is documented on stela Cairo JE 39410.[324] It is an unknown location in the region.

ID:	NOME:	BANK: NA	GEOREF: NA
ThIP_UE.125	A–A (HH)		

ArabicNAME: NA **AEN_Hiero:** 𓉐𓏤𓂻𓈈𓏤𓏤𓊵𓂧𓏤𓊨 **AEN_Trans:** *dmi pꜣ iḥw*
šd-sw-ḫnsw

Discussion: 'The Village of the Military Camp/Stockyard/Storehouse/Stable of Shedsu-Khonsu' is documented on Cairo JE 39410.[325] It is an unknown location in the region.

ID:	NOME:	BANK: NA	GEOREF: NA
ThIP_UE.126	A–A (HH)		

ArabicNAME: NA **AEN_Hiero:** 𓉐𓏤𓈖𓃀𓏤𓏛 **AEN_Trans:** *iꜣt n wꜥbw*

Discussion: 'The Mound of the Pure' is documented on Cairo JE 39410.[326] It is an unknown location in the region.

ID:	NOME:	BANK: NA	GEOREF: NA
ThIP_UE.127	A–A (HH)		

ArabicNAME: NA **AEN_Hiero:** 𓉐𓏤𓂻𓈅𓂋𓏤𓏤𓅡𓊨 **AEN_Trans:** *dmi tꜣ iꜣt pꜣ*
bꜣ ꜣst

Discussion: 'The Village of the Mound of the Ba of Isis' is documented on Cairo JE 39410.[327] The transcription of the toponym 'The Village of the Mound of the Ba of Isis' is uncertain, but it may be a play on words between 'The Ba of Isis' (*bꜣ st*) and the Goddess Bastet (*bꜣstt*).[328]

ID:	NOME:	BANK: NA	GEOREF: NA
ThIP_UE.128	A–A (HH)		

ArabicNAME: NA **AEN_Hiero:** 𓉐𓏤𓈅𓊨𓂋𓊪 **AEN_Trans:** *iꜣt šꜣis r pt*

Discussion: 'The Mound of Sharope' is documented on Cairo JE 39410.[329] It is an unknown location in the region.

ID:	NOME:	BANK: NA	GEOREF: NA
ThIP_UE.129	A–A (HH)		

ArabicNAME: NA **AEN_Hiero:** 𓉐𓏤𓈅𓍿𓏤𓏛 **AEN_Trans:** *tꜣ iꜣt tꜣty*

Discussion: 'The Mound of the Vizier' is documented on Cairo JE 39410.[330] It is an unknown location in the region.

ID:	NOME:	BANK: NA	GEOREF: NA
ThIP_UE.130	A–A (HH)		

ArabicNAME: NA **AEN_Hiero:** 𓉐𓏤𓂝𓏏𓈉𓂋𓏤𓀜 **AEN_Trans:** *tꜣ-ꜥt-pꜣ-*
ḳn-pꜣ-mšꜥ

Discussion: 'The House of the Brave of the Army' is documented on Cairo JE 39410.[331] It is an unknown location in the region.

ID:	NOME:	BANK: NA	GEOREF: NA
ThIP_UE.131	A–A (HH)		

ArabicNAME: NA   **AEN_Hiero:**   **AEN_Trans:** *dmi t3 šꜥꜥ r s3*

Discussion: 'The Village of the Granary of the Rear' is documented on Cairo JE 39410.[332] It is an unknown location in the region.

ID:	NOME:	BANK: NA	GEOREF: NA
ThIP_UE.132	A–A (HH)		

ArabicNAME: NA   **AEN_Hiero:**   **AEN_Trans:** *t3 st n ib-ndm*

Discussion: 'The Place of Ib-nedjem' is documented on Cairo JE 39410.[333] It is an unknown location in the region.

ID:	NOME:	BANK: NA	GEOREF: NA
ThIP_UE.133	A–A (HH)		

ArabicNAME: NA   **AEN_Hiero:**   **AEN_Trans:** *dmi pr-nbit*

Discussion: Nebyouy, 'The Village of the House of the Flame', is documented on Cairo JE 39410. This toponym may be identified with the toponym Nebyouy on P. Wilbour.[334] On the western wall of the west Osirian chapel at Dendera there is mention of a Goddess of Nebyouy who presides in the Domain of Nebyouy.[335] It may be that this Nebyouy should be equated with the Heracleopolitan Nebyouy.

ID:	NOME:	BANK: NA	GEOREF: NA
ThIP_UE.134	A–A (HH)		

ArabicNAME: NA   **AEN_Hiero:**   **AEN_Trans:** *dmi nkrw*

Discussion: 'The Village of Nekeru' is documented on Cairo JE 39410.[336] It is an unknown location in the region.

ID:	NOME:	BANK: NA	GEOREF: NA
ThIP_UE.135	A–A (HH)		

ArabicNAME: NA   **AEN_Hiero:**   **AEN_Trans:** *ḥwt-mntw*

Discussion: 'The Village of the House of Montu' is documented on Cairo JE 39410.[337] It is an unknown location in the region.

ID:	NOME:	BANK: NA	GEOREF: NA
ThIP_UE.136	A–A (HH)		

ArabicNAME: NA   **AEN_Hiero:**   **AEN_Trans:** *dmi ḥwt ndst*

Discussion: 'The Village of the Little House' is documented on Cairo JE 39410.[338] It is an unknown location in the region.

ID:	NOME:	BANK: NA	GEOREF: NA
ThIP_UE.137	A–A (HH)		

ArabicNAME: NA   **AEN_Hiero:**   **AEN_Trans:** *dmi ḥwt nbs*

Discussion: 'The Village of the House of the Jujube Tree' is documented on Cairo JE 39410.[339] There is mention of a House of the Jujube Tree on P. London UC 32201 from Lahun,[340] and in Tomb 5 belonging to Ahanakht at el-Bersheh.[341]

ID: ThIP_UE.138   **NOME:** A–A (HH)   **BANK:** NA   **GEOREF:** NA

ArabicNAME: NA   **AEN_Hiero:** 𓉐 ...   **AEN_Trans:** *dmi pr ḥw-it.f*

Discussion: 'The Village of the House of the One who Protects his Father' is documented on Cairo JE 39410.[342] It is an unknown location in the region.

ID: ThIP_UE.139   **NOME:** A–A (HH)   **BANK:** NA   **GEOREF:** NA

ArabicNAME: NA   **AEN_Hiero:** ...   **AEN_Trans:** *pr-ḥnw*

Discussion: 'The House of the Henu Barque' is documented on the Year 6 stela of Pedubast I, from Kom el-Qala (Memphis).[343] A second attestation to this toponym was found on a coffin from Lahun.[344] This religious location was most likely situated to the north of Heracleopolis in the region of the Twenty-First Upper Egyptian Nome. It is again mentioned in P. Louvre I 3079.[345]

ID: ThIP_UE.140   **NOME:** A–A (HH)   **BANK:** NA   **GEOREF:** NA

ArabicNAME: NA   **AEN_Hiero:** ...   **AEN_Trans:** *sw*

Discussion: 'Sou' is mentioned on Cairo JE 39410.[346] This was the principal cult site of Seth. The site should be in the region to the north of Heracleopolis between Medinat el-Faiyum and Atfih, as P. Harris lists Sou after Heracleopolis and Medinat el-Faiyum, but before Atfih.[347] This is confirmed by P. Wilbour.[348]

ID: ThIP_UE.141   **NOME:** A–A (HH)   **BANK:** NA   **GEOREF:** NA

ArabicNAME: NA   **AEN_Hiero:** ...   **AEN_Trans:** *dmi t3 wḥyt ḥd*

Discussion: *dmi t3 wḥyt ḥd* is documented on Cairo JE 39410.[349] It is an unknown location in the region.

ID: ThIP_UE.142   **NOME:** A–A (HH)   **BANK:** NA   **GEOREF:** NA

ArabicNAME: NA   **AEN_Hiero:** ...   **AEN_Trans:** *dmi t3 wḥyt kn*

Discussion: *dmi t3 wḥyt kn* is documented on Cairo JE 39410.[350] It is an unknown location in the region.

ID: ThIP_UE.143   **NOME:** A–A (21st Capital)   **BANK:** Faiyum   **GEOREF:** 29°18′31.64″N 30°50′36.30″E

ArabicNAME: Medinat el-Faiyum   **AEN_Hiero:** ...   **AEN_Trans:** *pr-sbk*

Discussion: *pr-sbk* (classical: Crokodopolis-Arsinoe) is the ancient name for the capital of the Faiyum (Medinat el-Faiyum). Third Intermediate Period evidence is limited but a statue of proposed Twenty-Second Dynasty date comes from Medinat el-Faiyum,[351] and the settlement is mentioned on the Piankhy Stela.

ID: ThIP_UE.144   **NOME:** A–A (21st)   **BANK:** Faiyum   **GEOREF:** 29°31'7.72"N 30°54'15.75"E

ArabicNAME: Kom Aushim   **AEN_Hiero:** NA   **AEN_Trans:** NA

Discussion: Two cartonnage mummy cases, each in an anthropoid wooden coffin without lid, were said to have been found during excavations at Kom Aushim (classical: Karanis) in the 1980s.[352]

ID: ThIP_UE.145   **NOME:** A–A (21st)   **BANK:** Faiyum   **GEOREF:** 29°11'34.83"N 30°38'35.43"E

ArabicNAME: Medinat Maadi   **AEN_Hiero:** NA   **AEN_Trans:** NA

Discussion: At Medinat Maadi (classical: Narmouthis), the Middle Kingdom temple (Temple A) has a preserved decoration of a King Osorkon in the portico (Second Hypostyle Hall).[353]

ID: ThIP_UE.146   **NOME:** A–A (21st)   **BANK:** NA   **GEOREF:** NA

ArabicNAME: NA   **AEN_Hiero:** 𓏏𓊖𓆓𓈖𓏏𓈉   **AEN_Trans:** *dmi t3 wḥyt sw*

Discussion: *dmi t3 wḥyt sw* is documented on Cairo JE 39410,[354] and may have been a secondary settlement to the main cult centre of 𓈉 *sw* located between Medinat Maadi and Atfih.

ID: ThIP_UE.147   **NOME:** A–A (21st)   **BANK:** West   **GEOREF:** 29°12'4.28"N 30°57'7.75"E

ArabicNAME: Gurob   **AEN_Hiero:** 𓏠𓂋𓏤   **AEN_Trans:** *mr-wr*

Discussion: *mr-wr* 'The Great Channel' is listed on the Onomasticon of Amenemope,[355] and is the modern-day Gurob located to the west of the Bahr Yusef. There is evidence of Third Intermediate Period tomb re-use and all come from Brunton and Engelbach's Cemetery W, which formed part of the large New Kingdom cemetery that had been thoroughly plundered by the time Engelbach and Brunton got to work. The cemetery was likely extensively re-used during the Third Intermediate Period.[356] The re-used tombs have been dated to between the ninth and eighth century BCE,[357] and therefore this cemetery has been defined as broad cemetery date. In addition to the cemetery usage, a land donation stela of Osorkon III was found at Gurob.[358]

ID: ThIP_UE.148   **NOME:** A–A (21st)   **BANK:** West   **GEOREF:** 29°23'17.17"N 31°9'31.52"E

ArabicNAME: Meidum   **AEN_Hiero:** 𓏠𓏏𓈖𓏤   **AEN_Trans:** *mr-tm*

Discussion: Meidum was mentioned on the Piankhy Stela, and the Old Kingdom necropolis was seemingly re-used in the Third Intermediate Period, though the publication of these intrusive burials is poor.[359] They were from a poor section of society and were rarely provided with grave goods. Many tomb groups were dated to the Twenty-Second Dynasty, but none of these seems to have been published so they cannot be confirmed.[360]

ID: ThIP_UE.149   **NOME:** A–A (21st)   **BANK:** West (west of Bahr Yusef)   **GEOREF:** 29°8'32.13"N 30°54'1.55"E

ArabicNAME: Sedment   **AEN_Hiero:** NA   **AEN_Trans:** NA

Discussion: Several Third Intermediate Period burials were found in 1892–3,[361] and incorrectly dated to the Ptolemaic–Roman Period.[362]

ID: **NOME:**   **BANK:** West   **GEOREF:** 29°14′18.78″N
ThIP_UE.150   A–A (21ˢᵗ)   30°59′5.97″E
ArabicNAME: Lahun   **AEN_Hiero:** ◁𓎛𓈖𓈖   **AEN_Trans:** *r ḥnt*

Discussion: *r ḥnt* is the ancient name of Lahun. The site is mentioned on the Piankhy
Stela. The term *r ḥnt* literally means 'The Mouth of the *ḥnt* (Pool/Lake)',[363] and this
may relate not just to Lahun but to the entirety of the Faiyum mouth to the Valley.[364] It
was proposed that the cemetery site of Lahun had been abandoned at the end of the
Middle Kingdom and was reutilised between the Twenty-Second and Twenty-Fifth
Dynasty, being used for the burials of the people of the fortress of Per
Sekhemkheperre.[365] Only one such military burial was found in the necropolis, while
no monument from Lahun mentions Per Sekhemkheperre.[366] These so-called
Twenty-Second to Twenty-Fifth Dynasty burials have been re-dated to no earlier than
the seventh century BCE, which would place them right at the end of the Third
Intermediate Period, probably sometime in the Twenty-Fifth Dynasty.[367] Also found at
Lahun was a wooden door of Osorkon I.[368]

ID: **NOME:**   **BANK:** West   **GEOREF:** 29°13′55.17″N
ThIP_UE.151   A–A (21ˢᵗ)   31°3′1.04″E
ArabicNAME: Haraga   **AEN_Hiero:** NA   **AEN_Trans:** NA

Discussion: Three intrusive burials have been tentatively dated to the Twenty-
Second to Twenty-Third Dynasty but were heavily plundered.[369]

ID: **NOME:**   **BANK:** West   **GEOREF:** 29°16′17.03″N
ThIP_UE.152   A–A (21ˢᵗ)   30°53′57.38″E
ArabicNAME: Hawara   **AEN_Hiero:** NA   **AEN_Trans:** NA

Discussion: The reputed Third Intermediate Period burials all appear to have been
intrusive within the Middle Kingdom tombs around Petrie's crocodile tomb chapels to
the north of the pyramid of Amenemhat III.[370] One of the burials has been dated based
on Theban stylistic developments to ca. 930–730 BCE.[371]

ID: **NOME:**   **BANK:** West   **GEOREF:** 29°18′5.89″N
ThIP_UE.153   A–A (21ˢᵗ)   31°15′18.12″E
ArabicNAME: Riqqeh   **AEN_Hiero:** NA   **AEN_Trans:** NA

Discussion: Nine cemeteries were discovered at Riqqeh.[372] Three of them (B, E, and F)
were said to have been re-used in the Third Intermediate Period. Based on burial objects,
Cemetery B had burials dating to the Twenty-Third to Twenty-Fifth Dynasty,[373] while
Cemetery F had a general Third Intermediate Period date attributed to it.[374]

ID: **NOME:**   **BANK:** West   **GEOREF:** 29°26′40.52″N
ThIP_UE.154   A–A (21ˢᵗ)   31°11′50.04″E
ArabicNAME: Girza   **AEN_Hiero:** NA   **AEN_Trans:** NA

Discussion: Third Intermediate Period amulets along with a scarab of Shoshenq III
and Pedubast I suggest that an Eighteenth Dynasty cemetery near Girza was re-used
during this period.[375] In the early excavation of 1912,[376] it is unclear whether these
scarabs were found in association with burials or found in the top sand.[377]

ID: **NOME:**   **BANK:** West   **GEOREF:** 29°19′52.68″N
ThIP_UE.155   A–A (21ˢᵗ)   31°8′16.76″E
ArabicNAME: Kom Abu Radi   **AEN_Hiero:** NA   **AEN_Trans:** NA

Discussion: There is possible evidence of a funerary stela from Kom Abu Radi which
is located to the north-east of Abusir el-Meleq and 6 km south of Meidum.[378]

ID: **NOME:** **BANK:** West **GEOREF:** 29°14′53.57″N
ThIP_UE.156 A–A (21ˢᵗ) 31°4′57.08″E
ArabicNAME: Abusir el-Meleq **AEN_Hiero:** 𓉻𓊪𓄿𓊖 **AEN_Trans:** *dmi pr wsir*

Discussion: *dmi pr wsir* (modern: Abusir el-Meleq) is mentioned on Cairo JE 39410.³⁷⁹ The excavations of the cemetery brought to light several burials dating from the Saite to Byzantine times.³⁸⁰ The original dating of the intact tomb group of Tadja, around the Twenty-Fifth Dynasty ca. 700 BCE, is probably a little too early and it should be dated to the Saite Period.³⁸¹

ID: **NOME:** **BANK:** NA **GEOREF:** NA
ThIP_UE.157 A–A (21ˢᵗ)
ArabicNAME: NA **AEN_Hiero:** See below **AEN_Trans:** See below.

Discussion: This was a fortified location founded by Osorkon I just to the north of Heracleopolis, located in the Twenty-First Upper Egyptian Nome.³⁸² The toponyms for Per Sekhemkheperre do not specifically refer to a fortified foundation. This designation is based upon the military titles of the individuals who were associated with it,³⁸³ but the Piankhy Stela does mention 𓊚𓃀𓏭 *sзwt.f* 'its walls' and 𓈖𓎡𓏭 *ḥtm.f* 'its citadel'. Some scholars locate the fortress just to the north of Heracleopolis,³⁸⁴ while others place it closer to Lahun.³⁸⁵

ID: **NOME:** **BANK:** East **GEOREF:** 29°24′28.07″N
ThIP_UE.158 A–A (22ⁿᵈ 31°15′10.87″E
  Capital)
ArabicNAME: Atfih **AEN_Hiero:** 𓊖𓃘 **AEN_Trans:** *pr-nbt-tp-iḥw*

Discussion: *pr-nbt-tp-iḥw*, is equated with the modern Atfih and is documented on the Bubastite Gate at Karnak and the Piankhy Stela. Several monuments have been found from the Third Intermediate Period, including blocks dating from the Twenty-First Dynasty and the reign of Osorkon the Elder that were found re-used in the cow necropolis;³⁸⁶ a statuette found at Atfih dated to the reign of Osorkon I;³⁸⁷ a statue of a Year 22 of Shoshenq V;³⁸⁸ two Twenty-Fifth Dynasty statues;³⁸⁹ a statue from the Michaelidis collection;³⁹⁰ and a stela dated to either the Twenty-Fifth or Twenty-Sixth Dynasty, possibly from Atfih.³⁹¹

LOWER EGYPT

1. *Memphite Area*

ID: ThIP_LE.1 **GEOREF:** NA
ArabicNAME: NA **AEN_Hiero:** 𓈐𓏏𓏤 **AEN_Trans:** *it̠ tзwy*

Discussion: The Middle Kingdom capital of *it̠ tзwy* is mentioned on the Piankhy Stela as being one of the besieged settlements. It is likely to be in the region of modern-day Lisht, but this is not certain.³⁹²

ID: ThIP_LE.2 **GEOREF:** 29°34′27.57″N 31°13′34.61″E
ArabicNAME: Lisht **AEN_Hiero:** NA **AEN_Trans:** NA
(North)

Discussion: At Lisht North a small group of houses were built against the face of the pyramid of Amenemhat III. These houses were active from the end of the Twentieth Dynasty and continued to be used throughout the Twenty-First Dynasty. They were finally abandoned at some time during the Twenty-Second Dynasty.[393] The abandonment of this area of Lisht may reflect a possible movement of the settlement nearer to Itj-Tawy as it appears to have been an active and important site during the Third Intermediate Period, being documented as one of the main locations that Piankhy besieged on his invasion of Egypt. This part of Lisht may even have been part of the wider suburb of *it t3wy*; however, this cannot be confirmed and therefore this site has been given a unique identifier.

ID: ThIP_LE.3   **GEOREF:** 29°50′51.88″N 31°15′27.17″E
ArabicNAME: Mit   **AEN_Hiero:** 𓏶𓊹𓏤𓊖   **AEN_Trans:** *mnf*
Rahinah

Discussion: In the Twenty-First Dynasty the ancient capital of 𓏶𓊹𓏤𓊖 *mnf* Memphis,[394] like the rest of the north of Egypt, lay under the control of the Tanite pharaohs. Later in the Third Intermediate Period there is no evidence of a local dynasty of autocratic rulers which is seen elsewhere in the Delta and northern Egypt. The kings of the Twenty-Fifth Dynasty made Memphis the focal point for their religious and political aspirations, and there is no doubt that the Twenty-Fifth Dynasty rulers adopted Memphis as their principal residence in Egypt, despite the religious importance of Thebes in the south.[395] An assessment of the Manethoic king list, which has a Memphite bias, indicates that several Twenty-Second Dynasty Libyan 'kings' who are expected to be recognised at Memphis are absent from the list. Apart from Shoshenq I, there are no other Shoshenqs listed, but there are unquestionable attestations to Shoshenq III and Shoshenq V in the Serapeum Stela from Saqqara.[396] Neither Piankhy nor Tefnakht is listed, despite both men fighting for control of the settlement. Jurman states that if one looks to find a truth in the king list of Manetho, after the 'Battle for Memphis' control of the settlement must have resided with one of the local eastern Delta rulers, before Bakenrenef managed to regain control of the settlement, only to be later displaced by Shebitku. The well-known kings of the Twenty-Second Dynasty are only attested at Memphis through indirect evidence from royal monuments, and the Memphite priesthood therefore accepted the mentioned kings as legitimate overlords of Memphis.[397] Several elite burials have been found at Memphis. The burials V–Z found in the south-west corner of the small temple of Ptah built by Ramesses II were originally dated to the beginning of the Twenty-First Dynasty,[398] and then subsequently to the Twenty-Second Dynasty.[399] A recent reassessment of these tomb groups shows they should be dated to the New Kingdom, probably the Twentieth Dynasty.[400] The later burials at Memphis are more securely dated to the members of the Twenty-Second Dynasty royal family. These five burials – Shoshenq D, his son, the Great Chief of the Ma, Takeloth B, his grandsons, Pediese A and Harsiese, together with Tabakhtenaskhet – were all interred in a grave complex of individual chambers closely aligned to one another and the neighbouring cult temple of Ptah.[401]

ID: ThIP_LE.4   **GEOREF:** 29°56′14.65″N 31°18′59.18″E
ArabicNAME: Turah   **AEN_Hiero:** 𓏶𓈖𓂋𓉐𓊖   **AEN_Trans:** *tr3w*

Discussion: The quarry site of *tr3w* is listed on the Onomasticon of Amenemope.[402] These were the quarries on the East Bank of the Nile and could indicate an economic reason for its incorporation on the settlement list of Amenemope as it provided access to resources. There is no more evidence after the Twenty-First Dynasty for quarry activity at Turah during the Third Intermediate Period.

ID: ThIP_LE.5   **GEOREF:** 29°50′59.38″N 31°13′7.59″E
ArabicNAME: Saqqara   **AEN_Hiero:** Multiple different   **AEN_Trans:** NA
                          hieroglyphic designations for the
                          cemeteries of Saqqara

Discussion: There has so far been little evidence of burials that have been dated to the Third Intermediate Period, though references to supposed examples are frequent within Egyptological literature.[403] There must have been sustained activity in the burial grounds at Saqqara though, particularly at the Serapeum, as many Apis Bull stelae were left by rulers, together with many donated statues in the local shrines, while the pottery provides evidence that there was continued activity at the Anubieion.[404]

ID: ThIP_LE.6   **GEOREF:** 29°58′36.37″N 31°8′0.17″E
ArabicNAME: Giza   **AEN_Hiero:** NA   **AEN_Trans:** NA

Discussion: A small temple to 'Isis Mistress of the Pyramids' may have incorporated an additional small-scale priestly community to house those who worked in it. There must have been several Third Intermediate Period interments at Giza given the presence of chance finds, yet there is no evidence of tomb structures. The chance finds include fragments of coffins and ushabtis, but they all remain unpublished.[405]

ID: ThIP_LE.7   **GEOREF:** NA
ArabicNAME: NA   **AEN_Hiero:** 𓉔𓄑𓆓𓈖𓃩𓇳   **AEN_Trans:** *ḥwt-šd-ꜣbd*

Discussion: *ḥwt-šd-ꜣbd* is documented on the Onomasticon of Amenemope and located in the capital zone geographically south of the settlement of 𓉔𓈖𓀭𓏏𓉐 *pr-ḥꜤpy* (modern: Atar en-Naby).[406]

ID: ThIP_LE.8   **GEOREF:** 29°59′13.48″N 31°14′56.59″E
ArabicNAME: Atar en-   **AEN_Hiero:** 𓉔𓈖𓀭𓏏𓉐   **AEN_Trans:** *pr-ḥꜤpy*
Naby

Discussion: *pr-ḥꜤpy* (modern: Atar en-Naby) is listed on the Onomasticon of Amenemope.[407] *pr-ḥꜤpy* continues to be active and is documented on the Piankhy Stela in a more abbreviated form 𓉔𓉐𓇳.[408] The Piankhy Stela documents *pr-ḥꜤpy* as one of the sites used as a residence or ruled over by Count Pebes.

ID: ThIP_LE.9   **GEOREF:** 30°0′21.31″N 31°13′47.38″E
ArabicNAME: Old Cairo **AEN_Hiero:** 𓉐𓊖   **AEN_Trans:** *ḥr-ꜤḥꜤ*

Discussion: *ḥr-ꜤḥꜤ* (classical: Babylon) is in Old Cairo. Babylon was the access point into the eastern Delta.[409] 𓉔𓏏𓏏𓏏 *pr-psḏt* 'The House of the Ennead' was most likely another name for the site of Babylon.[410] The Piankhy Stela documents *ḥr-ꜤḥꜤ* as being ruled over by Count Pebes in addition to *pr-ḥꜤpy*.

ID: ThIP_LE.10   **GEOREF:** NA
ArabicNAME: NA   **AEN_Hiero:** 𓄿𓏏𓊖   **AEN_Trans:** *ḫnt-nfr*

Discussion: In the south of the Memphite Nome was the settlement of 𓄿𓏏𓊖 *ḫnt-nfr*. This was a cult settlement for the god Amun.[411] *ḫnt-nfr* was ruled by Count Djedkhu as documented on the Piankhy Stela.

ID: ThIP_LE.11   **GEOREF:** NA
ArabicNAME: NA   **AEN_Hiero:** 𓉔𓄿𓆓   **AEN_Trans:** *pr-pgꜣ*

Discussion: The location of this settlement and the subsequent district is in the south of Memphis, to the north of Heracleopolis.[412] It is related to the wider geographical district of 𓄿𓄿𓆓 *w pgꜣ* 'The District of Pega', documented on a block statue of

Nespaqashuty dated to Shoshenq III from Thebes,[413] in which Nespaqashuty is called the High Priest of Osiris of 'the District of Pega'.[414] *pr-pg3* has been proposed to be equated with the φωχη of the Archives of Zenon.[415] This papyrus listed the localities in the south of the Memphite Nome. *pr-pg3* must have been in the south of the Memphite Nome to the north of Heracleopolis.[416]

ID: ThIP_LE.12   **GEOREF:** NA
ArabicNAME: NA   **AEN_Hiero:** 𓉐𓃀𓈎𓏏𓏥𓏥𓏥   **AEN_Trans:** *3t-t3mt*

Discussion: On the statue of Shedsunerfertum A the High Priest of Ptah in Memphis under Shoshenq I, there is mention of a location called 𓉐𓃀𓈎𓏏𓏥𓏥𓏥 *3t-t3mt*.[417] The location is so far unidentified but it should be located in the vicinity of Memphis.[418]

ID: ThIP_LE.13   **GEOREF:** 30°7'45.87"N 31°18'22.98"E
ArabicNAME: Ain Shams   **AEN_Hiero:** 𓉺𓊖   **AEN_Trans:** *iwnw*
(Cairo suburb), multiple
suburbs of north-east Cairo
(ancient Heliopolis)

Discussion: The ancient site of 𓉺𓊖 *iwnw* (classical: Heliopolis) is now located in the modern Cairo suburb of Ain Shams, and is no doubt under several expanding suburban areas of north-eastern Cairo. Little is known about this important political and religious centre during the Third Intermediate Period, but architectural fragments from the reign of Shoshenq I point to activity in the settlement.[419] A number of monuments that come from the region around the ancient settlement include several Twenty-Second to Twenty-Third Dynasty objects including a donation stela,[420] an early Twenty-Second Dynasty royal family block statue,[421] a block of King Pamiu found in the fortress of Bab el-Nasr,[422] a stela of the Great Chief Nesptah dated to the Twenty-Second to Twenty-Fourth Dynasty,[423] a group figure of Hapiemhab and Ankheseniset in the Boreax Collection,[424] and a re-used stela of Kuki.[425] Almost nothing is known about the wider settlement of the Third Intermediate Period, but additional toponyms that made up the urban fabric, including religious and cultic settlement toponyms, included 𓈎𓏤𓏤𓏤𓈗𓆭𓃀𓈎𓊖 *šci-k3-m-iwnw* 'The High Sand of Heliopolis' documented on the Piankhy Stela.[426] Finally, 𓉐𓂋𓏤 *pr rc* 'The House of Re' (the main temple to the god Re of Heliopolis) is again mentioned on the Piankhy Stela, which tells us that the territory of the ruler Bakennefi A included Heliopolis in conjunction with Athribis.

ID: ThIP_LE.14   **GEOREF:** NA
ArabicNAME: NA   **AEN_Hiero:** 𓁷𓏤𓏤�𓉐𓏤𓏤𓊖   **AEN_Trans:** *ḥry-p3-dmi*

Discussion: *ḥry-p3-dmi* (lit. 'The Village of Height') is documented on the Piankhy Stela.[427]

ID: ThIP_LE.15   **GEOREF:** NA
ArabicNAME: NA   **AEN_Hiero:** 𓂝𓏤𓃀𓏏𓏏𓏤𓏤𓊖   **AEN_Trans:** *p3-bḥn-n-byw*

Discussion: The military site of *p3-bḥn-n-byw* is first mentioned on the Piankhy Stela and later on a Year 6 stela of Taharqa (ca. 685 BCE).[428] The stela was erected 5 km to the west of the pyramid of Pepy II on a desert road used for manoeuvres of the Egyptian army under Taharqa and Psammetik I. The road led from Memphis via Dashur and into the Faiyum. The stela records how Taharqa inspected the troops of the camp of Bia, which is identical to Byw.

ID: ThIP_LE.16   **GEOREF:** NA
ArabicNAME: NA   **AEN_Hiero:** 𓈍𓏥𓈖𓏥   **AEN_Trans:** *t3-whyt-byt*

Discussion: *t3-whyt-byt* was a location in the Memphite Nome documented on the Piankhy Stela but so far not located.

2 West of Classical Sebennytic

ID: ThIP_LE.17   **GEOREF:** NA
ArabicNAME: NA   **AEN_Hiero:** 𓆓𓎡   **AEN_Trans:** *ḥꜥpy*

Discussion: *ḥꜥpy* is documented on the Piankhy Stela. *ḥꜥpy* is in the territory of the later provinces of Sais and Prosopis,[429] the double province of Neith.[430]

ID: ThIP_LE.18   **GEOREF:** 30°52′57.02″N 30°19′43.40″E
ArabicNAME: Kom el-Abqa'in   **AEN_Hiero:** NA   **AEN_Trans:** NA

Discussion: Kom el-Abqa'in was one of the western Delta fortresses of Ramesses II.[431] After it had fallen out of use as a fortress, it continued to be used in the Twenty-First Dynasty for domestic purposes, like that of Kom Firin.[432]

ID: ThIP_LE.19   **GEOREF:** 30°57′53.96″N 30°46′4.29″E
ArabicNAME: Sa el-Hagar (Kom Rebwa)   **AEN_Hiero:** 𓋴𓏏𓈖   **AEN_Trans:** *s3.t*

Discussion: *s3.t* (classical: Sais) is now the modern Sa el-Hagar. Early Third Intermediate Period domestic occupation has been identified on the east of the Kom Rebwa mound,[433] while tenth- to seventh-century BCE domestic occupation has been identified on the west of the mound.[434] Other monuments of the Third Intermediate Period include early Twenty-Second Dynasty armbands of Prince Nimlot, probably from Sais,[435] and a donation stela in Athens of King Tefnakht.[436] A statue of the Chief of the Ma, Pamiu, son of the Lord of the Two Lands, Shoshenq, beloved of Amun, was said to come from Sa el-Hagar (Sais).[437] The inscription would, however, suggest that it actually derives from Heracleopolis and dates to the end of the Third Intermediate Period, as there is no indication as to which Shoshenq this refers to.[438]

ID: ThIP_LE.20   **GEOREF:** 31°11′43.70″N 30°44′32.25″E
ArabicNAME: Tell el-Fara'in   **AEN_Hiero:** 𓉐𓃒𓈖𓏏   **AEN_Trans:** *pr wꜣḏt*

Discussion: Buto is documented on the Onomasticon of Amenemope.[439] At Buto, there is extensive evidence of Third Intermediate Period settlement layers after the reoccupation of the site at the start of the Third Intermediate Period, attested by coring, up to 2 m deep in some areas. The excavations at the western edge of the site show that most of the surviving physical remains of walls and settlement contexts were destroyed by later Saite buildings built through these remains.[440] Two elite tombs were found at Buto and were overbuilt by Saite Period constructions dated to around the time of Iuput II.[441]

ID: ThIP_LE.21   **GEOREF:** 31°13′3.81″N 30°48′18.28″E
ArabicNAME: Kom el-Asfar   **AEN_Hiero:** NA   **AEN_Trans:** NA

Discussion: Drill cores[442] and survey work[443] conducted at Kom el-Asfar show that activity on this site dates back as far as the Third Intermediate Period.

ID: ThIP_LE.22   **GEOREF:** 31°5′8.87″N 30°56′56.27″E
ArabicNAME: Sakha   **AEN_Hiero:** 𓇋𓎸𓈖𓈖𓊖   **AEN_Trans:** *ḫ3sww*

Discussion: *ḫ3sww* (modern: Sakha) is listed on the Onomasticon of Amenemope[444] and on the Piankhy Stela in relation to the overall Nome of Xois. *ḫ3sww* was ruled over by the Count and Chief of the Ma, Nesnaisu.

ID: ThIP_LE.23   **GEOREF:** 30°47′44.58″N 30°36′0.49″E
ArabicNAME: Kom   **AEN_Hiero:** 𓌡𓂋𓈖𓊖   **AEN_Trans:** *im3w*
el-Hisn

Discussion: The ancient site of *im3w* is equated with modern Kom el-Hisn. Several blocks from a gateway of Shoshenq III were found in the Ramesside temple.[445] Four blocks with his cartouche have been found at the site approximately 50 m to the east of the earlier Ramesside statues found within the temple enclosure.[446] The find spot of the blocks would place them along the east–west axis in front of the Ramesside statues, if they were still in their original positions in the temple. This positioning indicates that Shoshenq III may have added a monumental gateway to the pre-existing temple of Ramesses II.

ID: ThIP_LE.24   **GEOREF:** NA
ArabicNAME: NA   **AEN_Hiero:** 𓉐𓋞𓊖   **AEN_Trans:** *pr-nwb*

Discussion: *pr-nwb* 'The House of Gold' has not been identified with certainty, but it is most likely in the western Delta.[447] There was a *pr-nwb* in the vicinity of Sais.[448] The same place is mentioned in the titulary of the General Petisis who was prophet of the goddess Hathor at the same time as being a priest at Sais and Buto.[449] It is also suggested that this toponym should be linked with the toponym of *Punubu* documented in the Annals of Assurbanipal.[450]

ID: ThIP_LE.25   **GEOREF:** 30°43′17.28″N 30°56′48.50″E
ArabicNAME: Bindariya   **AEN_Hiero:** NA   **AEN_Trans:** NA

Discussion: A block from a temple of Shoshenq III comes from Bindariya.[451]

ID: ThIP_LE.26   **GEOREF:** 30°35′51.66″N 31°8′33.92″E
ArabicNAME: Tell Umm   **AEN_Hiero:** 𓌩𓏤𓊖   **AEN_Trans:** *msdt*
Harb (Mosdai)

Discussion: *msdt* is equated with the modern site of Mosdai/Tell Umm Harb about 15 km to the north-west of Athribis. A block of Shoshenq III was found at this site, indicating some form of religious structure was built here during his reign.[452]

ID: ThIP_LE.27   **GEOREF:** 30°51′52.26″N 30°29′24.73″E
ArabicNAME: Kom Firin   **AEN_Hiero:** NA   **AEN_Trans:** NA

Discussion: A settlement of the early Third Intermediate Period was found at Kom Firin,[453] along with several donation stelae.[454]

ID: ThIP_LE.28   **GEOREF:** 30°25′44.67″N 30°49′8.45″E
ArabicNAME: Kom Abu   **AEN_Hiero:**   **AEN_Trans:** *pr ḥwt ḥr nbt*
Billo   𓉐𓎟𓏏𓂋𓈖𓊖𓏤𓏤𓏤𓋴   *mfkt*

Discussion: A hieratic donation stela from Year 19 of Shoshenq V records the donation of ten arourae of fields to the House of Hathor Lady of Mefket.[455]

ID: ThIP_LE.29   **GEOREF:** NA
ArabicNAME: NA   **AEN_Hiero:**   **AEN_Trans:** *dmi pꜣ sbk*

Discussion: The Village of the Crocodile is recorded on a donation stela and is in the region of Kom Abu Billo.[456] It cannot be said if it was a new foundation of the Third Intermediate Period, or an already existing settlement.

ID: ThIP_LE.30   **GEOREF:** NA
ArabicNAME: NA   **AEN_Hiero:**   **AEN_Trans:** *dmi r-bꜣ-gr*

Discussion: In connection with the site of Kom Firin, a toponym is documented on the donation stela of ⸗ *ti-tꜣ-rw*, called ⸗ *dmi r-bꜣ-gr*, which can be read Rabager, or Rasager.[457] The toponym is probably of a Libyan proper name relating to the Chief of Dancers who donated the stela, or the actual name of the settlement itself.[458] This toponym has not yet been identified but must have been near the site of Kom Firin.

ID: ThIP_LE.31   **GEOREF:** 30°7′24.62″N 31°8′9.80″E
ArabicNAME: Ausim   **AEN_Hiero:** ⸗   **AEN_Trans:** *sḥm / ḥm*

Discussion: The ancient name of Letopolis (modern: Ausim) ⸗ *sḥm / ḥm* is located to the west of Imbaba, approximately 13 km north-west of Cairo in the western fringes of the western Delta, on the left bank of the modern Rosetta branch.[459] Letopolis is named on the Piankhy Stela, but little else is known about this settlement for the Third Intermediate Period, apart from the fact that it was ruled by the Prophet of Horus Pedihorsomtus in the late Third Intermediate Period.

ID: ThIP_LE.32   **GEOREF:** NA
ArabicNAME: NA   **AEN_Hiero:** ⸗   **AEN_Trans:** *pr-sḥmt-nbt-sꜣt/ist*

Discussion: *pr-sḥmt-nbt-sꜣt/ist* is documented on the Piankhy Stela, but there are no further attestations to this toponym prior to or after the Third Intermediate Period. The Piankhy Stela records that *pr-sḥmt-nbt-sꜣt/ist* was ruled by Count Harbes. This settlement may be located either at the modern village of el-Zeidieh or at Kafr Sa'id Moussa, but neither is certain.

ID: ThIP_LE.33   **GEOREF:** NA
ArabicNAME: NA   **AEN_Hiero:**   **AEN_Trans:** *pr-sḥmt-nbt-rḥsꜣw*

Discussion: *pr-sḥmt-nbt-rḥsꜣw* is documented on the Piankhy Stela and was ruled by Count Harbes like *pr-sḥmt-nbt-sꜣt/ist*. The settlement is not yet located, but must be in the area of Letopolis or at either el-Zeidieh or Kafr Sa'id Moussa. This location may have been the modern village of el-Rahawi to the north-west of Letopolis.[460] There are no further attestations to this toponym after the Third Intermediate Period.

ID: ThIP_LE.34   **GEOREF:** NA
ArabicNAME: NA   **AEN_Hiero:**   **AEN_Trans:** *sḥbt*

Discussion: The settlement of *sḥbt* 'Sachebu' is recorded on a block of a King Shoshenq.[461] The settlement is not yet located. It is recorded on monuments and texts of the Hyksos Period, the New Kingdom, the Twenty-Sixth Dynasty, and the Ptolemaic–Roman Period up until the reign of the Emperor Trajan.[462] Further attestations to this site are found on a sphinx of Pinudjem I at Karnak.[463] Two stelae from the Ptolemaic Period relate to priests and their titles in the region of Memphis and Letopolis.[464] This may indicate that the location of Sachebu may be found in the region. The evidence from just to the north of this region at Kom el-Hisn and Kom Firin during the Twenty-Second to Twenty-Fourth Dynasty shows the development of the western Delta by both Shoshenq III and Shoshenq V, and Sachebu may have undergone renovations by one of these Shoshenqs during this period.

3 East of Classical Sebennytic

ID: ThIP_LE.35   **GEOREF:** 31°3′25.99″N 31°34′53.09″E
ArabicNAME: Tell Tebilla   **AEN_Hiero:** ⊙⌇⊗   **AEN_Trans:** rꜥ-nfr

Discussion: Shoshenq I constructed a temple at Tell Tebilla. In the late Third Intermediate Period, Tell Tebilla was ruled by a King Osorkon along with the settlement at Bubastis.

ID: ThIP_LE.36   **GEOREF:** 30°56′59.67″N 31°26′10.04″E
ArabicNAME: El-Baqliya   **AEN_Hiero:** ⌐⌐⸗⸗⌣⎸⎸⊗   **AEN_Trans:** pr-ḏḥwtÿ-wp-rḥwy

Discussion: pr-ḏḥwtÿ-wp-rḥwy is equated with the classical Hermopolis Parva. To the south of the modern village of el-Baqliya a cluster of three low mounds make up the area of the ancient settlement.

1 Tell el-Naqus (north-east mound), only 2–3 m higher than the surrounding cultivation, comprises part of a rectangular 15 m thick, 10 m high enclosure wall, probably of Thirtieth Dynasty date, and a sacred lake. The mound has been used by the Egyptian military since the 1970s.

2 Tell el-Zereiqi/Kom Baqliya (west mound), 200 m in diameter, is separated from Tell el-Naqus by cultivated land and a modern roadway. This mound was a cemetery and an Ibis necropolis.

3 Tell el-Ahmar/Rub'a (south-west of Baqliya village), 1.5 km west of Tell el-Zereiqi, comprises Romano-Coptic material. There was also a headless statue of Nectanebo I and a possible naos of Apries from this site.[465]

The monumental remains that come from these mounds indicate the site's importance in the New Kingdom and the Late Period onwards. Third Intermediate Period evidence is lacking, with the only known evidence being from the Piankhy Stela, which states pr-ḏḥwtÿ-wp-rḥwy was ruled over by the eldest son of Count Djedameniuefankh, Ankhhor.[466]

ID: ThIP_LE.37   **GEOREF:** NA
ArabicNAME: NA   **AEN_Hiero:** ⎓⎹⎺⌐⌐⊙⎸   **AEN_Trans:** tꜣ-šwnt-rꜥ

Discussion: The Piankhy Stela documents that tꜣ-šwnt-rꜥ was ruled over by Count Djedameniuefankh. The settlement is not identified with a modern Arabic settlement. Thmuis, the partner settlement of Mendes, may have been ⎓⎹⎺⌐⌐⊙⎸ 'The Granary of Re'. There is a connection between Tell el-Timai (Thmuis) and the God Re, as the later Demotic story cycle of Pedubast, 'The Breastplate of Inaros', alludes to a southern fortress, naming Mendes and another location (the southern fortress) collectively as 'The Two Chicks of Re'.[467] This fortress was most likely established on the east bank of the Mendesian branch as a southern fortress of the Mendesian chiefs during the later Third Intermediate Period. The location would allow the Mendesian chiefs to control access to the grain and suggests that the late Third Intermediate Period fortress indicated on later documents could have been erected to secure the large granary. The inclusion of a town's name in conjunction with a granary facility indicates a consolidation and control of commodities at a local Mendesian level, an arrangement that is seen in the late Old Kingdom and First Intermediate Period, when the local nomarchs consolidated these local structures.[468] The position of the Mendesian branch at the time of the Third Intermediate Period may support this theory, as Herodotus mentions a Thmuite Nome with Tell el-Timai (Thmuis) as its capital, separate from the Mendesian Nome. This would indicate that a natural boundary (i.e. the Nile) separated the two cities, thus creating the ideal conditions for the Mendesian chiefs to fortify both the east and west banks of the Mendesian branch. The site of 𓂋𓏤𓃀𓏏𓊹𓇳 'The Granary of Re' remains elusive, and so far, there is no archaeological evidence from Thmuis for a Third Intermediate Period occupation.

ID: ThIP_LE.38   **GEOREF:** 30°57′15.87″N 31°31′5.17″E
ArabicNAME: Tell el-   **AEN_Hiero:** 𓉐𓃀𓎟𓆓�   **AEN_Trans:** *pr-bꜣ-nb-ḏd*
Rub'a

Discussion: The site of Mendes, modern-day Tell el-Rub'a, is recorded on the Onomasticon of Amenemope.[469] There is evidence for both burial activity and some form of settlement, along with temple building activity, in the city during the period, particularly under its Libyan chiefs. The Piankhy Stela recorded that Mendes was ruled over by Count Djedameniuefankh in the late Third Intermediate Period. Several donation stelae have also been found here that record donations of land to the city temple.[470] In addition to royal temple building, two blocks said to come from Tell el-Timai (Thmuis) (probably mistaken for Mendes) date to the late Twenty-Second to Twenty-Third Dynasty. The first records the name of Nesubanebdjed IV,[471] and the second records Hornakht B.[472]

ID: ThIP_LE.39   **GEOREF:** 30°40′58.70″N 31°21′15.54″E
ArabicNAME: Tell   **AEN_Hiero:** 𓏏𓈖𓏤𓏭   **AEN_Trans:** *tꜣ-rmw / ṯnt-*
Muqdam   *rmw*

Discussion: *tꜣ-rmw / ṯnt-rmw* is the classical Leontopolis, and the modern-day Tell Muqdam.[473] Tell Gadiya is part of the ancient site of Tell Muqdam and has been taken as a collective of the overall site.[474] The Piankhy Stela documents that Tell Muqdam was ruled over by a King Iuput in the late Third Intermediate Period. A statue from the reign of Shoshenq I was found at Tell Muqdam.[475] The burial of Karomama B (ca. 830 BCE) was also found at Tell Muqdam.[476] Other monuments of the period from Tell Muqdam include a seated statue of Senwosret III which was usurped by Osorkon II.[477] A bronze door hinge of Iuput II was found at Tell Muqdam.[478] Not far from Tell Muqdam is Mit Yaish. A donation stela found here is likely to have derived from Tell Muqdam.[479]

ID: ThIP_LE.40   **GEOREF:** NA
ArabicNAME: NA   **AEN_Hiero:** 𓈖𓊖   **AEN_Trans:** *tꜣ-ꜥn*

Discussion: In association with Leontopolis is the site of 𓈖𓊖 *tꜣ-ꜥn*. It is not located with certainty, but may be a variation of the later toponym 𓈖𓊖 *tꜣ-iri-tꜣ* documented on a stela of Year 8 of Psammetik I from Horbeit.[480] This is not localised with any certainty. It may be that Ta'an may be equated with the toponym 𓈖𓊖 *tꜣ-iri-tꜣ* found on a Year 8 stela of Psammetik I from Horbeit.[481] The site of *tꜣ-iri-tꜣ* was mentioned in connection with other place names and is located to the south of the site of Horbeit.[482] It is not certain that *tꜣ-iri-tꜣ* is the name of a settlement. It may have been just a field or the name of a field that was in the area of Horbeit The settlement must have been near Tell Muqdam as it was within the territory of Iuput II.

ID: ThIP_LE.41   **GEOREF:** NA
ArabicNAME: Ezbet   **AEN_Hiero:** NA   **AEN_Trans:** NA
Razaiqa

Discussion: Documented as EES Delta Survey 466. Ezbet Razaiqa is now completely levelled and the location is now unknown.[483] Pottery collected by the Amsterdam University survey of the eastern Delta provided evidence of Third Intermediate Period ceramics.[484]

ID: ThIP_LE.42   **GEOREF:** 30°27′48.11″N 31°10′53.62″E
ArabicNAME: Tell Atrib   **AEN_Hiero:** 𓉐   **AEN_Trans:** *ḥwt ḥry ib*

Discussion: This is the classical site of Athribis, the modern Tell Atrib (Benha), and is documented on the Piankhy Stela.[485] Additional toponyms in association with the site of Athribis documented on the Piankhy Stela include *mryt nt km-wr* 'The Harbour of Athribis'.

ID: ThIP_LE.43   **GEOREF:** 30°57′59.25″N 31°14′54.21″E
ArabicNAME: Sammanud   **AEN_Hiero:**   **AEN_Trans:** *ṯb-nṯr (t)*

Discussion: *ṯb-nṯr (t)* is the modern settlement of Sammanud, the capital of the Twelfth Lower Egyptian Nome. It lies on the West Bank of the modern Damietta Nile branch,[486] and the Piankhy Stela documents that it was ruled over by Count Akanosh.

ID: ThIP_LE.44   **GEOREF:** 31°1′40.06″N 31°17′19.88″E
ArabicNAME: Behbeit el- **AEN_Hiero:** or **AEN_Trans:** *nṯr, pr-ḥbit*
Hagar

Discussion: *nṯr* or *pr-ḥbit* is not located with certainty, but is regarded as being related to the region of Buto.[487] Netjer is related to Pediese on two statues of a Late Period date and deemed, like Tefnakht, to be taken in relation to Buto or Sais, but not at Sammanud (Sebennytos).[488] Netjer has been proposed to be located at Behbeit el-Hagar (the Iseum, or Isidis of the classical geographers).[489] The use of *pr-ḥbit* is the toponym for the modern Behbeit el-Hagar (Iseopolis).[490] Behbeit el-Hagar, based on this association of the toponym, was, according to the Piankhy Stela, ruled over by Count Akanosh.

ID: ThIP_LE.45   **GEOREF:** 30°52′54.21″N 31°14′5.12″E
ArabicNAME: Abu **AEN_Hiero:**   **AEN_Trans:** *pr-wsi*
Sir Bana   *r-nb-ḏdw*

Discussion: *pr-wsir-nb-ḏdw* 'The House of Osiris Lord of Djedu' (Greek: Βούσιρις; Coptic: Ⲡⲟⲩⲥⲓⲣⲉ), which is the modern town of Abu Sir Bana, is located on the West Bank of the modern Damietta branch of the Nile about 5.5 km south of Sammanud.[491] It was the capital of the Ninth Lower Egyptian Nome *'nḏty* Andjety.[492] The settlement of Busiris during the Third Intermediate Period is poorly understood, beyond the setting up of a donation stela in the reign of Shoshenq III[493] and the mention on the Piankhy Stela of Busiris being ruled over by the Count and Chief of the Ma, Pamiu.

ID: ThIP_LE.46   **GEOREF:** 31°15′37.15″N 31°34′22.64″E
ArabicNAME: Tell el- **AEN_Hiero:**   **AEN_Trans:** *sm3-bḥdt*
Balamun

Discussion: Tell el-Balamun is documented on the Onomasticon of Amenemope under the writing of *p3 iw n imn* 'The Island of Amun'.[494]

ID: ThIP_LE.47   **GEOREF:** 30°51′35.84″N 31°55′3.80″E
ArabicNAME: Nebesheh   **AEN_Hiero:** ⟨hieroglyphs⟩   **AEN_Trans:** *imt*
(Tell Fara'un)

Discussion: The cemetery at Nebesheh dates to the second half of the eleventh century BCE, which would place it in the Twenty-First Dynasty[495] and corresponds to the dating of the mention on the Onomasticon of Amenemope.[496] Further evidence of Third Intermediate Period settlement activity was identified at the site by the Supreme Council of Antiquities excavations.[497]

ID: ThIP_LE.48   **GEOREF:** 30°47′59.05″N 31°50′10.87″E
ArabicNAME: Qantir   **AEN_Hiero:** ⟨hieroglyphs⟩   **AEN_Trans:** *pr rᶜmssw mry ᶜmn ᶜ. w. s*

Discussion: *pr rᶜmssw mry ᶜmn ᶜ. w. s* 'The House of Ramesses II' is equated with the modern area of Qantir and is listed on the Onomasticon of Amenemope.[498] At Qantir (Site Q IV) a child pot burial of the tenth century BCE contained a child of ten months.[499] There continued to be some form of settlement activity at Qantir in Area IV in the area of the Royal Horse Stud during the early Third Intermediate Period based on the discovery of ceramics.[500]

ID: ThIP_LE.49   **GEOREF:** 30°58′39.58″N 32°10′31.00″E
ArabicNAME: Tell Belim   **AEN_Hiero:** ⟨hieroglyphs⟩   **AEN_Trans:** *šdḥrw*

Discussion: *šdḥrw* was the ancient Sethroe, with Sethroe being equated with classical Heracleopolis Parva in the eastern Delta.[501] The site of Tell Belim can be identified with the class Heracleopolis Parva. The position of *šdḥrw* on the Onomasticon of Amenemope[502] before Tanis and after Tell Nebesheh would appear to confirm the location of Tell Belim, which is between these two sites, as the correct identification of the site. Third Intermediate Period settlement remains have been identified at Tell Belim around the main temple.[503]

ID: ThIP_LE.50   **GEOREF:** 30°58′37.55″N 31°52′49.83″E
ArabicNAME: San el-Hagar   **AEN_Hiero:** ⟨hieroglyphs⟩   **AEN_Trans:** *ḏᶜnt*

Discussion: The ancient settlement of *ḏᶜnt* (classical: Tanis; modern: San el-Hagar) was one of the main religious and political centres of the Third Intermediate Period.[504]

ID: ThIP_LE.51   **GEOREF:** 30°34′10.96″N 31°30′57.93″E
ArabicNAME: Tell Basta   **AEN_Hiero:** ⟨hieroglyphs⟩   **AEN_Trans:** *pr-bꜣstt*

Discussion: Tell Basta is the ancient Bubastis. So far only the cemetery of the Middle and New Kingdom has been found; the Third Intermediate Period cemetery has not been discovered. A single pyramidion of Harhotep, which has been attributed through internal inscriptional references to Bubastis,[505] was dated on stylistic and epigraphic grounds to the Twenty-Second Dynasty.[506] There must have been a large cemetery at the site, which has not yet been discovered. From the middle of the Twenty-Second Dynasty onwards Bubastis began having land donated to it.[507] In the late Third Intermediate Period the Piankhy Stela documents that Bubastis was ruled by a King Osorkon.

ID: ThIP_LE.52   **GEOREF:** 30°37′31.48″N 31°38′8.69″E
ArabicNAME: El-Alaqma   **AEN_Hiero:** NA   **AEN_Trans:** NA

Discussion: The now-levelled site of el-Alaqma had Third Intermediate Period ceramics.[508]

ID: ThIP_LE.53   **GEOREF:** 30°39'40.04"N 31°44'0.40"E
ArabicNAME: Gezirat   **AEN_Hiero:** NA   **AEN_Trans:** NA
el-Tawila

Discussion: At Gezirat el-Tawila, Third Intermediate Period ceramics were identified.[509] A temple of Ramesses II was added to by Siamun as blocks of his were identified by the SCA in the local fields.[510]

ID: ThIP_LE.54   **GEOREF:** 30°44'22.71"N 31°45'16.35"E
ArabicNAME: Tell   **AEN_Hiero:** NA   **AEN_Trans:** NA
Fadadna/Tell Mindar

Discussion: Evidence of Third Intermediate Period ceramics were found in the surface survey by Amsterdam University.[511]

ID: ThIP_LE.55   **GEOREF:** 30°50'55.53"N 31°41'1.15"E
ArabicNAME: Tell   **AEN_Hiero:** NA   **AEN_Trans:** NA
Gherier

Discussion: Evidence of Third Intermediate Period ceramics were found in the surface survey by Amsterdam University.[512]

ID: ThIP_LE.56   **GEOREF:** 30°56'3.69"N 31°53'31.74"E
ArabicNAME: Tell   **AEN_Hiero:** NA   **AEN_Trans:** NA
Zuwelein

Discussion: A cemetery was discovered at Tell Zuwelein in the 1880s, but the necropolis had been plundered by the local inhabitants. The finds included a ushabti of Ankesesnese.[513] The burials in the necropolis date from the ninth to seventh century BCE.[514]

ID: ThIP_LE.57   **GEOREF:** 30°53'33.59"N 31°53'14.14"E
ArabicNAME: Tell   **AEN_Hiero:** NA   **AEN_Trans:** NA
Gumaiyima

Discussion: Tell Gumaiyima had a Third Intermediate Period temple and mud-brick enclosure.[515] Satellite images suggest that the enclosure that Griffith identified has now been built over by the modern village.

ID: ThIP_LE.58   **GEOREF:** 30°51'11.97"N 31°49'51.62"E
ArabicNAME: Tell   **AEN_Hiero:** NA   **AEN_Trans:** NA
Ibrahim Awad

Discussion: The western part of the Tell Ibrahim Awad mound had Third Intermediate Period ceramics.[516]

ID: ThIP_LE.59   **GEOREF:** 30°51'10.75"N 31°45'57.28"E
ArabicNAME: Tell   **AEN_Hiero:** NA   **AEN_Trans:** NA
Iswid (S)

Discussion: Tell Iswid (S), also known as Tell Haddadin, preserved Third Intermediate Period ceramics.[517]

ID: ThIP_LE.60   **GEOREF:** NA
ArabicNAME: NA   **AEN_Hiero:** 𓉐𓊪𓏏𓎛𓊖   **AEN_Trans:** *pr-ptḥ*

Discussion: There is a settlement that is known to have been active during the Twenty-First Dynasty called 𓉐𓊪𓏏𓎛𓊖 *pr-ptḥ* 'The House of Ptah'.[518] It was proposed that it was linked with 𓈖𓏭𓇋𓇋𓏏𓉐𓊖 *nȝy tȝ ḥwt* 'Tell el-Yahudiyah' as an overall reference to

Memphis,[519] but this has since been rejected.[520] There are numerous cults of the god Ptah in the Delta, with whom one of the western Delta waterways is also associated (the Water of Ptah). There is a temple called the temple of Ptah-Tanan located on that river bank, while in the Roman Period there was a town named Hephaestus (the Roman designation of Ptah).[521] Place names that relate to the god Ptah may be called Sanhur in Arabic.[522] A later Saite statue of a priest from Kafr ed-Deir (ancient Per Weret Hekau in the Twenty-Sixth Dynasty) in the north-eastern Delta mentions the owner being a Prophet of Ptah.[523] Using Gardiner's suggested association of ancient place names relating to the god Ptah with modern Arabic places with Sanhur in their names does not allow for the site of Per Ptah to be located in the neighbourhood of Kafr ed-Deir, as no such locations with Sanhur are to be found.[524] To the south of Kafr ed-Deir, there is a village called Sanhut el-Birak or 'Sanhut of the Swamps', which was a considerable small town at the end of the nineteenth century, by which time some of the ancient mounds had become swamps; the site has since been mined for sebakh.[525] Based on settlement maps and associated waterways, the site of Sanhut el-Birak would be located near both the Pelusiac and Tanitic branches, that is approximately 16.09 km upstream of the Pelusiac branch from the settlement of Zagazig and approximately 16.09 km upstream on the Tanitic branch from the settlement of Zagazig. The town was thus about 3.2 km from the banks of both projected Tanitic and Pelusiac courses. Beyond this there is no other evidence that would confirm that Sanhut el-Birak was the ancient Per Ptah.

ID: ThIP_LE.61   **GEOREF:** 30°17′32.01″N 31°19′54.04″E
ArabicNAME: Tell   **AEN_Hiero:** 𓈖𓇼𓏏𓉐𓊖   **AEN_Trans:** *nꜣy tꜣ ḥwt*
el-Yahudiyah

Discussion: *nꜣy tꜣ ḥwt* is the modern Tell el-Yahudiyah. The settlement is listed on the Onomasticon of Amenemope.[526] Tomb groups dating from the twelfth to eleventh century BCE, the eleventh to tenth century BCE, the tenth to ninth century BCE, and eighth century BCE have been found at the site.[527] Other monuments from Tell el-Yahudiyah include a bronze statue from the reign of Osorkon I;[528] Twenty-Second Dynasty block statues of the Head Doctor Pa'an-meni;[529] two granite fragments from the reign of Shoshenq V now in the British Museum;[530] and finally, a granite socle from Tell el-Yahudiyah from the reign of Iuput II.[531]

ID: ThIP_LE.62   **GEOREF:** 30°33′14.15″N 31°36′37.01″E
ArabicNAME: Saft   **AEN_Hiero:** 𓉐𓊃𓊪𓂧𓅱𓊖   **AEN_Trans:** *pr-spdw*
el-Henna

Discussion: *pr-spdw* is the modern site of Saft el-Henna and was the capital of the Twenty-Second Lower Egyptian Nome.[532] The cemetery at Saft el-Henna was used during this period, but the burials that were excavated by Duncan Garrow were poorly published. They were divided into different types, no such photos or drawings were provided, and any conclusions must be drawn from Garrow's own descriptions.[533] The groups that provided sufficient evidence for dating included sand pit graves, which, based on the presence of bronze bells and double-faced pendants, may link these burials with Petrie's class 4 Wadjet eye burials from Tell el-Yahudiyah, dated by Aston to the ninth century BCE; and brick-lined graves, one example of which is dated to the ninth–eighth century BCE.[534] Monuments of the Twenty-Second to Twenty-Fourth Dynasty include a group statue of Senwaset,[535] a scribe statue of the General Hor and Senwaset,[536] and a block statue of Mehnefertum.[537] The Piankhy Stela documents that Saft el-Henna was ruled over by Patjenfi, Count and Chief of the Ma in the late Third Intermediate Period.

ID: ThIP_LE.63   **GEOREF:** 30°31′46.48″N 31°37′13.42″E
ArabicNAME: Suwa   **AEN_Hiero:** NA   **AEN_Trans:** NA

Discussion: Suwa may have been a separate site or was possibly an extension of the Saft el-Henna mound and an additional cemetery location for Saft el-Henna during the period. Ceramics of the Third Intermediate Period have been identified at Suwa.[538]

ID: ThIP_LE.64   **GEOREF:** 30°33′12.88″N 32°5′56.41″E
ArabicNAME: Tell el-   **AEN_Hiero:** NA   **AEN_Trans:** NA
Maskhuta

Discussion: A temple of Shoshenq I was built at Tell el-Maskhuta, see Appendix 2. Other monuments from Tell el-Maskhuta include a Twenty-Second Dynasty (reign of Osorkon II) block statue with naos of Ankhkherednefer,[539] and a Twenty-Second to Twenty-Fourth Dynasty head of a block statue of Wekermen.[540]

ID: ThIP_LE.65   **GEOREF:** 30°32′53.49″N 31°57′53.62″E
ArabicNAME: Tell   **AEN_Hiero:** NA   **AEN_Trans:** NA
el-Retaba

Discussion: For temple building at Tell el-Retaba, see Appendix 2. A Polish–Slovak mission to Tell el-Retaba has uncovered the remains of Third Intermediate Period housing, workshops, and stables.[541] Other monuments from Tell el-Retaba include a seated statue of a man holding a shrine in front of him, dated to the reign of Osorkon II,[542] and a granite fragment of Shoshenq I.[543] Just to the north of the settlement site, Petrie located the cemetery, which contained several burials that can be dated to the Third Intermediate Period. All the tombs had been plundered in ancient times and the grave goods scattered over a wide area. The cemetery was not completely cleared, and the results were only partially published.[544] The tombs were in groups of brick chambers like those from Nebesheh.[545] The burials have been dated from the eleventh to seventh century BCE, therefore encompassing the entire period.[546]

ID: ThIP_LE.66   **GEOREF:** 30°40′52.31″N 31°38′27.03″E
ArabicNAME: Tukh el-   **AEN_Hiero:** 𓂧𓎡𓇌𓏤𓊖   **AEN_Trans:** dḳyt, bhnw
Qaramus   or 𓃀𓉔𓈖𓅱𓏤𓊖

Discussion: A donation stela dated to Year 10, Day 20 of the reign of Shoshenq III was found at Tukh el-Qaramus.[547] In the text there is mention of two toponyms called 𓂧𓎡𓇌𓏤𓊖 dḳyt and 𓃀𓉔𓈖𓅱𓊖 bhnw. The gods mentioned on this stela are Amun-Re 𓇋𓏥𓊹 nb pr b3w 'Lord of the Ba's' (a sanctuary in the Delta in an unknown locality), the great Mut, Mistress of 𓂝𓈖𓏤 Šnᶜ that was probably an epithet of Mut, and their son Khonsu.[548] These deities are found together on a Ptolemaic stela from Saqqara.[549] The writing of bhnw from the stela of Shoshenq III should be equated with the writing of 𓃀𓉔𓈖𓏤𓊖 bhnt from the later Ptolemaic stela.[550] The site of bhnt has not yet been located with certainty. It was proposed that the settlement should be located in the vicinity of Mit Ghamr[551] or Sakha,[552] but a proposal associating it with the area around Sakha was met with criticism.[553] The associated second and third order sites mentioned on donation stela are to be found in the local hinterland of the main settlement mentioned in the text; therefore the placing of 𓃀𓉔𓈖𓏤𓊖 almost 37.62 km to the north-west, across the proposed Tanitic and Mendesian trajectories in the region of the now modern Damietta branch, is untenable. Identification of the settlement and the connection with the location of the stela at Tukh el-Qaramus would indicate that it is to be found in the region Tukh el-Qaramus. The inscription of Piankhy documents a wr ᶜ3 n m p3-n-t3-bhnt 𓂧𓃀𓉔𓈖𓏤𓊖 (The Man of t3 bhnt).[554] This man is known as a Chief of the Meshwesh in the eastern Delta. Gomaà proposed that this was the name of a separate settlement. In the list of chiefs and governors of the Delta, this man and another, 𓊪𓈖𓅡𓏏𓊖 *pn-tȝ-wrt*, are the only ones who are not associated with an area of power.[555] Yoyotte suggested that these chiefs had been expelled from their cities just before Piankhy invaded. The Piankhy Stela therefore records the names of the cities where they had previously ruled, one being *wrt* and the other *bḥnt*. The toponym *bḥnt* or *bḥnw* is to be located in the eastern Nile delta and not in the region of Mit Ghamr or Sakha. The name *bḥnw* is not a village name but refers to the noun *bḥn* meaning castle or fortress.[556] Another toponym in association with the region of Tukh el-Qaramus is 𓂧𓏏𓊖 *dḳyt*.[557] Both *bḥnw* and *dḳyt* may refer to the same site, with Tukh el-Qaramus acting as one of the eastern military bases of the Libyan chiefs.[558] Finally, a faience vessel from the reign of Shoshenq III was found in the temple area of Tukh el-Qaramus.[559]

ID: ThIP_LE.67   **GEOREF**: NA
ArabicNAME: NA   **AEN_Hiero**: 𓅡𓏏𓊖   **AEN_Trans**: *wrt*

Discussion: See the entry above for Tukh el-Qaramus, which discusses the possibility of this being a settlement somewhere in the eastern Delta related to the man described on the Piankhy Stela as 𓊪𓈖𓅡𓏏𓊖 *pn-tȝ-wrt*. Another settlement in the eastern Delta with the name of *tȝ-wrt* is not known; there is a region called *wryt* in the region of Tanis, but this is only noted in the Ramesside Period and no links between the two toponyms can be provided.[560] If both 𓊪𓈖𓏏𓊖 and 𓊪𓈖𓅡𓏏𓊖 are the names of individual cities, this has an impact on the political geography of the Delta at the time of Piankhy's invasion[561] and would imply that the eastern Delta was much more fragmented than was previously thought.

ID: ThIP_LE.68   **GEOREF**: 30°42′29.86″N 31°37′48.14″E
ArabicNAME: Horbeit   **AEN_Hiero**: 𓍲𓏏𓊖   **AEN_Trans**: *šdnw*

Discussion: The ancient settlement of *šdnw*, the classical Pharbaitos, is poorly known for the Third Intermediate Period, but it had its own line of Libyan chiefs who ruled over it.[562]

ID: ThIP_LE.69   **GEOREF**: 30°44′43.07″N 31°40′17.49″E
ArabicNAME: Gezirat Sultan Hassan   **AEN_Hiero**: NA   **AEN_Trans**: NA

Discussion: Ceramics of the Third Intermediate Period have been identified at Gezirat Sultan Hassan.[563]

ID: ThIP_LE.70   **GEOREF**: 30°47′1.75″N 31°48′31.47″E
ArabicNAME: El-Khataana   **AEN_Hiero**: NA   **AEN_Trans**: NA

Discussion: Some form of settlement activity continued at el-Khataana in the Twenty-First Dynasty as a block of Siamun has been found there.[564]

ID: ThIP_LE.71   **GEOREF**: 30°47′12.26″N 31°49′26.34″E
ArabicNAME: Tell el-Daba   **AEN_Hiero**: NA   **AEN_Trans**: NA

Discussion: Some form of settlement activity continued at Tell el-Daba.[565]

ID: ThIP_LE.72   **GEOREF**: 30°55′8.01″N 32°3′0.98″E
ArabicNAME: Tell Ginn   **AEN_Hiero**: NA   **AEN_Trans**: NA

Discussion: Tell Ginn is located 3 km to the east of Minshat Abu Omar, and surface survey found Third Intermediate Period ceramics of an undefined dynastic phase.[566]

ID: ThIP_LE.73   **GEOREF**: 30°57′56.01″N 32°25′25.16″E
ArabicNAME: Tell el-Ghaba   **AEN_Hiero**: NA   **AEN_Trans**: NA
Discussion: A Third Intermediate Period settlement has been identified at Tell el-Ghaba.[567]

ID: ThIP_LE.74   **GEOREF**: 30°56′14.20″N 32°22′31.83″E
ArabicNAME: Tell   **AEN_Hiero**:   **AEN_Trans**: *pr ḥtm n iзrw*
Heboua
Discussion: *pr ḥtm n iзrw* is listed on the Onomasticon of Amenemope.[568] This toponym can now be identified with the modern Tell Heboua.[569]

ID: ThIP_LE.75   **GEOREF**: 31°4′44.24″N 31°45′57.85″E
ArabicNAME: Tell   **AEN_Hiero**: NA   **AEN_Trans**: NA
Buweib
Discussion: At Tell Buweib a late New Kingdom mud-brick temple was identified. The temple was founded at a low level and its presence may have been the primary factor in the creation of the settlement on the mound in which it is now buried. There was an accumulation of collapse and erosion of the temple's brickwork and above this accumulation were fills of late Third Intermediate Period ceramics, which date the abandonment of the temple.[570]

ID: ThIP_LE.76   **GEOREF**: 30°47′1.10″N 31°28′2.76″E
ArabicNAME: Barakim   **AEN_Hiero**: NA   **AEN_Trans**: NA
Discussion: Surface surveys of the site have identified Third Intermediate Period ceramics.[571]

ID: ThIP_LE.77   **GEOREF**: NA
ArabicNAME: NA   **AEN_Hiero**:   **AEN_Trans**: *pr-grr*
Discussion: This place name is mentioned on a Demotic papyrus in the Cairo Museum.[572] The location of the settlement is controversial. Several identifications have been proposed, including Phagroriopolis and Kom el-Schuqafa (south of Tell el-Kebir).[573] It cannot be said if *pr-grr* can be identified with Kom el-Schuqafa. *pr-grr* must be situated in the eastern Delta and it was ruled over by the Count and Chief of the Ma, Nakhthornashenu, documented on the Piankhy Stela.

ID: ThIP_LE.78   **GEOREF**: NA
ArabicNAME: NA   **AEN_Hiero**:   **AEN_Trans**: *nb pr bзw*
Discussion: 'Lord of the Ba's' is recorded on a donation stela from Tukh el-Qaramus dated to Year 10, Day 20 of the reign of Shoshenq III.[574] The gods mentioned on this stela include Amun-Re *nb pr bзw* 'Lord of the Ba's'. This was a sanctuary in the Delta in an unknown locality.

ID: ThIP_LE.79   **GEOREF**: NA
ArabicNAME: NA   **AEN_Hiero**:   **AEN_Trans**: *šnwt tз - inb - ḥd*
Discussion: *šnwt tз - inb - ḥd* 'The Granary of Memphis' was ruled over by Patjenfi as documented on the Piankhy Stela. The writing of *pn* in the name is most likely a scribal error for *tз*. The settlement is probably located in the region of Saft el-Henna,[575] or simply in the eastern Delta.[576]

ID: ThIP_LE.80   **GEOREF:** NA

ArabicNAME: NA   **AEN_Hiero:** 𓄋𓊪𓏏𓇯𓈖𓉐   **AEN_Trans:** *wsi n pt*

Discussion: On a Twenty-Second to Twenty-Fourth Dynasty statue of
Djedbastefankh, the toponym *wsi n pt* (lit. Window of Heaven) is recorded.[577] The
statue owner is recorded as the Infantry Commander of *wsi-n-pt*, indicating its role as
a military settlement in the eastern Delta.

ID: ThIP_LE.81   **GEOREF:** NA

ArabicNAME: NA   **AEN_Hiero:** 𓎡𓐠𓈖𓏌   **AEN_Trans:** *kꜣhni*

Discussion: To the south of the settlement of Athribis in the Delta was the toponym of
kꜣhni. The location of this toponym is likely to be equated with the modern settlement
of Qaha about halfway between Cairo and Benha, or the village of Kafr Muies, 5 km to
the south of Athribis. However, these suggestions are not supported.[578]

ID: ThIP_LE.82   **GEOREF:** NA

ArabicNAME: NA   **AEN_Hiero:** 𓉔𓊪𓄿   **AEN_Trans:** *hpw*

Discussion: *hpw* 'Khapu' was a settlement that rose to prominence in the Twenty-
First Dynasty and was most likely located in the region of Tanis.[579]

ID: ThIP_LE.83   **GEOREF:** NA

ArabicNAME: NA   **AEN_Hiero:**   **AEN_Trans:** *pꜣ-sbtỷ-n-ššnḳ*
𓊠𓏏𓈎𓊪𓈖𓈙𓈙𓏌𓎡

Discussion: In the reign of Shoshenq III, one of his sons, Bakennefi A, is known
from a stela found near Heliopolis, mentioning the foundation of 𓊠𓏏𓈎𓊪𓈖𓈙𓈙𓏌𓎡
pꜣ-sbtỷ-n-ššnḳ 'The Wall of Shoshenq'.[580] The noun *sbty* has the meaning of 'wall' or
'fortification'.[581] The writing of the word *sbty* does not indicate that it was a simple
temple enclosure. It is therefore likely that 'The Wall/Fortification of Shoshenq (III)'
was a military foundation set up in the eastern Delta not far from Heliopolis where the
stela was erected. The Egyptian term *pꜣ sbty* is rendered into Greek as ψωβθις.[582] Arabic
place names preserved the memory of these small, fortified establishments in the form
Saft.[583] There are several instances of the Arabic toponym Saft in Middle Egypt that
relate to ancient military centres,[584] and two such locations are known with the
toponym Saft in the Nile Delta. They are Saft el-Laban on the West Bank of the Nile to
the south of Imbaba in the Giza Governate, and the site of Saft el-Henna located to the
south-east of Bubastis and near the entrance of the Wadi Tumilat. The location of Saft
el-Henna in the entrance to the Wadi Tumilat would have provided a strong strategic
location for the control of this access point into the eastern Delta. Three statues of non-
royal individuals come from Saft el-Henna that are dated to the Twenty-Second to
Twenty-Fourth Dynasty. The first was a statue of the General Senwaset,[585] dated to the
Twenty-Second Dynasty;[586] the second was a scribe statue of the General Hor, the son
of Senwaset;[587] while the third statue was a block statue of Mehnefertum.[588] Further
material comes from Twenty-Fifth Dynasty activity at Saft el-Henna, with a seated
figure of Kheru[589] and an unnamed block statue.[590] Saft el-Henna preserves the
remains of a burial ground dated to the Third Intermediate Period, but it was too
poorly published to define phases of burial activity further.[591] The statue of Senwaset
lists several military titles, while his son Hor is named as general, indicating that the site
of Saft el-Henna at this period was the home to several military personnel. None of the
associated texts mention the toponym of 'The Wall of Shoshenq (III)' in association
with Saft el-Henna. In conclusion, the presence of military personnel at Saft el-Henna
in the period of Shoshenq III, the strategic location in relation to the Wadi Tumilat,
and the single association of the term Saft in the eastern Delta with preserved Third
Intermediate Period remains would strongly argue for 'The Wall of Shoshenq (III)'

being located at, or near, Saft el-Henna, but as this cannot be confirmed the location has been given a unique identifier.

GEOGRAPHICAL ZONES AND GEOLOGICAL AND HYDROLOGICAL FEATURE LOCATIONS

ID: ThIP_GeoZon.1   **RG:** 3rd UE Nome
ArabicNAME: Edfu   **AEN_Hiero:** ⊇⊪⊛   **AEN_Trans:** *bḥd.t*
Discussion: ⊇⊪⊛ *bḥd.t* is the overall name for the settlement and its districts at Edfu.

ID: ThIP_GeoZon.2   **RG:** North-east Nile Delta
ArabicNAME: The   **AEN_Hiero:**   **AEN_Trans:** *p3-ṯwf*
Ballah Lake Region   𓆰𓆱⟜𓎡𓆰𓈉
Discussion: The toponym 𓆰𓆱⟜𓎡𓆰𓈉 *p3-ṯwf* 'The Papyrus Marshes' is recorded on the Onomasticon of Amenemope.[592] The toponym is recorded earlier in the Nineteenth Dynasty on P. Chester Beatty II.[593] In Papyrus Anastasi, the Nile Valley is compared to a large ox that is 'Standing in Tell el-Balamun and the top of its tail rests upon the Papyrus Marshes'.[594] The toponym is therefore likely to indicate a region standing in between the site of Tell el-Balamun and the Mediterranean coast, probably that of Lake Menzaleh. Other texts indicate a more restricted area in the Menzaleh region.[595] The Papyrus Marshes have been associated with the Hebrew *yām sûp* or the Re(d) Sea of the biblical Exodus tradition, and the etymological relationship between these two locations has been confirmed.[596] 'The Papyrus Marshes' is written in association with the site of Tjaru/Sile which is located at Tell Heboua in the northern Sinai,[597] and therefore must be in close proximity to it. The writing of 'The Papyrus Marshes' with the settlement determinative indicates a circumscribed topographical area.[598] New linguistic evidence now supports the identification of 'The Papyrus Marshes' with the Ballah Lakes.[599] The ancient name is preserved in the modern site of Tell Abu Sefeh, the site that was likely the Ptolemaic–Roman Sile.[600] Arabic place names often preserve some variation of the original ancient toponym, but this is not the case with Tell Abu Sefeh and Sile. Linguistic evidence shows that Abu Sefeh preserved the name of the ancient lake (Ballah) adjacent to Sile, i.e. The Papyrus Marshes.

ID: ThIP_GeoZon.3   **RG:** In the Mendesian hinterland, near the site of Tell Tebilla
ArabicNAME: NA   **AEN_Hiero:** 𓃀𓃀𓏏𓊖𓈉   **AEN_Trans:** *ww r⁽-nfr*
Discussion: The *ww* 'district' documented in Piankhy in relation to the settlement of *r⁽-nfr* is likely to indicate the area around the site of Tell Tebilla. The district is also documented on a Twenty-Second to Twenty-Fourth Dynasty block of a King Hedjkhepere.[601]

ID: ThIP_GeoZon.4   **RG:** In the region of Tell Atrib
ArabicNAME: NA   **AEN_Hiero:** 𓂿𓏏𓏤𓊪𓃒   **AEN_Trans:** *mṯn nt sp3*
Discussion: *mṯn nt sp3* is translated as 'The Road of Sepa'. This was possibly an overland route. Sepa was a god in the region of Heliopolis who was associated with Osiris.[602]

ID: ThIP_GeoZon.5   **RG:** In the region of Heliopolis
ArabicNAME: NA   **AEN_Hiero:** 𓏏𓈗   **AEN_Trans:** *iti*
Discussion: *iti* designates a canal located in the modern area of Heliopolis.[603] The *iti* branch of the Nile is distinguished from the 'Waters of Pre'.[604]

ID: ThIP_GeoZon.6 **RG:** Tanitic hinterland
ArabicNAME: NA **AEN_Hiero:** **AEN_Trans:** *rꜣ-ꜣḥt*

Discussion: *rꜣ-ꜣḥt* 'The Opening of the Fields' is documented on the Twenty-Second Dynasty statue of Gerew from the time of Shoshenq I, found at Tanis.[605]

ID: ThIP_GeoZon.7 **RG:** Memphite Area
ArabicNAME: NA **AEN_Hiero:** **AEN_Trans:** *r-n-itr*

Discussion: 'Mouth of the River' is recorded on the Onomasticon of Amenemope and may link to the toponym of *pr-ḥꜥpy*, the modern Atar en-Naby which was believed to be the entrance to the Nile Delta.[606]

ID: ThIP_GeoZon.8 **RG:** Western Delta
ArabicNAME: NA **AEN_Hiero:** **AEN_Trans:** *itrw imntt*

Discussion: For a discussion of this river course in the western Delta, see Chapter 2.

ID: ThIP_GeoZon.9 **RG:** Western Delta
ArabicNAME: NA **AEN_Hiero:** **AEN_Trans:** *ḫns*

Discussion: For a discussion of this river course in the western Delta, see Chapter 2.

ID: ThIP_GeoZon.10 **RG:** Central Delta
ArabicNAME: NA **AEN_Hiero:** **AEN_Trans:** *itrw ꜥꜣ*

Discussion: For a discussion of the hydrology of the central Delta during the Third Intermediate Period, see Chapter 2.

ID: ThIP_GeoZon.11 **RG:** The Tanite Hinterland
ArabicNAME: NA **AEN_Hiero:** **AEN_Trans:** *spꜣt ḫpwt*

Discussion: A Late Period statue of a man called Mermay documents the District of Khapuwt and the associated town of Khapu.[607] The statue is dedicated to the Goddess Merit-Re and Weret Hekau, Mistress of the Palace, residing in the 'District of Khapuwt'.[608] The statue mentions *Per Weret Hekau*, which is the ancient name for the modern settlement of Kafr ed-Deir.[609] The 'District of Khapuwt' that is mentioned by this Twenty-Sixth Dynasty statue has no more textual references and no indications as to where it may have been located. The 'District of Khapuwt' is the civil name for the region,[610] and the Saite settlement of Per Weret Hekau is to be associated with this district. In the Twenty-First Dynasty there is a mention of a settlement called 'Khapu' on a statue dedicated to Osiris by Ankhefenamun, who was the Great Chamberlain and the royal scribe to Psusennes I.[611] Ankhefenamun was buried at Tanis in a lavish tomb.[612] The statue was found at a site halfway between Tanis and Kafr Sakr. Khapu must have been the main administrative settlement for the 'District of Khapu' mentioned later in the Saite Period. The locations of the 'District of Khapuwt' and the settlement of 'Khapu' are somewhat challenging. The find spot of the statue of Ankhefenamun mentioning Khapu was a site somewhere between Tanis and Kafr Sakr. This would place the site in the area of the proposed Tanitic Nile branch region. The site of Kafr ed-Deir that mentions the district of Khapuwt lies on the upstream section of the Tanitic branch of the Nile proposed by Bietak, which runs approximately on the course of the modern Bahr Muweis waterway. Each of the sites of Kafr ed-Deir and Kafr Sakr are to be found in the region of the proposed Tanitic branch. The first mention of Khapu in the Twenty-First Dynasty and its association with elite members at Tanis would indicate that this settlement came to prominence in the Twenty-First

Dynasty or was itself a new foundation of the period, as it is not mentioned prior to the Third Intermediate Period. The connection of the town location of Khapu and its associated district of Khapuwt within the area of the Tanitic Nile branch and the elite members at Tanis would seem to indicate that the district of Khapuwt formed part of the large area between the cities of Tanis and Kafr Sakr and onwards to the site of Kafr ed-Deir. The location of Khapu may therefore be in the area of the Tanitic hinterland and most likely in the area of the proposed Tanitic Nile course. Between Kafr Sakr and Tanis there are only two sites that provide evidence of Third Intermediate Period ceramics, namely Tell Gherier and Tell Iswid South. No inscriptions have come to light that can determine whether the sites of Tell Gherier or Tell Iswid South are to be equated with Khapu. The existence of this region suggests that smaller parcels of land bounded by waterways were an important method of dividing the landscape, with these few mentions perhaps representing a general practice for the way in which land and settlement relationships were organised.

ID: ThIP_GeoZon.12   **RG:** Western Delta near Kom el-Hisn
ArabicNAME: NA   **AEN_Hiero:** 🔲   **AEN_Trans:** ꜥn / ꜥyn
Discussion: This was an area of wetlands or marshes in the area of Imau, the capital of the province of the west.[613] Evidence of the environment in the Kom el-Hisn hinterland is documented on the Piankhy Stela with the toponym 🔲 ꜥyn (Canal),[614] indicating another 'canal' from the western Delta riverine landscape.[615] The mention of this location on the stela must indicate that Piankhy felt it was an important feature of the western Delta landscape.

ID: ThIP_GeoZon.13   **RG:** In the 12th/13th Upper Egyptian Nome
ArabicNAME: NA   **AEN_Hiero:**   **AEN_Trans:** ww-n-wḥꜥ
🔲
Discussion: ww-n-wḥꜥ 'The Area/District of Fishing and Catching Birds' is recorded on the Onomasticon of Amenemope.[616] It is unknown whether the site is to be located within either the Twelfth or Thirteenth Upper Egyptian Nome, but this settlement that was active in the Twenty-First Dynasty could be bounded geographically by the sites of Asyut and el-Atawla, as indicated by its relative position on the Onomasticon of Amenemope.

ID: ThIP_GeoZon.14   **RG:** The Memphite Region
ArabicNAME: NA   **AEN_Hiero:**   **AEN_Trans:** pny-nꜣ-ywꜥ
🔲
Discussion: The reading of 🔲 is possibly dmi-pn-inꜣiw.[617] It may also be read as pꜣ=nni-iw 'The Place where the Inundation Stops',[618] where there is a Memphite location dedicated to Sekhmet.[619] However, 'The Place where the Inundation Stops' is only attested later on in the Ptolemaic Period.[620] The location may be also seen as designating a geographical feature linked to the Nile, most likely that of whirlpools.[621]

ID: ThIP_GeoZon.15   **RG:** The Memphite Region
ArabicNAME: NA   **AEN_Hiero:** 🔲   **AEN_Trans:** ww pgꜣ
Discussion: On a block statue of Nespaqashuty dated to Shoshenq III from Thebes, the toponym of 🔲 ww pgꜣ 'The District of Pega' is documented, and Nespaqashuty is called the High Priest of Osiris of 'The District of Pega'.[622] This toponym is again met with on the Piankhy Stela in which there is specific reference to a 🔲 pr-pgꜣ. The location of this town and the subsequent district is in the south of the Memphite Nome, just to the north of Heracleopolis.[623]

ID: ThIP_GeoZon.16   **RG:** The Memphite Region
ArabicNAME: NA   **AEN_Hiero:**   **AEN_Trans:** *ꜣ ꜥt n ḥr*

𓈙𓏏𓎆𓃀𓈖𓎡𓆱𓏤𓊌

Discussion: See Appendix 3, The House of Millions of Years of Shoshenq I.

ID: ThIP_GeoZon.17   **RG:** 21ˢᵗ Upper Egyptian Nome: The Faiyum
ArabicNAME: The   **AEN_Hiero:** See   **AEN_Trans:** See
Faiyum   discussion below   discussion below

Discussion: There are several different designations for the Faiyum during the Third Intermediate Period and they have been recorded here. They do not constitute an individual site but a wider geographical area.

𓈗𓏤𓇼𓏏𓈖 *š* 'The Lake' Twenty-First Dynasty.[624]

𓈗𓈖 *ꜣ š* 'The Lake' from a re-inscribed Middle Kingdom statue possibly found at Crocodopolis.[625]

𓈗𓏥 *Tꜣ š* 'The Lake'. Reign of Shoshenq III, Year 39, 1ˢᵗ Month of Shemu, Day 26. Karnak.[626]

𓈗𓊖 *ꜣ š* 'The Lake': possible designation for the Faiyum. Possibly dated to the Third Intermediate Period inscription found on the cartonnage of a mummy at Lahun.[627]

𓎛𓈗𓏤 *wpt š* 'The Opening of the Lake', i.e. the entrance to the Faiyum.[628]

APPENDIX 2

TEMPLE BUILDING OF THE TWENTY-SECOND TO TWENTY-FOURTH DYNASTY

Unlike the main Third Intermediate Period site gazetteer (Appendix 1), Appendix 2 includes temple building in the Oases. This appendix focuses on the built remains and decoration of new and existing temples and temple elements in the Twenty-Second to Twenty-Fourth Dynasty, and when temple building is indicated within texts. For other royal monuments, see Appendix 1 for documentation and further reference, including temple building in the Twenty-First Dynasty.

SHOSHENQ I

1 Tanis

Two monumental blocks of Shoshenq I were re-used in the new gateway of Shoshenq III which cut through the earlier mud-brick temenos wall of Psusennes I.[1] A pillar from the Mut temple complex bears his name,[2] along with a cavetto cornice block from the Great Temple of Amun.[3] Furthermore, two sphinxes of Amenemhat II,[4] which were originally re-inscribed by Merenptah,[5] were usurped by Shoshenq I, and most probably came from the Ramesside capital of Piramesse. Of the blocks documented above, only one from the Shoshenq III gateway and the other from the Mut temple complex can confidently be said to have come from Tanis as they both name the local Tanite triad of Amun, Mut, and Khonsu.[6]

2 Tell el-Maskhuta

A granite fragment of Shoshenq I from the temple of Tell el-Maskhuta has the remains of two offering scenes.[7]

3 Bubastis

The only evidence from the reign of Shoshenq I at Bubastis or in its vicinity is a quartzite relief,[8] and maybe a limestone block with two partial cartouches.[9] A limestone lintel discovered at Bubastis was once suggested to be the joint work of Psusennes II and Shoshenq I, but is now assigned to Tut-kheper-Re Shoshenq IIb and is documented below.

4 Athribis

A single limestone fragment bearing the name of Shoshenq I was found at Athribis.[10]

5 Tell Tebilla

Several temple blocks bearing the prenomen *ḥd-[ḥpr]-rꜥ stp-[n-r']* were found at Tell Tebilla.[11] This is the prenomen used for Smendes I, Shoshenq I, Takeloth I, Harsiese, and Takeloth II.[12] The best candidate for the builder of the temple is Shoshenq I owing to the relative proximity to both Tanis and Bubastis, and the widespread building programme of Shoshenq I in the Delta.[13] The blocks were unprovenanced on the site, but in the 1990s the SCA found an intact stretch of limestone paving, column bases, and drainage channel from a destroyed temple which was probably the same temple from which the blocks came.[14]

6 Memphis

Shoshenq I built widely at Memphis.[15] A cavetto cornice block of his was found in the Ptah temple.[16] The cavetto cornice was probably from a new monumental gateway or pylon.[17] This new gateway was added on to the existing Ptah temple in front of the pylon and hypostyle hall of Seti I and Ramesses II, and probably represents Shoshenq's 'House of Millions of Years'.[18] Other monuments include two column fragments[19] and a carved limestone block depicting a scene of offerings by Nile gods,[20] which may have originally come from the Ptah complex and not from Saqqara where it was found, as 'Chosen of Ptah' and not 'Chosen of Re' was used in the prenomen of Shoshenq I.[21] Finally, what is probably a lintel from the embalming house of the Apis Bull at Kom el-Fakri is known.[22]

7 Heliopolis

There is a possible attribution of a block of Shoshenq I from Heliopolis.[23] However, both the pharaoh and the provenance cannot be stated with certainty.[24]

8 Heracleopolis

Some cultic activity was resumed at Heracleopolis under Shoshenq's son Nimlot for the cult of Heryshef.[25] However, it is not known if additions to the temple were made at the same time.

9 El-Hibeh

Shoshenq I constructed a new temple to Amun which is now destroyed.[26] The temple dimensions were 17.65 x 30 m. It consisted of a hypostyle hall of two by four pillars, an offering chamber, and a barque sanctuary with four side rooms for the cult images, and it was finely carved.[27]

10 Thebes

After the campaign of Shoshenq I in the Levant, he planned to construct a grand new pylon and make a festival hall for Amun-Re, surrounded with statues and a colonnade. The project was called 'The Mansion of Hedjkhepere Setepenre in Thebes'.[28] Before the Second Pylon of the Great Amun temple a vast court was added with lateral colonnades, which was probably enclosed by a pylon gateway where the pylon of Nectanebo now stands (Pylon I). Fragments of blocks with the cartouche of Shoshenq I have been found in the foundations of the rostrum of the First Pylon.[29] By the southern exit from the court, along the south face of Pylon II, was engraved the huge triumphal scenes of the king's campaign to Palestine. Next to these scenes was constructed the great Bubastite Gateway, and its side pilasters were decorated on the north side with three scenes of Shoshenq I, Iuput, and the gods, while the architrave was adorned with the titles of Shoshenq I, engraved in large scale.[30] Shoshenq I died suddenly, and his works were left unfinished.[31]

OSORKON I

During the first four years of the reign of Osorkon I, he bestowed large gifts of gold and silver vessels and furnishings upon the temples of the major deities of Egypt, including Re-Horakhty, Hathor Nebet-hetepet, Mut, Heryshef, All (?) of Heliopolis, Thoth of Hermopolis, Bast of Bubastis, and Amen-Re.[32]

1 Bubastis

At Bubastis, an inscription recording the donations to the temples of Egypt by Osorkon I was recorded on broken fragments of a granite pillar in the Atum temple, which was probably an enlargement, or a renewal, of the existing Ramesside structure by Osorkon I 600 m away from the main precinct and therefore likely outside the main precinct of Bubastis.[33] In the main precinct of the Bastet enclosure, Osorkon I built extensively inside the enclosure no doubt because the temple had fallen into disrepair.[34] Osorkon I renewed the main sanctuary, but his works are so heavily destroyed that the original layout is unknown.[35] The debris mounds indicate Osorkon I began a new construction of a temple house and a court. The gates and columns were built of granite, while the walls were probably of limestone. The front part of the temple consisted of a hypostyle hall with a central row of 8.55 m high papyrus bundle columns of granite, which were probably flanked by smaller 6.71 m high palm columns. The hypostyle hall probably had a higher central nave, but nothing is known regarding the temple house behind.[36]

2 Memphis

At Memphis half of a lintel of Osorkon I was found from a large shrine of Bast.[37]

3 Atfih

Osorkon I constructed a small chapel (?) at the temple of Isis at Atfih.[38]

4 El-Hibeh

The temple of Shoshenq I was continued under Osorkon I by the addition of five offering scenes in the north half of the rear wall of the temple.[39]

5 Quft

Osorkon I added his name to a doorway of Thutmose III in the north chapel at Quft.[40]

6 Thebes

At Karnak, offering scenes were added by Osorkon I to the Bubastite Gate.[41]

SHOSHENQ IIB

1 Bubastis

A block of Shoshenq IIb was found in the great temple at Bubastis, indicating he conducted some building work there.[42]

OSORKON II

1 Tanis

Osorkon II enlarged the temple of Amun by adding two pylons and associated courts on the front of Siamun's works.[43] The temple was now doubled in length at 234 m long. The emplacement of all the pylons at Tanis is based on the position of fallen obelisks usurped from Piramesse. In front of the first pylon of Osorkon II stood obelisks 1 and 2. In the court behind were 3 and 4. This court enclosed the two colossal sphinxes of Shoshenq I usurped from Amenemhat II.[44] This court was attributed to Osorkon II by the finding of foundation deposits in the north-west and south-west corners of the Amun temple.[45]

2 Bubastis

Osorkon II continued the work of Osorkon I at Bubastis. He added a new hypostyle hall of granite pillars with Hathor heads. The higher central row was probably flanked by smaller ones like the previous court of Osorkon I. This hypostyle hall was built in connection with the new Sed Festival Gate, and probably stood at the front of the court which led to the hypostyle hall. The gate was decorated on the front, interior, and inside the doorway with several registers depicting the rites. The door width was ca. 5 m and the total height was ca. 15 m.[46] Osorkon II built a small Mahes temple ca. 60 m north behind the Bastet temple,[47] which may have been a version of an early birth house (mammisi) as Mahes was the child of Bastet and Atum.[48] A large granite naos was dedicated to Bastet by Osorkon II.[49]

3 Leontopolis

A large building project of Osorkon I may be indicated at Leontopolis as a block naming this king and his officer Harmose was found here.[50] Furthermore, the re-inscribing of one of two statues of Senwosret III[51] may have been in connection with this new chapel or temple, which may be attributed to Mahes, who was the son of Bastet, or Sekhmet.[52]

4 Thebes

A block of Osorkon I from the south wall of the northern courtyard near the Sixth Pylon at Karnak has eight columns of a decree for the temple of Amun.[53] Remains of a small chapel of Horemheb at the sacred Lake of Karnak were renewed by Osorkon II.[54] Re-used blocks of a door of Osorkon II were found in the Montu temple.[55] A chapel (Chapel E) was constructed at Karnak North with scenes of Osorkon II and Queen Karomama in Room I.[56] There was wall decoration added to Chapel J (the Isis Chapel) in Karnak East.[57]

HARSIESE

1 *Thebes*

Little survives of the religious building activity from the reign of Harsiese, but all his works have been recovered from the Theban region. He had himself represented on the gateway of the south wing of the Fourth Pylon at Karnak,[58] while his cartouche appears in the forecourt of the Khonsu temple at Karnak above columns 18 and 19.[59] Finally, a block of his was re-used in a gate of the Ptolemaic enclosure wall at the small temple of Deir el-Medina.[60]

TAKELOTH II

1 *Thebes*

Takeloth II commissioned a restoration text in the sixth gateway of the Ptah temple at Karnak North.[61] In addition, wall reliefs of Takeloth II and the Gods Wife Karomama Meyrtmut were added to Chapel E in Karnak North.[62]

SHOSHENQ III

1 *Tanis*

At Tanis, Shoshenq III built a new western gateway for the Great Temple of Amun. This was a large pylon gateway of granite built through the enclosure wall of Psusennes I. The new gateway became the main processional route into the Great Amun temple at Tanis. Shoshenq III also re-used works from Piramesse.[63] The dating of this new western gateway was further confirmed by the location of two foundation plaques of Shoshenq III found in the south-east corner of the gateway.[64]

2 *Memphis*

Three blocks of Shoshenq III were found belonging to either a Ptah or Sekhmet chapel.[65]

3 *Tell Mostai (Tell Umm Harb)*

Re-used blocks of Ramesses II were used for the construction of a new sanctuary by Shoshenq III.[66]

4 *Bindariya*

A block of Shoshenq III was found at Bindariya,[67] indicating a small sanctuary, possibly like the one at Tell Mostai (Tell Umm Harb).

5 *Mendes*

Blocks were found from a building, most likely another chapel of Shoshenq III.[68]

6 Tell el-Balamun

Foundation deposits of Shoshenq III were found under the north-west wing of the Second Pylon.[69]

7 Kom el-Hisn

Blocks from a gateway of Shoshenq III were found at the front of the temple of Ramesses II.[70]

PEDUBAST

1 Dakhleh Oasis

A sunken relief block of Pedubast showing the king facing right and wearing the crown of Tatenen was found in the Dakhleh Oasis.[71]

2 Bubastis

A limestone fragment, possibly part of a panelled wall, with a fragmentary cartouche of Pedubast, was found at Bubastis.[72]

3 Thebes

Other attestations to royal monuments of Pedubast are few and limited to Thebes. They consist of Nile level inscriptions,[73] and a vestibule door to the tenth pylon at Karnak.[74]

SHOSHENQ IV

1 Thebes

At Karnak, a lintel with the throne name of Shoshenq IV[75] was added to the chapel of Osiris Ruler of Eternity at Karnak.[76]

PAMIU

1 Tanis

Temple building work was conducted by Pamiu at Tanis. The blocks show finely carved reliefs. However, the buildings have not survived, and the blocks were later re-used in the Sacred Lake.[77]

2 Heliopolis

A temple block from Heliopolis bearing Pamiu's name was re-used in the medieval fortifications at Bab el-Nasr.[78]

SHOSHENQ V

1 Tanis

Shoshenq V dedicated a new temple to Khonsu in the great temenos of Tanis, perhaps in the north-eastern quarter.[79] This area was later turned into the Sacred Lake. From the walls and colonnades of this temple some two hundred blocks were re-used in the Sacred Lake. Shoshenq V added a jubilee gateway or chapel to this temple. Only twenty fragments have been found.[80]

OSORKON III

1 Thebes

Osorkon III had reliefs installed in the Khonsu temple,[81] while a door jamb was found in Chapel U, south-east of the Sacred Lake.[82] Osorkon III is also shown in the chapel of Osiris Ruler of Eternity.[83]

2 Hermopolis

Four hundred and twenty-five fragments of a quartzite stela from Year 15 of Osorkon III records the foundation of a chapel at Hermopolis.[84]

TAKELOTH III

1 Thebes

At Karnak, there are reliefs of Takeloth III in the chapel of Osiris Ruler of Eternity. Takeloth is shown ten times in the decoration, and appears in corresponding, or symmetrically opposed, scenes.[85]

RUDAMUN

1 Thebes

At Karnak, painted cartouches of Rudamun appear on the southern and northern walls of the inner room of the temple of Osiris Ruler of Eternity at Karnak, but no representations of the king survive in this chapel.[86]

OSORKON IV

1 Tanis

Blocks of Osorkon IV have been found at Tanis, and come from the temple area, most likely representing a small chapel or temple.[87]

SANKHTAWY SEKHEMKARA, SHEPSESKARA IRENRA
GEMENEFKHONSBAK, AND NEFERKARE P . . .

1 Tanis

Several blocks from Tanis mention these three kings and were found re-used in the Sacred Lake, indicating that they erected religious structures at Tanis.[88]

APPENDIX 3

UNIDENTIFIED TOMB, MORTUARY TEMPLE, AND PALACE LOCATIONS

THE RESIDENCE OF SHOSHENQ I

The location of the residence of Shoshenq I and the subsequent Twenty-Second Dynasty pharaohs has long been regarded as Bubastis, based on the dynastic segmentation system of Manetho, or at the site of Tanis, as this was the location of the capital of the preceding Twenty-First Dynasty and the latter part of the Twenty-Second Dynasty. No known text from the reign of Shoshenq I explicitly names either Tanis or Bubastis as the residence of Shoshenq I.[1] A stela from the quarry at Gebel el-Silsila in the Nile Valley records that in Year 21 of Shoshenq I he ordered the reopening of the quarry when he was in 'the Residence of the Temple Estate of Per Iset (the House of Isis), the Great Ka of Re Horakhty'.[2] This location cannot be equated with Bubastis, as the town was the home to the cult centre of the cat goddess Bastet and not Isis.[3] The entire region of the upper Pelusiac Nile branch has long been associated with Isis.[4] The residence is unlikely to be located at Tanis as evidence for the reign of Shoshenq I is absent.[5] On the other hand, there are similarities between the name of Piramesse and the residence of Shoshenq I. The location of the residence should be located, therefore, in the north-eastern Nile Delta, but not at Piramesse itself.[6] Kitchen suggested that the new residence should be looked for to the south of Tanis and on the northern side of Piramesse.[7] Several tell sites are located between the sites of Tanis and Piramesse. These are Tell Gumaiyima, Tell Zuwelein, and Gezirat el-Rimal. As noted in the main body of the text and in Appendix 2, both Tell Zuwelein and Tell Gumaiyima have late New Kingdom and Third Intermediate Period burial activity at the same time as Tanis developed into the Third Intermediate Period capital. Both the sites do not appear to have come into prominence until after the start of the Twenty-First Dynasty. It appears Tell Zuwelein was primarily a burial site for Tanis, while Tell Gumaiyima had a sustained occupation from the late Ramesside Period into the Ptolemaic–Roman Period. Excavations at Tell Gumaiyima documented a large enclosure of Ptolemaic–Roman date, but there was evidence that this was constructed over an earlier Third Intermediate Period foundation. No evidence of Third Intermediate Period activity has been found at Gezirat el-Rimal, and therefore, based on the available evidence, the site of Tell Gumaiyima provides the strongest case to be the lost residence of Shoshenq I. This residence may have been subsequently dismantled and built over in the Saite and Ptolemaic–Roman Period.

THE HOUSE OF MILLIONS OF YEARS OF SHOSHENQ I

Shoshenq I constructed his 'House of Millions of Years of the King of Upper and Lower Egypt, Hedj-Kheper-Re, Chosen of Re, Son of Re, Shoshenq, Beloved of Amun, that is in Hut-Ka-Ptah' at Memphis. This foundation is mentioned on an oracular decree from Karnak.[8] Shoshenq I built several monuments at Memphis, among them almost certainly a pylon and forecourt of the Ptah temple fronting the pylon and hypostyle hall of Seti I and Ramesses II. The pylon and forecourt are considered to be the House of Millions of Years of Shoshenq I.[9] The Memphite House of Millions of Years was made in parallel to the 'House of Hedj-Kheper-Re-in-Waset', which is known to be the forecourt and first pylon (which was later replaced by the Thirtieth Dynasty first pylon) of the Great Temple of Amun at Karnak. A Serapeum stela[10] dating to the late Twenty-Second Dynasty mentions personnel associated with the Memphite funerary cult of the 'House of Millions of Years of Shoshenq I, Beloved of Amun', revealing that the cult was still functioning several generations after its establishment at the Ptah temple.[11] Another Twenty-Second Dynasty stela from the reign of Pedubast I mentions a priest of Heryshef Lord of Heracleopolis.[12] The stela is fragmented, but there is an association with the god 'Osiris of the House of Millions of Years of King Shoshenq' in the neighbourhood of 𓊹𓏏𓎼𓈔𓈖𓊖 *B ꜥt n Br*. This toponym has been equated with several sites including *B-ꜥt-nt-Brt* on the Twenty-Sixth Dynasty Nitocris Stela, between Per Manaw (in the region of Kom el-Hisn) and Tanis,[13] Tjaru (Sile),[14] and an allusion to a toponym in the region of Sebennytos.[15] However, none of these suggestions can be regarded as certain. The stela is dated to the reign of Pedubast; therefore the temple establishment documented on the stela probably belongs to Shoshenq I.[16] It is suggested that this toponym should be equated with the House of Millions of Years of Shoshenq I at Memphis, in the close vicinity of the main settlement temple of Ptah.[17]

THE TOMB OF OSORKON III AT THEBES

As Osorkon III was a Theban/Heracleopolitan king, it is likely that he was buried at Thebes.[18] In the Late Period, papyri from the reigns of Necho II (Papyrus Louvre E.7858), Amasis (Turin 231.2), and Darius I (Papyrus Louvre E.7128) refer to a tomb of a King Osorkon located on the Theban West Bank.[19] This tomb probably belonged to Osorkon III, as his monuments are only known from Upper Egypt, while those of Osorkon I, II, and IV are found exclusively in the Delta at Tanis and Bubastis.[20] The tomb is not yet located, but based on the surviving evidence was located in a temple precinct on the West Bank of Thebes where the enclosure wall was either already destroyed by the reign of Necho II, or there were domestic residences inside the enclosure wall and the monument was easily recognisable by the inhabitants of Thebes as a royal tomb.[21] The architecture of the tomb was possibly similar to that of Harsiese A, which was a tomb with a small pyramid.[22]

NOTES

1. Taylor, 2000: 330.
2. For discussions on the HPA succession in the late Twentieth and early Twenty-First Dynasty, see Broekman, 2012; Egberts, 1997: 23–5; 1998: 93–108; Gnirs, 1996: 199–201; Gregory, 2013; Gundlach, 1994: 133–8; James and Morkot, 2010; Jansen-Winkeln, 1992; Kitchen, 1996: xiv–xix; 2009: 192–5; Mladjov, 2017; Niwiński, 1995: 346–7; Palmer, 2014; Taylor, 1998: 1143–55; Von Beckerath, 1995: 49–53. For recent discussions on Herihor, see Gregory, 2014.
3. There is general scholarly agreement on the number and reigns of the Twenty-First Dynasty, and a precise idea of the parallel sequence of HPA at Thebes and northern pharaohs. For a wider discussion of the Twenty-First Dynasty High Priests of Amun, see Jansen-Winkeln, 2006a: 224–32.
4. For recent discussions of the early Twenty-Second Dynasty, see Dodson, 2012: 83–111; Kitchen, 2009: 165. For debate on the chronology of the mid-Twenty-Second Dynasty onwards, see Broekman, 2005; Dodson, 1993; 2000; 2012: 114–38; Jansen-Winkeln, 1995; 2006a; 2007b; Kitchen, 1996: xxiii–xxiv; 2009: 168–91; Von Beckerath, 1997: 94–9; 2003. Dates for the table taken from Aston, 2009b: 22, with utilisation of Krauss' lunar date 845 BCE for Takeloth II Year 1.
5. Aston, 2009b: 26, with utilisation of Krauss' lunar date 834 BCE for Takeloth II Year 1.
6. Aston, 2009b: 24, with utilisation of Krauss' lunar date 845 BCE for Takeloth II Year 1.
7. Aston, 2009b: 26, with utilisation of Krauss' lunar date 834 BCE for Takeloth II Year 1.
8. Aston, 2009b: 23, with utilisation of Krauss' lunar date 845 BCE for Takeloth II Year 1.
9. Aston 2009b: 26–7, with utilisation of Krauss' lunar date 834 BCE for Takeloth II Year 1.
10. Aston, 2009b: 25.
11. Aston, 2009b: 25, with utilisation of Krauss' lunar date 834 BCE for Takeloth II Year 1.
12. For chronological discussions on the Twenty-Fourth Dynasty, see Dodson, 2012: 136–7, 146–8, 153–4.

1   TERMINOLOGY AND CHRONOLOGY

1. Kitchen, 1996: §206.
2. Sagrillo, 2009: 343–6.
3. Taylor, 2000: 330.
4. Broekman, 2010: 85–99; Leahy, 1985: 59; O'Connor, 1983: 183–278; Ritner, 2009a: 327–40.
5. Lantzas, 2012: 10; Nelson, 2007: 192.
6. Kitchen, 1996: §207.
7. Kitchen, 1996: §207.
8. Kitchen, 1996: §208.
9. Lantzas, 2012: 16.
10. Tainter, 1999: 988.
11. Aston, 2009a: 19.
12. N. Spencer, 2007: 7.
13. Lantzas, 2012: 9.
14. Lantzas, 2012: 10; Shanks and Tilley, 1992: 8.
15. Lantzas, 2012: 10; Redman, 1999: 48.
16. Aldred, 1956: 7.
17. Steindorff, 1946: 17.
18. Romer, 2016: 538.
19. Kitchen, 1996.
20. Desborough, 1972: 12; Lantzas, 2012: 16.
21. Taylor, 2000: 333.
22. Kitchen, 1996: §328.
23. For discussions on the sequences of kings and officials of the Third Intermediate Period, see most recently, Aston, 2009b; Dodson, 2012; Kitchen, 2009.
24. Jansen-Winkeln, 2006a: 235.

25. Jurman, 2009: 115.
26. Taylor, 2000: 331.
27. Broekman, 2012: 197.
28. Ritner, 2009a.
29. Kitchen, 2009: 193.
30. Kitchen, 2009: 195.
31. Jansen-Winkeln, 1992.
32. Gnirs, 1996: 199–201; Kitchen, 1996: xiv–xix; 2009: 192–5; Niwiński, 1995: 346–7; Von Beckerath, 1995: 49–53.
33. Egberts, 1997: 23–5; 1998: 93–108; Gundlach, 1994: 133–8; Taylor, 1998: 1143–55.
34. Broekman, 2012; Gregory, 2013; James and Morkot, 2010; Mladjov, 2017; Palmer, 2014; for recent discussions on Herihor, see Gregory, 2014.
35. Broekman, 2012.
36. Kitchen, 2009: 191.
37. Krauss, 2005: 43–8.
38. Stela Louvre IM 2846.
39. Jansen-Winkeln, 2006a: 234.
40. Dodson, 2012: 113–14; Jansen-Winkeln, 2006a: 234, n.1.
41. Aston, 1989.
42. Aston, 2009b: 1.
43. Aston, 2009a.
44. Broekman, 2005; Dodson, 1993; 2000; 2012: 114–38; Jansen-Winkeln, 1995; 2006a; 2007b; Von Beckerath, 1997: 94–9; 2003.
45. Kitchen, 1996: xxiii–xxiv; 2009: 168–91.
46. Cairo, JE 41013, Jansen-Winkeln, 2007b: 336; Leclant, 1963: 74–8, fig. 1.
47. Dunham, 1950: 2–3.
48. Kitchen, 1996: §320.
49. Kitchen, 1996: §320.
50. Kitchen, 1996: §321.
51. Kahn, 2009: 139; Yoyotte, 1961b: 151–4.
52. Kitchen, 1996: §324.
53. Kitchen, 1996: §328.
54. Kitchen, 1996: §332.
55. Kitchen, 1996: §337.
56. For recent discussions on the orders of the Kushite kings Shebitku and Shabaka, see Banyai, 2013; Banyai et al., 2015; Broekman, 2015; 2017a; 2017b; Jansen-Winkeln, 2017; Jurman, 2017; Payraudeau, 2014.
57. Kitchen, 2009: 161.
58. Kitchen, 1996: §356.
59. Kitchen, 1996: §352–4.
60. Kitchen, 1996: §354.
61. Kitchen, 1996: §355.
62. Kitchen, 1996: §359–64.

2   SETTLEMENT PATTERNS AND LAND POLICY

1. Leclère, 2008: 3.
2. N. Spencer, 2007: 22.
3. P. Spencer, 2007: 38.
4. P. Spencer, 2007: 56.
5. Bagnall, 1993: 6; Bietak, 1979a: 159; 1979b: 97–8; Franke, 1994: 29; Haeny, 1979: 86–8; Leclère, 2008: 4; Parlebas, 1977: 50; Smith, 1972: 705.
6. Hoffman, Hamroush, and Allen, 1986: 181; Jeffreys and Malek, 1988: 19–23; von der Way, 1984: 297–328; 1986: 191–212.
7. Yoyotte, 1961b.
8. Gomaà, 1974.
9. Meffre, 2015.
10. Meffre, 2015: 365–77.
11. O'Connor, 1983: 246–7.
12. Wilkinson, 2003: 4–8.
13. Hillier, Bunbury, and Graham, 2007: 1011.
14. Bunbury, 2011: 211.
15. Stanley and Warne, 1993.
16. Hillier, Bunbury, and Graham, 2007: 1011.
17. Bunbury, 2011: 211.
18. Hassan, 1996.
19. Bunbury, 2011: 211; Jeffreys and Tavares, 1994.
20. Graham, 2010: 138.
21. Bickel, 2009; Daressy, 1896a; Jansen-Winkeln, 2007a: 298–301.
22. Bickel, 2009: 51.
23. Bickel, 2009: 52.
24. Bickel, 2009: 51.
25. Butzer, 1976: 29.
26. Graham, 2010: 125.
27. Graham, 2010: 125.
28. Graham, 2010: 139; Jeffreys, 1996: 290, 292.
29. Graham, 2010: 139.
30. Bietak, 1979b: 102.
31. Hoffman, Hamroush, and Allen, 1986: 177.
32. Bietak, 1979b: 102.
33. Wilson, 2012: 99.
34. Wilson, 2012: 99.
35. Bietak, 1979b: 102.
36. Bietak, 1979b: 102.
37. Bietak, 1979b: 102.
38. Bunbury, 2011: 211.
39. Hillier, Bunbury, and Graham, 2007: 1011.
40. Bunbury, 2011: 212.
41. Cooper, 2014: 101.
42. Bunbury, 2011: 212.

43. Butzer, 1976.
44. The positions of the Ptolemaic–Roman towns and villages in the region of Akhmim suggest that the Nile ran west of a series of prominent levees in Hellenistic times, and the course of the Nile was ca. 3 km west of the position of the modern Nile, see Hassan, 2010: 134.
45. Cartographic studies and analysis of satellite imagery in the region of Sohag in Middle Egypt confirm that from 1798 CE to the present day the Nile has migrated to the east, see Butzer, 1976.
46. Results from Memphis show an eastern Nile migration, see Jeffreys, 1985: 48–51. Lutley and Bunbury, 2008, have demonstrated that GoogleEarth satellite imagery and field surveys can detect movements in the Nile in the Memphite area which suggest the Nile flowed alongside the western margin of the floodplain, having shifted at a rate of up to 9 km per 1,000 years/9 m per year.
47. Hillier, Bunbury, and Graham, 2007: 1013, have analysed the channels around the Qamula-Danfiq bend south of Luxor and shown the switching of a river channel around an island (1 km wide) takes approximately two hundred years. If island creation takes as long as channel switching, this provides a migration rate on the order of 1 km in 400 years, or 2.5 km per 1,000 years. This rate is greater than the 1–2 km per 1,000 years suggested in the Sohag region, the 250 m per 1,000 years estimated at Thebes (Karnak), and the 1 km per 1,000 years near Memphis. This shows the Nile exhibited a range of morphologies and rates of migration in different regions. The results from the Theban region show a westward Nile drift see Graham and Bunbury, 2005, while results from the Qamula-Danfiq bend suggest an eastward shift of the Nile based on a sequence of river levees, see Hillier, Bunbury, and Graham, 2007.
48. Cooper, 2014: 101.
49. Meffre, 2015: 374, fig. 1.
50. Cooper, 2014: 101.
51. Butzer, 1976: 82.
52. Butzer, 1976: 92; Westermann, 1917.
53. Butzer, 1976: 82.
54. Zalla et al., 2000: 9.
55. Fahmy, 1998: 152.
56. Zalla et al., 2000: 9.
57. Adriansen, 2009: 664.
58. El-Shakry, 2006: 76.
59. El-Shakry, 2006: 76.
60. Zalla et al., 2000: 10.
61. Zalla et al., 2000: 10.
62. Adriansen, 2009: 666; Zalla et al., 2000: 10.
63. Http://gain.fas.usda.gov/Recent%20GAIN%20Publications/Egyptian%20Land%20Reclamation%20Efforts_Cairo_Egypt_5–16-2016.pdf.
64. Bailey, 1999: 211.
65. Bailey, 1999: 212; Coulson and Leonard, 1982a: 364; Nibbi, 1979.
66. Habachi, 1943: 369.
67. Bailey, 1999: 212.
68. Bailey, 1999: 212; Maspero, 1912: 51–3.
69. Bailey, 1999: 213.
70. Bailey, 1999: 213; Maspero, 1912: 310–11.
71. Awad and Zohary, 2005.
72. Http://data.un.org/CountryProfile.aspx?crName=egypt.
73. Http://data.un.org/CountryProfile.aspx?crName=egypt.
74. Http://data.un.org/CountryProfile.aspx?crName=egypt.
75. Http://gain.fas.usda.gov/Recent%20GAIN%20Publications/Egyptian%20Land%20Reclamation%20Efforts_Cairo_Egypt_5–16-2016.pdf.
76. Hole and Heizer, 1973: 86–7.
77. Binford, 1964: 431.
78. Dunnell, 1992: 22.
79. Dunnell, 1922.
80. Trampier, 2010: 10.
81. Tainter, 1983.
82. Tainter, 1983.
83. Trampier, 2010: 15–49.
84. Trampier, 2010: 41.
85. Trampier, 2010: 41.
86. Www.deltasurvey.ees.ac.uk/gadiya.html.
87. Jansen-Winkeln, 2006b: 308–10.
88. Ur, 2002b.
89. Wright, 2004: 118.
90. Wilkinson, Ur, and Casana, 2004: 192.
91. Ur, 2002a; Wilkinson, 1982; Wilkinson, Ur, and Casana, 2004: 193.
92. Ur, 2003; Wilkinson, 1993; Wilkinson, Ur, and Casana, 2004: 192–3.
93. Miller-Rosen, 1986: 52; Tassie and Owens, 2010: 113.
94. Miller-Rosen, 1986: 51; Tassie and Owens, 2010: 113.
95. Steinberg, 1996; Tassie and Owens, 2010: 113.
96. Tassie and Owens, 2010: 113.

97. Abdel-Fattah, 2002.
98. Tassie and Owens, 2010: 113.
99. Redman and Watson, 1970: 280; Tassie and Owens, 2010: 112.
100. Tassie and Owens, 2010: 112–13.
101. Miller-Rosen, 1986; Tassie and Owens, 2010: 114.
102. A. J. Spencer, 1994: 318; Tassie and Owens, 2010: 114.
103. Hodder and Orton, 1976: 69–73.
104. Wright, 2004: 118.
105. Hartung et al., 2009.
106. Trampier, 2010: 15.
107. Trampier, 2010: 15.
108. Trampier, 2010: 15–16.
109. Trigger, 2006: 68.
110. Trigger, 2006: 68.
111. Baines and Malek, 2000: 107.
112. Trigger, 2006: 68.
113. Murray, 1950.
114. Trampier, 2010: 34.
115. Wilson and Grigoropoulos, 2009: 3.
116. N. Spencer, 2007: 1–31.
117. P. Spencer, 2007: 33–65.
118. Hogarth, 1904; Wilson and Grigoropoulos, 2009: 3.
119. Bernand, 1970.
120. Timm, 1984–92.
121. Bietak, 1975.
122. Coulson, 1988; 1996; Coulson and Leonard, 1979; 1982a; 1982b; Coulson, Leonard, and Wilkie, 1982.
123. Snape, 1986.
124. Van den Brink, 1987; 1988.
125. Chlodnicki, Fattovich, and Salvatori, 1992.
126. Valbelle et al., 1992.
127. Ballet and von der Way, 1993.
128. Brewer et al., 1996.
129. Trampier, 2009; 2010; 2014; Trampier et al., 2013.
130. Kenawi, 2014.
131. Blue and Khalil, 2011.
132. Jucha and Buszek, 2011; Jucha et al., 2010.
133. Http://giscenter.gov.eg/home.
134. Wilson, 1998.
135. Www.ees.ac.uk/deltasurvey/ds-home.html; Wilson and Grigoropoulos, 2009: 4.
136. Spencer and Spencer, 2000: 25.
137. Spencer and Spencer, 2000: 26.
138. Rowland, 2007; Rowland and Billing, 2006; Rowland and Spencer, 2011; Rowland and Wilson, 2006: 1–13; Rowland et al., 2009; A. J. Spencer, 2002b: 6–7; Wilson, 2003: 1–8.
139. Parcak, 2006: 57.
140. Herbich, 2003.
141. Herbich, 2012a: 11.
142. Herbich, 2012a: 11.
143. Deletie, Lemoine, and Montluçon, 1989; Herbich, 2004; 2012b; 2013; Herbich and Hartung, 2004; Pavlish, 2004; Pavlish, Mumford, and D'Andrea, 2003; Pusch, Becker, and Fassbinder, 1999a; A. J. Spencer, 2011.
144. Herbich, 2001; Herbich and Richards, 2006; Hussain, 1983.
145. Herbich and Smekalova, 2001; Smekalova, Mills, and Herbich, 2003.
146. Parcak, 2004.
147. Parcak, 2009.
148. Parcak, 2007.
149. Hoffman, Hamroush, and Allen, 1986: 181; Jeffreys and Malek, 1988: 19–23; von der Way, 1984: 297–328; 1986: 191–212.
150. Bunbury and Graham, 2005; Bunbury, Graham, and Hunter, 2008; Graham, 2010.
151. Rowland and Strutt, 2012.
152. For general publications on the funerary papyri of the Third Intermediate Period, see Lucarelli, 2006; Niwiński, 1989; Piankoff and Rambova, 1957; Rössler-Köhler, 1999; Sadek, 1985.
153. Lucarelli, 2009.
154. Gardiner, 1947; Herbin, 1986.
155. Jansen-Winkeln, 2007b: 4–7, no. 15; Meffre, 2010: 221–34; 2015: 48–63, no. 7; Ritner, 2009b: 180–6; Tresson, 1935–8.
156. Vleeming, 1993.
157. Gasse, 1988: 23.
158. Gasse, 1988: 50.
159. Kitchen, 1969–70: 59.
160. Cairo Museum JE 48862, 47086–9, Goedicke, 1998; Grimal, 1981; Jansen-Winkeln, 2007b: 337–50; Meffre, 2015: 143–50, doc.56.
161. Verreth, 1999.
162. Wilkinson, 2003: 8.
163. Gasse, 1988.
164. Vleeming, 1993.
165. The methodology for the collection of New Kingdom toponyms follows the same approach as those of the Third Intermediate Period corpus. The EES Delta survey website http://deltasurvey.ees.ac.uk/dsintro.html provides detailed discussions of individual site entries for the Delta. For detailed lists of New Kingdom sites, see Brugsch, 1879; Davies, 1943: II, pl. XXXII; Gardiner, 1947; 1941–8; Gauthier, 1925–9; Montet, 1957; 1961; Otto,

1952. For other specific reports to New Kingdom sites, see also Bernand, 1970, IV, 933–61; Bietak, 1975; Bunbury, Graham, and Strutt, 2009; Daressy, 1910: 64; 1912: 206; 1920b: 162; Edgar, 1907: 279 [bottom]; 1911: 278; 1914: 279; Gardiner, 1912: pl. IV, 49–57; Grandet, 1994: I: 2, 58; Griffith, 1888; Habachi, 1954: 515; Lefebvre, 1908; 1912: 82–3; Müller, 2009; P. Anastasi VI, 2.2, 3; P. Anastasi VI, 4.8; PM IV: 58; V, 1937: 1–4, 16, 36–7, 106; Posener, 1940; Sauneron, 1950; 1955; N. Spencer, 2008: 7–8; Thomas, 2000; Urk IV, 555; van den Brink, 1987; 1988: 65–114; Weigall, 1908: 111–12 [16]; Wilson, 2006: 13–14; Yoyotte, 1950; 1959.

166. Church and Bell, 1988.
167. Bevan and Wilson, 2013.
168. Tassie and Owens, 2010: 113.
169. Bunbury, Graham, and Strutt, 2009.
170. Bunbury, Graham, and Strutt, 2009: 5.
171. Sullivan, 2013.
172. El-Saghir, 1988.
173. Cairo Stela 3/12/24/2.
174. Ritner, 2009b: 136–7.
175. Hölscher, 1954.
176. Aston, 1996a: 53–6; 2009a: 260–8.
177. Snape, 2014: 40.
178. Snape, 2014: 40.
179. Snape, 2014: 40.
180. Pierrat-Bonnefois, 2000.
181. Bouriant, 1886: 126–8.
182. Kamal, 1909: 63.
183. Gardiner, 1941–8, II: table II.
184. Gardiner, 1941–8, III: 33.
185. Aston, 2009a: 108–11; Pérez-Die, 2009; 2010.
186. Aston, 1996a, 36–7; Mace, 1921.
187. Aston, 2009a: 111–12; Hanasaka, 2011: 9–11; Kawanishi and Tsujimura, 2013: 5–15; Tsujimura, 2011: 4–9.
188. Aston, 1996a: 39–40; 2009a: 107–8; Naville, 1894: 13, pls. vii–viii, xi; Petrie and Brunton, 1924a: pl. xv.25–6; 1924b, pls. lxvii, lix.35, lx.40–3.
189. Aston, 1996a: 39; 2009a: 107; Brunton and Engelbach, 1927; Kemp, 1978; Loat, 1905: 8, pls. xviii (2), xix; PM IV, 1934: 114.
190. Aston, 2009a: 94–107.
191. Aston, 2009a: 94; Engelbach, 1923: 2–3, pl. xxi.200, 204–5, 218–19, pl. lxiii; Petrie, 1914b: 186.
192. Aston, 2009a: 92; Petrie, 1912: 36, pl. xxxi.
193. Aston, 2009a: 90–2; Mackay, 1910: 22, 24, 35, pl. xxviii.135–9; Petrie, 1892: 14, 19, 20–1;

194. Beni Suef Inspectorate 32–987, Meffre, 2015: doc.137.
195. Yoyotte, 1961a: 94; 1963: 90, n.3.
196. Meffre, 2015: 375.
197. Taylor, 2009: 382.
198. Davoli, 1998: 228; Meffre, 2015: doc.15.
199. Baltimore, Walkers Art Museum 22.202, Steindorff, 1946: 26–7, no. 42, pl. X and CXI no. 42; Zecchi, 1999: 70–1, no. 292.
200. Gardiner, 1947: II, 130–1.
201. Gardiner, 1947: II, 131.
202. Gardiner, 1947: II, 141–2.
203. Zivie-Coche, 1991: 295.
204. Gardiner, 1947: II, 120–2; Gomaà, 1974: 51.
205. Cairo CG 42232, now Luxor J 152, Jansen-Winkeln, 2007b: 205–7; Legrain, 1914b: 78–80, pls. 40–1; PM II, 1929: 149.
206. Bietak, 1975: 118.
207. Bietak, 1975: 118.
208. Gardiner, 1924: 92; 1947: II, 153–71.
209. Bunbury, Hughes, and Spencer, 2014: 12.
210. Bunbury, Hughes, and Spencer, 2014: 12; Trampier, 2010: 12.
211. Trampier, 2010: 325.
212. Bunbury, Hughes, and Spencer, 2014: 12.
213. Bunbury, Hughes, and Spencer, 2014: 12.
214. Daressy, 1916b: 243; Gomaà, 1974: 23; Montet, 1961: 66.
215. Trampier, 2010: 324.
216. Trampier, 2010: 325.
217. Trampier, 2010: 328.
218. Wilkinson, 2003: 97.
219. Wilkinson, 2003: 99.
220. Trampier, 2010: 328.
221. Berlin Museum 7344.
222. Cairo Museum, JdE 30872.
223. Wilson, 2006: 9, fig. 2.
224. Wilson, 2006: 11.
225. Wilson, 2006: 11.
226. El-Gamili and el-Khedr, 1989.
227. Wilson, 2006: 12.
228. Schiestl, 2012; 2014; Wunderlich and Ginau, 2016.
229. Wilson, 2011.
230. Hartung et al., 2009: 172–90.
231. BM 14594–5.
232. Jansen-Winkeln, 2007b: 85, no. 3; Meffre, 2015: 65.
233. Cooper, 2014: 33.
234. Stanley, 1988.
235. Mumford, 2013.

236. Bietak, 1975: 173–4, 217.
237. Blouin, 2014: 95.
238. Blouin, 2014: 95; Redford, 2010: 24, 37, fig. 3.18.
239. Blouin, 2014: 95; Redford, 2010: 105.
240. Bietak, 1975: plan 4.
241. Bietak, 1975: plan 4.
242. Bietak, 1975: plan 4.
243. Bietak, 1975.
244. Hassan, 2010: 141.
245. Cooper, 2014: 30.
246. Cooper, 2014: 32.
247. Cooper, 2014: 33.
248. Cooper, 2014.
249. Cooper, 2014.
250. Gauthier, 1925–9, I: 200; Gomaà, 1974: 107–8.
251. Hannig, 2000: 208.
252. Montet, 1957: 199.
253. Montet, 1957: 199.
254. Bietak, 1975: plan 4.
255. Bietak, 1975: plan 4.
256. Bietak, 1975: plan 4.
257. Bietak, 1975: 109.
258. Leclant, 1973: 396.
259. Aston, 2009a: 62.
260. Ashmawy, 2006.
261. Griffith, 1888: 41.
262. Wilkinson, 2003: 99.
263. Wilkinson, 2003: 99.
264. Aston, 1996a: 26; Foucart, 1902: 58–9, figs. 7–8; van den Brink, 1987.
265. Snape, 2014: 212.
266. Bietak, 1975: 102–3.
267. Bietak, 1975: plan 4.
268. Bietak, 1975: plan 4.
269. Taylor, 2000: 349.
270. Jansen-Winkeln, 2007a: 81; Römer, 1994: 579 (54).
271. Jansen-Winkeln, 2007a: 25.
272. Aston, 1996b; Jaritz, 1986. Identified as a 'fortified townsite'.
273. Kitchen, 1996: §226.
274. Jansen-Winkeln, 2007a: 417; Osing et al., 1982: pl. 9, no. 45.
275. Yoyotte, 1950.
276. Müller, 2009: 260–1.
277. Chabân, 1907: 223, no. IV.
278. Jansen-Winkeln, 2006b: 308–10.
279. Gardiner, 1941–8, III: 35.
280. Meffre, 2015: 58, doc.7, Face D, x+20.
281. Meffre, 2015: 58, doc.7, Face D, x+21.
282. Medjay, *Wb.* II, 186.9–13, translated as *Wüstenpolizisten*, 'Desert Police'.
283. Cairo JE 39410, Face D, x+21.
284. Cairo JE 39410, Face D, x+22.
285. Cairo JE 39410, Face D, x+21.
286. Gauthier, 1925–9, II: 30.
287. Yoyotte, 1962: 93.
288. Gardiner, 1941–8, III: 35.
289. Meffre, 2015: 371.
290. Meffre, 2015: 372.
291. Wilkinson, 2003: 42.
292. Vleeming, 1993.
293. Gasse, 1988.
294. Vleeming, 1993: 13–44.
295. Sullivan, 2013: 154.
296. Gardiner, 1941–8, II: 9.
297. Liszka, 2010.
298. Bennett, 2015.
299. Gardiner, 1947: II, 49.
300. Krauss, 2005.
301. N. Spencer, 2014: 24–7.
302. Meeks, 1979: 622.
303. Meeks, 2009. The only example so far from the Twenty-First Dynasty is dated to the reign of Pinudjem I; see Uchida, 1995: 299–301.
304. For the corpus of Twenty-Fifth Dynasty Abnormal Hieratic land leases and discussions on legal terminology in Abnormal Hieratic and early Demotic land leases, see Donker van Heel, 1997; 1998; 1999; Hughes, 1973; van Saane, 2015.
305. Kitchen, 1969–70: 59.
306. Meeks, 1979: 638.
307. Meeks, 1979: 608.
308. One aroura of land has been calculated at 2,735 m², see Gardiner, 1941–8, II: 60.
309. Meeks, 1979: 617.
310. Meeks, 1979: 618–19.
311. Meeks, 1979: 619, 621.
312. Sullivan, 2013: 156.
313. Aston, 2007b: 70; Jacquet, 1965: 47, 48, fig. 3, pl. 9; Nicholson, 1993: 115, 116, fig. 117.
314. Jacquet, 1965: 47.
315. Aston, 2007b: 70.
316. Aston, 2007b: 70.
317. Bourriau, Nicholson, and Rose, 2000: 136.
318. Varille and Robichon, 1935: fig. 1.
319. Anthes et al., 1965: 129–31, nos. 258–94; Aston, 2007b: 76; Bakry, 1959: 48–9, nos. 225–39; el-Sayed Mahmud, 1978: 13.
320. Aston, 2007b: 76; Petrie, 1909: 11.
321. Aston, 2007b: 76.

322. Anthes et al., 1965: 109–10; Aston, 2007b: 76.
323. Giddy, 1999: 177, pl. 39.
324. Thomas, 1981: I, 32–3, nos. 8–18, II, pls. 1.8–10, 14.
325. Bacquerisse, 2015: 382–3.
326. Tsujimura, 2012.
327. A. J. Spencer, 1993: pl. 31, nos. 59–60.
328. Mace, 1914: fig. 4.
329. Tsujimura, 2012: 15.

3 SETTLEMENT DEVELOPMENT AND BUILT REMAINS OF THE THIRD INTERMEDIATE PERIOD

1. El-Saghir, 1988.
2. Sullivan, 2013.
3. Cairo Stela 3/12/24/2.
4. Ritner, 2009b: 136–7.
5. *P.BM* 10068.
6. Brunton, 1948.
7. Spencer and Bailey, 1985, pls. 3, 92; A. J. Spencer, 1993: 50.
8. A. J. Spencer, 1993.
9. A. J. Spencer, 1993: 50.
10. A. J. Spencer, 1993: 50.
11. A. J. Spencer, 1993: 72.
12. Jeffreys, 2007: 7.
13. Jeffreys, 2007: 7.
14. Jeffreys, 2007: 8.
15. N. Spencer, 2008: 43–5, 47–8.
16. N. Spencer, 2014: 35.
17. Redford, 2004: 35; 2010: 106.
18. Redford, 2010: 106.
19. Redford, 2004: 35.
20. Kirby, Orel, and Smith, 1998: 33–4, 37–8, figs. 7, 40, 41–2.
21. Kirby, Orel, and Smith, 1998.
22. Kirby, Orel, and Smith, 1998: 34.
23. A. J. Spencer, 1999: 19, 59–60.
24. A. J. Spencer, 1996: 63.
25. A. J. Spencer, 1996: 64.
26. Sullivan, 2013: figs. 6.3–6.4.
27. A. J. Spencer, 1993: 50.
28. N. Spencer, 2014: 35.
29. A. J. Spencer, 1996: 63.
30. A. J. Spencer, 1996: 63.
31. A. J. Spencer, 1996: 36–42.
32. Brissaud, Chauvet, and Hairy, 1998: 87; Lézine, 1951.
33. N. Spencer, 2006: 41.
34. Montet, 1966.
35. Moeller, 2004; 2016.
36. Kemp, 2004: 259–60.
37. Mumford, 2013: table 1; Spence, 2004a: 265.
38. Spence, 2004a: 265.
39. Spence, 2004a: 270.
40. Spence, 2004a: 265.
41. Spence, 2004a: 266.
42. Caminos, 1964: 95–6; Gardiner, 1947: II, 213; Grimal, 1981: 16, n.26; Mumford, 2013: 52; P. Spencer, 1981: 270–8; Yoyotte, 1963: 108, n.5.
43. *Wb.* IV, 95.10–96.
44. P. Spencer, 1981: 238.
45. P. Spencer, 1981: 239–40.
46. Cairo Stela, 3/12/24/2.
47. *Wb.* IV, 210.2–10.
48. *Wb.* IV, 210.6–7; Thiers, 1995: 496.
49. Thiers, 1995: 496.
50. Thiers, 1995: 497.
51. Daressy, 1916a: 61–2; Jansen-Winkeln, 2007b: 196–7; Meeks, 1979: 668 (doc.22.8.14); Yoyotte, 1961b: 134, 163–4.
52. Grimal, 1981; Lichtheim, 1980: 66–84.
53. *Urk.* III. 6, 7.
54. *Urk.* III. 17, 32.
55. *Urk.* III. 29, 88; 31, 90.
56. *Urk.* III. 26, 83.
57. *Urk.* III. 26, 14; P. Spencer, 1981: 239.
58. *Wb.* IV, 14.4–14.
59. Grimal, 1981: ll. 5, 77, 91, 92, 95.
60. *Urk.* III. 16, 28.
61. *Urk.* III. 24, 77.
62. *Urk.* III. 5.5.
63. *Urk.* III. 30, 89; 31, 91; 32, 92.
64. *Urk.* III. 34, 95.
65. P. Spencer, 1981: 210.
66. P. Spencer, 1981: 210.
67. Breasted, 1906: 308; Daressy, 1888: 136–7.
68. *Wb.* I, 159–7.
69. *Wb.* I, 93.2–14.
70. Traunecker, 1975: 151–2.
71. P. Spencer, 1981: 288.
72. Leclère, 2008: §9.6.
73. Leclère, 2008: §9.6.
74. Lawrence, 1965: 91.
75. Coulon, Leclère, and Marchand, 1995: 223–5, pl. XIIIb; Thiers, 1995: 497.
76. Cairo Stela, 3/12/24/2.
77. Coulon, Leclère, and Marchand, 1995: 224–5.

78. Von Pilgrim, 2010: 12–13.
79. Hall, 1928: 44, pl. xl.
80. Kemp, 2004: 259.
81. Kitchen, 1996: §208.
82. Kitchen, 1996: §276.
83. Shaw, 2012: 96, fig. 7.3.
84. *Wb.* I, 54.3, lit. Tower of Movement. They were used by Piankhy to go up against the walls, see *Urk.* III. 15, 28. as the determinative indicates the siege tower was constructed of wood.
85. *Wb.* v, 388.3. This term was a semitic loan word, see Hoch, 1994: no. 548. They were constructed against the walls of Hermopolis, see *Urk.* III. 17, 32.
86. Siege platforms were used in the battle of Hermopolis for archers, javelin, and slinger troops to attack over the walls and in effect reduce the effect of the high defensive walls, see *Urk.* III. 31, 91.
87. Rowlands, 1972: 448.
88. Rowlands, 1972: 448.
89. Rowlands, 1972: 447.
90. Pinder, 2011: 72.
91. Tracey, 2000: 5.
92. Pinder, 2011: 72.
93. Traunecker, 1975.
94. Cairo JE 44665.
95. Cairo JE 36410, Traunecker, 1975: 146.
96. *Wb.* IV, 351.7–353.17.
97. O'Connor, 1989: 74; Sullivan, 2013: 67.
98. O'Connor, 1991: 171–2; Sullivan, 2013: 67.
99. Jurman, 2007: 172.
100. O'Connor, 1989: 78; 1995: 270–1, 281–2; Sullivan, 2013: 67.
101. Sullivan, 2013: 68.
102. Lacovara, 1997: 24.
103. Sullivan, 2013: 68.
104. *Wb.* I, 214.10–21.
105. *Wb.* I, 516.2–12.
106. *Wb.* IV, 340.11–341.11.
107. *Wb.* I, 513.3–5.
108. Jurman, 2007: 173.
109. Ritner, 2009b: 101–4.
110. Caminos, 1952: pl. 13; Jansen-Winkeln, 2007b: 22 (12.27).
111. *Urk.* III. 18, 34; 21, 62; 54, 150–3.
112. Jurman, 2007: 173.
113. Stadelmann, 1996: 228, 230.
114. Redford, 2010: 106–8.
115. Redford, 2010: 108.
116. Redford, 2010: 110.
117. Lichtheim, 1980: 72–3.
118. Arnold, 1999: 28.
119. Arnold, 1999: 43.
120. Arnold, 1999: 30.
121. Arnold, 1999: 30.
122. Ingold, 2000: 187–8; N. Spencer, 2015: 202.
123. N. Spencer, 2015: 201.
124. N. Spencer, 2015: 200.
125. N. Spencer, 2015: 203.
126. N. Spencer, 2015: 203.
127. Kamp, 2000: 91.
128. N. Spencer, 2015: 203.
129. Correas Amador, 2013.
130. Rainville, 2015: 4; Steadman, 2004: 527, 531–7.
131. Rainville, 2015: 4.
132. Rainville, 2015: 8.
133. Spence, 2015: 85.
134. Hölscher, 1954: 3.
135. Brunton, 1948: 60.
136. Rainville, 2015: 8.
137. Kamp, 2000: 86.
138. N. Spencer, 2015: 203.
139. Rainville, 2015: 8–9.
140. Spence, 2015: 83.
141. Lang, 2005: 12.
142. Lang, 2005: 13.
143. Müller, 2015: xvi.
144. Parker and Foster, 2012; Yasur-Landau, Ebeling, and Mazow, 2011.
145. Parker and Foster, 2012.
146. Von Pilgrim, 1996.
147. Koltsida, 2007.
148. Arnold, 1998; Crocker, 1985; Endruweit, 1994; Kóthay, 2001; Meskell, 1998; 2002; Samuel, 1999; Spence, 2004b; 2010; Tietze, 1985; 1986; 2008a; 2008b.
149. Mühs, 2015.
150. Aston, 1996a.
151. Anus and Sa'ad, 1971.
152. Masson, 2007.
153. Anus and Sa'ad, 1971: 219.
154. Traunecker, 1993: 83.
155. Masson, 2007: 607–12.
156. Aston, 1996a: 56.
157. Aston, 1996a: 56.
158. Masson, 2007.
159. Masson, 2007: 618–19.
160. Anthes et al., 1965: 92–6, pl. 31.
161. Kitchen, 1996: §225.
162. Jeffreys, 1985: 71.
163. Aston, 2007a: 68.

164. Nevett, 1999: 39–50; N. Spencer, 2015: 172.
165. Aston, 2007b: 69.
166. Hölscher, 1954: 4.
167. Hölscher, 1954: 5.
168. Lacovara, 1997: 61.
169. Bietak, 1996: 37, fig. 1; Lacovara, 1997: 56.
170. Lacovara, 1997: 22–3.
171. Crocker, 1985; Shaw, 1992; Spence, 2015: 86.
172. Spence, 2015: 86–7.
173. Borchardt and Ricke, 1980, plan I; Frankfort and Pendlebury, 1933: pls. xii–xiv; Peet and Woolley, 1923: pl. iii; Sullivan, 2013: 63.
174. Spence, 2004b; 2015: 87.
175. Lacovara, 1997: 71, states the house style reverted to the traditional styles of the Middle Kingdom, of which he cited the Karnak priestly houses as an example. As discussed, the construction and occupation date for these houses is debatable and they were subject to considerable adaptation over time.
176. Pusch, 1999b: 15; Pusch, Becker, and Fassbinder, 1999: 160–1, figs. 1–2.
177. Hölscher, 1941: fig. 53.
178. Lacovara, 1997: 61.
179. Sullivan, 2013.
180. Lacovara, 1997: 61.
181. Kemp, 1977: 127.
182. Giddy, 1999: 2–3.
183. Kemp, 1995: 446–8.
184. Hölscher, 1954: 6–7, 14, figs. 4–6, 19.
185. Arnold, 1996: 20.
186. Mace, 1922: 14.
187. Arnold, 1996: 20.
188. Mace, 1914; 1921; 1922.
189. Mace, 1922: 13–14.
190. Arnold, 1996: 20.
191. El-Saghir, 1988: 80.
192. El-Saghir, 1988: 80.
193. El-Saghir, 1988: 79–81.
194. Sullivan, 2013: 64.
195. Hölscher, 1954: fig. 19.
196. Hölscher, 1954: 8.
197. Aston, 2007b: 69; Jeffreys, 1996: 290.
198. Petrie, 1909: 11, pl. xxvii.
199. Aston, 2007b: 69; Hölscher, 1954: 6–8; Kemp, 1995: 446–8.
200. Aston, 2007b: 69.
201. Jeffreys, 2007.
202. N. Spencer, 2008; 2014: 46.
203. Hölscher, 1954: 8.
204. Rzepka, 2011: 135–6.
205. Jarmužek and Rzepka, 2014.
206. Roeder, 1959.
207. Aston, 1996a: 41.
208. Aston, 1996a: 42.
209. A. J. Spencer, 1993: 13.
210. Marouard, 2014.
211. A. J. Spencer, 1993: 18, the Level 3 house.
212. Hölscher, 1954: 7–8, 14.
213. N. Spencer, 2014: 42.
214. Snape, 2014: 80.
215. N. Spencer, 2014: 55.
216. Giddy, 1999: 305, EES 275.
217. N. Spencer, 2014: 55.
218. Giddy, 1999: 156, EES 366, 400, 543, 865.
219. Peet and Woolley, 1923: 62–3, fig. 10, pl. XVII.3.
220. Hölscher, 1954: 11.
221. N. Spencer, 2014: 55.
222. N. Spencer, 2014: 55.
223. N. Spencer, 2014: 55.
224. Brunton, 1948.
225. A. J. Spencer, 1993: 15.
226. Brunton, 1948: 60.
227. Jarmužek and Rzpeka, 2014: 87.
228. Snape, 2014: 78.
229. Kemp, 2000: 84; A. J. Spencer, 1979.
230. Emery and Morgenstein, 2007.
231. Kemp, 2000: 84.
232. Kemp, 2000: 84.
233. A. J. Spencer, 1979: 147–8, pls. 41–4.
234. Raue, 2010.
235. N. Spencer, 2014: 31.
236. Kemp, 2006: 178–9.
237. Kemp, 2006: 178–9. The capacity estimates for Third Intermediate Period grain silos are likely to be on the maximum estimate. The estimates provided in this study have been calculated based on the silos filled exclusively with wheat or barley to the maximum capacity to feed a population of the settlement over the course of a year. The silos may have operated a surplus and could be replenished in line with the harvest season, and they may have been used to store other commodities. These figures do not account for fluctuations in the harvest yield, in times of bumper harvests or times of drought, which may affect the amount of grain being stored in the silos at any one time, the moisture content, and the size of grain.

238. Brunton, 1948: pl. XLV.
239. Kemp, 2006: 171.
240. Lichtheim, 1980: 75.
241. Jarmužek, 2011.
242. Herold, 1999; Pusch, 1999a.
243. Penelope Wilson, Durham University, personal communication.
244. Bertini, 2014: table 1.
245. Szpakowska, 2008: 19.
246. Bertini, 2014: 306.
247. Tsujimura, 2013: 15.
248. Tsujimura, 2011: 8.
249. Bertini, 2014: 309.
250. Szpakowska, 2008: 20.
251. Wilson, 2011: 15.
252. Wilson, 2011: 15.
253. Malleson, 2011: 269.
254. Wilson, 2011: 15.
255. A. J. Spencer, 1993: 31.
256. Miller, 1990: 137.
257. Miller, 1990: 130; Schadewaldt, 1983: 68–80.
258. Szpakowska, 2008: 92.
259. Miller, 1990: 125.
260. Arnold, 1989: 78–81.
261. Arnold, 2015: 159.
262. Arnold, 1989: 84–8, fig. 3.
263. Arnold, 2015: 160; Kemp, 1987: 40–6.
264. A. J. Spencer, 1993: 14.
265. Jarmužek and Rzepka, 2014: 86.
266. Wilson, 2011: 15.
267. Miller, 1990: 125.
268. Miller, 1990: 126.
269. Miller, 1990: 126.
270. Darby, Ghalioungui, and Grivetti, 1977: 186–7, figs. 4.8–4.9.
271. Miller, 1990: 126.
272. Miller, 1990: 130.
273. Donald, 1984: 56–7; Miller, 1990: 130.
274. Bertini, 2014: 306–8.
275. Allbaugh, 1953: 279; Bökönyi, 1989: 23; Miller, 1990: 126.
276. Miller, 1990.
277. N. Spencer, 2014.
278. If we take the eleven cemeteries in the Theban necropolis as separate sites, the number rises to forty, which gives Thebes a 27.5 per cent cemetery density in Upper Egypt.
279. Aston, 2009a: 398.
280. Aston, 2009a: 398.
281. Aston, 2009a: 398.
282. Redford, 2004: 5; 2010: 110.
283. Arnold, 1998: 33–5.

4   DOMESTIC MATERIAL CULTURE OF THE THIRD INTERMEDIATE PERIOD

1. Aston, 2003; Bourriau, 2010: 2; Hope, 1989.
2. Bourriau, 2010: 2.
3. Aston, 1996a: 15.
4. Bourriau, 2010: 2.
5. For a recent study on the development of ceramics during the Third Intermediate Period and a detailed overview, see Boulet, 2018: 338–46.
6. Boulet, 2018: 338.
7. For studies on the pottery of the transition between the Twentieth and Twenty-First Dynasty, see Aston, 1996a; 2009a; Boulet, 2016b.
8. Aston, 2009a: 307; Boulet, 2018: 338.
9. Boulet, 2018: 338. For assemblages of this phase, see the chapel of Osiris Wennefer Neb-djefau at Karnak (Boulet, 2017: 53–62) and the Mut temple at Karnak (Sullivan, 2013: 76–143, 190–239).
10. Boulet, 2016a: 213–16.
11. Boulet, 2018: 340.
12. Aston, 1999: 4.
13. Boulet, 2018: 341–2.
14. Boulet, 2018: 343.
15. Boulet, 2018: 344.
16. Aston, 1996a: 88.
17. Aston, 1996a: 88.
18. Boulet, 2018: 344.
19. Boulet, 2018: 346; Defernez, 2015.
20. Bourriau, Smith, and Serpico, 2001.
21. Hankey and Aston, 1995.
22. Eriksson, 2001; 2007; Merrillees, 1968.
23. Bourriau, 2010: 113–46; Smoláriková, 2014: 51.
24. A. J. Spencer, 1993: 47.
25. Aston, 2009a: 27.
26. Wilson, 2011: 178–9.
27. Aston, 2009a: 318–19.
28. French, 2013: 21.
29. Kohen, 2015: 309.
30. Kohen, 2015: 309.
31. Tyson-Smith, 2003: 50–2.
32. Wilson, 2011: 31–43.
33. Smoláriková, 2014: 48.
34. Aston, 1999: 169.
35. Sullivan, 2013: 178, Type L.
36. A. J. Spencer, 1993.
37. Sullivan, 2013: 120.

38. Giddy, 1999: 259, pl. 55, EES 502, and 288, pl. 63, EES 408; A. J. Spencer, 1993: 32–3, pl. 27, nos. 13–18; Wilson, 2011: 102–3.

39. Aston, 1994: 159, types 202–6.

40. Giddy, 1999: 259, pl. 55, EES 502.

41. Giddy, 1999: 259, 263.

42. Giddy, 1999: 265–76.

43. Giddy, 1999: 265–76, pls. 58–9; A. J. Spencer, 1993: 36–7, pl. 33.

44. N. Spencer, 2008: 68.

45. Cairo JE 59785, Hölscher, 1954: 11; N. Spencer, 2008: 68.

46. Giddy, 1999: 265–76. Whole vessels, or fragments of faience vessels, are found in more than twenty Third Intermediate Period burials at Tell Zuwelein, Tell el-Balamun, Tell el-Retaba, Abusir el-Meleq, Lahun, Matmar, Qau, at the Ramesseum, Riqqeh, Hawara, and intrusively in TT 99 at Thebes, see Aston, 2009a: 377.

47. Schlick-Nolte, 1999: 37–42; Tait, 1963: 96–103.

48. Aston, 2007b: 76.

49. Aston, 2009a: 377.

50. A. J. Spencer, 1993: 36, pl. 32, nos. 95–106.

51. Only a single undecorated blue glazed example comes from Hermopolis and is dated to 700–600 BCE, but may have been an intrusive Twenty-Sixth Dynasty object.

52. Aston, 2009a: 378.

53. Giddy, 1999: 276, pl. 59.

54. Aston, 2009a: 384.

55. Giddy, 1999: 306, pls. 67, 92, EES 262.

56. A. J. Spencer, 1993: 34, pls. 28, 31, no. 40, 950–850 BCE house phase. The inscription reads 'May my father (ancestor?) live', followed by a cartouche, which may have contained the name of the person in question. A limestone statue of a seated monkey, roughly carved with little attention to detail, was found underneath the plaster floor of the 700–600 BCE house, but above the earlier 850–750 BCE house at Hermopolis and was probably dumped there by the builders of the new house phase. Whether this statue once belonged to the 850–750 BCE house phase cannot be said with certainty, see A. J. Spencer, 1993: pl. 30, no. 33.

57. Aston, 2009a: 387.

58. Aston, 2009a: 387.

59. Giddy, 1999: 88–9.

60. Anthes et al., 1965: 133; Aston, 2007b: 78; Bakry, 1959: 48, nos. 214–21.

61. Aston, 2009a: 380.

62. Giddy, 1999: 98.

63. Zivie-Coche, 2000: 111–12, pl. IV.

64. Giddy, 1999: 103, pls. 22, 85.

65. Wilson, 2011: 114, pl. 14.9.

66. Aston, 2009a: 380.

67. Wilson, 2011: 140.

68. N. Spencer, 2014: pl. 275.

69. A. J. Spencer, 1993: 35, pl. 32, no. 68.

70. Aston, 2009a: 385.

71. Aston, 2009a: 385.

72. N. Spencer, 2014: pl. 275.

73. Aston, 2009a: 385.

74. Aston, 2009a: 385.

75. Bacquerisse, 2015: 371.

76. Bacquerisse, 2015: 371.

77. Giddy, 1999: 121–2.

78. Giddy, 1999: 129–30.

79. N. Spencer, 2014: 57.

80. Teeter, 2010: 5.

81. Teeter, 2010: 5.

82. Page-Gasser and Wiese, 1997; Schulte and Arnold, 1978, no. 97; Seipel, 1989: 42, no. 7.

83. Pinch, 1993; Schulte and Arnold, 1978: nos. 182–3.

84. N. Spencer, 2008: 66.

85. Teeter, 2010: 6.

86. Teeter, 2010: 6.

87. Kemp and Stevens, 2010; Peet and Woolley, 1923; Stevens, 2006.

88. Szpakowska, 2003: 113–14.

89. Giddy, 1999.

90. N. Spencer, 2008; 2014.

91. Wilson, 2011.

92. Hanasaka, 2012: 4–14.

93. Szpakowska, 2003: 113–14.

94. Only one example of a cobra figurine was found in the fill of a pit overlying the Ramesside strata, see Giddy, 1999: 22, pl. 2, EES 517, and the material from these levels could not be securely dated to the Third Intermediate Period. Overall eight examples were found in Level 0, a series of silt deposits covering the Kom Rabia excavation areas. The material in which the cobra figurines were found was not in situ and could have been brought up from much earlier levels as objects dating from the reigns of Amenhotep

III to Ramesses II were also contained in it, see Giddy, 1999: pl. 15 (127) and (171).

95. Giddy, 1999: 17.

96. Wilson, 2011: 116–25. Those found in the upper strata, according to Penelope Wilson (personal communication), are likely to have been brought up from and are residual of earlier New Kingdom levels. Excavations at Sais of settlement layers of the tenth century BCE onwards would appear to confirm the cessation of cobra figurine manufacture and usages after the New Kingdom as none have been found.

97. N. Spencer, 2008: 66.

98. Giddy, 1999: 310, pl. 68, EES 343.

99. N. Spencer, 2014: 54, figs. F197, F686, F741, F198, F596.

100. Wilson, 2011: pl. 21 (5.1000, L2-4, S.019).

101. Teeter, 2010: 111–23.

102. A. J. Spencer, 1993: 39–40.

103. Bacquerisse, 2015: 358–60, figs. 7–11.

104. Terracotta animals were found at Karnak (Mut temple), see Sullivan, 2013: 240–1, but they are described as 'animal' and it cannot be said whether they represented quadrupeds.

105. N. Spencer, 2008: 67.

106. N. Spencer, 2008: 67.

107. Giddy, 1999: 310; Teeter, 2010: 111.

108. Vandier d'Abbadie, 1937: pls. 19–23; 1946, pls. 104–7.

109. Teeter, 2010: 11.

110. Bailey, 2008: 16.

111. Teeter, 2010: 111.

112. Wilson, 2011: 200.

113. *Urk.* III. 21.64–5, 22.66.

114. Bacquerisse, 2015: 358–60.

115. Heidorn, 1997: 106.

116. Weidner, 1941–4: 42, ll. 8–11.

117. Fuchs, 1994: 80, ll. 66–7, 186, l. 450, 245, ll. 183–4; Luckenbill, 1989: 39, §74, 44, §87.

118. Borger, 1956: 99, §65, l. 44, 114, §80, col. ii, 16; Luckenbill, 1989: 227, §580.

119. Streck, 1914: 14, col. ii, ll. 28–16, col. ii, l. 48

120. N. Spencer, 2014: 175.

121. Coulson, 1996: 141–3 (12), pl. 17 (I).

122. Redford, 2004: 130–1, figs. 83–4.

123. De Linage and Michalowski, 1938: 119–20, pl. 38.

124. Thomas, 2016: 41.

125. Martin, 1987: 71; Teeter, 2010: 26.

126. Teeter, 2010: 26.

127. Hornblower, 1929: 29–47.

128. Desroches-Noblecourt, 1953: 7–47.

129. Bruyère, 1939: 109–50; Petrie, 1927; Pinch, 1993: 198–209.

130. Munro, 1973.

131. Teeter, 2010: 6.

132. Anthes et al., 1965: 127–8.

133. Wilson, 2011: 120.

134. Teeter, 2010: 157.

135. Teeter, 2010: 157.

136. Teeter, 2010: 158.

137. Teeter, 2010: 159.

138. Teeter, 2010: 167.

139. Teeter, 2010: 168.

140. Teeter, 2010: 168.

141. Teeter, 2010: 168.

142. Teeter, 2010: 168.

143. Teeter, 2010: 168.

144. Backhouse, 2012.

145. Teeter, 2010: 168.

146. Teeter, 2010: 154.

147. Teeter, 2010: 154.

148. Teeter, 2010: 154.

149. Hanasaka, 2012: 12.

150. Hanasaka, 2012: 12.

151. Parkinson, 1991: 125.

152. Teeter, 2003: 14.

153. Hornung and Staehelin, 1976: 26–9.

154. Schlick-Nolte and von Droste zu Hülshoff, 1990: 92–3, no. 5, 94–6, no. 57.

155. Ben-Tor, 1993; Brunner-Traut and Brunner, 1981; Teeter, 2003.

156. Teeter, 2003: 14.

157. Keel, 1980; 1997; 2004; 2010a; 2010b; 2013; 2016.

158. Teeter, 2003: 14.

159. Hayes, 1951: 234; Teeter, 2003: 14.

160. Hornung and Staehelin, 1976: 41–87; Jaeger, 1982: 94, 184–253; Teeter, 2003: 14.

161. Aston, 2009a: 384.

162. Droiton, 1957; Hornung and Staehelin, 1976: 60–4, 174–8; Jaeger, 1982: 94; Satzinger, 1974; Teeter, 2003: 14.

163. Lupo, 2015b: 389–90.

164. N. Spencer, 2014: 57, pl. 286, F720.

165. A. J. Spencer, 1993: 37, pl. 36, no. 143.

166. Teeter, 2003: 45 (47).

167. Aston, 2009a: 384.

168. Aston, 2009a: 384.

169. Aston, 2009a: 384.

170. Malaise, 1978: 75.

171. Petrie, 1917a: 29.

172. A pale blue faience scarab bore the motif of symmetrically opposed uraei flanking a kheper-sign and sun disc, see N. Spencer, 2008: 104; 2014: 57, no. F676, pl. 72.

173. A scarab with an identical design to that at Kom Firin is known from Akoris, see Hanasaka, 2011: 9–10, fig. 6 (2). A further five scarabs in blue and green faience and steatite were also found at Akoris in the Third Intermediate Period layers, including versions with the Menkheperre motif. Another example had a monkey or a human with a stick on it and the final example had a simple lattice design, see Kawanishi and Tsujimura, 2013: 12, fig. 9, nos. 1–4.

174. Scarabs were common in the Hermopolis domestic assemblages. The Hermopolis scarab corpus from the pre-eighth century BCE shows a preference for steatite scarabs with three examples, see A. J. Spencer, 1993: 38, pl. 36, nos. 147–9. One was a perforated scarab with clear details on the back, undercut between the legs and the body. The design on the back was a hieroglyphic inscription, 'The Judge, Amenhotep', which is a reference to Amenhotep son of Hapu, see A. J. Spencer, 1993: 38. From the eighth century BCE onwards at Hermopolis, the materials used for scarabs become more diversified. Eleven examples from the Level 2b–1a phases of occupation consisted of scarabs made of serpentine, green faience, Egyptian blue, green jasper, and blue glass, with steatite being the main material used, see A. J. Spencer, 1993: 37–8, nos. 137–46, 150–1.

175. The name 'Menkheperre' was a common motif in the Third Intermediate Period. Examples of scarabs with the name have been found at Tell el-Ghaba, see Lupo, 2015b: 389–90, and those from Kom Firin have the name flanked by the *Maat* feathers and a *nb* (Lord) sign, see N. Spencer, 2014: 57, pl. 286, F720. At Hermopolis, the motif of Menkheperre was used often, see A. J. Spencer, 1993: 37, pl. 36, no. 143, with one scarab having the sign *mn* repeated, see A. J. Spencer, 1993: 38, pl. 36, no. 149. Decorative Menkheperre scarabs were found at Medinat Habu, which indicates scarabs of this type were not just used in the Eighteenth Dynasty, see Teeter, 2003: 45 (47),

similar to Kom Firin where there was no Eighteenth Dynasty occupation, see N. Spencer, 2014: 57.

176. Aston, 2009a: 374.

177. Andrews, 1994; Herrmann, 1985; 1990; 1994; 2002; 2003; 2006; 2007; 2015; 2016; Müller-Winkler, 1987; Petrie, 1914a.

178. Aston, 2009a.

179. Aston, 2009a: 374.

180. Anthes et al., 1965: 121–4, 135–8; Aston, 2007b: 77–8; Bakry, 1959: 50–7.

181. Bacquerisse, 2015.

182. A. J. Spencer, 1993: 35, pl. 34, no. 71.

183. Bacquerisse, 2015: 360; A. J. Spencer, 1993: 35, pl. 34, no. 83.

184. A. J. Spencer, 1993: 35, pl. 34, no. 85.

185. A. J. Spencer, 1993: 35, pl. 34, no. 86.

186. Giddy, 1999: 81, pl. 19, EES 1117.

187. A. J. Spencer, 1993: 35, pl. 32, no. 82; Zivie-Coche, 2000: 126, pls. II, F–G, and XXI, G.

188. Anthes et al., 1965: 121.

189. Bacquerisse, 2015: 360.

190. Bacquerisse, 2015: 362–3.

191. Zivie-Coche, 2000: 125, pl. II, D.

192. Spalinger, 2005: 227.

193. Tillmann, 1992: 93, pl. 23.1.

194. Graves-Brown, 2015: 44.

195. Giddy, 1999: 227, 233–4, nos. 951/69, 1066.

196. Graves-Brown, 2015: 45.

197. Roeder, 1931–2: 108, fig. 3.

198. Graves-Brown, 2015: 43.

199. Aston, 2009a: 142–3.

200. Aston, 2009a: 382.

201. Petrie, 1917b: pl. xxxix.

202. Aston, 2009a: 149.

203. Leclère, 2014: 73, pl. 26, EA 23943.

204. Aston, 2007b: 76.

205. Prell, 2011; Tillmann, 1992; 2007.

206. Thomas, 1981, I: 31, nos. 4–6; II: pl. I.4–6.

207. Peet and Woolley, 1923: I, pls. xiii, 6, xiv, I, LIV, 518.

208. Bruyère, 1939: xliii, 3.

209. Brunton, 1948: 71, pl. LII, 20, 78, 79.

210. Aston, Harrell, and Shaw, 2000: 28.

211. Wilson, 2011: 104–8, pls. 7–10.

212. N. Spencer, 2014: 56, pls. 220, 268–74.

213. Aston, 2007b: 76–7; Giddy, 1999: 226–43.

214. A. J. Spencer, 1993: 33, pls. 27–9, nos. 20–30 (a–o).

215. Hanasaka, 2011: 10, fig. 6, no. 21; Kawanishi and Tsujimura, 2013: 14, fig. 9, no. 21.

216. Wilson, 2011: 105.
217. Wilson, 2011: 105.
218. Graves-Brown, 2015: 50.
219. Copper tweezers are found in the late New Kingdom/early Third Intermediate Period settlement at Lisht North, see Mace, 1914: fig. 4, along with what appears to be some possibly corroded hair curlers, like an example from a mid- to late Eighteenth Dynasty level at Memphis, see Giddy, 1999: 175, pl. 36.
220. Copper bodkins and needles were used at Lisht North, see Mace, 1914: fig. 4. At Hermopolis, bodkins and metal tools of the same types used for piercing were found in all the occupation phases. The use of iron for bodkins was found in both the pre- and post-eighth century BCE phases.
221. Wilson, 2011: 109–10.
222. N. Spencer, 2008: 70; 2014: 58.
223. In the overburden of the early Third Intermediate Period level at Sais, there was found a copper alloy fragment which may have been a chisel or awl like an example from Kom Firin, see Wilson, 2011: 110, pl. 12.5,.
224. Crist, Dunn-Vaturi, and de Voogt, 2016: 53.
225. Crist, Dunn-Vaturi, and de Voogt, 2016: 60.
226. Wilson, 2011: 46, fig. 70.
227. Pusch, 1979: 320–1.
228. Piccione, 1990: 436–7.
229. Crist, Dunn-Vaturi, and de Voogt, 2016: 59.
230. Leclère, 2014: 48, pl. 30, nos. 22323, 22803, 23802.
231. N. Spencer, 2014: 55, pl. 169.
232. Szpakowska, 2008: 115.
233. Wilson, 2011: 128.
234. Kemp and Vogelsang-Eastwood, 2001: 306; Redford, 2004: 120, fig. 73 (742); N. Spencer, 2014: 55; Sullivan, 2013: 241, fig. 9, no. 50, fig. 10, no. 53.
235. Wilson, 2011: 128.
236. Wilson, 2011: 128–30.
237. Wilson, 2011: 128.
238. Hanasaka, 2011: 9.
239. Sullivan, 2013: 241, fig. 10, no. 53.
240. Zivie-Coche, 2000: 113, pls. V, A–D, and XXII, E.
241. N. Spencer, 2014: 55, pl. 167, F828.
242. N. Spencer, 2014: 55, pl. 168, F827.
243. N. Spencer, 2014: 460.
244. Giddy, 1999: 88–95.
245. A. J. Spencer, 1993: 37, nos. 125–9.
246. Szpakowska, 2008: 114, fig. 6.4.
247. Giddy, 1999: pl. 71, no. 1254.
248. A. J. Spencer, 1993: 34, no. 48, pl. 31.
249. Leclère, 2014: 87, pl. 30, no. 18463.
250. Bacquerisse, 2015: 380–1.
251. Bader, 2001: 218–19.
252. Wilson, 2011: 131.
253. For a typology of different shapes of ceramic counter, see Brissaud and Cotelle, 1987. For a discussion of tesson in the Aegean, see Papadopoulos, 2002.
254. Wilson, 2011: 131–5.
255. N. Spencer, 2008: 67; 2014: 54.
256. A. J. Spencer, 1993: 38, pl. 37, no. 166.
257. Zivie-Coche, 2000: 113, pls. V, E and XXII, F.
258. Giddy, 1999: 324–30.
259. Giddy, 1999: 325–6.
260. Peña, 2007: 154–7; Wilson, 2011: 132.
261. Giddy, 1999: 325.
262. Giddy, 1999: 325.
263. Kemp and Vogelsang-Eastwood, 2001: 83.
264. Wilson, 2011: 132.
265. N. Spencer, 2014: 54.
266. Aston, 2016, in his study of more than 750 ceramic tesson from Hyksos levels at Tell el-Dab'a, argues convincingly that ceramic 'tessons' were used as gaming counters, while it must be noted that after their primary use as gaming counters they could have taken on secondary functions.
267. Leclère, 2014: pl. 30, no. 23802.
268. Leclère, 2014: pl. 30, nos. 23835–8.
269. Ritner, 2009a.
270. Lillios, 1999: 235.
271. Lillios, 1999: 236.
272. Lillios, 1999: 236.
273. Steel, 2013.
274. Lillios, 1999: 236.
275. Steel, 2013.
276. Steel, 2013.
277. Teeter, 2010: 6.
278. Teeter, 2010: 6.
279. Andrews, 1994: 8.
280. Andrews, 1994: 174–9.

5 CONCLUSIONS: TRANSITION AND CONTINUITY IN THE THIRD INTERMEDIATE PERIOD

1. Seidlmayer, 2000: 120.
2. Seidlmayer, 2000: 121.

3. Seidlmayer, 2000: 121.
4. Jansen-Winkeln, 2012.
5. For discussions of 'city-state' cultures, see Hansen, 2000.
6. Petersen, 1977; Yoyotte, 1972.
7. Taylor, 2009.
8. Aston, 1996a; Boulet, 2018; Boulet and Defernez, 2014.

APPENDIX 1   GAZETTEER OF THIRD INTERMEDIATE PERIOD SITES

1. Gauthier, 1914: 290 (277).
2. For discussions on the Third Intermediate Period activity at the site of Balat in the Dakhleh Oasis, see Minault-Gout, 1983: 117; Mills, 1983: 128, and for excavations at the temple and settlement of Mut el-Kharab, see Hope, 2001: 29–46; Hope et al., 2008: 49–73; 2009: 47–86; Kaper, 2009.
3. Gardiner, 1947, II: 1, On.Am.314.
4. Jansen-Winkeln, 2007a: 81; Römer, 1994: 579 (54).
5. Gauthier, 1914: 245, VII; Jansen-Winkeln, 2007a: 25.
6. Jansen-Winkeln, 2007b: 120; Seidlmayer, 1982: 329–34, taf. 72.
7. Jansen-Winkeln, 2007b: 172; Junge, 1987: 62–3 (5, 2), taf. 38.
8. Jansen-Winkeln, 2007b: 254, 413, 472; Junge, 1987: 61–3, taf. 35 e–f; Payraudeau, 2003: 203.
9. Cairo JE 41013, Jansen-Winkeln, 2007b: 336; Leclant, 1963: 74–8, fig. 1.
10. Krekeler, 1988: 170–4; 1993: 172, 174, Abb. 13.
11. Aston, 1996b; Jaritz, 1986.
12. Aston, 2009a: 154–5; Jansen-Winkeln, 2004; 2007a: 94; Wenig, 1968.
13. PM VI, 1939: 199.
14. Caminos, 1952.
15. Winlock, 1920.
16. Gardiner, 1947, II: 6.
17. Alliot, 1934: 201–10; Jansen-Winkeln, 2007b: 472, n.154; Sternberg-el Hotabi, 1999, I: 50, 82, 84, 86; II: 25.
18. PM V, 1937: 204.
19. BM 1225, PM V, 1937: 204.
20. Leclant, 1987: 349; Leclant and Clerc, 1986: 287.

21. Cairo Mus Ent. 46916.
22. Engelbach, 1921: 190–2, fig. 2; PM V, 1937: 204.
23. Henne, 1925: 15.
24. Moeller, 2010: 87.
25. Davies and O'Connell, 2011a: 105, figs. 22–6.
26. Davies and O'Connell, 2011b: 6.
27. Gardiner, 1947, II: 7, On.Am.320.
28. Cairo JE 89125, Jansen-Winkeln, 2007a: 195; Quaegebeur, 1989: 121–33.
29. Gardiner, 1947, II: 8.
30. Kitchen, 1996: §232.
31. Leclant and Clerc, 1997: 311.
32. Limme, 2008: 23–4, fig. 35.
33. Gardiner, 1947, II: 9, On.Am.322.
34. Gardiner, 1947, II: 10, On.Am.323.
35. Cairo CG 70007, Daressy, 1889: 81, xxiii; Roeder, 1914: pls. 7, 25–8.
36. Garstang, 1907: 132–48.
37. Aston, 2009a: 153.
38. Downes, 1974.
39. Aston, 2009a: 153.
40. Aston, 2009a: 154.
41. Aston, 2009a: 154.
42. Gardiner, 1947, II: 13, On.Am.324.
43. Cairo CG 42221, Jansen-Winkeln, 2007b: 243–5, n.51; Legrain, 1914b: 47–50, pl. 29; PM II, 1929: 149.
44. Gardiner, 1947, II: 14–15, On.Am.325.
45. Cairo Mus Ent. 38269, PM V, 1937: 165; Vikentiev, 1930.
46. Baines and Malek, 2000: 82; Snape, 2014: 36.
47. Gardiner, 1947, II: 15–17, On.Am.326.
48. Cairo CG 42221.
49. Gardiner, 1947, II: 16.
50. Berlin 9679.
51. Berlin 8516 and 8517.
52. Aston, 2009a: 153.
53. Breasted, 1906: §627–30, listed as the Gebelein Stela; Daressy, 1888; Kitchen, 1996: §213.
54. Gardiner, 1947, II: 21, On.Am.330.
55. Fraser, 1892–3: pl. 5 (xxi), opposite pp. 494, 498; Schiaparelli, 1921: 126–7.
56. Gardiner, 1947, II: 20, On.Am.330.
57. Gardiner, 1947, II: 21, On.Am.332–3.
58. Florence Museum 7632, Pellegrini, 1898: (29); PM V, 1937: 161.
59. Gauthier, 1914: 387 (2, A), 388 (XVIII, 2); Legrain, 1906: 44.
60. Pierrat-Bonnefois, 2000.
61. The Third Intermediate Period funerary landscape of the Theban West Bank is dealt with in

detail by Aston, 2009a: 157–268. For documentation of the Third Intermediate Period settlement inside the walls of Medinat Habu, see Hölscher, 1954.

62. Yoyotte, 1950: 63–6.

63. Block Statue Cairo CG 42232: JE 36665: Karnak Cachette, NR. 99; now in Luxor Museum Nr J 152.

64. Kitchen, 1996: §171.

65. Gardiner, 1947, II: 24, On.Am.334.

66. P. Berlin 3141, 3111.

67. Otto, 1952: 79.

68. P. BM 10230, IV, I.

69. Otto, 1952: 80.

70. Yoyotte, 1950.

71. Gardiner, 1947, II: 24, On.Am.335–6.

72. For the Karnak temples, see PM II, 1929: 1–301, and for Luxor temple, see PM II, 1929: 301–39.

73. El-Saghir, 1988; Sullivan, 2013.

74. Gardiner, 1947, II: 26, On.Am.337.

75. Jansen-Winkeln, 2007a: 81 n.21; A. J. Spencer, 1979: 145, pl. 34 (82).

76. PM V, 1937: 144.

77. Gardiner, 1947, II: 27, On.Am.338.

78. BM EA 13368, PM VIII/2, 1999: 546; Turin Museo Egizio Cat 3087, PM VIII/2, 1999: 550.

79. Davies, 1923: 79.

80. Wolf, 1929: 31.

81. Davies, 1923: 83.

82. Cairo Museum JE 1221, Borchardt, 1934: 116–17, pl. 170; Hamada, 1947: 20; Northampton, Spiegelberg, and Newberry, 1908: 7; PM II, 1929: 422–3.

83. PM II, 1929: 422–3.

84. Cairo Museum JE 44670, Gauthier, 1914: 269, xxiii (A); Jansen-Winkeln, 2007a: 80 n.20; A. J. Spencer, 1979: 145, pl. 35 (92).

85. Gardiner, 1947, II: 27, On.Am.339.

86. Moscow I.1.a. 1934 (2083).

87. Hodjash and Berlev, 1982: 156, 157 (103); Jansen-Winkeln, 2007b: 413.

88. Gardiner, 1947, II: 28, On.Am.341.

89. London UC 16824, Römer, 1994: 467–8.

90. Cairo JE 71902, Abdallah, 1984: pls. 16–17; Jansen-Winkeln, 2007a: 25.

91. Jansen-Winkeln, 2007b: 52; Kitchen, 1996: §263; Petrie, 1896: 17, pl. 13 (5–7); PM V, 1937: 26; Traunecker, 1992: §9, 62.

92. Cairo JE 37516, Carter and Legrain, 1905: 123–4; Daressy, 1913: 143; Gauthier, 1914: 349 (viii, x), 380 (x); Jansen-Winkeln, 1995: 137; 2007b: 155–6; PM V, 1937: 133; Yoyotte,

1977–8: 163–9; 1979–80: 194–7, 90; 1981–2, 189–92.

93. Cairo JE 48400, Jansen-Winkeln, 2009: 61–3; PM V, 1937: 130; Vikentiev, 1930: 1–8, 15–49, pls. 1, 3–4.

94. Kawa V, Copenhagen AEIN 1712, Jansen-Winkeln, 2009: 135–8; Leclant and Yoyotte, 1952: 15–29.

95. Gardiner, 1947, II: 29, On.Am.342.

96. Gardiner, 1947, II: 30, On.Am.343.

97. Marchand, 2000: 268–9; Zignani, Marchand, and Morisot, 1998: 483–4, figs. 19, 23, nos. 1–2, 6–8.

98. Marchand, 2000; Zignani, Marchand, and Morisot, 1998: 483.

99. Chicago OIM 10729, Jansen-Winkeln, 2007b: 407.

100. Ashmolean Mus. 2403.

101. Petrie, 1900: 11, 31.

102. Aston, 2009a: 153.

103. Gardiner, 1947, II: 31, On.Am.344; Gauthier, 1925–9, III: 69.

104. Gardiner, 1951: 123.

105. Gardiner, 1947, II: 32, On.Am.345.

106. Gardiner, 1947, II: 33, On.Am.346; Gauthier, 1925–9, IV: 45, 129, 226.

107. Collombert, 1997: 16–24; Jansen-Winkeln, 2007b: 471.

108. Stela Harvard 1902.16.9 = 2321, Collombert, 1998: 239–42; Jansen-Winkeln, 2009: 393.

109. London BM 386, Collombert, 1997: 30–4; Jansen-Winkeln, 2009: 393–4.

110. Stela San Jose RC 1817, Collombert, 1997: 40–4; Jansen-Winkeln, 2009: 394.

111. Gardiner, 1947, II: 35, On.Am.347.

112. Loret, 1916–17: 61.

113. Mariette, 1880: pl. 51 as pl. 57; PM V, 1937: 59.

114. Cairo JE 39410, l. 27.

115. Meffre, 2015: doc.7.

116. Gardiner, 1947, II: 35, On.Am.348.

117. Vatican Museuo Gregoriano Egizio 22692, PM VIII, 1999: 770.

118. Gardiner, 1933; Jansen-Winkeln, 2007b: 23–6 (12.28).

119. Krauss, 2005.

120. Kaper, 2009: 148.

121. Krauss, 2005.

122. Gardiner, 1947, II: 36, On.Am.349.

123. Gardiner, 1947, II: 36; Gauthier, 1925–9, III: 66.

124. Gardiner, 1947, II: 36.

125. Gardiner, 1947, II: 36, On.Am.351.

126. BM EA 642.
127. Aston, 2009a: 141–2.
128. Gardiner, 1947, II: 276.
129. Turin Cat no. 2074.
130. Černy, 1955: 29–30.
131. Gardiner, 1947, II: 37, On.Am.352.
132. Kees, 1937: 78.
133. Gardiner, 1947, II: 36, On.Am.350.
134. O'Connor, 2009.
135. Mace's Cemetery D; Garstang's Cemetery E; Peet's Cemeteries B, F, X; the Pennsylvania–Yale excavations; and in part of the areas worked by Amélineau.
136. Aston, 2009a: 148–50.
137. Aston, 2009a: 141–8.
138. Aston, 1996a: 46–7, figs. 137–137a; Budka, 2010: 49.
139. Budka, 2010: 51.
140. Budka, 2010: 52.
141. Gardiner, 1947, II: 38, On.Am.353.
142. P. Louvre E. 25363 recto 4, Müller, 2009: 257.
143. Other forms of the toponym appear on P. Strasbourg 31+ 40XXII, 10–12, P. Strasbourg 26 + 271 + 29VII + 44IV, 4–7, P. Strasbourg 39 recto 5–6, P. Berlin 23233 recto x+4, P. Strasbourg 31+ 44III, P. Aberdeen 169c + 172i + o, P. Strasbourg 33 and P. Berlin 8524, while P. Berlin 8524 recto x+8 has the apposition [hieroglyphs] 'the Island of the Valley', see Müller, 2009: 257.
144. Müller, 2009: 257.
145. Müller, 2009: 261.
146. Gardiner, 1947, II: 41, On.Am.355.
147. Gardiner, 1947, II: 41.
148. Gardiner, 1947, II: 40, On.Am.354.
149. El-Masry, 2008: 235.
150. El-Masry, 2008: 236.
151. Sarcophagus Berlin 8505–6, Jansen-Winkeln, 2007a: 213.
152. Cairo JE 26097 (TN 20/6/24/10), Bouriant, 1889: 367–70; Jansen-Winkeln, 2007b: 481–2; PM V, 1937: 20; von Bissing, 1914: taf. 98.
153. Gardiner, 1947, II: 41; Maspero, 1889: 578.
154. Gardiner, 1947, II: 46; On.Am.356; Gauthier, 1925–9, II: 129.
155. Gardiner, 1947, II: 46–7; Gauthier, 1925–9, VI: 111.
156. Gardiner, 1947, II: 45.
157. Yoyotte, 1959: 23–33.
158. Gardiner, 1941: 39.
159. Bologne K.S. 1813, Gabolde, 1994: 261–75.
160. Gardiner, 1947, II: 39.

161. Gasse, 1988.
162. Gasse, 1988.
163. Gasse, 1988.
164. Gardiner, 1947, II: 358, On.Am.358; Gauthier, 1925–9, IV: 139.
165. Gardiner, 1947, II: 7; Gasse, 1988: 32.
166. Gardiner, 1947, II: 49–55, On.Am.361.
167. Gardiner, 1947, II: 49–55.
168. Brunton, 1930: pl. xxxviii.
169. Aston, 2009a: 140.
170. Aston, 2009a: 141.
171. P. Louvre AF 6345 col. VI, l.16, Gasse, 1988: pl. 6.
172. P. Louvre AF 6345 col.VI, l.18, Gasse, 1988: pl. 6.
173. Gardiner, 1941–8, table II, n.80; Gasse, 1988: 32, n.47.
174. P. Louvre AF 6345 col. VI, l.19, Gasse, 1988.
175. P. Louvre AF 6345 col.VI, ll.22, 24, Gasse, 1988.
176. P. Louvre AF 6345 col. VI, l.26, Gasse, 1988.
177. P. Louvre AF 6345 col. XII, ll.12, 14, Gasse, 1988.
178. P. Louvre AF 6345 col. II, ll.9, 10, 11, Gasse, 1988.
179. Gardiner, 1947, II: 49, On.Am.360.
180. Gardiner, 1947, II: 55–62, On.Am.362.
181. Gasse, 1988.
182. Gomaà, 1986: 241–3; Malek, 1978.
183. Gardiner, 1947, II: 62–4, On.Am.363–4.
184. Gasse, 1988.
185. Caminos, 1958.
186. Gasse, 1988.
187. Gardiner, 1947, II: 64–6, On.Am.365.
188. P. BM 10052 verso 12, 4, Gasse, 1988: 35.
189. Gardiner, 1947, II: 66, On.Am.366.
190. P. Louvre AF 6345 col. II, l.13, Gasse, 1988: 60.
191. P. Louvre AF 6345 col. XII, 13, Gasse, 1988: 60.
192. Gasse, 1988: 38, n.87.
193. P. Louvre AF 6345 col. XIV D, I, Gasse, 1988: 60.
194. Gasse, 1988: 41, n.112.
195. P. Louvre AF 6345 col. VII, 2, Gasse, 1988: 60.
196. P. Louvre AF 6345 col. XI, 9, Gasse, 1988: 60.
197. P. Louvre AF 6345 col. XIII, 13, Gasse, 1988: 60.
198. P. Louvre AF 6345 col. II.3, 25, Gasse, 1988: 8, 9, 57, 60.
199. P. Louvre AF 6346 Frag. G, 3, Gasse, 1988: 80, 84.

200. P. Louvre AF 6345 col. VI, l.22, 24, Gasse, 1988: 8, 9, 57.

201. P. Louvre AF 6346 Frag. G, 2, Gasse, 1988: 80, 84.

202. P. Louvre AF 6345 col. II, 7, Gasse, 1988: 5, 60.

203. P. Louvre AF 6345 col. VI, 2, Gasse, 1988: 8, 60.

204. Gardiner, 1947, II: 67, On.Am.367; Gauthier, 1925–9, V: 107.

205. London, Petrie Museum 14352, Weigall, 1907: 219, ix.

206. BM EA 14466, Hall, 1930: 1–2, pls. I–II.

207. P. BM EA 10554, 87, Maspero, 1889: 578.

208. Aston, 1996a: 44–5; 2009a: 140; Aston and Bader, 1998: 23–6; Brunton, 1948: 73–8, pls. LIV–LVI.

209. Gardiner, 1947, II: 73, On.Am.370.

210. Gardiner, 1947, II: 74–5, On.Am.371.

211. BM EA 47609, 47610, Aston, 2009a: 114.

212. Jansen-Winkeln, 2009: 257; Leahy, 1999.

213. Gardiner, 1947, II: 75, On.Am.372.

214. Gardiner, 1947, II: 76–7, On.Am.373.

215. Gardiner, 1947, II: 77, On.Am.374.

216. Gardiner, 1947, II: 77, On.Am.375.

217. Kemp, 1995.

218. Kessler, 1981.

219. Willems and Muhammad, 2010.

220. Aston, 2009a: 114.

221. Aston, 1996a.

222. A. J. Spencer, 1993: 13–50.

223. Jansen-Winkeln, 2007b: 294–5, n.8; Meffre, 2015: 118; Sheikholeslami, 2009: 515–29; P. Spencer, 1989: 57–62, pls. 100–110.

224. Meffre, 2015: 120.

225. Meffre, 2015: 121.

226. Perdu, 2002b: 157–8.

227. BM EA 43070, A. J. Spencer, 1988: 232, pl. XXX.

228. Wild, 1972: 209–15.

229. Aston, 2009a: 113–14; A. J. Spencer, 2007.

230. Gardiner, 1947, II: 83, On.Am.378.

231. Maspero, 1890–1: 516.

232. Smith and Smith, 1976: 71, fig. 2.

233. Montet, 1961: 152.

234. Gardiner, 1947, II: 83.

235. Kessler, 1981.

236. Lichtheim, 1980: 68, 81 n.27.

237. Research by Graves, 2013 added weight to the original hypothesis of Kessler, 1981 that the site of Jarris was indeed that of Neferusy, but stated that many other mounds around Jarris could be possible locations, while Graves' research discounted the identification with Itlidem.

238. Gardiner, 1947, II: 84–7, On.Am.379.

239. Gardiner, 1947, II: 88, On.Am.380; Gauthier, 1925–9, I: 212; II: 73.

240. Kessler, 1981.

241. Garstang, 1907: 200–10.

242. Taylor, 2009: 384–5.

243. Gardiner, 1947, II: 90–2, On.Am.382.

244. Wainwright, 1927.

245. Chabân, 1907.

246. Gardiner, 1947, II: 90–2, On.Am.383.

247. For a discussion on the Third Intermediate Period tomb groups from Akoris, see Aston, 2009a: 111–12.

248. Jansen-Winkeln, 2007b: 296.

249. Gardiner, 1947, II: 96, On.Am.384.

250. Gardiner, 1947, II; On.Am.387.

251. Gardiner, 1947, II: 98–103, On.Am.385.

252. Gardiner, 1947, II: 103, On.Am.386.

253. Grimal, 1981: §3, 12, 17 n.34.

254. Gomaà, Müller-Wollermann, and Schenkel, 1991: 177.

255. Gomaà, Müller-Wollermann, and Schenkel, 1991: 177; Vandier d'Abbadie, 1963: 20, taf. 7.1.

256. Gomaà, Müller-Wollermann, and Schenkel, 1991: 177; PM IV, 1934: 126; Wessetzky, 1977: 133; 1981: 107; Wilbour, 1936: 566.

257. Gomaà, Müller-Wollermann, and Schenkel, 1991: 178; PM IV, 1934: 125; Schenkel, 1987: 154.

258. Gomaà, 1983: 135; Gomaà, Müller-Wollermann, and Schenkel, 1991: 178.

259. Gomaà, Müller-Wollermann, and Schenkel, 1991: 178.

260. Collombert, 2014: 1–27.

261. Gomaà, Müller-Wollermann, and Schenkel, 1991: 75; Grenfell and Hunt, 1902: 4.

262. Gomaà, 1983: 137; Gomaà, Müller-Wollermann, and Schenkel, 1991: 75.

263. Gomaà, Müller-Wollermann, and Schenkel, 1991: 75.

264. Gardiner, 1947, II: 107; Kees, 1958: 173.

265. Gomaà, 1983: 143; Zibelius, 1978: 154.

266. Gomaà, Müller-Wollermann, and Schenkel, 1991: 76.

267. Saint Petersburg Museum Hermitage 5528, Grimal, 1981: §3, 12, 16, n.33; Jansen-Winkeln, 2007b: 393–4, n.26; Meffre, 2015: doc.116.

268. Gomaà, Müller-Wollermann, and Schenkel, 1991: 79; Timm, 1984–92, I: 1207. For the temple of Shoshenq I from el-Hibeh, see Jansen-Winkeln, 2007b: 7–10; Meffre, 2015: 35–48, doc.6.

269. Gardiner, 1947, II: 93; Gauthier, 1925–9, IV: 38–9; Gomaà, 1974: 47; Yoyotte, 1961b: 151.

270. Coffin Florence 10568, a, b, has decoration from chapters 125 and 146 of the Book of the Dead arranged in the manner characteristic of the late Twenty-Second Dynasty Theban coffins, see Botti, 1958: 58–68, tav. XV. 2–4; Taylor, 2009: 384, n. 59, while Coffins Florence 10501–2 have archaising features which are suggestive of the Twenty-Fifth Dynasty, with false door designs and scenes of Old Kingdom type, see Botti, 1958: tav. II. 1–3.

271. Grimal, 1981: §3, 12, 16, n.31.

272. Gomaà, Müller-Wollermann, and Schenkel, 1991: 100; Timm, 1984–92, I: 558–60.

273. Gardiner, 1947, II: 110–11, On.Am.388.

274. Recorded on Cairo JE 94748 from Heracleopolis and dated to the second half of the Twenty-First Dynasty or start of the Twenty-Second Dynasty, see Aston, 2009a: 405; Jansen-Winkeln, 2006b: 307; Meffre, 2015: doc.65; Pérez-Die, 2010, I: 331–3, figs. 313–20; Pérez-Die and Vernus, 1992: doc.17.

275. Cairo Museum CG 42228 from the reign of Osorkon II found at Karnak, see Brandl, 2008, I: 50–1, doc.0-2.4, II, pl. 12; Meffre, 2015: doc.23. Beni Suef Museum MAE 85–174, Register Book 641, from a door from Tomb 4 at the Third Intermediate Period necropolis, see Meffre, 2015: doc.81; Pérez-Die, 2010, I: 274, figs. 104, 245–7, 280–1; Pérez-Die and Vernus, 1992: doc.22; and a tablet from the Ivanovitsch Collection, Cairo 1882, see Meffre, 2015: doc.93; Wiedemann, 1890–1: 36.

276. Díaz-Iglesias Llanos, 2012.

277. Cairo Museum JE 94748.

278. Cairo CG 9430, Daressy, 1903b: 37–9, pl. XI; Moje, 2014: 255; Yoyotte, 1988: 155–6, 171–4.

279. Meffre, 2015: 189, n.354.

280. Meffre, 2015: 365–7.

281. Cairo JE 39410, Meffre, 2015: 52, 57, doc.7. face D, x+18.

282. Unknown Number, Jansen-Winkeln, 2006b: 308–10; Kessler, 1975: 130–1, doc.D; Meffre, 2015: 152, doc.59, l.4; Petrie, 1905: 22, n.1 and pl. XXVII, I; PM IV, 1934: 119.

283. Meffre, 2015: 366.

284. Meffre, 2015: 366, doc.A.

285. It is now listed as under the authority of the prophet Pentaweret, see P. Wilbour, B 22, 27–22, 30, Meffre, 2015: 366, doc.B.

286. P. BM EA 10068, IV, 16, Meffre, 2015: 366, doc.C; Peet, 1930: 90.

287. Meffre, 2015: 367.

288. Kessler, 1975: 134, n.170.

289. Grandet, 1994.

290. Meffre, 2015: 367–8.

291. Unknown number, Meffre, 2015: 151, doc.58; Petrie, 1905: 22, n.2, pl. XXVII, 2; PM IV, 1934: 119.

292. Cairo JE 39410, Meffre, 2015: 55, doc.7, l.x +13. The Touher were a group of foreign soldiers of Asiatic origin within the Fortress of Usermaatre (Ramesses II), Wb 5, 322.10-14.

293. Meffre, 2015: 368.

294. Meffre, 2015: 369.

295. MAE 86–368, 86–369, 89–321 and b, Jansen-Winkeln, 1994: 84; 2006b: 307; 2007b: 166; Meffre, 2015: 154–5, doc.63; Pérez-Die, 2010: 131, 139–40, 146, figs. 25, 29, 63; Pérez-Die and Vernus, 1992: doc.15.

296. Cairo JE 94748, Aston, 2009a: 405; Jansen-Winkeln, 2006b: 307; Meffre, 2015: 155–8, doc.65; Pérez-Die, 2010: 331–3, figs. 313–20; Pérez-Die and Vernus, 1992: doc.17.

297. Jansen-Winkeln, 2006b: 308–10.

298. Meffre, 2015: 370; Winnicki, 2009: 81–3.

299. Meffre, 2015: 370.

300. Jansen-Winkeln, 2006b: 308–10; Kessler, 1975: 130–1, doc.D; Meffre, 2015: 152–3, doc.59; Petrie, 1905: 22, n.1, pl. XXVII:1; PM IV, 1934: 119.

301. Jansen-Winkeln, 1994: 91; 2001: 170, n.99. This restoration is also followed by Lull, 2006: 238.

302. Cairo JE 39410.

303. Jansen-Winkeln, 2006b: 308–10.

304. Jansen-Winkeln, 2006b: 309; Meffre, 2015: 370.

305. Atfih site numbers 46 and 131, el-Enany, 2012: 131; el-Nagger, 1991; Meffre, 2015: 81, doc.16; Perdu, 2009: 462.

306. Meffre, 2015: 293; von Beckerath, 1999: 152–3, 158–61, 166–7, 170–1.

307. Meffre, 2015: 293.

308. Cairo JE 39410, Face D, x+21, Meffre, 2015: 58, n.85.

309. Gomaà, Müller-Wollermann, and Schenkel, 1991: 88.

310. Cairo JE 39410, Face D, x+22, Meffre, 2015.

311. Cairo, JE 39410, Face D, x+21, Meffre, 2015.

312. Gomaà, Müller-Wollermann, and Schenkel, 1991: 118.

313. Meffre, 2015: 58, doc.7, Face D, l.X+20.

314. P. Wilbour B 23, 15, Gardiner, 1941–8, II: 35.

315. Gardiner, 1941–8, III, 177–8; Meffre, 2015: 58, n.80.

316. Meffre, 2015: 58, doc.7, Face D, l.X+21.

317. P. Wilbour B 14, 24; 16, 16; 18, 7; 20, 13, Gardiner, 1941–8, II: 31, n.8, 35; Meffre, 2015: 58, n.84.

318. Meffre, 2015: 58, n.84.

319. Vernus, 1967: 166–9.

320. Gardiner, 1947, II: 115, On.Am.391.

321. Gomaà, Müller-Wollermann, and Schenkel, 1991: 130, 138, 156, 165.

322. Cairo Museum JE 45948, Daressy, 1917: 43–5; Fazzini, 2002: 357–8, 362; Jansen-Winkeln, 2007b: 333–4; Meeks, 1979: n. 23IX.10a; Meffre, 2015: 125–6, doc.43; Moje, 2014: 382.

323. For this stela, see Tresson, 1935–8: 817–40; Meffre, 2015: 61, doc.7, Face D, x+25.

324. Meffre, 2015: 61, doc.7, Face D, x+25.

325. Meffre, 2015: 61, doc.7, Face D, x+25.

326. Meffre, 2015: 60, n.88, doc.7, Face D, x+22.

327. Meffre, 2015: doc.7, x+22.

328. Meffre, 2015: 59, n.88.

329. Meffre, 2015: doc.7, Face D, x+23.

330. Meffre, 2015: doc.7, Face D, x+24.

331. Meffre, 2015: doc.7, Face D, x+20.

332. Meffre, 2015: doc.7, Face D, x+22.

333. Meffre, 2015: doc.7, Face D, x+28.

334. P. Wilbour B 24, 21.

335. Cauville, 1997: 415.

336. Meffre, 2015: 61, n.102.

337. Meffre, 2015: 60, n.95.

338. Meffre, 2015: 61, n.100.

339. Meffre, 2015: 60–1, n.99.

340. Collier and Quirke, 2002: 104–5.

341. Brovarski, 1981: 18; Griffith and Newberry, 1894: pl. XIII.

342. Meffre, 2015: 59.

343. Cairo JE 45530, Jansen-Winkeln, 2007b: 209–10, n.10; Meeks, 1979: doc.23.1.6; Meffre, 2015: doc.34; Schulman, 1966: 33–9, pl. 13, fig. 2; Yoyotte, 1961a: 93–4.

344. London UC 16026, Jansen-Winkeln, 2007b: 433–4, n.82; Meffre, 2015: doc.115; Petrie, 1890: pl. xxv, 21–3; Taylor, 2009: 382, 392, 394–5, 401, 405, fig. 1, pl. IV, 1–1a; Yoyotte, 1961a, 94, n.c.

345. Goyon, 1967: 106, 152.

346. Meffre, 2015: doc. 7.

347. Grandet, 1994, I: 311; II: 204 n.835.

348. Gardiner, 1948: 124–8, §4–30.

349. Meffre, 2015: doc.7, Face D, x+24.

350. Meffre, 2015: doc.7, Face D, x+23.

351. Baltimore Walkers Art Museum 22.202, Steindorff, 1946: 26–7, n.42, pls. X, CXI, n.42; Zecchi, 1999: 70–1, n.292.

352. Taylor, 2009: 382.

353. Davoli, 1998: 228; Meffre, 2015: doc.15; Schott, 1937: 19, 35.

354. Meffre, 2015: doc.7, Face D, x+20.

355. Gardiner, 1947, II: 115–16, On.Am.393.

356. Aston, 2009a: 107.

357. Aston, 2009a: 107.

358. Jansen-Winkeln, 2007b: 312.

359. Aston, 2009a: 90–2.

360. Aston, 2009a: 91–2.

361. Naville, 1894: pls. vii–viii, xi.

362. Aston, 2009a: 107.

363. *Wb.* III, 105.1–5.

364. Meffre, 2015: 373–4.

365. Yoyotte, 1961a; 1963: 90, n.3.

366. Meffre, 2015: 375.

367. Aston, 2009a.

368. Cairo Museum TR 20/5/24/4, Meffre, 2015: 74, doc.14; Petrie, 1891: 24–5.

369. Aston, 2009a: 94.

370. Aston, 2009a: 92; Petrie, 1890: 8; 1912: 36, pl. xxxi.

371. Aston, 2009a: 92.

372. Engelbach, 1915.

373. Aston, 2009a: 90.

374. Aston, 2009a: 90.

375. Aston, 2009a: 89.

376. Wainwright, 1912.

377. Aston, 2009a: 89–90.

378. Beni Suef Inspectorate 32–987, Meffre, 2015: doc.137.

379. Cairo JE 39410 x+20, Meffre, 2015.

380. Rubensohn and Knatz, 1904: 1–21.

381. Aston, 2009a: 93.

382. The chronological list of attestations follows that of Meffre, 2015.

   Bronze statue plinth of Osorkon II, from Memphis (Santa Barbara, California World Institute for World Archaeology, Senusret Collection MET.XL.00174), see Meffre, 2015: doc.19. Year 16 stela of Osorkon II from Tell el-Minieh and el-Shurafa (Cairo Museum JE 45327), see Daressy, 1915: 140–3; Iversen, 1941: 4–18, pl. 1; Jansen-Winkeln, 2007b: 131–3, n.69; Meeks, 1979: doc.22.05.16; Meffre,

2015: doc.18 l.5; Moje, 2014: 373; PM IV, 1934: 75. ⬚ stela of Osorkon II from Heracleopolis (Cairo Museum JE 65841), see Gauthier, 1937: 16–24; Jansen-Winkeln, 2007b: 297, n.11; Meffre, 2015: 371, doc.68; Moje, 2014: 376–7; Mokhtar, 1983: 130, pl. XXIV. ⬚ Vase of Osorkon II from Assur but taken by the Assyrians from the palace of King Abdimilkutti of Sidon (Berlin, Staatliche Museen VA Ass 2258), see Gamer-Wallert, 1978: 23, 27, 42–3, 226, pls. 8–10; Jansen-Winkeln, 1989: 151–3, n.5; 2007b: 297, n.12; Meffre, 2015: 165, 371, doc.70, n.319; Moje, 2014: 376; Vittmann, 2003: 55–6, pl. 3a. ⬚ Bubastite Gate, Karnak, Theban Twenty-Third Dynasty, reign of Takeloth II, completed under Shoshenq III, see Caminos, 1958; Jansen-Winkeln, 2007b: 161–8, n.20.7, 189–96, n.22.21; Meffre, 2015: doc.33; Perdu, 2003: 129–42. ⬚ Theban Twenty-Third Dynasty, Pedubast I, Year 6 Stela, from Memphis (Kom el-Qala) (Cairo Museum JE 45530), see Jansen-Winkeln, 2007b: 209–10, n.10; Meeks, 1979: doc.23.1.6; Meffre, 2015: doc.34; Schulman, 1966: 33–9, pl. 13, fig. 2; Yoyotte, 1961a: 93–4. ⬚ Pedubast I Stela (Hanover, Museum August Kestner 1935.200.208), found at Gurob, re-used in the area of the animal cemetery, see Jansen-Winkeln, 2007b: 312, n.32; Loat, 1905: 8, n.16, pls. XVIII, 2, XIX; Malek (PM viii), 1999: 803–065-400; Meeks, 1979: doc.23.1.0; Meffre, 2015: 162, doc.69, n.309; Moje, 2014: 377–8. ⬚ Blocks of unknown date from the royal necropolis (Tomb 4) at Heracleopolis (Beni Suef, Museum MAE 85–174 (Register Book 641)), see Jansen-Winkeln, 2007b: 223, n.5; Meffre, 2015: doc.81; Pérez-Die, 2010: 276, fig. 108; Pérez-Die and Vernus, 1992: doc.21. ⬚ Piankhy Stela (Cairo Museum JE 48862, 47086–47089, l.4, 77), Year 21 of Piankhy, from Gebel Barkal, see Goedicke, 1998; Grimal, 1981; Jansen-Winkeln, 2007b: 337–50, n.1; Meffre, 2015: doc.56.

383. Meffre, 2015: 372.

384. Caminos, 1958: 147, §230, n.ff; Grimal, 1981: §3, 12, 16, n.28; Kitchen, 1996: §263, 304, n.339; Schulman, 1966: 35, n.e; Yoyotte, 1961b: 135, n.1; 1963: 90, n.3.

385. Breasted, 1906: 419, n.g; Meffre, 2015: 373–4.

386. Mission égypto-française d'Atfih, 2010; Meffre, 2015: doc.5.

387. Atfih site nos. 46, 131, el-Enany, 2012: 131.d; el-Nagger, 1991; Meffre, 2015: doc.16; Perdu, 2009: 462.

388. London UC 14534, Jansen-Winkeln, 2007b: 291–2, n.47; Malek (PM VIII), 1999: 803–063-200; Meffre, 2015: doc.31; Stewart, 1983: 4–5, n.6, pl. 5.

389. Atfih site no. 41, el-Enany, 2012: 130–7; Meffre, 2015: doc.147.

390. Michaelidis Collection, Cairo 1944, Droiton, 1944: 91–8; Malek (PM VIII), 1999: 801–643-770; Meffre, 2015: doc.148.

391. London UC 14510, Meffre, 2015: doc.149; Petrie, 1909: 13, pl. XXXIII; Stewart, 1983: 5, pl. 6, no. 7.

392. For a discussion of the location of *It tswy*, see Malleson, 2007.

393. Mace, 1914; 1921; 1922.

394. For a list of royal monuments from the Twenty-Second to Twenty-Fifth Dynasty at Memphis, see Jurman, 2009.

395. Jurman, 2009: 113.

396. Jurman, 2009: 115.

397. Jurman, 2009: 115.

398. Anthes, 1959: 68–9; 1965: 18.

399. Smith, Jeffreys, and Malek, 1983: 34, fig. 3 'Twenty-Second Dynasty', 41, 'Twenty-First to Twenty-Second Dynasty'.

400. Aston, 2009a: 77–8.

401. Aston, 2009a: 78–82.

402. Gardiner, 1947, II: 126–30, On.Am.395.

403. Aston, 2009a: 82; Firth and Gunn, 1926: 5–6, 67; Leclant, 1952: 239; Quibell, 1907: 8–11; 1923; Quibell and Hayter, 1927: 305; Raven, 1991; Smith and Jeffreys, 1980: 18.

404. French, 2013: 217–356.

405. Aston, 2009a: 76; Zivie-Coche, 1991: 270–81.

406. Gardiner, 1947, II: 130–1, On.Am.396.

407. Gardiner, 1947, II: 131, On.Am.397.

408. Gauthier, 1925–9, II: 110; Gomaà, 1974: 155; Montet, 1957: 164.

409. Gardiner, 1947, II: 131; Gomaà, 1974: 155; Grimal, 1981: 136, n.398; Hamza, 1937: 233.

410. Gardiner, 1947, II: 141–2.

411. Gardiner, 1947, II: 120–2; Gomaà, 1974: 51.

412. Grimal, 1981: 38, no. 90.

413. Cairo CG 42232, now Luxor J 152, Jansen-Winkeln, 2007b: 205–7; Legrain, 1914b: 78–80, pls. 40–1; PM II, 1929: 149.

414. Breasted, 1906: 424–5, n.g; Gauthier, 1925–9, II: 78; III: 149; Maspero, 1898: 123–5.

415. *PSI*, v, 544; P. London, I, 99, 55, Grimal, 1981: 38, n.90; Yoyotte, 1962: 78, n.2.

416. Grimal, 1981: 38, no. 90.
417. Cairo CG 741/JE 29858, Kitchen, 1996: §152; Schulman, 1980: 311.
418. Zivie-Coche, 1991: 295.
419. Alexandria no. 360, Daressy, 1904a: 115–16; Jansen-Winkeln, 2007b: 4, doc.13; Yoyotte, 2003: 240–51, pls. 16–18.
420. New York MMA 10.176.42.
421. Vienna 5791.
422. Bickel, Gabolde, and Tallet, 1998: 31–56; Jansen-Winkeln, 2007b: 259–61.
423. Cairo JE 67846.
424. Cairo JE 92591.
425. Cairo TN 16/3/64/1.
426. Grimal, 1981: §19, l.102. For the location of this toponym at Heliopolis, see Gardiner, 1947, II: 145.
427. Breasted, 1906: 435; Montet, 1961: 37, 47.
428. Altenmüller and Moussa, 1981: 63–5, fig. 2; Pierce and Török, 1994.
429. Kitchen, 1996: §324, n.691.
430. Breasted, 1906: 419; Grimal, 1981: 12, 16, n.15; Yoyotte, 1961b: §52, 155–6.
431. Bernand, 1970: 1043–4; Daressy, 1904b; Habachi, 1954: 482–4; PM IV, 1934: 50.
432. Thomas, 2000: 371–6; Trampier, 2014: 89–108.
433. Wilson, 2011.
434. Penelope Wilson, personal communication.
435. BM EA 14594–5, Jansen-Winkeln, 2007b: 84.
436. Jansen-Winkeln, 2007b: 372.
437. CG 9430, Daressy, 1894: 48.
438. Meffre, 2015: 185–90, PM IV, 1934: 46, dates it to the Twenty-Third Dynasty. PM IV, 1934: 46, also records a base of a statuette of Isis the Scorpion, in the name of a priest (?) called Pamiu, possibly dated to the Twenty-Third Dynasty.
439. Gardiner, 1947, II: 187–99, On.Am.415.
440. Aston, 1996a: 23, figs. 26–7 (phase 1); Faltings et al., 2000: 14–15; French, 1996: 8–12; 2003; French and Bourriau, 1996; Hartung et al., 2003: 203, 209–11, 220, fig. 4; Ziermann, 2002: 463, 494–6, figs. 2, 14, pls. 52–3.
441. For documentation and discussions of Gräber J2/67 and J2/89, see Aston, 2009a: 73; Ballet, 2009; Effland, 2009; Kitagawa, 2009.
442. Schiestl, 2010: 7–11.
443. Leclant and Clerc, 1985: 343; von der Way, 1984: 323.
444. Gardiner, 1947, II: 181–2, On.Am.414.
445. Jansen-Winkeln, 2007b.
446. Daressy, 1903a: 283–4; 1914a: 86; Gauthier, 1914: 366, §xxii; Kitchen, 1996, §304; PM IV, 1934: 51.
447. Kitchen, 1996: §324, n.694.
448. Breasted, 1906: 419; Brugsch, 1879: 325; Grimal, 1981: §3, 12, 16, n.18.
449. Sarcophagus Berlin 29 dated to the Thirtieth Dynasty–early Ptolemaic Period, Yoyotte, 1958: 414–15; 1961b: 156, n.4.
450. Yoyotte, 1952: 213.
451. Daressy, 1912: 206.
452. Gauthier, 1925–9, III: 62; Grimal, 1981: §22, l.122; Montet, 1957: 100–1.
453. For discussions of Kom Firin and the domestic settlement reports from Kom Firin during the Third Intermediate Period, see N. Spencer, 2008; 2014.
454. Cairo JE 85647, Bakir, 1943; Jansen-Winkeln, 2007b: 275; Meeks, 1979: 669, doc.22.10.00a. Stela IFAO Store Registration no. 14456, Berlandini, 1978: 147–63, pls. 49–50; Jansen-Winkeln, 2007b: 275–6; Meeks, 1979: 666, doc.22.0.30. Stela Brooklyn Museum 67.119, Kitchen, 1969–70: 64–7, fig. 4; Meeks, 1979: 670, doc.22.10.15; Yoyotte, 1961b: 144, pl. 1.2. Stela British Museum EA 73965, Jansen-Winkeln, 2007b: 274. In addition to the four stelae documented above, there is a fifth from Kom Firin from Year 8 of another Shoshenq, possibly Shoshenq V, see Yoyotte, 1961b: 143. This stela represented three people, at least two of whom wear the Libyan feather before Sekhmet and Heka. The first person is labelled as 'The Great Chief of the Libu [N]im(a)-teped', the name of the second is partly preserved as Wa-tir-...-y.
455. Cairo JE 30972, Gomaà, 1974: 27–8; Kitchen, 1996: §311; Yoyotte, 1961b: 125, n.14, doc.E.
456. Cairo JE 30972, Gauthier, 1925–9, II: 41; Gomaà, 1974: 28.
457. Brooklyn no. 67.119, Jansen-Winkeln, 2007b: 274, n.18.
458. Kitchen, 1969–70: 65, n.32.
459. Gardiner, 1947, II: 161; Gauthier, 1925–9, V: 45–6; Gomaà, 1974: 51.
460. Ramzi, 1953: 268.
461. Jansen-Winkeln, 2007b: 410–11; Sauneron, 1955: 61–2, pl. 1.
462. Sauneron, 1955: 64.
463. Monnet, 1954: 32, D.
464. Stela Vienna, Sauneron, 1950: 65, E, and Stela Cherchal, Monnet, 1954: 30, B.

465. EES Delta Survey, Baqliya, EES 79: 2016.
466. Kitchen, 1996: §328, n.714.
467. Yoyotte, 1960–3: 5–9.
468. Papazian, 2013: 63–4.
469. Gardiner, 1947, II: 151–3, On.Am.404.
470. Stela Brooklyn Mus. 67–118, de Meulenaere and MacKay, 1976: 205, pl. 30, no. 106; Jansen-Winkeln, 2007b: 198–9; Kitchen, 1969–70: fig. A, 1–3; Meeks, 1979: 688, doc.22.8.22. Stela Art Sale, Cairo, Stela Geneva MAH 23473, Chappaz, 1982; Jansen-Winkeln, 2007b: 370–1; Kitchen, 1996: §449; Meeks, 1979: 671, doc.23.2.21. Stela Strasbourg 1379, de Meulenaere and MacKay, 1976: 205, pl. 30a (105); Jansen-Winkeln, 2007b: 199–200; Meeks, 1979: 669, doc.22.8.30; Spiegelberg, 1903: 197.
471. Cairo JE 43359, Jansen-Winkeln, 2007b: 387.
472. Cairo JE 43359, Jansen-Winkeln, 2007b: 387–8.
473. Gomaà, 1974: 113–14, 117, 124; Grimal, 1981: §21, l.114; Lichtheim, 1980: 78, 83 n.64, n.84; Urk. III, 3 (8), 11 (18), 36 (99), 45 (114).
474. EES Delta Survey, Gadiya, EES 510, 2016.
475. Brandl, 2008, I: 256–7; II: pl. 21, doc.M-3.1; Jansen-Winkeln, 2006b: 300–1, 313–16, pls. XXXI–XXXVI; Meffre, 2015: 64, doc.9.
476. Aston, 2009a: 64–5. For other Twenty-Second Dynasty burial objects from Tell Muqdam from the reign of Osorkon II, see Jansen-Winkeln, 2007b: 127–8.
477. BM EA 1146, Jansen-Winkeln, 2007b: 116; Naville, 1894: 29–31, pls. 4, 12.
478. Cairo JE 38261, Daressy, 1908; Jansen-Winkeln, 2007b: 370; A. J. Spencer and P. Spencer, 1986: 200, fig. 3 (Twenty-Third Dynasty).
479. Cairo JE 46789, Daressy, 1922: 77; Jansen-Winkeln, 2007b: 128–9; Meeks, 1979: 666, doc.22.5.00.
480. Gomaà, 1974: 118; Revillout, 1891: 238.
481. Gomaà, 1974: 118; Revillout, 1891: 238.
482. Gomaà, 1974: 118.
483. EES Delta Survey, Ezbet Razaiqa, EES 466: 2016.
484. Aston, 1996a: 26; van den Brink, 1987: 7, 21, 23.
485. For monuments and attestations to the site of Tell Atrib during the Twenty-Second to Twenty-Fifth Dynasty, see the detailed list and documentation by Vernus, 1978.
486. Gauthier, 1925–9, VI: 74; Gomaà, 1974: 68; Montet, 1957: 104.
487. Yoyotte, 1961b: 154–5. This identification with the region of Buto is also followed by Lichtheim, 1980: 80 and Kitchen, 1996: §324.
488. Kitchen, 1996: §365, n.941.
489. Grimal, 1981, while Favard-Meeks, 2002, has studied the connection of the toponym with Behbeit el-Hagar. Breasted, 1906: 419, also states that this location was in the central Delta near the modern Behbeit el-Hagar.
490. Gauthier, 1925–9, II: 110–11; Gomaà, 1974: 49, 69; Montet, 1949: 43; 1957: 107; Yoyotte, 1961b: 154–5, §51.
491. Gomaà, 1974: 60.
492. Gardiner, 1947, II: 176–80; Gauthier, 1925–9, II: 70–1; On.Am.412; Gomaà, 1974: 52, 60–8, 70, 75, 87, 101, 103, 112, 156–7, 159; Montet, 1957: 98.
493. London UC 14533, Meeks, 1979: 668, doc.22.8.15; Stewart, 1983: 4, pl. 4 (5).
494. Gardiner, 1947, II: 180–1, On.Am.413.
495. Aston, 2009a: 62–4.
496. Gardiner, 1947, II: 170–1, On.Am.409.
497. Mostafa, 1986: 8–12, no. 8.
498. Gardiner, 1947, II: 171, On.Am.410.
499. Aston, 1998: 694–5; 2009a: 64; Pusch, 1989: 74–5.
500. Aston and Pusch, 1999; Laemmel, 2008; Pusch, 1999c.
501. Golenischeff, 1902–3: 105; A. J. Spencer, 2002a: 39.
502. Gardiner, 1947, II: 175, On.Am.411.
503. A. J. Spencer, 2002a: 40.
504. For detailed and comprehensive discussions on the settlement of Tanis throughout the Third Intermediate Period, see Leclère, 2008: §9.
505. Aston, 2009a: 64.
506. Quaegebeur, 1982: 181–206.
507. For temple building at Bubastis during the Third Intermediate Period, see Appendix 2.
508. Aston, 1996a: 26; van den Brink, 1987.
509. Van den Brink, 1987.
510. EES Delta Survey, Gezirat el-Tawila, EES 537, 2016.
511. Aston, 1996a: 26; van den Brink, 1987.
512. Aston, 1996a: 26; van den Brink, 1987.
513. Griffith, 1888: 46, pl. i.
514. Aston, 2009a: 61–2.
515. Griffith, 1888: 41.
516. Van den Brink, 1992.
517. Aston, 1996a: 26; van den Brink, 1987.
518. Gardiner, 1947, II: 149, On.Am.402.
519. Gauthier, 1925–9, IV: 216.

520. Gardiner, 1947, II: 149.
521. Gardiner, 1947, II: 155, 158; Habachi, 1967: 37.
522. Gardiner, 1947, II: 149.
523. Cairo, Temp No. 20–10–48–15.
524. Habachi, 1967: 37.
525. Habachi, 1967: 37, n.2.
526. Gardiner, 1947, II: 146, On.Am.401.
527. Aston, 2009a: 65–71.
528. Brooklyn 57.92, from Schibin el-Qanatir, see Hill, 2004: 154–5, pl. 11 (10); Jansen-Winkeln, 2007b: 49.
529. Brandl and Jansen-Winkeln, 2008; Jansen-Winkeln, 2007b: 131.
530. Daressy, 1915: 145; Jansen-Winkeln, 2007b: 269.
531. Jansen-Winkeln, 2007b: 370.
532. Gauthier, 1925–9, II: 127–8; Gomaà, 1974: 76, 87, 94, 101–4, 108, 112, 128, 135–6, 144, 157; Montet, 1957: 206–7.
533. Aston, 2009a: 71.
534. Aston, 2009a: 71.
535. Cairo JE 46600 + Munich 6296, Jansen-Winkeln, 2007b: 418.
536. Cairo JE 41664, Jansen-Winkeln, 2007b: 420.
537. Paris Louvre N.3670, Jansen-Winkeln, 2007b: 421.
538. Aston, 1996a: 29; Petrie, 1906: 47–52.
539. BM EA 1007, Jansen-Winkeln, 2007b: 126; Naville, 1885: 15–16, pl. 4.
540. Ismalia 2408, Jansen-Winkeln, 2007b: 430.
541. Jarmužek, 2011; Jarmužek and Rzepka, 2014; Rzepka, 2011.
542. BM 1007, Naville, 1885: 15–16, frontispiece and pl. 4.
543. Naville, 1885: pl. 4.
544. Aston, 2009a: 74; Petrie, 1906: 32–4.
545. Petrie, 1906: 32.
546. Aston, 2009a: 74–6.
547. Cairo Mus. 11/1/25/13.
548. Gauthier, 1925–9, V: 136; Gomaà, 1974: 91.
549. Cairo JdE 8392, Kamal, 1905: 146–7, no. 22161, pl. XLIX.
550. Gomaà, 1974: 91.
551. Gomaà, 1974: 91.
552. Brugsch, 1879: 201–2.
553. Habachi, 1956: 462.
554. Gomaà, 1974: 92; Ranke, 1935: 111, no. 19.
555. Gomaà, 1974: 157.
556. Gardiner, 1947, II: 204–5; Godron, 1959: 83; Gomaà, 1974: 92, n.10; *Wb.* I, 471 (6–8).
557. Gauthier, 1925–9, VI: 101; Gomaà, 1974: 91.
558. Snape, 2014: 211–12.
559. Cairo CG 3842, Jansen-Winkeln, 2007b: 20.
560. Gomaà, 1974: 107–8.
561. Grimal, 1981: 157, no. 472.
562. Daressy, 1922; Kitchen, 1996: §328, n.717.
563. Aston, 1996a: 26; van den Brink, 1987.
564. Naville, 1887: 21, pl. 9E.
565. Aston, 1996a: 26; Bietak, 1986: 271; Naville, 1887, pl. 9E.
566. EES Delta Survey, Tell Ginn, EES 203, 2016.
567. Lupo, 2015a.
568. Gardiner, 1947, II: 202–3, On.Am.419.
569. El-Maksoud, 1987; 1998.
570. EES Delta Survey, Tell Buweib, EES 160, 2016.
571. EES Delta Survey, Barakim, EES 497, 2016.
572. Cairo Mus. 31169, Daressy, 1910–11: 166–7; Gomaà, 1974: 105; Spiegelberg, 1906–8: 270.
573. Breasted, 1906: 440, §878 n.h, identified the settlement with that of Phagroriopolis, known in Strabo, XVII 508, see Ball, 1942: 65, 123, 173, 178; Gomaà, 1974: 105.
574. Cairo Mus. 11/1/25/13.
575. Gauthier, 1925–9, V: 141.
576. Gomaà, 1974: 102; Kitchen, 1996: §328, 716; Yoyotte, 1961b: 133.
577. Cairo CG 39217, Barta, 1968: 180; Daressy, 1905: 302–3, pl. LVII; Jansen-Winkeln, 2007b: 421–2; Lange, 1925: 20; Meeks, 2006: 109.
578. Gauthier, 1925–9, V: 192; Gomaà, 1974.
579. For a discussion of Khapu and the district of Khapu, see below, ThIP_GeoZon.11.
580. Daressy, 1916a: 61–2; Kitchen, 1996: §305.
581. *Wb.* IV, 95.10–96.4.
582. Meffre, 2015: 375.
583. Yoyotte, 1963: 106–14.
584. Meffre, 2015: 375–6.
585. Cairo JE 46600 + Munich ÄS 6296, Daressy, 1920b: 123–8; Davoli, 1993; 2001: 35–6 (4) tav. 8; Jansen-Winkeln, 2007b: 418–20.
586. Davoli, 1993.
587. Cairo JE 41664, Daressy, 1911: 142–4; Davoli, 2001: 36 (5) tav. 9; Jansen-Winkeln, 2007b: 420.
588. Paris Louvre N.3670, Jansen-Winkeln, 2007b: 421; Schulz, 1992: 594.
589. Sammlung Weill, Davoli, 2001: 42–3 (13); Jansen-Winkeln, 2009: 388; Schumacher, 1988: 199, 202–3, 222; Weill, 1914: 95–7.
590. Jerusalem 67.30.426, earlier Cairo CG 535, Borchardt, 1925: 85–6; Daressy, 1898: 76–7

(1); Davoli, 2001: 36–7 (6) tav. X; Giveon, 1975: 19–21, pls. 9–12; Jansen-Winkeln, 2009: 388–9.

591. Aston, 2009a: 71–2.

592. Gardiner, 1947, II: 201, On.Am.418; Gauthier, 1925–9, VI: 72.

593. P. BM EA 10682.

594. P. Anastasi III, 2, 11–12.

595. P. Sallier, I, 4.9; P. Anastasi VIII, 3.3f., Gardiner, 1947, II: 201.

596. Gardiner, 1947, II: 201; Hoffmeier and Moshier, 2006: 169; Muchiki, 1999: 251–2; Müller, 1887–8: 467–77; Ward, 1974: 339–49.

597. El-Maksoud, 1987: 13–16; 1998: 61–5; Hoffmeier and Moshier, 2006: 170–1.

598. Gardiner, 1947, II: 201.

599. Hoffmeier and Moshier, 2006: 170–1.

600. El-Maksoud, 1998: 61–5; Hoffmeier and Moshier, 2006: 170.

601. Cairo TN 25/11/18/6, Jansen-Winkeln, 2007b: 411; *Urk.* III, 11 (19), 45, 114.

602. Vandier, 1961: 240–1, n.974.

603. Gauthier, 1925–9, I: 113, 217; Grimal, 1981: §19, l.101. Breasted, 1906: 436 n.a, calls it the Heliopolitan canal.

604. Bietak, 1975: 126.

605. Montet, 1957: 199.

606. Gardiner, 1947, II: 144, On.Am.398–9.

607. Cairo Temp no. 20–10–48–15.

608. Habachi, 1967.

609. Habachi, 1967: 64.

610. Habachi, 1967: 35.

611. Habachi, 1947.

612. Kitchen, 1996: §222.

613. Grimal, 1981: §3, 12, 16, n.17; Kitchen, 1996: §324, n.693; Lichtheim, 1980: 68, 81, n.7; Yoyotte, 1961b: 156.

614. *Wb.* I, 189.17, 'Canal'.

615. Grimal, 1981: §3, 12, 16, n.7; Kitchen, 1996: §324, n.693; Lichtheim, 1980: 68, 81, n.7; Yoyotte, 1961b: 156.

616. Gardiner, 1947, II: 73, On.Am.369.

617. Gauthier, 1925–9, I: 169; II: 49; Grimal, 1981: 128.

618. Montet, 1957: 37.

619. Gauthier, 1925–9, I: 31, 215.

620. Grimal, 1981: 128.

621. Grimal, 1981: 128.

622. Cairo CG 42232, now Luxor J 152, Jansen-Winkeln, 2007b: 205–7; Legrain, 1914b: 78–80, pls. 40–1; PM II, 149.

623. Grimal, 1981: 38, no. 90.

624. Gardiner, 1947, II: 114–15, On.Am.390.

625. Baltimore, Walters Art Museum 22.202, Meffre, 2015: doc.138, l.1; Steindorff, 1946: 26–7, no. 42, pls. X, CXI no. 42; Zecchi, 1999: 70–1, n.292.

626. Cairo Museum JE 36493, Fragment 7 of the Karnak Priestly Annals, Jansen-Winkeln, 2007b: 203–4, n.38; Kruchten, 1989: 59–61, pls. 4, 19–20; Meffre, 2015: doc.28, l.4; Moje, 2014: 374–5.

627. Oxford Ashmolean Museum 1889.1038, Meffre, 2015: doc.135; also see Aston, 2009a: 95; Petrie, 1890: pl. XXV, 9–12, 16; 1891: 26–7; Taylor, 2009: 383.

628. Piankhy Stela l.76.

APPENDIX 2   TEMPLE BUILDING OF THE TWENTY-SECOND TO TWENTY-FOURTH DYNASTY

1. Jansen-Winkeln, 2007b: 1 (12.1).

2. Jansen-Winkeln, 2007b: 1 (12.2).

3. Yoyotte, 1987: 68.

4. Louvre A23: JE 37478 + CG 639, Fay, 1995: 75–9; 1996; Jansen-Winkeln, 2007b: 1–2 (12.3–4).

5. Sagrillo, 2009: 351.

6. Sagrillo, 2009: 351.

7. Jansen-Winkeln, 2007b: 2 n.6; Naville, 1885: 4, 15.

8. Edinburgh Royal Museum 1967.2, Jansen-Winkeln, 2007b: 26–7.

9. Gomàa, 1974: 127; Naville, 1891: 46.

10. El-Alfi, 1987: 190–1; Jansen-Winkeln, 2007b: 2 n.7; Kamel, 1968: 71, pl. Xb; Vernus, 1978: 58 (63).

11. Edgar, 1914: 275.

12. Jansen-Winkeln, 1987; Mumford, 2013: 62, n.33.

13. Mumford, 2013: 62, n.33.

14. Mumford, 2013: 40.

15. For a full list of temple building by Shoshenq I at Memphis, see Jansen-Winkeln, 2007b: 2–3; Jurman, 2009: 117; Sagrillo, 2009: 357, n.128.

16. Jansen-Winkeln, 2007b: 2 (12.8).

17. Arnold, 1999: 33.

18. Sagrillo, 2009: 357–8.

19. Daressy, 1900: 143; Jansen-Winkeln, 2007b: 2–3; Maystre, 1992: 364–5 (172).

20. Jansen-Winkeln, 2007b: 3; Yoyotte, 1989: 33–5.

21. Sagrillo, 2009: 357, n.128.
22. Jansen-Winkeln, 2007b: 3 (12.10); Jones, 1990: pl. 6; Sagrillo, 2009: 357, n.128.
23. Architectural Fragment Alexandria N.360.
24. Jansen-Winkeln, 2007b: 4.
25. Recorded on Cairo JE 39410, Jansen-Winkeln, 2007b: 4–6; Meffre, 2015: doc.7; Tresson, 1935–8: 817–40.
26. For blocks of the temple, see Jansen-Winkeln, 2007b: 7–10; Meffre, 2015: 35–48, doc.6.
27. Arnold, 1999: 33; Feucht, 1978.
28. Kitchen, 1996: §260.
29. Jansen-Winkeln, 2007b: 10.
30. Jansen-Winkeln, 2007b: 11–19; Kitchen, 1996: §260.
31. Kitchen, 1996: §260.
32. Kitchen, 1996: §262.
33. Arnold, 1999: 36; Jansen-Winkeln, 2007b: 38–42; Kitchen, 1996: §262; Naville, 1891: 60–2, pls. 51–2; PM IV, 1934: 32.
34. Arnold, 1999: 36.
35. Arnold, 1999: 36.
36. Arnold, 1999: 36.
37. Munich Gl.78, Jansen-Winkeln, 2007b: 49–50; Kitchen, 1996: §262; PM III/2, 1931: 227.
38. Kitchen, 1996: §263; Petrie and Mackay, 1915: pl. 40; PM IV, 1934: 76.
39. Jansen-Winkeln, 2007b: 50–2.
40. Jansen-Winkeln, 2007b: 52; Kitchen, 1996: §263; Petrie, 1896: 17, pl. 13 (7); Traunecker, 1992: §9, 62.
41. Jansen-Winkeln, 2007b: 52–4; PM II, 1929: 36 (129).
42. Jansen-Winkeln, 2006a: 237; 2007b: 75 (15.1); Lange, 2004: 65–72; Sagrillo, 2009: 342.
43. Arnold, 1999: 38.
44. Arnold, 1999: 38.
45. Jansen-Winkeln, 2007b: 108; Montet, 1947: 257–8; 1952: 136–8.
46. Arnold, 1999: 38. For the blocks and inscriptions, see Lange, 2009; Naville, 1892.
47. Habachi, 1957: 46–55, pls. 12–13; Jansen-Winkeln, 2007b: 114–15; Naville, 1891: pl. 41, E–H.
48. Arnold, 1999: 39.
49. Cairo CG 70006, Daressy, 1901: 132; Jansen-Winkeln, 2007b: 115; PM IV, 1934; Roeder, 1914: 24–5.
50. Gauthier, 1921: 23, 26–7; Kitchen, 1996: §276.
51. BM 1146.
52. Arnold, 1999: 39.
53. Jansen-Winkeln, 2007b: 118–19; PM II, 1929: 92 (264); Vernus, 1975: 2, 20–6, pl. 2.
54. Goyon and Traunecker, 1978–81: 355–66; Jansen-Winkeln, 2007b: 119.
55. Jansen-Winkeln, 2007b: 119.
56. Jansen-Winkeln, 2007b: 119; Kitchen, 1996: §278, n.422; PM II, 1929: 15 (56).
57. Chevrier, 1951: 554, pl. 2; Jansen-Winkeln, 2007b: 119–20; Leclant, 1951: 462–4, pl. 54; PM II, 1929: 203–4; Redford, 1986: 1–15.
58. Barguet, 1962: 92; Jansen-Winkeln, 2007b: 154; PM II, 1929: 78.
59. Jansen-Winkeln, 2007b: 154; PM II, 1929: 232.
60. Hölscher, 1939: 37; 1954: 8, n.34; Jansen-Winkeln, 2007b: 154; PM II, 1929: 772.
61. Jansen-Winkeln, 2007b: 160; Kitchen, 1996: §289; Legrain, 1902: 66; PM II, 1929: 199 (g).
62. Jansen-Winkeln, 2007b: 160; Kitchen, 1996: §289.
63. Jansen-Winkeln, 2007b: 175; Kitchen, 1996: §304.
64. Jansen-Winkeln, 2007b: 175.
65. Daressy, 1920a; PM III/2, 1931: 873. Kitchen, 1996: §304, only mentions them belonging to Sekhmet.
66. Daressy, 1912: 209–13; Edgar, 1911: 164–9; Jansen-Winkeln, 2007b: 179–81; Kitchen, 1996: §304; PM IV, 1934: 44.
67. Daressy, 1912: 206.
68. Cairo JE 38272, de Meulenaere and MacKay, 1976: 193 (20); Jansen-Winkeln, 2007b: 181; Kitchen, 1996: §304.
69. Jansen-Winkeln, 2007b: 181–2; A. J. Spencer, 1999: 13–15, 83–6, 90–1.
70. Daressy, 1903a: 283–5; Jansen-Winkeln, 2007b: 182; Kitchen, 1996: §304, n.564; PM IV, 1934: 51.
71. Jansen-Winkeln, 2007b: 209; Kaper, 2009: 151, fig. 3.
72. Excavation Record KF 533, 7.4.1994, Jansen-Winkeln, 2007b: 209, 479.
73. Jansen-Winkeln, 2007b: 208; von Beckerath, 1966.
74. Barguet, 1962: 246; Jansen-Winkeln, 2007b: 208; Kitchen, 1996: §299; Legrain, 1914a: 14, 39–40; PM II, 1929: 189.
75. Jansen-Winkeln, 2007b: 219.
76. Bonhême, 1987: 126 (5); Legrain, 1900.
77. Jansen-Winkeln, 2007b: 259; Kitchen, 1996: §308; Montet, 1966: 44, pls. 5–6; Yoyotte, 1988: 162–4, pl. 3.
78. Bickel, Gabolde, and Tallet, 1998: 31–56; Jansen-Winkeln, 2007b: 259–61.
79. Jansen-Winkeln, 2007b: 268–9; Kitchen, 1996: §315; Montet, 1966: 44–56, nos. 27–211.

80. Jansen-Winkeln, 2007b: 269; Kitchen, 1996: §315; Montet, 1966: 57–61, nos. 212–29, pls. 28–9.
81. Fazzini, 1988: 19, 32, pl. 16; Goyon, 1983: 2–9; Jansen-Winkeln, 2007b: 294.
82. Berlin 2101/2102, Jansen-Winkeln, 2007b: 294; PM II, 1929: 223.
83. Ayad, 2009: 31; Jansen-Winkeln, 2007b: 330–9; Jurman, 2006.
84. Jansen-Winkeln, 2007b: 294–6; P. A. Spencer, 1989: 57–62, pls. 100–10.
85. Ayad, 2009; Jansen-Winkeln, 2007b: 313–19; Legrain, 1900: 128–34, 146–9; Redford, 1973: 16–30.
86. Ayad, 2009: 31; Jansen-Winkeln, 2007b: 330–1; Jurman, 2006.
87. Brissaud and Cranson, 2010; Dodson, 2014.
88. Montet, 1966: 68.

APPENDIX 3 UNIDENTIFIED TOMB, MORTUARY TEMPLE, AND PALACE LOCATIONS

1. Sagrillo, 2009: 350.

2. Stela 100, Caminos, 1952: pl. 13; Jansen-Winkeln, 2007b: 22 (12.27).
3. Caminos, 1952: 55; Sagrillo, 2009: 350.
4. Redford, 1986: 307–8; Sagrillo, 2009: 352.
5. Redford, 1986: 309, n.82; Sagrillo, 2009: 350.
6. Caminos, 1952: 55, n.40; Sagrillo, 2009: 351.
7. Kitchen, 1996: §259, n.314.
8. Vernus, 1975: 13–20.
9. Sagrillo, 2009: 357.
10. Stela 18417, Saqqara Register Book no. 11 in Magazine 4 at Saqqara.
11. Sagrillo, 2009: 354–8.
12. Ny Carlsberg Glyptotek AEIN 917 (l.3).
13. Caminos, 1964: 76 pl. x; Perdu, 2002a: 25.
14. Von Beckerath, 1995: 10, n.3.
15. Yoyotte, 1988: 174–5.
16. Meffre, 2015: 118.
17. Meffre, 2015: 118.
18. Aston, 2014; for a detailed discussion on the location and architecture of the tomb, see Ohshiro, 2017: 301–2.
19. Griffith, 1909: III. 19 (14), 28 (48); Malinine, 1953: 85–8; Donker van Heel, 2014: 201.
20. Aston, 2014: 21–3.
21. Ohshiro, 2017: 305.
22. Aston, 2014: 23.

BIBLIOGRAPHY

EES DELTA SURVEY INTERNET RESOURCES

Third Intermediate Period Delta Sites

EES Delta Survey, Baqliya, EES 79: (2016), Accessed from http://deltasurvey.ees.ac.uk/baqliya80.html.

EES Delta Survey, Barakim, EES 497: (2016), Accessed from http://deltasurvey.ees.ac.uk/baramkin.html.

EES Delta Survey, Ezbet Razaiqa, EES 466: (2016), Accessed from http://deltasurvey.ees.ac.uk/451-480.html.

EES Delta Survey, Gezirat el-Tawila, EES 537: (2016), Accessed from http://deltasurvey.ees.ac.uk/tawila537.html.

EES Delta Survey, Tell Buweib, EES 160: (2016), Accessed from http://deltasurvey.ees.ac.uk/ginn203.html.

EES Delta Survey, Tell el-Abassiya, EES 593: (2016), Accessed from http://deltasurvey.ees.ac.uk/abis593.html.

EES Delta Survey, Tell Gadiya, EES 510: (2016), Accessed from http://deltasurvey.ees.ac.uk/gadiya.html.

EES Delta Survey, Tell Ginn, EES 203: (2016), Accessed from http://deltasurvey.ees.ac.uk/ginn203.html.

New Kingdom Delta Sites

EES Delta Survey, Arab el-Sheikh Mubarak, EES 586: (2016), Accessed from http://deltasurvey.ees.ac.uk/61-90.html.

EES Delta Survey, Barakim, EES 497: (2016), Accessed from http://deltasurvey.ees.ac.uk/121-150.html.

EES Delta Survey, Dimeiyin, EES 565: (2016), Accessed from http://deltasurvey.ees.ac.uk/181-210.html.

EES Delta Survey, el-Birkawi, EES 673: (2016), Accessed from http://deltasurvey.ees.ac.uk/151-180.html.

EES Delta Survey, el-Kifriya, EES 578: (2016), Accessed from http://deltasurvey.ees.ac.uk/451-480.html.

EES Delta Survey, el-Salatna, EES 590: (2016), Accessed from http://deltasurvey.ees.ac.uk/451-480.html.

EES Delta Survey, el-Shagamba, EES 330: (2016), Accessed from http://deltasurvey.ees.ac.uk/481-510.html.

EES Delta Survey, Gezirat el-Faras, EES 351: (2016), Accessed from http://deltasurvey.ees.ac.uk/241-270.html.

EES Delta Survey, Gezirat Sineita, EES 566: (2016), Accessed from http://deltasurvey.ees.ac.uk/241-270.html.

EES Delta Survey, Gezirat Sultan Hassan, EES 562: (2016), Accessed from http://deltasurvey.ees.ac.uk/541-570.html.

EES Delta Survey, Kom el-Ahmar, EES 190: (2016), Accessed from http://deltasurvey.ees.ac.uk/ahmar190.html.

EES Delta Survey, Kom el-Ghuzz, EES 609: (2016), Accessed from http://deltasurvey.ees.ac.uk/ghuzz609.html.

EES Delta Survey, Kom Hamrit, EES 638: (2016), Accessed from http://deltasurvey.ees.ac.uk/hamrit.html.

EES Delta Survey, Kom Zimran/Zumran, EES 741: (2016), Accessed from http://deltasurvey.ees.ac.uk/571-608.html.

EES Delta Survey, Quiesna, EES 639: (2016), Accessed from http://deltasurvey.ees.ac.uk/queisna.html.

EES Delta Survey, Sidi Ahmed Tawil, EES 587: (2016), Accessed from http://deltasurvey.ees.ac.uk/511-540.html.

EES Delta Survey, Sinitris, EES 560: (2016), Accessed from http://deltasurvey.ees.ac.uk/sintiris560.html.

EES Delta Survey, Suwa, EES 327: (2016), Accessed from http://deltasurvey.ees.ac.uk/541-570.html.

EES Delta Survey, Tell Abu Shafei, EES 533: (2016), Accessed from http://deltasurvey.ees.ac.uk/31-60.html.

EES Delta Survey, Tell Abu Sulliman, EES 352: (2016), Accessed from http://deltasurvey.ees.ac.uk/31-60.html.

EES Delta Survey, Tell Awlad Moussa, EES 316: (2016), Accessed from http://deltasurvey.ees.ac.uk/awladmous316.html.

EES Delta Survey, Tell Bahr Mahed, EES 323: (2016), Accessed from http://deltasurvey.ees.ac.uk/bahrmahed323.html.

EES Delta Survey, Tell Buweib, EES 160: (2016), Accessed from http://deltasurvey.ees.ac.uk/buweib.html.

EES Delta Survey, Tellein, EES 521: (2016), Accessed from http://deltasurvey.ees.ac.uk/tellein521.html.

EES Delta Survey, Tell el-Abassiya, EES 593: (2016), Accessed from http://deltasurvey.ees.ac.uk/abis593.html.

EES Delta Survey, Tell el-Abiad, EES 540: (2016), Accessed from http://deltasurvey.ees.ac.uk/abiad540.html.

EES Delta Survey, Tell el-Awaya, EES 596: (2016), Accessed from http://deltasurvey.ees.ac.uk/91-120.html.

EES Delta Survey, Tell el-Iswid (N), EES 184: (2016), Accessed from http://deltasurvey.ees.ac.uk/301-330.html.

EES Delta Survey, Tell el-Samuni, EES 541: (2016), Accessed from http://deltasurvey.ees.ac.uk/481-510.html.

EES Delta Survey, Tell el-Shuhada, EES 585: (2016), Accessed from http://deltasurvey.ees.ac.uk/511-540.html.

EES Delta Survey, Tell Fauziya, EES 557: (2016), Accessed from http://deltasurvey.ees.ac.uk/fauziya557.html.

EES Delta Survey, Tell Ibrahim Awad, EES 535: (2016), Accessed from http://deltasurvey.ees.ac.uk/ibawad535.html.

EES Delta Survey, Tell Zaazi, EES 543: (2016), Accessed from http://deltasurvey.ees.ac.uk/571-608.html.

SECONDARY SOURCES

Abdallah, A. O. A., 1984. 'An unusual private stela of the Twenty-First Dynasty from Coptos', *JEA* 70, pp. 65–72.

Abdel-Fattah, A., 2002. 'The question of the presence of pharaonic antiquities in the city of Alexandria and its neighbouring sites (Alexandria pre-Alexander the Great)', in Hawass, Z. (ed.), *Egyptology at the dawn of the twenty-first century: proceedings of the Eighth International Congress of Egyptologists, Cairo, 2000, vol. II: history and religion* (Cairo, American University in Cairo Press), pp. 63–71.

Adriansen, H. K., 2009. 'Land reclamation in Egypt: a study of life in the new lands', *Geoforum* 40, pp. 664–674.

Aldred, C., 1956. 'The Carnarvon statuette of Amūn', *JEA* 42, pp. 3–7.

Allbaugh, L. G., 1953. *Crete: a case study of an undeveloped area* (Princeton, Princeton University Press).

Alliot, M., 1934. 'Une stèle magique d'Edfou', in Anonymous (ed.), *Mélanges Maspero I: Orient ancient, vol. I* (Cairo, IFAO), pp. 201–210.

Altenmüller, H., and A. M. Moussa, 1981. 'Die Inschriften der Taharkastele von der Dahschurstraße', *SAK* 9, pp. 57–84.

Andrews, C., 1994. *Amulets of ancient Egypt* (London, British Museum Press).

Anthes, R., 1959. 'Summary and conclusions', in Anthes, R., *Mit Rahineh 1955* (Philadelphia, University Museum, University of Philadelphia), pp. 65–73.

1965. 'General report on the excavation', in Anthes, R., *Mit Rahineh 1956* (Philadelphia, University Museum, University of Pennsylvania), pp. 1–44.

Anthes, R., H. H. K. Bakry, H. G. Fischer, and W. K. Simpson, 1965. 'The catalogue of finds', in Anthes, R., *Mit Rahineh 1956* (Philadelphia, University Museum, University of Pennsylvania), pp. 71–161.

Anus, P., and R. Sa'ad, 1971. 'Habitations de prêtres dans le temple d'Amon de Karnak', *Kêmi* 21, pp. 217–238.

Arnold, D., 1999. *Temples of the last pharaohs* (Oxford, Oxford University Press).

Arnold, F., 1989. 'A study of Egyptian domestic buildings', *VA* 5, pp. 75–93.

1996. 'Settlement remains at Lisht-North', in Bietak, M. (ed.), *Haus und Palast im Alten Ägypten* (DGÖAW 14/UZK 14; Vienna, Verlage der Österreichischen Akademie der Wissenschaften), pp. 13–21.

1998. 'Die Priesterhäuser der Chentkaues in Giza. Staatlicher Wohnungsbau als Interpretation der Wohnvorstellungen für einen "Idealmenschen"', *MDAIK* 54, pp. 1–18.

2015. 'Clean and unclean space: domestic waste management at Elephantine', in Müller, M. (ed.), *Household studies in complex societies: (micro) archaeological and textual approaches* (OIS 10; Illinois, Oriental Institute of the University of Chicago), pp. 151–168.

Ashmawy, A. A., 2006. 'Tell Gemaiyemi "Gomaimah": more than 100 years after Griffith's excavation', in Czerny, E., I. Hein, H. Hunger, D. Melman, and A. Schwab (eds.), *Timelines: studies in honour of Manfred Bietak, vol. 1* (OLA 149; Leuven, Peeters), pp. 55–64.

Aston, B. G., 1994. *Ancient Egyptian stone vessels: materials and forms* (SAGA 5; Heidelberg, Heidelberger Orientverlag).

Aston, B. G., J. A. Harrell, and I. Shaw, 2000. 'Stone', in Nicholson, P. T., and I. Shaw (eds.), *Ancient Egyptian materials and technology* (Cambridge, Cambridge University Press), pp. 1–77.

Aston, D. A., 1989. 'Takeloth II: a king of the "Theban Twenty-Third Dynasty"?', *JEA* 75, pp. 139–153.

1996a. *Egyptian pottery of the late New Kingdom and Third Intermediate Period (twelfth–seventh centuries BC): tentative footsteps in a forbidding terrain* (SAGA 13; Heidelberg, Heidelberger Orientverlag).

1996b. 'Sherds from a fortified townsite near Abu 'Id', *CCÉ* 4, pp. 19–45.

1998. *Die Keramik des Grabungsplatzes Q I. Teil 1: corpus of fabrics. Forschungen in der Ramses-Stadt: die Grabungen des Pelizaeus-Museums Hildesheim in Qantir – Pi-Ramesse, 1* (Mainz am Rhein, Philipp von Zabern).

1999. *Elephantine XIX: Pottery from the Late New Kingdom to the Early Ptolemaic Period* (AVDAIK 95; Mainz am Rhein, Philipp von Zabern).

2003. 'New Kingdom pottery phases as revealed through well-dated tomb contexts', in Bietak, M. (ed.), *The synchronisation of civilisation in the eastern Mediterranean in the second millennium BC, II: proceedings of the SCIEM 2000 EuroConference Haindorf, 2nd May–7th May 2001* (CCEM 4; Vienna, Österreichischen Akademie der Wissenschaften), pp. 135–62.

2007a. 'Section 2: Pottery of the twelfth to seventh centuries BC', in Aston, D. A., and D. G. Jeffreys, *The survey of Memphis III: the Third Intermediate Period levels* (EES EM 81; London, Egypt Exploration Society), pp. 17–57.

2007b. 'Section 3: Memphis in the Third Intermediate (Libyan) Period', in Aston, D. A., and D. G. Jeffreys, *The survey of Memphis III: the Third Intermediate Period levels* (EES EM 81;

London, Egypt Exploration Society), pp. 61–82.

2009a. *Burial assemblages of D–ynasty 21-25: chronology – typology – developments* (CCEM 21; Vienna, Österreichische Akademie der Wissenschaften).

2009b. 'Takeloth II, a king of the Herakleopolitan/Theban Twenty-Third Dynasty revisited: the chronology of Dynasties 22 and 23', in Broekman, G. P. F., R. J. Demarée, and O. E. Kaper (eds.), *The Libyan Period in Egypt: historical and cultural studies into the 21st–24th Dynasties. Proceedings of a conference at Leiden University, 25–27 October 2007* (EgUit 23; Nederlands Instituut voor het Nabije Oosten, Leuven, Peeters), pp. 1–28.

2014. 'Royal burials at Thebes during the first millennium BC', in Pischikova, E., J. Budka, and K. Griffin (eds.), *Thebes in the first millennium BC* (Newcastle upon Tyne, Cambridge Scholars Publishing), pp. 15–59.

2016. 'A possible twenty-square game (?) and other varia from L81', in Franzmeier, H., T. Rehren, and R. Schulz (eds.), *Mit archäologischen Schichten Geschichte schreiben Festschrift für Edgar B Pusch zum 70. Geburtstag* (Forschungen in der Ramses-Stadt 10; Hildesheim, Gerstenberg), pp. 7–10.

Aston, D. A., and B. Bader, 1998. 'Einige Bemerkungen zum späten Neuen Reich in Matmar', *MDAIK* 54, pp. 19–48.

Aston, D. A., and E. Pusch, 1999. 'The pottery from the royal horse stud and its stratigraphy', *Ä&L* 9, pp. 37–76.

Awad, A., and A. Zohary, 2005. 'The end of Egypt population growth in the 21st century: challenges and aspirations', in *The 35th Annual Conference on Population and Development Issues Current Situation & Aspirations*; Cairo Demographic Center, 20–22 December, 2005, Cairo.

Ayad, M. F., 2009. 'The transition from Libyan to Nubian rule: the role of the God's Wife of Amun', in Broekman, G. P. F., R. J. Demarée, and O. E. Kaper (eds.), *The Libyan period in Egypt: historical and cultural studies into the 21st–24th Dynasties. Proceedings of a conference at Leiden University, 25–27 October 2007* (EgUit 23; Nederlands Instituut voor het Nabije Oosten, Leuven, Peeters), pp. 29–49.

Backhouse, J., 2012. 'Figured ostraca from Deir el-Medina', in Abd el-Gawad, H., N. Andrews, M. Correas-Amador, V. Tamorri, and J. Taylor (eds.), *Current research in Egyptology 2011: proceedings of the twelfth annual symposium which took place at Durham University, United Kingdom, March 2011* (Oxford, Oxbow Books), pp. 25–39.

Bacquerisse, C., 2015. 'Small finds at Tell el-Ghaba', in Lupo, S. (ed.), *Tell el-Ghaba III: a Third Intermediate–Early Saite Period site in the Egyptian eastern Delta; excavations 1995–1999 and 2010 in areas I, II, VI and VIII* (BAR IS 2756; Oxford, Archaeopress), pp. 357–385.

Bader, B., 2001. *Tell el-Dab'a XIII. Typologie und Chronologie der Mergel C-Ton Keramik: Materialien zum Binnenhandel des Mittleren Reiches und der Zweiten Zwischenzeit* (Denkschriften der Gesamtakademie 22: Untersuchungen der Zweigstelle Kairo des Österreichischen Archäologischen Instituts 19; Vienna, VÖAW).

Bagnall, R. S., 1993. *Egypt in Late Antiquity* (Princeton, Princeton University Press).

Bailey, D. M., 1999. 'Sebakh, sherds and survey', *JEA* 85, pp. 211–218.

2008. *Ptolemaic and Roman terracottas from Egypt: catalogue of terracottas in the British Museum* (London, British Museum Press).

Baines, J. and J. Malek, 2000. *Cultural atlas of ancient Egypt* (revised edition) (New York, Checkmark).

Bakir, A. el-M., 1943. 'A donation-stela of the Twenty-Second Dynasty', *ASAE* 43, pp. 75–81.

Bakry, H. S. K., 1959. 'Various finds', in Anthes, R., *Mit Rahineh 1955* (Philadelphia, University Museum, University of Philadelphia), pp. 41–61.

Ball, J., 1942. *Egypt in the classical geographers* (Cairo, Ministry of Finance, Egypt, Survey of Egypt, Government Press).

Ballet, P., 2009. 'Elitegräber der 3. Zwischenzeit im Nordwesten Butos (Grabungsfläche J2)', in Hartung, U., P. Ballet, A. Effland et al., 'Tell el-Fara'in – Buto 10. Vorbericht', *MDAIK* 65, pp. 94–107.

Ballet, P., and T. von der Way, 1993. 'Exploration archéologique de Bouto et de sa région (époques romaine et byzantine)', *MDAIK* 49, pp. 1–22.

Banyai, M., 2013. 'Ein Vorschlag zur Chronologie der 25. Dynastie in Ägypten', *JEgH* 6, pp. 46–129.

2015. 'Die Reihenfolge der kuschitischen Könige', *JEgH* 8, pp. 115–180.

Barguet, P., 1962. *Le temple d'Amon-Rê à Karnak: essai d'exégèse* (RAPH 21; Cairo, IFAO).

Barta, W., 1968. *Aufbau und Bedeutung der altägyptischen Opferformel* (ÄF 24; Glückstadt, Augustin).

Bennett, J. E., 2015. 'Some comments on the dating of the compilation of the Onomasticon of Amenemope', *GM* 245, pp. 5–8.

Ben-Tor, D., 1993. *The scarab: a reflection of ancient Egypt* (Jerusalem, Israel Museum).

Berlandini, J., 1978. 'Une stèle de donation du dynaste libyen Roudamon', *BIFAO* 78, pp. 147–163.

Bernand, A., 1970. *Le delta égyptien d'après les textes grecs* (MIFAO 91; Cairo, IFAO).

Bertini, L., 2014. 'Faunal remains at Kom Firin', in Spencer, N., *Kom Firin II:* the urban fabric and landscape (British Museum Research Publication 192; London, British Museum Press), pp. 306–312.

Bevan, A., and A. Wilson, 2013. 'Models of settlement hierarchy based on partial evidence', *JAS* 40 (5), pp. 2415–2427.

Bickel, S., 2009. 'The inundation inscription in Luxor temple', in Broekman, G. P. F., R. J. Demarée, and O. E. Kaper (eds.), *The Libyan Period in Egypt: historical and cultural studies into the 21st–24th Dynasties. Proceedings of a conference at Leiden University, 25–27 October 2007* (EgUit 23; Nederlands Instituut voor het Nabije Oosten, Leuven, Peeters), pp. 51–55.

Bickel, S., M. Gabolde, and P. Tallet, 1998. 'Des annales héliopolitaines de la Troisième Période Intermédiaire', *BIFAO* 98, pp. 31–56.

Bietak, M., 1975. *Tell el-Dab'a II: der Fundort im Rahmen einer archäologisch-geographischen Untersuchung über das ägyptische Ostdelta* (DGÖAW 4/UZK 1; Vienna, VÖAW).

1979a. 'The present state of Egyptian archaeology', *JEA* 65, pp. 156–160.

1979b. 'Urban archaeology and the "town problem" in ancient Egypt', in Weeks, K. R. (ed.), *Egyptology and the social sciences: five studies. Papers originally presented at a conference on ancient Egypt: problems of history, sources and methods, Cairo, 1975* (Cairo, American University in Cairo Press), pp. 97–144.

1986. *Avaris and Piramesse: archaeological exploration in the eastern Nile Delta* (London, British Academy).

1996. 'Zum Raumprogramm ägyptischer Wohnhäuser des Mittleren und des Neuen Reiches', in Bietak, M. (ed.), *Haus und Palast im alten Ägypten* (DGÖAW 14/UZK 14; Vienna, Verlage der Österreichischen Akademie der Wissenschaften), pp. 23–43.

Binford, L., 1964. 'A consideration of archaeological research design', *AmerAnt* 29 (4), pp. 425–441.

Blouin, K., 2014. *Triangular landscapes: environment, society, and the state in the Nile Delta under Roman rule* (Oxford Studies on the Roman Economy; Oxford, Oxford University Press).

Blue, L., and E. Khalil, 2011. *A multidisciplinary approach to Alexandria's economic past: the Lake Mareotis Research Project* (BAR IS 2285; Oxford, Archaeopress).

Bökönyi, S., 1989. 'Definitions of animal domestication', in Clutton-Brock, J. (ed.), *The walking larder: patterns of domestication, pastoralism, and predation* (One World Archaeology; London, Unwin Hyman), pp. 22–27.

Bonhême, M.-A., 1987. *Les noms royaux dans l'Égypte de la Troisième Période Intermédiaire* (BdE 98; Cairo, IFAO).

1995. 'Les Chechanqides: qui, combien?', *BSFE* 134, pp. 54–5.

Borchardt, L., 1925. *Statuen und Statuetten von Königen und Privatleuten im Museum von Kairo. Nr 381–653*, vol. II (CGC 1–1294; Berlin, Reichsdruckerei).

1934. *Statuen und Statuetten von Königen und Privatleuten im Museum von Kairo. Nr 951–1294*, vol. IV (CGC 1–1294; Berlin, Reichsdruckerei).

Borchardt, L., and H. Ricke, 1980. *Die Wohnhäuser in Tell El-Amarna, Ausgrabungen der Deutschen Orient-Gesellschaft in Tell El-Amarna 5* (WVDOG 91; Berlin, Mann).

Borger, R., 1956. 'Die Inschriften Asarhaddons, Königs von Assyrien', *AfO* 9.

Botti, G., 1958. *Le casse di mummie e i sarcofagi da el Hibeh nel Museo Egizio di Firenze* (AttiFir 5; Firenze, L. S. Olschki).

Boulet, S., 2016a. 'La chapelle d'Osiris Ounnefer Neb-Djefaou à Karnak. Nouvelles avancées sur les développements des productions céramiques entre la Troisième Période Intermédiaire et la Basse Epoque', *BCE* 26, pp. 213–226.

2016b. 'Les productions céramiques de la Troisième Période Intermédiaire', *EAO* 81, pp. 31–38.

2017. 'Les productions céramiques de la 25e dynastie dans le secteur du temple de Ptah à Karnak', *BCE* 27, pp. 53–62.

2018. 'Ceramic industry developments in the Theban area during the Twenty-Fifth Dynasty: between traditions and innovations', in Pischikova, E., J. Budka, and K. Griffin (eds.), *Thebes in the first millennium BC: art and archaeology of the Kushite Period and beyond* (GHP Egyptology 27; London, Golden House), pp. 335–356.

Boulet, S., and C. Defernez, 2014. 'Ceramic production in the Theban area from the Late Period: recent discoveries from Karnak', in Pischikova, E., J. Budka, and K. Griffin (eds.), *Thebes in the first millennium BC* (Newcastle upon Tyne, Cambridge Scholars Publishing), pp. 603–624.

Bouriant, U., 1886. 'Petits monuments et petits textes recueillis en Égypte', *RT* 7, pp. 114–132.

1889. 'Rapport au Ministre de l'Instruction Publique sur une mission dans la Haute-Égypte (1884–1885)', *MMAF* 1 (3), pp. 367–408.

Bourriau, J. D., 2010. *The survey of Memphis IV. Kom Rabia: the New Kingdom pottery* (EES EM 93; London, Egypt Exploration Society).

Bourriau, J. D., P. T. Nicholson, and P. J. Rose, 2000. 'Pottery', in Nicholson, P. T., and I. Shaw (eds.), *Ancient Egyptian materials and technology* (Cambridge, Cambridge University Press), pp. 121–148.

Bourriau, J. D., L. M. V. Smith, and M. Serpico, 2001. 'The provenance of Canaanite amphorae found at Memphis and Amarna in the New Kingdom', in Shortland, A. (ed.), *The social context of technological change: Egypt and the Near East, 1650–1150 BC* (Oxford, Oxbow Books), pp. 113–146.

Brandl, H., 2008. *Untersuchungen zur steinernen Privatplastik der dritten Zwischenzeit: Typologie, Ikonographie, Stilistik*, 2 vols. (Berlin, MBV).

Brandl, H., and K. Jansen-Winkeln, 2008. 'Fünf Denkmäler des Obersten Arztes *P3-ʿn-mnj* aus der 22. Dynastie', *MDAIK* 64, pp. 15–34.

Breasted, J. H. 1906. *Ancient records of Egypt: Historical documents from the earliest times to the Persian conquest: the Twentieth to the Twenty-Sixth Dynasties, vol. IV* (Chicago, University of Chicago Press).

Brewer, D. J., R. J. Wenke, J. Isaacson, and D. Haag, 1996. 'Mendes regional archaeological survey and remote sensing analysis', *Sahara* 8, pp. 29–42.

Brissaud, P., and L. Cotelle, 1987. 'À propos de tessons retaillés en forme de jetons', in Brissaud, P. (ed.), *Cahiers de Tanis I* (Paris, Editions Recherche sur les Civilisations), pp. 101–105.

Brissaud, P., and S. Cranson, 2010. 'Dans les profundeurs de lac sacré', *Archaeologia* 476, pp. 26–35.

Brissaud, P., V. Chauvet, and I. Hairy, 1998. 'Deux siècles de fouilles à Tanis: analyse des divers modes d'intervention sur le site', in Brissaud, P., and C. Zivie-Coche (eds.), *Tanis: travaux récents sur le Tell Sân el-Hagar, Mission Française des Fouilles de Tanis, 1987–1997* (Paris, Éditions Noêsis), pp. 71–100.

Broekman, G. P. F., 2005. 'The reign of Takeloth II, a controversial matter', *GM* 205, pp. 21–35.

2010. 'Libyan rule over Egypt: the influence of the tribal background of the ruling class on political structures and developments during the Libyan Period in Egypt', *SAK* 39, pp. 85–99.

2012. 'The Theban high-priestly succession in the first half of the Twenty-First Dynasty', *JEA* 98, pp. 195–209.

2015. 'The order of succession between Shabaka and Shabataka: a different view on the chronology of the Twenty-Fifth Dynasty', *GM* 245, pp. 17–31.

2017a. 'Genealogical considerations regarding the kings of the Twenty-Fifth Dynasty in Egypt', *GM* 251, pp. 13–20.

2017b. 'Some consequences of the reversion of the order Shabaka–Shabataka', *GM* 253, pp. 1–8.

Brovarski, E., 1981. 'Ahanakht of Bersheh and the Hare nome in the First Intermediate Period and Middle Kingdom', in Simpson, W. K., and W. M. Davis (eds.), *Studies in ancient Egypt, the Aegean, and the Sudan: essays in honor of Dows Dunham on the occasion of his 90th birthday, June 1, 1980* (Boston, MA, Department of Egyptian and Ancient Near Eastern Art, Museum of Fine Arts), pp. 14–30.

Brugsch, H., 1879. *Dictionnaire géographique de l'ancienne Égypte: contenant par ordre alphabétique la nomenclature comparée des noms propres géographiques qui se rencontrent sur les monuments et dans les papyrus, notamment les noms des préfectures et de leurs chefs-lieux, des temples et sanctuaires, des villes, bourghs et nécropoles, des mers, du nil et de ses embouchures, des lacs, marais, canaux, bassins et ports, des vallées, grottes, montagnes, des îles et îlots, etc* (Leipzig, Librairie J. C. Hinrichs).

Brunner-Traut, E., and H. Brunner, 1981. *Die ägyptische Sammlung der Universität Tübingen*, 2 vols. (Mainz am Rhein, Philipp von Zabern).

Brunton, G., 1930. *Qau and Badari, vol. III* (BSAE/ERA 50; London, Bernard Quaritch).

1948. *Matmar* (British Museum Expedition to Middle Egypt, 1929–1931; London, Bernard Quaritch).

Brunton, G., and R. Engelbach, 1927. *Gurob* (BSAE/ERA 41; London, Bernard Quaritch).

Bruyère, B., 1939. *Rapport sur les fouilles de Deir el Médineh (1934–1935).* (FIFAO 16; Cairo, IFAO).

Budka, J., 2010. 'The use of pottery in funerary contexts during the Libyan and Late Period: a view from Thebes and Abydos', in Bareš, L., F. Coppens, and K. Smoláriková (eds.), *Egypt in transition: social and religious development of Egypt in the first millennium BCE: proceedings of an international conference: Prague, September 1–4, 2009* (Prague, Czech Institute of Egyptology, Charles University in Prague), pp. 22–72.

Bunbury, J., 2011. 'The development of the capital zone within the Nile floodplain', in Subías, E., P. Azara, J. Carruesco, I. Fiz, and R. Cuesta (eds.), *The space of the city in Graeco-Roman Egypt: image and reality* (Documenta 22; Tarragona, Institut Català d'Arqueologia Clàssica), pp. 211–217.

Bunbury, J., and A. Graham, 2005. 'The ancient landscapes and waterscapes of Karnak', *EA* 27, pp. 17–19.

Bunbury, J., A. Graham, and M. A. Hunter, 2008. 'Stratigraphic landscape analysis: charting the Holocene movements of the Nile at Karnak through ancient Egyptian time', *Geoarchaeology* 23 (3), pp. 351–373.

Bunbury, J., A. Graham, and K. D. Strutt, 2009. 'Kom el-Farahy: a New Kingdom island in an evolving Edfu floodplain', *BMSAES* 14, pp. 1–23.

Bunbury, J., E. Hughes, and N. Spencer, 2014. 'Ancient landscape reconstruction at Kom Firin', in Spencer, N., *Kom Firin II: the urban fabric and landscape* (British Museum Research Publication 192; London, British Museum Press), pp. 11–16.

Butzer, K. W., 1976. *Early hydraulic civilization in Egypt: a study in cultural ecology* (Prehistoric Archeology and Ecology series; Chicago, University of Chicago Press).

Caminos, R. A., 1952. 'Gebel es-Silsilah no. 100', *JEA* 38, pp. 46–61.

1958. *The Chronicle of Prince Osorkon* (AnOr 37; Rome, Pontifical Biblical Institute).

1964. 'The Nitocris Adoption Stela', *JEA* 50, pp. 71–101.

Carter, H., and G. Legrain, 1905. 'Report of work done in Upper Egypt (1903–1904)', *ASAE* 6, pp. 112–129.

Cauville, S., 1997. *Dendara: les chapelles osiriennes*, 2 vols. (Dendara X; Cairo, IFAO).

Černý, J., 1955. 'The storehouses of This', in *Università di Pisa, Studi in memoria di Ippolito Rosellini nel primo centenario della morte (4 giugno 1843–4 giugno 1943)* 2 (Pisa, Lischi), pp. 27–31.

Chabân, M., 1907. 'Fouilles à Achmounéin', *ASAE* 8, pp. 211–223.

Chappaz, J.-L., 1982. 'Une stèle de donation de l'an 21 de Ioupout II au Musée d'Art et d'Histoire', *Genava* 30, pp. 71–81.

Chevrier, H., 1951. 'Rapport sur les travaux de Karnak, 1950–1951', *ASAE* 51, pp. 549–572.

Chlodnicki, M., R. Fattovich, and S. Salvatori, 1992. 'The Italian archaeological mission of the CSRL-Venice to the eastern Nile Delta: a preliminary report of the 1987–1988 field seasons', *CRIPEL* 14, pp. 45–62.

Church, R. L., and T. H. Bell, 1988. 'An analysis of ancient Egyptian settlement patterns using location-allocation covering models', in *Ann Assoc Am Geogr* 78 (4), pp. 701–714.

Collier, M., and S. Quirke, 2002. *The UCL Lahun papyri: letters* (BAR IS 1083; Oxford, Archaeopress).

Collombert, P., 1997. 'Hout-Sekhem et le septième nome de Haute-Égypte II: les stèles tardives', *RdE* 48, pp. 15–70.

——— 1998. 'La stèle de Nesmin (complément à Revue d'égyptologie 48 (1997), 15–70)', *RdE* 49, pp. 239–242.

——— 2014. 'Le [glyphs] toponyme et la géographie des 17e et 18e nomes de Haute Égypte', *RdE* 65, pp. 1–27.

Cooper, J. P., 2014. *The medieval Nile: route, navigation, and landscape in Islamic Egypt* (Cairo, American University in Cairo Press).

Correas-Amador, M., 2013. *Ethnoarchaeology of Egyptian mudbrick houses: towards a holistic understanding of ancient Egyptian domestic architecture* (Ph.D. thesis, Durham University).

Coulon, L., F. Leclère, and S. Marchand, 1995. 'Catacombes' osiriennes de Ptolémée IV à Karnak', *Karnak* 10, pp. 205–251.

Coulson, W. D. E., 1988. 'The Naukratis survey', in van den Brink, E. C. M. (ed.), *The archaeology of the Nile Delta, Egypt: problems and priorities. Proceedings of the seminar held in Cairo, 19–22 October 1986, on the occasion of the fifteenth anniversary of the Netherlands Institute of Archaeology and Arabic Studies in Cairo* (Amsterdam, Netherlands Foundation for Archaeological Research in Egypt), pp. 259–263.

——— 1996. *Ancient Naukratis, vol. II: the survey at Naukratis and environs, part I: the survey at Naukratis* (OMS 60; Oxford, Oxbow Books).

Coulson, W. D. E., and A. Leonard Jr, 1979. 'A preliminary survey of the Naukratis region in the western Nile Delta', *JFA* 6, pp. 151–168.

——— 1982a. 'Investigations at Naukratis and environs, 1980 and 1981', *AJA* 86, pp. 361–380.

——— 1982b. 'The Naukratis survey', in *L'égyptologie en 1979: axes prioritaires de recherches* (Paris, Éditions du Centre National de la Recherche Scientifique), pp. 203–220.

Coulson, W. D. E., A. Leonard Jr, and N. Wilkie, 1982. 'Three seasons of excavations and survey at Naukratis and environs', *JARCE* 19, pp. 73–109.

Crist, W., A.-E. Dunn-Vaturi, and A. de Voogt, 2016. *Ancient Egyptians at play: board games across borders* (London, Bloomsbury).

Crocker, P. T., 1985. 'Status symbols in the architecture of El-'Amarna', *JEA* 71, pp. 52–65.

Darby, W. J., P. Ghalioungui, and L. Grivetti, 1977. *Food: the gift of Osiris*, 2 vols. (London, Academic Press).

Daressy, G., 1888. 'Les carriers de Gebelein et le roi Smendés', *RT* 10, pp. 133–139.

——— 1889. 'Remarques et notes', *RT* 11, pp. 79–95.

——— 1894. 'Notes et remarques', *RT* 16, pp. 42–60.

——— 1896. 'Une inundation à Thèbes sous le règne d'Osorkon II', *RT* 18, pp. 181–186.

——— 1898. 'Notes et remarques', *RT* 20, pp. 72–78.

——— 1900. 'Notes et remarques', *RT* 22, pp. 137–143.

——— 1901. 'Notes et remarques', *RT* 23, pp. 125–133.

——— 1903a. 'Rapport sur Kom el-Hisn', *ASAE* 4, pp. 281–285.

——— 1903b. *Textes et dessins magiques* (CGC 9401–9449; Cairo, IFAO).

——— 1904a. 'Inscriptions hiéroglyphiques du Musée d'Alexandrie', *ASAE* 5, pp. 113–128.

——— 1904b. 'Rapport sur Kom el-Abq'ain', *ASAE* 5, pp. 129–130.

——— 1905. *Statues de divinités, vol. II* (CGC 38001–39384; Cairo, IFAO).

——— 1908. 'Le roi Auput et son domaine', *RT* 30, pp. 202–208.

——— 1910. 'Litanies d'Amon du temple de Louxor', *RT* 32, pp. 62–69.

1910–11. 'La liste géographique du papyrus no. 31169 du Caire', *Sphinx* 14, pp. 155–171.

1911. 'Une statue de Saft-el-Henneh', *ASAE* 11, pp. 142–144.

1912. 'À travers les koms du Delta', *ASAE* 12, pp. 169–213.

1913. 'Notes sur les XXIIe, XXIIIe et XXIVe Dynasties', *RT* 35, pp. 129–150.

1914a. 'Le nom d'Horus du roi Chéchanq III', *ASAE* 13, p. 86.

1914b. 'À travers les koms du Delta', *ASAE* 13, pp. 1–4, 179–186.

1915. 'Trois stèles de la période bubastide', *ASAE* 15, pp. 140–147.

1916a. 'Le fils aîné de Chéchanq III', *ASAE* 16, pp. 61–62.

1916b. 'Une Inscription d'Achmoun et la Géographie du Nome Libyque', *ASAE* 16, pp. 221–246.

1917. 'Stèle du roi Pefnifdubast', *ASAE* 17, pp. 43–45.

1920a. 'Fragments memphites', *ASAE* 20, pp. 167–171.

1920b. 'Un groupe de Saft el Henneh', *ASAE* 20, pp. 123–128.

1922. 'Une stèle de Mit Yaich', *ASAE* 22, p. 77.

Davies, N. de G., 1923. *The tomb of Puyemrê at Thebes (2): the chapels of hope* (New York, Metropolitan Museum of Art).

1943. *The tomb of Rekh-mi-Re at Thebes* (New York, Plantin Press).

Davies, W. V., and E. R. O'Connell, 2011a. 'British Museum expedition to Elkab and Hagr Edfu, 2010', *BMSAES* 16, pp. 101–132.

2011b. 'British Museum expedition to Elkab and Hagr Edfu, 2011', *BMSAES* 17, pp. 1–29.

Davoli, P., 1993. 'Il gruppo statuario di Senuaset (Cairo J.E. 46600 + Monaco ÄS 6296)', *SEAP* 12, pp. 17–37.

1998. *L'archeologia urbana nel Fayyum di età ellenistica e romana* (Missione Congiunta delle Università di Bologna e di Lecce in Egitto 1; Naples, Procaccini, Athenaeum).

2001. *Saft el-Henna: archeologia e storia di una citta del Delta orientale.* (Archeologia e storia della civiltà egiziana e del vicino Oriente antico – Materiali e studi 6; Bologna, Edizione La Mandragora Imola).

Defernez, C., 2015. 'Premiers résultats d'un programme de prospections céramologiques dans la zone centrale du tell de Tanis: campagne 2014 (Mission française des fouilles *DE* Tanis)', *BCE* 25, 77–100.

Deletie, P., Y. Lemoine, and J. Montluçon, 1989. 'Site de Tanis: prospection géophysique 1987', *BSFFT* 2–3, pp. 53–91.

de Linage, J., and M. Michałowski, 1938. 'Catalogue des objets', in Michałowski, K., J. de Linage, J. Manteuffel, and J. Sainte Fare Garnot, *Tell Edfou 1938* (Cairo, IFAO, Uniwersytet Józefa Piłsudskiego w Warszawie), pp. 32–135.

de Meulenaere, H., and P. MacKay, 1976. *Mendes II*, ed. Bothmer, B.V., and E. Swan Hall (Warminster, Aris and Phillips).

Desborough, V. R. d'A., 1972. *The Greek dark ages* (London, Ernest Benn).

Desroches-Noblecourt, C., 1953. '"Concubines du mort" et mères de famille au Moyen Empire', *BIFAO* 53, pp. 7–47.

Díaz-Iglesias Llanos, L., 2012. 'Nareref/ Naref: una cualidad de Osiris y un espacio para el dios en la provincia heracleopolitana', in Araújo, L. M. de, and J. des Candeias Sales (eds.), *Novos trabalhos de Egiptologia Ibérica: IV Congresso Ibérico de Egiptologia, vol. 1* (Lisbon, Instituto Oriental e Centro de História da Facultade de Letras da Universidade de Lisboa), pp. 375–392.

Dodson, A., 1993. 'A new king Shoshenq confirmed?', *GM* 137, pp. 53–58.

2000. 'Towards a mininum chronology of the New Kingdom and Third Intermediate Period', *BES* 14, pp. 7–18.

2002. 'Die Dauer der Dritten Zwischenzeit – III', in Van der Veen, P., and U. Zerbst (eds.), *Biblische Archäologie am Scheideweg? Für und Wider einer Neudatierung archäologischer Epochen im alttestamentlichen Palästina* (Edition 'Pascale'; Darmstadt, Hänssler-Verlag Holzgerlingen), pp. 77–78.

2012. *Afterglow of empire: Egypt from the fall of the New Kingdom to the Saite renaissance* (Cairo, American University in Cairo Press).

2014. 'The coming of the Kushites and the identity of Osorkon IV', in Pischikova, J., J. Budka, and K. Griffin (eds.), *Thebes in the first millennium BC* (Newcastle upon Tyne, Cambridge Scholars Publishing), pp. 1–12.

Donald, C. R., 1984. 'Examination of the archaeological samples supplied by Barry J. Kemp from the Tell el-'Amarna site', in Kemp, B. J. (ed.), *Amarna Reports I* (EES OP 1; London, Egypt Exploration Society), pp. 56–59.

Donker van Heel, K., 1997. 'Papyrus Louvre E 7852: a land lease from the reign of Taharka', *RdE* 48, pp. 81–93.

1998. 'Papyrus Louvre E 7856 verso and recto: leasing land in the reign of Taharka', *RdE* 49, pp. 91–104.

1999. 'Papyrus Louvre E 7851 verso and recto: two more land leases from the reign of Taharka', *RdE* 50, pp. 135–146.

2014. *Mrs Tsenhor: a female entrepreneur in ancient Egypt* (Cairo, American University in Cairo Press).

Downes, D., 1974. *The excavations at Esna, 1905–1906* (Warminster, Aris and Phillips).

Droiton, É., 1944. 'Une statuette-bloc de la XIXe dynastie', *ASAE* 44, pp. 91–98.

1957. 'Trigrammes d'Amon', *WZKM* 54, pp. 11–33.

Dunham, D., 1950. *El Kurru: the Royal Cemeteries of Kush I* (Cambridge, MA, Harvard University Press).

Dunnell, R. C., 1992. 'The notion site', in Rossignol, J., and L. Wandsnider (eds.), *Space, time and archaeological landscapes* (Interdisciplinary Contributions to Archaeology; New York, Plenum Press), pp. 21–43.

EAIS GIS, 2016. http://giscenter.gov.eg/home. Accessed 3/4/2017.

Edgar, C. C., 1907. 'The sarcophagus of an unknown queen', *ASAE* 8, pp. 276–280.

1911. 'Report on an excavation at Tell Om Harb', *ASAE* 11, pp. 164–169.

1914. 'Notes from my inspectorate', *ASAE* 13, pp. 277–284.

EES Delta Survey, 2016. http://deltasurvey.ees.ac.uk/dsintro.html. Accessed 1/8/2016.

Effland, A., 2009. 'Der usurpierte Sarkophag aus dem Grab J2/89', in Hartung, U., P. Ballet, A. Effland et al., 'Tell el-Fara'in – Buto 10. Vorbericht', *MDAIK* 65, pp. 108–112.

Egberts, A., 1997. 'Piankh, Herihor, Dhutmose and Butehamun: a fresh look at O. Cairo CG 25744 and 25745', *GM* 160, pp. 23–25.

1998. 'Hard times: the chronology of "The Report of Wenamun" revised', *ZÄS* 125, pp. 93–108.

el-Alfi, M., 1987. 'Varia athribica', *VA* 3 (3), pp. 189–194.

el-Enany, K., 2012. 'Une statuette sistrophore d'Atfih', *BIFAO* 112, pp. 129–137.

el-Gamili, M. M., and H. H. el-Khedr, 1989. 'Geophysical investigations for Holocene palaeohydrography in the northwestern Nile Delta', in Nibbi, A. (ed.), *Proceedings of colloquium 'The archaeology, geography and history of the Egyptian Delta in pharaonic times': Wadham College, 29–31 August, 1988,*

Oxford (Discussions in Egyptology Special Number 1; Oxford, Eynsham), pp. 125–154.

el-Maksoud, M. Abd, 1987. 'Une nouvelle forteresse sur la route d'Horus: Tell Heboua 1986 (Nord Sinaï)', *CRIPEL* 9, pp. 13–16.

1998. 'Tjarou, porte de l'Orient', in Valbelle, D., and C. Bonnet (eds.), *Le Sinaï durant le'antiquité et le Moyen-Age: 4000 ans d'histoire pour un desert: actes du colloque 'Sinaï' qui s'est tenu à l'UNESCO du 19 au 21 septembre 1997* (Paris, Errance), pp. 61–65.

el-Masry, Y., 2008. 'Evidence of building activities of certain monarchs from inscribed material in Akhmim', *MDAIK* 64, pp. 207–237.

el-Nagger, M., 1991. 'Sacred cow unearthed', *Al-Ahram Weekly*, 7 November.

el-Saghir, M., 1988. 'The EAO excavations at Abou el-Gud, Luxor', *JACF* 2, pp. 79–81.

el-Sayed Mahmud, A., 1978. *A new temple for Hathor at Memphis* (Egyptology Today 1; Warminster, Aris and Phillips).

el-Shakry, O., 2006. 'Cairo as capital of socialist revolution?', in Singerman, D., and P. Amar (eds.), *Cairo cosmopolitan: politics, culture, and urban space in the new globalized Middle East* (Cairo, American University in Cairo Press), pp. 73–98.

Emery, V. L., and M. Morgenstein, 2007. 'Portable EDXRF analysis of a mud brick necropolis enclosure: evidence of work organization, el Hibeh, Middle Egypt', *JAS* 34 (1), pp. 111–122.

Endruweit, A., 1994. *Städtischer Wohnbau in Ägypten: Klimagerechte Lehmarchitektur in Amarna* (Berlin, Gebr. Mann Verlag).

Engelbach, R., 1915. 'Riqqeh, 1914', in Engelbach, R., M. A. Murray, and W. M. F. Petrie, *Riqqeh and Memphis*

VI (BSAE/ERA 25; London, Bernard Quaritch).

1921. 'Notes of inspection, April 1921', *ASAE* 21, pp. 188–196.

1923. *Harageh* (BSAE/ERA 28; London, Bernard Quaritch).

Eriksson, K. O., 2001. 'Cypriot ceramics in Egypt during the reign of Tuthmosis III: the evidence of trade for synchronising the late Cypriot cultural sequence with Egypt at the beginning of the late Bronze Age', in Åström, P. (ed.), *The chronology of base-ring ware and bichrome wheel-made ware: proceedings of a colloquium held in the Royal Academy of Letters, History and Antiquities, Stockholm, May 18–19, 2000* (Kungl. Vitterhets Historie och Antikvitets Akademien Konferenser 54; Stockholm, Almqvist & Wiksell), pp. 51–68.

2007. 'Using Cypriot red lustrous wheel-made ware to establish cultural and chronological synchronisms during the late Bronze Age', in Hein, I. (ed.), *The lustrous wares of late Bronze Age Cyprus and the eastern Mediterranean* (CCEM 13/DGÖAW 41; Vienna, Österreichische Akademie der Wissenschaften), pp. 51–60.

Fahmy, K., 1998. 'The era of Muhammad 'Ali Pasha, 1805–1848', in Daly, M. W. (ed.), *The Cambridge history of Egypt, vol. II: modern Egypt, from 1517 to the end of the twentieth century* (Cambridge, Cambridge University Press), pp. 139–179.

Faltings, D., P. Ballet, F. Förster, P. French, C. Ihde, H. Sahlmann, J. Thomalsky, C. Thumshirn, and A. Wodzinska, 2000. 'Zweiter Vorbericht über die Arbeiten in Buto von 1996 bis 1999', *MDAIK* 56, pp. 131–179.

Favard-Meeks, C., 2002. 'Les toponymes Nétjer et leur liens avec Behbeit El-Hagara et Coptos', in Boussac, M.-F., M. Gabolde, and G. Galliano (eds.),

Autour de Coptos: actes du colloque organisé au Musée des Beaux-Arts de Lyon (17–18 mars 2000) (Topoi orient-occident, Supplément 3; Paris, De Boccard), pp. 29–45.

Fay, B., 1995. 'The Louvre sphinx, A 23', in Anonymous (ed.), Kunst des Alten Reiches: Symposium im Deutschen Archäologischen Institut Kairo am 29. und 30. Oktober 1991, SDAIK 28, pp. 75–79.

1996. *The Louvre sphinx and royal sculpture from the reign of Amenemhat II* (Mainz, Verlag Philipp von Zabern).

Fazzini, R. A., 1988. *Egypt: Dynasty XXII–XXV* (Leiden, Brill).

2002. 'Some reliefs of the Third Intermediate Period in the Egyptian Museum, Cairo', in Eldamaty, M., and M. Trad (eds.), *Egyptian museum collections around the world: studies for the centennial of the Egyptian Museum, Cairo*, vol. 1 (Cairo, Supreme Council of Antiquities), pp. 351–362.

Feucht, E., 1978. 'Zwei Reliefs Scheschonqs I. aus el-Hibeh', *SAK* 6, pp. 69–77.

Firth, C. M., and B. Gunn, 1926. *Teti pyramid cemeteries* (Cairo, IFAO).

Foucart, G., 1902. 'Extraits des rapports adressés pendant une inspection de la Basse-Égypte en 1893–1894', *ASAE* 2, pp. 44–83.

Franke, D., 1994. 'Zur Bedeutung der Stadt in altägyptischen Texten', in Jansen, M., J. Hoock, and J. Jarnut (eds.), *Städtische Formen und Macht: 1. Symposium, 2.–4. Juli 1993 Paderborn. Festschrift zur Vollendung des 65. Lebensjahres von Werner Jöel* (Veröffentlichungen der Interdisziplinären Arbeitsgruppe Stadtkulturforschung 1; Aachen, Frank), pp. 29–51.

Frankfort, H., and J. D. S. Pendlebury, 1933. *The city of Akhenaten, part II: The north suburb and the desert altars* (EES EM 40; London, Egypt Exploration Society).

Fraser, G. W., 1892–3. 'El Kab and Gebelên', *PSBA* 15, pp. 494–500.

French, P., 1996. 'Buto: Tell al-Fara'in. A pottery assemblage of the 8th century BC', *BCE* 19, pp. 8–12.

2003. 'Phase dating at Buto in the Third Intermediate Period and Late Dynastic Periods', in Hartung, U., P. Ballet, F. Béguin et al., 'Tell el Fara'in – Buto 8. Vorbericht', *MDAIK* 59, pp. 219–221.

2013. *The Anubieion at Saqqara III: pottery from the Archaic to the Third Intermediate Period* (EES EM 103; London, Egypt Exploration Society).

French, P., and J. Bourriau, 1996. 'Buto: Tell al-Fara'in: Third Intermediate to Late Period', *BCE* 19, p. 5.

Fuchs, A., 1994. *Die Inschriften Sargons II. aus Khorsabad* (Göttingen, Cuvillier).

Gabolde, M., 1994. 'La statue de Merymaât gouverneur de Djâroukha (Bologne K.S. 1813)', *BIFAO* 94, pp. 261–275.

Gamer-Wallert, I., 1978. *Ägyptische und ägyptisierende Fundes von der Iberischen Halbinsel* (B. TAVO 21; Wiesbaden, Reichert).

Gardiner, A. H., 1912. 'The stele of Bilgai', *ZÄS* 50, pp. 49–57.

1924. 'The geography of the Exodus: an answer to Professor Naville and others', *JEA* 10 (2), pp. 87–96.

1933. 'The Dakhleh Stela', *JEA* 19, pp. 19–30.

1941. 'Ramesside texts relating to the taxation and transport of corn', *JEA* 27, pp. 19–73.

1947. *Ancient Egyptian Onomastica*, vols. I–III (Oxford, Oxford University Press).

1941–8. *The Wilbour Papyrus*, 3 vols.: vol. I: *Plates* (1941); vol. II: *Commentary* (1948); vol. III: *Translation* (1948) (Oxford, Oxford University Press).

1951. 'A protest against unjustified tax-demands', *RdE* 6, pp. 128–133.

Garstang, J., 1907. 'Excavations at Hierakonpolis, at Esna, and in Nubia', *ASAE* 8, pp. 132–148.

Gasse, A., 1988. *Données nouvelles adminis- tratives et sacerdotales sur l'organisation du domaine d'Amon: XXe–XXIe Dynasties, à la lumière des papyrus Prachov, Reinhardt et Grundbuch (avec édition prin- ceps des papyrus Louvre AF 6345 et 6346– 7), vol. 1* (BdE 104; Cairo, IFAO).

Gauthier, H., 1914. *Le livre des rois d'Égypte, recueil de titres et protocoles royaux, 3, de la XIXe à la XXIVe Dynastie* (MIFAO 19; Cairo, IFAO).

——— 1921. 'À travers la Basse-Égypte', *ASAE* 21, pp. 17–39.

——— 1925–1929. *Dictionnaire des noms géographiques contenus dans les textes hiéroglyphiques*, 6 vols. (Cairo, Société Royale de Géographie d'Égypte).

——— 1937. 'Un curieux monument des dynasties boubastites à Héracléopolis Magna', *ASAE* 37, pp. 16–24.

Giddy, L., 1999. *Survey of Memphis II: Kom Rabi'a: the New Kingdom and Post-New Kingdom objects* (EES EM 64; London, Egypt Exploration Society).

Giveon, R., 1975. 'A late Egyptian statue from the eastern Delta', *JARCE* 12, pp. 19–21.

Gnirs, A. M., 1996. *Militär und Gesellschaft: ein Beitrag zur Sozialgeschichte des Neuen Reiches* (SAGA 17; Heidelberg: Heidelberger Orientverlag).

Godron, G., 1959. 'Un fragment de stèle au nom du sḏm-aš ḥꜥy[-m]-bhnt', *BIFAO* 58, pp. 81–85.

Goedicke, H., 1998. *Pi(ankh)y in Egypt: a study of the Pi(ankh)y Stela* (Baltimore, Halgo).

Golenischeff, W., 1902–1903. 'Offener Brief an Herrn Professor G. Steindorff', *ZÄS* 40, pp. 101–106.

Gomaà, F., 1974. *Die libyschen Fürstentümer des Deltas vom Tod Osorkons II. bis zur Wiedervereinigung Ägyptens durch Psametik I.* (B.TAVO 6; Wiesbaden, Reichert).

——— 1983. 'Bemerkungen Zur Nekropole von El-Kom El-Aḥmar Sawaris', *WdO* 14, pp. 135–146.

——— 1986. *Die Besiedlung Ägyptens Während des Mittleren Reiches I: Oberägypten und das Fayyūm*, vol. 1 (B. TAVO 66; Wiesbaden, Reichert).

Gomaà, F., R. Müller-Wollermann, and W. Schenkel, 1991. *Mittelägypten zwischen Samalūṭ und dem Gabal Abū Ṣīr: Beiträge zur historischen Topographie der pharaonischen Zeit* (B. TAVO 69; Wiesbaden, Reichert).

Goyon, J.-C., 1967. 'Le cérémonial de glorification d'Osiris du papyrus du Louvre I. 3079 (colonnes 110 à 112)', *BIFAO* 65, pp. 89–156.

——— 1983. 'Aspects thébains de la confirma- tion du pouvoir royal: les rites lunaires', *JSSAE* 13 (1), pp. 2–9.

Goyon, J.-C., and C. Traunecker, 1978– 81. 'La chapelle de Thot et d'Amon au sud-ouest du Lac Sacré', *Karnak* 7, pp. 355–366.

Graham, A., 2010. 'Islands in the Nile', in Bietak, M., E. Czerny, and I. Forstner-Müller (eds.), *Cities and urbanism in ancient Egypt: papers from a workshop in November 2006 at the Austrian Academy of Sciences* (DGÖAW 60/UZK 35; Vienna, VÖAW), pp. 125–143.

Graham, A., and J. Bunbury, 2005. 'The ancient landscapes and waterscapes of Karnak', *Egyptian Archaeology* 27, pp. 17–19.

Grandet, P., 1994. *Le papyrus Harris I (BM 9999)*, 2 vols. (BdE 109; Cairo, IFAO).

Graves, C., 2013. 'The problem with Neferusi: a geoarchaeological approach', in Graves, C., G. Heffernan, L. McGarrity, E. Millward, and M. Sfakianou Bealby (eds.), *Current research in Egyptology 2012: proceedings of the thirteenth annual symposium, University of Birmingham 2012* (Oxford, Oxbow Books), pp. 70–83.

Graves-Brown, C., 2015. 'Flint and forts: the role of flint in late Middle–New Kingdom Egyptian weaponry', in

Harrison, T. P., E. B. Banning, and S. Klassen (eds.), *Walls of the prince: Egyptian interactions with southwest Asia in antiquity: essays in honour of John S. Holladay, Jr.* (CHANE 77; Leiden, Brill), pp. 37–59.

Gregory, S., 2013. Piankh and Herihor: art, ostraca, and accession in perspective. *Birmingham Egyptology Journal* 1, pp. 5–18.

—— 2014. *Herihor in art and iconography: kingship and the gods in the ritual landscape of late New Kingdom Thebes* (London, Golden House).

Grenfell, B. P., and A. S. Hunt, 1902. 'Excavations in the Fayûm and at el Hîbeh', *Archaeological Report 1901–1902*, pp. 2–5.

Griffith, F. Ll., 1888. 'Gemaiyemi', in Petrie, W. M. F., A. S. Murray, and F. Ll. Griffith, *Nebesheh (Am) and Defenneh (Tahpanhes)* (EEF 4; London, Trübner), pp. 37–47.

—— 1909. *Catalogue of the demotic papyri in the John Rylands Library, Manchester: with facsimiles and complete translations, vols. I–III* (Manchester, Manchester University Press).

Griffith, F. Ll., and P. E. Newberry, 1894. *El-Bersheh Part II* (EES ASE 4; London, Egypt Exploration Fund).

Grimal, N., 1981. *La stèle triomphale de Pi ('ankh)y au Musée du Caire. JE 48862 et 47086–47089* (Études sur la Propagande Royale Égyptienne 1; Cairo, IFAO).

Gundlach, R., 1994. 'Das Königtum des Herihor: zum Umbruch in der ägyptischen Königsideologie am Beginn der 3. Zwischenzeit', in Minas, M., and J. Zeidler (eds.), *Aspekte spätägyptischer Kultur: Festschrift für Erich Winter zum 65. Geburtstag* (Mainz: Philipp von Zabern), pp. 133–138.

Habachi, L., 1943. 'Sais and its monuments', *ASAE* 42, pp. 369–407.

—— 1947. 'A statue of Osiris made for Ankhefenamun, prophet of the house of Amun in Khapu and his daughter', *ASAE* 47, pp. 261–282.

—— 1954. 'Khatâ'na-Qantîr: importance', *ASAE* 52 (2), pp. 443–562.

—— 1956, 'Notes on the Delta Hermopolis, capital of the XVth nome of Lower Egypt', *ASAE* 53 (2), pp. 441–480.

—— 1957. *Tell Basta* (ASAE Supplément 22; Cairo, IFAO).

—— 1967. 'Per-Ra'et and Per-Ptah in the Delta', *CdE* 42 (83), pp. 30–40.

Haeny, G., 1979. 'New Kingdom architecture', in Weeks, K. R. (ed.), *Egyptology and the social sciences: five studies. Papers originally presented at a conference on ancient Egypt: problems of history, sources and methods, Cairo, 1975* (Cairo, American University in Cairo Press), pp. 85–94.

Hall, H. R., 1928. *Babylonian and Assyrian sculpture in the British Museum* (Paris and Brussels, Éditions G. van Oest).

—— 1930. 'The bronze statuette of Khonserdaisu in the British Museum', *JEA* 16, pp. 1–2.

Hamada, A., 1947. 'Statue of the fan-bearer Amenmosi', *ASAE* 47, pp. 15–21.

Hamza, M., 1937. 'The statue of Meneptah I found at Athar en-Nabi and the route of Pi'ankhi from Memphis to Heliopolis', *ASAE* 37, pp. 233–242.

Hanasaka, T., 2011. 'Archaeological investigations: finds from the South Area', in Kawanishi, H., S. Tsujimura, and T. Hanasaka (eds.), *Preliminary report, Akoris, 2010* (History and Anthropology; Tsubuka, University of Tsubuka), pp. 9–11.

—— 2012. 'Clay cobra figurines unearthed from Akoris (Tihna el-Gabal)', in Kawanishi, H., S. Tsujimura, and T. Hanasaka (eds.), *Preliminary report, Akoris, 2011* (History and Anthropology; Ibaraki, University of Tsubuka), pp. 4–14.

Hankey, V., and D. A. Aston, 1995. 'Mycenaean pottery at Saqqara: finds from excavations by the Egypt Exploration Society of London and the Rijksmuseum van Oudheden, Leiden, 1975–1990', in Carter, J. B., and S. Morris (eds.), *The ages of Homer: a tribute to Emily Townsend Vermeule* (Austin, TX, Van Siclen Books), pp. 67–91.

Hannig, R., 2000. *Großes Handwörterbuch Deutsch-Ägyptisch (2800–950 v. Chr.): die Sprache der Pharaonen* (KAW 86; Mainz am Rhein, Philipp von Zabern).

Hansen, M. H., 2000. 'Introduction: the concepts of city-state and city-state cultures', in Hansen, M. H. (ed.), *A comparative study of thirty city-state cultures: an investigation conducted by the Copenhagen Polis Centre* (Historisk filosofiske Skrifter 21: Copenhagen, Royal Danish Academy of Sciences and Letters), pp. 11–35.

Hartung, U., P. Ballet, F. Béguin et al., 2003. 'Tell el-Fara'in – Buto: 8. Vorbericht', *MDAIK* 59, pp. 199–267.

Hartung, U., P. Ballet, A. Effland et al., 2009. 'Tell El-Fara'in – Buto: 10. Vorbericht', *MDAIK* 65, pp. 83–190.

Hassan, F. A., 1996. 'Abrupt Holocene climatic events in Africa', in Pwiti, G., and R. Soper (eds.), *Aspects of African archaeology: papers from the 10th Congress of the PanAfrican Association for Prehistory and Related Studies* (Harare, University of Zimbabwe Publications), pp. 83–89.

2010. 'Climate change, Nile floods and riparia', in Hermon, E. (ed.), *Riparia dans l'empire romain: pour la définition du concept. Proceedings of the Quebec seminar, 29–31 October 2009* (BAR IS 2066; Oxford, Archaeopress), pp. 131–150.

Hayes, W. C., 1951. 'Inscriptions from the palace of Amenhotep III', *JNES* 10, pp. 35–56, 82–112, 156–183, 231–242.

Heidorn, L. A., 1997. 'The horses of Kush', *JNES* 56 (2), pp. 105–114.

Henne, H., 1925. *Rapport sur les fouilles de Tell Edfou (1923 et 1924)* (FIFAO 2.3; Cairo, IFAO).

Herbich, T., 2001. 'Qasr el-Sagha: magnetic survey, 1999', *PAM* 12, pp. 181–184.

2003. 'Archaeological geophysics in Egypt: the Polish contribution', *APol* 41, pp. 13–55.

2004. 'Magnetic survey at Tell el-Farkha or how to interpret a magnetic map', in Hendrickx, S., R. F. Friedman, K. M. Cialowicz, and M. Chlodnicki (eds.), *Egypt at its origins [1]: studies in memory of Barbara Adams. Proceedings of the international conference 'Origin of the State: Predynastic and Early Dynastic Egypt', Kraków, 28th August–1st September 2002* (OLA 138; Leuven, Peeters), pp. 389–398.

2012a. 'Geophysical methods and landscape archaeology', *EA* 41, pp. 11–14.

2012b. 'Magnetic survey', in Cialowicz, K. M., and A. Mączyńska (eds.), *Tell El-Farkha I: excavations 1998–2011. Polish archaeological expedition to the eastern Nile Delta* (Poznań and Kraków, Poznan Archaeological Museum, Institute of Archaeology, Jagiellonian University), pp. 383–391.

2013. 'Geophysical survey at Tell el-Ghaba, 2010', *PAM* 22, pp. 121–130.

Herbich, T., and U. Hartung, 2004. 'Geophysical investigations at Buto (Tell el-Farain)', *EA* 24, pp. 14–17.

Herbich, T., and J. Richards, 2006. 'The loss and rediscovery of the vizier Iuu at Abydos: magnetic survey in the middle cemetery', in Czerny, E., I. Hein, H. Hunger, D. Melman, and A. Schwab (eds.), *Timelines: studies in honour of Manfred Bietak, vol. I*

(OLA 149; Leuven, Peeters), pp. 141–149.

Herbich, T., and T. N. Smekalova, 2001. 'Dakhleh Oasis: magnetic survey 1999–2000', *PAM* 12, pp. 259–262.

Herbin, F.-R., 1986. 'Une version inachevée de l'onomasticon d'Aménémopé (P. BM 10474 vo)', *BIFAO* 86, pp. 187–198.

Herold, A., 1999. 'Ein Kindergrab im Königlichen Marstall?', *Ä&L* 9, pp. 85–100.

Herrmann, C., 1985. *Formen für ägyptische Fayencen: Katalog der Sammlung des Biblischen Instituts der Universität Freiburg Schweiz and einer Privatsammlung* (OBO 60; Freiburg and Göttingen, Universitätsverlag and Vandenhoeck & Ruprecht).

1990. 'Die Sammlung von Modeln für ägyptische Fayencen', in Keel, O., and C. Uehlinger (eds.), *Altorientalische Miniaturkunst: die ältesten visuellen Massenkommunikationsmittel. Ein Blick in die Sammlungen des Biblischen Instituts der Universität Freiburg Schweiz* (Mainz, Zabern), pp. 119–123.

1994. *Ägyptische Amulette aus Palästina/ Israel [I]: mit einem Ausblick auf ihre Rezeption durch das Alte Testament* (OBO 138; Freiburg and Göttingen, Universitätsverlag and Vandenhoeck & Ruprecht).

2002. *Ägyptische Amulette aus Palästina/ Israel II* (OBO 184; Freiburg and Göttingen, Universitätsverlag and Vandenhoeck & Ruprecht).

2003. *Die ägyptischen Amulette der Sammlungen BIBEL + ORIENT der Universität Freiburg, Schweiz: anthropomorphe Gestalten und Tiere* (OBO Series Archaeologica 22; Freiburg and Göttingen, Universitätsverlag and Vandenhoeck & Ruprecht).

2006. *Ägyptische Amulette aus Palästina, Israel III* (OBO Series Archaeologica 24; Freiburg and Göttingen, Universitätsverlag and Vandenhoeck & Ruprecht).

2007. *Formen für ägyptische Fayencen aus Qantir, Band II: Katalog der Sammlung des Franciscan Biblical Museum, Jerusalem und zweier Privatsammlungen* (OBO 225; Freiburg and Göttingen, Universitätsverlag and Vandenhoeck & Ruprecht).

2015. *Corpus der Formen für ägyptische Fayencen aus Qantir* (Gachnang, Christian Herrmann).

2016. *Ägyptische Amulette aus Palästina/ Israel IV: vonder Spätbronzezeit IIB bis in die römische Zeit* (OBO Series Archaeologica 38; Freiburg and Göttingen, Universitätsverlag and Vandenhoeck & Ruprecht).

Hill, M., 2004. *Royal bronze statuary from ancient Egypt: with special attention to the kneeling pose* (EM 3; Leiden, Brill).

Hillier, J. K., J. M. Bunbury, and A. Graham, 2007. 'Monuments on a migrating Nile', *JAS* 34 (7), pp. 1011–1015.

Hoch, J. E. 1994. *Semitic words in Egyptian texts of the New Kingdom and Third Intermediate Period* (Princeton, Princeton University Press).

Hodder, I., and C. Orton, 1976. *Spatial analysis in archaeology* (New Studies in Archaeology; Cambridge, Cambridge University Press).

Hodjash, S., and O. Berlev, 1982. *The Egyptian reliefs and stelae in the Pushkin Museum of Fine Arts, Moscow* (Leningrad, Aurora Art).

Hoffman, M. A., H. A. Hamroush, and R. O. Allen, 1986. 'A model of urban development for the Hierakonpolis region from predynastic through Old Kingdom times', *JARCE* 23, pp. 175–187.

Hoffmeier, J. K., and S. O. Moshier, 2006. 'New paleo-environmental evidence from north Sinai to complement Manfred Bietak's map of the eastern Delta and some historical implications', in Czerny, E., I. Hein, H. Hunger, D. Melman, and A. Schwab (eds.), *Timelines: studies in honour of Manfred Bietak, vol. II* (OLA 149; Leuven, Peeters), pp. 167–176.

Hogarth, D., 1904. 'Three north Delta nomes', *JHS* 24, pp. 1–19.

Hole, F., and R. F. Heizer, 1973. *An introduction to prehistoric archaeology* (New York, Holt Rinehart & Winston).

Hölscher, U., 1939. *The excavation of Medinet Habu, vol. II: the temples of the Eighteenth Dynasty* (OIP 41; Chicago, University of Chicago Press).

1941. *The excavation of Medinet Habu: the mortuary temple of Ramesses III, part 1, vol. III* (OIP 54; Chicago, University of Chicago Press).

1954. *The excavation of Medinet Habu: the post-Ramesside remains, vol. V* (OIP 66; Chicago, University of Chicago Press).

Hope, C. A., 1989. 'Pottery of the Ramesside Period', in Hope, C. A. (ed.), *Pottery of the Egyptian New Kingdom: three studies* (Victoria College Archaeology Research Unit, Occasional Papers 2; Burwood (Victoria), Victoria College Press), pp. 45–84.

2001. 'Egypt and Libya: the excavations at Mut el-Kharab in Egypt's Dakhleh Oasis', *Artefact* 24, pp. 29–46.

Hope, C. A., G. E. Bowen, J. Cox, W. Dolling, J. Milner, and A. Pettman, 2009. 'Report on the 2009 season of excavations at Mut El-Kharab, Dakhleh Oasis', *BACE* 20, pp. 47–86.

Hope, C. A., G. E. Bowen, W. Dolling, E. Healey, J. Milner, and O. E. Kaper, 2008. 'The excavations at Mut El-Kharab, Dakhleh Oasis in 2008', *BACE* 19, pp. 49–72.

Hornblower, G. D., 1929. 'Predynastic figures of women and their successors', *JEA* 15, pp. 29–47.

Hornung, E., and E. Staehelin, 1976. *Skarabäen und andere Siegelamulette aus Basler Sammlungen* (ÄeDs 1; Mainz, Philipp von Zabern).

Hughes, G. R., 1973. 'Notes on Demotic Egyptian leases of property', *JNES* 32, pp. 152–160.

Hussain, A. G., 1983. 'Magnetic prospecting for archaeology in Kom Oshim and Kiman Faris, Fayoum, Egypt', *ZÄS* 110, pp. 36–51.

Ingold, T., 2000. *The perception of the environment: essays in livelihood, dwelling and skill* (London, Routledge).

Iversen, E., 1941. *Two inscriptions concerning private donations to temples* (Copenhagen, Historisk-filologiske meddelelser).

Jacquet, J., 1965. 'The architect's report', in Anthes, R., *Mit Rahineh 1956* (Philadelphia, University Museum, University of Pennsylvania), pp. 45–59.

Jaeger, B., 1982. *Essai de classification et datation des scarabées Menkhéperrê* (OBO Series Archaeologica 2; Göttingen, Vandenhoeck & Ruprecht).

James, P., and R. Morkot, 2010. 'Herihor's kingship and the high priest of Amun Piankh', *JEgH* 3 (2), pp. 231–260.

Jansen-Winkeln, K., 1987. 'Thronname und Begräbnis Takeloths I', *VA* 3 (3), pp. 253–258.

1989. 'Zu einigen "Trinksprüchen" auf ägyptischen Gefäßen', *ZÄS* 116, pp. 143–153.

1992. 'Das Ende des Neuen Reiches', *ZÄS* 119, pp. 22–37.

1994. 'Der Beginn der Libyschen Herrschaft in Ägypten', *BN* 71, pp. 78–97.

1995. 'Historische Probleme Der 3. Zwischenzeit', *JEA* 81, pp. 129–149.

1997. 'Die thebanischen Gründer der 21. Dynastie', *GM* 157, pp. 49–74.

2001. 'Der Thebanische "Gottesstaat"', *Orientalia* 70, pp. 153–182.

2004. 'Zu Einer Sekundärbestattung Der 21. Dynastie in Kom Ombo', *GM* 202, pp. 71–78.

2006a. 'The chronology of the Third Intermediate Period: Dyns. 22–24', in Hornung, E., R. Krauss, and D. A. Warburton (eds.), *Ancient Egyptian chronology* (HdO 1; Leiden, Brill), pp. 234–265.

2006b. 'Die Libyer in Herakleopolis Magna', *Orientalia* 75 (4), pp. 297–316.

2007a. *Inschriften der Spatzeit, Teil 1: Die 21 Dynastie* (Wiesbaden, Harrassowitz Verlag).

2007b. *Inschriften der Spätzeit. Teil 2: Die 22.-24. Dynastie* (Wiesbaden, Harrassowitz Verlag).

2009. *Inschriften der Spätzeit, Teil 3: Die 25. Dynastie* (Wiesbaden, Harrassowitz Verlag).

2012. 'Libyer und Ägypten in der Libyerzeit', in Zivie-Coche, C., and I. Guermeur (eds.), *Parcourir l'éternité, hommages à Jean Yoyotte, vol. II* (BEHE 156; Turnhout, Brepols), pp. 618–622.

2017. 'Beiträge zur Geschichte der Dritten Zwischenzeit', *JEgH* 10, pp. 23–42.

Jaritz, H., 1986. 'Three townsites in the Upper Thebaid', *CRIPEL* 8, pp. 37–39.

Jarmužek, L., 2011. 'Third Intermediate Period stable', in Rzepka, S., A. Wodzińska, C. Malleson et al., 'New Kingdom and the Third Intermediate Period in Tell el-Retaba: results of the Polish–Slovak Archaeological Mission, seasons 2009–2010', *Ä&L* 21, pp. 129–135 (129–184).

Jarmužek, L., and S. Rzepka, 2014. 'Third Intermediate Period, Settlement Area 9', in Rzepka, S., et al., 'Tell el-Retaba from the Second Intermediate Period till the Late Period: results of the Polish–Slovak

Archaeological Mission, seasons 2011–2012', *Ä&L 24*, pp. 86–92.

Jeffreys, D. G., 1985. *The survey of Memphis, part one: the archaeological report* (EES OP 3; London, Egypt Exploration Society).

1996. 'House, palace and islands at Memphis', in Bietak, M. (ed.), *Haus und Palast im Alten Ägypten* (DGÖAW 14/UZK 14; Vienna, Verlage der Österreichischen Akademie der Wissenschaften), pp. 287–294.

2007. 'Section 1: post-Ramesside levels at Kom Rabia', in Aston, D. A., and D. G. Jeffreys, *The survey of Memphis, III: the Third Intermediate Period levels* (EES EM 81; London, Egypt Exploration Society), pp. 1–15.

Jeffreys, D. G., and J. Malek, 1988. 'Memphis 1986, 1987', *JEA* 74, pp. 15–29.

Jeffreys, D. G., and A. Tavares, 1994. 'The historic landscape of Early Dynastic Memphis', *MDAIK* 50, pp. 143–173.

Jones, M., 1990. 'The temple of Apis in Memphis', *JEA* 76, pp. 141–147.

Jucha, M. A., and A. Buszek, 2011. 'Tell el-Murra (north-eastern Nile Delta survey): season 2008', *PAM* 20, pp. 177–182.

Jucha, M. A., K. Blaszczyk, A. Buszek, and G. Pryc, 2010, 'Tell el-Murra (Northeastern Nile Delta Survey): season 2010', *PAM* 22, pp. 105–120.

Junge, F., 1987. *Elephantine XI: Funde und Bauteile. 1.–7. Kampagne, 1969–1976* (AVDAIK 49; Mainz am Rhein, Philipp von Zabern).

Jurman, C., 2006. 'Die Namen des Rudjamun in der Kapelle des Osiris-Hekadjet. Bemerkungen zu Titulaturen der 3. Zwischenzeit und dem Wadi Gasus-Graffito', *GM* 210, pp. 69–91.

2007. 'bw hri hm=f the place where his majesty dwells: some remarks about the localisation of royal palace, residence and central administration in Late Period Egypt', in Endreffy, K., and A. Gulyás (eds.), *Proceedings of the Fourth Central European Conference of Young Egyptologists: 31 August–2 September 2006, Budapest* (StudAeg 18; Budapest, ELTE Régészeti Tanszek), pp. 171–193.

2009. 'From the Libyan dynasties to the Kushites in Memphis: historical problems and cultural issues', in Broekman, G. P. F., R. J. Demarée, and O. E. Kaper (eds.), *The Libyan Period in Egypt: historical and cultural studies into the 21st–24th Dynasties. Proceedings of a conference at Leiden University, 25–27 October 2007* (EgUit 23; Nederlands Instituut voor het Nabije Oosten, Leuven, Peeters), pp. 113–138.

2017. 'The order of the Kushite kings according to sources from the Eastern Desert and Thebes. Or: Shabataka was here first!', *JEgH* 10, pp. 124–151.

Kahn, D., 2009. 'The transition from Libyan to Nubian rule in Egypt: revisiting the reign of Tefnakht', in Broekman, G. P. F., R. J. Demarée, and O. E. Kaper (eds.), *The Libyan Period in Egypt: historical and cultural studies into the 21st–24th Dynasties. Proceedings of a conference at Leiden University, 25–27 October 2007* (EgUit 23; Nederlands Instituut voor het Nabije Oosten, Leuven, Peeters), pp. 139–148.

Kamal, A. B., 1905. *Stèles ptolémaiques et romaines* (CGC 22001–22208; Cairo, IFAO).

1909. *Tables d'offrandes* (CGC 23001–23256; Cairo, IFAO).

Kamel, I., 1968. 'A bronze hoard at Athribis', *ASAE* 60, pp. 65–71.

Kamp, K., 2000. 'From village to tell: household ethnoarchaeology in Syria', *NEA* 63 (2), pp. 84–93.

Kaper, O. E., 2009. 'Epigraphic evidence from the Dakhleh Oasis in the Libyan Period', in Broekman, G. P. F., R. J. Demarée, and O. E. Kaper (eds.), *The Libyan Period in Egypt: historical and cultural studies into the 21st–24th Dynasties. Proceedings of a conference at Leiden University, 25–27 October 2007* (EgUit 23; Nederlands Instituut voor het Nabije Oosten, Leuven, Peeters), pp. 149–159.

Kawanishi, H., and S. Tsujimura, 2013. 'Archaeological investigation', in Kawanishi, H., S. Tsujimura, and T. Hanasaka (eds.), *Preliminary report, Akoris, 2012* (History and Anthropology; Tsubuka, University of Tsubuka), pp. 5–15.

Keel, O., 1980. 'La glyptique', in Briend, J. and J.-B. Humbert (eds.), *Tell Keisan (1971–1976): une cité phénicienne en Galilée* (Freiburg and Göttingen, Universitätsverlag and Vandenhoeck & Ruprecht), pp. 257–295.

1997. *Corpus der Stempelsiegel-Amulette aus Palästina/Israel: von den Anfängen bis zur Perserzeit. Katalog Band I: von Tell Abu Farağ bis 'Atlit* (OBO 13; Freiburg and Göttingen, Universitätsverlag and Vandenhoeck & Ruprecht).

2004. 'Scarabs, stamp seal-amulets and impressions', in Ussishkin, D. (ed.), *The renewed archaeological excavations at Lachish (1973–1994), vol. III* (Tel Aviv, Emery and Claire Yass Publications in Archaeology), pp. 1537–1571.

2010a. *Corpus der Stempelsiegel-Amulette aus Palästina/Israel: von den Anfängen bis zur Perserzeit. Katalog Band II: von Bahan bis Tel Eton* (OBO 29; Freiburg and Göttingen, Universitätsverlag and Vandenhoeck & Ruprecht).

2010b. *Corpus der Stempelsiegel-Amulette aus Palästina/Israel: von den Anfängen bis zur Perserzeit. Katalog Band III: von Tell el Far'a Nord bis Tell el-Fir* (OBO 31; Freiburg and Göttingen, Universitätsverlag and Vandenhoeck & Ruprecht).

2013. *Corpus der Stempelsiegel-Amulette aus Palästina/Israel: von den Anfängen bis zur Perserzeit. Katalog Band IV: von Tel Gamma bis Chirbet Husche* (OBO 33; Freiburg and Göttingen, Universitätsverlag and Vandenhoeck & Ruprecht).

2016. 'The glyptic material', in Herzog, Z., and L. Singer-Avitz (eds.), *Beer-Sheba III: the Early Iron IIA enclosed settlement and the late Iron IIA–Iron IIB cities*, vol. III (Winona Lake, Eisenbrauns), pp. 1048–1061.

Kees, H., 1937. 'Die Laufbahn des Hohenpriesters Onhurmes von Thinis', *ZÄS* 73, pp. 77–90.

1958. 'Der Gau von Kynopolis und seine Gottheit', *MIO* 6, pp. 157–175.

Kemp, B. J., 1977. 'The city of el-Amarna as a source for the study of urban society in ancient Egypt', *WorldArch* 9, pp. 124–139.

1978. 'The Harim-Palace at Medinet el-Ghurab', *ZÄS* 105, pp. 122–133.

1987. 'Appendix: general review of the Workmen's Village houses', in Kemp, B. J. (ed.), *Amarna reports IV* (EES OP 5; London, Egypt Exploration Society), pp. 40–46.

1995. 'Outlying temples at Amarna', in Kemp, B. J. (ed.), *Amarna reports VI* (EES OP 10; London, Egypt Exploration Society), pp. 411–462.

2000. 'Soil (including mud-brick architecture)', in Nicholson, P.T., and I. Shaw (eds.), *Ancient Egyptian materials and technology* (Cambridge, Cambridge University Press), pp. 78–104.

2004. 'Egypt's invisible walls: introduction', *CAJ* 14 (2), pp. 259–260.

2006. *Ancient Egypt: anatomy of a civilization* (2nd edition) (Abingdon, Routledge).

2018. *Ancient Egypt: anatomy of a civilization* (3rd edition) (Abingdon, Routledge).

Kemp, B. J., and A. Stevens, 2010. *Busy lives at Amarna: excavations in the main city (Grid 12 and the house of Ranefer, N49.18)*, vol. II: *the objects* (EES EM 91; London, Egypt Exploration Society).

Kemp, B. J., and G. Vogelsang-Eastwood, 2001. *The ancient textile industry at Amarna* (EES EM 68; London, Egypt Exploration Society).

Kenawi, M., 2014. *Alexandria's hinterland: archaeology of the western Nile Delta, Egypt* (Oxford, Archaeopress).

Kessler, D., 1975. 'Eine Landschenkung Rameses' III. Zugunsten eines "Grossen der thrw" aus mr-mšꜥ.f', *SAK* 2, pp. 103–134.

1981. *Historische Topographie der Region Zwischen Mallawi und Samaluṭ* (B. TAVO 30; Wiesbaden, Reichert).

Kirby, C. J., S. E. Orel, and S. T. Smith, 1998. 'Preliminary report on the survey of Kom el-Hisn, 1996', *JEA* 84, pp. 23–43.

Kitagawa, C., 2009. 'Comment on the cat burial from Tomb J2/89', in Hartung U., P. Ballet, A. Effland et al., 'Tell el-Fara'in – Buto 10. Vorbericht', *MDAIK* 65, pp. 112–115.

Kitchen, K. A., 1969–70. 'Two donation stelae in the Brooklyn Museum', *JARCE* 8, pp. 73–78.

1996. *The Third Intermediate Period in Egypt (1100–650 BC)* (3rd edition with supplement) (Warminster, Aris and Phillips).

2009. 'The Third Intermediate Period in Egypt: an overview of fact and fiction', in Broekman, G. P. F., R. J. Demarée, and O. E. Kaper (eds.), *The Libyan Period in Egypt: historical and cultural studies into the 21st–24th Dynasties. Proceedings of a conference at Leiden University, 25–*

27 October 2007 (EgUit 23; Nederlands Instituut voor het Nabije Oosten, Leuven, Peeters), pp. 161–202.

Kohen, C. I., 2015. 'Imported pottery types', in Lupo, S. (ed.), *Tell el-Ghaba III: a Third Intermediate–Early Saite Period site in the Egyptian eastern Delta; excavations 1995–1999 and 2010 in areas I, II, VI and VIII, 309–326* (BAR IS 2756; Oxford, Archaeopress), pp. 309–326.

Koltsida, A., 2007. *Social aspects of ancient Egyptian domestic architecture* (BAR IS 1608; Oxford, Archaeopress).

Kopp, P., C. von Pilgrim, F. Arnold, E. Kopp, E. Laskowska-Kusztal, and D. Raue, 2010. *Elephantine, report on the 40th season* (pdf). Accessed from www.dainst.org/documents/10180/3 84618/Elephantine+-+Report+on+t he+40th+Season+(ENGLISH)/7a936 239-6ace-4f45-8690-dba33b475326;js essionid=E09107174292E5AC6782C CC27584093F?version=1.0. Accessed 20/3/2019.

Kóthay, K.A., 2001. 'Houses and households at Kahun: bureaucratic and domestic aspects of social organization during the Middle Kingdom', in Győry, H. (ed.), *'Le lotus qui sort de terre': mélanges offerts à Edith Varga* (BMusHongr, Supplément 2001; Budapest, Musée Hongrois des Beaux-Art), pp. 349–368.

Krauss, R., 2005. 'Das wrš-Datum aus Jahr 5 von Sheshonq [I]', *DE* 62, pp. 43–48.

Krekeler, A., 1988. 'Untersuchungen im Stadtgebiet nordwestlich des Späten Chnumtempels', *MDAIK* 44, pp. 170–174.

1993. 'Stadt und Tempel von Elephantine 19./20. Grabungsbericht. VIII. Stadtgebiet nordwestlich des Späten Chnumtempels: spates Neue Reich bis Spätantike', *MDAIK* 49, pp. 170–181.

Kruchten, J.-M., 1989. *Les annales des prêtres de Karnak (XXI–XXIIImes dynasties) et autres textes contemporains*

relatifs à l'initiation des prêtres d'Amon (OLA 32; Leuven, Peeters).

Lacovara, P., 1997. *The New Kingdom royal city* (New York, Kegan Paul International).

Laemmel, S., 2008. 'Preliminary report on the pottery from Area Q IV at Qantir/Pi-Ramesse: excavations of the Roemer-Pelizaeus Museum, Hildesheim', *Ä&L* 18, pp. 173–202.

Lang, F., 2005. 'Structural change in archaic Greek housing', in Ault, B. A., and L. C. Nevett (eds.), *Ancient Greek houses and households: chronological, regional and social diversity* (Philadelphia, University of Pennsylvania Press), pp. 12–36.

Lange, E. R., 2004. 'Ein neuer König Schoschenk in Bubastis', *GM* 203, pp. 65–72.

2009. 'The sed-festival reliefs of Osorkon II at Bubastis: new investigations', in Broekman, G. P. F., R. J. Demarée, and O. E. Kaper (eds.), *The Libyan Period in Egypt: historical and cultural studies into the 21st–24th Dynasties. Proceedings of a conference at Leiden University, 25–27 October 2007* (EgUit 23; Nederlands Instituut voor het Nabije Oosten, Leuven, Peeters), pp. 203–218.

Lange, H. O., 1925. *Das Weisheitsbuch des Amenemope: aus dem Papyrus 10,474 des British Museum* (Historisk-filologiske meddelelser 11, no. 2; Copenhagen, Høst).

Lantzas, K., 2012. *Settlement and social trends in the Argolid and the Methana peninsula, 1200–900 BC* (BAR IS 2421; Oxford, Archaeopress).

Lawrence, A.W., 1965. 'Ancient Egyptian fortifications', *JEA* 51, pp. 69–95.

Leahy, A., 1985. 'The Libyan Period in Egypt: an essay in interpretation', *LibStud* 16, pp. 51–65.

1999. 'More fragments of the Book of the Dead of Padinemty', *JEA* 85, pp. 230–232.

Leclant, J., 1951. 'Fouilles et travaux en Égypte, 1950–1951. 1', *Orientalia* 20, pp. 453–475.

1952. 'Fouilles et travaux en Égypte, 1950–1951. 2', *Orientalia* 21, pp. 233–249.

1963. 'Kashta, pharaon, en Egypte', *ZÄS* 90, pp. 74–81.

1973. 'Fouilles et travaux en Égypte et au Soudan, 1971–1972', *Orientalia* 42, pp. 393–440.

1987. 'Fouilles et travaux en Égypte et au Soudan, 1985–1986', *Orientalia* 56, pp. 292–389.

Leclant, J., and G. Clerc, 1985. 'Fouilles et travaux en Égypte et au Soudan, 1983–1984', *Orientalia* 54, pp. 337–415.

1986. 'Fouilles et travaux en Égypte et au Soudan, 1984–1985', *Orientalia* 55, pp. 236–319.

1997. 'Fouilles et travaux en Égypte et au Soudan, 1995–1996', *Orientalia* 66, pp. 222–363.

Leclant, J., and J. Yoyotte, 1952. 'Notes d'histoire et de civilisation éthiopiennes: à propos d'un ouvrage récent', *BIFAO* 51, pp. 1–39.

Leclère, F., 2008. *Les villes de Basse Égypte au Ier millénaire av. J.-C.: analyse archéologique et historique de la topographie urbaine*, 2 vols. (BdE 144; Cairo, IFAO).

2014. 'Catalogue of objects from Tell Dafana in the British Museum', in Leclère, F., and A. J. Spencer (eds.), *Tell Dafana reconsidered: the archaeology of an Egyptian frontier town* (Research Publication 199; London, British Museum), pp. 51–89.

Leclère, F., and S. Marchand, 1995. 'Données complémentaires sur les structures de briques crues rubéfiées du Musée de Plein Air de Karnak', *Karnak* 10, pp. 349–380.

Lefebvre, M. G., 1908. 'Notes sur Khawaled', *ASAE* 9, pp. 158–161.

1912. 'A travers la Moyenne-Égypte: documents et notes', *ASAE* 12, pp. 81–94.

Legrain, G., 1900. 'Le temple et les chapelles d'Osiris à Karnak', *RT* 22, pp. 125–136.

1902. 'Le temple de Ptah Rîs-anbou-f dans Thèbes', *ASAE* 3, pp. 38–66.

1906. *Statues et statuettes de rois et de particuliers* (CGC 42001–42138; Cairo, IFAO).

1914a. 'Au pylône d'Harmhabi à Karnak (Xe pylône)', *ASAE* 14, pp. 13–44.

1914b. *Statues et statuettes de rois et de particuliers* (CGC 42192–42250; Cairo, IFAO).

Lézine, A., 1951. 'Le temple du nord à Tanis', *Kêmi* 12, pp. 46–58.

Lichtheim, M., 1980. *Ancient Egyptian literature: a book of readings, III: the Late Period* (Los Angeles, University of California Press).

Lillios, K., 1999. 'Objects of memory: the ethnography and archaeology of heirlooms', *J Archaeol Method Th* 6 (3), pp. 235–262.

Limme, L., 2008. 'Elkab, 1937–2007: seventy years of Belgian archaeological research', *BMSAES* 9, pp. 15–50.

Liszka, K., 2010. '"Medjay" (no. 188) in the onomasticon of Amenemope', in Hawass, Z., and J. H. Wegner (eds.), *Millions of jubilees: studies in honor of David P. Silverman*, vol. 1 (Cairo, Supreme Council of Antiquities), pp. 315–331.

Loat, W. L. S., 1905. *Gurob* (BSAE/ERA 10; London, Bernard Quaritch).

Loret, V., 1916–17. 'Le ⌐⌐⌐ titre', *RT* 38, pp. 61–68.

Lucarelli, R., 2006. *The Book of the Dead of Gatseshen: ancient Egyptian funerary religion in the 10th century BC* (Leiden, Peeters).

2009. 'Popular beliefs in demons in the Libyan Period: The evidence of the oracular amuletic decrees', in Broekman, G. P. F., R. J. Demarée, and O. E. Kaper (eds.), *The Libyan Period in Egypt: historical and cultural studies into the 21st–24th Dynasties.*

Proceedings of a conference at Leiden University, 25–27 October 2007 (EgUit 23; Nederlands Instituut voor het Nabije Oosten, Leuven, Peeters), pp. 231–239.

Luckenbill, D. D., 1989. *Ancient records of Assyria and Babylonia, vol. II: historical records of Assyria from Sargon to the end* (Chicago, University of Chicago Press).

Lull, J., 2006. *Los sumos sacerdotes de Amón tebanos de la wḥm mswt y dinastía XXI (ca. 1083–945 c. C.)* (BAR IS 1469; Oxford, Archaeopress).

Lupo, S., 2015a. 'Egyptian pottery typology in Nile and marl clay', in Lupo, S. (ed.), *Tell el-Ghaba III: a Third Intermediate–Early Saite Period site in the Egyptian eastern Delta; excavations 1995–1999 and 2010 in areas I, II, VI and VIII* (BAR IS 2756; Oxford, Archaeopress), pp. 139–308.

2015b. 'Scarabs, scaraboids and plaques at Tell el-Ghaba', in Lupo, S. (ed.), *Tell el-Ghaba III: a Third Intermediate–Early Saite Period site in the Egyptian eastern Delta; excavations 1995–1999 and 2010 in areas I, II, VI and VIII* (BAR IS 2756; Oxford, Archaeopress), pp. 387–394.

Lutley, K., and J. Bunbury, 2008. 'The Nile on the move', *EA* 32, pp. 3–5.

Mace, A. C., 1914. 'The Egyptian expedition: excavations at the North Pyramid of Lisht', *BMMA* 9 (10), pp. 207–222.

1921. 'The Egyptian expedition 1920–1921: excavations at Lisht', *BMMA* 16 (11.2), pp. 5–19.

1922. 'The Egyptian expedition 1921–1922: excavations at Lisht', *BMMA* 17 (12.2), pp. 4–18.

Mackay, E., 1910a. 'The great western tombs', in Petrie, W. M. F., E. Mackay, and G. A. Wainwright, *Meydum and Memphis III* (BASE/ERA 18; London, British School of Archaeology in Egypt), pp. 22–24.

1910b. 'The southern mounds and tombs', in Petrie, W. M. F., E. Mackay, and G. A. Wainwright, *Meydum and Memphis III* (BASE/ERA 18; London, British School of Archaeology in Egypt), pp. 35–36.

Malaise, M., 1978. *Les scarabées de coeur dans l'Égypte ancienne* (MRE 4; Brussels, Fondation Égyptologique Reine Élisabeth).

Malek, J., 1978. 'A new sculpture from Mgbt, the town of Mut', *GM* 29, pp. 71–77.

1999. *Topographical bibliography of ancient Egyptian hieroglyphic texts, statues, reliefs and paintings VIII: objects of provenance not known. Part 2: private statues (Dynasty XVIII to the Roman Period), statues of deities* (Oxford, Ashmolean Museum).

Malinine, M., 1953. *Choix de textes juridiques en hiératique 'anormal' et en démotique (XXVe–XXVIIe dynasties): première partie: traduction et commentaire philologique* (BEHE SHP 300; Paris, Honoré Champion).

Malleson, C., 2007. 'Investigating ancient Egyptian towns: a case study of Itj-tawy', in Mairs, R., and A. Stevenson (eds.), *Current research in Egyptology 2005: proceedings of the sixth annual symposium, University of Cambridge, 6–8 January 2005* (Oxford, Oxbow Books), pp. 90–104.

2011. 'Sais archaeobotanical report 2007', in Wilson, P., *Sais I: the Ramesside-Third Intermediate Period at Kom Reba* (EES EM 98; London, Egypt Exploration Society), pp. 267–272.

Marchand, S., 2000. 'Le survey de Dendara (1996–1997)', *CCÉ* 6, pp. 261–297.

Mariette, A., 1880. *Catalogue général des monuments d'Abydos découverts pendant les fouilles de cette ville* (Paris, Imprimerie Nationale).

Marouard, G., 2014. 'Maison-tours et organisation des quartiers domestiques sans les agglomerations du Delta: l'example de Bouto de la Basse Époque aux premiers Laguides', in Marchi, S. (ed.), *Les maison-tours en Égypte durant la Basse-Époque, les périods Ptólemaïque et Romaine. Actes de la table-ronde de Paris. Université Paris-Sorbonne (Paris IV), Novembre 2012* (NeHeT Revue numérique d'Égyptologie 2; Paris), pp. 29–30.

Martin, G. T., 1987. 'Erotic figurines: the Cairo Museum material', *GM* 96, pp. 71–84.

Maspero, G., 1889. *Les momies royales de Déir El-Baharî* (MMAF 1 (4); Paris, Ernest Leroux), pp. 511–787.

1890–1. 'Notes au jour le jour', *PSBA* 13, pp. 298–315, 407–437, 496–525.

1898. 'Notes au jour le jour', *PSBA* 20, pp. 123–144.

1912. *Rapports sur la marche du Service des Antiquités de 1899 à 1910* (Gouvernement Égyptien; Cairo, Imprimiere Nationale).

Masson, A., 2007. 'Le quartier des prêtres du temple de Karnak: rapport préliminaire de la fouille de la Maison VII, 2001–2003', *Karnak* 12 (2), pp. 593–655.

Maystre, C., 1992. *Les grands prêtres de Ptah de Memphis* (OBO 113; Göttingen, Vandenhoeck & Ruprecht).

Meeks, D., 1979. 'Les donations aux temples dans l'Égypte du Ier millénaire avent J.-C.', in Lipiński, E. (ed.), *State and temple economy in the ancient Near East: proceedings of the international conference organized by the Katholieke Universiteit Leuven from the 10th to the 14th of April 1978* (OLA 5; Leuven, Department Orientalistiek), pp. 605–687.

2006. *Mythes et légendes du Delta d'après le papyrus Brooklyn 47.218.84* (MIFAO 125; Cairo, IFAO).

2009. 'Une stèle de donation de la Deuxième Période intermédiaire', *ENiM* 2, pp. 129–154.

Meffre, R., 2010. 'Un nouveau nom d'Horus d'or de Sheshonq Ier sur le bloc Caire JE 39410', *BIFAO* 110, pp. 221–234.

2015. *D'Héracléopolis à Hermopolis: la Moyenne Égypte durant la Troisième Période Intermédiaire (XXIe–XXIVe Dynasties)* (Passé présent; Paris, Presses de l'Université Paris-Sorbonne).

Merrillees, R. S., 1968. *The Cypriote Bronze Age pottery found in Egypt* (SMA 18; Lund, P. Åström).

Meskell, L., 1998. 'An archaeology of social relations in an Egyptian village', *J Archaeol Method Th* 5 (3), pp. 209–243.

2002. *Private life in New Kingdom Egypt* (Princeton, Princeton University Press).

Miller, R. L., 1990. 'Hogs and hygiene', *JEA* 76, pp. 125–141.

Miller-Rosen, A., 1986. *Cities of clay: the geoarchaeology of tells* (Prehistoric and Ecology Series; Chicago, University of Chicago Press).

Mills, A. J., 1983. 'The Dakhleh Oasis Project: report on the fifth season of survey, October, 1982–January, 1983', *JSSEA* 13 (3), pp. 121–141.

Minault-Gout, A., 1983. 'Rapport préliminaire sur la quatrième campagne de fouilles du mastaba II à Balat (oasis de Dakhleh): neuf tombes du secteur nord', *ASAE* 69, pp. 113–119.

Mission égypto-française d'Atfih, 2010. 'Atfih, la zone central de l'Hésateum (zone A). Travaux dans la nécropole des vaches sacrées (1) (Octobre 2008, November 2009), *ENiM* 3, pp. 137–165.

Mladjov, I., 2017. 'The transition between the Twentieth and Twenty-First dynasties revisited', *Birmingham Egyptology Journal* 5, pp. 1–23.

Moeller, N., 2004. 'Evidence for urban walling in the third millennium BC', *CAJ* 14 (2), pp. 260–265.

2010. 'Tell Edfu: preliminary report on season 2005–2009', *JARCE* 46, pp. 81–111.

2016. *The archaeology of urbanism in ancient Egypt: from the predynastic period to the end of the Middle Kingdom* (Cambridge, Cambridge University Press).

Moje, J., 2014. *Herrschaftsräume und Herrschaftswissen ägyptischer Lokalregenten: Soziokulturelle Interaktionen zur Machtkonsolidierung vom 8. Bis zum 4. Jahrhundert v. Chr.* (TOPOI 21; Berlin, Walter de Gruyter).

Mokhtar, M. G. E., 1983. *Ihnâsya el-Medina (Hérakleopolis Magna), its importance and its role in pharaonic history* (BdE 40; Cairo, IFAO).

Monnet, J., 1954. 'Nouveaux documents relatifs à l'Horus-Rê de Sakhebou', *Kêmi* 13, pp. 28–32.

Montet, P., 1947. 'La quatorzième campagne de fouilles à Sân el Hagar', *ASAE* 47, pp. 249–260.

1949. 'Les divinités du temple de Behbeit el-Hagar', *Kêmi* 10, pp. 43–48.

1952. *Les énigmes de Tanis* (Bibliothèque historique; Paris, Payot).

1957. *Géographie de l'Égypte ancienne, première partie : To-Mehou, la Basse Égypte* (Paris, Imprimerie Nationale).

1961. *Géographie de l'Égypte ancienne, deuxième partie: To-Chemâ, la Haute Égypte* (Paris, Librairie C. Klincksieck).

1966. *Le lac sacré de Tanis* (Paris, Imprimerie Nationale).

Mostafa, I. A., 1986. 'Tell Fara'on-Imet', *BCE* 11, pp. 8–12.

Muchiki, Y., 1999. *Egyptian proper names and loanwords in North-West Semitic* (SBL Dissertation Series 173; Atlanta, Society of Biblical Literature).

Mühs, B. P., 2015. 'Property title, domestic architecture, and household lifecycles in Egypt', in Müller, M. (ed.), *Household studies in complex societies: (micro) archaeological and textual*

approaches (OIS 10; Illinois, Oriental Institute of the University of Chicago), pp. 321–339.

Müller, M., 1887–8. 'A contribution to the Exodus geography', *PSBA* 10, pp. 467–477.

Müller, M., 2009. 'The "el-Hibeh" Archive: introduction and preliminary information', in Broekman, G. P. F., R. J. Demarée, and O. E. Kaper (eds.), *The Libyan Period in Egypt: historical and cultural studies into the 21st–24th Dynasties. Proceedings of a conference at Leiden University, 25–27 October 2007* (EgUit 23; Nederlands Instituut voor het Nabije Oosten, Leuven, Peeters), pp. 251–265.

2015. 'Introduction: household studies in complex societies: (micro) archaeological and textual approaches', in Müller, M. (ed.), *Household studies in complex societies: (micro) archaeological and textual approaches* (OIS 10; Illinois, Oriental Institute of the University of Chicago), pp. xiii–xlii.

Müller-Winkler, C., 1987. *Die ägyptischen Objekt-Amulette: mit Publikation der Sammlung des Biblischen Instituts der Universität Freiburg Schweiz, ehemals Sammlung Fouad S. Matouk* (OBO 5; Göttingen, Vandenhoeck & Ruprecht).

Mumford, G., 2013. 'A Late Period riverine and maritime port town and cult center at Tell Tebilla (Ro-nefer)', *JAEI* 5 (1), pp. 38–67.

Munro, P., 1973. *Die spätägyptischen Totenstelen* (ÄF 25; Glückstadt, J. J. Augustin).

Murray, G. W., 1950. (ed.), *Survey of Egypt: 1898–1948* (Cairo, Survey Department Paper).

Naville, E., 1885. *The store-city of Pithom and the route of the Exodus* (MEEF 1; London, Trübner).

1887. *The shrine of Saft el Henneh and the land of Goshen (1885)* (MEEF 5; London, Trübner).

1891. *Bubastis (1887–1889)* (MEEF 8; London, Kegan Paul, Trench, Trübner & Co.).

1892. *The festival-hall of Osorkon II in the great temple of Bubastis (1887–1889)* (MEEF 10; London, Kegan Paul, Trench, Trübner & Co.).

1894. *Ahnas el Medineh* (MEEF 11; London, Egypt Exploration Fund).

Nelson, J. L., 2007. 'Dark ages', *HWJ* 63, pp. 191–201.

Nevett, L. C., 1999. *House and society in the ancient Greek world* (Cambridge, Cambridge University Press).

Nibbi, A., 1979. 'Some rapidly disappearing and unrecorded sites in the eastern Delta', *GM* 35, pp. 41–46.

Nicholson, P. T., 1993. *Egyptian faience and glass* (SE 18; Princes Risborough, Shire).

Niwiński, A., 1989. *Studies on the illustrated funerary papyri of the 11th and 10th centuries BC* (Göttingen, Vandenhoeck & Ruprecht).

1995. 'Le passage de la XXe à la XXIIe dynastie: chronologie et histoire politique', *BIFAO* 95, pp. 329–360.

Northampton, Marquis of, W. Spiegelberg, and P. E. Newberry, 1908. *Report on some excavations in the Theban necropolis during the winter of 1898–9* (London, Constable).

O'Connor, D., 1983. 'New Kingdom and Third Intermediate Period, 1552–664 BC' in Trigger, B. G., B. J. Kemp, D. O'Connor, and A. B. Lloyd (eds.) *Ancient Egypt: a social history* (Cambridge, Cambridge University Press), pp. 183–279.

1989. 'City and palace in New Kingdom Egypt', *CRIPEL* 11, pp. 73–87.

1991. 'Mirror of the cosmos: the palace of Merenptah', in Bleiberg, E., and R. Freed (eds.), *Fragments of a shattered visage: the proceedings of the International Symposium of Ramesses the Great* (Monographs of the Institute of Egyptian Art and Archaeology; Memphis, Memphis State University), pp. 167–198.

1995. 'Beloved of Maat, the horizon of Re: the royal palace in New Kingdom Egypt', in O'Connor, D., and D. P. Silverman (eds.), *Ancient Egyptian kingship* (PdÄ 9; Leiden, Brill), pp. 263–300.

2009. *Abydos: Egypt's first pharaohs and the cult of Osiris* (New Aspects of Antiquity; London, Thames and Hudson).

Ohshiro, M., 2017. 'Searching for the tomb of the Theban King Osorkon III', in Jurman, C., B. Bader, and D. A. Aston (eds.), *A true scribe of Abydos: essays on first millennium Egypt in honour of Anthony Leahy* (Leuven, Peeters), pp. 299–317.

Osing, J., M. Moursi, D. Arnold, O. Neugebauer, R. A. Parker, D. Pingree, and M. A. Nur el-Din, 1982. *Denkmäler der Oase Dachla: aus dem Nachlass von Ahmed Fakhry* (AVDAIK 28; Mainz am Rheim, Philipp von Zabern).

Otto, E., 1952. *Topographie des Thebanischen Gaues* (UGAAe 16; Berlin, Akademie-Verlag).

Page-Gasser, M., and A. Wiese, 1997. *Ägypten: Augenblick der Ewigkeit: Unbekannte Schätze aus schweizer Privatbesitz* (Mainz am Rhein, Philipp von Zabern).

Palmer, J., 2014. 'The high priests of Amun at the end of the Twentieth Dynasty', *Birmingham Egyptology Journal* 2, pp. 1–22.

Papadopoulos, J., 2002. 'A contextual approach to pessoi (gaming pieces, counters or convenient wipes?)', *Hesperia* 71, pp. 423–427.

Papazian, H., 2013. 'The central administration of the resources in the Old Kingdom: departments, treasuries, granaries and work centers', in

Moreno García, J. C. (ed.), *Ancient Egyptian administration* (HdO erste Abteilung: Der Nahe und Mittlere Osten 104; Leiden, Brill), pp. 41–83.

Parcak, S., 2004. 'Satellite remote sensing resources for Egyptologists', *GM* 198, pp. 63–78.

2006. 'Fieldwork, 2005–06: the Middle Egypt Survey Project, 2004–06', *JEA* 92, pp. 57–61.

2007. 'Satellite remote sensing methods for monitoring archaeological tells in the Middle East', *JFA* 32, pp. 65–81.

2009. 'The skeptical remote senser: Google Earth and Egyptian archaeology', in Ikram, S., and A. Dodson (eds.), *Beyond the horizon: studies in Egyptian art, archaeology and history in honour of Barry J. Kemp* (Cairo, Supreme Council of Antiquities), pp. 362–382.

Parker, B. J., and C. P. Foster, 2012. 'Introduction: household archaeology in the Near East and beyond', in Parker, B. J., and C. P. Foster (eds.), *New perspectives on household archaeology* (Winona Lake, Eisenbrauns), pp. 1–12.

Parkinson, R. B., 1991. *Voices from ancient Egypt: an anthology of Middle Kingdom writings* (London, British Museum Press).

Parlebas, J., 1977. 'Les Égyptiens et la ville d'après les sources littéraires et archéologiques', *Ktèma* 2, pp. 49–57.

Pavlish, L. A., 2004. 'Archaeometry at Mendes: 1990–2002', in Knoppers, G. N., and A. Hirsch (eds.), *Egypt, Israel, and the ancient Mediterranean world: studies in honor of Donald B. Redford* (PdÄ 20; Leiden, Brill), pp. 61–112.

Pavlish, L. A., G. Mumford, and A. C. D'Andrea, 2003. 'Geotechnical survey at Tell Tabilla, northeastern Nile Delta, Egypt', in Hawass, Z., and L. Pinch Brook (eds.), *Egyptology at the dawn of the twenty-first century:*

proceedings of the Eighth International Congress of Egyptologists, Cairo, 2000 (Cairo, American University in Cairo Press), pp. 361–368.

Payraudeau, F., 2003. 'Harsiésis, un vizir oublié de l'Époque Libyenne?', *JEA* 89, pp. 199–205.

2014. 'Retour sur la succession Shabaqo–Shabataqo', *NeHet* 1, pp. 115–127.

Peet, T. E., 1930. *The great tomb-robberies of the Twentieth Egyptian Dynasty: being a critical study, with translations and commentaries, of the papyri in which these are recorded* (Oxford, Clarendon Press).

Peet, T. E., and L. Woolley, 1923. *The city of Akhenaten, part 1: excavations of 1921 and 1922 at El-'Amarneh* (MEES 38; London, Egypt Exploration Society).

Pellegrini, A., 1898. 'Glanures', *RT* 20, pp. 86–99.

Peña, J. T., 2007. *Roman pottery in the archaeological record* (Cambridge, Cambridge University Press).

Perdu, O., 2002a. *Recueil des inscriptions royales saïtes, vol. 1: Psammétique Ier* (ÉdÉ 1; Paris, Cybele).

2002b. 'Le roi Roudamon en personne!', *RdE* 53, pp. 157–158.

2003. 'De la "chronique d'Osorkon" aux annales héliopolitaines de la Troisème Période Intermédiare', in Grimal, N., and M. Baud (eds.), *Événement, récit, histoire officielle: l'écriture de l'histoire dans les monarchies antiques: actes du colloque du College de France 2002* (Paris, Cybele), pp. 129–142.

2009. 'Une sistrophore d'un nouveau genre au nom du fameux Montouemhat', in Claes, W., H. de Meulenaere, and S. Hendrickx (eds.), *Elkab and beyond: studies in honour of Luc Limme* (OLA 191; Leuven, Peeters), pp. 457–475.

Pérez-Die, M. C., 2009. 'The Third Intermediate Period necropolis at Herakleopolis Magna', in

Broekman, G. P. F., R. J. Demarée, and O. E. Kaper (eds.), *The Libyan Period in Egypt: historical and cultural studies into the 21st–24th Dynasties. Proceedings of a conference at Leiden University, 25–27 October 2007* (EgUit 23; Nederlands Instituut voor het Nabije Oosten, Leuven, Peeters), pp. 265–275.

2010. (ed.), *Heracleópolis Magna (Ehnasya el Medina, Egipto): la necrópolis 'real' des Tercer Período Intermedio y su reutilización* (Madrid, Gobierno de Espana, Ministerio de Cultura).

Pérez-Die, M. C., and P. Vernus, 1992. *Excavaciones en Ehnasya el Medina (Heracleópolis Magna): introducción general, inscripciones* (Informes Arqueológicos, Egipto 1; Madrid, Ministerio de Cultura, Dirección General de Bellas Artes y Archivos, Instituto de Conservación y Restauración de Bienes Culturales).

Petersen, B., 1977. 'Gesicht und Kunststil. Ein Reportorium der ägyptischen Kunstentwicklung der Spätzeit anhand von Grabfiguren', *Medelhavsmuseet Bulletin* 12, pp. 12–37.

Petrie, W. M. F., 1890. *Kahun, Gurob and Hawara* (London, Kegan Paul, Trench, Trübner, and Co.).

1891. *Illahun, Kahun and Gurob, 1889–90* (London, David Nutt).

1892. *Medum* (London, David Nutt).

1896. *Koptos* (London, Bernard Quaritch).

1900. *Dendereh, 1898* (MEEF 17; London, Egypt Exploration Fund).

1905. *Ehnasya, 1904* (MEEF 26; London, Egypt Exploration Fund).

1906. *Hyksos and Israelite cities* (BSAE 12; London, Bernard Quaritch).

1909. *Memphis I* (BSAE/ERA 15; London, Bernard Quaritch).

1912. 'The tombs of the XIIth Dynasty', in Petrie, W. M. F., G. A. Wainwright, and E. Mackay, *The labyrinth, Gerzeh and Mazghuneh* (BSAE/ERA 21; London, Bernard Quaritch), pp. 35–37.

1914a. *Amulets: illustrated by the Egyptian collection in University College, London* (London, Constable).

1914b. *Tarkhan II* (BSAE/ERA 26; London, Bernard Quaritch).

1917a. *Scarabs and cylinders with names* (BSAE/ERA 29; London, Constable, Bernard Quaritch).

1917b. *Tools and weapons: illustrated by the Egyptian collection in University College, London* (BSAE/ERA 30; London, Constable, Bernard Quaritch).

1927. *Objects of daily use with over 1800 figures from University College, London* (BSAE/ERA 42; London, Bernard Quaritch).

Petrie, W. M. F., and G. Brunton, 1924a. *Sedment I* (BSAE/ERA 34; London, Bernard Quaritch).

1924b. *Sedment II* (BSAE/ERA 35; London, Bernard Quaritch).

Petrie, W. M. F., and E. Mackay, 1915. *Heliopolis, Kafr Ammar and Shurafa* (BSAE/ERA 24; London, Bernard Quaritch).

Piankoff, A., and N. Rambova, 1957. *Mythological papyri* (New York, Pantheon).

Piccione, P. A., 1990. *The historical development of the game of Senet and its significance for Egyptian religion*, 2 vols. (Ann Arbor, MI, UMI).

Pierce, R. H., and L. Török, 1994. 'Stela of Taharqo on the race of his soldiers from the Dashur road', in Eide, T., T. Hägg, R. H. Pierce, and L. Török (eds.), *Fontes Historiae Nubiorum. Textual sources for the history of the middle Nile region between the eighth century BC and the sixth century AD, vol. 1: from the eighth to the mid-fifth century BC* (Bergen, University of Bergen, Department of Classics), pp. 158–163.

Pierrat-Bonnefois, G., 2000. 'La céramique dynastique et ptolémaïque des fouilles du Louvre à Tôd: 1989–1991', *CCÉ* 6, pp. 299–342.

Pinch, G., 1993. *Votive offerings for Hathor* (Oxford, Griffith Institute, Ashmolean Museum).

Pinder, I., 2011. 'Constructing and deconstructing Roman city walls: the contribution of urban enceintes to an understanding of the concept of borders', in Mullin, D. (ed.), *Places in between: the archaeology of social, cultural and geographical borders and borderlands* (Oxford, Oxbow Books).

Porter, B., and R. L. B. Moss, 1929. *Topographical bibliography of ancient Egyptian hieroglyphic texts, reliefs, and paintings, vol. II: Theban temples* (Oxford, Clarendon Press).

—— 1931. *Topographical bibliography of ancient Egyptian hieroglyphic texts, reliefs, and paintings, vol. III: Memphis, part 2: Saqqâra to Dahshûr* (Oxford, Oxford University Press).

—— 1934. *Topographical bibliography of ancient Egyptian hieroglyphic texts, reliefs, and paintings, vol. IV: Lower and Middle Egypt (Delta and Cairo to Asyût)* (Oxford, Clarendon Press).

—— 1937. *Topographical bibliography of ancient Egyptian hieroglyphic texts, reliefs, and paintings, vol. V: Upper Egypt: sites (Deir Rîfa to Aswân, excluding Thebes and the temples of Abydos, Dendera, Esna, Edfu, Kôm Ombo and Philae)* (Oxford, Clarendon Press).

—— 1939. *Topographical bibliography of ancient Egyptian hieroglyphic texts, reliefs, and paintings, vol. VI: Upper Egypt chief temples* (Oxford, Oxford University Press).

Posener, G., 1940. '*ḏkᶜpyr*, Métropole du IVe nome de basse-égypte', *RdE* 4, pp. 228–229.

Prell, S., 2011. *Einblicke in der Werkstätten der Residenz. Die Stein und Metallwerkzeuge des Grabungsplatz Q1* (Forshungen in der Ramses Stadt 8; Hildesheim, Gerstenberg).

Pusch, E. B., 1979. *Das Senet-Brettspiel im alten Ägypten: Teil 1. Das inschriftliche und archäologische Material* (MÄS 38, Munich, Deutscher Kunstverlag).

—— 1989. 'Bericht über die sechste Hauptkampagne in Qantir/Piramesse-Nord: Herbst 1988', *GM* 112, pp. 67–90.

—— 1999a. 'Tausret und Sethos II in der Ramses-Stadt', *Ä&L* 9, pp. 101–109.

—— 1999b. 'Towards a map of Piramesse', *EA* 14, pp. 13–15.

—— 1999c. 'Vorbericht über die Abschlußkampagne am Grabungsplatz Q IV 1997', *Ä&L* 9, pp. 19–37.

Pusch, E. B., H. Becker, and J. Fassbinder, 1999. 'Wohnen und Leben. Oder: weitere Schritte zu einem Stadtplan der Ramses-Stadt', *Ä&L* 9, pp. 155–170.

Quaegebeur, J., 1982. *Studia Paulo Naster oblata II: orientalia antiqua* (OLA 13; Departement Orientalistiek/ Uitgeverij, Leuven, Peeters).

—— 1989. 'Le petit obélisque d'Elkab et la Dame du terroir d'en haut', *CdÉ* 64, pp. 121–133.

Quibell, J. E., 1907. *Excavations at Saqqara (1905–1906)* (Cairo, IFAO).

—— 1923. *Excavations at Saqqara (1912–1914): archaic mastabas* (Cairo, IFAO).

Quibell, J. E., and A. G. K. Hayter, 1927. *Excavations at Saqqara: Teti pyramid, north side* (Cairo, IFAO).

Rainville, L., 2015. 'Investigating traces of everyday life in ancient households: some methodological considerations', in Müller, M. (ed.), *Household studies in complex societies: (micro) archaeological and textual approaches* (OIS 10; Chicago, Oriental Institute of the University of Chicago), pp. 1–27.

Ramzi, M., 1953. *Das Geographische Wörterbuch der Ägyptischen Städte und Dörfer* (Cairo).

Ranke, H., 1926. *Koptische Friedhöfe bei Karara und der Amontempel Scheschonks*

I bei El-Hibe, Bericht über die badischen Grabungen in Ägypten in den Wintern 1913 und 1914 (Berlin, Walter de Gruyter).

1935. *Die Ägyptischen Personennamen. I, Verzeichnis Der Namen* (Glückstadt, Augustin).

Raue, D., 2010. 'Third Intermediate Period: King Ini on Elephantine', in Arnold, F., et al., 'Report on the 37th season of excavation and restoration on the island of Elephantine', *ASAE* 84, pp. 343–362.

Raven, M. J., 1991. *The tomb of Iurudef: a Memphite official in the reign of Ramesses II* (EES EM 57; London, Egypt Exploration Society).

Redford, D. B., 1973. 'An interim report on the second season of work at the temple of Osiris', *JEA* 59, pp. 16–30.

1986. 'New light on Temple J at Karnak', *Orientalia* 55, pp. 1–15.

2004. *Excavations at Mendes, vol. 1: the royal necropolis* (CHANE 20; Leiden, Brill).

2010. *City of the Ram-Man: the story of ancient Mendes* (Princeton, Princeton University Press).

Redman, C. L., 1999. 'The development of archaeological theory: explaining the past', in Barker, G. (ed.), *Companion encyclopaedia of archaeology, vol. i* (London, Routledge), pp. 48–80.

Redman, C. L., and P. J. Watson, 1970. 'Systematic intensive surface collection', *AmerAnt* 35, pp. 279–291.

Revillout, E., 1891. 'Un papyrus bilingue du temps de Philopator', *PSBA* 14, pp. 60–97, 120–132, 229–255.

Ritner, R. K., 2009a. 'Fragmentation and re-integration in the Third Intermediate Period', in Broekman, G. P. F., R. J. Demarée, and O. E. Kaper (eds.), *The Libyan Period in Egypt: historical and cultural studies into the 21st–24th Dynasties. Proceedings of a conference at Leiden University, 25–27 October 2007* (EgUit

23; Nederlands Instituut voor het Nabije Oosten, Leuven, Peeters), pp. 327–340.

2009b. *The Libyan Anarchy: inscriptions from Egypt's Third Intermediate Period* (Atlanta, Society of Biblical Literature).

Roeder, G., 1914. *Naos* (CGC 70001–70050; Leipzig, Breitkopf & Härtel).

1931–2. *Vorläufiger Bericht über die Ausgrabungen in Hermopolis, 1929–1932* (Vienna, Druck von Adolf Holzhausens Nachfolger).

1959. *Hermopolis, 1929–1939: Ausgrabungen der Deutschen Hermopolis-Expedition in Hermopolis, Ober-Ägypten* (Pelizâus-Museum zu Hildesheim – Wissenschaftliche Veröffentlichung 4; Hildesheim, Verlag Gebrüder Gerstenberg).

Romer, J., 2016. *A history of ancient Egypt, vol. ii: From the Great Pyramid to the fall of the Middle Kingdom* (Harmondsworth, Penguin Books).

Römer, M., 1994. *Gottes- und Priesterherrschaft in Ägypten am Ende des Neuen Reiches: Ein Religionsgeschichtliches Phänomen und Seine Sozialen Grundlagen* (ÄUAT 21; Wiesbaden, Otto Harrassowitz Verlag).

Rössler-Köhler, U., 1999. *Zur Tradierungsgschichte des Totenbuches zwischen der 17. und 22. Dynastie* (Bonn, Otto Harrassowitz Verlag).

Rowe, A., 1931. 'The Eckley B Coxe Jr expedition excavations at Meydûm', *UPMJ* 22, pp. 5–46.

Rowland, J., 2007. 'The Delta survey: Minufiyeh province, 2006–7', *JEA* 93, pp. 65–77.

Rowland, J., and N. Billing, 2006. 'The EES Delta survey: Minufiyeh 2005', *EA* 28, pp. 3–6.

Rowland, J., and A. J. Spencer, 2011. 'The EES Delta survey in spring 2011', *EA* 39, pp. 3–5.

Rowland, J., and K. D. Strutt, 2012. 'Geophysical survey and sub-surface investigations at Quesna and Kom el-Ahmar (Minuf), governorate of Minufiyeh: an integrated strategy for mapping and understanding sub-surface remains of mortuary, sacred and domestic contexts', in Belova, G. A., and S. V. Ivanov (eds.), *Achievements and problems of modern Egyptology: proceedings of the international conference held in Moscow on September 29–October 2, 2009* (Moscow, Russian Academy of Sciences), pp. 328–345.

Rowland, J., and P. Wilson, 2006. 'Fieldwork: the Delta survey, 2004–05', *JEA* 92, pp. 1–13.

Rowland, J., K. Edinborough, R. Phillipps, and A. el-Senussi, 2009. 'The Delta survey: Minufiyeh province, 2008–9', *JEA* 95, pp. 35–49.

Rowlands, M. J., 1972. 'Defense: a factor in the organization of settlements', in Ucko, P. J., R. Tringham, and G. W. Dimbleby (eds.), *Man, settlement and urbanism: proceedings of a meeting of the Research Seminar in Archaeology and Related Subjects held at the Institute of Archaeology, London University* (London, Duckworth), pp. 447–462.

Rubensohn, O., and F. Knatz, 1904. 'Bericht über die Ausgrabungen bei Abusir el Mäläq im Jahre 1903', *ZÄS* 41, pp. 1–21.

Rzepka, S., 2011. 'Third Intermediate Period houses and workshops', in Rzepka, S., A. Wodzińska, C. Malleson et al., 'New Kingdom and the Third Intermediate Period in Tell el-Retaba: results of the Polish–Slovak Archaeological Mission, seasons 2009–2010', *Ä&L* 21, pp. 135–138 (129–184).

Sadek, A. A., 1985. *Contribution à l'étude de l'Amdouat. Les variantes tardives dans les papyrus du Musée du Caire* (Freiburg, Vandenhoeck & Ruprecht).

Sagrillo, T. L., 2009. 'The geographic origins of the "Bubastite" Dynasty and possible locations for the royal residence and burial place of Shoshenq I', in Broekman, G. P. F., R. J. Demarée, and O. E. Kaper (eds.), *The Libyan Period in Egypt: historical and cultural studies into the 21st–24th Dynasties. Proceedings of a conference at Leiden University, 25–27 October 2007* (EgUit 23; Nederlands Instituut voor het Nabije Oosten, Leuven, Peeters), pp. 341–361.

Samuel, D., 1999. 'Bread making and social interactions at the Amarna workmen's village, Egypt', *WorldArch* 31 (1), pp. 121–144.

Satzinger, H., 1974. 'Zu den Men-cheper-Rēꜥ-Skarabäen', *StudAeg* 1, pp. 329–337.

Sauneron, S., 1950. 'La ville de sAXbw', *Kêmi* 11, pp. 63–72.

——— 1955. 'Sakhebou (troisième article)', *BIFAO* 55, pp. 61–64.

Schadewaldt, H., 1983. 'Von der Cloaca maxima bis zur modernen Kläranlage-historische Aspeckte zur Abfallbeseitigung', *Zentralblatt für Bakteriologie, Mikrobiologie und Hygiene, I. Abt. Orig. B* 178, pp. 68–80.

Schenkel, W., 1987. 'Über den Umgang mit Quellen: Al-Kōm al-Aḥmar/ Šꜣarūna', in Assmann, J., V. Davies, and G. Burkard (eds.), *Problems and priorities in Egyptian archaeology* (London, Kegan Paul International), pp. 149–173.

Schiaparelli, E., 1921. 'La missione italiana a Ghebelein', *ASAE* 21, pp. 126–128.

Schiestl, R., 2010. *Regional Survey Governorate Kafr esh-Shaikh: report on the first season, spring 2010*, pp. 1–20 (pdf) accessed from: www.academia.edu/1871573/Regiona l_Survey_around_Buto_-_First_Repor t_Spring_2010 Accessed on 8/1/2017.

——— 2012. 'Investigating ancient settlements around Buto', *EA* 40, pp. 18–20.

——— 2014. 'Field boundaries and ancient settlement sites: observations from the regional survey around Buto, western Delta', *MDAIK* 68, pp. 175–190.

Schlick-Nolte, B., 1999. 'Ägyptische Fayence und Ägyptisch Blau im Alten Ägypten', in Busz, R., and P. Gercke (eds.), *Türkis und Azur: Quarzkeramik im Orient und Okzident* (Wolfratshausen, Edition Minerva), pp. 12–51.

Schlick-Nolte, B., and V. von Droste zu Hülschoff, 1990. *Skarabäen, Amulette und Schmuck* (Liebieghaus, Museum Alter Plastik, Ägyptische Bildwerke, 1; Gutenberg, Melsungen).

Schott, S., 1937. In Vogliano, A., *Secondo rapport degli scavi condotti della missione archeologica d'Egitto della R. Università di Milano nella zona di Madinet Madi (campagna inverno e primavera 1936–1937)* (Milan, Pubblicazioni della regia università di Milano).

Schulman, A. R., 1966. 'A problem of Pedubasts', *JARCE* 5, pp. 33–41.

1980. 'Two unrecognized monuments of Shedsunefertem', *JNES* 39 (4), pp. 303–311.

Schulte, A. R., and D. Arnold, 1978. *Meisterwerke altägyptischer Keramik: 5000 Jahre Kunst und Kunsthandwerk aus Ton und Fayence: 16. September bis 30. November 1978, Höhr-Grenzhausen, Rastal Haus* (Höhr-Grenzhausen, Keramikmuseum Westerwald).

Schulz, R., 1992. *Die Entwicklung und Bedeutung des kuboiden Statuentypus: eine Untersuchung zu den sogenannten 'Würfelhockern'* (HÄB; Hildesheim, Gerstenberg), pp. 33–34.

Schumacher, I. W., 1988. *Der Gott Sopdu: der Herr der Fremdländer* (OBO 79; Göttingen, Vandenhoeck & Ruprecht).

Seidlmayer, S., 1982. 'Stadt und Tempel von Elephantine: Neunter/Zehnter Grabungsbericht', *MDAIK* 38, pp. 271–345.

2000. 'The First Intermediate Period (*c.*2160–2055 BC)', in Shaw, I. (ed.), *The Oxford history of ancient Egypt* (Oxford, Oxford University Press), pp. 108–137.

Seipel, W., 1989. *Ägypten: Götter, Gräber und die Kunst: 4000 Jahre Jenseitsglaube* (Katalogue des Oberösterreichischen Landesmuseums 22; Linz, Landesmuseum).

Shanks, M., and C. Tilley, 1992. *Re-constructing archaeology* (2nd edition) (London, Routledge).

Shaw, I., 1992. 'Ideal homes in ancient Egypt: the archaeology of social aspiration', *CAJ* 2 (2), pp. 147–166.

2012. *Ancient Egyptian technology and innovation: transformations in pharaonic material culture* (London, Bloomsbury Academic Press).

Sheikholeslami, C. M., 2009. 'Breast or paw? Thoughts on the Osorkon III stela from Ashmunein', in Magee, D., J. Bourriau, and S. Quirke (eds.), *Sitting beside Lepsius: studies in honour of Jaromir Malek at the Griffith Institute* (OLA 185; Leuven, Peeters), pp. 515–529.

Smekalova, T. N., A. J. Mills, and T. Herbich, 2003. 'Magnetic survey at 'Ain el-Gazzareen', in Bowen, G. E., and C. A. Hope (eds.), *The oasis papers 3: proceedings of the Third International Conference of the Dakhleh Oasis Project* (Oxford, Oxbow Books), pp. 131–135.

Smith, H. S., 1972. 'Society and settlement in ancient Egypt', in Ucko, P. J., R. Tringham, and G. W. Dimbleby (eds.), *Man, settlement and urbanism: proceedings of a meeting of the Research Seminar in Archaeology and Related Subjects held at the Institute of Archaeology, London University* (London, Duckworth), pp. 705–719.

Smith, H. S., and D. G. Jeffreys, 1980. 'The "Anubieion", north Saqqâra: preliminary report, 1978–9', *JEA* 66, pp. 17–27.

Smith, H. S., and A. Smith, 1976. 'A reconsideration of the Kamose Texts', *ZÄS* 103, pp. 48–76.

Smith, H. S., D. G. Jeffreys, and J. Malek, 1983. 'The survey of Memphis, 1981', *JEA* 69, pp. 30–42.

Smoláriková, K., 2014. 'Ceramics from the Ramesside enclosure', in Spencer, N., *Kom Firin II: the urban fabric and landscape* (British Museum Research Paper 192; London, British Museum Press), pp. 47–53.

Snape, S., 1986. *Six archaeological sites in Sharqiyeh province* (Liverpool, Liverpool University Press).

——— 2014. *The complete cities of ancient Egypt* (London, Thames and Hudson).

Spalinger, A. J., 2005. *War in ancient Egypt* (Ancient World at War Series; Maldon, Blackwell).

Spence, K., 2004a. 'Royal walling projects in the second millennium BC: beyond an interpretation of defence', *CAJ* 14 (2), pp. 265–271.

——— 2004b. 'The three-dimensional form of the Amarna House', *JEA* 90, pp. 123–152.

——— 2010. 'Settlement structure and social interaction at El-Amarna', in Bietak, M., E. Czerny, and I. Forstner-Müller (eds.), *Cities and urbanism in ancient Egypt: papers from a workshop in November 2006 at the Austrian Academy of Sciences* (DGÖAW 60/UZK 35; Vienna, VÖAW), pp. 289–298.

——— 2015. 'Ancient Egyptian houses and households: architecture, artifacts, conceptualization, and interpretation', in Müller, M. (ed.), *Household studies in complex societies: (micro) archaeological and textual approaches* (OIS 10; Chicago, Oriental Institute of the University of Chicago), pp. 83–101.

Spencer, A. J., 1979. *Brick architecture in ancient Egypt* (Warminster, Aris and Phillips).

——— 1988. 'A glazed composition sistrum handle inscribed for Amenrud', *JEA* 74, p. 232.

——— 1993. *Excavations at el-Ashmunein, III: the town* (British Museum Expedition to Middle Egypt; London, British Museum Press).

——— 1994. 'Mud brick: its decay and detection in Upper and Lower Egypt', in Eyre, C., A. Leahy, and L. Montagno Leahy (eds.), *The unbroken reed: studies in the culture and heritage of ancient Egypt in honour of A. F. Shore* (EES OP 11; London, Egypt Exploration Society), pp. 315–320.

——— 1996. *Excavations at Tell el-Balamun, 1991–1994* (London, British Museum Press).

——— 1999. *Excavations at Tell el-Balamun, 1995–1998* (London, British Museum Press).

——— 2002a. 'The exploration of Tell Belim, 1999–2002', *JEA* 88, pp. 37–51.

——— 2002b. 'Fieldwork, 2001–02: the Delta survey, 2001', *JEA* 88, pp. 6–7.

——— 2003. *Excavations at Tell el-Balamun 3: 1999–2001* (London, British Museum Press).

——— 2007. 'The possible existence of Third Intermediate Period elite tombs at el-Ashmunein', *BMSAES* 8, pp. 49–51.

——— 2009. *Excavations at Tell el-Balamun, 2003–2008* (pdf), available at www.britishmuseum.org/pdf/Book%201.pdf.

——— 2011. 'Tell el-Balamun 2010', *BMSAES* 16, pp. 149–168.

Spencer, A. J., and D. M. Bailey, 1985. *British Museum expedition to Middle Egypt: Ashmunein (1984)* (British Museum Occasional Paper 61; London, British Museum).

Spencer, A. J., and P. Spencer, 1986. 'Notes on late Libyan Egypt', *JEA* 72, pp. 198–201.

——— 2000. 'The EES Delta Survey', *EA* 16, pp. 25–27.

Spencer, N., 2006. *A Naos of Nekhthorheb from Bubastis: religious iconography and temple building in the 30th Dynasty* (British

Museum Research Publication 156; London, British Museum Press).

2007. 'Naville at Bubastis and other sites', in Spencer, P. (ed.), *The Egypt Exploration Society: the early years* (EES OP 16; London, Egypt Exploration Society), pp. 1–31.

2008. *Kom Firin I: the Ramesside temple and the site survey* (British Museum Research Publication 170; London, British Museum Press).

2014. *Kom Firin II: the urban fabric and landscape* (British Museum Research Publication 192; London, British Museum Press).

2015. 'Creating a neighbourhood within a changing town: household and other agencies at Amara West in Nubia', in Müller, M. (ed.), *Household studies in complex societies: (micro) archaeological and textual approaches* (OIS 10; Chicago, Oriental Institute of the University of Chicago), pp. 169–210.

Spencer, P., 1981. 'Studies in the lexicography of ancient Egyptian buildings and their parts' (PhD thesis, University College London).

1989. 'The stela of Osorkon', in Spencer, A. J., *Excavations at el-Ashmunein II: the temple area* (London, British Museum Press), pp. 57–62.

2007. 'Petrie in the Delta', in Spencer, P. (ed.), *The Egypt Exploration Society: the early years* (EES OP 16; London, Egypt Exploration Society), pp. 33–65.

Spiegelberg, W., 1903. 'Die Tefnachthosstele des Museums von Athen', *RT* 25, pp. 190–198.

1906–8. *Die demotischen Denkmäler, II: Die demotischen Papyrus* (CGC 30601–31270, 50001–50022; Strasburg, M. Dumont Schauberg).

Stadelmann, R., 1996. 'Temple palace and residential palace', in Bietak, M. (ed.), *Haus und Palast im Alten Ägypten* (DGÖAW 14/UZK 14; Vienna,

Verlage der Österreichischen Akademie der Wissenschaften), pp. 225–230.

Stanley, J. D., 1988. 'Subsidence in the northeastern Nile Delta: rapid rates, possible causes and consequences', *Science* 240, pp. 497–500.

Stanley, J. D., and A. G. Warne, 1993. 'Nile Delta: recent geological evolution and human impact', *Science* 260, pp. 628–634.

Steadman, S., 2004. 'The architecture of family and society in early sedentary communities on the Anatolian plateau', *J Anthropol Res* 60 (4), pp. 515–558.

Steel, L., 2013. *Materiality and consumption in the Bronze Age Mediterranean* (Routledge Studies in Archaeology 7; London, Routledge).

Steinberg, J. M., 1996. 'Ploughzone sampling in Denmark: isolating and interpreting site signals from disturbed contexts', *Antiquity* 70 (286), pp. 268–292.

Steindorff, G., 1946. *Catalogue of the Egyptian sculpture in the Walters Art Gallery* (Baltimore, The Trustees of the Walters Art Gallery).

Sternberg-El Hotabi, H., 1999. *Untersuchungen zur Überlieferungsgeschichte der Horusstelen: ein Beitrag zur Religionsgeschichte Ägyptens im 1. Jahrtausend v. Chr.* (ÄA 62; Wiesbaden, Harrassowitz).

Stevens, A., 2006. *Private religion at Amarna: the material evidence* (BAR IS 1587; Oxford, Archaeopress).

Stewart, H. M., 1983. *Egyptian stelae, reliefs and paintings from the Petrie Collection, part 3: the Late Period* (Warminster, Aris and Phillips).

Streck, M., 1914. *Assurbanipal und die letzen assyrischen Könige bis zum Untergange Niniveh's* (Vorderasiatische Bibliothek 7; Leipzig, Hinrichs).

Sullivan, E. A., 2013. *A glimpse into ancient Thebes: excavations at South Karnak*

(2004–2006) (BAR IS 2538; Oxford, Archaeopress).

Szpakowska, K., 2003. *Behind closed eyes: dreams and nightmares in ancient Egypt* (Swansea, Classical Press of Wales).

2008. *Daily life in ancient Egypt: recreating Lahun* (Oxford, Blackwell).

Tainter, J. A., 1983. 'Settlement behavior and the archaeological record: concepts for the definition of "archaeological site"', *Contract Abstracts and CRM Archeaology* 3 (2), pp. 130–133.

1999. 'Post-collapse societies', in Barker, G. (ed.), *Companion encyclopaedia of archaeology, vol. II* (London, Routledge), pp. 988–1039.

Tait, G. A. D., 1963. 'The Egyptian relief chalice', *JEA* 49, pp. 93–139.

Tassie, G. J., and L. S. Owens, 2010. *Standards of archaeological excavation: a fieldguide* (ECHO Monograph Series 1; London, Garden House).

Taylor, J. H., 1998. 'Nodjmet, Payankh and Herihor: the end of the New Kingdom reconsidered', in Eyre, C. J. (ed.), *Proceedings of the Seventh International Congress of Egyptologists, Cambridge, 3–9 September 1995* (Leuven, Peeters), pp. 1143–1155.

2000. 'The Third Intermediate Period', in Shaw, I. (ed.), *The Oxford history of ancient Egypt* (Oxford, Oxford University Press), pp. 330–368.

2009. 'Coffins as evidence for a "north–south divide" in the 22nd–25th Dynasties', in Broekman, G. P. F., R. J. Demarée, and O. E. Kaper (eds.), *The Libyan Period in Egypt: historical and cultural studies into the 21st–24th Dynasties. Proceedings of a conference at Leiden University, 25–27 October 2007* (EgUit 23; Nederlands Instituut voor het Nabije Oosten, Leuven, Peeters), pp. 375–416.

Teeter, E., 2003. *Scarabs, scaraboids, seals, and seal impressions from Medinat Habu*

(OIP 118; Chicago, Oriental Institute of the University of Chicago).

2010. *Baked clay figurines and votive beds from Medinet Habu* (OIP 133; Chicago, Oriental Institute of the University of Chicago).

Thiers, C., 1995. 'Civils et militaires dans les temples: occupation illicite et expulsion', *BIFAO* 95, pp. 493–516.

Thomas, A. P., 1981. *Gurob: a New Kingdom town*, 2 vols. (Egyptology Today 5; Warminster, Aris and Phillips).

Thomas, R. L., 2016. *Naukratis: Greeks in Egypt: Egyptian Late Period figures in terracotta and limestone* (pdf), accessed from www.britishmuseum.org/pdf/Thomas_Egyptian_figures_final.pdf. Accessed 20/3/2019.

Thomas, S., 2000. 'Tell Abqa'in: a fortified settlement in the western Delta: preliminary report of the 1997 season', *MDAIK* 56, pp. 371–376.

Tietze, C., 1985. 'Amarna: Analyse der Wohnhäuser und soziale Struktur der Stadtbewohner', *ZÄS* 112, pp. 48–84.

1986. 'Amarna (Teil II): Analyse der ökonomischen Beziehungen der Stadtbewohner', *ZÄS* 113, pp. 55–78.

2008a. 'Ökonomische Beziehungen der Bewohner der Südstadt', in Tietze, C., *Amarna: Lebensräume – Lebensbilder – Weltbilder* (Potsdam, Universitätsverlag), pp. 124–139.

2008b. 'Wohnhäuser und Bewohner der Südstadt', in Tietze, C. (ed.), *Amarna: Lebensräume – Lebensbilder – Weltbilder* (Potsdam, Universitätsverlag), pp. 86–109.

Tillmann, A., 1992. 'Die Steinartefakte des dynastischen Ägypten, dargestellt am Beispiel der Inventare aus Tell el-Dab'a und Qantir' (PhD thesis, University of Tübingen).

2007. *Neolithikum in der Späten Bronzezeit. Steingeräte des 2. Jahrtausend aus Auaris-*

Piramesse (Forschungen in der Ramses-Stadt 4; Hildesheim, Gerstenberg).

Timm, S., 1984–92. *Das christlich-koptische Ägypten in arabischer Zeit: eine Sammlung christlicher Stätten in Ägypten in arabischer Zeit, unter Ausschluss von Alexandria, Kairo, des Apa-Mena-Klosters (Dēr Abū Mina), des Skētis (Wādi n-Naṭrūn) und der Sinai-Region*, 6 vols. (B.TAVO 41; Wiesbaden, Reichert).

Tracey, J. D., 2000. 'To wall or not to wall: evidence from medieval Germany', in Tracey, J. D. (ed.), *City walls: the urban enceinte in global perspective* (Cambridge, Cambridge University Press), pp. 71–87.

Trampier, J., 2009. 'Expanding archaeology in the Nile floodplain: a non-destructive, remote sensing-assisted survey in the western Delta landscape', *Bulletin of the American Research Center in Egypt* 194, pp. 21–24.

2010. 'The dynamic landscape of the western Nile Delta from the New Kingdom to the Late Roman periods' (PhD thesis, University of Chicago).

2014. *Landscape archaeology of the western Nile Delta* (Wilbour Studies in Egypt and Ancient Western Asia; Atlanta, Lockwood).

Trampier, J., A. Simony, W. Toonen, and J. Starbird, 2013. 'Missing Koms and abandoned channels: the potential of regional survey in the western Nile Delta landscape', *JEA* 99, pp. 217–240.

Traunecker, C., 1975. 'Une stèle commémorant la construction de l'enceinte d'un temple de Montou', *Karnak* 5, pp. 141–158.

1992. *Coptos: hommes et dieux sur le parvis de Geb* (OLA 43; Leuven, Peeters).

1993. 'Les résidents des rives du Lac Sacré: le cas d'Ankhefenkhonsou', *CRIPEL* 15, pp. 83–93.

Tresson, P., 1935–8. 'L'inscription de Chéchanq Ier, au muse du Caire: un frappant exemple d'impôt progressif en matière religieuse', in *Mélanges Maspero*, 1/2 (MIFAO 66; Cairo, IFAO), pp. 817–840.

Trigger, B. G., 2006. *A history of archaeological thought* (2nd edition) (Cambridge, Cambridge University Press).

Tsujimura, S., 2011. 'Archaeological investigations: South Area', in Kawanishi, H., S. Tsujimura, and T. Hanasaka (eds.), *Preliminary report: Akoris 2010* (History and Anthropology; Tsukuba, University of Tsukuba), pp. 4–9.

2012. 'Fishing in Akoris', in Kawanishi, H., S. Tsujimura, and T. Hanasaka (eds.), *Preliminary report: Akoris 2012* (History and Anthropology; Tsukuba, University of Tsukuba), pp. 14–18.

2013. 'Faunal remains in the South Area', in Kawanishi, H., S. Tsujimura, and T. Hanasaka (eds.), *Preliminary report: Akoris 2012* (History and Anthropology; Tsukuba, University of Tsukuba), pp. 15–17.

Tyson-Smith, S., 2003. *Wretched Kush, ethnic identities, and boundaries in Egypt's Nubian empire* (London, Routledge).

Uchida, S., 1995. 'Fragmentary relief of Pinudjem I', in Paleological Association of Japan Egyptian Committee (ed.), *Akoris: report of the excavations at Akoris in Middle Egypt, 1981–1992* (Kyoto, Koyo Shobo), pp. 299–301.

UN Data, 2015. *Egypt, Country Profile*. Available at http://data.un.org/CountryProfile.aspx?crName=egypt. Accessed 1/8/2016.

Ur, J. A., 2002a. 'Settlement and landscape in northern Mesopotamia: the Tell Hamoukar Survey, 2000–2001', *Akkadica* 123, pp. 57–88.

2002b. 'Surface collection and offsite studies at Tell Hamoukar, 1999', *Iraq* 64, pp. 15–44.

2003. 'CORONA satellite photography and ancient road networks: a northern Mesopotamian case study', *Antiquity* 77, pp. 102–115.

USDA Foreign Agricultural Service, 2016. *Egyptian land reclamation efforts* (pdf). Available at https://gain.fas.usda.gov /Recent%20GAIN%20Publications/ Egyptian%20Land%20Reclamation% 20Efforts_Cairo_Egypt_5-16-2016. pdf. Accessed 1/8/2016.

Valbelle, D., F. Le Saout, M. Chartier-Raymond, M. Abd el-Samie, C. Traunecker, G. Wagner, J.-Y. Carrez-Maratray, and P. Zignani, 1992. 'Reconnaissance archéologique à la pointe orientale du Delta: rapport préliminaire sur les saisons 1990 et 1991', *CRIPEL* 14, pp. 11–22.

van den Brink, E. C. M., 1987. 'A geo-archaeological survey in the north-eastern Nile Delta', *MDAIK* 43, pp. 7–31.

1988. 'The Amsterdam University Survey expedition to the northeastern Nile Delta (1984–1986)', in van den Brink, E. C. M. (ed.), *The archaeology of the Nile Delta, Egypt: problems and priorities. Proceedings of the seminar held in Cairo, 19–22 October 1986, on the occasion of the fifteenth anniversary of the Netherlands Institute of Archaeology and Arabic Studies in Cairo* (Amsterdam, Netherlands Foundation for Archaeological Research in Egypt), pp. 65–110.

1992. 'Preliminary report on the excavations at Tell Ibrahim Awad, seasons 1988–1990', in van den Brink, E. C. M. (ed.), *The Nile Delta in transition: 4th–3rd millennium BC. Proceedings of the seminar held in Cairo, 21–24 October 1990, at the Netherlands Institute of Archaeology and Arabic Studies* (Tel Aviv, E. C. M. van den Brink), pp. 43–68.

van Saane, M., 2015. 'Land leases and the legal lexicon: examining legal terminology in abnormal hieratic and early demotic land leases' (MA thesis, Leiden University).

Vandier, J., 1961. *Le papyrus Jumilhac* (Paris, Centre National de la Recherche Scientifique).

Vandier d'Abbadie, J., 1937. *Catalogue des ostraca figurés de Deir el Médineh: nos 2001–2733* (DFIFAO 2 (1); Cairo, IFAO).

1946. *Catalogue des ostraca figurés de Deir el Médineh* (DFIFAO 2 (3); Cairo, IFAO).

1963. *Nestor L'Hôte (1804–1842): choix de documents conservés à la Bibliothèque Nationale et aux Archives du Musée du Louvre* (Documenta et monumenta Orientis antiqui 11; Leiden, Brill).

Varille, A., and C. Robichon, 1935. 'Quatre nouveaux temples thébains', *CdE* 10, pp. 237–242.

Vernus, P., 1967. 'Une localité de la région d'Héracléopolis', *RdE* 19, pp. 166–169.

1975. 'Inscriptions de la Troisième Période Intermédiaire (I): Les inscriptions de la cour péristyle nord du VIe pylône dans le temple de Karnak', *BIFAO* 75, pp. 1–66.

1978. *Athribis: textes et documents relatifs à la géographie, aux cultes et à l'histoire d'une ville du Delta égyptien à l'époque pharaonique* (BdE 74; Cairo, IFAO).

Verreth, H., 1999. 'The Egyptian eastern border region in Assyrian sources', *JAOS* 119 (2), pp. 234–247.

Vikentiev, V., 1930. *La haute crue du Nil et l'averse de l'an 6 du roi Taharqa: le dieu 'Hemen' et son chef-lieu 'Hefat'* (Cairo, IFAO).

Vittmann, G., 2003. *Ägypten und die Fremden im ersten vorchristlichen Jahrtausend* (KAW 97; Mainz am Rhein, Philipp von Zabern).

Vleeming, S. P., 1993. *Papyrus Reinhardt: an Egyptian land list from the tenth century BC* (= Hieratische Papyri aus den Staatlichen Museen zu Berlin –

Preussischer Kulturbesitz, 2; Berlin, Akademie Verlag).

von Beckerath, J., 1966. 'The Nile level records at Karnak and their importance for the history of the Libyan Period (Dynasties XXII and XXIII)', *JARCE* 5, pp. 49–55.

1994. 'Zur Rückeninschrift der Statuette Kairo CG 42192', *Orientalia* 63, pp. 84–87.

1995. 'Beiträge zur Geschichte der Libyerzeit', *GM* 144, pp. 7–13.

1997. *Chronologie des pharaonischen Ägypten: die Zeitbestimmung der ägyptischen Geschichte von der Vorzeit bis 332 v. Chr.* (Münchner Ägyptologische Studien 46; Munich: Philipp von Zabern).

1999. *Handbuch der ägyptischen Königsnamen* (2nd revised edition) (MÄS 49; Mainz, Philipp von Zabern).

2003. 'Über das Verhältnis der 23. zur 22. Dynastie', in Kloth, N., K. Martin, and E. Pardey (eds.), *Es werde niedergelegt als Schriftstück: Festschrift für Hartwig Altenmüller zum 65. Geburtstag* (Hamburg, Buske), pp. 31–36.

von Bissing, Fr. W., 1914. *Denkmäler Ägyptischer Sculptur, vol. III* (Munich, Bruckmann).

von der Way, T., 1984. 'Untersuchungen des Deutschen Archäologischen Instituts Kairo im nördlichen Delta zwischen Disûq und Tida', *MDAIK* 40, pp. 297–328.

1986. 'Tell el-Fara'in – Buto: 1. Bericht', *MDAIK* 42, pp. 191–212.

von Pilgrim, C., 1996. *Elephantine XVIII. Untersuchungen in der Stadt des Mittleren Reiches und der Zweiten Zwischenzeit* (AVDAIK 91; Mainz am Rhein, Philipp von Zabern).

2010. 'Chronology of the town wall', in Kopp, P., C. von Pilgrim, F. Arnold, E. Kopp, E. Laskowska-Kusztal, and D. Raue, *Elephantine, report on the 40th season* (pdf). Accessed from www.dai

nst.org/documents/10180/384618/Elephantine+-+Report+on+the+40th+Season+(ENGLISH)/7a936239-6ace-4f45-8690-dba33b475326;jsessionid=E09107174292E5AC6782CCC27584093F?version=1.0. Accessed 20/3/2019.

Wainwright, G. A., 1912. In Petrie, W. M. F., G. A. Wainwright, and E. Mackay, *The labyrinth, Gerzeh and Mazghuneh* (BSAE/ERA 21; London, Bernard Quaritch).

1927. 'El-Hiba and Esh Shurafa and their connection with Herakleopolis and Cusae', *ASAE* 27, pp. 76–104.

Ward, W. A., 1974. 'The Semitic biconsonantal root sp and the common origin of Egyptian čwf and Hebrew sûp: "marsh(-plant)"', *Vetus Testamentum* 24 (3), pp. 339–349.

Weidner, E. F., 1941–4. 'Šilkan(he)ni, König von Muṣri, ein Zeitgenosse Sargons II., nach einem neuen Bruchstück der Prisma-Inschrift des assyrischen Königs', *AfO* 14, pp. 40–53.

Weigall, A. E. P., 1907. 'Some inscriptions in Prof. Petrie's collection of Egyptian antiquities', *RT* 29, pp. 216–222.

1908. 'Upper Egyptian notes', *ASAE* 9, pp. 103–112.

Weill, R., 1914. 'Monuments égyptiens divers', *RT* 36, pp. 83–101.

Wenig, S., 1968. 'Eine Grabkammer des Mittleren Reiches aus Kom Ombo', *Forschungen und Berichte* 10, pp. 71–94.

Wenke, R. J., 1984. 'Introduction', in Wenke, R. J., *Archaeological investigations at El-Hibeh 1980: preliminary report* (American Research Center in Egypt Reports 9; Malibu, Undena), pp. 1–10.

Wessetzky, V., 1977. 'Reliefs aus dem Tempel Ptolemaios I. in Kom el-Ahmar-Sharuna in der Budapester und Wiener Ägyptischen Sammlung', *MDAIK* 33, pp. 133–141.

1981. *Egyiptomi Művészet a Szépművészeti Múzeumban* (Budapest, Képzőművészeti alap kiadóvállalata).

Westermann, W. L., 1917. 'Land reclamation in the Fayum under Ptolemies Philadelphus and Euergetes I', *Classical Philology* 12 (4), pp. 426–430.

Wiedemann, A., 1890–1. 'Stela at Freiburg in Baden', *PSBA* 13, pp. 31–39.

Wilbour, C. E., 1936. *Travels in Egypt [December 1880 to May 1891]: letters of Charles Edwin Wilbour, edited by Jean Capart* (New York, Brooklyn Museum).

Wild, H., 1972. 'Une statue de la XII dynastie utlisée par le roi hermopolitain Thot-em-hat de la XXIIIe', *RdE* 24, pp. 209–215.

Wilkinson, T. J., 1982. 'The definition of ancient manured zones by means of extensive sherd-sampling techniques', *JFA* 9, pp. 323–333.

1993. 'Linear hollows in the Jazira, Upper Mesopotamia', *Antiquity* 67, pp. 548–562.

2003. *Archaeological landscapes of the Near East* (Tucson, University of Arizona Press).

Wilkinson, T. J., J. A. Ur, and J. Casana, 2004. 'From nucleation to dispersal: trends in settlement patterns in the northern Fertile Crescent', in Cherry, J., and S. Alcock (eds.), *Side-by-side survey: comparative regional surveys in the Mediterranean world* (Oxford, Oxbow Books), pp. 189–205.

Willems, H., and W. H. Muhammad, 2010. 'A note on the origin of the toponym Al-Barshā', *JEA* 96, pp. 232–236.

Wilson, P., 1998. 'Fieldwork, 1997–8: Delta survey', *JEA* 84, pp. 1–22.

2003. 'Fieldwork, 2002–03: the Delta survey, 2002', *JEA* 89, pp. 1–8.

2006. *The survey of Saïs (Sa el Hagar), 1997–2002* (EES EM 77; London, Egypt Exploration Society).

2011. *Saïs I: the Ramesside–Third Intermediate Period at Kom Rebwa* (EES EM 98; London, Egypt Exploration Society).

2012. 'Waterways, settlements and shifting power in the north-western Nile Delta', *Water History* 4 (1), pp. 95–117.

Wilson, P., and D. Grigoropoulos, 2009. *The west Nile Delta regional survey, Beheira and Kafr El-Sheikh provinces* (EES EM 86; London, Egypt Exploration Society).

Winlock, H., 1920. 'Stela of Pernesbastet from Hassaïa', *JEA* 6 (3), pp. 209–211.

Winnicki, J. K., 2009. *Late Egypt and her neighbours: foreign population in Egypt in the first millennium BC* (Journal of Juristic Papyrology, Supplement 12; Warsaw).

Wolf, W., 1929. 'Der Berliner Ptah-Hymnus (P 3048, II–XII)', *ZÄS* 64, pp. 17–44.

Wright, J. C., 2004. 'Comparative settlement patterns during the Bronze Age in the Peloponnesos', in Cherry, J., and S. Alcock (eds.), *Side-by-side survey: comparative regional studies in the Mediterranean world* (Oxford, Oxbow Books), pp. 114–131.

Wunderlich, J., and A. Ginau, 2016. 'Paläoumweltwandel im Raum Tell el Fara'in/Buto: Ergebnisse und Perspektiven geoarchäologischer Forschung', *MDAIK* 70–71, pp. 485–497.

Yasur-Landau, A., J. R. Ebeling, and L. B. Mazow, 2011. (eds.), *Household archaeology in ancient Israel and beyond* (CHANE East 50; Leiden, Brill).

Yoyotte, J., 1950. 'La localité *p3imy-r m$^{š\varsigma}$n t3dhwty st mry*, établissement militaire du temps de Merenptah', *RdE* 7, pp. 63–66.

1952. 'Quelques toponymes égyptiens mentionnés dans les "Annales d'Assurbanipal" (Rm. I, 101–105)', *RA* 46 (4), pp. 212–214.

1958. 'Notes de toponymie égyptienne', *MDAIK* 16, pp. 414–430.

1959. 'Le bassin de Djâroukha', *Kêmi* 15, pp. 23–33.

1960–3. 'A propos des "terrains neufs" et de Thmouis (Toponymie de l'Égypte pharaonique III [2])', *GLECS* 9, pp. 5–9.

1961a. 'Études géographiques, I: la "Cité des Acacias" (Kafr Ammar)', *RdE* 13, pp. 71–105.

1961b. 'Les principautés du Delta au temps de l'anarchie libyenne', in *Mélanges Maspero I: Orient Ancien 4* (Cairo, IFAO), pp. 121–181.

1962. 'Études géographiques, II: les localités méridonales de la région memphite et le "Pehou d'Héracléopolis"', *RdE* 14, pp. 75–111.

1963. 'Études géographiques, II: les localités méridionales de la région memphite et le "Pehou d'Héracléopolis"', *RdE* 15, pp. 87–119.

1972. 'Les adoratrices de la Troisième Periode Intermédiaire. À propos d'un chef-d'ouvre rapport par Champollion', *BSFE* 64, pp. 31–52.

1977–8. 'Religion de l'Égypte ancienne', *Annuaire, École Pratique Des Hautes Études: Ve Section – Sciences Religieuses* 86, 163–171.

1979–80. 'Religion de l'Égypte ancienne', *Annuaire, École Pratique Des Hautes Études: Ve Section – Sciences Religieuses* 88, pp. 193–199.

1981–2. 'Religion de l'Égypte ancienne', *Annuaire, École Pratique Des Hautes Études: Ve Section – Sciences Religieuses* 90, pp. 189–195.

1987. 'Une nouvelle figurine d'Amon voilé et le culte d'Amenopé à Tanis', in Brissaud, P. (ed.), *Cahiers de Tanis 1* (Paris, Editions Recherche sur les Civilisations), pp. 61–69.

1988. 'Des lions et des chats: contribution à la prosopographie de l'époque libyenne', *RdE* 39, pp. 155–178.

1989. 'Note sur le bloc de Sheshonq I découvert par la mission archéologique à Saqqara de l'Université de Pisa', *EVO* 12, pp. 33–35.

2003. 'Un nouveau souvenir de Sheshanq I et un muret héliopolitain de plus', *RdE* 54, pp. 219–265.

Zalla, T., M. A. Fawzy, Y. Ishak, A. H. Y. Saad, M. Road, and H. M. el-Noubi, 2000. *Availability and quality of agricultural data for the new lands of Egypt* (Impact Assessment Report 12; Cairo, Ministry of Agriculture and Land Reclamation).

Zecchi, M., 1999. *Prosopografia dei sacerdoti del Fayyum: dall'Antico Regno al IV secolo a. C. Archeologia e storia della civiltà egiziana e del vicino Oriente antico* (Materiali e studi 4; Imola, La Mandragora).

Zibelius, K., 1978. *Ägyptische Siedlungen nach Texten des Alten Reiches* (B. TAVO 19; Wiesbaden, Reichert).

Ziermann, M., 2002. 'Tell el-Fara'in – Buto: Bericht über die Arbeiten am Gebäudekomplex der Schicht V und die Vorarbeiten auf dem Nordhügel (site A)', *MDAIK* 58, pp. 461–499.

Zignani, P., S. Marchand, and C. Morisot, 1998. 'Deux sondages sur les fondations du temple d'Hathor à Dendera', *BIFAO* 98, pp. 463–496.

Zivie-Coche, C., 1991. *Giza au premier millénaire: autour du temple d'Isis Dame des Pyramides* (Boston, Museum of Fine Arts).

2000. 'Les objets provenant de la structure elliptique', in Brissaud, P., and C. Zivie-Coche (eds.), *Tanis: travaux récents sur le Tell Sân el-Hagar 2* (MFFT 1997–2000; Paris, Noesis), pp. 109–154.

INDEX